Benchmark Papers
in Geology

Series Editor: Rhodes W. Fairbridge
Columbia University

Benchmark Papers in Geology

ENVIRONMENTAL GEOMORPHOLOGY AND LANDSCAPE CONSERVATION
Volume 1: Prior to 1900

Edited by
DONALD R. COATES
State University of New York at Binghampton

Dowden, Hutchinson & Ross, Inc.
Stroudsburg, Pennsylvania

To Jeanne,
who made this volume possible

Acknowledgments
and Permissions

ACKNOWLEDGMENTS

The Government Printing Office—THE YEARBOOK OF AGRICULTURE, 1955
"The Story of Water as the Story of Man"

The Government Printing Office—U.S. GEOLOGICAL SURVEY
"Preliminary Report of the United States Geological Survey of Montana and Portions of Adjacent Territories"

The Government Printing Office—U.S. GEOLOGICAL SURVEY PROFESSIONAL PAPER, 105
"Hydraulic Mining Debris in the Sierra Nevada"

The Government Printing Office—U.S. GEOGRAPHICAL SURVEY; U.S. ARMY, ENGINEER DEPARTMENT
"Report Upon United States Geographical Surveys West of the One Hundredth Meridian"

The Government Printing Office—SMITHSONIAN INSTITUTE ANNUAL REPORT
"Lessons from the Old World to the Americas in Land Use"

The Government Printing Office—U.S. DEPARTMENT OF AGRICULTURE MISCELLANEOUS PUBLICATION (256)
"Early Erosion-Control Practices in Virginia"

The Government Printing Office—HOUSE OF REPRESENTATIVES EXECUTIVE DOCUMENT
"Report on the Lands of the Arid Region of the United States with a More Detailed Account of the Lands of Utah"

Henry Holt & Co.—INFLUENCES OF GEOGRAPHIC ENVIRONMENT
"Chapter XV, Mountain Barriers and Their Passes"

Scribner, Armstrong & Co.—THE EARTH AS MODIFIED BY HUMAN ACTION; a new edition of MAN AND NATURE

American Academy for the Advancement of Science—SCIENCE
"Salt and Silt in Ancient Mesopotamian Agriculture"

PERMISSIONS

The following papers have been reprinted with the permission of the authors, publishers and the present copyright owners.

The University of Chicago Press—MAN'S ROLE IN CHANGING THE FACE OF THE EARTH
"The Hydraulic Civilizations"

National Council for Geographic Education—JOURNAL OF GEOGRAPHY
"The Relation of Geography to the Writing and Interpretation of History"

Cornell University—NEW YORK'S FOOD AND LIFE SCIENCES QUARTERLY
"Examples of Ancient and Modern Use and Abuse of Soils"
"Some Implications of Soils for Civilizations"

The Academy of Political Science—POLITICAL SCIENCE QUARTERLY
  "Rome's Fall Reconsidered"

Harvard University Press—THE QUARTERLY JOURNAL OF ECONOMICS
  "Climatic Changes and Agricultural Exhaustion as Elements in the Fall of Rome"

The American Meteorological Society—BULLETIN OF THE AMERICAN METEOROLOGICAL
  SOCIETY
  "Possibility of Major Climatic Modifiations and Their Implications: Northwest India, a Case for Study"

Archeological Institute of America—AMERICAN JOURNAL OF ARCHEOLOGY
  "The Dark Ages in Ancient History: I. The First Dark Age in Egypt"

Washington Academy of Science—WASHINGTON ACADEMY OF SCIENCE JOURNAL
  "Why the Mayan Cities of the Petén District, Guatemala, Were Abandoned"

The University of New Mexico—SOUTHWESTERN JOURNAL OF ANTHROPOLOGY
  "Ecological and Geochemical Archeology in the Southern Maya Lowlands"

Yale University—AMERICAN JOURNAL OF SCIENCE
  "Recent Stream Trenching in the Semi-arid Portion of Southwestern New Mexico, a Result of Removal
  of Vegetation Cover"

American Association for the Advancement of Science—SCIENCE
  "Ancient Agriculture in the Negev"

Royal Geographical Society—GEOGRAPHICAL JOURNAL
  "Water and Soil from the Deserts: Some Ancient Agricultural Achievements in the Central Negev"

Series Editor's Preface

The philosophy behind the "Benchmark Series" is one of collection, sifting and rediffusion. Scientific literature today is so vast, so dispersed and, in the case of old papers, so inaccessible for readers not in the immediate neighborhood of major libraries, that much valuable information has become ignored— by default. It has become just so difficult, or time consuming, to search out the key papers in any basic area of research that one can hardly blame a busy man for skimping on some of his "homework."

The "Benchmark Series" has been devised, therefore, to make a practical contribution to this critical problem. The geologist, perhaps even more than any other type of scientist, often suffers from twin difficulties—isolation from central library resources and an immensely diffused source of material. New colleges and industrial libraries simply cannot afford to purchase complete runs of all the world's earth science literature. Specialists simply cannot locate reprints or copies of all their principal reference materials. So it is that we are now making a concentrated effort to gather into single volumes the critical material needed to reconstruct the background to any and every major topic of our discipline.

We are interpreting "Geology" in its broadest sense: the fundamental science of the Planet Earth, its materials, its history and its dynamics. Because of training and experience in "earthy" materials, we also take in astrogeology, the corresponding aspect of the planetary sciences. Besides the classical core disciplines such as mineralogy, petrology, structure, geomorphology, paleontology, or stratigraphy, we embrace the newer fields of geophysics and geochemistry, applied also to oceanography, geochronology, and paleoecology. We recognize the work of the mining geologists, the petroleum geologists, the hydrologists, the engineering and environmental geologists. Each specialist needs his working library. We are endeavoring to make his task a little easier.

Each volume in the series contains an Introduction prepared by a specialist, the volume editor—and a "state-of-the-art" opening or a summary of the objects and content of the volume. The articles selected, usually some 30–50 reproduced either in their entirety or in significant extracts, attempt to scan the field from the key papers of the last century until fairly recent years. Where the original references may be in foreign languages, we have endeavored to locate or commission translations. Geologists, because of their global subject, are often acutely aware of the oneness of our world. Its literature, therefore, cannot be restricted to any one country and, whenever possible, an attempt has been made to scan the world literature.

To each article, or group of kindred items, some sort of "Highlight Commentary" is usually supplied by the volume editor. This should serve to bring that article into historical perspective and to emphasize its particular role in the growth of the field. References or citations, wherever possible, will be reproduced in their entirety; for by this means the observant reader can assess the background material available to that particular author, or, if he wishes, he too can double check the earlier sources.

A "benchmark," in surveyor's terminology, is an established point on the ground, recorded on our maps. It is usually anything that is a vantage point, from a modest hill to a mountain peak. From the historical viewpoint, these benchmarks are the bricks of our scientific edifice.

Rhodes W. Fairbridge

Author List

Contents

V. LANDSCAPE CONSERVATION

Introduction

I became an environmentalist about 35 years ago while watching the soils of my friends' farms in Nebraska blow away during the dry season. These "dust bowl" events set in motion a chain reaction of academic-professional studies that provided the impetus for this book, the first in a three-volume series entitled "Environmental Geomorphology and Landscape Conservation." Whereas this first book concerns itself with activities before 1900, subsequent volumes will concentrate on nonurban and on urban aspects of the field during the 20th century. When it became apparent that a single volume would be inadequate to present the vast amount of material on the subject, various approaches were taken in attempts to provide a meaningful separation of information. All except one were rejected as being too artificial and contrived; including those based on geomorphic process, climate, and geographic setting. Thus, a temporal division is made in this first volume as emphasizing differences between the past centuries and situations of the present.

As a basic tenet it must be understood that man has acted on, with, and against his environment during his tenure on planet Earth. It is likewise obvious that the environmental *law of reciprocity* has always acted throughout time: namely, the environment affects man, and man also changes his environment. Furthermore the environment has always posed problems for man, and there never has been, nor ever will be any totally satisfying panacea for the future resolution of the mutually disturbing forces. Nevertheless there seem to be some major differences that have appeared during the 20th century that require special treatment. One is that most problems are now being aggravated at an accelerating rate—a difference in magnitude and not kind. The accelerating (three-fold) increase in the earth's population is a major cause in the scale of man-induced environmental distortion. The projected exponentially rising population curve (Fig. 1) points to the urgency of this problem.

A second change in the environment is occurring from the mechanization, industrialization, and mobilization of society. An entirely new array of inventions, machines, and resources has placed unusual stresses on the environment and in many cases

1

created a new family of problems that were largely nonexistent before the 20th century—a difference in kind. For example, the automobile has created the need for a dense network of highways which in turn has necessitated massive terrain modification. The rapid growth and development of fluid fuels such as diesel oil, gasoline, and natural gas have aided the multiplication of new types of machines and transport facilities. The new energy has led to the drilling of deep water wells, thus opening new areas for grazing, settlement, and irrigation. The new machines facilitate the mining of mineral resources by open-pit methods in coal, copper, and iron but have irreparably scarred the landscape. Therefore this new energy provides a mobility into new regions that previously were relatively unpopulated. In this way many new problems of large scope have arisen in the 20th century; they include, in addition, such things as land subsidence by withdrawal of fluids, salinization of coastal aquifers due to ground water "mining," and in general a mammoth pollution of the lands, water, and air.

A third major change occurring in the 20th century concerns the urbanization process and the style of living and societal attitudes. These have produced new considerations on the political-governmental-public affairs scene. There has been a greater government involvement in environmental matters that includes the establishment of such agencies in the United States as the Bureau of Reclamation, Soil Conservation Service (U.S. Department of Agriculture), and new mandates for the Corps of Engineers (U.S. Army). Comparable developments have occurred in numbers of other countries. New legislation on local, state, and federal levels provides fresh insight into the necessity for improving environmental management, resulting in a different dimension of man's awareness of the environment and his attempts to minimize his degradation of it. Because urbanization is the most important sector in the change in man's habitation pattern, it has become necessary to separate his arena of activity in this setting from his actions in the nonurban region. Such matters comprise the content for Volumes 2 and 3 of this series.

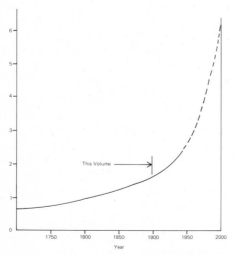

Figure 1, World population growth curve since 1700 (data from Durand, 1967).

The title for these volumes was selected to clarify their content and to portray the unity necessary when evaluating the interrelationships of man and the land–water ecosystem. Environmental geomorphology is a topic that has greater coherence and can be handled in books of shorter length than those on environmental geology in general. The latter would have needed inclusion of such major fields as petroleum geology, mining geology, and engineering geology along with much material in areas such as geochemistry and geophysics.

The expression "environmental geology" first became current in the 1960's, whereas "environmental geomorphology" was not used until 1971 (Coates). According to McGee (1893), John Wesley Powell was the first to use the term "geomorphology" back in the 1880's. Definitions of what constitute the geomorphology field have not been consistent during the past 80 years but most specialists are now in agreement that its study involves both terrain analysis and investigation of those processes which shape landforms. (See also Fairbridge, 1968.) Man's involvement with the earth's surface creates changes, so that professional scrutiny of these activities also falls within the realm of geomorphology. Environmental geomorphology combines and clarifies these relationships and includes: (1) study of geomorphic processes and terrain that affect man, including hazard phenomena such as floods and landslides; (2) analysis of problems when man plans to disturb or has already degraded the land–water ecosystem; (3) man's utilization of geomorphic agents or products as resources, such as water or sand and gravel; and (4) how the science of geomorphology can be used in environmental planning and management.

The companion feature of these volumes, landscape conservation, portrays constructive elements in man's attempt to live more harmoniously with his environment. Often they involve helping nature to help itself. Man's practices and policies for preventing or remedying destructive tendencies are discussed and conservation is used in the broadest sense to include both preservation (protection) and reclamation. In like manner "landscape" is not narrowly conceived as meaning only the land. Instead it takes on full meaning only when considered along with water and the matrix of ideas associated with their relationship.

Considered in this manner the subject matter for these volumes transcends traditional disciplines and shows the interdisciplinary harmony needed in such fields as geomorphology, hydrogeology, geography, and agronomy.

Therefore, although the subject matter shows a wide range in these volumes and includes topics often considered the province of separate disciplines, the purpose is to show how environmental affairs encompass many fields necessitating the cooperation of many sciences. It is only recently that discipline-splitting and super specialization has occurred, resulting in not only problems in semantics, but creating gaps in communications. It is hoped that this series can blend and provide some harmony for mutual problems. Studies of the environment provide not only a unique challenge to scholars, but a ray of hope that it may be the avenue through which there can be a new growth of scientific union and interdependence. In order to provide as comprehensive understanding as possible it has been necessary to include environmental appraisals by scientists in many different fields.

This volume is largely a compilation of what constitutes some of the best literature dealing with the most significant aspects of man's involvement with surface features of the earth. Since the stature for such a book depends on the included articles, a discussion of problems and criteria used in their selection should prove informative. It is obvious that a single volume cannot be complete and include, or even represent all important literature, ideas, and practices for this long period of man's history. I have, however, attempted to assemble a sampling of significant works and concepts. Most of them contain original work or compiled data and ideas that were very important when written and provided answers to problems or stimulated others and aided in scientific progress. Since this is a three-volume series, certain topics and geographic areas have been reserved for future volumes, but each volume contains examples drawn from many different parts of the world. The articles selected also represent a wide variety of different books, journals, and bulletins from private and governmental sources. In addition they come from many different disciplines such as geology, geography, anthropology, meteorology, political science, economics, etc. This book would also be incomplete without inclusion of works from some scientists who are recognized as being giants of their time and who greatly influenced others such as Grove Karl Gilbert, George Perkins Marsh, and John Wesley Powell. Since unanimity does not always occur on such matters as the scope or the impact of man's influence on the environment and on certain cause–effect relationships, it is necessary to show various approaches to such contradictions. Thus selections are included upon such debatable issues as the cause for the Fall of Rome, demise of Mayan civilization, resource engineering in the Negev, and arroyo initiation in the American Southwest. It should not be construed that these articles represent the view of the editor, or that they are necessarily correct. They are all achievements of their time however, and contributed significantly to the advancement of knowledge. These articles include coverage of both man's environmental insight and his disregard, or lack of understanding, of nature. The topical materials chosen also illustrate a variety of geomorphic processes and man-made terrain alterations, including the largest single land sea transformation—the Netherlands landscape. Some emphasis in this volume is placed on soil erosion and its conservational aspects. Future volumes will provide greater detail on such problems as coastal erosion, floods, landslides, subsidence, and also degradation in abnormally fragile environments as the arctic and tropical regions. The utility of this book should be enhanced by the use of examples and selections from rare or obscure sources such as Columella, Sorsby, Sinclair, and Nickols, because too many source-book volumes fall into a pattern of repeating the same literature and quotations. Earth scientists should also become more aware of the importance of work done in allied fields and journals such as those in anthropology and archeology.

For reader convenience and understanding this volume is divided topically into five unequal parts. The book opens with Part I, Importance of Water to Man: this illustrates the all-encompassing significance of water in the destiny and works of man. Water is so fundamental in landscape considerations and all ramifications of surficial earth processes that it forms the cornerstone of the science of geomorphology.

Part II, Influence of Terrain on Man, explores man's relationships in the entire setting of the land–water ecosystem. In this section the first of two aspects of the duality of environment is illustrated, namely, the manner in which topography has influenced the behavior, history, and settlement patterns of man. The reciprocal

4

of this process, the impact of man on his environment, provides the theme for Part IV

Part III, Physical Environmental Descriptions of the United States, presents views of early travellers and scientists in America and shows how they evaluated the environment. Such articles provide not only interesting historical guidelines but gave contemporaries insight for personal plans and environmental policies of the future.

Part IV, Environmental Degradation by Man, documents the destructive tendencies of man and shows his lack of understanding and inability to cope with natural processes.

Part V, Landscape Conservation, emphasizes constructive elements in the activity of mankind and his attempts to prevent erosion and restore land. Some selections show the use of certain practices to alleviate imbalances, and others provide suggestions for planning and future operations.

Each of the five parts is prefaced with materials that should provide continuity and relevance of the selections. Additional bibliographic information is given to assist the reader in further study.

The composition, style, and material coverage of this volume (and its partners) is not duplicated by any other single work or group of books. This unusual format attempts to blend coordinate disciplines whose cooperation is of importance. Geomorphology by its very nature must be interdisciplinary in character and thus provides the perfect entree to this field. It is hoped that some new dimensions of unity and insight have been provided and brought into clearer focus. It is necessary that this first volume should be historical and provide some insight into past failures and successes, because only with such analysis can the progress of mankind be weighed. We need to remind ourselves of the old adage that those who don't read history have a greater likelihood of repeating mistakes. Therefore, the purpose of these volumes is to provide for the reader some new perspectives in understanding. As Aldo Leopold remarked in his preface to *A Sand County Almanac* (1949), "We abuse land as a commodity belonging to us. When we see land as a community to which we belong, we may begin to use it with love and respect."

Importance of Water to Man

I

Although this section emphasizes the vital role of water to man and his history, the entire book is actually a testimony to its significance. Water is not only the life blood of man himself, but societies and nations have risen and fallen depending upon their level of understanding of this basic resource. Indeed it is the fundamental building block of our planet and the commodity that provides uniqueness among all others in the solar system. The person who named our planet "earth" perpetrated a grave injustice with this misnomer, because water is the indispensable property of our globe. Perhaps this illustrates the egotism of man; since his abode was usually on land, this came to be equated with earth. It is an interesting coincidence that water comprises about 70 percent of the human body and covers about 70 percent of the surface of the earth.

It is the many unusual, and the nearly unique, properties of water that make it the most coveted of all natural resources. Many of these are pointed out in the articles selected for this part, those by Bernard Frank and by Karl Wittfogel. In addition it is the only material that exists in all three physical states at the earth's surface—liquid, solid, and gas. In liquid form it is colorless and odorless when pure. Its property of transparency permits light penetration so that aqueous plants and animals can live, and its fluid property, with just the proper amount of surface tension allows animals and land plants to survive. Water has one of the highest capacities for specific heat retention of all substances, thus providing a tremendous storehouse of energy. Upon freezing it possesses the unusual quality of expanding, a characteristic shared by only a few natural materials. Such a quality has made it possible for man to live in regions that would otherwise have been uninhabitable. As a resource it is different from others because there is no second crop for such elements as iron, copper, and petroleum. Thus the hydrologic cycle, a marvelous self-perpetuating machine, permits water to be replenishable and this process must be classed as one of the wonders of the earth.

7

It is easy to eulogize water and myriads of words have been written extolling it in a great variety of ramifications, and the Frank and Wittfogel articles summarize some of this information. Water is needed in the physiology of man, and in his external endeavors involving agricultural, municipal, and industrial usages. Man's water needs are well illustrated by some of the earliest laws for its use and regulation from the time of Hammurabi's Code to the present time (Volumes 2 and 3). Man's settlement patterns and life style, especially in the ancient world, were determined by considerations for water. Owing to new discoveries of water, of powerful pumps that can mine ground water at great depths, and such innovations as desalinization, 20th century man can now inhabit in greater numbers regions that formerly could sustain only a small society at subsistence levels. Several chapters in Semple (1911) are devoted to man and water such as her chapters, "Man's Relation to the Water" and "Anthropogeography of Rivers." She describes such factors as the use of water as protection, economic aspects in irrigation, navigation and commerce. Lakes have also had a political and ethnic control where they became the nuclei for such societies as the Swiss federation of states, and the focus for the Inca empire owes its beginning to Lake Titicaca.

Since water is a man-required resource in many different spheres and ways, its use, and commonly abuse, has caused him trouble throughout history. Water plays a dual role in its relation to man, and thereby can be considered to contain schizophrenic tendencies. When water is used properly and managed efficiently and harmoniously it is a wonderful servant to man. However, when improperly used, misunderstood, or neglected, it becomes a tyrant that can do great damage and cause man's destruction. Attempting to provide an appropriate balance between these ends of the spectrum will be a recurring theme in these volumes.

A major difference in the behavioral attitudes of man towards water (especially in industrialized countries) exists when the 20th century posture is compared with earlier attitudes. It has become common to consider water as a natural heritage and take it for granted. When the tap is turned on little thought is given and everyone expects to have good clean clear water come pouring forth. Certainly its rather ubiquitous character mesmerizes and enhances this attitude of the general population in temperate regions. Such human attitudes are similar to those as regards health: a person rarely counts his blessings while he is healthy and only when he becomes violently ill does he realize how wonderful it was to feel well. In the words of Lord Byron, "Til taught by pain, men know not what good water's worth." In a sense, ancient man probably realized the importance of water and respected it more than a great many people do in the 20th century. In similar fashion it has taken massive educational efforts to alert the American population to the respect water deserves. Too often man has always assumed that works created by the engineering mind can solve any problem. The trinity of problems that lead to damages and cause large expenditures in solution attempts has become severely acute in the 20th century—too much water; too little water; and too poor water quality. Such aspects will be treated in greater detail in Volumes 2 and 3.

Dr. Karl A. Wittfogel was born in Germany (1896) and received his Ph.D. (1928) from the University of Frankfort, where he was a research associate until 1933. From 1934 until the present he has largely been associated with the University of Washington and Columbia University in Chinese History programs. He has a variety of publications which include the book *Oriental Despotism: A Comparative Study of Total Power* (1957). His article "The Hydraulic Civilizations" documents the crucial role that water has played in the development and evolution of society and civilization. The demographic aspect of water's importance sometimes poses perplexing problems in several disciplines. Woodbury's study (1961) of Hohokam works in the Salt River Valley of Arizona provides ideas about the scope of irrigation and the size of communities that were flourishing more than 700 years ago. He states (p. 556) "The scale of prehistoric Hohokam canals is sufficient to raise the possibility of an incipient 'hydraulic society' having been in the process of development." In this example, however, he found no support for Wittfogel's thesis that large magnitude hydraulic works require a hierarchically ordered society which controls the labor force by central authority. Hack (1942) in a classic paper on the physical environment of the Hopi Indians emphasizes how "water supply is probably the most important environmental factor determining the concentration of population" (p. 10). Hodge and Duisberg (1963) also emphasize the extraordinary significance of water in the arid areas.

In: *Water: The Yearbook of Agriculture, 1955, The Government Printing Office, pp. 1–8*

1

The Story of Water as the Story of Man

BERNARD FRANK

The Story of
Water as the
Story of Man

Bernard Frank

You could write the story of man's growth in terms of his epic concerns with water.

Through the ages people have elected or have been compelled to settle in regions where water was deficient in amount, inferior in quality, or erratic in behavior. Only when supplies failed or were made useless by unbearable silt or pollution or when floods swept everything before them were centers of habitation abandoned. But often the causes lay as much in the acts or failures of men themselves as in the caprices of Nature. So, too, man's endeavors to achieve a more desirable relationship with the waters of the earth have helped mold his character and his outlook toward the world around him.

People always have preferred to meet their water troubles head-on rather than quit their places of abode and industry. So people have applied their creative imagination, and utilized their skills, and cleased heroic energy. The ancient wells, aqueducts, and reservoirs of the Old World, some still serviceable after thousands of years, attest to the capacity for constructive thinking and cooperative ventures, which

had a part in human advancement.

Fifty centuries ago the Mohan-Jo-Daro civilization of the Indus Valley in India enjoyed the benefits of well-designed water supply and drainage systems and even public swimming pools and baths. Excavated ruins of that period have revealed a surprising variety of waterworks, including tanks and irrigation canals.

The people of Assyria, Babylonia, Egypt, Israel, Greece, Rome, and China built similar facilities long before the Christian era. Egypt has the world's o'dest known dam, a rock-fill structure built 5,000 years ago to store drinking and irrigation water and perhaps also to hold back floodwaters. Its length was 355 feet, and its crest was 40 feet above the riverbed. Apparently it was poorly designed, for it failed soon after, and no other was erected for 3,000 years afterward. Jacob's well was excavated through rock to a depth of 105 feet. The well is reported to be still in use. About 950 B. C., Solomon directed the construction of sizable aqueducts to provide for the needs of man, beast, and field. Ancient Arabia's enterprising farmers utilized extinct volcanic craters to store surface flows for irrigation and drove deep wells to get drinking water. Babylonia's King Hammurabi supervised the digging of an extensive network of irrigation canals and promulgated laws for their repair.

Among the early Greeks, Hippocrates recognized the dangers to health of

1

polluted drinking water and recommended that water be filtered and boiled. The Romans used their poorer waters for irrigation and fountains.

The Tukiangyien system, built in China some 2,200 years ago, is another tribute to the genius and toil of ancient peoples. This skillfully designed multipurpose engineering project was intended to divert the flows of the Min River, a tumultuous stream that rises on the high plateau of Tibet. By building a series of dams and dikes on the main river where it first enters the broad plain from the mountain canyon, the farmers divided its flow into many parts so they could irrigate one-half million fertile acres. The structures—composed of bamboo frames weighted down by rocks—also reduced greatly the heavy toll of life and property from spring and summer floods.

THE HABITS OF MEN and the forms of their social organizations have been influenced more by their close association with water than with the land by which they earned their bread. This association is reflected in the Psalms of the Hebrew poets and in the laws, regulations, and beliefs among the civilizations of the Near East, the Far East, and South America.

Read, in the Old Testament: ". . . A good land, a land of brooks of water, of fountains and depths that spring out of valleys and hills . . ." (Deuteronomy 8: 7). "I did know thee in the wilderness, in the land of great drought." (Hosea 13: 5). "Drought and heat consume the snow waters . . ." (Job 24: 19). "He sendeth the springs into the valleys, which run among the hills. They give drink to every beast of the field: the wild asses quench their thirst. By them shall the fowls of the heaven have their habitation, which sing among the branches. He watereth the hills from his chambers . . . He causeth the grass to grow for the cattle, and herb for the service of man . . ." (Psalm 104: 10–14).

Property in water long antedated property in land in the arid lands of antiquity. Property rights were associated primarily with the uses of water—first for drinking, next for irrigation. Mohammed saw water as an object of religious charity. He declared that free access to water was the right of every Moslem community and that no Moslem should want for it. The precept of the Holy Koran, "No one can refuse surplus water without sinning against Allah and against Man," was the cornerstone of a whole body of social traditions and of regulations governing the ownership, use, and protection of water supplies.

All persons who shared rights to a watercourse were held responsible for its maintenance and cleaning. The whole community was responsible for the care of large watercourses. Cleaning was to start at the head of the stream or canal, descending in order to each waterside family. All users shared the cost in proportion to their irrigation rights.

Even marriage might be influenced by the difficulties of obtaining water. The inhabitants of one rural community in southeastern Asia must walk 9 miles to the nearest sources of drinking water—a group of wells. Local custom decrees that wives must fetch the water. One wife can make only one trip a day with her bucket—not enough for the family's needs—and so a man finds it desirable to have several wives.

ALL LIFE DEPENDS ON WATER. For us today water is as necessary for life and health as it was for our prehistoric ancestors. Like air, water is bound up with man's evolution—and doubtless his destiny—in countless ways. One of the basic conditions for life on earth is that water be available in liquid form.

The origin of all life on our planet is believed to be the sea, and today, after millions of years of evolution, modern man's tissues are still bathed in a saline solution closely akin to that of the sea when the earlier forms of life first left it to dwell on the land.

Every organic process can occur only in the watery medium. The embryo floats in a liquid from conception to birth. Breathing, digestion, glandular activities, heat dissipation, and secretion can be performed only in the presence of watery solutions. Water acts as a lubricant, helps protect certain tissues from external injury, and gives flexibility to the muscles, tendons, cartilage, and bones.

The role of water in metabolism, in regulating body temperature, and in nourishing the tissues, explains why we could not long survive without adequate amounts of water. Yet our direct bodily needs for water are relatively small in terms of our total body weight (itself more than 71 percent water) and infinitesimal in relation to the total demands upon water by human societies, even among primitive cultures.

The average person in the Temperate Zone can get along with about 5.5 pints of water a day if he is moderately active. Slightly more than 2 pints are taken in with a normal mixed diet or created in the body by the oxidation of food, especially sugars, starches, and fats. Another 3 pints are taken in as fluids. Altogether it takes 5 or 6 pints to replace the daily losses in perspiration, exhalation, and excretion.

The amount for a given individual varies with his weight, age, activity, health, and other factors, but basic needs must be satisfied if life is to go on. The consumption of lesser amounts than those needed to replace losses will lead to a diminished appetite and eventually to undernutrition. A man in good health might be able to survive without water for a few days in a desert if he is only slightly active. If he tried to be more active he might not last a single day, because the consequent losses of water—as much as 10 pints an hour—from the body would greatly exceed the losses incurred under slight activity. Unless water were promptly made available, the losses would cause dehydration, incapacity, and painful death. By contrast, in the parts of the Tropics where high temperature and high humidity prevail, high rates of activity cannot be

maintained even if abundant water were available, since the body is unable to dissipate heat and rid itself of waste products fast enough to prevent a breakdown in body functions.

WATER SERVES in many other ways to maintain life, health, vigor, and social stability. The nutritive value of food crops may be affected by the amount of moisture available to them when they are in active growth. Because the minerals in the soil can be taken up by plants only when they are in solution, the amounts thus made available are greatest when the soil is moist.

The oceans, lakes, and flowing waters and their shores furnish food and clothing. Men always have looked to such places for a goodly part of their diet of proteins and carbohydrates.

The gathering of fish, lobsters, crabs, and other crustacea, the waterfowl, fur bearers, and other wildlife that frequent riparian environments, and the stems, roots, bulbs, or fruits of bulrush, watercress, marshmarigold, water chinquapin, wildrice, and other water-loving vegetation have furnished sustenance to people the world over.

The occurrence of water in a locality confers advantages on the people who own or use the lands. The lakes, beaver ponds, the waterfalls, cascades, bogs, swamps, springs, or snowfields that feature wilderness, park, and the other recreational places and the colorful plants and wildlife that thrive there provide an appeal that attracts many people to the outdoors.

NATURAL WATERWAYS—oceans, lakes, and rivers—have greatly facilitated the worldwide spread of population and of commerce. Most of the permanent settlements in the arid regions—today as in antiquity—have concentrated along river valleys. Even along the seacoasts, habitation clustered around or near the convenient sources of fresh water.

The early Egyptians along the Nile and the Incas at Lake Titicaca in Peru employed rafts cleverly constructed of native plants. Solid logs filled with double outriggers and platforms made seaworthy craft in Africa and Polynesia; later craft were constructed from logs hollowed out by fire and crude tools.

Inland transportation since early times has been facilitated by canals, first for irrigation and later for transport, as among the early Assyrians, Egyptians, and Chinese. The Grand Canal, built in China in the 13th century, served irrigation needs and also provided an important artery of commerce for the products of its millions of people. European countries, notably Holland, France, and England, later developed extensive systems of canals between natural waterways. So, too, in the Andes region of South America, rivers are the arteries on which rubber, lumber, and other products of the interior are carried to the coast.

Early settlement in the United States, at first restricted to the coastal strips, soon moved westward through the mountains by utilizing such streams as the Mohawk River in New York, the upper Potomac in Maryland and West Virginia, and the Ohio. By 1790, shortly after our country achieved independence, all but 5 percent of the 4 million inhabitants still lived along the Atlantic seaboard, but the way westward was rapidly being charted. River craft had navigated up the coastal rivers to the fall line. Canals to bypass the unnavigable parts of rivers were already built in Pennsylvania—connecting the town of Reading on the Schuylkill River with Middletown on the Susquehanna—and around the rapids at Harpers Ferry, W. Va., on the Potomac. Following the successful tests of steam-propelled craft, large fleets began to haul wheat, coal, and iron on the Ohio River, the Great Lakes, and the Mississippi.

As the country expanded and prospered, eyes turned increasingly to the opportunities on the major rivers. Today, notwithstanding the intensive networks of railroads, highways, and airways, our improved navigation waterways—developed largely by the Corps of Engineers—total more than 25,000 miles and in 1953 carried a volume of raw and manufactured products amounting to nearly 225 million tons. It is possible to travel by boat from the Gulf of Mexico to Sioux City, Iowa, a distance of 2,030 miles.

MODERN CIVILIZATION imposes heavy demands on water. Merely to sustain life takes relatively little water. But even in pastoral or other simple societies, additional amounts are needed in preparing food and washing our bodies and clothes. The total daily requirement for all purposes, including drinking, in ancient villages may have averaged 3 to 5 gallons a person. Now a person uses 60 gallons or more each day for household and lawn-watering purposes in the average electrified farm or urban home in the United States! The figures are for homes with running water; the corresponding average for homes without that convenience is only 10 gallons a person a day.

At the minimum comfort level of 5 gallons a day—corresponding to the needs of primitive living conditions—our country's 165 million people would have few serious water difficulties. That daily total consumption of 825 millions of gallons would represent 0.07 percent of the Nation's average daily runoff of 1,160 billion gallons a day and 1.2 percent of the amount used up (not available for reuse) in the United States.

But our technological civilization could not have been attained at a level of water consumption geared to the requirements of primitive societies, even in our humid sections, where the need for irrigating crops is relatively slight. The steady rise in the consumption of water in industrially advanced countries explains why we now regard our water supplies with great concern.

The impact of new inventions and new developments and growth in population and industry has not commonly been given the attention it has merited.

Many critical local water shortages

therefore have occurred that could have been forestalled. For example, rural electrification has brought about such heavy increases in the use of water for household and production purposes that the limited well-water supplies of many farms have been severely strained.

Similarly, factories have been built without prior studies to determine whether water would be available to operate the factories and to provide for the communities around them.

Towns, cities, industries, and farms have kept expanding beyond the safe limits of available water. Often makeshift efforts have been necessary to meet emergencies, especially in years of low rainfall. Such efforts have often hastened the depletion of the limited reserves in underground reservoirs, generated disputes with other cities or industries drawing on the same sources of water, introduced conflicts with the use of water for recreation, and threatened the permanent flooding of lands valuable for farming, forestry, wilderness, or wildlife.

To meet the difficulties, more thought is being given to the advance planning of storage reservoirs, aqueducts, canals, methods of recharging ground water, reclamation of waste waters, and other devices. Still the search for more and better water goes on. Use continues to rise; advancing standards of health and comfort, the application of more intensive farming practices, and the development of new products all impose additional demands. In fact, the proportion of our total economic and recreational activity—both in rural and urban areas—that depends on handy and abundant supplies of clean, safe water is greater than ever before in our history.

OUR WATER NEEDS are indeed great. Yet they do not begin to compare with the needs of the millions of people in Asia Minor, India, Africa, and South America who must still scoop up water from shallow pools or foul streams or haul it up by hand from wells. Travelers relate how in Madagascar the women carry water home in jars on their heads across miles of hot sands. In parts of the Egyptian Sudan, water is stored in the trunks of large, hollow trees. The openings are sealed with wet clay to keep it uncontaminated. Thousands of these small reservoirs—which hold 300 to 1,000 gallons each—appear along routes of travel. In one province all the trees are registered and the contents noted for information on the extent of the water resource.

Among the early pioneers, especially in the southern Appalachian Mountains, the ownership and control of a clean, abundantly flowing spring was considered an indispensable prerequisite to staking out a homestead. Once chosen, the spring was cherished. It meant cleanliness, health, and comfort. It was sheltered against contamination and protected against trespassers.

How far have most of us strayed from the old family spring! Generations of men and women have grown up without experiencing the joy of satisfying their thirst from cool, sparkling, spring water. Modern living standards have made it necessary to rely upon water supplies of far greater volumes than the one-family—or even the community—spring could furnish. Many of us have lost contact with the land and the pure waters that came from its depths. We must get water from distant rivers or reservoirs and then only after it has been made safe by filtration and chemicals.

THE TASK OF FINDING, developing, and maintaining suitable water supplies has not been limited to modern times. It has had to be faced wherever large numbers of people have crowded together in small spaces.

Paul B. Sears, discussing climate and civilization (in the book *Climatic Change*, edited by Harlow Shapley), wrote that the highly developed civilization of Babylon finally disintegrated because "for centuries the operation of agriculture had been increasingly burdened by heavy loads of silt in the life-giving [irrigation] canals." He added: "So much labor was required for their annual cleaning that little leisure remained for anything else, and the long piles of silt . . . grew steadily in height and volume. Presumably this was due to increasing pressure, through cutting and grazing, upon the vegetation of the highlands whose runoff supplied the water. Under those conditions, the landscape became increasingly vulnerable to the effects of climate with its infrequent but violent rains and dry-season winds."

During the several centuries of stability under the Roman Empire, vast and intricate systems of waterworks had been constructed to provide the millions of people with safe supplies. Disposal of sewage was well developed for the times, and, in general, the value of clean household water and of sanitation was well understood. But when the empire disintegrated, chaos reigned, and the hard-won gains were rapidly dissipated. The constant warfare and political disturbances broke down the social concerns over water supplies, among other important public services. As ignorance and poverty increased, sanitary precautions came to mean less and less, and in time cleanliness was frowned upon as evidence of wicked thoughts and self-indulgence. Bathing, formerly widely practiced for its therapeutic values, was abandoned. The citizens no longer took pride in clean homes and streets, which became filthier and filthier. Worst of all, the water, obtained mostly from wells, eventually became so fouled as to be unfit for use.

Illness and death from waterborne diseases have plagued one country after another down to the present time. And not only were the poor people struck down. Records indicate that many famous characters of history also fell victim to waterborne diseases. Among them was King Louis VIII of France, Charles X of Sweden, Prince Albert of England, his son Edward VII, and his grandson George V. George Washington was known to have suffered from dysentery. And Abigail Adams, wife of the second President of the United States; Zachary Taylor; and—ironically enough—Louis Pasteur's two daughters are said to have died of typhoid fever.

Apparently the popular indifference toward safe, clean water prevailed well into the 19th century, even in England and the United States, where the dangers from the polluted supplies were generally known.

The effects of polluted waters now are considered to be the foremost obstacle to raising the living standards of underdeveloped countries.

BERNARD FRANK *is assistant chief of the Division of Watershed Management Research of the Forest Service. He has written extensively on water-resources and watershed management.*

For further reading:

Jasper B. Draffin: *The Story of Man's Quest for Water*, The Garrard Press, Champaign, Ill., 1939.

Jonathan Forman and Ollie E. Fink (editors): *Water and Man: A Study in Ecology*, Friends of the Land, Columbus, Ohio, 1950.

A. Haddow (editor): *Biological Hazards of Atomic Energy*, Oxford University Press, London, 1952.

Charles R. Hursh: *Water from the Family Spring*, The Living Wilderness, No. 39, Winter 1951–52.

Kenneth A. MacKichan: *Estimated Use of Water in the United States, 1950*, U. S. Geological Survey Circular 115, May 1951.

Charles G. Rogers: *Textbook of Comparative Physiology*, McGraw-Hill Book Co., Inc., New York, 1927.

Harlow Shapley (editor): *Climatic Change*, Harvard University Press, Cambridge, Mass., 1953.

A. K. (Dad) Short: *References from Ancient and Modern Agriculture*, The Naylor Co., San Antonio, Tex., 1938.

C. P. Straub: *Effect of Radioactive Materials on Environmental Health*, Department of Health Education, and Welfare, Public Health Service Report 67, No. 3, March 1952.

The Physical and Economic Foundation of Natural Resources, part II. The Physical Basis of Water Supply and Its Principal Uses, Interior and Insular Affairs Committee, House of Representatives, U. S. Congress, 1952.

Water Laws in Moslem Countries, FAO Development Paper No. 43, Food and Agriculture Organization of the United Nations, Rome, Italy, March 1954.

E. L. Waterman: *Elements of Water Supply Engineering*, John Wiley & Sons, New York, 1938.

In: *Man's Role in Changing the Face of the Earth (W. L. Thomas, Ed.), 1956, Chicago University Press, pp. 152–164*

The Hydraulic Civilizations

2

KARL A. WITTFOGEL*

THE HYDRAULIC AND THE URBAN REVOLUTION

A great deal has recently been said about the "urban revolution"—a process of differentiation that split an originally village-centered agrarian society into an urban and a rural sector: town and village. The distinction between town and village considerably interested certain classical economists (Smith, 1937, pp. 373 ff.), including Marx (1953, pp. 381, 382 ff.; 1919, I, 317; III, Part I, 318). Properly employed, it opens up important sociohistorical vistas.

However, those who use it today, either as part of a general developmental scheme or as a means for juxtaposing urban and rural ("folk") culture, tend to disregard two essential methodological precautions. Stress on the revolutionary character of the rise of the town one-sidedly accents what at the most is only one among several features of cultural change. For instance, Childe, who is eager to accustom his readers to the idea of revolution (1952, p. 19), thus promotes historical views that are highly problematic. And his unqualified emphasis on urbanization as a develop-

mental feature bulwarks the thesis of a general evolution in agrarian civilization that is manifestly false. This thesis, which culminates in the concept of a unilinear and necessarily progressive development of society, clearly contradicts the facts of history. It also contradicts the views of the classical economists, who with varying consistency recognized that the higher agrarian civilizations of the "Orient" and their urban and rural conditions followed a pattern of development decidedly unlike that of the West.

A juxtaposition of rural and urban institutions will promote our analysis of agrarian history to the extent to which we realize that there are at least two major types of rural-urban agrarian civilizations—hydraulic and non-hydraulic—and that the primitive farmers who started on an agrohydraulic course initiated a revolution that, structurally and for a whole epoch, split the higher civilizations into two different parts. Prior to the urban revolution and with extraordinary consequences, the fate of agricultural man was profoundly shaped by what may be suitably called the "hydraulic revolution."

* Dr. Wittfogel is Professor of Chinese History, University of Washington, Seattle, and Director of the Chinese History Project, co-sponsored by the University of Washington and Columbia University. He is author of *Wirtschaft und Gesellschaft Chinas*, 1931, and co-author, with Fêng Chia-shêng, of *History of Chinese Society, Liao (907–1125)*, 1949. A recently completed book, *Oriental Despotism and Hydraulic Society* is scheduled for publication in 1956.

MAJOR EFFECTS OF THE HYDRAULIC REVOLUTION

Hydraulic Agriculture

The peculiarities of agrohydraulic civilization become apparent as soon as we realize the role that the management of water has played in the subsistence economy of certain agrarian societies.

To be sure, water is no more essential to agriculture than several other basic factors, such as temperature, the lay of the land, the fertility of the soil, and the character of the cultivable plants. But water is specific in that, among the manipulative essentials, it is the only element which tends to agglomerate in bulk (Wittfogel, 1956, chap. ii). In its agriculturally most precious occurrence —as the water of rivers and large streams in arid or semiarid regions—it therefore defied the small-scale approach which, under preindustrial conditions, was so effective in the treatment of soil and plants. In order to bring fertility to large water-deficient areas by the management of substantial sources of water supply, man had to create large-scale enterprises that usually were operated by the government. The emergence of big productive water works (for irrigation) was frequently accompanied by the emergence of big protective water works (for flood control), and at times the latter even surpassed the former in magnitude and urgency. I suggest that this type of agrarian economy be called "hydraulic agriculture" to distinguish it from rainfall farming and hydroagriculture.

It is customary to apply the term "rainfall agriculture" to a situation in which a favorable climate permits cultivation on the basis of natural precipitation. The term "hydroagriculture" may be applied to a situation in which the members of a farming community resort to irrigation but, because of the scarcity and fragmentation of the available moisture, to irrigation on a small scale only. The term "hydraulic agriculture" may be applied to a situation in which the dimension of the available water supply leads to the creation of large productive and protective water works that are managed by the government.

Institutional Essence of Hydraulic Civilization

Irrigation was practiced in parts of Greece to compensate for the deficiencies of a semiarid climate and in Japan for the cultivation of an aquatic plant— rice. But in both countries a broken terrain permitted the growth of only small irrigation works, which could be handled without government direction. This fact has had far-reaching sociohistorical consequences. Japan established a simple variant of the same feudal society which, in a more complex form, emerged in medieval Europe (Wittfogel, 1956, chap. x). And Greece, prior to the Hellenistic period, developed aristocratic and democratic ways of life. In each case hydroagriculture encouraged the evolution of a multicentered society, an institutional conformation that assumed great significance in the rainfall-based civilizations of feudal Europe.

The contrast between this development and that of the agrohydraulic world is striking. Where agriculture required substantial and centralized works of water control, the representatives of the government monopolized political power and societal leadership, and they dominated their country's economy. By preventing the growth of strong competitive forces, such as a feudal knighthood, an autonomous church, or self-governing guild cities, they were able to make themselves the sole masters of their society. It is this combination of a hydraulic agriculture, a hydraulic government, and a single-centered society that constitutes the institutional essence of hydraulic civilization.

Differentiations

Within the orbit of hydraulic civilization immense cultural differences occur; but this essay cannot elaborate on them.

19

An inquiry dealing with man's impact upon his natural environment may content itself with discussing certain subdivisions of the general institutional order that concern this man-nature relation.

Development in political structure is most consequential when the primitive governments of hydraulic tribes, managed largely by part-time functionaries, evolve into statelike organizations, managed by a body of full-time officials. The hydraulic state provides more comprehensive opportunities for imposing hydraulic installations upon the natural environment, but it also gives the men of the state apparatus the opportunity to neglect water works which will benefit the people, in order to build huge palaces and tombs and process precious organic and inorganic materials which will benefit the rulers.

Development in the patterns of property may lead from a predominance of state control over land and over professional handicraft and trade (simple hydraulic society) to a configuration in which mobile property in industry and trade is largely private, while land remains government controlled (semicomplex hydraulic society), or to a configuration in which private property in land is also widespread (complex hydraulic society). The rise of a semicomplex hydraulic order tends to differentiate the individual producer's interaction with nature; and it furthers the processes of locomotion which overcome difficulties of space and terrain. The rise of private property in land (tenancy as well as ownership) tends to stimulate careful agriculture. The intensive farmers of the ancient Near East were mainly tenants of public (state and temple) lands or of private estates. In China the transition to private land-ownership evoked the comment that the peasants worked less carefully on the public fields than on their own land (Lü, 1936, ch. 17). Chinese peasant farming, which for over two thousand years has been based on private property of land, represents perhaps the most advanced form of intensive agriculture prior to the machine age.

Development in the spatial expansion of the hydraulic state is equally consequential. It is a historical fact that certain non-hydraulic *constructional* patterns and the major *organizational* and *acquisitive* patterns of hydraulic ("Oriental") despotism advanced far beyond the area of hydraulic economy proper. In "loose" hydraulic civilizations, such as China, India, and pre-Spanish Mexico, the monopolistic state apparatus controlled wide areas that had no comprehensive water works and in some cases not even small-scale irrigation.

This aspect was readily accepted by earlier analysts of "Asiatic" society, from the classical economists to Max Weber. But little effort has been made to explain the underlying mechanics of power. Still less analytic attention has been given to the fact that, either through a breakoff from a hydraulic regime proper (later Byzantium) or through institutional transfer (Mongol and post-Mongol Russia and probably Maya society), there may be governments which fulfil few or no agrohydraulic functions but which utilize the organizational methods of hydraulic despotism (such as record-keeping, census-taking, centralized armies, a state system of post and intelligence) as well as its acquisitive methods (such as general labor service, general and heavy taxation, and periodic confiscations) and its legal and political methods (such as fragmentative laws of inheritance and the suppression of independent political organizations) to keep private property weak and the non-bureaucratic forces of society politically impotent.

In fact, so strong were the devices of hydraulic statecraft and social control that they operated successfully in "mar-

ginal" areas without those large-scale water works which persisted in the hydraulic core areas and which apparently were an essential feature in the genesis of all historically relevant agrarian monopoly despotisms. From the standpoint of man's relation to man, the institutional periphery of the hydraulic world has been important in that it enormously widened the range of this despotic order. From the standpoint of man's relation to nature, it has been important in that, like the hydraulic core area, it frustrated the development of a big mechanized industry—the most profound recent change in man's attitude toward his natural environment.

MAN AND NATURE IN HYDRAULIC CIVILIZATION

Having considered the institutional setting of hydraulic civilization, we are now ready to contemplate more closely the specific relations between man and nature within it. These relations involve a peculiar system of mass labor in one segment of the economic order and a peculiar system of intensive work in another.

Government-directed Preparatory Operations: Division of Labor and Co-operation, Bureaucracy, Astronomical and Mathematical Sciences

Hydraulic civilization came into being not through a technological but through an organizational revolution. Its rise necessitated the establishment of a new system of division of labor and co-operation.

Economic historians, when dealing with this matter, frequently assert that until recent times agriculture, in contrast to industry, involved little division of labor and no significant co-operation (Seligman, 1914, p. 350; Sombart, 1927, II, 825 ff.; Marshall, 1946, p. 290; for pioneer formulations see Smith, 1937, p. 6; and Marx, 1919, I, 300, 322 ff.). By and large, this view is justified with regard to the conditions of non-hydraulic farming. But it does not fit the operational pattern of hydraulic agriculture. A major separation between "preparatory labor" (for this term see Mill, 1909, p. 31) and production proper is held to have occurred first in the industrial revolution. Actually, it took place much earlier and on an enormous scale in the hydraulic revolution.

Comprehensive preparatory activities were necessary to make cultivation either possible (in arid areas) or safe and rewarding (in semiarid areas) or specific (in humid areas suitable for the growth of aquatic plants, such as rice and wet taro). The difference between this type of preparatory labor and the preparatory labor employed in modern industry is obvious. In industry preparatory labor provides the ultimate producer with raw material, with auxiliary material (e.g., coal for fuel and oil for lubrication), and also with special tools (machinery). In hydraulic economy preparatory labor consisted essentially in the gathering, conducting, and distributing of one auxiliary material— water. In modern industry the workers who engage in preparatory activities, such as mining, the making of machinery, etc., tend to work full time at their various jobs. In agrohydraulic economy division of labor proceeded differently. The great mass of the men who made and maintained the canals and dikes and who watched for floods did not do so full time and for the greater part of the year but part time and for as short a period as possible. In their overwhelming majority they were farmers, and the very authorities who mobilized them for hydraulic and other *corvée* duties were eager to have them return in good time to their villages to attend properly to the cultivation of their fields.

Thus, like modern industry, hydraulic agriculture involves significant division of labor; but, unlike modern industry, it involves no significant division of laborers. And while the organizers of preparatory work in industry endeavor to achieve their purpose with as small a labor force as possible, the organizers of the hydraulic *corvée* are interested in mobilizing as large a labor force as circumstances permit.

In hydraulic tribes, such as the Suk and Chagga of East Africa and the Pueblo Indians of New Mexico, all able-bodied males participated as a matter of course in the ditch work. In small, state-centered hydraulic civilizations, such as Bali and the early Mesopotamian and Indian city-states, the same mobilization pattern seems to have been customary (Wittfogel, 1956, chap. ii). A list of canal workers in ancient Lagash includes one corviable person from each commoner family (Schneider, 1920, pp. 108 ff.). In an irrigation conflict which, according to a pious legend, led to the Buddha's personal interference, the whole laboring population of the towns involved is said to have engaged in the hydraulic work (Anonymous, n.d., *Jātakam*, p. 441). Even clusters of territorial states may, at times, have gathered their combined populations to execute a big hydraulic task. This appears to have been the case in the Mexican federation prior to the arrival of the Spaniards. And it may have been a recurring trend in countries such as Egypt, where all villages depended on one huge source of irrigation water and where, therefore, their labor forces could be called up, either simultaneously or in shifts, to dig, dam, and watch for floods (Wittfogel, 1956, chap. ii).

In larger hydraulic civilizations varying regional conditions suggested varying patterns of state-directed *corvée* labor, but its mass character remained unchanged. The underlying mobilization principle is drastically formulated by a historian of Mogul economy, Pant (1930, p. 70): "The King by his *firman* (order) could collect any number of men he liked. There was no limit to his massing of labourers, save the number of people in his Empire." Pant was speaking of Mogul India, but his statement is valid for all analogous periods and countries. In hydraulic economy man extended his power over the arid, the semiarid, and certain humid parts of the globe through a government-directed division of labor and a mode of co-operation not practiced in agrarian civilizations of the non-hydraulic type.

The development of such a work pattern meant more than the agglomeration of large numbers of men. To have many persons co-operate periodically and effectively, there had to be planning, record-keeping, communication, and supervision. There had to be organization in depth. And above the tribal level this involved permanent offices and officials to man them—bureaucrats.

Of course, there were scribes in the city-states of ancient Greece and Rome and on the manorial estates, at the courts, and in the church centers of medieval Europe. But there was no national managerial network. In the great Oriental civilizations a hydraulic bureaucracy (*Wasserbau-Bureaukratie* [Weber, 1921–22, p. 117]) emerged together with the new type of organization in depth.

It was in these same Oriental (hydraulic) civilizations that man, in seeking a more rational approach to nature, laid the foundations for several sciences: astronomy, algebra, and geometry. Significantly, Greek mathematics and astronomy drew their early inspiration from the Oriental Near East, and they reached their climax under Euclid, Heron, and Ptolemy, not in Greece, but in one of the foremost centers of hydraulic culture—Egypt (Wittfogel, 1931, p. 682).

To be sure, neither the bureaucratic nor the scientific possibilities of hydraulic civilization were always exhausted. Some simpler hydraulic civilizations did not advance far. But the major hydraulic centers created elaborate administrations, and their astronomical and mathematical accomplishments were impressive. Thus any attempt to define hydraulic man's relation to nature must also consider the organizational (bureaucratic) and the scientific aspects of hydraulic economy.

Irrigation Farming with Intensive Labor and Special Operations of Tillage

Government management of the great hydraulic works is supplemented by intensive farming based on irrigation. As stated above, irrigation farming also occurs in certain non-hydraulic societies, and to this extent the subsequent statements have validity beyond the borders of hydraulic civilization. But, while irrigation farming occurs occasionally in the non-hydraulic agricultural world, it is essential in the core areas of hydraulic civilization.

Irrigation demands a treatment of soil and water that is not customary in rainfall farming. The typical irrigation peasant has (1) to dig and re-dig ditches and furrows; (2) to terrace the land if it is uneven; (3) to raise the moisture if the level of the water supply is below the surface of the fields; and (4) to regulate the flow of the water from the source to the goal, directing its ultimate application to the crop. Tasks (1) and (4) are essential to all irrigation farming proper (inundation farming requires damming rather than ditching). Task (3) is also a frequent one, for, except at the time of high floods, the level of water tends to lie below that of the cultivated fields.

The type and amount of work involved in these operations become clear when we contrast the labor budget of an Oriental irrigation farmer with that of a rainfall farmer of medieval Europe. The medieval peasant usually plowed his field once or twice, then he sowed

(Parain, 1942, p. 142; cf. Maitland, 1921, pp. 398 ff.; Lamprecht, 1886, p. 557), and he harvested his crop at the end of the season. As a rule he spent no time watering.

The irrigation farmer, who, of course, plows, sows, and harvests, is in addition burdened with a number of other chores. In regions like Egypt, which depended mainly on inundation, these activities were insignificant, yet such regions were not very numerous. In others, such as ancient Mesopotamia, inundation was supplemented by canal irrigation. In this case a considerable amount of time was devoted to the watering of the fields (Meissner, 1920, pp. 192, 194). In modern India the husbandmen of a Punjab village spend much time irrigating their crops, wheat receiving three to four waterings in January, February, and March during more than twenty days. This work period is the most time-consuming item listed in the year's agricultural calendar (Singh, 1928, pp. 33–36, 38). Sugar cane is an old Indian crop, requiring a great deal of water. In certain Deccan villages favoring its cultivation, the total cost of plowing, harrowing, planting, harvesting, and related operations is about 97 rupees as against 157 rupees for watering (Mann and Kanitkar, 1920, p. 86). In a South Gujarat village, studied by Mukhtyar (1930, p. 96), watering is by far the heaviest expense item in the labor budget of the grower of sugar cane.

Concerning Chinese traditional irrigation economy, Buck has provided us with valuable numerical data. In 1923, 152 farms in Pinghsiang (in present Hopeh Province) grew wheat as their main crop. Of the time devoted to this crop, the peasant spent 10.2 per cent in plowing, 1.7 per cent in harrowing, 9.2 per cent in harvesting, or altogether 21.1 per cent, as against 58.5 per cent in irrigating (Buck, 1930, p. 306). In 1924 two groups of farmers in Kiangsu Province spent 21 and 25.1 per cent, respectively, in plowing, harrowing, and harvesting their main rice crop, as against 18.1 and 39.6 per cent in its irrigation (*ibid.*, p. 310). As may be expected, the labor budgets show great variation in detail, but they all reveal that the amount of work involved in watering operations is commonly far in excess of the combined operations of a non-irrigation farmer.

Repeated preparatory tillage—plowing or hoeing—was also undertaken by the rainfall farmers of feudal Europe (Cole and Mathews, 1938, pp. 324 ff.). But it was primarily on the manorial domain that the fields were "worked" three or four times, while the "poor peasants could often only work their land once to the detriment of the yield" (Parain, 1942, p. 141; cf. Lamprecht, 1886, p. 557).

Except for some cutting of thistles (Parain, 1942, pp. 144 ff.; Kulischer, 1928, p. 160), intertillage was then, as now, technically impossible for grain crops, because, under conditions of rainfall farming, these "can be grown satisfactorily and most economically by planting them in solid stands so that they cover all the ground equally." As a rule, they are today "given no tillage while they are growing" (Cole and Mathews, 1938, p. 327).

Plants grown in rows are easily approached and easily cultivated. But the most important of these, corn and potatoes, appeared in Europe only after the discovery of America, and even after the sixteenth century their economic importance remained definitely secondary to that of the cereals. In the West the modern dry farmer still hesitates to cultivate grain crops in rows. After an early harrowing he frequently lets nature take its course (Widtsoe, 1913, pp. 163 ff.).

Irrigation agriculture requires a row-like arrangement of the seeds not only for crops such as corn and potatoes but also for cereals. Plants can be watered by ditches only if proper space for the distributing furrows is provided. The layout of the fields differs in accordance with economic experience, crops, and terrain, but all patterns aim at making the plants accessible to the irrigation farmer, who may work the soil and the crop as thoroughly as he wishes.

Intensive techniques are not limited to the period between sowing and harvesting. Frequently the soil is plowed or harrowed several times before the sowing. Nor are these techniques limited to the fields for which irrigation water is available. In semiarid areas (under conditions of full aridity cultivation ends where the water supply ends) the farmers are eager to grow not only crops which they can water but also crops which may mature without the benefit of irrigation.

Chinese farmers in the province of Kiangsu who had sufficient water for two main crops only, rice and vegetables, used to grow wheat and barley without irrigation. However, they treated the last two as intensively as the first two. Of all labor devoted to wheat, intertillage accounted for over 20 per cent; in the case of barley, it accounted for almost 33 per cent; and in the case of kaoliang, which in some parts of Hopeh is grown without irrigation, it accounted for more than 40 per cent (Buck, 1930, p. 306).

In India certain Deccan villages grow their main cereal crop, *bajri*, also without irrigation. But, like the irrigated cereals, it is planted in rows and intensively cultivated. It gets one plowing and four harrowings before sowing and further treatment after sowing (Mann and Kanitkar, 1920, pp. 72 ff.).

The good Aztec farmer made beds for his corn, pulverized the soil, and kept his crop free of weeds (Sahagun, 1938, p. 39). He irrigated whenever this was possible, but he obviously was expected to farm intensively under any circumstances. The Mayan peasants of Yucatán, who did not water their crops, weeded them as carefully as did the inhabitants of the highland regions in which irrigation farming was customary.

Thus, as the political patterns of hydraulic civilization spread far beyond the areas of hydraulic economy, so the techniques of irrigation farming spread far beyond the irrigated fields. These techniques established an agronomical relation among man, soil, and plants that, in terms of a given amount of land, was much more rewarding than the agriculture of preindustrial Europe. Early in the twentieth century a European agronomist found the Indian peasants, who by and large followed their traditional pattern of cultivation, quite as good as the average modern British farmer and in some respects better (Anonymous, 1909, p. 6). The father of organic chemistry, Justus von Liebig, in comparing nineteenth-century German agriculture with contemporary Chinese farming, viewed the former as the procedure of "a child compared to that of a mature and experienced man" (Liebig, 1878, p. 453).

Demographic Consequences

In some ways Liebig's statement touches upon problems that lie outside the concern of the biochemist. But he was quite right in noting the greater refinement—and better results—of hydraulic agriculture as practiced in China. Whatever its deficiencies, this method of farming produced great quantities of food on a given acreage, and it permitted the individual peasant to support his family on a very small farmstead. For this reason the areas of intensive hydraulic farming came to support extremely dense populations.

In preconquest America relatively small hydraulic regions comprised about 75 per cent of America's total population (Kroeber, 1939, p. 166; Ro-

senblat, 1945, pp. 188 ff., 202 ff.; Kubler, 1946, p. 339; for a considerably higher estimate of the population of the Inca Empire see Rowe, 1946, p. 185). Beloch's classical estimates (1886, p. 507) for the time of Augustus assume a much greater density for the Asian provinces of the Roman Empire (thirty persons per square kilometer) than for the European provinces (ten persons per square kilometer). The contrast becomes even more spectacular when we juxtapose his figures for Augustan Greece (eleven) and Italy (twenty-four) with those of Egypt (one hundred and seventy-nine). More recent studies (Premerstein, 1936, p. 56; Rostovtzeff, 1941, II, 1138; III, 1605) suggest a still higher figure for Egypt, namely, about two hundred and eighty persons per square kilometer.

The population distribution in contemporary Han China was not unlike that of the Roman Empire. The old Chinese territories of the north seem to have been as densely populated as Rome's eastern provinces, while the hydraulic core areas of the Han world showed demographic trends similar to those of their western counterparts, Egypt and Babylonia (Lao, 1935, pp. 216 ff.).

The dimension of the Oriental cities expresses both the productivity of hydraulic agriculture and the acquisitive power of its administrative centers. While, in classical days, Athens may have had 120,000 inhabitants, Corinth 70,000, and the majority of all Greek cities between 5,000 and 10,000 persons (Beloch, 1886, p. 478), Hellenistic Ephesus may have harbored 225,000 people (*ibid.*, p. 231), Antioch 500,000 (*ibid.*, p. 479; Kahrstedt, 1924, p. 663; Rostovtzeff, 1941, I, 498), Seleuceia 600,000 (Beloch, 1886, p. 479; Rostovtzeff, 1941, I, 498; II, 1140), and Alexandria at the end of the Hellenistic period the same number (Rostovtzeff, 1941, II, 1139 ff.). The recently published "gerusia acts" lead Rostovtzeff (*ibid.*, p. 1139; cf. Premerstein, 1936, p. 56) to conclude that for A.D. 37 the total population of the Egyptian capital "must be estimated at one million at least."

It is also illuminating to compare these figures with estimates for metropolitan populations in pre-Spanish America and feudal Europe. Prevailing expert opinion credits Cuzco with 200,-000 and Mexico City with 300,000 inhabitants (Rosenblat, 1945, pp. 205, 191). Some cities of Moorish Spain may have housed several hundred thousand persons, and the capital, Cordova, at its peak, a million (Wittfogel, 1956, chap. vi; cf. also al-Makkari, 1840, pp. 214 ff.). In contrast, in the fourteenth century the most populous city north of the Alps seems to have had 35,000 inhabitants (London), while other major English cities comprised 11,000 (York), 9,500 (Bristol), or between 7,000 and 5,000 persons (Rogers, 1884, p. 117). At the beginning of the fifteenth century the foremost city of the Hanseatic League, Lübeck, had 22,300 inhabitants and Frankfurt 10,000. Other big German towns of this century sheltered between 20,000 and 10,000 persons, Leipzig 4,000 and Dresden 3,200 (Büchner, 1922, p. 382).

Chinese census data have been discussed at length. What should be remembered is that these data were compiled primarily for fiscal reasons. Since tax payments had to agree with the announced population, the census records tended to represent not the actual but the admitted population, that is, the lowest figures the regional officials dared to submit (Wittfogel and Fêng, 1949, p. 53). Weak regimes got understatements, and tougher and more effective governments more realistic accounts. Two decades ago Buck, on the basis of a comprehensive rural survey, obtained population figures about 23 per cent higher than the official data.

He hesitated to press his findings, but he stated that, if his higher figures were used, "the total would be over 600 million" (1937, p. 363). The first census taken by the new Communist government claims a total mainland population of almost 600 million persons.

Much more could be said on this subject. But the just-cited data fit with our other information on Oriental demography. Obviously, the hydraulic way of life permitted an accumulation of rural and urban populations which, though paralleled in a few non-hydraulic territories of small-scale irrigation, such as Japan, has not been matched by the higher agrarian civilizations based on rainfall farming.

DIMENSIONS OF HYDRAULIC CIVILIZATION IN TIME, SPACE, AND MANPOWER

According to conservative estimates, hydraulic civilizations took shape in the ancient Near East not later than the fourth millennium B.C., and they persisted until very recent times. It may therefore be said safely that in this area hydraulic civilization endured for about five millenniums.

The great hydraulic civilizations of India and China maintained themselves for some three or four millenniums. And recent archeological finds suggest that in certain areas of the Western Hemisphere, such as Peru, hydraulic civilizations may have existed at least since the first millennium B.C., that is, for more than two millenniums prior to the arrival of the Spaniards.

Neither ancient Greece nor feudal Europe nor Japan can equal these figures. Greek agrarian civilization seems to have lasted for a millennium until Hellenistic despotism put an end to its non-Oriental pattern. The societies of feudal Europe and Japan had an even shorter duration.

The core areas and the margins of the hydraulic civilizations covered the greater part of western, southern, and eastern Asia. The Hellenistic regimes, the Orientalized Roman Empire, the Arab conquests of Spain and Sicily, and the Byzantine, Turkish, and Russian expansions imposed Orientally despotic regimes on large areas of Europe.

In Africa north of the Sahara, a hydraulic way of life prevailed for millenniums. A thousand years ago it seems to have spread temporarily from Lake Tanganyika and Kenya to Rhodesia (Huntingford, 1933, pp. 153, 159 ff.; Wilson, 1932, pp. 252 ff.; Hall and Neal, 1904, pp. 356 ff.; Randall-MacIver, 1906, pp. 12 ff.). In recent times it was observed among the Chagga and a few other tribes of central East Africa.

Hydraulic agriculture and government persisted in some major Pacific islands, such as Hawaii. In pre-Columbian America hydraulic developments spread beyond the Rio Grande in the north. In the Meso-American highlands and in the lowlands of Yucatán, clusters of loose and marginal hydraulic civilizations emerged. And in the south hydraulic expansion reached its maximum on the eve of the Spanish conquest. Early in the sixteenth century the Inca Empire stretched from Peru to Ecuador in the north and to Bolivia and Chile in the west and south. It co-ordinated practically all important centers of higher agrarian development in South America. Clearly, hydraulic civilizations covered a vastly larger proportion of the surface of the globe than all other significant agrarian civilizations taken together.

The demographic dimension of the hydraulic world has already been indicated. According to our present information, it would seem that, prior to the commercial and industrial revolution, the majority of all human beings lived within the orbit of hydraulic civilization.

COSTS AND PERSPECTIVES OF HYDRAULIC CIVILIZATION

Manifestly, then, this civilization was an eminently successful "going concern." It stimulated organization in depth. It gave birth to certain sciences. And it refined farming and handicraft. Yet, in terms of human affairs, it was as costly as it was tenacious. While such scientific aids to counting and measuring as astronomy and mathematics emerged, these developments eventually stalled, and the experimental sciences never gained significance. Masses of men were co-ordinated for public works and warfare, but the patterns of integration were crude, and they improved little throughout the centuries. Farming techniques were subtle, but from the standpoint of the main protagonist, the peasant, their one-sidedly labor-intensive development was frustrating. Hydraulic agriculture made the cultivator till his fields with a minimum of labor-saving tools and animals and with a maximum of human labor. Being politically without influence, the hydraulic farmer maintained a man-nature relation that involved unending drudgery on a socially and culturally depressing level.

Aristotle's vision of a society of free men based on the advance of the mechanical arts is increasingly being realized in the multicentered industrial societies of the West. It never materialized in hydraulic society. For reasons inherent in this institutional conformation, the masters of hydraulic civilization succeeded in perpetuating the economic and technological order which was the *raison d'être* for their existence.

REFERENCES

Anonymous
1909　*Imperial Gazetteer of India,* Vol. III. Oxford: Clarendon Press. 520 pp.

N.d.　*Jātakam: Das Buch der Erzählungen aus früheren Existenzen Buddhas,* Vol. V. Trans. by Julius Dutoit. Munich: Oskar Schloss. 608 pp.

Beloch, Julius
1886　*Die Bevölkerung der griechisch-römischen Welt.* Leipzig: Duncker & Humblot. 520 pp.

Buck, John Lossing
1930　*Chinese Farm Economy.* Nanking: University of Nanking; Chicago: University of Chicago Press. 476 pp.

1937　*Land Utilization in China.* Chicago: University of Chicago Press. 494 pp.

Bücher, Karl
1922　*Die Entstehung der Volkswirtschaft,* Vol. I. Tübingen: H. Laupp. 475 pp.

Childe, V. Gordon
1952　*Man Makes Himself.* New York: Mentor Books. 192 pp.

Cole, John S., and Mathews, O. R.
1938　"Tillage," pp. 321–28 in U.S. Department of Agriculture, *Soils and Men: Yearbook of Agriculture.* Washington, D.C.: Government Printing Office. 1232 pp.

Hall, Richard Nicklin, and Neal, W. S.
1904　*The Ancient Ruins of Rhodesia.* London: Methuen & Co. 404 pp.

Huntingford, G. W. B.
1933　"The Azanian Civilization of Kenya," *Antiquity,* VII, No. 26, 153–65.

Kahrstedt, Ulrich
1924　"Die Bevölkerung des Altertums," *Handwörterbuch der Staatswissenschaften,* II, 655–70. 4th ed. Jena.

Kroeber, A. L.
1939　*Cultural and Natural Areas of Native North America.* Berkeley: University of California Press. 242 pp.

Kubler, George
1946　"The Quechua in the Colonial World," pp. 331–410 in Steward, Julian H. (ed.), *Handbook of South American Indians,* Vol. II. (Smithsonian Institution, Bureau of American Ethnology, Bulletin No. 143.) Washington, D.C.: Government Printing Office. 976 pp.

Kulischer, Josef
1928　*Allgemeine Wirtschaftsgeschichte des Mittelalters und der Neuzeit,* Vol. I: *Das Mittelalter.* Munich and Berlin: R. Oldenbourgh. 351 pp.

Lamprecht, Karl G.
1886　*Deutsches Wirtschaftsleben im Mittelalter: Untersuchungen über die Entwicklung der materiellen Kultur des platten Landes auf Grund der Quellen zunächst des Mosellandes,* Vol. I, No. 1. Leipzig: Alphons Dürr. 663 pp.

Lao Kan
1935　"Liang Han chün-kuo mien-chi chih ku-chi chi k'ou-shu tsêng-chien chih t'ui-ts'ê," *Academia sinica,* V, No. 2, 215–40. Peking.

Liebig, Justus von
1878　*Chemische Briefe.* 6th ed. Leipzig and Heidelberg: Carl Winters. 479 pp.

[Lü]
1936　*Lü-shih ch'un-ch'iu* ("Mr. Lü's Spring and Autumn Annals"), in *Ssǔ-pu Pei-yao.* Chung-hua ed. Shanghai. 770 pp.

Maitland, Frederic William
1921　*Domesday Book and Beyond.* Cambridge: Cambridge University Press. 527 pp.

al-Makkari, Ahmed ibn Mohammed
1840　*The History of the Mohammedan Dynasties in Spain: extracted from the "Nafhu-t-tíb min Ghosni-l-Andalusi-r-rattíb wa Táríkh Lisánu-d-dín Ibni-l-khattíb,"* Vol. I. Trans. from the Arabic by Pascual de Gayangos y Arce. London: Oriental Translation Fund. 548 pp.

Mann, Harold H., and Kanitkar, N. V.
1920　*Land and Labour in a Deccan Village.* ("University of Bombay Economic Series," No. III.) London and Bombay: H. Milford and Oxford University Press. 182 pp.

Marshall, Alfred
1946　*Principles of Economics.* London: Macmillan & Co. 871 pp.

MARX, KARL
1919   *Das Kapital*, Vols. I and III, Part I. Hamburg. Otto Meissner. 739+ 448 pp.
1953   *Grundrisse der Kritik der politischen Oekonomie (Rohentwurf)*. Berlin: Dietz. 1,102 pp.

MEISSNER, BRUNO
1920   *Babylonien und Assyrien*, Vol. I. Heidelberg: Carl Winters. 466 pp.

MILL, JOHN STUART
1909   *Principles of Political Economy*. London and New York: Longmans, Green & Co. 1,013 pp.

MUKHTYAR, G. C.
1930   *Life and Labour in a South Gujarat Village*. Ed. C. N. VAKIL. London and New York: Longmans, Green & Co. 304 pp.

PANT, D.
1930   *The Commercial Policy of the Moguls*. Bombay: D. B. Taraporevala Sons & Co. 281 pp.

PARAIN, CHARLES
1942   "The Evolution of Agricultural Technique," pp. 118–68 in CLAPHAM, J. H. and POWER, E, (eds.), *Cambridge Economic History*, Vol. 1. 2 vols. Cambridge: Cambridge University Press.

PREMERSTEIN, ANTON VON
1936   *Alexandrinische Geronten vor Kaiser Gajus*. ("Mitteilungen der Papyrussammlung der Giessener Universitätsbibliothek," Monograph V.) Giessen. 71 pp.

RANDALL-MACIVER, DAVID
1906   *Mediaeval Rhodesia*. London and New York: Macmillan & Co. 106 pp.

ROGERS, JAMES E. THOROLD
1884   *Six Centuries of Work and Wages*. New York: G. P. Putnam's Sons. 591 pp.

ROSENBLAT, ÁNGEL
1945   *La Población indígena de América desde 1492 hasta la actualidad*. Buenos Aires: Institución Cultural Española. 295 pp.

ROSTOVTZEFF, M.
1941   *The Social and Economic History of the Hellenistic World*. 3 vols. Oxford: Clarendon Press. 1,779 pp.

ROWE, JOHN HOWLAND
1946   "Inca Culture at the Time of the Spanish Conquest," pp. 183–330 in STEWARD, JULIAN H. (ed.), *Handbook of South American Indians*, Vol. II. (Smithsonian Institution, Bureau of American Ethnology, Bulletin No. 143.) Washington, D.C.: Government Printing Office. 976 pp.

SAHAGUN, BERNARDINO DE
1938   *Historia general de las cosas de Nueva España*, Vol. III. Mexico, D.F.: Pedro Robredo. 390 pp.

SCHNEIDER, ANNA
1920   *Die Anfänge der Kulturwirtschaft: Die sumerische Tempelstadt*. Essen: G. D. Baedeker. 120 pp.

SELIGMAN, EDWIN R. A.
1914   *Principles of Economics*. New York and London: Longmans, Green & Co. 711 pp.

SINGH, SARDAR GIAN
1928   *An Economic Survey of Gaggar Bhana, a Village in the Amritsar District of the Punjab*. (Board of Economic Inquiry, Punjab, Conducted by . . . under the Supervision of M. KING . . . [Rural Section Publication No. 16], "Punjab Village Survey," Vol. I.) Lahore. 235 pp.

SMITH, ADAM
1937   *An Inquiry into the Nature and Causes of the Wealth of Nations*. New York: Modern Library. 976 pp.

SOMBART, WERNER
1927   *Das Wirtschaftsleben im Zeitalter des Hochkapitalismus*. 2 vols. Munich and Leipzig: Duncker & Humblot. 1,064 pp.

WEBER, MAX
1921–22   *Wirtschaft und Gesellschaft: Grundriss der Sozialökonomik*. 2 vols. Tübingen: J. C. B. Mohr. 840 pp.

WIDTSOE, JOHN A
1913   *Dry-Farming: A System of Agriculture for Countries under a Low Rainfall*. New York: Macmillan Co. 445 pp.

WILSON, G. E. H.
1932   "The Ancient Civilization of the Rift Valley," *Man*, XXXII, No. 298, 250–57.

WITTFOGEL, KARL A.
  1931 *Wirtschaft und Gesellschaft Chinas.* Leipzig: C. L. Hirschfeld. 768 pp.
  1956 *Oriental Despotism and Hydraulic Society.* (In press.)
WITTFOGEL, KARL A., and FÊNG CHIA-SHÊNG

  1949 *History of Chinese Society, Liao (907–1125).* (*Transactions of the American Philosophical Society,* Vol. XXXVI.) New York: Macmillan Co. 752 pp.

Influence of Terrain on Man
II

Weaving through the fabric of nature is the repetitive theme of duality. One of the fundamental laws of physics, the second law of thermodynamics, indicates that for every action there is an equal and opposite reaction. In chemistry there are positive and negative particle charges, and in the realm of astrophysics there is much discussion about matter and antimatter. Man's relation to nature also has components of this reciprocal phenomenon, because not only does nature greatly influence man's activities and his history, but man also modifies and transforms nature. In this part the manner in which man is influenced by nature is explored, whereas in a later section the impact of man on nature will be discussed. The articles by H. E. Barnes and by E. C. Semple are provided to illustrate some of the typical large-scale adjustments and decisions by man when nature dominates the decision-making process (see also Brunhes, 1952). However, nature can play other roles in the constitution of man, and influence his spirit and even perhaps his constitution.

The usual view of conservation relates the concept in a physical sense, but nature has also had an indelible imprint on man in a literal sense of the human spirit and been preserved in myths, stories, religion, habits, and life styles of people. In much of the ancient world nature was given god-like qualities in a superanthropomorphic manner. This mental control of nature over man caused him to make a wide range of decisions in which the slightest signs and omens were watched in the sun, moon, stars, wind, weather, etc., for the most propitious time to take a trip, plant seed, harvest, set sail, etc. In his book *Landscape in History,* Sir Archibald Geikie discusses this duality of nature, and states:

> The landscapes of a country, the form, height, and trend of mountain-ranges, the position and extent of its plains and valleys, the size and direction of its rivers, the varying nature of its soils and climate, the presence or absence of useful minerals, nearness to or distance from the sea, the shape of the coast-line whether rocky or precipitous, or indented with creeks

31

and harbors—all these and other aspects of the scenery of the land have contributed their share to the moulding of national history and character. (pp. 1–2)

Hence the problems presented by the more impressive details of the scenery of the earth's surface were in truth among the earliest with which the human race began to deal. If we try to discover how they were first approached, and how their treatment varied, not only with peculiarities of race and national temperament, but with conditions of climate and variations of topography, we are led backward into the study of some of the most venerable efforts of the human imagination, which, though now in large measure faded or vanished, may yet be in some slight degree recovered from the oldest mythologies and superstitions. In many of the earlier myths we may recognize primitive attempts to account for some of the more prominent features of landscape or of climate. (p. 29–30)

Typical of such myths are some of those in India where Pillai and Panikar (1965, p. 14) report: "Popular mythology has it that the whole of Kerala was reclaimed from the sea by the legendary hero Parasurama. The accounts of Kerala in the writings of early geographers like Pliny and Ptolemy lend colour to the view that large parts of Kerala were once submerged under water."

Geikie (1905) points out that in time myths gave way to new forms of literary expression, and:

From that time onward the influence of scenery on the human imagination took a different course. The gods were dethroned, and the invisible spirits of nature no longer found worshippers; but it was impossible that the natural features which had prompted the primeval beliefs should cease to exercise a potent influence on the minds of men. This influence has varied in degree and in character from generation to generation . . . in the literature of successive periods. (p. 31)

To illustrate these points Geikie shows how the "placid scenery" of the eastern lowlands of England influenced the literary progress of the nation.

The simple child-like delight in Nature, so characteristic of Chaucer, and the influence of cultivated scenery, so conspicuous in him, are readily traceable among his successors. Shakespeare throughout his plays presents us with not a few reminiscences of his youth among the Warwickshire woodlands. In Milton we see how the placid rural quiet of the Colne valley inspired the two finest lyrics in the English tongue. (p. 83)

In similar manner Geikie shows the influence of the English–Scotch border country with its rivers, glens, and dales.

These streams, with their endless changes of aspect, their variations from season to season, their play of sunshine and shadow . . . had a strong hold on the affections of Robert Burns. His best inspiration came to him from them.

'We'll gar our streams and burnies shine
     Up wi' the best
We'll sing auld Coila's plains an' fells,
Her moors red-brown wi' heather-bells,
Her banks an' braes, her dens an' dells.'

For the first time in English literature the burning ardour of a passionate soul went out in tumultuous joy towards Nature. The hills and woods, the streams and dells were to Burns not merely enjoyable scenes to be visited and described. They became part of his very being. (p. 96–97)

A different aspect of the environmental influence on man concerns his own physical characteristics and racial traits. Such topics are complex and controversial, but one of the first to give such ideas respectability was Hippocrates (c. 460–370 B.C.,), a Greek born on the island of Cos. He became known as the founder of the school of the scientific art of healing and instituted the first beginnings in comparative ethnography. He gathered and described medical traditions of his time while traveling throughout Greece and the 72 works that bear his name contain both practical and theoretical aspects of a wide range of topics dealing with man, his illnesses, diseases, and character. The Hippocratic Oath, although written before his time, embodies his ideals and is a tribute to the esteem he obtained as the leading physician of the ancient world. In his "Airs, Waters, Places" (Jones, 1957) Hippocrates discusses how those who wish to pursue the science of medicine must consider such features as effects of seasons, of hot and cold winds, properties of the waters, position of the winds and risings of the sun.

> He must consider with greatest care both these things and how the natives are off for water, whether they use marshy, soft waters, or such as are hard and come from rocky heights, or brackish and harsh. The soil too, whether bare or dry or wooded and watered, hollow and hot or high and cold. (p. 71)

He discusses "the dwellers on the Phasis" who live in marshes and make little use of walking, drink stagnant water, and eat imperfect fruit.

> For these causes, therefore, the physique of the Phasians is different from that of other folk. They are tall in stature, and of a gross habit of body, while neither joint nor vein is visible. Their complexion is yellowish, as though they suffered from jaundice. (p. 113)

Hippocrates describes how the Scythians live where the plains are high and bare and the climate rigors change very little throughout the year.

> They are stunted owing to the severe climate and the bareness of the land, where there is neither warmth nor shelter. And the changes of the seasons are neither great nor violent, the seasons being uniform and altering little. Wherefore the men also are like one another in physique . . . (p. 121–123)

He also contrasts Europeans with Asians, and believed Europe had more climatic variation.

In such a climate arise wildness, unsociability and spirit. For the frequent shocks to the mind impart wildness, destroying tameness and gentleness . . . For uniformity engenders slackness, while variation fosters endurance in both body and soul. Wherefore Europeans are more warlike, and . . . their institutions . . . not being under kings as are Asiatics. (p. 133)

He concludes his treatise by stating:

These are the most important factors that create differences in men's constitutions; next come the land in which a man is reared, and the water. For in general you will find assimilated to the nature of the land both the physique and the characteristics of the inhabitants. For where the land is rich, soft, and well-watered, and the water is very near the surface, so as to be hot in summer and cold in winter, and if the situation be favourable as regards the seasons, there the inhabitants are fleshy, ill-articulated, moist, lazy, and generally cowardly in character. Slackness and sleepiness can be observed in them, and as far as the arts are concerned they are thickwitted, and neither subtle nor sharp. But where the land is bare, waterless, rough, oppressed by winter's storms and burnt by the sun, there you will see men who are hard, lean, well-articulated, well-braced, and hairy; such natures will be found energetic, vigilant, stubborn and independent in character and in temper, wild rather than tame, of more than average sharpness and intelligence in the arts, and in war of more than average courage. The things also that grow in the earth all assimilate themselves to the earth. Such are the most sharply contrasted natures and physiques. Take these observations as a standard when drawing all other conclusions, and you will make no mistake. (p. 137)

The following two articles were selected to illustrate man's involvement and preoccupation with his physical world. The Barnes paper provides a generalized treatment of the topic throughout history and includes the evaluation of past events in the environmental framework. This contrasts with the Semple chapter which describes in depth how a certain range of landforms has controlled man's societal patterns, settlement locations, and fortunes.

Harry E. Barnes (1889–1968) was born in Cooperstown, New York, and received his Ph.D. (1918) from Harvard University. He taught at several institutions including Columbia University, Clark University, Amherst College, and Smith College. He was a specialist in the history of western thought and culture, and so his article provides a fine review of environmental influences on the affairs of man and how they are chronicled.

Ellen C. Semple (1863–1932) was born in Louisville, Kentucky. She served on the faculty at the University of Chicago from 1906–1923, and then became Professor of Anthropogeography at Clark University until her death. She coauthored another book (Semple and Jones, 1933) which details the environmental influences on the history and development of man's settlement patterns and affairs in the United States—including military events. The book from which the following selection is taken is one of the earliest and most comprehensive English treatments on the influence of terrain and water on decisions of man. Her style is patterned after Ratzel who initiated the school of thought that became known as "anthropogeography."

The JOURNAL *of* GEOGRAPHY

VOLUME XX   DECEMBER, 1921   NUMBER 9

THE RELATION OF GEOGRAPHY TO THE WRITING AND INTERPRETATION OF HISTORY*

HARRY ELMER BARNES, PH. D.

Professor of History, Clark University

BRIEF SKETCH OF THE THEORIES REGARDING THE INFLUENCE OF GEOGRAPHY UPON THE HISTORICAL DEVELOPMENT OF PEOPLES

Many historians have been startled by what they regarded as the unique and original doctrines of Ellsworth Huntington calling attention to the relation between geography and certain aspects of history, but, as a matter of fact, this approach to the interpretation of the progress of society is as old as history itself.[1]   The subject was first systematically discussed by the contemporary of Herodotus and Thucydides, the phsyician Hippocrates of Cos (c. 460-370 B.C.), in his work on "Airs, Waters, and Places."   While primarily concerned with the relation between environment and the patho-genesis of disease, Hippocrates digressed into a discussion of the relation of geographical surrounding to the character of peoples, and presented an interesting account of the effect of climate and topography upon the physical characteristics and the political tendencies of the peoples of Asia and southeastern Europe.[2]   Aristotle found a geographical explanation for the assumed superiority of the Greeks over the barbarians.   He contended that by virtue of their intermediate geographical position the Greeks were able to combine the superior mental attainments of southern peoples and the greater bravery of northerners, while escaping the fickleness of the southerners and the stupidity of the inhabitants of cold climates.[3]   Strabo (64 B.C.–19 A.D.) was

---

* Revision of a paper prepared for the spring meeting of the New England Teachers' Association, Clark University, March 19, 1921.

[1] A brief and ill-proportioned survey of the history of this subject is contained in A. H. Koller's, The Theory of Environment.   The authoritative survey is in preparation by J. Franklin Thomas.   Much of value on the earlier period is to be found in A. Meuten's Bodin's Theorie von der Beinflussung des politischen Lebens durch ihre geographische Lage.

[2] Works of Hippocrates, trans. by Adams, London, 1841, Vol. I, pp. 190-222.

[3] Politics, Jowett's translation, II, 7.

not only the greatest geographer of antiquity; he also contributed much of value on the theory of the relation between topography, climate and civilization, as well as presenting much descriptive material on the environments of the leading contemporary peoples.[4]

The Roman writers made use of environmental doctrine to explain the alleged superiority of the Roman polity and culture. Cicero (106–43 B.C.) pointed to the excellent strategic position and the topographic advantages of the city of Rome, while Vitruvius (c. 30 B.C.) commented upon the favorable climate and astral influences of Italy.[5] Vegetius (c. 375 A.D.) attempted to explain the military prowess of various nations on the basis of the influences radiating from their differing geographical environments.[6] Paul the Deacon (725-800) in his "History of the Lombards" discussed the relation of geographical environment to the characteristics of the Germanic barbarians.[7]

In the medieval period St. Thomas Aquinas (1227-1274) revived the doctrines of Aristotle on the question of environmental influences and gave them vogue among scholastic philosophers.[8] The Arab historian, Ibn Khaldun (1332-1406), combined the Arabian appropriation of Aristotle with the progress of geographical science among the Arabs in what was the most thoro analysis of geographical influences upon human society which had appeared down to his time.[9] The French political philosopher and historian, Jean Bodin (1530-1596), contended that their geographic situation had made the French the foremost nation of the world, and analyzed in some detail the effect of topography and climate upon the inhabitants of a geographical region.[10] The chief defect in these early doctrines was that they were based upon fallacious scientific postulates, namely the Greek physical philosophy and physiological chemistry and the belief in astrology. When they attempted an ultimate explanation of geographical influences these writers resorted to the doctrine of the four elements in

---

[4] H. F. Tozer: History of Ancient Geography; Selections from Strabo; and the English translation of Strabo's Geography in the Bohn library.

[5] Cicero: De republica, 1, 3; Vitruvius: The Ten Books on Architecture, trans. by Morgan, Book VI, Chap. I.

[6] Vegetius: De re militari, 1, 2.

[7] Paul the Deacon: History of the Langobards, trans. by W. D. Foulke.

[8] Aquinas: De regimine principum, II, i-iv.

[9] Ibn Khaldun: Prolégomènes historiques, trans. by M. G. De Slane. Cf. R. Flint: History of the Philosophy of History in France, 1894, pp. 158 ff.

[10] Jean Bodin: The Six Bookes of a Commonweale, trans. by Richard Knolles, Book V, Chap. I, Cf. Meuten, op. cit. Fournol, Bodin, prédécesseur de Montesquieu; Flint: op. cit. pp. 190–200.

man's bodily constitution, the four humors which determined his health, and the influence of astral bodies on the constitution and the destiny of man.   Between the time of Bodin and that of Montesquieu (1689-1755), Boyle, Stahl and other seventeenth century scientists had destroyed the grotesque body of Greek physical philosophy and established the inductive or experimental method in science.   Tycho Brahe, Galileo and Kepler had discredited astrology.   Hence, tho Montesquieu may have in part formulated his doctrines of geographic determinism from experimentation as to the effect of heat and cold upon a sheep's tongue, such procedure marked a great advance over Empedocles and astrological hypotheses.   Richard Mead, an English physician of note, under the influence of Isaac Newton's scientific discoveries, composed the first modern treatise on the effect of the atmosphere upon human conduct and vitality, "The Power of the Sun and Moon over Human Bodies" (1704).   An even more comprehensive and suggestive work was John Arbuthnot's "Essay on the Effects of Air on Human Bodies" (1733), which is said by Dedieu to have furnished Montesquieu with most of his views with respect to the effect of climate on man.   The brilliant young Dutch physician, Bernhardus Varenius (1622-50), in his "Geographia generalis" not only created the framework for the modern science of geography, but also foreshadowed the work of Ritter in comparative geography.   The "Travels" of Sir John Chardin (1667-1735) did much to popularize the knowledge of extra-European lands, particularly the near orient, and were widely used later by such writers as Montesquieu.   Finally, Vico (1668-1744) in his "Scienza nuova" anticipated Montesquieu in his appropriation of these advances for social science.

The beginning of scientific anthropogeography is conventionally associated with the appearance in 1817-18 of the first edition of Karl Ritter's "Die Erdkunde im Verhältniss zur Natur und zur Geschichte der Menschen."[11]   A number of phases of progress in geographical and other sciences served to make possible Ritter's monumental work and to give its views wide currency.   Montesquieu discussed the importance of a knowledge of geographical environment, particularly climate, in understanding the customs, laws and civilization of peoples, and the school of historians, led by Heeren, who adhered to his views, naturally emphasized the significance of geographical factors.[12]

[11] The significant portions of Ritter's work are translated by W. L. Gage in a work entitled "Ritter's Geographical Essays."

[12] Montesquieu: The Spirit of Laws, Books XIV, XVII; Heeren: Ideen über die Politik, den Verkehr, und den Handel der vornehmsten Völker der Alten Welt (trans. by Tolboys, 1833).

Montesquieu's work was subjected to constructive criticism by Turgot (1727-1781) and Charles Comte (1782-1837).[13] Romanticism was foreshadowed by Herder who inquired at length into the geographical elements which entered into the shaping of national character.[14] The progress and utilization of geographical discovery, best typified perhaps by the work of Alexander von Humboldt, vastly increased the body of geographical data and helped to shape the subject of physical geography.[15] The Darwinian hypothesis of the evolutionary development of living matter thru the reciprocal action of environment and organism, while not utilized by Ritter, served later to give acceptance and added significance to his doctrines. Wilhelm Riehl and Gustav Freytag, in attempting to reconstruct the social history of Germany, made wide use of geographical material in interpreting the development of the German people.[16] Buckle, in his effort to reduce history to an exact science, held that one must accept the doctrine of the influence of geography on culture, especially in the earlier periods of human development.[17] F. Hellwald in his "Kulturgeschichte in ihrer natürlichen Entwickelung" (1874) worked out a universal history in which he assigned large place to geographical influences. Finally, the impulse to systematic anthropogeography, which had been initiated by Ritter, was carried further by Peschel, Ratzel, Kirchoff, Semple, Vallaux, Reclus, and Brunhes. It is of significance in any study of the relation between geography and history to note that such important writers as Heeren, Ritter, Buckle, Hellwald, Ratzel and Semple were professionally quite as much historians as students of geography.

Some More Notable Contributions of Anthropogeography to History

A brief catalogue of the more significant works on various phases of anthropogeography will suffice to indicate the large amount of relevant material which this group of writers has put at the disposal of historians. Peschel, Ratzel and Kirchoff in Germany; Reclus, Vallaux

[13] Cf. Flint: op. cit., pp. 286-7, 577-9.

[14] Herder: Ideen zur Philosophie der Geschichte der Menschheit, trans. by Churchill, 1800. Cf. Flint: History of the Philosophy of History, (1874 edition), pp. 375-386.

[15] Humboldt: Ansichten der Natur (English trans. 1850); also Cosmos, Vol. I.

[16] W. Riehl: Die Naturgeschichte des Volkes als Grundlage einer deutschen Sozialpolitik, Vol. I, (Land und Leute); G. Freytag: Bilder aus der deutschen Vergangenheit. Cf. Gooch: History and Historians in the Nineteenth Century, pp. 574-80.

[17] H. T. Buckle: History of Civilization in England, Chap. II. Cf. J. M. Robertson: Buckle and His Critics.

and Brunhes in France; and Miss Semple in the United States have contributed systematic works on anthropogeography which deal with nearly every phase of geographic influences on man.[18] Fully as important as the systematic works upon the subject are the writings of those who have considered special aspects of environmental influences. The influence of topography in its general implications has been discussed by Demolins, Cowan and Vallaux. Demolins has pointed out the relation of natural routes of travel and communication to the movements, habitats and culture of peoples.[19] Cowan has combined the environmental doctrine with the theory of group-conflict as the chief progressive force in society. Holding that progress can come only where there is enough social mixture and conflict to prevent cultural stagnation, and yet not so great a degree of invasion as to produce continuous warfare and destruction, he has attempted to prove that the great historic nations have evolved in those districts where the topography secured protection without at the same time causing isolation.[20] Vallaux contends that progress is possible only where there is an adequate degree of social differentiation and division of labor, and he holds that this condition can exist only in a region of variegated topography and climate.[21] The importance of rivers, of the sea and the ocean for the movements of peoples and the expansion of civilization has been touched upon by Metchnikoff and Mackinder, and systematically studied by Vallaux.[22] The historical significance of the great oriental river basins has been studied by Léon Metchnikoff, who has tried to demonstrate that they supplied the sole conditions of fertility of soil and concentration of population under which man could make his first steps towards civilization. He further contends that the chief stages of civilization have been those founded upon a river, then a sea or thalassic, and finally an oceanic environment.[23] Le Play and Geddes have analyzed the river basin as a natural geographic region which has been the unit of cultural evolution and should constitute

---

[18] F. Ratzel: Anthropologie; and Politische Geographie. The best summary of Ratzel's views is contained in Chap. III of Vol. I of Helmholt's Weltgeschichte, of which an English translation is available. An excellent brief sketch of Ratzel's contributions is contained in Brunhes' Human Geography, pp. 31-35. A. Kirchhoff: Mensch und Erde (English translation, 1914); E. Reclus: Nouvelle géographie universelle; C. Vallaux: Géographie sociale; le sol et l' état; J. Brunhes: La Géographie humaine (English translation, 1920); E. C. Semple: The Influences of Geographic Environment.

[19] E. Demolins: Comment la route crée le type social.

[20] A. R. Cowan: Master Clues in World History.

[21] Vallaux: op. cit., pp. 174 ff., 244 ff.

[22] C. Vallaux: Géographie sociale: la mer.

[23] L. Metchnikoff: La Civilisation et les grandes fleuves historiques.

the basic unit for social reconstruction.[24] The relation of strategic geographical position to political and economic power has been pointed out by Ratzel and Cowan, but has been most strikingly worked out by H. J. Mackinder. In particular he has contended that the pivotal area in the old world is the great Eurasiatic steppe region and he maintains that the state possessing this district has the key to the domination of the eastern hemisphere.[27] Climate, in both its static and dynamic aspects has claimed the attention of Ellsworth Huntington in several daring and original volumes. He has not only attempted to correlate culture and civilization with the presence of certain specific climatic conditions, but, following out the suggestions of Holdich and Kropotkin, has also made an effort to connect great historic changes with what he assumes to be marked climatic oscillations.[26] Less spectacular but more reliable work has been done in this field by R. D. C. Ward.[27] The relation of climatic influences to international relations has been discussed by Ripley and Woodruff, particularly with reference to the possibility of the white race inhabiting the tropics as permanent occupants. Ripley contends that this is still an open question, but Woodruff is confident that climatic and solar influences will operate to prevent permanent large-scale white settlement in the tropics.[28] Ripley has further produced a monumental work on the relation between physical environment and racial characteristics.[29] Leffingwell has sought to correlate seasonal changes with certain aberrations of conduct.[30] Dexter has contributed the most thoro study of the effect of temporary oscillations of the weather upon human conduct, energy and vitality.[31] An even more comprehensive study has been undertaken by W. Hellpach in his "Die Geopsychischen Erscheinungen." Finally, Brunhes has insisted that any comprehensive account of environmental influences must include a consideration of the artificial environment which man has contributed.

[24] F. Le Play: La Réforme sociale; P. Geddes: Cities in Evolution; Geddes and Branford: The Coming Polity.

[25] H. J. Mackinder: The Geographical Pivot of History in *Geographical Journal*, April, 1904; Democratic Ideals and Reality; Cf. Teggart: Processes of History, Chap. II.

[26] E. Huntington: The Pulse of Asia; Civilization and Climate; World Power and Evolution.

[27] R. D. C. Ward: Climate. The standard reference work on climate is J. Hann's Handbuch der Klimatologie.

[28] W. Z. Ripley: The Races of Europe; Chap. XXI; C. E. Woodruff: The Effect of Tropical Light on White Man; and Medical Ethnology.

[29] Ripley: op. cit.

[30] A. Leffingwell: The Influence of Seasons upon Conduct.

[31] E. G. Dexter: Conduct and the Weather; and Weather Influences.

Henry Holt & Co., New York, 1911, 683 pp.

4

Influences of Geographic Environment

ELLEN C. SEMPLE

CHAPTER XV

MOUNTAIN BARRIERS AND THEIR PASSES

THE important characteristic of plains is their power Man as part of the mobile envelope of the earth. to facilitate every phase of historical movement; that of mountains is their power to retard, arrest, or deflect it. Man, as part of the mobile envelope of the earth, like air and water feels always the pull of gravity. From this he can never fully emancipate himself. By an output of energy he may climb the steepest slope, but with every upward step the ascent becomes more difficult, owing to the diminution of warmth and air and the increasing tax upon the heart.[1] Maintenance of life in high altitudes is always a struggle. The decrease of food resources from lower to higher levels makes the passage of a mountain system an ordeal for every migrating people or marching army that has to live off the country which it traverses. Mountains therefore repel population by their inaccessibility and also by their harsh conditions of life, while the lowlands attract it, both in migration and settlement. Historical movement, when forced into the upheaved areas of the earth, avoids the ridges and peaks, seeks the valleys and passes, where communication with the lowlands is easiest.

High massive mountain systems present the most effective Inaccessibility of mountains. barriers which man meets on the land surface of the earth. To the spread of population they offer a resistance which long serves to exclude settlers. The difficulty of making roads up steep, rocky slopes and through the forests usually covering their rain-drenched sides, is deterrent enough; but in addition to this, general infertility, paucity of arable land, harsh climatic conditions, and the practical lack of communication with the outside world offer scant basis for subsistence. Hence, as a rule, only when pressure of population in the lowlands becomes too great under prevailing economic methods, do clearings and cabins begin to creep up the slopes. Moun-

42

tains are always regions of late occupation. Even in the Stone Age, we find the long-headed race of Mediterranean stock, who originally populated Europe, distributed over the continent close up to the foot of the high Alps, but not in the mountains themselves, and only scantily represented in the Auvergne Plateau of France. The inhospitable highlands of Switzerland, the German Alps, and the Auvergne received their first population later when the Alpine race began to occupy western Europe.[2] The *Mittelgebirge* of Germany were not settled till the Middle Ages. In the United States, the flood of population had spread westward by 1840 to the ninety-fifth meridian and the north-south course of the Missouri River; but out of this sea of settlement the Adirondack Mountains, a few scattered spots in the Appalachians, and the Ozark Highlands rose as so many islands of uninhabited wilderness, and they remain to-day areas of sparser population. In 1800, the "bare spots" in the eastern mountains were more pronounced. [See map page 156.] Great stretches of the Rocky Mountains, of the Laurentian Highlands of Canada, like smaller patches in the Scandinavian and Swiss Alps, are practically uninhabited.

Mountains as transit regions.

Mountain regions, like deserts and seas, become mere transit districts, which man traverses as quickly as possible. Hence they often lie as great inert areas in the midst of active historical lands, and first appear upon the historical stage in minor rôles, when they are wanted by the plains people as a passway to desirable regions beyond. Then, as a rule, only their transit routes are secured, while the less accessible regions are ignored. Cæsar makes no mention of the Alps, except to state that he has crossed them, until some of the mountain tribes try to block the passage of Roman merchants or armies; then they become important enough to be conquered. It was not till after the Cimbri in 102 B. C. invaded Italy by the Brenner route, that the Romans realized the value of Rhaetia (Tyrol) as a thoroughfare from Italy to Germany, and began its conquest in 36 B. C. This was the same value which the Tyrol so long had for the old German Empire and later for Austria,—merely to secure connection with the Po Valley. The need of land communication with the

Rhone Valley led the Romans to attack the Salyes, who inhabited the Maritime Alps, and after eighty years of war to force from them the concession of a narrow transit strip, twelve stadia or one and a half miles wide, for the purpose of making a road to Massilia.[3]   The necessity of controlling such transit lands has drawn British India into the occupation of mountain Baluchistan, Kashmir and Sikkim, just as it has caused the highlands of Afghanistan to figure actively in the expansion policy of both India and Russia. The conquest of such transit lands has always been attended by road building, from the construction of the Roman highway through the Brenner Pass to the modern Russian military road through the Pass of Dariel across the Caucasus, and the yet more recent Indian railroad to Darjeeling, with the highway extension beyond to the Tibetan frontier through Himalayan Sikkim.

Such mountain regions attain independent historical importance when their population increases enough to form the nucleus of a state, and to acquire additional territory about the highland base either by conquest or voluntary union, while they utilize their naturally protected location and their power to grant safe transit to their allies, as means to secure their political autonomy.   Therefore to mountain regions so often falls the rôle of buffer states.   Such were medieval Burgundy and modern Savoy, which occupied part of the same territory, Navarre which in the late Middle Ages controlled the important passway around the western end of the Pyrenees, and Switzerland which commands the passes of the central Alps.   The position of such mountain states is, however, always fraught with danger, owing to the weakness inherent in their small area and yet smaller allowance of productive soil, to their diverse ethnic elements, and the forces working against political consolidation in their deeply dissected surface.   Political solidarity has a hard, slow birth in the mountains.

In view of the barrier character of mountains, a fact of immense importance to the distribution of man and his activities is the rarity of abrupt, ungraded forms of relief on the earth's surface.   The physiographic cause lies in the

Transition forms of relief between highlands and lowlands.

elasticity of the earth's crust and the leveling effect of weathering and denudation. Everywhere mountains are worn down and rounded off, while valleys broaden and fill up to shallow trough outlines. Transition forms of relief abound. Human intercourse meets therefore few absolute barriers on the land; but these few reveal the obstacles to historical movement in perpendicular reliefs. The mile-high walls of the Grand Cañon of the Colorado are an insuperable obstacle to intercourse for a stretch of three hundred miles. The glacier-crowned ridge of the Bernese Alps is crossed by no wagon road between the Grimsel Pass and the upper Rhone highway around their western end, a distance of 100 kilometers (62 miles). The Pennine Alps have no pass between the Great St. Bernard and the Simplon, a distance of 90 kilometers (54 miles).

portance
transi-
n
pes.

Gentle transition slopes or terrace lands facilitate almost everywhere access to the lowest, most habitable and therefore, from the human standpoint, most important section of mountains. They combine the ease of intercourse characteristic of plains with many advantages of the mountains, and especially in warm climates they unite in a narrow zone both tropical and temperate vegetation. The human value of these transition slopes holds equally of single hills, massive mountain systems, and continental reliefs. The earth as a whole owes much of its habitability to these gently graded slopes. Continents and countries in which they are meagerly developed suffer from difficulty of intercourse, retarded development and poverty of the choicest habitable areas. This is one disadvantage of South Africa, emphasized farther by a poor coastline. The Pacific face of Australia would gain vastly in historical importance, if the drop from the highlands to the ocean were stretched out into a broad slope, like that which links our Atlantic coastal plain with the Appalachian highlands. There each river valley shows three characteristic anthropo-geographical sub-divisions—the active seaports and tide-water tillage of its lower course, the contrasted agriculture of its hilly course, the upland farms, waterpower industries and mines of its headstream valleys, each landscape giving its population distinctive characteristics.

45

The same natural features, with the same effect upon human activities and population, appear in the long seaward slopes of France, Germany and northern Italy.

At the base of the mountains themselves, where the bold relief begins, is always a piedmont zone of hilly surface but gentler grade, at whose inner or upland edge every phase of the historical movement receives a marked check. Here is a typical geographical boundary, physical and human. It shifts slightly in different periods, according to the growing density of population in the plains below and improved technique in industry and road-making. It is often both an ethnic and cultural boundary, because at the rim of the mountains the geologic and economic character of the country changes.[4] The expanding peoples of the plains spread over the piedmont so far as it offers familiar and comparatively favorable geographic conditions, scatter their settlements along the base of the mountains, and here fix their political frontier for a time, though later they may advance it to the crest of the ridge, in order to secure a more scientific boundary. The civilized population of the broad Indus Valley spread westward up the western highlands, only so far as the shelving slopes of the clay and conglomerate foothills, which constitute the piedmont of the Suleiman and Kirthar Mountains, afforded conditions for their crops. Thus from the Arabian Sea for 600 miles north to the Gomal River, the political frontier of India was defined by the line of relief dividing the limestone mountains from the alluvial plain, the marauding Baluch and Afghan hill tribes from the patient farmers of the Sind.[5] This line remained the border of India from pre-British days till the recent annexation of Baluchistan.

These piedmont boundaries are most clearly defined in point of race and civilization, where superior peoples from the lowlands are found expanding at the cost of retarded mountain folk. Romans and Rhaetians once met along a line skirting the foot of the eastern Alps, as Russians to-day along the base of the Caucasus adjoin the territories of the heterogeneous tribes occupying that mountain area.[6] [See map page 225.] The plains-loving Magyars of Hungary have

Piedmont belts as boundary zones.

46

pushed up to the rim of mountainous Siebenburgen or Transylvania from Arad on the Maros River to Sziget on the upper Theiss, while the highland region has a predominant Roumanian population.   A clearly defined linguistic and cultural boundary of Indo-Aryan speech and religion, both Hindu and Mohammedan, follows the piedmont edges of the Brahmaputra Valley, and separates the lowland inhabitants from the pagans of Tibeto-Burman speech occupying the Himalayan slope to the north and the Khasia Mountains to the south. The highland race is Mongoloid, while the Bengali of an Aryan, Dravidian and Mongoloid blend fill the river plain.[7] Such piedmont boundary lines tend to blur into bands or zones of ethnic intermixture and cultural assimilation.   The western Himalayan foothills show the blend of Mongoloid and Aryan stocks, where the vigorous Rajputs of the plains have encroached upon the mountaineer's land.[8]   Of almost every mountain folk it can be assumed that they once occupied their highlands to the outermost rim of the piedmont, and retired to the inner rim of this intermediary slope only under compulsion from without.

The piedmont boundary also divides two areas of contrasted density of population.   Mountain regions are, as a rule, more sparsely settled than plains.   The piedmont is normally a transition region in this respect; but where high mountains rise as climatic islands of adequate water supply out of desert and steppes, they concentrate on their lower slopes all the sedentary population, making their piedmonts zones of greatest density.   Low mountains in arid regions become centers of population; here their barrier nature vanishes.   In the Sudanese state of Darfur, the Marra Mountains are the district best watered and most thickly populated.   Nowhere higher than 6000 feet (1850 meters), they afford running water at 4000 feet elevation and water pools in the sandy beds of their wadis at 3200 feet.   Below this, water disappears from the surface, and can be found only in wells whose depth and scarcity increase with distance from the central mountains.[9]   The neighboring kingdom of Wadai shows similar conditions and effects.[10]   In the heart of Australia, where utter desert reigns, the Macdonnell Ranges form the nucleus of the northern area occupied by the Arunta tribe of natives; farther north the Murchison Range, usually abounding in water-holes, is the center and stronghold of the Warramunga tribe.[11]

Mineral wealth or waterpower in the mountains serves to collect an urban and industrial population along their rim, as we see it about the base of the Erz Mountains in Saxony, the Riesen range in Silesia, the coal-bearing Pennine Mountains of northwestern England, and the highlands of southern Wales, all which piedmont zones show a density of over 150 to the square kilometer (385 to the square mile). Hence the original Swiss Confederation, which included only the mountain cantons of Schwyz, Uri and Unterwalden, was greatly strengthened by the accession of the piedmont cantons of Lucerne, Zurich, Zug and Bern in the early fourteenth century, as later by St. Gall, Aargau and Geneva. These marginal cantons to-day show a density of population exceeding 385 to the square mile, and rising to 1356 in the canton of Geneva.

Piedmont belts tend strongly towards urban development, **Piedmont** even where rural settlement is sparse. Sparsity of popula- **towns and** tion and paucity of towns within the mountains cause main **roads.** lines of traffic to keep outside the highlands, but close enough to their base to tap their trade at every valley outlet. On the alluvial fans or plains of these valley outlets, where mountain and piedmont road intersect, towns grow up. Some of them develop into cities, when they command transverse routes of communication quite across the highlands. The ancient *Via Aemilia* traced the northern base of the Apennines from Ariminum on the Adriatic to Dertona at the foot of the Ligurian range back of Genoa, and connected a long line of Roman colonies. The modern railroad follows almost exactly the course of the old Roman road,[12] while a transverse line southward across the Apennines, following an ancient highway over the Poretta Pass to the Arno Valley, has maintained the old preëminence of Bologna. A line of towns, connected by highways or railroads, according to the economic development of the section, defines the bases of the Pyrenees, Alps, Jura, Apennines, Harz, Vosges, Elburz and

48

numerous other ranges. Along the Elburz piedmont runs the imperial road of Persia from Tabriz through Teheran to Meshed. In arid regions these piedmont roads are an unfailing feature, but their towns shrink to rural settlements, except at the junction of transmontane routes.

Piedmont termini of transmontane routes.

Piedmont cities draw their support from plain, mountain and transmontane region, relying chiefly on the fertile soil of the level country to feed their large populations. Sometimes they hug the foot of the mountains, as Bologna, Verona, Bergamo, Zurich, Denver and Pittsburg do; sometimes, like Milan, Turin, and Munich, they drop down into the plain, but keep the mountains in sight. They flourish in proportion to their local resources, in which mineral wealth is particularly important, and to the number and practicability of their transmontane connections. Hence they often receive their stamp from the mountains behind them as well as from the bordering plain. The St. Gotthard route is flanked by Lucerne on the north and Milan on the south. The Brenner has its urban outlets at Munich and Verona. Narbonne and Barcelona form the termini of the route over the eastern Pyrenees; Toulouse commands the less used central passes, and Bayonne the western. Tiflis is situated in the great mountain trough connecting the Black Sea and the Caspian; but over the Caucasus by the Pass of Dariel come the influences which make it a Russian town. Peshawar, situated in the mountain angle of the Punjab, depends more upon the Khaibar Pass and its connections thereby with Central Asia than upon the plains of the Indus; its population, in appearance and composition nearly as much Central Asiatic as Indian, is engaged in traffic between the Punjab and the whole trans-Hindu Kush country.[13]

Where a mountain system describes a semi-circular course, its transit routes tend to converge on the inner side, and at their foci fix the sites of busy commercial centers. Turin draws on a long series of Alpine and Apennine routes from the Pass of Giovi (1548 feet or 472 meters) leading up from Genoa on the south, to the Great St. Bernard on the north. Milan gets immense support from the St. Gotthard and Simplon railroads over the Alps, besides wagon routes over several minor passes.   Kulm, Balkh and Kunduz in the piedmont of northern Afghanistan are fed by twenty or more passes over the Hindu Kush and Pamir.   Bukhara is the remoter focus of all these routes, and also of the valley highways of the western Tian Shan.   It therefore occupies a location which would make it one of the great emporiums of the world, were it not for the expanse of desert to the west and the scantiness of its local water supply, which is tapped farther upstream for the irrigation of Samarkand.   In its bazaars are found drugs, dyes and teas from India; wool, skins and dried fruit from Afghanistan; woven goods, arms, and books from Persia; and Russian wares imported by rail and caravan.   English goods, which formerly came in by the Kabul route from India, have been excluded since Russia established a protectorate over the province of Bukhara. Across the highlands to the east, the cities of Kashgar and Yarkand, situated in that piedmont zone of vegetation where mountain and desert meet, are enclosed by a vast amphitheater formed by the Tian Shan, the Pamir Highlands, and the Karakorum range.   Stieler's atlas marks no less than six trade routes over the passes of these mountains from Kashgar to the headstreams of the Sir-daria and Oxus, and six from Yarkand to the Oxus and Indus.   Kashgar is a meeting ground of many nationalities.   To its bazaars come traders from China, India, Afghanistan, Bukhara, and Russian Turkestan."   The Russian railway up the Sir-daria to Andizhan brings European goods within relatively easy reach of the Terek Davan Pass, and makes serious competition for English wares entering by the more difficult Karakorum Pass from India.[15]

Where mountains drop off into a desert, as these Central Asiatic ranges do, their piedmont cities are confined to a narrow zone between mountains and arid waste.   Bordering two transit regions of scant population and through travel, they become natural outfitting points, centers of exchange rather than production.   Where mountains drop off into the sea and the piedmont therefore becomes a coastal belt, again it borders two transit regions; but here the ports of the desert are replaced by maritime ports, which command the world

Cities of coastal piedmonts.

thoroughfare of the ocean. They therefore tend to concentrate population and commerce wherever a good harbor coincides with the outlet of a transmontane route, as in Genoa and Bombay.

Piedmonts
as colonial
or back-
woods
frontiers.
Since mountains are inhospitable to every phase of the historical movement, they long remain regions of retardation. Hence to their bordering plains they sustain the relation of young undeveloped lands, so that life in their piedmont belts tends to show for a long time all the characteristics of a new colonial frontier. The rim of the Southern Appalachians abundantly illustrates this principle even to-day. During the westward expansion of the American people from 1830 to 1850, the eastern rim of the Rocky Mountains was dotted with trading posts like that of the Missouri Fur Company at the forks of the Missouri River, Forts Laramie and Platte on the North Fork of the Platte, Vrain's Fort and Fort Lancaster on the South Fork, Bent's Fort at the mountain exit of the Arkansas River, and Barclay's in the high Mora Valley of the upper Canadian. These posts gathered in the rich pelts which formed the one product of this highland area susceptible of bearing the cost of transportation to the far away Missouri River. Though they developed into way-stations on the overland trails, when the movement of population to California and Oregon in the forties and fifties made the Rocky Mountains a typical highland transit region, yet they long remained frontier posts.[16] Later the abundant water supply of this piedmont district, as compared with the arid plains below, and the mineral wealth of the mountains concentrated here an agricultural and industrial population.

In Sze Chuan province of western China, the piedmont of a vast highland hinterland shows a similar development. Here the towns of Matang, Sungpan, Kuan Hsien, and even the capital Chengtu, situated in the high Min Valley at the foot of the mountains walling them in on the west, are emporiums for trade with the Tibetans, who bring hither furs, hides and wool from their plateau pastures, and musk from the musk deer on the Koko Nor plains.[17] Just to the north, Sian (Singan), capital of the highland province of Shensi, concentrates the fur trade of a large mountain wilderness to the west. Several blocks on the main street form a great fur market for the sale of mink and other skins used to line the official robes of mandarins.[18]

Like seas, deserts, and other geographical transit regions, mountains too under primitive conditions develop their professional carriers. These collect in the piedmont, where highway and mule train cease, and where the steep track admits only human beasts of burden, trained by their environment to be climbers and packers. These mountain carriers are found on the Pacific face of the coast ranges of North and South America from the peninsula of Alaska to the Straits of Magellan. They are able to pack from 100 to 160 pounds up a steep grade. The Chilkoot Indians, men, women and children, did invaluable service on the White Horse and Chilkoot passes during the early days of the Klondike rush. They had devised a well-arranged harness, which enabled them better to carry their loads. Farther south in British Columbia the piedmont tribes had once a like importance; there they operated especially from the town of Hope on the lower Frazer River as a distributing center. The Mexican carrier is so efficient and so cheap that he enters into serious competition with modern schemes to improve transportation, especially as the rugged relief of this country makes those schemes expensive.[19] The Indians of the eastern slope of the Andes pack India rubber, in loads of 150 pounds each, from the upper Purus and Madeira rivers up to the Andean plateau at a height of 15,000 feet, and there transfer their burdens to mules for transport down to the Peruvian port of Mollendo.[20]

The retarded mountain peoples on the borders of the Central Asia plateau employ the same primitive means of transportation. The roads leading from the Sze Chuan province of western China over the mountain ranges to Tibet are traversed by long lines of porters, men, women and children, laden with bales of brick tea,[21] the strongest of them shouldering 350 pounds. The Bhutia coolies of Sikkim act as carriers on military and commercial expeditions on the track across the Himalayas between Darjeeling and Shigatze. Colonel Younghusband found that these Bhutias, who were

Mountain carriers.

52

paid by the job, would carry a pack of 250 to 300 pounds, or three times the usual burden of a Central Asia carrier. Landon cites the case of a Bhutia lady who was said to have carried a piano on her head from the plains up to Darjeeling (7150 feet).[22] In Nepal, women and girls, less often men, have long been accustomed to carry travellers and merchandise over the Himalayan ranges.[23] In the marginal valleys of the Himalayas, like Kashmir and Baltistan, the natives are regularly impressed for *begar* or carrier service on the English military roads to strategic points on the high mountain frontier of the Indian Empire.[24] So the Igorots of the Luzon province of Benguet pack all goods and supplies from Naguilian in the lowlands up 4000 feet in a distance of 25 miles to their little capital of Baguio; for this service they are now paid one peso (46 cents in 1901) a day with food, or ten times as much as under the Spanish rule.[25]

Power of mountain barriers to block or deflect.

If the historical movement slackens its pace at the piedmont slope, higher up the mountain it comes to a halt. Only when human invention has greatly improved communication across the barrier are its obstacles in part overcome. The great highland wall stretching across southern Europe from the Bay of Biscay to the Black Sea long cut off the solid mass of the continent from the culture of the Mediterranean lands. Owing to these mountains Central Europe came late into the foreground of history, not till the Middle Ages. Even the penetrating civilization of Greece reached it only by long detours around the ends of the mountain barrier: by Massilia and the Rhone, by Istria and the Danube, Greek commerce trickled through to the interior of the continent.

Where mountains fail to check, they deflect the historical movement. The wall of the Carpathians, bulwark of Central Europe, split the westward moving Slav hordes in the 6th century, diverting one southward up the Danube Valley to the Eastern Alps, and turning one northward along the German lowlands.[26] The northward expansion of the Romans, rebuffed by the high double wall of the Central Alps, was bent to the westward over the Maritime, Cottine and Savoy Alps, where the barrier offered the shortest and

53

easiest transmontane routes.   Hence Germany received the elements of Mediterranean culture indirectly through Gaul, second-hand and late.   The ancient Helvetians, moving southward from northern Switzerland into Gaul, took a route skirting the western base of the Alps by the gap at Geneva, and thus threatened Roman Provincia.   Cæsar's campaigns into northern Gaul were given direction by the massive Central Plateau of France.[27]   The rugged and infertile area of the Catskills long retarded the westward movement in colonial New York and deflected it northward through the Mohawk depression, which therefore had its long thin line of settlements when the neighboring Catskills were still a "bare spot."

In their valleys, mountains lose something of their barrier nature, and approximate the level of the plains.   Here they harbor oases of denser population and easier intercourse. Valleys favor human settlement through the milder climate of their lower elevation, the accumulation of soil on their floors, their sheltered environment, and their command of such routes of communication as the highlands afford.   They are the avenues into and within a mountain system, and therefore radically influence its history by their direction and location.   The Central Plateau of France, through the valleys of the Alliers and upper Loire, is most accessible from the north; therefore in that direction it has maintained its most important historical connections,[28] from the days of Cæsar and Vercingetorix.   The massive highland region of Transylvania, which opens long accessible valleys westward toward the plains of the Theiss and Danube, has since the eleventh century received thence Hungarian immigration and political dominion.[29] Its dominant Roumanian population, however, seems to have fled thither from the Tartar-swept plains to the southeast.

The anthropo-geography of mountain valleys depends upon the structure of the highlands themselves, whether they are fold mountains, whose ranges wall in longitudinal valleys, or dissected plateaus, whose valleys are mostly transverse river channels leading from the hydrographic center out to the rim of the highlands.   Longitudinal valleys are not only long, but also broad as a rule and often show a nearly level

Significance of mountain valleys.

floor.[30]   They therefore form districts of considerable size, fertility, and individuality, and play distinct historical rôles in the history of their respective highlands.   Such are the upper Rhone Valley with its long line of flourishing towns and villages, the Hither Rhine, the Inn of the Tyrol and the Engadine, the fertile trough of the meandering Isère above Grenoble,[31] the broad Orontes-Leontes valley between the Lebanon and Anti-Lebanon where Kadesh and Baalbec were once the glory of northern Syria.   Such is the central trough of the Appalachian Mountains, known as the Great Appalachian Valley, seventy-five miles wide, subdivided into constituent valleys of similar character by parallel, even-crested ridges following the trend of the mountains.   These are drained by broad, leisurely rivers, bordered by fertile farms and substantial towns.   Transverse valleys, on the other hand, are generally narrow, with steep slopes rising almost from the river's edge and supporting only small villages and farms.   A comparison of the spacious, smooth-floored valley of Andermatt with the wild Reuss gorge, of the fertile and populous Shenandoah Valley in the Southern Appalachians with the cañon of the Kanawha in the Cumberland Plateau, makes the contrast striking enough.

Longitudinal valleys.   Longitudinal valleys, by reason of their length and their branching lateral valleys, are the natural avenues of communication within the mountains themselves.   They therefore give a dominant direction to such phases of the historical movement as succeed in passing the outer barrier.   The series of parallel ranges which strike off from the eastern end of the Tibetan plateau southward into Farther India have directed along their valleys the main streams of Mongolian migration and expansion, heading them toward the river basins of Burma and Indo China, and away from India itself.[32] While Tibetan elements have during the ages slowly welled over the high Himalayan brim and trickled down toward the Gangetic plain, Burma has been deluged by floods of Mongolians pouring down the runnels of the land. A carriage road follows the axis of the Central Alps from Lake Geneva to Lake Constance by means of the upper Rhone, Andermatt, and upper Rhine valleys, linked by the Furca and

Oberalp passes. The Roman and Medieval routes north-ward across the Central Alps struck the upper Rhine Valley above Coire, (the ancient Curia Rhaetorum); this natural groove gave them a northeastward direction, and made them emerge from the mountains directly south of Ulm, which thereby gained great importance. The trade routes from Damascus and Palmyra which once entered the Orontes-Leontes trough in the Lebanon system found their Mediterranean termini south near Tyre or north near Antioch, and thus contributed to the greatness of those ancient emporiums. The Great Appalachian Valley used to be a highway for the Iroquois Indians, when they took the warpath against the Cherokee tribes of Tennessee. Later it gave a distinct southwestward trend to pioneer movements of population within the mountains, blending in its common channel the Quakers, Germans and Scotch-Irish from Pennsylvania, with the English and Huguenot French of the more southern colonies. In the Civil War its fertile fields were swept by marching armies, all the way from Chattanooga to Gettysburg.

The barrier nature of mountains depends upon their height and structure, whether they are massive, unbroken walls like the Scandinavian Alps and the Great Smoky range; or, like the Welsh Highlands and the Blue Ridge, are studded with low passes. The Pyrenees, Caucasus and Andes, owing to the scarcity and great height of their passes, have always been serious barriers. The Pyrenees divide Spain from France more sharply than the Alps divide Italy from France; owing to their rampart character, they form the best and most definite natural boundary in Europe.[33] Epirus and Aetolia, fenced in by the solid Pindus range, took little part in the common life of ancient Greece; but the intermittent chains of Thessaly offered a passway between Macedon and Hellas. The Alps have an astonishing number of excellent passes, evenly distributed for the most part. These, in conjunction with the great longitudinal valleys of the system, offer transit routes from side to side in any direction. The Appalachian system is some three hundred miles broad and thirteen hundred miles long, but it has many easy gaps among its parallel ranges, so that it offered natural though cir-

Passes in mountain barriers.

56

cuitous highways to the early winners of the West. The long line (400 miles) of the Hindu Kush range, high as it is, forms no strong natural boundary to India, because it is riddled with passes at altitudes from 12,500 to 19,000 feet.[34] The easternmost group of these passes lead down to Kashmir, and therefore lend this state peculiar importance as guardian of these northern entrances to India.[35] The Suleiman Mountains along the Indo-Afghan frontier are an imperfect defence for the same reason. They are indented by 289 passes capable of being traversed by camels. The mountain border of Baluchistan contains 75 more, the most important of which focus their roads upon Kandahar. Hence the importance to British India of Kandahar and Afghanistan. Across this broken northwest barrier have come almost all the floods of invasion and immigration that have contributed their varied elements to the mixed population of India. Tradition, epic and history tell of Asiatic highlanders ever sweeping down into the warm valley of the Indus through these passes; Scythians, Aryans, Greeks, Assyrians, Medes, Persians, Turks, Tartars, and Mongols have all traveled these rocky roads, to rest in the enervating valleys of the peninsula.[36]

Breadth of mountain barriers. Mountains folded into a succession of parallel ranges are greater obstructions than a single range like the Erz, Black Forest, and Vosges, or a narrow, compact system like the Western Alps, which can be crossed by a single pass. Owing to this simple structure the Western Alps were traversed by four established routes in the days of the Roman Empire. These were: 1. The *Via Aurelia* between the Maritime Alps and the sea, where now runs the Cornice Road. II. The *Mons Matrona* (Mont Genevre Pass, 6080 feet or 1854 kilometers) between the headstream of the Dora Riparia and that of the Durance, which was the best highway for armies. III. The Little St. Bernard (7075 feet or 2157 meters), from Aosta on the Dora Baltea over to the Isère and down to Lugdunum (Lyons). IV. The Great St. Bernard (8109 feet or 2472 meters) route, which led northward from Aosta over the Pennine Alps to Octodurus at the elbow of the upper Rhone, where Martigny now stands. Across the broad double rampart of the Central Alps the Roman used chiefly the Brenner route, which by a low saddle unites the deep reën-trant valleys of the Adige and Inn rivers, and thus surmounts the barrier by a single pass. However, a short cut north-ward over the Chalk Alps by the Fern Pass made closer connection with Augusta Vindelicorum (Augsburg). The Romans seem to have been ignorant of the St. Gotthard, which, though high, is the summit of an unbroken ascent from Lake Maggiore up the valley of the Ticino on one side, and from Lake Lucerne up the Reuss on the other.

Mountains which spread out on a broad base in a series of parallel chains, and through which no long transverse valleys offer ready transit, form serious barriers to every phase of intercourse. The lofty boundary wall of the Pyre-nees, a folded mountain system of sharp ranges and difficult passes, has successfully separated Spain from continental Europe; it has given the Iberian Peninsula, in the course of a long history, closer relations with Morocco than with its land neighbor France. It thus justifies the French saying that "Africa begins at the Pyrenees." The Andalusian fold mountains stretching across southern Spain in a double wall from Trafalgar to Cape Nao, accessible only by narrow and easily defended passes, enabled the Moors of Granada to hold their own for centuries against the Spaniard Christians. The high thin ridges of the folded Jura system, poor in soil and sparsely populated, broken by occasional "cluses" or narrow water-gaps admitting the rivers from one elevated longitudinal valley to another, have always been a serious hindrance to traffic.[87]

Such mountains can be crossed only by circuitous routes from pass to pass, ascending and descending each range of the system. The Central Alps, grooved by the longitudinal valleys of the upper Rhone, Rhine and Inn, make transit travel a series of ups and downs. The northern range must be crossed by some minor pass like the Gemmi, (7553 feet) or Panixer (7907 feet) to the longitudinal valleys, and the southern range again by the Simplon (6595 feet), San Bernadino (6768 feet), Splügen (6946 feet) or Septi-mer (7582 feet) to the Po basin. Across the corrugated

Circuitous routes through folded mountains.

highland of the Hindu Kush, lying between the plains of the Indus and the Oxus, the caravans of western Asia seek the market of the Punjab by a circuitous route through the Hajikhak Pass (12,188 feet) or famous Gates of Bamian over the main range of the Hindu Kush, by the Unai Pass over the Paghman Mountains to Kabul at 5740 feet, and then by gorges of the Kabul River and the Khaibar Pass (6825 feet) down to Peshawar. This road presents so many difficulties that caravans from Turkestan to India prefer another route from Merv up the valley of the Heri-Rud through the western hills of the Hindu Kush to Herat, thence diagonally southeast across Afghanistan to Kandahar, and thence by the Bolan Pass down to the Sind. The broad, low series of forested mountains consisting of the Vindhyan and Kaimur Hills, reinforced by the Satpura, Kalabet, Gawilgarh ranges, Mahadeo Hills, Maikal Range and Chutia Nagpur Plateau as a secondary ridge to the south, forms a double barrier across the base of peninsular India. It divides the Deccan from Hindustan so effectually that it has sufficed to set limits to any Aryan advance *en masse* southward. It kept southern India isolated, and admitted only later Aryan influences which filtered through the barrier. To people accustomed to treeless plains, these wide belts of wooded hills were barrier enough. Even a few years ago their passes were dreaded by cartmen; most of the carriage of the country was effected by pack-bullocks. Even when roads were cleared through the forests, they were likely to be rendered impassable by torrential rains.[38]

Dominant transmontane routes.
　　Where a broad, complex mountain system contracts to narrow compass, or is cut by deep reëntrant valleys leading up to a single pass, the transmontane route here made by nature assumes great historical importance. The double chain of the mighty Caucasus, from 120 to 150 miles wide and 750 miles long, stretches an almost insuperable barrier between the Black Sea and the Caspian. But nearly midway between these two seas it is constricted to only 60 miles by a geographical and geological gulf, which penetrates from the steppes of Russia almost to the heart of the system.[39] This gulf forms the high valley of the Terek River, beyond

whose headstream lies the Dariel defile (7503 feet or 2379 meters), which continues the natural depression across to the short southern slope.   All the other passes of the Caucasus are 3000 meters or more high, lie above snow line and are therefore open only in summer.   The Dariel Pass alone is open all the year around.[40]   Here runs the great military road from Vladicaucas to Tiflis, which the Russians have built to control their turbulent mountaineer subjects; and here are located the Ossetes, the only people among the variegated tribes of the whole Caucasus who occupy both slopes.   All the other tribes and languages are confined to one side or the other.[41]   Moreover, the Ossetes, occupying an exposed location in their highway habitat, lack the courage of the other mountaineers, and yielded without resistance to the Russians. In this respect they resemble the craven-spirited Kashmiri, whose mountain-walled vale forms a passway from Central Asia down to the Punjab.

The Pass of Dariel, owing to its situation in a retarded **Brenner route.** corner of Asia, has never attained the historical importance which attaches to the deep saddle of the Brenner Pass (4470 feet) in the Central Alps.   Uniting the reëntrant valleys of the Inn and Adige rivers only 2760 feet above the Inn's exit from the mountains upon the Bavarian plateau, it forms a low, continuous line of communication across the Central Alps.   The Brenner was the route of the Cimbri invading the Po Valley, and later of the Roman forces destined for frontier posts of the Empire on the upper Danube.   In the Middle Ages it was the route for the armies of the German Emperors who came to make good their claim to Italy.   By this road came the artists and artisans of the whole north country to learn the arts and crafts of beauty-loving Venice.   From the Roman road-makers to the modern railroad engineer, with the concomitant civilization of each, the Brenner has seen the march of human progress.

Farther to the west, the wall of highlands stretching across **Pass of** southern Europe is interrupted by a deep groove formed **Belfort.** by the mountain-flanked Rhone Valley and the Pass of Belfort, or Burgundian Gate, which lies between the Vosges and Jura system, and connects the Rhone road with the long rift valley of the middle Rhine. This pass, broad and low (350 meters or 1148 feet) marks the insignificant summit in the great historic route of travel between the Mediterranean and the North Sea, from the days of ancient Etruscan merchants to the present. This was the route of the invading Teuton hordes which the Roman Marius defeated at Aquae Sextiae, and later, of the Germans under Ariovistus, whom Cæsar defeated near the present Mühlhausen. Four centuries afterward came the Alamannians, Burgundians and other Teutonic stocks, who infused a tall blond element into the population of the Rhone Valley.[42] The Pass of Belfort is the strategic key to Central Europe. Here Napoleon repeatedly fixed his military base for the invasion of Austria, and hither was directed one division of the German army in 1870 for the invasion of France. The gap is traversed to-day by a canal connecting the Doubs and the Rhine and by a railroad, just as formerly by the tracks of migrating barbarians.

Mohawk route.

The natural depression of the Mohawk Valley, only 445 feet (136 meters) above sea level, is the only decided break across the entire width of the long Appalachian system. This fact, together with its ready accessibility from the Hudson on the east and Lake Ontario on the west, lent it importance in the early history of the colonies, as well as in the later history of New York. It was an easy line of communication with the Great Lakes, and gave the colonists access to the fur trade of the Northwest, then in the hands of the French. So when French and English fought for supremacy in the New World, the Mohawk and Hudson valleys were their chief battleground; elsewhere the broad Appalachian barrier held them apart. Again in the Revolution, control of the Mohawk-Hudson route was the objective of the British armies mobilized on the Canadian frontier, because it alone would enable them to co-operate with the British fleet blockading the coast cities of the colonies. In the War of 1812, it was along this natural transmontane highway that supplies were forwarded to the remote frontier, to support Perry's fight for control of the Great Lakes. The war demonstrated the strategic necessity of a protected, wholly American line of water communication between the Hudson and our western

61

frontier, while the commercial and political advantage was obvious. Hence a decade after the conclusion of the war, this depression was traced by the Erie Canal, through which passed long lines of boats to build up the commercial greatness of New York City.

Other structural features being the same, mountains are barriers also in proportion to their height; for, with few exceptions, the various anthropo-geographic effects of up-heaved areas are intensified with increase of elevation. Old, worn-down mountains, like the Appalachians and the Ural, broad as they are, have been less effective obstacles than the towering crests of the Alps and Caucasus. The form of the elevation also counts. Easy slopes and flat or rounded summits make readier transit regions than high, thin ridges with escarpment-like flanks. Mountains of plateau form, though reaching a great altitude, may be relatively hospitable to the historical movement and even have a regular nomadic population in summer. The central and western Tian Shan system is in reality a broad, high plateau, divided into a series of smoothly floored basins and gently rolling ridges lying at an elevation of 10,000 to 12,000 feet above the sea. Its pamirs or plains of thick grass, nourished by the relatively heavy precipitation of this high altitude, and forming in summer an island of verdure in the surrounding sea of sun-scorched waste, attract the pastoral nomads from all the bordering steppes and deserts.[43] Thus it is a meeting place for a seasonal population, sparse and evanescent, but its uplifted mass holds asunder the few sedentary peoples fringing its piedmont. The corrugated dome of the Pamir highland, whose valley floors lie at an elevation of 11,000 to 13,000 feet, draws to its summer pastures Kirghis shepherds from north, east and west; and their flocks in turn attract the raids of the marauding mountaineers occupying the Hunza Valley to the south. The Pamir, high but accessible, was a passway in the tenth century for Chinese caravans bound from "Serica" or the "Land of Silk" to the Oxus River and the Caspian.

Height in mountain barriers.

NOTES TO CHAPTER XV

1. For physical effects, see Angelo Mosso, Life of Man on the High Alps. Translated from the Italian. London, 1898.

2. W. Z. Ripley, Races of Europe, pp. 463-465. New York, 1899.

3. Strabo, Book IV, chap. VI, 3.

4. W. Z. Ripley, Races of Europe, pp. 31-32. New York, 1899.

5. Sir Thomas Holdich, India, pp. 32-33. London, 1905.

6. W. Z. Ripley, The Races of Europe, Map p. 439. New York, 1899.

7. Imperial Gazetteer of India, Vol. I, pp. 294-295. Oxford, 1907. Sir Thomas Holdich, India, relief map on p. 171 compared with linguistic map p. 201. London, 1905.

8. Census of India for 1901, Risley and Gait, Vol. I, Part I, p. 2. Calcutta, 1903. B. H. Baden-Powell, The Indian Village Community, pp. 40, 130, 131. London, 1896.

9. Count Gleichen, The Egyptian Sudan, Vol. I, pp. 184, 185, 190. London, 1905.

10. Gustav Nachtigal, *Sahara und Sudan*, Vol. III, pp. 178, 188-192. Leipzig, 1889.

11. Spencer and Gillen, The Northern Tribes of Central Australia, pp. 6, 13. London, 1904.

12. W. Deecke, Italy, p. 365. London, 1904.

13. Sir Thomas Holdich, India, pp. 295-296. London, 1905. G. W. Steevens, In India, pp. 202-204. New York, 1899.

14. Francis Younghusband, The Heart of a Continent, pp. 138, 140, 145, 272-273. London, 1904.

15. E. Huntington, The Pulse of Asia, p. 87. Boston, 1907.

16. E. C. Semple, American History and Its Geographic Conditions, pp. 184-185. Boston, 1903.

17. Isabella Bird Bishop, The Yangtze Valley and Beyond, Vol. II, pp. 70-72, 88, 91. London, 1900.

18. Francis H. Nichols, Through Hidden Shensi, pp. 170-171. New York, 1902.

19. Otis T. Mason, Primitive Travel and Transportation, pp. 450-454, 474-475. Smithsonian Report, Washington, 1896.

20. Col. George E. Church, The Acre Territory and the Caoutchouc Regions of Southwestern Amazonia, *Geog. Jour.* May, 1904. London.

21. M. Huc, Journey through the Chinese Empire, pp. 39-40. New York, 1871.

22. Perceval Landon, The Opening of Tibet, pp. 54-55. New York, 1905.

23. Jean Baptiste Tavernier, Travels in India. Vol. II, p. 264. Translated from the French of 1676. London, 1889.

24. E. F. Knight, Where Three Empires Meet, pp. 231, 274, 276, 286-289. London, 1897.

25. Census of the Philippine Islands, Vol. I, p. 544. Washington, 1905.

26. Joseph Partsch, Central Europe, p. 134. London, 1903.

27. M. S. W. Jefferson, Cæsar and the Central Plateau of France, *Journal of Geog.*, Vol. VI, p. 113. New York, 1897.

28. P. Vidal de la Blache, *Tableau de la Géographie de la France*, p. 276. Paris, 1903.

29. E. A. Freeman, Historical Geography of Europe, Vol. I, p. 450-453. London, 1882.

30. William Morris Davis, Physical Geography, p. 183. Boston, 1899.

31. P. Vidal de la Blache, *Tableau de la Géographie de la France*, p. 260, map p. 261. Paris, 1903.

32. Indian Census for 1901, Risley and Gait, Vol. I, Part I, pp. 1, 2. Calcutta, 1903.

33. Hans Helmolt, History of the World, Vol. IV, p. 479. New York, 1902.

34. Sir Thomas Holdich, India, p. 67, cartogram of Hindu Kush orography. London, 1905.

35. *Ibid.*, pp. 102-104.

36. *Ibid.*, p. 26.

37. J. Partsch, Central Europe, p. 27. London, 1903.

38. B. H. Baden-Powell, The Indian Village Community, pp. 40-45, 111, 116. London, 1896.

39. H. R. Mill, International Geography, pp. 394-395. New York, 1902.

40. Gottfried Merzbacher, *Aus den Hochregionen des Kaukasus*, pp. 73-78. Leipzig, 1901.

41. W. Z. Ripley, The Races of Europe, p. 438. New York, 1899.

42. *Ibid.*, Maps pp. 143, 147, text p. 148.

43. E. Huntington, The Pulse of Asia, pp. 106-109. Boston, 1907.

Physical Environmental Descriptions
of the United States

III

Environmental descriptions have been written about most countries of the world. Such discussions include all aspects of the physical world such as the types of rocks, soils, and climate, the configuration of the lands and waters, and sometimes includes the relation that such features might have to man and his utilization of various resources. To cover such a phantasmagoric array of topics and places within limited pages would be both bewildering and capricious. Instead I have chosen to use the United States as an example, and to divide the materials with a view towards some type of comparison, between early descriptions in the eastern region and that in the western areas.

A. Eastern United States

There is a large literature that covers many descriptive features of the eastern United States. Reports, diaries, letters, articles, books, etc., were written by a great variety of people in many different professions. A large number of these materials contain only isolated phrases or sentences that are relevant and so are not suitable for incorporation as an entity in facsimile fashion. Included in such works are matters such as description of flora, fauna, and habits and customs of the people. Other written documents contain such disjointed happenings as personal matters, hardships of travel, and interactions with people that they are not appropriate. When such factors are considered the articles that are germane become reduced in number. Still it must be remembered that the impressions used here represent only a minute sampling of published works and ideas. Each of the selected items, however, has a purpose and meaning that is representative of a general class of literature.

The work and essays of Jared Eliot in the years 1748–1762 (Carman and Tugwell, 1934) provides one of the earliest accounts of husbandry practices, soils, and land usage in America. Eliot described the nature of the soils and lands in New England with remarks about what to plant, when and how, for example: "No fertility is to be expected from perfect sand, for every grain of sand is a pebble stone, and surely none can reasonably expect corn from stones alone, although these stones lye in never such good order: That a grain of sand is a pebble appears by being viewed in the microscope or magnifying glass; as also, that *sand* is one of the ingredients in the making of glass" (p. 122). Another early book on a similar topic was written by an anonymous English author (Carman, 1939) in 1775. Interest in the Colonies, stimulus for its agricultural development, and improvement of English agronomy were reasons why a large literature developed on these topics in the latter part of the 18th century. Typical of these and the best known was *American Husbandry* with the subtitle of "Containing an account of the soil, climate, production and agriculture of the British Colonies in North America and the West Indies." It contains a constant comparison of the state of agronomy and other practices in America with that in England, along with such descriptions as

Besides tracts which may come under this description, he is farther to examine the meadows which are composed of similar soils but without any trees, being covered with grass; these are to be judged by the height, thickness, and luxuriance of that grass. These tracts are common on the Ohio, and prove how valuable the country should be esteemed: they, like the woodlands, should be examined with the spade, in order to know the appearance of the soil. Besides these there are marshes or swamps, but not in great quantities as in the maritime parts of America: the value of these depend on two circumstances, the richness of the soil, and the ease of being drained: the former is seen by the products; cedars are good signs, though not very common; cypresses generally are found in them, and the excellency of the land [is] perceived from the tallness, size, and beauty of their stems: as to draining, it depends on the situation, and on examining the means of carrying off the water, as in all other countries. These swamps and marshes when drained, if the soil is stiff, are the proper lands for hemp, not that it will not thrive as well on fertile uplands; but they may be applied to other crops. There are, besides these, hilly tracts and the sides of mountains, generally of a gradual ascent, but sometimes sharp and rocky; on the latter vineyards may be planted . . . (p. 224)

Another group of writings was by governmental officials and one of the best descriptions was done by Thomas Pownall (see Mulkearn, 1949), a British administrator in America before the Revolutionary War. He was recognized as having greater sustained interest in Colonial affairs than most of his peers, and his descriptive terrain analysis was published in 1776 and revised in 1784. In speaking of mountains he said:

The Endless Mountains, so called from a Translation of the Indian Name bearing that Signification, come next in order. They are not confusedly scattered, and in loft Peaks overtopping one another, but stretch in long uniform ridges, scarce Half a Mile perpendicular in any Place above the intermediate Vallies. Their Name is expressive of their Extent, though, no doubt, not in a literal Sense. (p. 110)

And in describing water bodies:

> The Face of the Country, as already represented, determines the Nature of the Rivers. The flat Country (or Lower Plains) which lies between the Falls and the Sea, is everywhere interwoven with the most beautiful Bays, Rivers, and Creeks, navigable for all Sorts of Vessels; and is the Reason of so many fine Creeks spreading, on every Sod, from the Bays of Chesopeak and Delaware, For, as the Land has no Declivity, the Flux and Reflux of the Sea contribute to so wide extended Navigation. (p. 127)

One of the earliest geologic writers was William Maclure (1817) and such a section would be incomplete without providing remarks that typify his conclusions.

> On this earth, or in the page of history, it is probable no place can be found of the same extent, so well calculated to perpetuate a free and equal representative government, as the basin of the Mississippi, both from its physical advantages and the political constitutions on which the state of society is bottomed. (p. 89)

His outlook is summed up in the heading for Section IV that is entitled, "The probable effects, which the decomposition of the various classes of rocks may have on the nature and fertility of the soils of the different states of North America, in reference to the accompanying geological map." The following passages are representative of this section.

> Jersey consists of alluvial along the sea coast, which runs along the east bank of the Delaware from Cape May to Trenton; and from thence to Elizabethtown it is bounded by the red sandstone. It is of course partly formed by the sea and partly by the depositions of the Hudson and Delaware rivers, which touch two sides of it; the part of this alluvial, formed by the above mentioned rivers, consisting of depositions washed off the transition and secondary formations, is most probably good soil; but the part of it thrown up by the waves of the sea, will be thin and sandy. (pp. 70–71)
>
> The oldest red sandstone extends from the edge of the alluvial to the foot of the primitive mountains, and from the Hudson to the Delaware. Where the country is level, and consists of the red sandstone only, the soil is good; where it is covered with the greenstone trap, it is generally thin soil and stony. (p. 71)

In describing the area between Norristown and Reading, Maclure writes:

> The soil, through the whole of this tract, when level, is tolerably good; where formed by the alluvial of the rivers, it is generally rich and fertile, but the quartzy and siliceous aggregates, which most frequently occupy the mountains, depose into a light sandy soil, though the vallies between those mountains are rich and productive. (p. 72)

Sir Charles Lyell, who wrote the first English geology textbook, and who had also traveled in America in 1846 reported a 55-ft wide and 180-ft deep gully in Milledgeville,

Georgia, that had been caused by man-induced erosion. Other examples of the impact of man on the environment in America will be provided in Part IV.

The three facsimile reproductions in this section (Part III) were selected because they were written by influential men, who were not scientists, agriculturalists, or administrators, and each represents the view of a different nation. The earliest article, by Robert Beverley (1673–1722) is part of his book that was written as a direct response to a manuscript he had read by an English author. Beverley, a Virginia colonial historian and official with extensive land holdings, wrote his book to refute the many mistakes and misconceptions that were present in the English author's manuscript. It has been recorded that Beverley's book was an instant success and influential in providing Europeans an accurate account of America.

The second selection in this group is representative of the large number of Europeans who came to America after the Revolutionary War to see first hand the nature of the country. Isaac Weld (1774–1856) was an Irish author and topographic writer who viewed America with an unbiased eye and with the competence of a surveyor. He traveled widely throughout the northern states for three years, was well received in all strata of society, and met with George Washington. When printed in 1799 the book was so popular it sold out within the first year and a new edition had to be published. He was author of other books and articles such as *Illustrations of the Scenery of Killarney and the Surrounding Country* (1807).

It is more difficult to evaluate the writings of the last reproduction by C. F. Volney (1757–1820) because of his political ideas and prejudices. He traveled widely in Egypt and Syria and wrote a highly authoritative book *Voyage en Syrie et en Egypte* (1787) which was later used by Napoleon during his Egyptian invasion and occupation. Volney's renown led to his position as Secretary of the French National Assembly in 1790. Volney had a typical colonial bias towards undeveloped countries, but by 1797 he had become disenchanted with Europe and so he traveled to America where he expected to stay and live. In America, however, he again had a reversal of thought, became embittered and disillusioned, and returned to France in 1798. He became influential in France upon his return and was a senator under Napoleon in 1808. In the preface to his book on the United States he remarks:

> France and indeed Europe in general, presented to my view nothing but a gloomy and tempestuous prospect; a series of endless and obstinate wars, between aspiring prejudices and new born knowledges, between antiquated privileges and popular causes. Here [in America] I behold nothing but a splendid prospect of future peace and happiness, flowing from the wide extent of . . . territory.

Further in the preface, however, he explains his disenchantment and need to leave the country.

THE
HISTORY
OF
VIRGINIA,
In Four PARTS.

I. The HISTORY of the First Settlement of *Virginia*, and the Government thereof, to the Year 1706.

II. The natural Productions and Conveniencies of the Country, suited to Trade and Improvement.

III. The Native *Indians*, their Religion, Laws, and Customs, in War and Peace.

IV. The present State of the Country, as to the Polity of the Government, and the Improvements of the Land, the 10th of *June* 1720.

By a Native *and* Inhabitant *of the* PLACE.✝

The SECOND EDITION revis'd and enlarg'd by the AUTHOR.

LONDON:

Printed for F. FAYRAM and J. CLARKE at the *Royal-Exchange*, and T. BICKERTON in *Pater-Noster-Row*, 1722

Ⓦ

Of the NATURAL

Product and Conveniencies

OF

VIRGINIA:

IN ITS

Unimprov'd STATE, before the *English* went thither.

BOOK II.

CHAP. I.

Of the Bounds and Coast of Virginia.

§. 1. *V*IRGINIA, as you have heard before, was a Name at first given, to all the Northern Part of the Continent of *America*; and when the original Grant was made, both to the first and second Colonies, that is, to
those

those of *Virginia*, and *New-England*, they were both granted under the Name of *Virginia*. And afterwards, when Grants for other new Colonies were made, by particular Names, those Names for a long time served only to distinguish them, as so many Parts of *Virginia:* And until the Plantations became more familiar to *England*, it was so continued. But in Process of Time, the Name of *Virginia* was lost to all, except to that Tract of Land lying along the Bay of *Chesapeak*, and a little to the Southward, in which are included *Virginia* and *Maryland*; both which, in common Discourse, are still very often meant by the Name of *Virginia*.

The least Extent of Bounds in any of the Grants made to *Virginia*, since it was settled, and which we find upon Record there, is two hundred Miles North from Point *Comfort*, and two hundred Miles South; winding upon the Sea-Coast to the Eastward, and including all the Land West and North-West, from Sea to Sea; with the Islands on both Seas, within an hundred Miles of the Main. But these Extents both on the North and South, have been since abridg'd by the proprietary Grants of *Maryland* on the North, and *Carolina* on the South.

§. 2. The Entrance into *Virginia* for Shipping, is by the Mouth of *Chesapeak* Bay, which is indeed more like a River, than a Bay: For it runs up into the Land about two hundred Miles, being every where near as wide, as it is at the Mouth, and in many Places much wider. The Mouth thereof is about seven Leagues over, through which all Ships pass to go to *Maryland*.

The Coast is a bold and even Coast, with regular Soundings, and is open all the Year round: So that having the Latitude, which also can hardly be wanted, upon a Coast where so much clear

71

Weather is, any Ship may go in by Soundings alone, by Day or Night, in Summer or in Winter; and need not fear any Difaster, if the Mariners underftand any thing; for, let the Wind blow how it will, and chop about as fuddenly as it pleafes, any Mafter, tho' his Ship be never fo dull, has Opportunity (by the Evennefs of the Coaft) either of ftanding off, and clearing the Shoar; or elfe of running into fafe Harbour within the Capes. A bolder and fafer Coaft is not known in the Univerfe; to which Conveniencies, there's the Addition of good Anchorage all along upon it, without the Capes.

§. 3. *Virginia*, in the moft reftrain'd Senfe, diftinct from *Maryland*, is the Spot to which I fhall altogether confine this Defcription; tho' you may confider at the fame time, that there cannot be much Difference between this, and *Maryland*, they being contiguous one to the other, lying in the fame Bay, producing the fame Sort of Commodities, and being fallen into the fame unhappy Form of Settlements, altogether upon Country Seats, without Towns. *Virginia* thus confider'd, is bounded on the South by North *Carolina*; on the North by *Patowmeck* River, which divides it from *Maryland*; on the Eaft by the main Ocean, called the *Virginia* Seas; and on the Weft and North-Weft by the *Californian* Sea, whenever the Settlements fhall be extended fo far, or now by the River *Miffifippi*.

This Part of *Virginia* now inhabited, if we confider the Improvements in the Hands of the *Englifh*, it cannot upon that Score be commended; but if we confider its natural Aptitude to be improv'd, it may with Juftice be accounted one of the fineft Countries in the World. Moft of the natural Advantages of it therefore, I fhall endeavour to difcover, and fet in their true Light, together with its Inconveniencies; and afterwards proceed to the Improvements.

CHAP. II.

CHAP. II.

Of the WATERS.

§. 4. THE Largeness of the Bay of *Chesapeak* I have mention'd already. From one End of it to the other, there's good Anchorage, and so little Danger of a Wreck, that many Masters, who have never been there before, venture up to the Head of the Bay, upon the slender Knowledge of a common Sailor. But the Experience of one Voyage teaches any Master to go up afterwards, without a Pilot.

Besides this Bay, the Country is water'd with four great Rivers, *viz. James, York, Rappahannock,* and *Patowmeck* Rivers; all which are full of convenient and safe Harbours. There are also abundance of lesser Rivers, many of which are capable of receiving the biggest Merchant-Ships, *viz. Elizabeth* River, *Nansamond, Chickahomony, Pocoson, Pamunky, Mattapony,* (which two last are the two upper Branches of *York* River) *North* River, *Eastermost* River, *Corotoman, Wiccocomoco, Pocomoke, Chisseneffick, Pungotegue,* and many others : But because they are so well describ'd in the large Maps of *Virginia,* I shall forbear any farther Description of them.

These Rivers are of such Convenience, that, for almost every half dozen Miles of their Extent, there's a commodious and safe Road for a whole Fleet; which gives Opportunity to the Masters of Ships, to lye up and down straggling, according as they have made their Acquaintance, riding before that Gentleman's Door where they find the best Reception, or where 'tis most suitable to their Business.

§. 5. These

§. 5. Thefe Rivers are made up, by the Conflux of an infinite Number of chryftal Springs of cool and pleafant Water, iffuing every where out of the Banks, and Sides of the Valleys. Thefe Springs flow fo plentifully, that they make the River Water frefh, fifty, threefcore, and fometimes an hundred Miles below the Flux and Reflux of the Tides; and fometime within thirty or forty Miles of the Bay it felf. The Conveniencies of thefe Springs are fo many, they are not to be number'd: I fhall therefore content my felf to mention that one of fupplying the Country elfe where, except in the low Lands, with as many Mills as they can find Work for: And fome of thefe fend forth fuch a Glut of Water, that in lefs than a Mile below the Fountain-head, they afford a Stream fufficient to fupply a Grift-Mill; of which there are feveral Inftances.

§. 6. The only Mifchief I know belonging to thefe Rivers is, that in the Month of *June* annually, there rife up in the Salts, vaft Beds of Seedling-Worms, which enter the Ships, Sloops, or Boats where-ever they find the Coat of Pitch, Tar, or Lime worn off the Timber; and by degrees eat the Plank into Cells like thofe of an Honey-comb. Thefe Worms continue thus upon the Surface of the Water, from their Rife in *June,* until the firft great Rains, after the Middle of *July*; but after that, do no frefh Damage till the next Summer-Seafon, and never penetrate farther than the Plank or Timber they firft fix upon.

The Damage occafion'd by thefe Worms, may be four feveral Ways avoided.

1. By keeping the Coat, (of Pitch, Lime and Tallow, or whatever elfe it is,) whole upon the Bottom of the Ship or Veffel, for thefe Worms

never

never faſten nor enter, but where·the Timber is naked.

2. By anchoring the large Veſſels in the Strength of the Tide, during the Worm-Seaſon, and haling the ſmaller aſhore; for in the Current of a ſtrong Tide, the Worm cannot faſten.

3. By burning and cleaning immediately after the Worm-Seaſon is over; for then they are but juſt ſtuck into the Plank, and have not buried themſelves in it ; ſo that the leaſt Fire in the World deſtroys them entirely, and prevents all Damage, that would otherwiſe enſue from them.

4. By running up into the Freſhes with the Ship or Veſſel during the five or ſix Weeks, that the Worm is thus above Water : For they never enter, nor do any Damage in freſh Water, or where it is not very ſalt.

C H A P. III.

Of the E A R T HS, *and* S O I L.

§. 7. T H E Soil is of ſuch Variety, according to the Difference of Situation, that one Part or other of it, ſeems fitted to every Sort of Plant, that is requiſite either for the Benefit or Pleaſure of Mankind. And, were it not for the high Mountains to the North-Weſt, which are ſuppoſed to retain vaſt Magazines of Snow, and by that means cauſe the Wind from that Quarter to deſcend a little too cold upon them, 'tis believed, that many of thoſe delicious Summer Fruits, growing in the hotter Climates, might be kept there green all the Winter, without the Charge of Houſing, or any other Care, than what is due to the natural Plants of the Country, when tranſplanted into a Garden. But,

H as

as that would be no confiderable Charge, any Man that is curious might, with all the Eafe imaginable, preferve as many of them as would gratify a moderate Luxury; and the Summer affords genial Heat enough, to ripen them to Perfection.

There are three different Kinds of Land, according to the Difference of Situation, either in the lower Parts of the Country, the Middle, or that on the Heads of the Rivers.

1. The Land towards the Mouth of the Rivers is generally of a low moift and fat Mold, fuch as the heavier Sort of Grain delight in, as Rice, Hemp, *Indian* Corn, &c. This alfo is varied here and there with Veins of a cold, hungry, fandy Soil, of the fame Moifture, and very often lying under Water. But this alfo has its Advantages; for on fuch Land, generally grow the Huckle-berries, Cran-berries, Chinkapins, &c. Thefe low Lands are, for the moft part, well ftor'd with Oaks, Poplars, Pines, Cedars, Cyprefs, and Sweet-Gums; the Trunks of which are often thirty, forty, fifty, ·fome fixty or feventy Foot high, without a Branch or Limb. They likewife produce great Variety of Evergreens, unknown to me by Name, befides the beauteous Holly, Sweet-Myrtle, Cedar, and the Live-Oak, which for three Quarters of the Year is continually dropping its Acorns, and at the fame time budding, and bearing others in their Stead.

2. The Land higher up the Rivers throughout the whole Country, is generally a level Ground, with fhallow Vallies, full of Streams and pleafant Springs of clear Water, having interfpers'd here and there among the large Levels, fome fmall Hills, and extenfive Vales. The Mold in fome Places is black, fat, and thick laid; in others loofer, lighter, and thin. The Foundation of the Mold is alfo various; fometimes Clay, then Gravel and rocky Stones; and fome-

sometimes Marle. The Middle of the Necks, or Ridges between the Rivers, is generally poor, being either a light Sand, or a white or red Clay, with a thin Mold : Yet even these Places are stored with Chesnuts, Chinkapins, Acorns of the Shrub-Oak, and a reedy Grass in Summer, very good for Cattle. The rich Lands lye next the Rivers and Branches, and are stored with large Oaks, Walnuts, Hickories, Ash, Beech, Poplar, and many other Sorts of Timber, of surprising Bigness.

3. The Heads of the Rivers afford a Mixture of Hills, Vallies and Plains, some richer than other, whereof the Fruits and Timber-Trees are also various. In some Places lye great Plats of low and very rich Ground, well Timber'd ; in others, large Spots of Meadows and Savanna's, wherein are Hundreds of Acres without any Tree at all ; but yield Reeds and Grass of incredible Height : And in the Swamps and sunken Grounds grow Trees, as vastly big, as I believe the World affords, and stand so close together, that the Branches or Boughs of many of them, lock into one another ; but what lessens their Value is, that the greatest Bulk of them are at some Distance from Water-Carriage. The Land of these upper Parts affords greater Variety of Soil, than any other, and as great Variety in the Foundations of the Soil or Mold, of which good Judgment may be made, by the Plants and Herbs that grow upon it. The Rivers and Creeks do in many Places form very fine large Marshes, which are a convenient Support for their Flocks and Herds.

§. 8. There is likewise found great Variety of Earths for Physick, cleansing, scouring, and making all Sorts of Potters-Ware ; such as Antimony, Talk, yellow and red Oker, Fullers-Earth, Pipe-Clay,

H 2

Clay, and other fat and fine Clays, Marle, &c. In a Word, there are all Kinds of Earth fit for Use.

They have besides in those upper Parts, Coal for firing, Slate for covering, and Stones for building, and Flat-paving in vast Quantities, as likewise Pebble-Stones. Nevertheless, it has been confidently affirm'd by many, who have been in *Virginia*, that there is not a Stone in all the Country. If such Travellers knew no better than they said, my Judgment of them is, that either they were People of extream short Memories, or else of very narrow Observation. For tho' generally the lower Parts are flat, and so free from Stones, that People seldom shoe their Horses; yet in many Places, and particularly near the Falls of the Rivers, are found vast Quantities of Stone, fit for all kind of Uses. However, as yet there is seldom any Use made of them, because commonly Wood is to be had at much less Trouble. And as for Coals, it is not likely they should ever be used there in any thing, but Forges and great Towns, if ever they happen to have any; for, in their Country Plantations, the Wood grows at every Man's Door so fast, that after it has been cut down, it will in seven Years time, grow up again from Seed, to substantial Fire-Wood; and in eighteen or twenty Years 'twill come to be very good Board-Timber.

§. 9. For Mineral Earths, 'tis believed, they have great Plenty and Variety, that Country being in a good Latitude, and having great Appearances of them. It has been proved too, that they have both Iron and Lead, as appears by what was said before, concerning the Iron-Work, set up at *Falling-Creek* in *James* River, where the Iron proved reasonably good: But before they got into the Body of the Mine, the People were cut off in that fatal Massacre; and the Project has never been set on

Foot

Foot ſince, till of late; but it has not had its full Trial.

The Golden-Mine, of which there was once ſo much noiſe, may, perhaps, be found hereafter to be ſome good Metal, when it comes to be fully examined. But, be that as it will, the Stones, that are found near it in great Plenty, are valuable; their Luſtre approaching nearer to that of the Diamond, than thoſe of *Briſtol* or *Kerry*. There is no other Fault in them, but their Softneſs, which the Weather hardens, when they have been ſometime expoſed to it, they being found under the Surface of the Earth. This Place has now Plantations on it.

This I take to be the Place in *Purchaſe*'s fourth Book of his Pilgrim, called *Uttamuſſack*, where was formerly the principal Temple of the Country, and the Metropolitan Seat of the Prieſts, in *Powhatan*'s Time. There ſtood the three great Houſes, near ſixty Foot in Length, which he reports to have been fill'd with the Images of their Gods; there were likewiſe preſerved the Bodies of their Kings. Theſe Houſes they counted ſo holy, that none but their Prieſts and Kings durſt go into them, the common People not preſuming, without their particular Direction, to approach the Place.

There alſo was their great *Pawcorance*, or Altar-Stone, which, the *Indians* tell us, was a ſolid Chryſtal, of between three and four Foot Cube, upon which, in their greateſt Solemnities, they uſed to ſacrifice. This, they would make us believe, was ſo clear, that the Grain of a Man's Skin might be ſeen through it; and was ſo heavy too, that when they remov'd their Gods and Kings, not being able to carry it away, they buried it thereabouts: But the Place has never been yet diſcover'd.

H 3   Mr. *Alex.*

Mr. *Alexander Whittaker*, Minifter of *Henrico*, on *James* River, in the Company's Time, writing to them, fays thus: *Twelve Miles from the Falls, there is a Chryftal Rock, wherewith the* Indians *do head many of their Arrows; and three Days Journey from thence, there is a Rock and ftony Hill found, which is on the Top covered over with a perfect and moft rich Silver Ore. Our Men that went to difcover thofe Parts, had but two Iron Pickaxes with them, and thofe fo ill temper'd, that the Points of them turn'd again, and bow'd at every Stroke; fo that we could not fearch the Entrails of the Place: Yet fome Trial was made of that Ore with good Succefs.*

§. 10. Some People that have been in that Country, without knowing any thing of it, have affirm'd, that it is all a Flat, without any Mixture of Hills, becaufe they fee the Coaft to Seaward perfectly level: Or elfe they have made their Judgment of the whole Country, by the Lands lying on the lower Parts of the Rivers (which, perhaps, they had never been beyond) and fo conclude it to be throughout plain and even. When in truth, upon the Heads of the great Rivers, there are vaft high Hills; and even among the Settlements, there are fome fo topping, that I have ftood upon them, and view'd the Country all round over the Tops of the higheft Trees, for many Leagues together; particularly, there are *Mawborn* Hills in the Frefhes of *James* River; a Ridge of Hills about fourteen or fifteen Miles up *Mattapony* River; *Tolivers* Mount, upon *Rappahannock* River; and the Ridge of Hills in *Stafford* County, in the Frefhes of *Patowmeck* River; all which are within the Bounds of the *Englifh* Inhabitants. But a little farther backward, there are Mountains, which indeed deferve the Name of Mountains, for their Height and Bignefs; which by their difficulty in paffing,

✠ may

may eafily be made a good Barrier of the Country, againft Incurfions of the *Indians*, &c. and
fhew themfelves over the Tops of the Trees to
many Plantations, at 70 or 80 Miles diftance very
plain.

Thefe Hills are not without their Advantages ;
for, out of almoft every rifing Ground, throughout
the Country, there iffue Abundance of moft pleafant Streams, of pure and chryftal Water, than
which certainly the World does not afford any
more delicious. Thefe are every-where to be found
in the upper Parts of this Country ; and many of
them flow out of the Sides of Banks very high
above the Vales, which are the moft fuitable Places for Gardens : Where the fineft Water-works
in the World may be made, at a very fmall Expence.

There are likewife feveral Mineral Springs, eafily difcoverable by their Tafte, as well as by the
Soil, which they drive out with their Streams.
But I am not Naturalift fkilful enough, to defcribe
them with the Exactnefs they deferve.

TRAVELS

THROUGH

6   THE STATES

OF

NORTH AMERICA,

AND THE PROVINCES OF

UPPER AND LOWER CANADA,

DURING THE YEARS

1795, 1796, AND 1797.

―――――――

BY ISAAC WELD, JUN.

―――――――

FOURTH EDITION.
ILLUSTRATED AND EMBELLISHED WITH SIXTEEN PLATES.

――

IN TWO VOLUMES.
VOL. I.

―――――――

LONDON:

PRINTED FOR JOHN STOCKDALE, PICCADILLY.

1807.

We now come to New York, which enjoys the double advantages of an excellent harbour and a large navigable river, which opens a communication with the interior parts of the country; and here we find a flourishing city, containing forty thousand * inhabitants, and increasing beyond every calculation. The North or Hudson River, at the mouth of which New York stands, is navigable from thence for one hundred and thirty miles in large vessels, and in sloops of eighty tons burthen as far as Albany; smaller ones go still higher. About nine miles above Albany, the Mohawk River falls into the Hudson, by means of which, Wood Creek, Lake Oneida, and Oswego River, a communication is opened with Lake Ontario. In this route there are several portages, but it is a route which is much frequented, and numbers of boats are kept employed upon it, in carrying goods whenever the season is not too dry. In long droughts the waters fall so much, that oftentimes there is not sufficient to float an empty boat. All these obstructions however may, and will one day or other, be remedied by the hand of art. Oswego river, before it falls into Lake Ontario, communicates with

---

* Six inhabitants may be reckoned for every house in the United States.

the Seneka river, which affords in succession an entrance into the lakes Cayuga, Seneka, and Canadaqua. Lake Seneka, the largest, is about forty miles in length; upon it there is a schooner-rigged vessel of seventy tons burthen constantly employed. The shores of these lakes are more thickly settled than the other part of the adjacent country, but the population of the whole tract lying between the rivers Genesee and Hudson, which are about two hundred and fifty miles apart, is rapidly increasing. All this country west of the Hudson River, together with that to the east, comprehending the back parts of the states of Massachusets and Connecticut, and also the entire of the state of Vermont, are supplied with European manufactures and West Indian produce, &c. &c. by way of New York: not directly from that city, but from Albany, Hudson, and other towns on the North River, which trade with New York, and which are intermediate places for the deposit of goods passing to, and coming from the back country. Albany, indeed, is now beginning herself to import goods from the West Indies; but still the bulk of her trade is with New York. Nothing can serve more to shew the advantages which accrue to any town from an intercourse with the back country, than the sudden progress of these secondary places of trade upon the North River. At Al-

bany, the number of houses is increasing as fast
as at New York ; at present there are upwards
of eleven hundred ; and in Hudson city, which
was only laid out in the year 1783, there are
now more than three hundred and twenty
dwellings.   This city is on the east side of the
North River, one hundred and thirty miles
above its mouth.   By means also of the North
River and Lake Champlain, a trade is carried
on with Montreal in Canada.

But to go on with the survey of the towns
to the southward.   In New Jersey, we find
Amboy, situated at the head of Raritan Bay,
a bay not inferior to any throughout the United
States. The greatest encouragements also have
been held out by the state legislature, to merchants who would settle there; but the town,
notwithstanding, remains nearly in the state it
was in at the time of the revolution : sixty
houses are all that it contains.   New Brunswick, which is built on Raritan River, about
fifteen miles above its entrance into the bay,
carries on a small inland trade with the adjacent country ; but the principal part of New
Jersey is naturally supplied with foreign manufactures, by New York on one side, and by
Philadelphia on the other, the towns most hap-
pily situated for the purpose.   There are about
two hundred houses in New Brunswick, and

about the same number in Trenton on Delaware, the capital of the state.

Philadelphia, the largest town in the union, has evidently been raised to that state of preeminence by her extensive inland commerce. On one side is the river Delaware, which is navigable in sloops for thirty-five miles above the town, and in boats carrying eight or nine tons one hundred miles farther. On the other side is the Schuylkill, navigable, excepting at the falls, for ninety miles. But the country bordering upon these rivers, is but a trifling part of that which Philadelphia trades with. Goods are forwarded to Harrisburgh, a town situated on the Susquehannah, and from thence sent up that river, and dispersed throughout the adjoining country. The eastern branch of the Susquehannah is navigable for two hundred and fifty miles above Harrisburgh. This place, which in 1786 scarcely deserved the name of a village, now contains upwards of three hundred houses. By land carriage Philadelphia also trades with the western parts of Pennsylvania, as far as Pittsburgh itself, which is on the Ohio, with the back of Virginia, and, strange to tell, with Kentucky, seven hundred miles distant.

Philadelphia however does not enjoy the exclusive trade to Virginia and Kentucky; Baltimore, which lies more to the south, comes in for a considerable share, if not for the greatest part of it, and to that is indebted for her sudden rise, and her great superiority over Annapolis the capital of Maryland. Annapolis, although it has a good harbour, and was made a port of entry as long ago as the year 1694, has scarcely any trade now. Baltimore, situated more in the heart of the country, has gradually drawn it all away from her. From Baltimore nearly the entire of Maryland is furnished with European manufactures. The very flourishing state of this place has already been mentioned.

As the Patowmac river, and the towns upon it, are to come more particularly under notice afterwards, we may from hence pass on to the other towns in Virginia. With regard to Virginia, however, it is to be observed, that the impolitic laws which have been enacted in that state have thrown a great damp upon trade; the Virginians too have always been more disposed towards agriculture than trade, so that the towns in that state, some of which are most advantageously situated, have never increased as they would have done, had the country been inhabited by a different kind of people, and had different laws consequently existed ; still however we shall find that the most flourishing towns in the state, are those which are open to the sea, and situated most conveniently at the same time for trading with the people of the back country. On Rappahannock River, for instance, Tappahannock or Hobb's Hole was laid out at the same time that Philadelphia was. Fredericksburgh was built many years afterwards on the same river, but thirty miles higher up, and at the head of that part of it which was navigable for sea vessels ; the consequence of this has been, that Fredericksburgh, from being situated more in the heart of the country, is now four times as large a town as Hobb's Hole.

York River, from running so closely to James River on the one side, and the Rappahannock on the other, does not afford a good situation for a large town. The largest town upon it, which is York, only contains seventy houses.

Williamsburgh was formerly the capital of the state, and contains about four hundred houses; but instead of increasing, this town is going to ruin, and numbers of the houses at present are uninhabited, which is evidently on account of its inland situation. There is no navigable stream nearer to it than one mile and a half, and this is only a small creek which runs into James River. Richmond, on the contrary, which is the present capital of the state, has increased very fast, because it stands on a large navigable river ; yet Richmond is no more than an intermediate place for the deposit of goods passing to and from the back country, vessels drawing more than seven feet water being unable to come up to the town.

The principal place of trade in Virginia is Norfolk. This town has a good harbour, and is enabled to trade with the upper parts of the country, by means of James River, near the mouth of which it stands. By land also a brisk trade is carried on with the back parts of North Carolina, for in that state there are no towns of any importance. The entrances from the sea into the rivers in that state, are all impeded by shoals and sand banks, none of which afford more than eleven feet water, and the passage over some of them is very dangerous from the sand shifting. Wilmington, which is the greatest place of trade in it, contains only two hundred and fifty houses. In order to carry on their trade to North Carolina to more advantage, a canal is now cutting across the Dismal Swamp, from Norfolk into Albemarle sound, by means of the rivers that empty into which, a water communication will be opened ...

89

A VIEW.

OF

7   THE SOIL AND CLIMATE

OF THE

UNITED STATES OF AMERICA:

WITH SUPPLEMENTARY REMARKS

UPON FLORIDA; ON THE FRENCH COLONIES ON THE MISSISSIPPI
AND OHIO, AND IN CANADA; AND ON THE ABORIGINAL TRIBES
OF AMERICA.

———

BY C. F. VOLNEY,

MEMBER OF THE CONSERVATIVE SENATE, &c. &c.

——

TRANSLATED, WITH OCCASIONAL REMARKS,

BY C. B. BROWN.

———

WITH MAPS AND PLATES.

———

PHILADELPHIA,

PUBLISHED BY J. CONRAD & CO PHILADELPHIA; M. & J. CONRAD & CO.
BALTIMORE; RAPIN, CONRAD, & CO. WASHINGTON CITY; SOMERVELL
& CONRAD, PETERSBURG; AND BONSAL, CONRAD, & CO. NORFOLK.
PRINTED BY T. & G. PALMER, 116, HIGH STREET.

....

1804.

Face of the Country.

TO a traveller from Europe, and especially to one accustomed, as I had been, to the naked plains of Egypt, Asia, and the coasts of the Mediterranean, the most striking feature of America is the rugged and dreary prospect of an almost universal forest. This forest is first discerned on the coast, but continues thickening and enlarging from thence to the heart of the country. During a long journey, which I made in 1796, from the mouth of Delaware, through Pennsylvania, Maryland, Virginia, and Kentucky, to the Wabash, and thence northward, across the North-west territory, to Detroit, through Lake Erie to Niagara and Albany; and, in the following year, from Boston to Richmond, in Virginia, I scarcely passed, for three miles together, through a track of unwooded or *cleared* land.

I always found the roads, or rather the paths, bordered and obscured by copse or forest, whose silence, uniformity, and stillness was wearisome. The ground beneath it was sterile and rough, or encumbered with the fallen and decaying trunks of ancient trees. Clouds of gnats, mosquitoes, and flies hovered beneath the shade, and continually infested my peace. Such is the real state of these Elysian fields, of which, in the bosom of European cities, romancers entertain us with their charming dreams. On the sea coast there are, however, many open spaces, which the progress of cultivation and the vast consumption of fuel in the cities have occasioned. There are likewise considerable openings in the western regions especially between the Wabash and the Mississippi, on the banks of Lake Erie, and those of St. Laurence, in Tenessee and Kentucky, where the nature of the soil, or, more frequently, the annual or ancient conflagrations of the Indians, have opened vast deserts, called savannahs by the Spaniards, and prairies by the Canadians. These bear no resemblance to the arid plains of Arabia and Syria, but remind us rather of the *steps* or grassy wastes of Tartary and Russia. The prairies may be described as *steps*, covered with ligneous plants, growing very thick, and to the height of three or four feet. They display, in spring and autumn, a lively carpet of verdure and flowers, and such a scene is very rarely to be met with in the dry or stony plains of Arabia. In the rest of the country, especially among the inland mountains, trees are found in such numbers, and their prevalence is so little checked and circumscribed, that the United States, compared with such a country as France, may justly be denominated one vast forest.

If we subject this immense wilderness to a single comprehensive view, we shall be led to divide it into three regions or districts, each of which is distinguished from the rest by the nature of the timber it produces. The kind of tree, as the American observes, indicates the nature of the soil it grows upon.

The first of these districts I shall call the *southern forest*. It embraces the maritime parts of Virginia, the two Carolinas, Georgia, and Florida, and may be generally described as extending from the bay of Chesapeake to the river St. Mary, over a gravelly and sandy soil, spreading from a hundred to a hundred and fifty miles wide. All this space is thickly planted with the pine, fir, larch, cedar, cypress, and other resinous trees. It presents a scene of perpetual verdure, which, however, is only a cover for sterility, except in those spots which the course of rivers and alluvial depositions have fertilized, and which cultivation has made abundantly productive.

The *middle forest* comprehends the hilly parts of Carolina and Virginia, all Pennsylvania, the southern part of New York, all Kentucky, and the country north of the Ohio, as far as the Wabash. This whole extent is covered with the oak, ash, maple, hiccory, sycamore, acacia, mulberry, plum, birch, sassafras, and poplar. In the western part are found the cherry, horse chesnut, the sumac, &c. and all the kinds that indicate a rich soil, the only basis of the prosperity of this portion of the states. The resinous trees are mingled, in the plains and vallies, with those just mentioned, and form entire woods upon the mountains. They are met with in the chain called, in Virginia, the *south-west*, but, contrary to usual appearances, they here cover a red, deep, and fat soil.

The third district, or the *northern forest*, is likewise composed of the fir, pine, larch, cedar, and cypress. It spreads itself over the western parts of New York, and the inland countries of New England; exclusive, however, of the *inter-vales* and banks of rivers. It advances northward into Canada, and is lost at last among the deserts of the polar circle, where the trees dwindle down into thinly scattered junipers and other hardy plants, of stinted growth and scanty product.

Such is the general aspect of the territory of these states. The picture is composed of an almost universal forest, varied and broken by five vast lakes, or inland seas, in the north; by immense natural meadows, or *prairies*, in the west; and in the centre by a chain of mountains, whose ridges are parallel to the sea coast, at the distance of from fifty to a hundred and fifty miles, and which turn, to the east and west, rivers of a longer course, wider channel, and more ample stream, than we are accustomed to meet with in Europe*. These rivers are broken into cataracts, from twenty to

* M. Volney probably limits this comparison, in his own mind, to France or Britain, for the German, Polish, and Russian rivers fall not short of ours, in any of these circumstances. The American reader may listen with less dissatisfaction to our author's idea of an universal forest, when he is reminded that our present

one hundred and forty feet in height, and enter the sea in mouths that expand into gulphs. In the southern regions, the bogs or swamps extend above three hundred miles. In the north, the snows lie on the ground four or five months in the year. One one side, in a course of nine hundred miles, are scattered ten or twelve towns, built entirely of brick, or of painted wood, and containing from ten to sixty thousand souls. Without the cities are scattered farmhouses, built of unhewn logs, surrounded with a few small fields of wheat, tobacco, or maize, that are still encumbered with the half burnt stocks of trees, and are divided by branches laid across each other, by way of fence*. These rude dwellings and fields are

population consumes and exports the product of less than *one fiftieth* of the whole surface, and *fifty* acres of woodland would hardly be lessened to the eye, by cutting down *one* acre only. This diminution would be still less apparent, if the acre of wood thus removed were not one entire acre, but made up of trees scattered irregularly through the whole mass; but this has been pretty much the case in the settlement of North America. By an eye that could view the whole territory at a single glance, nothing would be seen but a *boundless contiguity of shade*. Very different, however, would be the face of things partially seen—TRANS.

* Those who are not enabled, by their own observation and experience, to qualify this general representation, will be led by it into great errors. In traversing New England, Jersey, and the eastern parts of Pennsylvania and Virginia, the scene is widely different from that above described. The picture is fully realized in those quarters only which are newly settled, and where attempts have just been commenced for reclaiming the wilderness. —TRANS.

B. Western United States

The exploration, opening, settlement, history, and chronicling of the West was quite different from that of the East. Although some early knowledge of it occurred, much was transmitted by word of mouth and became inaccurate in the final rendition. Many of the earliest visitors could not write, were not scholarly, and did not produce manuscripts. Much of the documented works, therefore, have taken an entirely different approach than was the case in the eastern United States. The pertinent literature of the West was generally government-sponsored, paid for by the federal government, and printed in governmental publications. Illustrative of the lack of good environmental and planning data of the West was the necessity of the Lewis and Clark Expedition (1804–1806) into the Northwest after the Louisiana Purchase (1803). The purpose of the expedition was to provide important information on the physical nature of the terrain and inhabitants of the region. The expedition produced only a series of short reports and diaries which were largely filled with day to day chores and experiences with the Indians. They did remark, however, on the customs of the inhabitants at length and observed carefully the flora and fauna. For example Cutright (1969) in his book refers to Lewis and Clark as the "pioneering naturalists." They also described some of the topographic characteristics of the region in such fashion:

> ... at 9. A.M. at the junction of the S.E. fork of the Missouri and the country opens suddonly to extensive and beatifull plains and meadows which appear to be surrounded in every direction with distant and lofty mountains; ... from E to S. between S.E. and middle forks a distant range of lofty mountains ran their snow clad tops above the irregular and broken mountains which lie adjacent to this beautifull spot. between the middle and S.E. forks near their junction with the S.W. fork there is a handsome site for a fortification. after making a draught of the connection and meanders of these streams I descended the hill and returned to the party. (DeVoto, 1937, p. 504)

John C. Fremont (1813–1890) sometimes called "The Pathfinder" and the West's greatest adventurer (Nevins, 1928) was a lieutenant in the Army Topographic Corps and did most of his western surveys between 1842–1845. The following is typical of some of his descriptive passages (as recorded in Smucker, 1856, p. 470–471).

> This account of the Great Basin, it will be remembered, belongs to the Alta California, and has no application to Oregon, whose capabilities may justify a separate remark. Referring to my journal for particular descriptions, and for sectional boundaries between good and bad districts, I can only say, in general and comparative terms, that, in that branch of agriculture which implies the cultivation of grains and staple crops, it would be inferior to the Atlantic States, though many parts are superior for wheat; while in the rearing of flocks and herds it would claim a high place. Its grazing capabilities are great; and even in the indigenous grass now there, an element of individual and national wealth may be found. In fact, the valuable grasses begin within one hundred and fifty miles of the Missouri frontier, and extend to the Pacific ocean. East of the Rocky mountains, it is the short

96

curly grass, on which the buffalo delights to feed, (whence its name of buffalo,) and which is still good when dry and apparently dead. West of those mountains it is a larger growth, in clusters, and hence called bunch-grass, and which has a second or fall growth. Plains and mountains both exhibit them; and I have seen good pasturage at an elevation of ten thousand feet. In this spontaneous product the trading or traveling caravans can find subsistence for their animals; and in military operations any number of cavalry men may be moved, and any number of cattle may be driven; and thus men and horses be supported on long expeditions, and even in winter, in the sheltered situations.

Commercially, the value of the Oregon country must be great, washed as it is by the North Pacific ocean—fronting Asia—producing many of the elements of commerce—mild and healthy in its climate—and becoming, as it naturally will, a thoroughfare for the East India and China trade.

Turning our faces once more eastward, on the morning of the 27th we left the Utah lake, and continued for two days to ascend the Spanish fork, which is dispersed in numerous branches among very rugged mountains, which afford few passes, and render a familiar acquaintance with them necessary to the traveler. The stream can scarcely be said to have a valley, the mountains rising often abruptly from the water's edge; but a good trail facilitated our traveling, and there were frequent bottoms, covered with excellent grass. The streams are prettily and variously wooded; and everywhere the mountain shows grass and timber.

The greatest chapter in the history of exploration, science, description, and topographic analysis and environmental impact resulted from four different, but somewhat competitive governmental surveys during the years 1867–1879. For brevity these surveys will be referred to respectively as the Hayden, King, Wheeler, and Powell Surveys. Each produced significant information and data, contained talented personnel, and performed prodigious feats. In their own way each was charged with obtaining valuable information that could be used for specific purposes in environmental planning.

1. The Hayden Survey (U.S. Geological Survey of the Territories, 1867–1879) was financed by General Land Office funds. It was led by Ferdinand V. Hayden (1829–1887) who received an M.D. degree (1853) and started geologic surveys of the West including Yellowstone and Missouri River badlands in 1856. During the Civil War he became Surgeon General and from 1865–1872 held the position of Professor of Geology at the University of Pennsylvania. The purpose of the Hayden Survey was to evaluate the lands and the geology of the region north of the 40th parallel. Hayden was a good organizer and administrator and by 1883 all 12 annual reports had been published along with many other documents. Although politically minded, he failed in his attempt to become first Director of the U.S. Geological Survey. He was influential, however, in paving the way so that the Yellowstone area became the first National Park:

> But no language can do justice to the wonderful grandeur and beauty of the cañon below the Lower Falls; the very nearly vertical walls, slightly sloping down to the water's edge on either side, so that from the summit the river appears like a thread of silver foaming over its rocky bottom; the variegated colors of the sides . . . (p. 83)

97

A glance at the map will show to the reader the geographical locality of the most beautiful lake in the world, set like a gem among the mountains. He will also see that the mountains that wall it in on every side form one of the most remarkable water-sheds on the continent. The snows that fall on the summits give origin to three of the largest rivers in North America . . . I have thus presented a brief history of the passage of this bill because I believe it will mark an era in the popular advancement of scientific thought, not only in this country, but throughout the civilized world. That our legislators, at a time when public opinion is so strong against appropriating the public domain for any purpose however laudable, should reserve, for the benefit and instruction of the people, a tract of 3,578 square miles, is an act that should cause universal joy throughout the land. (in making his tribute to the establishment of Yellowstone National Park, Hayden, 1872. p. 162)

2. The King Survey (Geological Survey of the 40th Parallel, 1867–1879) was led by Clarence King who in 1879 became the first Director of the U.S. Geological Survey. This survey was financed with Army funds and a major goal was terrain and geologic analysis of the lands that would serve as a route for the Union Pacific and Central Pacific railroads. King (1842–1901) was a complex man of many talents, scientific and otherwise, and who prided himself in the social graces. His survey was brilliantly planned and produced major accomplishments in such fields as paleontology and stratigraphy, and the first use of contour maps and of the petrographic microscope to corroborate field studies. The survey produced seven volumes and many other separate publications. Although King was reluctant to accept the directorship of the U.S. Geological Survey, he agreed to the position for the sake of science and to alleviate a damaging political battle that would have harmed the geologic image and perhaps hamstrung a fledgling new agency. Thus his introductory statement about the nature of the U.S. Geological Survey is reproduced here because it symbolizes such an important historical innovation.

3. The Wheeler Survey (U.S. Geographical Survey West of the One Hundredth Meridian, 1871–1879) was headed by George W. Wheeler, a Captain in the U.S. Army, and funded by the War Department. The main function of the expedition was to produce a geographic survey with accurate maps that might be required for any future military operation. Initially most personnel were in the army but later scientists were allowed to participate. A series of 75 topographic atlas sheets were made using the hachure method. Significant basic research, however, also emerged. For example, G. K. Gilbert received funds and his classic papers on Lake Bonneville and on the Great Basin were results of these studies. The reproduction selected for presentation is typical of parts of the seven volumes that were written for use by the War Department. Completion of the volume was postponed by Wheeler's illness and assignment to other priority jobs.

4. The Powell Survey (Geographical and Geological Survey of the Rocky Mountains, 1870–1878) was led by John Wesley Powell. Prior to 1872 various other names were used for this survey and during the first years it was financed by the Smithsonian Institute. After that time it was funded through the U.S. Department of the Interior. The purpose of the survey was to explore and do the topography and geology of

the Rocky Mountain region. From 1875–1880 eight volumes were published along with several separate publications. Although the volumes provided important structural geology and petrology concepts, they became best known for setting new insights into the geomorphology and hydrology of the West. Gilbert's classic work on the Henry Mountains (1877) was a great bonus from this work. Part of the outgrowth of his studies of the region are contained in the contributions by Powell in Part V.

The work and results of these four surveys cannot be overestimated. They provided a wealth of fundamental knowledge that was vital for an expanding nation. The descriptive work contained some of the first accurate accounts of the physical features of the West, and led to additional exploration for land, minerals, and exploitation of its resources. The surveys also gave a solid foundation in science and tipped the balance which up to that time had largely seen complete European domination in geology and geomorphology. Indeed, the surveys resulted in producing some of the finest literature of its day or any day.

PRELIMINARY REPORT

OF THE

UNITED STATES GEOLOGICAL SURVEY

OF

8 MONTANA

AND

PORTIONS OF ADJACENT TERRITORIES;

BEING A

FIFTH ANNUAL REPORT OF PROGRESS.

BY

F. V. HAYDEN,

UNITED STATES GEOLOGIST.

CONDUCTED UNDER AUTHORITY OF THE SECRETARY OF THE INTERIOR.

WASHINGTON:
GOVERNMENT PRINTING OFFICE.
1872.

100

GEOLOGICAL SURVEY OF THE TERRITORIES.

CHAPTER I.

FROM OGDEN, UTAH, TO FORT HALL, IDAHO.

In my previous reports I have endeavored to present such facts in regard to the geology of the country lying between Omaha and Salt Lake as my time and opportunities have enabled me to secure. In a subsequent chapter I shall pass this region again under review, adding such new matter as the investigations of the past seasons have brought to light.

In order that the results of the explorations of 1871 might be connected with those of preceding years, it was thought best to make Ogden the point of departure. The latitude and longitude of Salt Lake City are probably as well fixed as those of any point west of the Mississippi. The elevations taken along the line of the Pacific Railroad were assumed to be correct, and the geography as well as the geology of Salt Lake Valley were known in general terms. Our camp was located on a middle terrace one mile east of Ogden Junction, at an elevation above tide-water of 4,517 feet. Extending along the eastern side of the valley, with a trend nearly north and south, is a lofty and picturesque range of mountains—the northern section of the Wahsatch Range. Far southward, beyond the southern end of the Great Salt Lake, these mountains seem to extend, apparently growing more lofty and more picturesque, a gigantic wall inclosing one of the most beautiful valleys in the West. From the terraces, which form a conspicuous feature along the base of these mountains, one can obtain a full view of the wonderful body of water which has given name and character to this region. I will not attempt here to describe the scenic beauty of this region; it has already been done many times; it must be seen by the traveler to be understood, and once impressed upon the mind it becomes a perpetual pleasure thereafter.

The range of mountains which form so conspicuous and attractive a feature along the eastern shore of the lake, and north from Ogden, is composed mostly of quartzites and limestones, which present excellent examples of stratification. Just in the rear of our camp there is an illustration in which a thousand feet or more of layers of quartzite, varying from a few inches to several feet in thickness, are bent in the form of an arch (Fig. 1) as if the force had been applied from beneath, near the central portions, but that the sides or ends had lopped down for want of support.

101

Perhaps it will not be out of place for me here to make a suggestion in regard to a matter which deeply concerns the future welfare of the western half of the United States. As I have frequently stated, and as is now pretty generally known, irrigation is indispensable to cultivation of the soil throughout (with some very limited exceptions) all that part of the United States west of the one hundredth meridian. We also know from the history of those countries where irrigation is extensively practiced that it is absolutely necessary that the State shall take more or less control of this matter, upon which its prosperity, and, in fact, perpetuity rests. We may therefore predict, with confidence, that the day is not far distant when the States and Territories in the district where irrigation is necessary will have to take absolute control of the system of irrigation or keep a watchful eye over it and guard it well by laws, regulations, restrictions, &c.

As the development of the agricultural resources of these States and Territories and their prosperity depend upon irrigation and the extent to which this may be made available, therefore it is a subject of paramount importance, not only to those sections but also to the General Government. Unless proper and efficient steps are taken at an early day to adopt the best system of regulations, which will be adapted to an increased population, when the necessities demand such action in the future, it will cause much difficulty and inconvenience to lay aside one system and adopt another. This is, therefore, a matter well worthy the consideration of our national legislators while the Territories remain their wards; and if they can place these on the right footing now, it will greatly tend to accelerate their growth and prosperity. But the question is asked, How are they to do this? Is it possible for them to do this in accordance with their constitutional powers and without undue expense to the National Government? I am of the opinion there is a method by which this can be done, and I herewith submit the plan in a few words.

Let the General Government grant to the States and Territories in the region where irrigation is necessary—say, for example, all lying west of the one hundredth meridian, or perhaps the ninety-ninth, every alternate section of public land, with the condition that it be devoted entirely to the construction of irrigating canals and carrying on a system of irrigation. And the law making such grant should expressly reserve water privileges to those who may settle upon and occupy the remaining sections. By expressly providing that these lands should be applied solely to this purpose, it will be apparent to any one what an immense impetus it would give to the development of the agricultural resources of this section. All of the available water would thus be brought into use, and the reserved lands would also much sooner be brought into demand, as they would be as much entitled to the benefit of this measure as the lands thus granted. And in order to secure the grant from any improper diversion from the object contemplated in the grant, the law should provide that the States and Territories should refund to the General Government the value, at the minimum price, of all lands which the legislatures of these States and Territories should appropriate to any other purpose. The law should further provide that the grant should not include any portion of the reserved lands in lieu of those which might be occupied at the time of its passage, but should include only those employed. It should also provide that these State and territorial governments should not use any of the proceeds of these lands so granted for the payment of officers and other expenses of such registers, receivers, &c., as would necessarily have to be incurred in the sale, &c., of these lands, but should limit the application of the funds arising under this grant to the expenses belonging strictly to the system of irrigation. This should not apply of course to mineral lands, and a special provision may be made in regard to the timbered lands on the mountains which are not adapted to agricultural purposes. One-half of these might profitably be granted, with the provision that, as a return therefor, it should be the duty of these State and territorial governments to guard and preserve the forests on those lands not thus granted.

There would be some difficulty in regard to the survey of these mountain lands, but here the division need not be limited to alternate sections, but might be by townships, or in such a manner as the Commissioner of the General Land-Office might ascertain to be most practicable.

I think it cannot be denied that such a plan would result in more permanent benefit to these sections and to the General Government than any other which can possibly be adopted. It would at once prepare the way for the introduction of the best possible system of irrigation, and prevent the inconvenience and trouble which will hereafter arise when the introduction of such a system becomes absolutely necessary. It would rapidly bring into use the lands which require such extensive canals that individuals will not at present undertake it. There are millions of acres on the broad plateau bordering the Arkansas, Rio Grande, Plattes, Snake, Missouri, and other rivers which might be rendered excellent agricultural lands if an enlarged system of irrigation could be inaugurated. But individual effort is inefficient for this purpose. And though the granting of lands to railroads may partially accomplish this, yet it is evident that it falls infinitely short of that result which would be brought about by the system here proposed.

I submit these thoughts with the earnest request that you will give them such consideration as you think they merit. The object which the plan is proposed to accomplish I know to be one which you have long cherished, and for which you have so many years labored, and to which you now look forward with an earnest hope.

CHAPTER II.

THE GREAT BASIN.

As I have already given, in a former report, a description of the various valleys and arable tracts in Utah, I shall at present confine myself to a general view of the principal geographical features of the Great Basin, concluding the portion devoted to the Territory with a more minute account of that section visited in person the present season.

I use the term "Great Basin" in contradistinction to that of "Salt Lake Basin," to include that immense area lying between the Wahsatch Mountains on the east and the Sierra Nevada Range on the west, embracing the western part of Utah and the entire State of Nevada. In shape it is something like an ancient shield, the broad end being to the North, the southern extremity rounded to a point, its extreme width about 350 miles and its length north and south 300 miles. Having no outlet for its waters, by which they may be carried to the ocean, it forms an isolated and, as might be inferred from this fact, a somewhat peculiar district.

Although a basin in fact so far as its water-drainage is concerned, yet its surface does not sweep down from the surrounding rim to a central depression, but, on the contrary, its areas of greatest depression are to be found near the borders, especially along the eastern and western sides, while its central portion reaches a much greater elevation, and is broken into a series of detached ridges. This will be seen by an examination of the elevations along the line of the Central Pacific Railroad. For example, at Brigham Station, on the border of Salt Lake, it is 4,220 feet above the level of the sea, while at Pequop, the next station west of Toana, it reaches 6,184 feet; from this it again gradually descends to Desert, the second station east of Wadsworth, where it is only 4,017 feet, or about 200 feet below the level of Salt Lake. The highest ranges in it will probably exceed the greatest elevation here given as much as 1,500 or 2,000 feet. The elevations at the points of greatest depression in the southeastern and southwestern portions have not been accurately determined, but it is known that in the vicinity of Sevier Lake it is not more than 4,500 feet above the level of the sea. A comparison of these elevations with those of the broad mountain belt lying east from the Wahsatch Range to the Black Hills of Wyoming will bring out this feature more clearly and forcibly, and at the same time afford us a means of comparing the climate of the two sections, so far as influenced by elevation, in the same latitude. The highest point of the Union Pacific Railroad on the western side of this belt is at Wahsatch Station, 6,879 feet above the sea-level. The highest on the eastern side is at Sherman, 8,242 feet. The lowest point between the two is at Green River, where the elevation is 6,140 feet, or about 2,000 feet above the lowest level of the basin. Some of the intermediate ranges, as the Uintah Mountains, reach a height of 10,000 or 12,000 feet, and the peaks occasionally exceed 13,000 feet. That this difference in altitude must produce a considerable difference in the climate is evident. North the difference is not so great.

This depression below the general level is a fact of much importance in estimating the agricultural resources of this extensive interalpine region, as it indicates a very material moderation of climate. And that which might be inferred theoretically has been shown by extensive experiments to be true in fact, as can be seen from the list of the productions of Salt Lake Valley given in my last report.

MOUNTAINS.

The mountain features of this basin are somewhat peculiar, differing in some important respects from those of the sections lying east and north, and exerting a decided influence upon the channels of travel and internal commerce, and upon the lines of settlement and centers of population. The Wahsatch Range, which runs almost directly north and south near the one hundred and twelfth meridian, forms the eastern rim, and presents an immense terrace wall, bracing up the broad elevated table-land which stretches out eastward of it, and of which it may be said, with more than mere figure of speech, to form the western escarpment. It follows that its western slope presents a greater descent to reach the level of the lake than its eastern to reach the level of Green River. Except where cleft by the Ogden, Weber, and Provo Rivers, it presents a continuous ridge rising abruptly from the narrow plains, seldom sending out on this side foot-hills or slopes, but plunging abruptly down beneath the *débris* that presses against its surface. This character is especially prominent opposite Salt and Utah Lakes. The western face, though rocky, does not present that jagged, rugose appearance so characteristic of portions of the Rocky Mountains, but is marked by deep and sharp furrows, down which the little streams formed by the melting snow rush with impetuous speed to the valley below. These little rills and mountain brooks, though but small in volume, not combining to form any extensive streams, are perhaps of more value to the pioneer settler than the larger ones. And in our estimate of the irrigable land of this western country, especially if we pass through it in the latter part of summer or in autumn, we are apt to overlook or underestimate their value. I am satisfied that while in some instances I may have overestimated the capacity of large streams, I have paid too little regard to the small ones. My attention was called in a special manner to this subject while camped near Ogden the present season. Our tents were pitched on the high ground to the northeast of the town, which, to one traveling along one of the usual highways, would appear to be entirely beyond the reach of irrigation, the elevation being, as appears from the observations of Mr. Schönborn, the topographer of the expedition, over 300 feet above the level of the lake, and about 300 feet above Weber River at the railroad depot. Yet even here I noticed around and for some distance above camp several irrigating ditches well filled with water, from one of which we obtained a supply for camp use. I found, upon examination, that these were supplied with water from little streams running down the indentations in the mountain side to the north of us, fed by the patches of melting snow resting among the crevices along the summit. Although within two miles of the base, and the hot sun shining squarely against what appeared to be a bare and naked rocky wall, we could detect no stream flowing down it. Not until we had approached to the very base could we discover the silvery thread winding its way down among the bowlders and little fringe of bushes that lined its pathway. This stream furnished water sufficient to irrigate and supply the wants of a moderate sized farm. Multiply this by tens of thousands and we will have some idea of the importance of these minor and annual streams which generally pass unnoticed except by those immediately interested in them.

Passing to the interior of the basin, whether moving round the north or south end of the lake, we shall find a succession of "long, abrupt, detached, parallel ridges extending in a north and south direction." And this holds true not only on the eastern side, or Salt Lake Basin proper, but also throughout the greater portion of Nevada. That such is the case in the southeastern part of this State is expressly stated in the report of the expedition under Governor Blasdel to Pahranagat. Baron Richthoren alludes to the same character of the ranges in the southwest. These ridges are separated by intervening valleys of various width, and even where the valleys expand into broad open plains, as in the central and western part of Utah, their boundary walls retain the same general course. The valley of the Humboldt might, at first sight, appear to form a remarkable exception to this rule, but a closer examination will show this to be a mistake; for the greater part of its course it is formed by a series of openings through these ridges and across the intervening valleys. That this is true is clearly shown by the direction of the tributaries that flow into it. This uniformity in the direction of these minor ranges was noticed by Captain Stansbury, who states that even the northern rim of the basin partakes of the same character. "The northern rim of the Great Basin, or the elevated ground which divides it from the valley of the Columbia, does not consist, as has been supposed, of one continuous mountain range which may be flanked, but of a number of long, abrupt, detached parallel ridges extending in a north and south direction, and separated by intervening valleys, which constitute, as it were, so many summit levels, whence the waters flow north on the one side into the Columbia, and south on the other into the Great Basin." And in this opinion he is quite correct, for in passing from Cache Valley to Marsh Valley, the one lying south and the other north of this rim or divide, we found the two so united as to be continuous, but elevated at one point by a kind of broad cross-ridge which acted as a divide between the waters. I also know that such is the case with the Malade Valley.

In Utah this direction of the valleys holds good with a remarkable uniformity. Cache, Malade, Blue Spring, Hansee Spring, Jordan, Tooele, Tintic, San Pete, Rush, Lone Rock, and Upper Sevier Valleys all maintain this course almost direct, while the two parts of Salt Lake conform very nearly to it. From the head of Malade River to Utah Lake is one continuous valley, varying less than five degrees from a north and south course. Antelope and Frémont's Islands and Oquirrh Mountains lie in a direct line with the course of the promontory which separates the northern arms of the lake. Without any reference to this law which seems to govern the hills and valleys, I colored, upon a large map, the arable tracts of the Territory so far as at present known, especially those in which settlements have been made, when I was astonished to find that from the thirty-ninth parallel to the northern boundary almost every tract so colored would be included in a strip along the one hundred and twelfth meridian not exceeding fifty miles in width; Tooele, Rush, and Weber Valleys being the only exceptions. Another singular evidence of the force of this law which governed the formation of these ranges and valleys is shown in Cache Valley, which maintains the same direction, though closed at the lower end by a cross-range of broken hills which shoot out from the Wahsatch Range, and crossed at the north end in a diagonal manner by the valley of Bear River. A similar feature seems to govern the valleys of the western side of the basin. Baron Richthoren, speaking of the Washoe Mountains, says that they are separated from the steep slope of the Sierra Nevada by a continuous meridional depression, marked by the deep basins of Truckee Valley, Washoe Valley, and Carson Valley. Though irregular, a general direction may be traced in the summit range from north to south, where it slopes down to a smooth table-land, traversed from west to east by the Carson River, flowing in a narrow crevice, beyond which the Washoe Range is protracted in the more elevated Pine-Nut Mountains.

Notwithstanding this uniformity in the direction of the ridges and valleys, it exerts but little influence on the few leading streams, but, on the contrary, directs the course of all the minor streams. That it must have more or less influence upon the lines of travel and traffic, and the localities of the settlements of the Territory of Utah, is evident. A single railroad line from Corinne or Brigham City, in the north, to Saint George, in the extreme southwest, would have the principal agricultural areas strung so closely along it that a day's drive with a team would reach it from almost any settlement likely to be made for some years to come, (the chief exceptions being those already named and those lying north of its terminus.) It is, therefore, easy to predict where the chief highway of this Territory will be.

RIVERS AND LAKES.

The rivers of the basin are small, and, so far as the volume of water is concerned, of small importance, but in other respects play a conspicuous part in the development of the country. The principal ones are the Humboldt and Carson, in the western area, and the Bear and Jordan Rivers, in the eastern part. Sevier and Beaver Rivers, in the southwestern part of Utah, are considerable streams as compared with others of the section; but as little is accurately known in regard to them, I pass them without any special notice. Weber River, on account of its position, and as forming a gap through the mountain, is important. Provo (or Timpanogas) may be considered as a tributary to the Jordan.

As a list of the principal valleys of Nevada will be appended to this report, with a short notice of the agricultural resources of each, I shall omit further reference to that State at present, except the bearing the Humboldt River and Valley have upon the travel and commerce of the basin. This stream, rising in the northeast part of Nevada, runs a little south of west for about three hundred miles, where it suddenly disappears in what has been very significantly and appropriately termed the "Humboldt Sink," on the extreme western side of the State. Though a little stream of but few yards in width at its widest point, winding its way down the gradual descent through narrow valleys of a monotonous uniformity that soon tires the most enthusiastic traveler, wholly inadequate for navigation of any kind, yet it possesses an importance not to be overlooked. Its valley forms a natural channel for the great interoceanic highway, furnishing a natural and, we might say, the only, easy pathway and water-supply through a barren region of mountains and valleys for three hundred miles. This is certainly a consideration of no small moment, for it renders it really more valuable to the nation and the world than if, without this, it were navigable from head to mouth. Small as it is compared with the treeless ranges of hill and plain on each side, yet it will furnish the means of forming at least a narrow line of green fields through this comparatively barren section; for, to say the best we can of this region, although, perhaps, affording moderate grazing fields, yet outside of the immediate bottoms of the few streams it has a barren and uninviting appearance. This line assumes still more importance when we take into consideration the large mining area on each side, especially south, to which it forms the base of travel and commerce; and the prevailing direction of the ridges and valleys, before alluded to, lend additional force to this statement. It must ever be the chief axis of inland commerce and travel for the western portion of this great basin, and, consequently, a link in a through transverse line. Other lines of railroad may, and probably will, hereafter traverse the country north and south of this, but not so closely as to do away with its importance. Human genius and energy may make a pathway through the most rugged portions, but nature has prepared but one transverse channel in this region; longitudinally (north and south) there are many. But while the river is thus intimately connected with the development of the material resources of the country, on the contrary, the reservoir into which it pours its waters possesses no other than scientific interest—simply a marshy spot in a sandy plain, the extent of the water surface governed by the supply and capacity of the sands to drink it up and the atmosphere to evaporate it, the two latter generally being in excess of the former.

Bear River, the largest tributary to Salt Lake, takes its rise in Utah, near the southwest angle of Wyoming. After winding its way northward through the Wahsatch Mountains, about one hundred and fifty miles, extending even into the southern limits of Idaho, suddenly bends its course completely round, and flowing southward, pours its waters into Bear River Bay. As affording a supply of water for irrigating large areas of land in Cache and Malade Valleys, it assumes an importance of no little moment; but throughout its entire course, from its head to where it enters Cache Valley, (with the exception of a few miles where the railroad traverses it, and where the coal-mines are opened,) it exerts but little influence in the development of the country. Its volume of water is too small to admit of navigation; its course is too tortuous to be followed any great distance by any one line of travel; and its valley is too narrow and too closely hemmed in by rugged mountains to be of any great value as an agricultural section, yet not wholly without interest in this respect. As a means of conveying timber down from the mountains to the railroad and other accessible points, it may become a valuable accessory.

Weber River, though small, is remarkable as affording a gateway directly through the Wahsatch Range, Echo and Weber Cañons presenting, as is well known to all who have traveled on the Union Pacific Railroad, some of the grandest scenery in the West.

The Jordan forms an outlet for the fresh water of Utah Lake, and, running north some forty or fifty miles, empties into Salt Lake at its southeast angle. Insignificant in size, too small to be navigated, yet unlike the Oriental Jordan, from which it derived its name, it is of other value than simply a watering-place for thirsty man and beast. It and its tributaries afford water for irrigation, as shown in my last report, to an area capable, if properly and thoroughly cultivated, of supporting a population greater than the entire population of the Territory at this time.

The Provo, (or Timpanogas,) rising back in one of those mountain centers found in the mountain regions, rushes down through a narrow cañon, which cleaves the range at this point, and pours its waters into Utah Lake. In passing I would call attention to this mountain nucleus, situated about latitude 40°.30, longitude 111°, and culminating in Reed's Peak. This is doubtless formed by the junction of the Uintah Mountains with the Wahsatch Range. Here, within a small area, all the leading rivers of Salt Lake Basin proper take their rise, viz, Bear, Weber, and Provo; also the Uintah and White Rivers, which flow to the east and enter into Green River. The volume of water in the Provo is probably equal to any other belonging to the Salt Lake water system, except Bear River; and as its descent is very rapid it affords the means of irrigating all the table-lands lying in the vicinity of its exit from the mountains. It will afford excellent water-power for driving mills and machinery, and, being on the margin of the lake, must become of great value in this respect.

Sevier River rises in the southwest part of the Territory and runs a little east of north between two ranges of the Wahsatch Mountains for one hundred and fifty miles or more, when it breaks through the western rim of its narrow basin, and, turning southwest, flows into Sevier Lake. But as I have not visited this river I cannot speak very confidently in regard to its importance and the bearing it is likely to have upon the development of the country. Very little appears to be known in regard to the lake into which its waters flow.

FIRST ANNUAL REPORT

OF THE

UNITED STATES GEOLOGICAL SURVEY

9

TO THE

HON. CARL SCHURZ,

SECRETARY OF THE INTERIOR.

BY

CLARENCE KING,

DIRECTOR.

———•———

WASHINGTON:
GOVERNMENT PRINTING OFFICE.
1880.

ANNUAL REPORT

OF THE

UNITED STATES GEOLOGICAL SURVEY.

UNITED STATES GEOLOGICAL SURVEY,
OFFICE OF THE DIRECTOR,
November 1, 1880.

Hon. CARL SCHURZ,
Secretary of the Interior, Washington, D. C.:

SIR: I have the honor to present herewith the first annual report of the United States Geological Survey, covering the fiscal year ending June 30, 1880.

Congress having prescribed the mode of publishing the results of the survey, it is intended to confine these pages to a simple statement of the bureau organization, progress of field investigation, and results already attained.

The law creating the office of Director of the Geological Survey was enacted and approved March 3, 1879. On March 21, 1879, the President nominated me first Director of the Geological Survey, the Senate confirmed his action on April 3, 1879, and on May 24 I took the prescribed oath of office, and entered on my duties.

Congress expressed its determination to inaugurate the Geological Survey in a provision of law so brief, that I give it entire, in order to comprise in this report the history of the origin and organization of this bureau.

GEOLOGICAL SURVEY.

For the salary of the Director of the Geological Survey, which office is hereby established under the Interior Department, who shall be appointed by the President, by and with the advice and consent of the Senate, six thousand dollars: *Provided,* That this officer shall have the direction of the Geological Survey, and the classification of the public lands, and examination of the geological structure, mineral resources, and products of the national domain. And that the Director and members of the Geological Survey shall have no personal or private interests in the lands or mineral wealth of the region under survey, and shall execute no surveys or examinations for private parties or corporations; and the Geological and Geographical Survey of the Territories, and the Geographical and Geological Survey of the Rocky Mountain Region, under the Department of the Interior, and the Geographical Surveys west of the one hundredth meridian, under the War Department, are hereby discontinued, to take effect on the thirtieth day of June, eighteen hundred and seventy-nine. And all collections of rocks, minerals, soils, fossils, and objects of natural history, archæology, and ethnology, made by the Coast and Interior Survey, the Geological Survey, or by any other parties for the Government of the United States, when no longer needed for investigations in progress, shall be deposited in the National Museum.

For the expenses of the Geological Survey, and the classification of the public lands, and examination of the geological structure, mineral resources, and products of the national domain, to be expended under the direction of the Secretary of the Interior, one hundred thousand dollars. Enacted and approved March 3, 1879.

Prior to the above enactment, and at irregular intervals since the early years of this century, the national government had made various attempts

3

to acquire and diffuse information on the geological structure and mineral resources of the United States. Geologists were dispatched to report upon certain fields of mineral industry, and to nearly every military exploration or international boundary survey was attached some one more or less competent to delineate and describe the geological features of the land traversed. Instances of success in this line of expeditionary geological reconnaissance may be found in the reports of the Pacific Railroad and Colorado River surveys, executed under the Corps of Engineers of the Army, and those of the Mexican boundary surveys; while in the department of economical geology, Forster and Whitney's Lake Superior report stands almost alone.

Up to 1867, geology was made to act as a sort of camp-follower to expeditions whose main object was topographical reconnaissance. Charged with definite objects and missions, the leaders of these corps have tolerated geology rather as a hinderance than a benefit. In consequence, such subsidiary geological work amounts to little more than a slight sketch of the character and distribution of formations, valuable chiefly as indicating the field for future inquiry.

In the year 1867, however, Congress ordered the geological exploration of the fortieth parallel, a labor designed to render geological maps of the country about to be opened up by the Union and Central Pacific Railroads, then in process of construction. In this work, geology was the sole object. For the first time a government geologist found himself in independent command, able to direct the movements and guide the researches of a corps of competent professional assistants. At the same session of Congress, Dr. Hayden's "Geological and Geographical Survey of the Territories" was ordered, and a little later Maj. J. W. Powell's "Geological and Geographical Survey of the Rocky Mountain Region" was likewise placed in the field.

Eighteen hundred and sixty-seven, therefore, marks, in the history of national geological work, a turning point, when the science ceased to be dragged in the dust of rapid exploration and took a commanding position in the professional work of the country.

Congress, even then, hardly more than placed the Federal work on a par with that prosecuted by several of the wealthier States. During the years when the Federal geologists were following the hurried and often painful marches of the Western explorers, many States inaugurated and brought to successful issue State surveys whose results are of dignity and value.

Since 1867 the government work has been equal to the best State work, and in some important branches has taken the lead. The wisdom of the legislation which placed in the field those well-organized, well-equipped, and ably-manned corps is apparent in the improved and enlarged results obtained.

But there remained one more step necessary to give the highest efficiency and most harmonious balance to the national geological work. It was the discontinuance of the several geological surveys under personal leadership, and the foundation of a permanent bureau charged with the investigation and elucidation of the geological structure and mineral resources and productions of the United States.

The legislation above cited, and upon which the existence of this bureau is based, leaves some room for doubt as to the precise intention of Congress, both regarding the functions of the organization and its field. Two special and distinct branches of duty are imposed upon the Director of the Geological Survey. 1. The classification of the public land; and, 2. The examination of the geological structure and mineral resources.

As regards the classification of public lands, the text of the law leaves an uncertainty whether this classification is intended to be a scientific exposition of the kinds of lands embraced in the national domain, such as arable, irrigable, timber, desert, mineral, coal, iron, showing the practical values and adaptabilities of the various classes or kinds of soil and surface, or whether, on the other hand, it was intended to furnish a basis of classification, upon which the government should part title to portions of the public domain.

At present the General Land Office possesses the machinery for the survey, classification, and sale of the public lands. In that bureau the field-notes and maps of the various deputy surveyors are intended to convey sufficiently accurate information for the general guidance of the officers who execute the sales. The law also provides a method of proof as to the character of lands, which forms an indispensable stage in the process of sale. Any transaction as to a piece of public lands may be challenged before the proper officers, and its character may be determined by competent proof. The present method of sale of the public lands depends, therefore, chiefly upon a rule of law rather than the classification of experts in advance of the procedure of sale.

Upon examination of the existing land system, I have assumed that Congress, in directing me to make a classification of the public lands, could not have intended to supersede the machinery of the Land Office, and substitute a classification to be executed by another bureau of government, without having distinctly provided for the necessary changes within the Land Office, and adjustment of relations between the two bureaus.

The Public Lands Commission, created by Congress in the same law which organized the Geological Survey, carefully examined into the question of classification and disposition of the public lands. In the deliberate opinion of that body, it has been adjudged impracticable for the Geological Survey, or any other branch of the Interior Department, to execute a classification in advance of sale, without seriously impeding the rapid settlement of the unoccupied lands.

I have therefore concluded that the intention of Congress was to begin a rigid scientific classification of the lands of the national domain, not for purposes of aiding the machinery of the General Land Office, by furnishing a basis of sale, but for the general information of the people of the country, and to produce a series of land maps which should show all those features upon which intelligent agriculturists, miners, engineers, and timbermen might hereafter base their operations, and which would obviously be of the highest value for all students of the political economy and resources of the United States. Studies of this sort, entirely aside from the administration of the Land Office, can be made of the highest practical value; and to this end a careful beginning has been made.

A second ambiguity in the language of the law which I am called upon to execute, will be found in the use of the term "national domain." All operations of this bureau are, by the language of the law, intended to cover the "national domain."

That term was supposed by the first framers of the law to cover the entire United States. On the other hand, it might be held to mean simply the region of the public lands. It was of the utmost importance, before beginning to plan for any field operations, to know whether "national domain" meant the lands owned by the nation, or the area within its outer boundaries.

With the small appropriation given to begin the vast work of this bureau, I considered it best to confine the operations to the region of the public land, concerning which field there could be no question as to my legal authority. In the case, therefore, of the uncertainties arising from the language of the law, I have chosen to take the conservative side, and have neither invaded the functions of the General Land Office, nor placed my field parties outside the area of the public lands.

Former national geological surveys have been conducted by means of annual campaigns in the far West. The corps, when driven from the field by the snows of late autumn, have returned to Washington, there to await the accidents of appropriation; and, if provided for by Congress, to take the field at the close of Congressional sessions.

By this means a large amount of valuable time has been lost in breaking up the Western camps and removing the corps to Washington and again returning to the field the following year. Moreover, a very large item of transportation cost has been annually incurred.

GEOGRAPHICAL FIELD DIVISIONS.

I have entirely abandoned that plan, and have divided the region west of the 101st meridian into four geological districts. It will be seen by the map accompanying this report that these districts do not always coincide with political lines. On the contrary, they are outlined to embrace certain definite geological fields.

In passing westward the first division is that of the Rocky Mountains, which starts from the Mexican boundary on the Rio Grande, near its intersection with the 107th meridian. From that point the line follows the Texan boundary east to the 103d meridian, which it traces northward to the parallel of 37, and thence making a short jog eastward of a degree and a half of longitude, coincides with the eastern boundary of Colorado to the 41st parallel, and then continues along the meridian of the 102d to latitude 45. From that point a due west line is drawn to the 104th meridian, thence north along that line to the British boundary. The northern boundary of the district coincides with the British boundary to the meridian 116. From that point it follows the boundary line between Idaho and Montana southeasterly to its junction with the 111th meridian, and from that point south to the 41st parallel, thence east to the 109th meridian, and thence south to the Mexican boundary.

Embraced within these boundaries lie Colorado, New Mexico, Wyoming, and Montana, and a small part of Dakota; an area inclosing the whole great chain of the Rocky Mountains, whose geographical function is the dividing of the watershed of the Atlantic from that of the Pacific. This chain is made up of a great number of ranges and groups of mountains separated from each other by deep depressions, in which are either passes or inclosed lowlands known as parks. From the Mexican to the British boundary, the system is a geological unit, and should be studied as one, without reference to political lines.

One division of the survey corps, trained in any one part of this system, would have an immense advantage in deciphering the geological history of any other part. The same system of coal fields, the same types of economical mineral deposits—gold, silver, and iron ore-bodies—extend from one end to the other of this vast mountain district. In charge of this field I have placed Mr. S. F. Emmons, geologist-in charge, whose main office is fixed at Denver, Colo.

The Division of the Colorado embraces a remarkable plateau and cañon country unparalleled elsewhere in the world, which lies between the Rocky Mountains and the Great Basin. It is, in the main, a country drained by the great cañons of the Colorado River, and consists of elevated plateaus, above which arise isolated groups of mountains, and through which is traced a wonderful labyrinth of cañons from three to six thousand feet in depth.

This division has been for twelve or thirteen years the field of exploration of Maj. J. W. Powell, who has expended here over $300,000 in explorations and surveys, which are of the highest scientific value, and of which only the beginning has been published. His extensive work is inherited by the present bureau, and the Division of the Colorado is intended only as a temporary one until this work, already far advanced, can be brought to completion. The main portion of the division is most easily reached from Salt Lake City, and the headquarters of the division has been placed there in charge of Capt. C. E. Dutton, United States Ordnance Corps, geologist-in-charge.

The Division of the Great Basin is also a characteristic tract of country, differing essentially from the Rocky Mountains and the Colorado Plateau, which bound it on the east, and the country of the Sierra Nevada, Cascade, and Pacific coast ranges, which lie between it and the ocean on the west. It is for the most part a series of desert plains, interrupted by more or less parallel mountain chains. The chief peculiarity of three-quarters of the area is that its drainage never reaches the sea. Its geological characteristics, equally with its geographical ones, separate it from the surrounding country. It is a region to be studied by itself, and is of the highest importance from its abundant silver districts. Mr. G. K. Gilbert, geologist-in-charge, has been assigned to the direction of this division, with headquarters placed, for convenience of access, at Salt Lake; and it is designed that one office and one field laboratory will meet the requirements of this and the Colorado Division.

The Division of the Pacific embraces the whole of Washington Territory, that part of Oregon which lies west of the Blue Mountains, and all of California, except the desert region lying east of the Sierra Nevada and south of the thirty-eighth parallel, which, from its geological and physical characteristics, belongs, not to the series of Pacific coast mountains, but to the arid region of the Great Basin. The headquarters of the Pacific Division is placed at San Francisco; Mr. Arnold Hague, geologist in charge.

As soon as the work upon the cañons and plateaus of the Colorado is done it is intended to discontinue that division and to divide it on the line of the Colorado River between the Divisions of the Rocky Mountains and that of the Great Basin. Thus, after the space of four or five years, there will remain but three divisions west of the 102d meridian. The location and boundary of these divisions are clearly shown upon the map accompanying this report.

The Appropriation Committee of the House of Representatives were informed by me of the uncertainties as to the meaning of the term "national domain"; and they immediately caused to be offered House Resolution No. 116, extending the field of the geological survey over the whole United States. That resolution was promptly passed in the House, but is still pending in the Senate; but, in advance of the action of the Senate, I have laid down on the accompanying map the four divisions into which I would propose to district that part of the United States east of the 102d meridian.

Of the great Appalachian system of mountains, extending from New Brunswick to Alabama, I have made two divisions—one embracing Maryland, Delaware, Pennsylvania, New Jersey, New York, and the

New England States; the other embracing West Virginia, Virginia, North and South Carolina, Georgia, Florida, Alabama, Tennessee, and Kentucky.

These two areas will include the whole Appalachian mountain system in two parts of about equal geological importance; and, with the four divisions west of the 102d meridian, cover all the mountain country of the United States.

There remains, then, only the basin of the Mississippi, which, with all its enormous extent, is really one field and one geological problem. From its great size, however, I have thought best to divide it, as the lines upon the map will show, into two grand divisions; first, the Division of the North Mississippi, bounded west of the Mississippi on the south by a line including Missouri and Kansas, to the intersection of the 39th parallel with the 102d meridian. East of the Mississippi River the Ohio forms the dividing line between the Northern and Southern districts.

By placing each division under the charge of a geologist, whose personal experience and acquirements fit him to undertake the investigation of the chief problems of that division, and assigning to him a competent corps of assistants, a far better result will be obtained than by any plan of expeditionary operations, with parties moving from division to division. It is intended, on the contrary, to strictly confine each corps to its own division, and to keep it permanently at work there, except in case of certain technical economical investigations. In this respect the organization resembles that of the Army and the Coast and Geodetic Survey.

I have so arranged the initial work of the survey that special volumes on the most important geological subjects and mining industries in the four western divisions of the survey shall be brought to prompt publication. There can hardly be two opinions on the desirableness of immediately working out such problems in these great districts which in their past and present history offer examples of instructive geological structure and great bullion yield, and which have required of mining men special mechanical skill and large outlay of capital. Proper scientific reports on such typical districts become records of remarkable phenomena in the field of industrial geology and chronicles of distinguished success in the department of mining engineering. Among the great numbers of mining districts which merit rigid investigation I have chosen three, which more than others seemed to offer harvests of technical information, of which the mining population stands in immediate need. Leadville, the extraordinary district in Middle Colorado; Eureka, Nevada, which for fifteen years has been the most productive silver-lead district in America, and the incomparable Comstock Lode, are chosen as the first three districts to be illustrated by special monographs.

ENGINEER DEPARTMENT, U. S. ARMY.

REPORT

10

UPON

UNITED STATES GEOGRAPHICAL SURVEYS

WEST OF THE ONE HUNDREDTH MERIDIAN,

IN CHARGE OF

CAPT. GEO. M. WHEELER,

CORPS OF ENGINEERS, U. S. ARMY,

UNDER THE DIRECTION OF

THE CHIEF OF ENGINEERS, U. S. ARMY.

PUBLISHED BY AUTHORITY OF THE HONORABLE THE SECRETARY OF WAR,

IN ACCORDANCE WITH ACTS OF CONGRESS OF JUNE 23, 1874, AND FEBRUARY 15, 1875.

IN SEVEN VOLUMES AND ONE SUPPLEMENT, ACCOMPANIED BY ONE
TOPOGRAPHIC AND ONE GEOLOGIC ATLAS.

VOL. I.—GEOGRAPHICAL REPORT.

WASHINGTON:
GOVERNMENT PRINTING OFFICE.
1889.

INTRODUCTION.

The area within the United States west of the one hundredth meridian of longitude (1,443,360 square miles) embraces, entire, the basins of the Colorado (270,000 square miles), Interior (208,600 square miles), Coast (100,900 square miles), and Sacramento (64,300 square miles); also, that part of the Columbia (215,700 square miles) south of the forty-ninth parallel, and portions of the basins of the Missouri (338,200 square miles), Rio Grande (123,000 square miles), Arkansas (75,500 square miles), Brazos (34,800 square miles), and the Red River of the North (3,360 square miles).

Of the above approximation 993,360 square miles is of a mountainous structure, the many ranges surrounding interior plateaux and valleys, while the remainder (450,000 square miles) is composed of the "mauvaise terre" of the northern," plains" of the interior, and the "staked plains" of the southern, latitudes.

The approximate average elevation above sea of the total area west of the one hundredth meridian is approximately 4,225 feet, the volume of the mass above this level being 1,155,201 cubic miles, while the approximate average altitude of the area of 359,065 square miles covered by the survey is approximately 5,000 feet, or corresponding to a volume of 340,024 cubic miles.

The Colorado, Columbia, Missouri, Rio Grande, Arkansas, Sacramento, Brazos, Pecos, and Red Rivers are the principal lines of drainage of the fol-

9

117

lowing approximate total lengths and parts thereof comprised within the above area:

Name of river.	Total length.	Length west of 100th meridian.	Name of river.	Total length.	Length west of 100th meridian.
	Miles.	Miles.		Miles.	Miles.
1. Colorado	1,678	1,678	6. Sacramento	270	270
2. Columbia	1,350	1,350	7. Brazos	770	150
3. Missouri	2,824	1,600	8. Red River	1,200	175
4. Rio Grande	1,800	1,520	9. Pecos	600	600
5. Arkansas	1,539	500			

The Great Interior Basin that, on account of its present state of desiccation, is without outlet to the sea, has its own system of drainage and reservoirs, marked by a number of minor streams, such as the Humboldt, Sevier, Bear, Carson, Walker, Truckee, and Owens Rivers.

The following determined volumes have been noted for the streams given herewith:

No.	Name of river.	Total length, approximated.	Total drainage area, approximated.	Length in area west of 100th meridian.	Navigable west of 100th meridian. To what point.	Miles, approx.
		Miles.	Square miles.	Miles.		
1	Lower or main Mississippi	1,286	1,256,050	0	All east of 100th meridian	0
2	Yazoo	500	13,850	0	Not navigable	0
3	Saint Francis	380	10,500	0	...do	0
4	Red	1,200	97,000	175	Not navigable west of 100th meridian	0
5	Arkansas	1,514	189,000	500	...do	0
6	Upper Mississippi	1,330	169,000	0	All east of 100th meridian	0
7	Missouri	2,908	518,000	1,600	To Fort Benton	1,225
8	Columbia	1,350	215,700	1,350	To the Cascades	130
9	Sacramento	270	64,300	270	Tehama Rapids	233
10	Colorado of the West	1,678	279,000 (West of 100th meridian.)	1,678	Mouth of Grand Cañon	460
11	Rio Grande	1,800	123,000	1,520	Not navigable west of 100th meridian.	0

No.	Volumes of discharge. By—	Locality.	Date.	Velocity in feet per second.	Discharge per second.	Remarks.
					Cubic feet.	
1	Humphreys & Abbot				675,000	Physics and Hydraulics of Mississippi River, pages 92 and 93.
2	...do				43,000	Physics and Hydraulics of Mississippi River, page 92.
3	...do				31,000	Physics and Hydraulics of Mississippi River, page 92.
4	...do				57,000	3,300 square miles in area west of 100th meridian; Physics and Hydraulics of Mississippi River, page 92.
5	...do				63,000	75,500 square miles in area west of 100th meridian; Physics and Hydraulics of Mississippi River, page 92.
6	...do				105,000	
7	...do				120,000	2,824 miles to mouth of Three Forks; Physics and Hydraulics of Mississippi River, page 92.

118

No.	Volumes of discharge.					Remarks.
	By—	Locality.	Date.	Velocity in feet per second.	Discharge per second.	
8	Estimate of Board of Engineers.	....	....	....	*Cubic feet.* 300,000	(Mean). Sen. Ex. Doc. No. 13, 47th Cong., 2d sess., page 3.
9	W. H. Hall, State engineer of California.	Highest known. Ordinary high flood. } Discharge.{		205,000 cu.ft. 165,000 cu.ft.	(Average.) 30,000	Snag-boat has reached Red Bluff, 248 miles.
10	Lieutenant Bergland.	Stone's Ferry.....	Aug. 11, 1875	3,217	18,413.38	United States Geographical Surveys west of the 100th meridian.
	Do..............	Camp Mohave	Sept. 3, 1875	1,250	11,623.43	
	Do............	Fort Yuma .	Mar. 15, 1876	2,809	7,658.74	"
	P. W. Hamel	Near Camp Mohave.	Sept. 15, 1871	3,006	16,232.00	"
11	Lieutenant Michler...	Mouth Gila River.	Dec. —, 1854	3,000	6,249.00	Mexican Boundary Survey.
	L. Nell	Polonas, N. Mex ..	Sept. 19, 1878	2,560	856.40	Lowest water; United States Geographical Surveys west of the 100th meridian.
	Do..............	Fort Selden, N.M.	Oct. 3, 1878	2,222	640.75	"
	Lieutenant Bergland .	Del Norte, Colo...	June 22, 1877	5,300	4,685.50	High water. do.

NOTE.—The following measured discharges have been found for minor streams, a part or all of which lie west of the 100th meridian : (1) Kansas River, between Wamego and Saint Mary's, 2,500 cubic feet per second, in September, 1878, taken at stage of about 4 feet above low water; (2) Yellowstone, at Fort Keogh, near mouth of Tongue River, September, 1878, 14,462 cubic feet; at same point in October, 1879, 6,505 cubic feet per second; Willamette, at one-fourth mile below the northern boundary of Portland, in fall of 1876, at stage of 3½ to 4 feet above 0 or low water, 13,108 cubic feet per second, average velocity, 3.98 feet per second, and later at 9 feet (approximated) above low water, 51,590 cubic feet per second; (4) confluents of Great Salt Lake (Bear, Weber, and Jordan Rivers and miscellaneous), March and April, 1878, 4,386 cubic feet per second (during rising water and prior to commencement of irrigation); (5) Gunnison, below Tumichi Creek, November 5, 1875, 373.5 cubic feet per second.

For authority for the above see (1) A. R. C. of E. 1879, App. O, p. 1092, J. D. McKown, under Major Suter; (2) A. R. C. of E., 1880, App. R, p. 1476, Lieut. Maguire; (3) A. R. C. of E., 1877, App. JJ, p. 1009, R. A. Habersham, under Major Wilson; (4) A. R. Geographical Surveys, 1879, App. D, p. 229, Lieut. Young; (5) A. R. Geographical Surveys, 1878, App. A, p. 105, Lieut. Bergland.

The backbone of the continent within the boundaries of the United States, or the water-shed between the Interior and Pacific (approximately 1,850 miles in length), consists of a number of distinct ranges separated by noticeable passes easily approached from the eastward or westward, and to which the appellation "Rocky Mountains" has been given.

This name fades away as the true condition of its topography becomes known from actual surveys, and each of the several ranges claims a title.

The mother mass of this water-shed consists of the Saguache and Snowy Ranges in Colorado (about 425 miles in length) that, beginning at the head of the broad San Luis Valley, extend northwardly with a single break or marked depression at the head of the Arkansas, and become lost in the lower levels only as the ridges leading from Long's Peak reach the plains in this direction.

To this group of serrated ridges the name of "Sierra Madre" has been given, and no other mountain mass within our borders so well deserves the title, except perhaps the Sierra Nevada and Cascade Ranges, that within

United States territory are more local in their position, neither do they so truly form part of the great main line of continental uplift extending from the Isthmus of Darien to the Arctic Sea.

To describe the physical characteristics of the multitude of ranges as to their more important topographic relations alone, would fill volumes, and, indeed, even that could not be done for parts of the area that have not yet undergone instrumental survey.

Among the most important are the two just named, the Sierra Nevada, Cascades, Wahsatch, Uintah, Salmon River, Humboldt, Wind River, and many others.

The Coast Ranges of California and Oregon, and the large number of subordinate chains of the Great Basin, and other portions of the elevated plateau aggregate not less than 161 distinct ridges or mountain chains, with serrated axial profile of not less than 20 miles each in length, disposed according to political divisions as follows: Nevada, 49; Arizona, 15; New Mexico, 27; Utah, 25; California, 24; Colorado, 11; Wyoming, 4; Montana, 1; Idaho, 4; Oregon, 1 (part of Cascade Range only); Wyoming, 0; Texas, 0; Nebraska, 0; Dakota, 0; Kansas, 0; and Indian Territory, 0. Total, 161.

Of the above 143 distinct and separately named mountain ranges, distributed as follows: Nevada, 46; Arizona, 12; New Mexico, 25; Utah, 25; California, 20; Colorado, 11; Idaho, 3; and Oregon, 1; total, 143; independent of numbers of isolated groups of mountains as well as plateaux and mesas, have fallen within the area under survey.

Of the groups of named mountains, having no regular trend, there are found 103 within the surveyed area, and 93 exterior; and of the 41 principal plateaux, already named, lying west of the one hundredth meridian, 36 fall within the surveyed limits and 5 without

The aggregate number of ranges, mountain groups and plateaux (not including a number of minor subdivisions, that make up the Great Colorado Plateau) is three hundred and ninety-eight (398).

The ranges, mountains, and plateaux (37, 72, and 5 in numbers, respectively) lying outside the region surveyed, are taken from the names

120

given upon the latest edition of the Western Territory map of the Engineer Department, which number will doubtless be augmented when a detailed instrumental topographic survey of this territory is made.

The great mountain forms, which consist for the most part of upturned and corrugated strata, have been divided into ranges and mountains, the former confined to persistent ridges with distinct axial trend of not less than 20 miles in length each, the latter referring to the groups of mountain masses thrown above the general level with distinctive orographic features.

The plateaux are tabular shaped formations, usually of sedimentary character, although often volcanic capped, standing apart and above the general level, being of irregular form and height, showing usually bold escarpments along at least one well-marked portion of their perimeter.

An attempt has been made to confine where possible the adjective use of the word "Mount" to a single isolated structure, as "Mount Taylor," and attaching names to the summit of the peaks, the latter being a topographical feature, appreciable in extent, susceptible of exact geographical location, and more easily described with a definite individuality.

The passes from east to west are more limited in numbers, and yet the practicable ones for routes by rail or common roads are found to increase upon diligent search, while ranges considered impassable a decade since are now climbed by the narrow-gauge tracks in their search for mining and other markets found in the local objective points of these rugged regions.

The extended plateaux of the Colorado Basin and other localities west of the Continental Divide, and between it and the Sierra Nevada and Cascade Ranges, exceed in dimensions the plateaux and mesa system of Old Mexico, and the dry interior climate at elevations from 3,000 to 7,000 feet and above, south of the 40th parallel, is doubtless as lovely as any of the typical Mexican climes of the high interior valleys, and, when clearly understood as civilization advances, will furnish numerous spots noted for their climatic efficacy.

The Colorado Plateau, first named by the writer in 1868, covers, in its various mountain plateau and mesa forms, at least 100,000 square miles in Utah, Colorado, New Mexico, and Arizona.

The sub-plateaux, defined by the varying uplifts and subsequent denudations, are severally named. Erosion, through the sedimentaries that are the basis of its structure (and of the primitive rocks in some instances), has given rise to the Grand Cañon of the Colorado, a gorge without parallel, so far as known, for its high and nearly perpendicular walls, tortuous windings, and great length. Other cañons of extraordinary magnitude are the Glenn and Uinta of the Colorado River, the "Grand" of the Arkansas, the Cañon of the Yellowstone, while the Colorado, for the greater part of its length, is essentially a cañon river, and the Snake River flows through deep rocky gorges for much of its distance, and minor cañons of varied dimensions are to be found in or along the flanks of every prominent mountain range.

The principal falls are those in and around Yosemite Valley, more noted for their vertical dimensions than those of the Yellowstone, the Great and Little American on Snake River, and certain minor instances along the Columbia and Colorado Rivers.

The Yosemite Gorge has become justly famed as one of the most picturesque, and is especially unique at the season of high water.

The Yellowstone Park (so called) is one of the later wonders, on account of its geysers, mud and thermal springs, waterfalls, and beautiful lakes.

But few of these Western valleys are of erosion, and these comparatively narrow and occupying but a small area. The great detrital, plain-like valleys occupy the interior spaces between the positive ranges and plateaux, while the character of the extended plains, uniform as to elevation, the wrinkles of which are mostly from erosion, extending from the 100th meridian to the base of the mountains, is well known from descriptions of travelers and explorers of all grades.

The deserts (so called) are portions of the Lower Colorado Valley (now crossed by a railroad), the Mohave, Death Valley, Amargosa, Ralston, Humboldt, Quinn's River, and the Snake, thus reaching in patches from the Mexican border to the Columbia, between the meridinal limits of the Wahsatch and Sierra Nevada.

Sand dunes are noted particularly in the Colorado, Death, Amargosa, Termination, and San Luis Valleys.

Numbers of natural parks or extended glades have been discovered in the mountainous portions of Colorado, New Mexico, and Arizona, and especially by the writer in the area embraced by the heads of Little Colorado, Gila, San Francisco, and Salt Rivers.

The name has been erroneously applied in Colorado to those extended systems of detrital valleys inclosed by high encircling ridges called North, Middle, and South Parks, that are not particularly different from similar encompassed valleys, debouching abruptly in the direction of the flow of the waters, but wanting in that apparently artificial distribution of nature's bounties to be found in the glade-like parks above mentioned, and indeed others along the southeastern portion of the Great Colorado Plateau.

The number of peaks between 10,000 feet and 15,000 feet within the entire area, so far as now known, and measured and computed by this office, is (560) five hundred and sixty, Mount Whitney, or Fisherman's Peak, in the Southern Sierras, enjoying an elevation of 14,470 feet (barometric), being the highest that has been carefully measured barometrically. The number both measured and computed by the Survey within the limits between 5,000 feet and 10,000 feet can only be given quite approximately as (882) eight hundred and eighty-two.*

Areas of depression below the level of the sea are found in the Colorado Valley north and west from Fort Yuma, covering a space of approximately 1,600 square miles, and portions of Death Valley, in Eastern California.

The lakes of the Great Interior Basin, acting as reservoirs, are largely saline and alkaline, while the number in other localities is large, especially those little lakes near the crests of important mountain ranges. The most remarkable one, examined and called Crater or Mystic Lake, northwest of Fort Klamath, on the summit of the Cascades, evidently occupies an old eruptive vent, the surface of the water being not less than 900 feet from the lowest point of the rim of a number of lava beds of various colors and separate flows, that constitute the incasing walls of an oval of approximately

---

* These represent only a part of all existing peaks, as also but a portion of those determined in altitude. (See Appendix A and special volume Geographic Positions, &c., royal 8°.)

7 by 9 miles.   The greatest height of the almost perpendicular wall is about 2,200 feet.   A small conical extinct crater of basalt rises out of the western end of the water, which is pure and cool.   Although no visible outlet is known, yet one is possible, and the relative elevations permit that streams emerging from beneath the lava beds at both the eastern and western slopes of the Cascades should have their actual sources in this unique reservoir.

The sedimentary strata and crystalline rocks are broken through in many localities by basalts and older lavas, the vent points being marked in some instances by the residual typical cone, great fields of which are noted near San Francisco Mountain in Arizona, while the lines of eruption of the many overlying and intercalated masses of the more ancient lavas is naturally veiled from view.

The areas embraced by these lavas, except the basalts and trachytes, prove in most instances as indexes to deposits of the precious metals where search has been made, and will gradually become the alphabet of the more careful and intelligent prospecting of the future as mining advances into this extensive region.

The high mountain areas, that are perpetually covered with snow, are comparatively slight, and confined to the ravines sheltered from the sun's direct rays.   This is due largely to the relatively small amount of rain and snow fall existing at the present stage of desiccation of this portion of the continent, the elevation of many ranges being amply sufficient with proper humid conditions to justify the presence of extensive active glaciers.

The permanent source of supply from glacial masses, so efficacious in rendering certain the plans for irrigation in India and Italy that have the immense snow and ice storehouses of the Himalaya and the Alps, respectively, is wanting in the West; the winter snows melt rapidly and their moisture is soon transmitted below the lower levels, that most require irrigation, hence all plans looking to a successful recuperation of parched lands by the use of water must depend upon a larger than the usual modulus, upon the minimum of the running waters for the season, assuming a safe percentage of the additional volume that may be obtained by storage reservoirs.

Artesian wells may be made to increase the practicably arable areas by appreciable amounts at minor spots, but on no considerable scale.

Observations for the classification of the lands for map delineation into (1) Arable or agricultural, (2) timber, (3) pasturage or grazing, (4) arid or barren, having been conducted over an area exceeding 175,000 square miles in California, Nevada, Idaho, Wyoming, Utah, Colorado, New Mexico, and Arizona, there appears as a result the following approximate percentages: (1) Arable, 4.77 per cent.; (2) grazing, 49 37 per cent.; (3) timber, 26.94 per cent.; (4) arid, 16.95 per cent.; water and marsh, 1.01 per cent.; and chaparral, 0.96 per cent.

The locations of hundreds of points at which the precious and economic minerals occur but substantiate the belief gradually gaining ground of the almost unlimited prospective supply; the development of which is constantly being rendered more economic and certain.

The highest percentage reached for any single sheet by the "arid and barren" is 53.32, while the "arable," although relatively of meager amount (23.83 per cent. being the highest noted), will be increased somewhat by the artificial process of irrigation systematically conducted.

Evidences of extinct glacial action are numerous; and have been noted by observers for periods of years. The detrital floors of many of the valleys are the result of this action, and the detailed shapes of several prominent mountain ranges, especially in Colorado, Utah, New Mexico, and California, have been governed by the grand carving of glacial beds.

A possible connection between the lacustrine beach of the ancient Lake Bonneville, that once covered the present Salt Lake and Sevier Lake Basins entire, and the deep-fluted carvings along the eastern flanks of the Snake Range in Eastern Nevada was observed in 1872, indicating that glaciers existed during the period that portions of the Great Interior Basin were covered by extensive lakes draining toward the Pacific.

Mineral and thermal springs in considerable numbers have been noted in this region, and, up to 1875 not less than 120 had been located and reported upon. (See vol. 3, p. 150)

The lower levels of the detrital plain-like valleys, more especially of the Great Interior Basin, are marked by alkaline and saline flats, or mud lakes, of many square miles in extent, impassable in seasons of rain and snowfall, and the plague of these desert-like areas in times of drought.

2 WH—VOL I

Environmental Degradation by Man

IV

Although this topic comprises an enormous area of activity, the number of authors and writings prior to 1900 is surprisingly small. Contemporary ideas usually consisted of isolated statements and short essays rather than major articles or books. Much of the literature, therefore, that contains this important part of environmental geomorphology—analysis of man as a geomorphic process—is by 20th century reviewers who describe and evaluate with hindsight. A notable exception is the classic work of George Perkins Marsh who in 1864 wrote the first comprehensive book on the impact of man on nature and became an instant leader in the field.

Several different approaches are possible in treatment and organization of material on this topic. Although man causes chemical and biological deterioration of the environment the emphasis in this volume will be on the physical aberrations attributable to man's actions. Even in the ancient world man was a potent force on the landscape and in some cases may have destroyed the environment that had been providing his sustenance. Arnold Toynbee in several of his books uses this theme and in one book (1950, p. 169) quotes Plato on "The Denudation of Attica,"

> ... so that Attica has undergone the process observable in small islands, and what remains of her substance is like the skeleton of a body emaciated by disease, as compared with her original relief. All the rich, soft soil has moulted away, leaving a country of skin and bones. At the period, however, with which we are dealing, when Attica was still intact, what are now her mountains were lofty, soil-clad hills; her so-called shingle-plains of the present day were full of rich soil; and her mountains were heavily afforested—a fact of which there are still visible traces. There are mountains in Attica which can now keep nothing but bees, but which were clothed, not so very long ago, with fine trees producing timber suitable for roofing the largest buildings; and roofs hewn from this timber are still in existence. There were also many lofty cultivated trees, while the country produced boundless

127

pasture for cattle. The annual supply of rainfall was not lost, as it is at present, through being allowed to flow over the denuded surface into the sea, but was received by the country, in all its abundance . . .

Volumes 2 and 3 in this series will explore these topics more fully in the 20th century and show the sad tale that man has not always profited from past mistakes. A major difference, however, is that 20th century man has become more aware of his own rapaciousness and ability to destroy his physical habitat.

Man has interfered in the landscape in many different ways but this part will concentrate largely on his disruption that results in erosion and siltation. This approach should provide greater depth of understanding than a series of miscellaneous and disjointed changes. When the issue at hand is controversial, alternate views will be provided to aid the perspective of the problem. When analyzing past events it is not always easy to separate the variables and determine the importance of each. Even the cause–effect relationship can be difficult to decipher, and run the non sequitur risk. Several examples are provided. Thus the Fall of Rome, decline of the Mayan civilization, and initiation of the 19th century arroyo cycle in the Southwest need careful scrutiny in many different fields before the true pattern of man's involvement is solved. One omnipresent factor is climate, and its role in creating change is still only imperfectly known.

Space does not permit complete evaluation of early man and his environment but the reader is referred to such works as Stamp (1964) who in Britain traces some of the changes of earliest man including the time of the Romans and Anglo-Saxon kingdoms, and John Palmer writing on "Landforms, drainage and settlement in the vale of York" (in Eyre and Jones, 1966) reviews the history of the area and man's impact from earliest time in the Neolithic, Bronze, and Iron Ages.

Soil erosion is probably one of the most easily recognizable symptoms of man's use of the surface of the earth. As Lowdermilk (1943) points out it was always a problem in the Old World, and as Craven (1926) documents in his book, soil erosion-exhaustion became an immediate problem in the United States when agriculture became an important activity.

> . . . single crop production, poor plowing and draining, neglect of organic matters and fertilizers, and other harmful conditions have predominated and 'soil exhaustion' resulted . . . The agricultural life of Virginia and Maryland, from earliest colonial days well down to the eve of the Civil War, was carried on under conditions which gave wide play to the destructive forces of depletion. Physical surroundings were unusually favorable to the direct forces of 'exhaustion'; their economic life was begun under frontier conditions; markets and government regulations kept the life primarily agricultural and fixed habits that could not be easily shaken; low profits limited improvements, and a whole life was erected upon an exploitive agriculture, that had to be greatly changed before the economic effort which supported it could be altered. 'Soil exhaustion' and tobacco cultivation went hand in hand. (p. 24)

George Washington was very concerned about his lands and many of his letters and writing reflect his thoughts on erosion and conservation of soil.

Knowing as little as our farmers do, of the means of renovating lands, the longer they are cleared the less valuable, for the most part, they are. (Knight, 1847, p. 85)

... at present it is very much gullied, and if uncommon attention is not paid to it in the working ... it will be unfit hereafter for grass even ... (Letter to Anthony Whiting, January 27, 1793, in Fitzpatrick, 1940, V. 32, p. 319)

My lands are not congenial with [corn] and are much injured by the growth of it; having an understratum of hard clay impervious to water ... sweeps off the upper soil ... into injurious and eye-sore gullies. (Fitzpatrick, 1940, V. 36, p. 240)

Charles Fisher in a speech to the Rowan County Agricultural Society more than 100 years ago remarked:

We pursue a course of agriculture that takes all from the earth and returns nothing to it ... We completely exhaust our soil by an unvaried succession of crops; and when it can produce no longer, we turn it out into fields, let it wash into gullies ... defacing our country, and ruining our lands. (Cathey, 1966, pp. 16–17)

The concomitant problem and the doubly important reason why soil erosion is so troublesome concerns siltation, because when earth particles are removed from landslopes, they ultimately come to rest as a deposit and these sediments then pose another range of problems. Worthington (1946) in discussing the civilization of Babylon showed that the ever-increasing amounts of silt in the canals required so much labor there was little leisure time remaining. The silt increased in height and volume and was a direct result of population pressure's need for additional grazing in the uplands which made the slopes vulnerable to the infrequent, but violent rains.

It is appropriate that the first reproduction selection in this part should aid in memorializing George Perkins Marsh (1801–1882). Marsh had a remarkable and productive life that was set with financial reverses and personal tragedy. He graduated from Dartmouth College at the head of his class, and lived and worked out of Burlington, Vermont, for about 35 years where he had established a law practice and political career. He was a highly versatile man and an authority in several fields. For example he was such a fine architect that he was called in to solve the problem for determining the final proportions of the Washington Monument. He could read and translate many languages and it was his linguistic skills that gave him outstanding marks as a scholar of unusual depth. He was offered a professorship at Harvard University but turned it down because the salary was insufficient for his financial status. Some of his most famous books include *Lectures on the English Language* (1860) and *The Origin and History of the English Language, and of the Early Literature it Embodies* (1862). He was U.S. Ambassador in Turin, Florence, and Rome from 1861–1882, and the position afforded him great flexibility for travel and writing, which he did extensively throughout Egypt, Palestine, and Turkey. Thus diplomacy gave him leisure for

129

research, the locale provided the natural setting and incentive, and past positions such as State House Commissioner in Vermont including railroad commissioner and fish commissioner gave him knowledge and insight on man and his relation to the natural world.

His monumental book (Marsh, 1877) first published in 1864 had started to take form as early as 1847 when in a speech before the Agricultural Society of Rutland County he told how man in the clearing of hillsides, burning of woods, and damming of streams had caused significant changes. In the preface for his book he tells its purpose: "The object of the present volume is: to indicate the character and, approximately, the extent of the changes produced by human action . . . to point out the dangers of imprudence. . . to suggest the . . . importance of the restoration of disturbed harmonies and the material improvement of waste and exhausted regions . . ." His thesis that nature did not heal herself was contrary to much opinion of the day, but in spite of this the book was an immediate best seller and sold 1,000 copies in a few months. It was reprinted and revised several times. Although reprinted in 1908 it was largely overlooked until the 1930's at which time a new generation of conservationists was emerging. The last reprint was the 100th anniversary volume in 1964.

Scribner, Armstrong & Co., New York, 1877, 674 pp.

11

The Earth as Modified by Human Action: A New Edition of Man and Nature

G. P. MARSH

Destructiveness of Man.

Man has too long forgotten that the earth was given to him for usufruct alone, not for consumption, still less for profligate waste. Nature has provided against the absolute destruction of any of her elementary matter, the raw material of her works; the thunderbolt and the tornado, the most convulsive throes of even the volcano and the earthquake, being only phenomena of decomposition and recomposition. But she has left it within the power of man irreparably to derange the combinations of inorganic matter and of organic life, which through the night of æons she had been proportioning and balancing, to prepare the earth for his habitation, when in the fulness of time his Creator should call him forth to enter into its possession.

Apart from the hostile influence of man, the organic and the inorganic world are, as I have remarked, bound together by such mutual relations and adaptations as secure, if not the absolute permanence and equilibrium of both, a long continuance of the established conditions of each at any given time and place, or at least, a very slow and gradual succession of changes in those conditions. But man is everywhere a disturbing agent. Wherever he plants his foot, the harmonies of nature

131

are turned to discords.   The proportions and accommodations which insured the stability of existing arrangements are overthrown.   Indigenous vegetable and animal species are extirpated, and supplanted by others of foreign origin, spontaneous production is forbidden or restricted, and the face of the earth is either laid bare or covered with a new and reluctant growth of vegetable forms, and with alien tribes of animal life.   These intentional changes and substitutions constitute, indeed, great revolutions ; but vast as is their magnitude and importance, they are, as we shall see, insignificant in comparison with the contingent and unsought results which have flowed from them.

The fact that, of all organic beings, man alone is to be regarded as essentially a destructive power, and that he wields energies to resist which Nature—that nature whom all material life and all inorganic substance obey—is wholly impotent, tends to prove that, though living in physical nature, he is not of her, that he is of more exalted parentage, and belongs to a higher order of existences, than those which are born of her womb and live in blind submission to her dictates.

Human and Brute Action Compared.

It is maintained by authorities as high as any known to modern science, that the action of man upon nature, though greater in *degree*, does not differ in *kind* from that of wild animals. It is perhaps impossible to establish a radical distinction *in genere* between the two classes of effects, but there is an essential difference between the motive of action which calls out the energies of civilized man and the mere appetite which controls the life of the beast.   The action of man, indeed, is frequently followed by unforeseen and undesired results, yet it is nevertheless guided by a self-conscious will aiming as often at secondary and remote as at immediate objects.   The wild animal, on the other hand, acts instinctively, and, so far as we are able to perceive, always with a view to single and direct purposes. The back-woodsman and the beaver alike fell trees ; the man that he may convert the forest into an olive grove that will mature its fruit only for a succeeding generation, the beaver that he may feed upon the bark of the trees or use them in the construction of his habitation. The action of brutes upon the material world is slow and gradual, and usually limited, in any given case, to a narrow extent of territory. Nature is allowed time and oppor-tunity to set her restorative powers at work, and the destructive animal has hardly retired from the field of his ravages before nature has repaired the damages occasioned by his operations. In fact, he is expelled from the scene by the very efforts which she makes for the restoration of her dominion. Man, on the contrary, extends his action over vast spaces, his revolutions are swift and radical, and his devastations are, for an almost incal-culable time after he has withdrawn the arm that gave the blow, irreparable.

The form of geographical surface, and very probably the climate of a given country, depend much on the character of the vegetable life belonging to it. Man has, by domestication, greatly changed the habits and properties of the plants he rears ; he has, by voluntary selection, immensely modified the forms and qualities of the animated creatures that serve him ; and he has, at the same time, completely rooted out many forms of ani-

---

The difference between the relations of savage life, and of incipient civilization, to nature, is well seen in that part of the valley of the Missis-sippi which was once occupied by the mound builders and afterwards by the far less developed Indian tribes. When the tillers of the fields, which must have been cultivated to sustain the large population that once inhabited those regions, perished, or were driven out, the soil fell back to the normal forest state, and the savages who succeeded the more advanced race interfered very little, if at all, with the ordinary course of spontaneous nature.

mal if not of vegetable being.* What is there, in the influence of brute life, that corresponds to this? We have no reason to believe that, in that portion of the American continent which, though peopled by many tribes of quadruped and fowl, remained uninhabited by man or only thinly occupied by purely savage tribes, any sensible geographical change had occurred within twenty centuries before the epoch of discovery and colonization, while, during the same period, man had changed millions of square miles, in the fairest and most fertile regions of the Old World, into the barrenest deserts.

The ravages committed by man subvert the relations and destroy the balance which nature had established between her organized and her inorganic creations, and she avenges herself upon the intruder, by letting loose upon her defaced provinces destructive energies hitherto kept in check by organic forces destined to be his best auxiliaries, but which he has unwisely dispersed and driven from the field of action. When the forest is gone, the great reservoir of moisture stored up in its vegetable mould is evaporated, and returns only in deluges of rain to wash away the parched dust into which that mould has been converted. The well-wooded and humid hills are turned to ridges of dry rock, which encumbers the low grounds and chokes the watercourses with its débris, and—except in countries favored with an equable distribution of rain through the seasons, and a

---

* Whatever may be thought of the modification of organic species by natural selection, there is certainly no evidence that animals have exerted upon any form of life an influence analogous to that of domestication upon plants, quadrupeds, and birds reared artificially by man ; and this is as true of unforeseen as of purposely effected improvements accomplished by voluntary selection of breeding animals.

It is true that nature employs birds and quadrupeds for the dissemination of vegetable and even of animal species. But when the bird drops the seed of a fruit it has swallowed, and when the sheep transports in its fleece the seed-vessel of a burdock from the plain to the mountain, its action is purely mechanical and unconscious, and does not differ from that of the wind in producing the same effect.

moderate and regular inclination of surface—the whole earth, unless rescued by human art from the physical degradation to which it tends, becomes an assemblage of bald mountains, of barren, turfless hills, and of swampy and malarious plains. There are parts of Asia Minor, of Northern Africa, of reece, and even of Alpine Europe, where the operation of causes set in action by man has brought the face of the earth to a desolation almost as complete as that of the moon; and though, within that brief space of time which we call "the historical period," they are known to have been covered with luxuriant woods, verdant pastures, and fertile meadows, they are now too far deteriorated to be reclaimable by man, nor can they become again fitted for human use, except through great geological changes, or other mysterious influences or agencies of which we have no present knowledge, and over which we have no prospective control. The earth is fast becoming an unfit home for its noblest inhabitant, and another era of equal human crime and human improvidence, and of like duration with that through which traces of that crime and that improvidence extend, would reduce it to such a condition of impoverished productiveness, of shattered surface, of climatic excess, as to threaten the depravation, barbarism, and perhaps even extinction of the species.*

---

* ——" And it may be remarked that, as the world has passed through these several stages of strife to produce a Christendom, so by relaxing in the enterprises it has learnt, does it tend downwards, through inverted steps, to wildness and the waste again. Let a people give up their contest with moral evil; disregard the injustice, the ignorance, the greediness, that may prevail among them, and part more and more with the Christian element of their civilization; and in declining this battle with sin, they will inevitably get embroiled with men. Threats of war and revolution punish their unfaithfulness; and if then, instead of retracing their steps, they yield again, and are driven before the storm, the very arts they had created, the structures they had raised, the usages they had established, are swept away; 'in that very day their thoughts perish.' The portion they had reclaimed from the young earth's ruggedness is lost; and failing to stand fast against man, they finally get embroiled with nature, and are thrust down beneath her ever-living hand." —MARTINEAU'S Sermon, " The Good Soldier of Jesus Christ."

True, there is a partial reverse to this picture. On narrow theatres, new forests have been planted; inundations of flowing streams restrained by heavy walls of masonry and other constructions; torrents compelled to aid, by depositing the slime with which they are charged, in filling up lowlands, and raising the level of morasses which their own overflows had created; ground submerged by the encroachments of the ocean, or exposed to be covered by its tides, has been rescued from its dominion by diking; swamps and even lakes have been drained, and their beds brought within the domain of agricultural industry; drifting coast dunes have been checked and made productive by plantation; seas and inland waters have been repeopled with fish, and even the sands of the Sahara have been fertilized by artesian fountains. These achievements are more glorious than the proudest triumphs of war, but, thus far, they give but faint hope that we shall yet make full atonement for our spendthrift waste of the bounties of nature.†

† The wonderful success which has attended the measures for subduing torrents and preventing inundations employed in Southern France since 1865, and described in Chapter III., *post*, ought to be here noticed as a splendid and most encouraging example of well-directed effort in the way of physical restoration.

Jacobsen and Adams coauthored the next article which is a significant review of the problems of soil salinization and siltation in ancient Mesopotamia. They also provide new evidence and insight from their own field studies of the region. It should be noted that Marsh (1877, p. 468) had also remarked on the effects of salt in irrigated soils:

> The attentive traveller in Egypt and Nubia cannot fail to notice many localities, generally of small extent, where the soil is rendered infertile by an excess of saline matter in its composition . . . A saline efflorescence called 'Reh' and 'Kuller' is gradually invading many of the most fertile districts of Northern and Western India, and changing them into sterile deserts.

Thus it is important to realize that ancient man was capable of performing prodigious engineering feats for utilization of water (see also Wittfogel, 1956). Many of these works were on a massive scale and the dikes and canals were marvels of construction. In such enterprises, however, the early engineers either neglected or did not understand some of the fundamental laws of geomorphology. Irrigation in the "fertile crescent" eventually led to such major problems that it aided in causing the failure of the agrarian economy, and according to many such as Toynbee was the most important factor in causing the downfall of these civilizations. To be entirely objective, however, we must ask ourselves where would civilization have been, and what type of progress would have occurred, if man had never attempted and made such structures in the first place. Volume 2 will emphasize that similar problems continue to occur into the 20th century.

Thorkild Jacobsen (1904–   ) was born in Denmark and received his Ph.D. (1929) in Oriental Studies at the University of Chicago. He has been a professor at the University of Chicago, and since 1957 Director of the Diyala Institute. He is currently Professor in the Near Eastern Language and Literature program at Harvard University.

Robert M. Adams (1926–   ) received his Ph.D. (1956) in anthropology at the University of Chicago, and has taught there since 1954. He served as Professor and Director of the Oriental Institute. He is currently Professor of Anthropology and Near Eastern Archaeology and Dean of Social Sciences, Chicago University. He has written such books as *The Evolution of Urban Society: Early Mesopotamia and Prehistoric Mexico* (1966), and *Land Behind Baghdad* (1965).

21 November 1958, Volume 128, Number 3334

SCIENCE

12

Salt and Silt in Ancient Mesopotamian Agriculture

Progressive changes in soil salinity and sedimentation
contributed to the breakup of past civilizations.

Thorkild Jacobsen and Robert M. Adams

Under the terms of a farsighted statute, 70 percent of the oil revenues of the
Iraqi Government are set aside for a program of capital investment which is
transforming many aspects of the country's predominantly agricultural economy. As compared with the subsistence
agriculture which largely has characterized Iraq's rural scene in the past, new
irrigation projects in formerly uninhabited deserts are pioneering a rapid increase in land and labor productivity
through crop rotation, summer cultivation in addition to the traditional winter-
grown cereals, and emphasis on cash
crops and livestock.

But these and similar innovations often
have disconcerting effects in a semiarid,
subtropical zone—effects which cannot
be calculated directly from the results of
experiment in Europe and America. At
the same time, old canal banks and
thickly scattered ruins of former settlements testify to former periods of successful cultivation in most of the desert
areas now being reopened. The cultural
pre-eminence of the alluvial plains of
central and southern Iraq through much
of their recorded history provides still
further evidence of the effectiveness of
the traditional agricultural regime in
spite of its prevailing reliance on a simple system of fallow in alternate years.
Accordingly, the entire 6000-year record
of irrigation agriculture in the Tigris-
Euphrates flood plain furnishes an indispensable background for formulating
plans for future development.

At least the beginnings of a compre-

hensive assessment of ancient agriculture recently were undertaken on behalf
of the Government of Iraq Development
Board. In addition to utilizing ancient
textual sources from many parts of Iraq
which today are widely scattered in the
world's libraries and museums, this undertaking included a program of archeological field work designed to elucidate
the history of irrigation and settlement
of a portion of the flood plain that is
watered by a Tigris tributary, the Diyala
River (1). Here we cannot report all the
diverse findings of the project and its
many specialists, but instead will outline
some aspects of the general ecological
situation encountered by agriculturalists
in the Mesopotamian alluvium which
seem to have shaped the development of
irrigation farming. And, conversely, we
hope to show that various features of the
natural environment in turn were deci-
sively modified by the long-run effects of
human agencies.

Historical Role of Soil Salinization

A problem which recently has come to
loom large in Iraqi reclamation planning
is the problem of salinity. The semiarid
climate and generally low permeability
of the soils of central and southern Iraq
expose the soils to dangerous accumulations of salt and exchangeable sodium,
which are harmful to crops and soil texture and which can eventually force the
farmer off his land.

For the most part, the salts in the allu-

vial soils are presumed to have been
carried in by river and irrigation water
from the sedimentary rocks of the northern mountains. In addition, smaller
quantities may have been left by ancient
marine transgressions or borne in by
winds from the Persian Gulf. Beside the
dominant calcium and magnesium cat-
ions, the irrigation water also contains
some sodium. As the water evaporates
and transpires it is assumed that the calcium and magnesium tend to precipitate
as carbonates, leaving the sodium ions
dominant in the soil solution. Unless they
are washed down into the water table,
the sodium ions tend to be adsorbed by
colloidal clay particles, deflocculating
them and leaving the resultant structureless soil almost impermeable to water.
In general, high salt concentrations obstruct germination and impede the absorption of water and nutrients by plants.

Salts accumulate steadily in the water
table, which has only very limited lateral
movement to carry them away. Hence
the ground water everywhere has become
extremely saline, and this probably constitutes the immediate source of the salts
in Iraq's saline soils. New waters added
as excessive irrigation, rains, or floods
can raise the level of the water table
very considerably under the prevailing
conditions of inadequate drainage. With
a further capillary rise when the soil is
wet, the dissolved salts and exchangeable sodium are brought into the root
zone or even to the surface.

While this problem has received scientific study in Iraq only in very recent
years, investigation by the Diyala Basin
Archeological Project of a considerable
number and variety of ancient textual
sources has shown that the process of
salinization has a long history. Only the
modern means to combat it are new:
deep drainage to lower and hold down
the water table, and utilization of chemical amendments to restore soil texture.
In spite of the almost proverbial fertility
of Mesopotamia in antiquity, ancient
control of the water table was based only
on avoidance of overirrigation and on
the practice of weed-fallow in alternate

Dr. Jacobsen is a professor in the Oriental Institute, University of Chicago. Dr. Adams is an assistant professor in the department of anthropology
and a research associate in the Oriental Institute,
University of Chicago.

years. As was first pointed out by J. C. Russel, the later technique allows the deep-rooted *shoq* (*Proserpina stephanis*) and *agul* (*Alhagi maurorum*) to create a deep-lying dry zone against the rise of salts through capillary action. In extreme cases, longer periods of abandonment must have been a necessary, if involuntary, feature of the agricultural cycle. Through evapotranspiration and some slow draining they could eventually reduce an artificially raised water table to safe levels.

As to salinity itself, three major occurrences have been established from ancient records. The earliest of these, and the most serious one, affected southern Iraq from 2400 B.C. until at least 1700 B.C. A milder phase is attested in documents from central Iraq written between 1300 and 900 B.C. Lastly, there is archeological evidence that the Nahrwan area east of Baghdad became salty only after A.D. 1200.

The earliest of these occurrences particularly merits description, since it sheds light on the northward movement of the major centers of political power from southern into central Iraq during the early second millennium B.C. It seems to have had its roots in one of the perennial disputes between the small, independent principalities which were the principal social units of the mid-third millennium B.C. Girsu and Umma, neighboring cities along a watercourse stemming from the Euphrates, had fought for generations over a fertile border district. Under the ruler Entemenak, Girsu temporarily gained the ascendancy, but was unable to prevent Umma, situated higher up the watercourse, from breaching and obstructing the branch canals that served the border fields. After repeated, unsuccessful protests, Entemenak eventually undertook to supply water to the area by means of a canal from the Tigris; access to that river, flowing to the east of Girsu, could be assured without further campaigning against Umma to the northwest. By 1700 B.C. this canal had become large and important enough to be called simply "the Tigris," and it was supplying a large region west of Girsu that formerly had been watered only by the Euphrates. As a result, the limited irrigation supplies that could be drawn from the latter river were supplemented with copious Tigris water. A corresponding increase undoubtedly occurred in seepage, flooding, and overirrigation, creating all the conditions for a decisive rise in groundwater level.

Several parallel lines of evidence allow the ensuing salinization to be followed quantitatively:

1) Beginning shortly after the reign of Entemenak, the presence of patches of saline ground is directly attested in records of ancient temple surveyors. In a few cases, individual fields which at that time were recorded as salt-free can be shown in an archive from 2100 B.C. to have developed conditions of sporadic salinity during the 300 intervening years of cultivation.

2) Crop choice can be influenced by many factors, but the onset of salinization strongly favors the adoption of crops which are more salt-tolerant. Counts of grain impressions in excavated pottery from sites in southern Iraq of about 3500 B.C., made by H. Helbaek, suggest that at that time the proportions of wheat and barley were nearly equal. A little more than 1000 years later, in the time of Entemenak at Girsu, the less salt-tolerant wheat accounted for only one-sixth of the crop. By about 2100 B.C. wheat had slipped still further, and it accounted for less than 2 percent of the crop in the Girsu area. By 1700 B.C., the cultivation of wheat had been abandoned completely in the southern part of the alluvium.

3) Concurrent with the shift to barley cultivation was a serious decline in fertility which for the most part can be attributed to salinization. At about 2400 B.C. in Girsu a number of field records give an average yield of 2537 liters per hectare—highly respectable even by modern United States and Canadian standards. This figure had declined to 1460 liters per hectare by 2100 B.C., and by about 1700 B.C. the recorded yield at nearby Larsa had shrunk to an average of only 897 liters per hectare. The effects of this slow but cumulatively large decline must have been particularly devastating in the cities, where the needs of a considerable superstructure of priests, administrators, merchants, soldiers, and craftsmen had to be met with surpluses from primary agricultural production.

The southern part of the alluvial plain appears never to have recovered fully from the disastrous general decline which accompanied the salinization process. While never completely abandoned afterwards, cultural and political leadership passed permanently out of the region with the rise of Babylon in the 18th century B.C., and many of the great Sumerian cities dwindled to villages or were left in ruins. Probably there is no historical event of this magnitude for

which a single explanation is adequate, but that growing soil salinity played an important part in the breakup of Sumerian civilization seems beyond question.

Silt and the Ancient Landscape

Like salt, the sources of the silt of which the alluvium is composed are to be found in the upper reaches of the major rivers and their tributaries. Superficially, the flatness of the alluvial terrain may seem to suggest a relatively old and static formation, one to which significant increments of silt are added only as a result of particularly severe floods. But in fact, sedimentation is a massive, continuing process. Silt deposited in canal beds must be removed in periodic cleanings to adjoining spoil banks, from which it is carried by rain and wind erosion to surrounding fields. Another increment of sediment accompanies the irrigation water into the fields themselves, adding directly to the land surface. In these ways, the available evidence from archeological soundings indicates that an average of perhaps ten meters of silt has been laid down at least near the northern end of the alluvium during the last 5000 years.

Of course, the rate of deposition is not uniform. It is most rapid along the major rivers and canals, and their broad levees slope away to interior drainage basins where accumulated runoff and difficult drainage have led to seriously leached soils and seasonal swamps. However, only the very largest of the present depressions seem to have existed as permanent barriers (while fluctuating in size) to cultivation and settlement for the six millennia since agriculture began in the northern part of the alluvium. More commonly, areas of swamp shifted from time to time. As some were gradually brought under cultivation, others formed behind newly created canal or river levees which interrupted the earlier avenues of drainage.

As the rate of sedimentation is affected by the extent of irrigation, so also were the processes of sedimentation – and their importance as an agricultural problem—closely related to the prevailing patterns of settlement, land-use, and even sociopolitical control. The character of this ecological interaction can be shown most clearly at present from archeological surveys in the lower Diyala basin, although other recent reconnaissance indicates that the same relation-

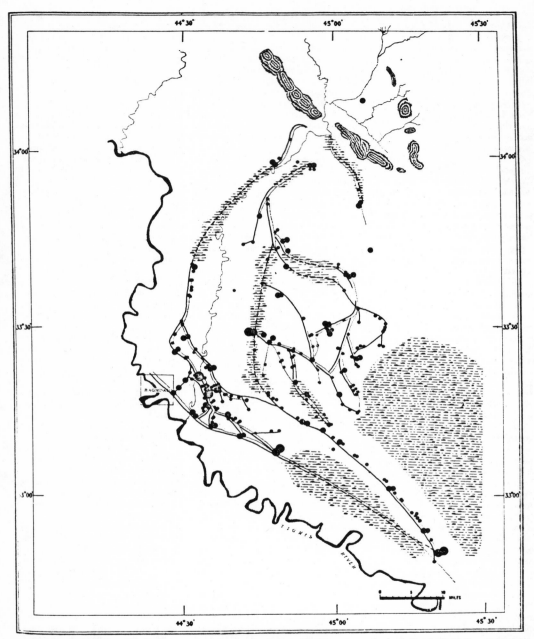

Fig. 1. **Early watercourses and settlements in the Diyala region.** The system shown in grey was in use during the Early Dynastic period, about 3000–2400 B.C. Sites and watercourses shown in black, slightly displaced so that the earlier pattern will remain visible, were occupied during the Old Babylonian period, about 1800–1700 B.C. In this and subsequent figures, size of circle marking an ancient settlement is roughly proportional to the area of its ruins. Modern river courses are shown in grey.

ships were fairly uniform throughout the northern, or Akkadian, part of the Mesopotamian plain (2). To what degree the same patterns occurred in the initially more urbanized (and subsequently more saline) Sumerian region further south, however, cannot yet be demonstrated.

The methods of survey employed here consisted of locating ancient occupational sites with the aid of large-scale maps and aerial photographs, visiting most or all of them—in this case, more than 900 in a 9000-square-kilometer area—systematically in order to make surface collections of selected "type fossils" of broken pottery, and subsequently determining the span of occupation at each settlement with the aid of such historical and archeological crossties as may be found to supplement the individual sherd collections (3). It then can be observed that the settlements of a particular period always describe networks of lines which must represent approximately the contemporary watercourses that were necessary for settled agricultural life. For more recent periods, the watercourses serving the settlements often still can be traced in detail as raised levees, spoil banks, or patterns of vegetation disturbance, but, owing in part to the rising level of the plain, all of the older watercourses so far have been located only inferentially.

A number of important and cumulative, but previously little-known, developments emerge from the surveys. By comparing the over-all pattern of settlement of both the early third and early second millennium B.C. (Fig. 1) with the prevailing pattern of about A.D. 500 (Fig. 2) these developments can be seen in sharply contrasting form. They may be summarized conveniently by distinguishing two successive phases of settlement and irrigation, each operating in a different ecological background and each facing problems of sedimentation of a different character and magnitude.

The earlier phase persisted longest. Characterized by a linear pattern of settlements largely confined to the banks of major watercourses, it began with the onset of agricultural life in the Ubaid period (about 4000 B.C.) and was replaced only during the final centuries of the pre-Christian era. In all essentials the same network of watercourses was in use throughout this long time-span, and the absence of settlement along periodically shifting side branches seems to imply an irrigation regime in which the water was not drawn great distances

inland from the main watercourses. Under these circumstances, silt accumulation would not have been the serious problem to the agriculturalist that it later became. The short branch canals upon which irrigation depended could have been cleaned easily or even replaced without the necessary intervention of a powerful, centralized authority. Quite possibly most irrigation during this phase depended simply on uncontrolled flooding through breaches cut in the levees of watercourses (like the lower Mississippi River) flowing well above plain level.

It is apparent from the map in Fig. 1 that large parts of the area were unoccupied by settled cultivators even during the periods of maximum population and prosperity that have been selected for illustration therein. An extended, historical study of soil profiles would be necessary to provide explanations for these uninhabited zones, but it is not unreasonable to suppose that some were seasonal swamps and depressions of the kind described above, while others were given over to desert because they were slightly elevated and hence not subject to easy flooding and irrigation. Still others probably were permanent swamps, since it is difficult to account in any other way for the discontinuities in settlement that appear along long stretches of some watercourses. One indication of the ecological shift which took place in succeeding millennia is that permanent swamps today have virtually disappeared from the entire northern half of the alluvium.

Considering the proportion of occupied to unoccupied area, the total population of the Diyala basin apparently was never very large during this long initial phase. Instead, a moderately dense population was confined to small regional enclaves or narrow, isolated strips along the major watercourses; for the rest of the area there can have been only very small numbers of herdsmen, hunters, fishermen, and marginal catch-crop cultivators. It is significant that most of the individual settlements were small villages, and that even the dominant political centers in the area are more aptly described as towns rather than cities (4).

An essential feature of the earlier pattern of occupation, although not shown in a summary map like Fig. 1, is its fluctuating character. There is good historical evidence that devastating cycles of abandonment affected the whole alluvium. The wide and simultaneous onset of these cycles soon after relatively peaceful and prosperous times suggests

that they proceeded from sociopolitical, rather than natural, causes, but at any rate their effects can be seen clearly in the Diyala region. For example, the numerous Old Babylonian settlements shown in Fig. 1 had been reduced in number by more than 80 percent within 500 years following, leaving only small outposts scattered at wide intervals along watercourses which previously had been thickly settled. An earlier abandonment not long after the Early Dynastic period that is shown in gray in Fig. 1, was shorter-lived and possibly affected the main towns more than the outlying small villages. Village life in general, it may be observed, remains pretty much of an enigma in the ancient Orient for all "historical" periods.

Under both ancient and modern Mesopotamian conditions, a clear distinction between "canals" and "rivers" is frequently meaningless or impossible. If the former are large and are allowed to run without control they can develop a "natural" regime in spite of their artificial origin. Some river courses, on the other hand, can be maintained only by straightening, desilting, and other artificial measures. Nevertheless, it needs to be stressed that the reconstructed watercourses shown in Fig. 2 followed essentially natural regimes and that at least their origins had little or nothing to do with human intervention. They were, in the first place, already present during the initial occupation of the area by prehistoric village agriculturalists who lacked the numbers and organization to dig them artificially. Secondly, the same watercourses persisted for more than three millennia with little change, even through periods of abandonment when they could not have received the maintenance which canals presuppose. Finally, the whole network of these early rivers describes a "braided stream" pattern which contrasts sharply with the brachiating canal systems of all later times, which are demonstrably artificial.

Specific features of the historic geography of the area are not within the compass of this article, but it should be noted that the ancient topography differed substantially from the modern. Particularly interesting is the former course of the Diyala River, flowing west of its present position and joining the Tigris River (apparently also not in its modern course) through a delta-like series of mouths. A branch that bifurcated from the former Diyala above its "delta" and flowed off for a long distance to the southeast before joining the Tigris has

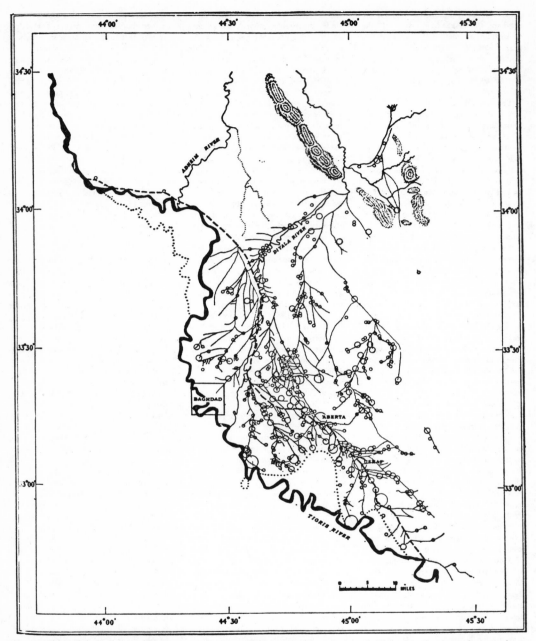

Fig. 2. Maximum extent of settlement and irrigation in the Diyala region. All canals shown by lines with minute serrations were in use during the Sassanian period, A.D. 226–637. However, expansion to the full limits came only with construction of the Nahrwan Canal (shown as a dashed black line) late in the period Settlements shown as black circles are also of Sassanian date. The different course probably followed in places by the Tigris River during the Sassanian period is suggested by black dotted lines.

142

been identified tentatively as the previously unlocated "River Dabban" that is referred to in ancient cuneiform sources.

The pattern of occupation illustrated in Fig. 2 began to emerge in Achaemenian times (539–331 B.C.), after nearly 1000 years of stagnation and abandonment. Perhaps the pace of reoccupation quickened with the conquest of Mesopotamia by Alexander, but the density of population reached during much older periods was attained again, and then surpassed, only in the subsequent Parthian period (about 150 B.C.–A.D. 226). New settlements large enough to be described as true cities, on the other hand, were introduced to the area for the first time by Alexander's Macedonian followers—demonstrating, if doubt could

otherwise exist, that the onset of urbanization depends more on historical and cultural factors than on a simple increase in population density.

A central feature of this second phase of settlement is the far more complete exploitation of available land and water resources for agriculture. There is some evidence that the irrigation capacity of the Diyala River was being utilized fully even before the end of the Parthian period, and yet both the proportion of land that was cultivated and the total population rose substantially further, reaching their maxima in this area, for any period, under the Sassanian dynasty (A.D. 226–637) that followed. A rough estimate of the total agricultural production in the area first becomes possible with records of tax collections under the early

Abbasids, perhaps 300 years after the maximum limits of expansion shown in Fig. 2 had been reached. From a further calculation of the potentially cultivable land it can then be shown that (with alternate years in fallow and assuming average yields) virtually the entire cultivable area must have been cropped regularly under both the Sassanians and early Abbasids.

Increased population, the growth of urban centers, and expansion in the area of cultivation to its natural limits were linked in turn to an enlargement of the irrigation system on an unprecedented scale. It was necessary, in the first place, to crisscross formerly unused desert and depression areas with a complex—and entirely artificial—brachiating system of branch canals, which is outlined in Fig.

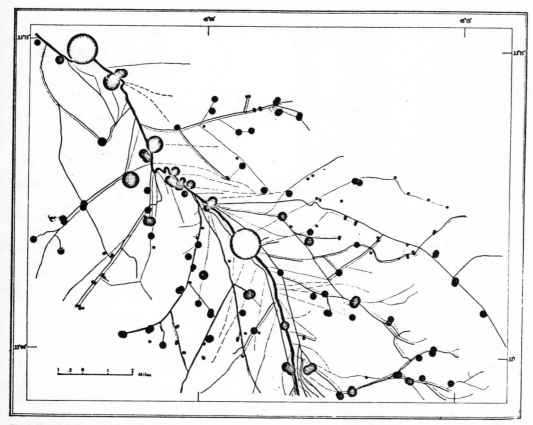

Fig. 3. Branch canal sequence along the Nahrwan. Branches shown as dashed grey lines date to the later Sassanian period (about A.D. 500–637). Settlements shown as grey circles and branch canals shown as continuous grey lines belong to the Early Islamic and Samarran periods, prior to about A.D. 900. Settlements and branch canals shown in black are those in use during the final phase of irrigation in the lower Nahrwan district, about A.D. 1100. The weir excavated by the project was located at the junction of numerous branch canals northwest of the city of Uskaf.

2. Expansion depended also on the construction of a large, supplementary feeder canal from the Tigris which, with technical proficiency that still excites admiration, and without apparent regard for cost, brought the indispensable, additional water through a hard, conglomerate headland, across two rivers, and thence down the wide levee left by the Dabban River of antiquity. Enough survives of the Nahrwan Canal, as the lower part of this gigantic system was called, even to play a key part in modern irrigation planning. Excavations carried out by the Diyala Basin Archeological Project at one of several known weirs along the 300-kilometer course of this canal provided a forceful illustration not only of the scale of the system but also of the attention lavished on such ancillary works as thousands of brick sluice gates along its branches. In short, we are dealing here with a whole new conception of irrigation which undertook boldly to reshape the physical environment at a cost which could be met only with the full resources of a powerful and highly centralized state (5).

In spite of its unrivaled engineering competence, there were a number of undesirable consequences of the new irrigation regime. For example, to a far greater degree than had been true earlier, it utilized long branch canals which tended to fill rapidly with silt because of their small-to-moderate slope and cross-sectional area. Only the Nahrwan Canal itself—and that only during the first two centuries or so of its existence—seems to have maintained its bed without frequent and costly cleaning. Silt banks left from Parthian, Sassanian, and Islamic canal cleaning are today a major topographic feature not only in the Diyala region but all over the northern part of the Mesopotamian alluvium; frequently they run for great distances and tower over all but the highest mounds built up by ancient towns and cities. Or again, while massive control installations were essential if such a complex and interdependent system was to operate effectively, they needed periodic reconstruction at great cost (six major phases at the weir excavated by the Diyala Project) and practically continuous maintenance. Moreover, the provision of control works of all sizes acted together with the spreading networks of canal branches and subbranches to reduce or eliminate flood surges which otherwise might have contributed to the desilting process.

None of these consequences, to be sure, vitiated the advantages to be obtained

with the new type of irrigation *so long as there remained a strong central authority committed to its maintenance.* But with conditions of social unrest and a preoccupation on the part of the political authorities with military adventures and intrigues, the maintenance of the system could only fall back on local communities ill equipped to handle it. These circumstances prevailed fairly briefly in late Sassanian times, leading to a widespread but temporary abandonment of the area. After an Islamic revival, they occurred again in the 11th and 12th centuries A.D., accompanied by such storm signals of political decay as the calculated breaching of the Nahrwan during a military campaign. On this occasion there was no quick recovery; it still remains for the modern Iraqis to re-establish the prosperity for which the region once was noted.

A closer look at the role of sedimentation along the Nahrwan during the years of political crisis under the later Abbasids is given in Fig. 3. In the first illustrated phase, in late Sassanian times, irrigation water was drawn from the Nahrwan at fairly uniform intervals and applied almost directly to fields adjoining its course. During a second phase, roughly coinciding with the rise of the Abbasid caliphate, irrigation water tended to be drawn off further upstream from the field for which it was destined. This is best exemplified by the increasing importance of the weir as a source for branch canals serving a considerable area. For some distance below the weir the level of the Nahrwan apparently no longer was sufficient to furnish irrigation water above the level of the fields.

By the time of the final phase, soon after A.D. 1100, practically all irrigation in the very large region below the weir had come to depend on branch canals issuing from above it; it is worth noting that two of the largest and most important of these branches simply paralleled the Nahrwan along each bank for more than 20 kilometers. The same unsuccessful struggle to maintain irrigation control is shown by the shrinkage or disappearance of town and city life along the main canal and the depopulation of the initial 5 to 10 kilometers along each major branch issuing from it, while lower-lying communities at the distal ends of the branches continued to flourish.

This cumulative change in the character of the system probably was a consequence of both natural and social factors. On the one hand, silt deposition

had raised the level of the fields by almost 1 meter over a 500-year period. Since the natural mechanisms for maintaining equilibrium between the bed of a watercourse and its alluvial levee were largely inoperative in such a complex and carefully controlled system, this rise in land surface may have reduced considerably the level of water available for irrigation purposes. At the same time, inadequate maintenance and subsequent siltation of the Nahrwan's own bed in time sharply reduced its flow and surely also reduced the head of water it could provide to its branches. But whatever the responsible factors were, the result was an especially disastrous one. At a time when the responsibility of the central government for irrigation was eroding away and when population had been reduced substantially by warfare and by prolonged disruption of the water supply, the heavy burden of desilting branch canals remained constant or even increased for the local agriculturalist. If the accumulation of silt was no more than a minor problem at the beginning of irrigation in the Diyala basin 5000 years earlier, by the late Abbasid period it had become perhaps the greatest single obstacle that a quite different irrigation regime had to deal with.

With the converging effects of mounting maintenance requirements on the one hand, and declining capacity for more than rudimentary maintenance tasks on the other, the virtual desertion of the lower Diyala area that followed assumes in retrospect a kind of historical inevitability. By the middle of the 12th century most of the Nahrwan region already was abandoned. Only a trickle of water passed down the upper section of the main canal to supply a few dying towns in the now hostile desert. Invading Mongol horsemen under Hulagu Khan, who first must have surveyed this devastated scene a century later, have been unjustly blamed for causing it ever since.

References and Notes

1. The Diyala Basin Archeological Project was conducted jointly by the Oriental Institute of the University of Chicago and the Iraq Directorate General of Antiquities, on a grant from the First Technical Section of the Development Board. It was directed by one of us (T. J.), with the other (R. M. A.) and Sayyid Fuad Safar, of the Directorate General of Antiquities, as associate directors. Excavations were under the supervision of Sayyid Mohammed Ali Mustafa, also of the Directorate General of Antiquities. Field studies of paleobotanical remains were undertaken in association with the project by Dr. Hans Helbaek, of the National Museum, Copenhagen, Denmark. Intensive study of the cuneiform and Arabic textual sources on agriculture was made possible through the collaboration of scholars of many countries. Especial thanks for assist-

1257

ance to the field program in Iraq, and for advice in the interpretation of its results, are due to Mr. K. F. Vernon, H. E. Dr. Naji al-Asil, Dr. J. C. Russel, and Sayyid Adnan Hardan.

2. R. M. Adams, *Sumer*, in press.

3. A preliminary application of this approximate methodology to conditions prevailing in Iraq was introduced by one of us (T. J.) in the Diyala basin in 1936–37, and the results of that earlier survey have been incorporated in the present study. Fortunately for the archeologist, there is sufficient disturbance from routine community activities (for example, foundation, well, and grave digging, and mud-brick manufacture, and so forth) for some traces of even the earli-

est of a long sequence of occupational periods to be detected on a mound's surface.

4. Partial town plans for the political capital of the region at Tel Asmar (ancient Eshnunna) and for two other slightly smaller centers are available from extensive Oriental Institute excavations carried out in the Diyala region between 1930 and 1937. See P. Delougaz, *The Temple Oval at Khafajah* [Oriental Inst. Publ. 53 (Univ. of Chicago Press, Chicago, 1940)]; P. Delougaz and S. Lloyd, *Pre-Sargonid Temples in the Diyala Region* [Oriental Inst. Publ. 58 (Univ. of Chicago Press, Chicago, 1942)]; and H. Frankfort, *Stratified Cylinder Seals from the Diyala Region* [Oriental Inst. Publ.

72 (Univ. of Chicago Press, Chicago, 1955)], plates 93–96. For recent general overviews of the history and culture of the earlier periods, see A. Falkenstein "La cité-temple Sumérienne" [*Cahiers d'Histoire Mondiale* 1 (1954)] and T. Jacobsen, "Early political developments in Mesopotamia" [*Z. für Assyriologie* (N.F.) 18 (1957)].

5. General accounts of political, social, and cultural conditions in Mesopotamia during the Persian dynasties and under the Caliphate are to be found in R. Ghirshman, *Iran* (Pelican, Harmondsworth, Middlesex, England, 1954) and P. K. Hitti, *History of the Arabs* (Macmillan, London, ed. 6, 1956).

145

The articles by Lowdermilk and by Olson cite case histories of terrain changes by man and suggest that by such studies modern man can become more enlightened. Lowdermilk's article provides a generalized treatment of man's impact on terrain, mostly destructive, whereas Olson concentrates on soil erosion with examples from Greece and Central America. They both indicate the two-sided character of erosion, loss of fertile soils on hillslopes and siltation in lowland areas (see also Cooke, 1931). Many additional places could be cited such as the ancient seaport of Tarsus. This city was a major harbor 2,000 years ago, the home of St. Paul and where the navies of Anthony and Cleopatra assembled prior to their fateful battle with Rome. Tarsus is now a small city, 10 miles inland, the result of sedimentation in the region, much from man-accelerated erosion of surrounding hillslopes. The Lowdermilk article also helps set the stage for the following Simkhovitch and Huntington articles by providing generalized information on the Fall of Rome and the relation of climate to history. He aids in providing perspective of man-made changes by showing they are not all a diabolical scheme to ruin the earth, but that some works are of a constructive reclamation nature. Thus Lowdermilk's article bridges the gap by giving entry into Part IV and linking these threads of man's activities.

Walter C. Lowdermilk (1888–   ) was born in Liberty, North Carolina, and received his Ph.D. (1929) from the University of California. His early professional life was spent with the U.S. Forest Service and he was Research Professor at the University of Nanking (1922–1927). In later years he worked for the U.S. Department of Agriculture and other governmental agencies and was instrumental in founding the San Dimas Experimental Forest in Hydrology. He has written many articles and some books which include *Conquest of Land Through 7,000 Years* (1939) and *Tracing Land Use Across Ancient Boundaries* (1940).

Gerald W. Olson (1932–   ) was born in Gothenberg, Nebraska, and received his Ph.D. (1962) from the University of Wisconsin. He is Associate Professor of Soil Science and Resource Development at Cornell University. His writings include more than 60 published soil survey and interpretative reports on many different aspects of soil genesis and morphology, waste disposal in soils, soil conservation, engineering applications, and watershed management.

Smithsonian Institute Annual Report, 1943, pp. 413–427

LESSONS FROM THE OLD WORLD TO THE AMERICAS IN LAND USE [1]

13

By WALTER CLAY LOWDERMILK
Assistant Chief, Soil Conservation Service, U. S. Department of Agriculture

[With 4 plates]

Lands of the Old World bear an indelible record written across landscape after landscape by resident populations. The longer the occupation, the deeper is the record written and the easier it is to read the story of man's stewardship of the earth, whether it be wasteful exploitation or use with conservation of the resource. One finds successful adjustments of populations to the land in remarkable terracing and reclamation works, as well as tragedies of land misuse, in gullied fields and alluvial plains, in rocky hills and mountain slopes washed bare of soils, in shifting soils and sands, in silted-up and abandoned irrigation reservoirs and canals, in ruins of great and prosperous cities and in ruins of olive presses and cisterns in desertlike landscapes. The effects of land use through the centuries are cumulative.

In the United States of America, we have in a comparatively short period written far and wide on the face of our country a story of wasteful exploitation and reckless use of abundant natural resources. We have grown wealthy by an economy of exploitation. The time has come with the occupation of all lands of the earth to change to an economy of conservation. It is of timely interest to the New World to read the story of land use as it has been written in the lands of the Old World, that we may profit by the experience of the past in its failures as well as its successes.

Western civilization had its beginnings in the Near East in the alluvial plains of the Nile Valley and of Mesopotamia. Early tillers of soil by irrigation and by selection of food plants produced more food than they themselves required. Surplus food supplies released other members of early societies to engage in useful activities other than food production. Division of labor thus began and increased the command over nature and progress in civilization.

---

[1] Reprinted by permission from Proceedings of the Eighth American Scientific Congress, vol. 5, 1942.

From these far-away lands of the Near East, western civilization has moved westward, until now its vanguard has reached the gleaming billows of the Pacific Ocean that wash the western sands of the Americas. For the first time in the history of the human race there are no more continents to discover, to colonize, and to exploit. The frontiers of new lands are gone forever. The nations of the Americas occupy the last frontier of western civilization.

A survey of land use throughout this westward march of civilization discloses successes and failures in the long use of land. The object of this survey was to profit by failures and achievements of the Old World in our national movement for the conservation of land. This survey covered 28,000 miles of overland travel by automobile from humid England to the margins of the deserts of Sahara and Arabia. Studies were made in consultation with fully a hundred specialists in 124 areas of special interest within 14 countries and dependencies in a period of 15 months of field work.

No attempt is made in this brief paper to account for the destruction or conservation of lands on economic grounds. To profit by the experience of the past it is important to know what has happened to the land after centuries and thousands of years of use. Complexity of causes cannot hide the menace to national welfare in soil erosion and the necessity for setting up national objectives to conserve basic resources of soils and waters in the land. Means of achieving the objectives of conservation will vary in accordance with the genius of peoples and their institutions. Soil erosion, if not controlled, has demonstrated its ability to undermine nations and civilizations regardless of what may have been the social or economic conditions that set it going or stimulated its destructiveness.

The land of special areas was examined for evidences—in changes of the original soil profiles insofar as they could be reconstructed; in the shifting of soils from slopes by erosion; and in the accumulation of sediments on valley floors and plains; in the shifting of sand dunes; in the cutting out of alluvial plains with deep gullies; in the filling cf stream channels with erosional debris producing marshy conditions; and in ruins of agricultural works for the control and conservation of waters for domestic and irrigation use; as well as evidences of changes or stability of climate. Furthermore, the fate of the physical body of the soil resource was given more attention in the survey than problems of fertility maintenance. For if the soil is maintained in place, liberty of action in use is assured to succeeding tillers of the soil, in applying more or less fertilizer, in growing this or that crop; but if the soil itself is destroyed, the present and succeeding generations are deprived of their basic heritage.

Throughout this broad expanse of land it became plain that the fate of land under use has been most influenced by slope. The hazard of soil erosion is low on flat lands, but it is critical on sloping lands. Flat lands have their problems, it is true, in the rise of water tables and in the accumulation of salts, but drainage is usually sufficient. Other problems occur in the formation of sand dunes, for which fixation with vegetation is the solution. But the tiller of soil has met his greatest problem throughout the ages in maintaining cultivation on sloping lands. We found failures and successes throughout this broad expanse of land.

ANCIENT PHOENICIA AND SLOPE FARMING

The Near East is believed by archeologists to be the scene of the beginnings of agriculture which made the growth of western civilization possible (11).[2] It is probable that irrigated agriculture preceded rain agriculture. The flat lands of the Nile Valley and Mesopotamia were irrigated before the slopes of ancient Phoenicia were cleared and cultivated. It is probable also that it was on the slopes of the originally forest-clad mountains of ancient Phoenicia that rain agriculture first began, and at the same time the tiller of soil of our western civilization first encountered the hazards of slope cultivation and of soil erosion. It is also probable that the tillers of soil first controlled erosion here with rock walls to terrace sloping lands.

In this connection, we must refer to the remarkable terraces of Peru. I am unaware if the age of the terraces of Peru has been determined. Certainly they were developed by the genius of a resourceful people in great antiquity and independently of the Phoenicians in the Near East, for which they deserve equal praise for a marvelous achievement.

About 5,300 years ago, the Phoenicians migrated from the desert and settled along the eastern shore of the Mediterranean Sea, establishing the harbor towns of Tyre and Sidon, Beyrouth and Byblos. They found their land mountainous, rising to a crest of 10,000 feet and heavily covered with forests, the greatest extent of which were the forests of the famous cedars of Lebanon. These forests became the timber supply for the treeless alluvial plains of the Nile and of Mesopotamia. This conclusion is inferred from inscriptions such as one on the Temple of Karnak, Egypt, placed at 2840 B. C., which announces the arrival in Egypt of 40 ships laden with timber of the cedars of Lebanon (2). Inscriptions found in excavations of Nineveh and of ancient Babylon refer to the use of "huge cedars from Mount Lebanon" in the construction of buildings (9).

In this mountainous land rising boldly out of the sea there was little flat land along the coast. The growing population doubtless soon exceeded the carrying capacity of these restricted flat lands and was

[2] Numbers in parentheses refer to literature cited.

faced with the alternatives of shipbuilding, trade, founding colonies, and the cultivation of slopes. As these slopes were cleared of forests and cultivated, they were subject to soil erosion under heavy winter rains, then as they would be now. The great area of terrace walls in various states of repair indicate that the ancient Phoenician slope farmer sought to retard or control erosion with rock walls across the slope, 40 or possibly 50 centuries ago.

The famous forests of the cedars of Lebanon, which are associated with the rise of civilization in the alluvial plains of the Near East, retreated before the ax and the hoe until today only a few remnants of the original forest of about 1,000 square miles are left. The best known relic is the Tripoli grove of cedars, consisting of about 400 trees, saved from vandalism by a church and from goat grazing by a stone wall. (Pl. 1, fig. 1.) Restocking of this grove within the protection of a stone wall against grazing signifies that under present climatic conditions the forest would spread and grow where soil enough has escaped the ravages of erosion. The disappearance of these famous forests is symbolic of the decline and deterioration of the resources of the country.

Today one may find on the mountains of ancient Phoenicia bare lime-stone slopes strewn with remnants of former terrace walls, showing that the battle with soil erosion sometimes was a losing fight (13); elsewhere one may find terraces that have been maintained for several thousand years. (Pl. 1, figs. 2 and 3.) Such astounding achievements demonstrate that when the physical body of the soil resource is maintained, it may be cultivated and made productive for thousands of years. Its yield in crops then depends upon its treatment.

The cost in human labor to level terrace slopes of 50 to 75 percent as were found in Beit-Eddine, Lebanon, works out at modern wage scales at 2,000 to 4,000 United States dollars per acre. Such costs are not justified when other lands are available; moreover these costs represent what may and sometimes must be paid in an economy of survival. Such remarkable works demonstrate to what lengths a people will go to survive, as well as the necessity of maintaining the soil resources to support a population. Such examples warn us to find ways of saving good lands before necessity drives a people to such extremes in costs of human effort.

A "HUNDRED DEAD CITIES"

Syria holds some of the grandest ruins to be found in the ancient world, such as Baalbek and Jerash. But to a soil conservationist the most striking ruins are found in the graveyard of a "hundred dead cities." (Pl. 2, fig. 3.) An area of about a million acres in North Syria lying between Aleppo, Antioch, and Hama exhibits soil erosion at its worst. Here are ruins of villages, market towns resting on the skeleton rock of limestone hills, from which 3 to 6 feet of soil have been swept off. Evidence of the depth of soil eroded from these slopes is found in doorsills of stone houses now 3 to 6 feet above the bare rock.

Here soil erosion has done its worst and spread a ghastly destruction over a formerly prosperous landscape, as judged by the ruins of splendid houses in villages and in cities, such as at El Bare, which we examined in the summer of 1939. In reality, these cities are dead, with no hope of resurrection; for the basis of their prosperity is gone. These cities have not been buried, but have been left high and stark by the removal of soil through the irreversible process of erosion. The good earth of terra rossa soils is completely gone from the slopes except in patches where it is held back by walls of ruined buildings or in pockets in the limestone. In these patches a few vines and olive trees stand as sad remnants of a former profitable use of land, which provided exports of olive oil and wine to Rome during the empire. Seminomads now inhabit repaired ruins in a few of the former cities.

As one travels in the desolation of this man-made desert today, amid the barren limestone hills once forested before they were converted to cultivated fields, I was moved by continuous astonishment to find ruins of dead cities which gave every evidence of former prosperity and well-being. (Pl. 2, fig. 1.) While buildings of some cities are tumbled amid their masses of overturned blocks, those of other cities stand upright, showing facades, towers, arches, and walls of convents and cathedrals, as well as details of houses, villas, shops, stores, public baths, hotels, and superb tombs such as those at El Bare. This area was flourishing from the third to the seventh century, without sign of decadence. The invasion of the Persians in 614 and the Arabs in 630 decimated the inhabitants, blotted out their culture, destroyed their cities, and even the traditions of their agriculture.

Today, after 13 centuries of neglect, of terraces overrun by herds and patch cultivation of grain by seminomadic descendants of the invaders, soil erosion has completed the destruction of the good earth with a thoroughness that has left this formerly productive land a man-made desert, generally void of vegetation, water, and soil. The cities could be made habitable again, but they will remain dead forever, because their soils are gone beyond hope of restoration. Here the "unpardonable sin" of land use has been committed.

THE "PROMISED LAND" OF PALESTINE

When Moses stood on Mount Nebo and looked across the Jordan to the "Promised Land" about 3,000 years ago, he described the land to his followers as a "land of brooks of water, of fountains and depths that spring out of valleys and hills; a land of wheat, and barley, and vines, and fig-trees and pomegranates; a land of oil-olive, and honey; a land wherein thou shalt eat bread without scarceness, thou shalt not lack any thing in it; a land whose stones are iron, and out of whose hills thou mayest dig brass" (1). The "Promised Land," as it is today, is a sad commentary on man's stewardship of the earth.

The "Promised Land" which 3,000 years ago was "flowing with milk and honey" has been so devastated by soil erosion that the soils have been swept off fully half the area of the hill lands. The soils have been washed off the hills into the valleys (pl. 2, fig. 2), where they are sorted: the finer particles are swept out in flood waters to change the beautiful blue of the Mediterranean to a dirty brown as far as the horizon; the coarser particles are spread out on former alluvium where they are still cultivated but in a progressively reduced area. Accelerated run-off from barren slopes continues to cut gullies through the alluvial valleys and to carry erosional debris out to choke up the channels of streams flowing through the coastal plains.

In times past, such erosional debris together with sand dunes blown in from the coast created marshes in the plains; then malaria came in, practically depopulating the lowlands. The hills also have been greatly depopulated as shown by the studies of Dr. Guy (5). A survey of ancient village sites abandoned and now occupied discloses how the hill lands of Palestine have been depopulated since the seventh century. The watershed of Wadi Musrara of 312 square miles draining the western slope from Jerusalem to Tel-Aviv was divided into three altitudinal zones: (1) the plain, 0–100 meters; (2) the foothills, 100–300 meters; (3) the hills, 300 meters and over. In the plains outside marshy areas, 32 sites are now occupied and 4 abandoned; in the foothills, 31 occupied and 65 abandoned; and in the hills, 37 occupied and 127 abandoned. The break-down of ancient terrace walls and the erosion of soils to bedrock on the upper slopes is sufficient reason to account for the reduction in population. Erosion in the hills as well as marshes with malaria in the coastal plain has been sufficient to reduce the population of the "Promised Land" to one-third of the Roman and Byzantine period.

Palestine can never be restored to its original condition as the "Promised Land"; it can be much improved over its present condition as the splendid works of the Jewish colonies on 5 percent of the total area have demonstrated, but the lands have been so devastated by the irreversible process of soil erosion in the uplands that they can never be restored to their original productivity as the "Promised Land"—it is too late. This case brings home the tremendous lesson that sloping lands may be damaged beyond full restoration; that unless suitable measures are taken in time, land resources are reduced in the face of increasing populations with their augmented demands.

The recent movement of Jewish colonization to redeem the wasted lands of Palestine is an excellent example of what can be done, but at great cost. (Pl. 1, fig. 4.) Works of reclamation of swamps and of reforestation of barren rocky slopes cost more than can be justified as commercial investments in land. The insidious nature of erosion is here made apparent. It reaches a point where the value of the lands will not justify their restoration as an investment for profit. This work can be justified only on the basis of survival of a people. Such expenditures fall into the category of national defense against a ruthless invader or destroyer; for land is the basis of life of a people.

ROMAN AFRICA

North Africa bristles with astounding ruins of opulent and populous cities and of thousands of villages and works of the Roman epoch. (Pl. 2, figs. 4 and 6.) A century or more after the destruction of Carthage by Scipio in 146 B. C. Rome began to colonize North Africa and in the course of time established several important and stately cities at the sites now known as Timgad, Sbeitla, Tebessa, Jemila, El Jem, and Lambesis. These cities were established at crossroads and along the southern edge of the great agricultural region, devoted principally to the growing of grain and olives.

The Roman city of Thydrus, at the present site of El Jem, was located in the midst of the great coastal plain of Tunisia. The most conspicuous remnant here is the ruin of a great coliseum to seat 60,000 spectators, which was second in size only to that at Rome. (Pl. 2, fig. 5.) Now a wretched village stands on the site of this great Roman city. This center was supported by intensive agriculture of grain fields and olive orchards; now this plain is sparsely covered with wild vegetation and isolated groves of olives overrun by herds of grazing animals.

The Roman city of Thamugadi, at the site called Timgad in Algeria, was one of the more famous centers of Roman power and culture. It was established by Emperor Trajan about A. D. 100 and was laid out in symmetrical pattern, equipped with a magnificent forum embellished with statuary and carved porticoes, with a public library, with 17 Roman baths adorned with beautiful mosaic floors, with a theater to seat some 2,500 and with marble flush latrines. Timgad was a stately city supported by extensive grain fields in the valley plains and olive orchards on the hills.

After the weakening of the Roman power by the Vandal invasion in A. D. 430 the Berbers captured the city, and after the Arab invasion of the seventh century it was lost to knowledge for 1,200 years, buried by dust, the product of wind erosion. Only a few columns and a portion of Trajan's arch stood above undulating mounds as tombstones to indicate that once a great city was here. There is no counterpart today of the magnificence of this ancient city. A wretched village of mud-wall houses sheltering a few hundred inhabitants is the only descendant of this center of Roman power and culture. Water erosion as well as wind erosion has been at work on the landscape. Gullies have cut through portions of the city and have exposed the aqueduct which supplied the city with water from a great spring some 3 miles away.

Ruins of the land are as impressive as the ruins of cities. The hills have been swept bare of soil, a story which may be read throughout the region. The original soil mantle is being washed off the slopes, often showing that the upper edge of the soil mantle is being gradually worked down slope by accelerated run-off from the bared upper slopes. Erosional debris has been deposited on the lower slopes and valley plain. Torrential storm waters cut great gullies into the alluvial plains. Water tables are lowered and rain waters quickly flow off the land leaving it dry and thirsty. The effects of desiccation of the land are brought about even if rainfall has not diminished.

Out toward the Sahara, 70 miles south of Tebessa, were found ruins of remarkable works for conserving and spreading storm run-off. Check dams were constructed to divert storm waters around the slopes and to spread them on a series of terraces, dating back to Roman or pre-Roman times. Why these terraces were constructed is not yet known. At any rate the French Government is rebuilding the works and is spreading storm waters out on these terraces to increase forage growth for the herds of the Arab nomads. These works of water conservation out so near the Sahara Desert might indicate that climate has changed or that all good lands were intensively utilized during the Roman epoch. All North Africa, as indicated by such a vast display of ruins and works in the midst of a sparsely settled and depressing land, must have had an agriculture of remarkable refinement in measures of soil and water conservation.

The striking contrast between the prosperous and populous condition of North Africa in Roman times and present decadence led early students to believe that an adverse change of climate was responsible for the decline of the granary of Rome. But the researches of Gsell (4), Gautier (3) and Leschi (7) discount an adverse change in climate since Roman times (6 and 10). The most telling evidence of unchanged climate in the past 2,000 years is the successful plantation of olive groves on the sites of ruins of Roman stone olive presses. An experimental grove planted at Timgad by Director Godet demonstrates that olive orchards would thrive today where soil still remains on slopes. The great plantation of more than 150,000 acres in the vicinity of Sfax, Tunisia, which now supports thriving enterprises at

Sfax, also discredits the change of climate theory. Moreover, in the vicinity of Sousse, Tunisia, there are a few Roman olive orchards which escaped the destructive invasions of the seventh century and survive to the present day. No pulsations of climate have been sufficiently adverse to kill off this remnant of the agriculture of Roman times.

The astounding decline in agriculture of the Near East and North Africa is not due primarily to adverse climatic change (14 and 12). It was begun by successful invasions of desert nomads during the seventh century and completed by soil erosion. This remarkable invasion, which not only destroyed a civilization, but its agriculture and, more important, the traditions of its agriculture, is another instance of the age-old struggle between Cain and Abel, between the shepherd and the farmer, between the tent dweller and the house dweller. The desert has always produced more people than it could feed. Farmers built up thriving cultures in the alluvial plains. From time to time the hungry tent dwellers swept into the valleys, when defenses were weak, and destroyed and robbed, sometimes passed on, and left destruction and carnage in their path. At other times they replaced the former population to become farmers and city dwellers themselves, only to be destroyed by another invasion of hungry denizens of the steppes or deserts.

These nomad invaders and their herds unleashed the forces of soil erosion by water and by wind which through centuries have reduced the capacity of the land to produce or to be restored to its former productivity, except in some alluvial valleys. The achievement of conservation of land resources by long and tedious methods was nullified by ruthless invasions and wars.

Such are some instances of the decline in the usefulness of the land due to the wastage of erosion and quickened run-off of storm waters, by the break-down of measures arrived at by long and slow experience of trial and error. The wisdom of the ages was nullified in a brief time, breaking into fragments the glories of the past.

It is also fitting to examine some of the recent works to reclaim lands damaged by inconsiderate and reckless use in the past.

RECLAMATION OF MARSHES

The climate of the Mediterranean sets the stage for land destruction by erosion if special precautions are not taken in cultivated fields and on grazed slopes. Heavy rains occur generally as erratic storms during the winter months—October to April. The remainder of the year is rainless and hot.

Where bold mountain ranges are bordered by comparatively broad coastal plains, as in Italy, Greece, Palestine and Algeria, cultivation of slopes unprotected by rock-wall terraces has induced serious soil erosion. Eroded soils and debris have choked up stream channels in the plains, converting these coastal plains into marshes. Malaria made the lowlands pestilential, weakened or practically depopulated extensive populous areas.

Such is the history of the Pontine Marshes in Italy, whose reclamation is an outstanding example of the application of the modern sciences of medicine, engineering, and agriculture to such problems. The Pontine Marshes were once well populated if we are to accept as evidence remains of 16 cities which predated Roman occupation. Following the rapid rise of Rome from the eighth century B. C., cultivation of the slopes of the Apennine Mountains took the same course as it did in Phoenicia. By the fourth century B. C. Appius Claudius undertook to drain the marshes, which had become a problem (pl. 3, fig. 1).

CONTROL OF TORRENTIAL FLOODS

Population pressures in Italy of 836 and in France of 547 per square mile of cultivated area have exceeded the carrying capacities of the flat lands and have pushed the cultivation line up slopes in the Alps to steep gradients as forests were cleared away. These mountains had been sculptured by glaciers of the Ice Age into deep gorges bordered by hanging valleys, which set the stage for torrential debris floods as slopes were cleared of forests for cultivation or heavily grazed.

France and Italy have been engaged for many years in the control of debris floods in mountain valleys. France has carried out for 60 years a comprehensive program of works, with notable achievements. The experience of 60 years of such works is especially valuable in meeting the increasing hazards of floods in mountainous areas of the New World. Debris floods bury fields, orchards, and villages in valley floors, interrupt communication, and destroy livestock and human life. Losses over the past century have reached enormous figures and have stimulated brilliant engineering and remarkable measures of erosion control and revegetation.

Correction of mountain torrents is most economically and effectively carried out as a gigantic chess game. It is man against nature, where man may perchance delay the inevitable long enough for his purposes. It takes time and daring as well to play this game, in addition to minute study of natural forces at work. As the torrent-control engineer builds each structure he waits to observe the responses of natural forces. These in turn determine his next move, whether to build another structure, or reinforce existing works, until in due time he is successful in checkmating torrential floods. The high costs of the control of torrents are justified by the protection of valley lands from damage, by the reduction of debris accumulations in stream channels, as a safeguard against rising water tables and marshy conditions in high-value alluvial lands, and by saving life.

Two essential principals are followed in all torrent-control works: establishment of base levels of cutting in torrent channels with permanent check dams, and revegetation of the catchment area. Similar work has been done in Bavaria in southern Germany, but it was not possible for me to continue the projected survey into Germany because of the outbreak of war in that fateful September.

FIXATION OF SAND DUNES

Problems of water-erosion control are most common on sloping lands, but those of wind-erosion control most often occur on flat lands. Sand dunes have been formed in semiarid regions by the sorting effect of wind erosion of cultivated lands. The wind sorts dry soils, lifting the fine and fertile particles to blow them away in dust clouds, whereas the heavier particles as sand are left behind to form hummocks and finally active sand dunes. Usually former farm lands of the Old World so damaged have been abandoned and left to their fate (8).

In southwestern France the government has carried out the classic and greatest achievement in the fixation of a vast area of a "moist Sahara" of sand dunes. A great pestilential sore spot in France, where dwelt poverty, malnutrition, and despair before the merciless march of gigantic sand dunes, was converted into a beautiful and productive forest and into a region of health resorts and prosperity. The destructive invasion of the Vandals in A. D. 407 set sand dunes on the march. By Napoleon's time they had covered 400,000 acres and had buried forests and farm villages, and dammed up the streams, causing a great area of coastal plain to overflow. Marshes brought in malaria, which diminished and weakened the resident population.

Work of fixation and control was begun by Bremontier in 1786 under the command of Napoleon. Reforestation of the dunes was made possible by creating a great littoral dune. This was done by means of a movable palisade of planks which were successively pulled up as the dune crest was raised. In time a dune was built up along the coast whose windward slope reached a grade too steep for the winds longer to blow sand over it. Thereupon, the slopes of the dune were fixed with sand grasses. Reforestation to the leeward and streams were thus safeguarded from further advance of dunes. Following the fixation of dunes, drainage of 2¼ million acres of lowlands was made possible under the direction of Chambrelent. By 1865 this memorable task was completed.

One dune, near d'Arcachon, however, was left uncontrolled for some reason (pl. 4, fig. 1). It is 2 miles long, ½ mile wide, and 300 feet high and is advancing on the forest at the rate of 60 to 65 feet a year. This active dune serves as a comparison of the present reclaimed dune area and gives some idea of the magnitude of the achievement of converting a devouring menace affecting 2½ million acres of land into a healing resource. It is estimated that the return from the resin crop alone from the pine plantations has been sufficient to pay off all the original costs of this classic example of reclamation of sand dunes and pestilential marshes.

THE INSIDIOUS NATURE OF EROSION

Our studies in lands long occupied by man disclose that soil erosion, i. e., man-induced erosion as distinguished from normal geologic erosion, is an insidious process that has destroyed lands and undermined progress of civilization and cultures. Achievements in the control of soil erosion and in adjustments of a lasting agriculture to sloping lands are steps in the march of civilization as momentous as the discovery of fire and the selection of food plants.

Solutions to problems of population pressure have too often in the past been sought in the conquest and destruction of the works of peoples rather than in conservation and improving the potential productivity of the earth, with provision for exchange of specialty products. The formula of exploitation and destruction has interrupted the orderly solutions to land-use problems in the past and has unleashed the forces of erosion to spread like the tentacles of an octopus through the lands of North China, North Africa, Asia Minor, and the Holy Lands, as well as in the United States and other countries of the New World.

One generation of people replaces another, but productive soils destroyed by erosion are seldom restorable and never replaceable. Conservation of the basic soil rescurce becomes more than a matter of individual interest; it becomes a matter of national interest necessary to the continuing welfare of a people. The day is gone when lands may be worn out with the expectation of finding new lands to the west. The economy of exploitation must give place to an economy of conservation if a people will survive into the unknown future. Peace among nations must rest upon such a policy.

158

In face of the limited area now available to the human race, the realization that enormous areas of land are still being destroyed by inconsiderate and wasteful methods must arouse thinking people to action. If man is making deserts out of productive lands, it is a matter not only of national, but of world-wide concern.

If Moses had foreseen how soil erosion induced by inconsiderate use of land would devastate the "Promised Land," as well as vast areas of the earth, resulting in man-made deserts and decadence of civilizations; if he had foreseen the impoverishment, revolution, wars, migrations, and social decadence of billions of people throughout thousands of years because of the exploitation and desolation of their lands by erosion, he doubtless would have been inspired to deliver an Eleventh Commandment to complete the trinity of man's responsibilities—to his Creator, to his fellow men, and to Mother Earth. Such a Commandment should read somewhat as follows:

Thou shalt inherit the holy earth as a faithful steward, conserving its resources and productivity from generation to generation. Thou shalt safeguard thy fields from soil erosion, thy living waters from drying up, thy forests from desolation, and protect thy hills from overgrazing by thy herds, that thy descendants may have abundance forever. If any shall fail in this stewardship of the land thy fruitful fields shall become sterile stony ground or wasting gullies and thy descendants shall decrease and live in poverty or perish from off the face of the earth.

Hitherto, mankind in its conquest of the land, except in very limited areas, has not been governed by such an injunction; on the contrary, mankind has been impelled by an economy of exploitation, looking to the discovery of new lands or new sources of food and materials as needs arise. The lands of the world are occupied and such a policy leads inevitably to conflict.

The solution of such conflicts in the past has been sought generally in a formula of war with destruction of property, works, and human lives as means of arriving at agreements. As this paper is being written fully half the human population of the earth, more than a billion human beings, have as their most absorbing purpose to destroy the achievements and works of generations and the annihilation of populations, soldiers and civilian men, women, and children. Civilization is committing suicide.

Sooner or later peoples engaged in modern warfare will become weary and exhausted by this hellish frenzy of destruction and carnage. Mankind may then be prepared to accept an alternative—a substitute for destruction in the conservation of the earth's resources, in maintaining and improving necessary supplies. Under scientific conservation, the earth will produce beyond the dreams of mankind.

Besides, the formula of destructive exploitation has failed miserably to solve problems of growing populations; it has only set back the same problem to come forth again with more insistence. The fate of lands devastated and despoiled by erosion, which is most often associated with war or conquest, stands as a warning to mankind to change from an economy of exploitation to an economy of conservation—of healing and saving conservation.

We must be fully prepared to defend our sovereignty and liberty of action against all aggressors. At the same time, the Americas are best situated to make the principle of conservation realistic in the use of land resources. Thus interpreted and reduced to works of saving soils and waters on the land as necessary to the conservation of human resources and values, the principle of conservation may be compelling and enticing enough to turn a war-weary world from a suicidal frenzy of destruction and carnage to a saving and healing conservation. The lands of the earth will record the decision of mankind as to this momentous question.

LITERATURE CITED

1. BIBLE.
   Deuteronomy VIII, 7–9.
2. BREASTED, JAMES H.
   1906.   Ancient records of Egypt, vol. 1, p. 146. Chicago.
3. GAUTIER, E. F.
   1935.   Sahara, the great desert, pp. 95–99. Translated by D. F. Mayhew. New York.
4. GSELL, STEPHANE.
   1913.   Histoire ancienne de l'Afrique du Nord, vol. 1.   Paris.
5. GUY, P. L. O.
   Unpublished notes.
6. KNIGHT, M. M.
   1928.   Water and the course of empire in North Africa. Quart. Journ. Econ., vol. 43, pp. 44–93, November.
7. LESCHI.
   Unpublished reports.
8. LOWDERMILK, W. C.
   1939.   Field notes.
9. LUCKENBILL, DANIEL D.
   1927.   Ancient records of Assyria and Babylonia, vol. 1, pp. 98, 194 f. Chicago.
10. MARTONNE, EMMANUEL DE.
    1930.   La degradation de l'hydrographie. Scientia, vol. 47, pp. 9–20, January.   (See p. 19.)
11. PEAKE, HAROLD J.
    1933.   Early steps in human progress. Philadelphia.

12. PLAYFAIR, SIR ROBERT L.
    1877.   Travels in the footsteps of Bruce in Algeria and Tunis, p. 155.
            London.
13. THOUMIN, R. L.
    1936.   Geographie humaine de la Syrie Centrale, p. 125.   Paris.
14. WOOLEY, C. LEONARD, and LAWRENCE, T. E.
    1914–1915.   The wilderness of Zin (archaeological report).   Palestine
            Exploration Fund.   London.

14

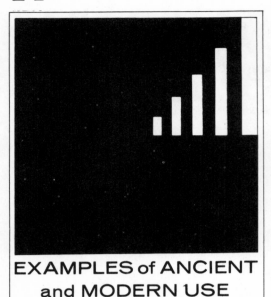

EXAMPLES of ANCIENT and MODERN USE and ABUSE of SOILS

by G. W. Olson, Department of Agronomy, Ithaca, and D. E. Puleston, University of Minnesota

Heavy structures as high as 200 feet were built at Tikal, Guatemala, more than 1,000 years ago. Intensive development in New York State is comparatively recent, but time and geographic differences shrink in the light of some considerations; ancient principles and problems in the use of soils are relevant to modern uses of soils.[1]

Archaeologists believe that Tikal was first settled some 2,500 years ago and in time became the prime city of the Maya people living on the Yucatan peninsula. This site in the lowland jungles of northeastern Guatemala held a remarkable civilization—a culture now largely dead and without links to the Old World.

The massive ruins of Tikal are surrounded by the 222-square-mile Tikal National Park, the first of its kind in Central America. The first official expedition to the site was made in 1848, but the University of Pennsylvania has been responsible for excavations at Tikal since 1956. The Tikal project has become a permanent field laboratory for research in archaeology, anthropology, American history, plant and animal life, geology, and climate.

Despite their totally different environment, Tikal soils have certain similarities to some in New York State. Poorly drained soils subject to shrinking and swelling,

for example, caused problems for pedestrians in ancient times and even now hinder airstrip development at Tikal (figure 1). Somewhat poorly drained soils subject to frost heaving in New York State also cause problems for vehicles on roads in modern suburban developments (figure 2). The causes of soil movement in these places are different, but the effects upon soil performance are similar.

A soil map (figure 3[2]) of part of Tikal illustrates some of the most modern concepts in the best use of soils now advocated by some planners in New York State. For example, soil areas labeled 10/A on the map have been avoided as construction sites. Like those shown in figure 1, they have poor trafficability and poor foundation-bearing strength. Modern planners similarly seek to delineate soils with poor characteristics for construction, reserving them for less intensive uses wherever possible.

Soils in areas labeled 4, 18, and 19 on A, B, C, D, and E slopes in figure 3 have good foundation support characteristics. Clustering of buildings on these desirable soils illustrates another modern concept of planning; clustering enables more efficient use of space than the oft-seen urban sprawl. The people who built Tikal more than 1,000 years ago did not use the wheel and had few traffic problems; some modern planners are experimenting with zones in inner cities where only pedestrians are allowed.

Building orientation, as well as location, is important in planning aesthetics for best use of different soils. Notice in figure 3 that most buildings are oriented in the cardinal directions. Planners today similarly point out that common orientation is much better than helter-skelter placement of buildings.

At Tikal most of the upland soils have soft limestone bedrock within two to four feet of the surface. Figure 4 is a view of a modern limestone quarry in an area that was quarried more than 1,000 years ago. Soil exposures at the edge of the quarry in the background indicate that original soils were buried, and new soils have formed in the overburden deposited on top of the original surface.

Highway excavations through hard limestone are typical in parts of New York State (figure 5). On some road-building projects this rock must be blasted and then moved with heavy equipment, in contrast to the softer limestone at Tikal that can be easily worked with hand tools. Shallow soils on hard limestone can be avoided for some highway routes; highway designers customarily use soil maps as guides to by-pass such excavations, or at least seek soil information to forewarn of the cost of bedrock cuts.

Soil-fertility problems are not as obvious as soil-construction and -trafficability problems, but they are just as important. At Tikal, maize yields average about 20 bushels per acre the first year after clearing the forest, then generally decline rapidly in successive years. These

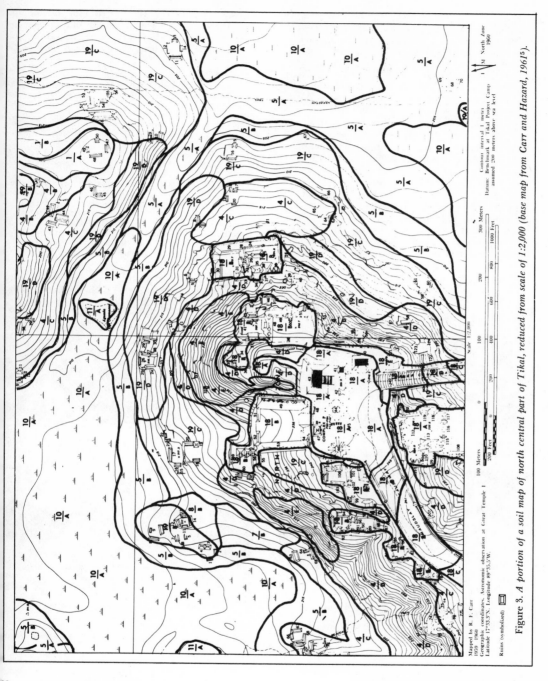

Figure 3. *A portion of a soil map of north central part of Tikal, reduced from scale of 1:2,000 (base map from Carr and Hazard, 1961[5]).*

yields are probably not much larger than those of 1,000 years ago. Perennial tree crops were probably harvested, in addition to annual crops.[3] But in New York, sustained yields of 100 bushels of corn per acre can be supported year after year on the best soils. Such wide yield differences are due to crop varieties, diseases, fertilizers, insects, management, and other factors in addition to soils.

At Tikal, soil erosion was a problem, especially in construction areas where the soil was bare. Sediments accumulated in water channels and reservoir bottoms and can be dated by pottery fragments. Similar accelerated erosion has been observed at modern construction sites[4], and some localities now have building codes that require soil conservation practices to reduce soil erosion during heavy construction periods. Prevention or control of erosion might have been the primary function of the great plaster floors at Tikal that covered plazas and many other apparently open areas.

Archaeological findings like those at Tikal indicate that some modern concepts are not really so new after all, and further that real benefits may be obtained from the experiences of past civilizations with soil use and abuse. Currently developing technology of course enables better use of our soil resources, but the varying soil properties that the ancients encountered are very similar to those of today.

This study was jointly financed by the Department of Agronomy of Cornell University, the University Museum of the University of Pennsylvania, and a Cornell University research grant to study relationships between man and soils.

[1]*Bartelli, L. J., et al. (Editors). 1966. Soil surveys and land use planning. American Society of Agronomy, Madison, Wisconsin. 196 pages.*

[2]*Olson, G. W. 1969. Descriptions and data on soils of Tikal, El Peten, Guatemala, Central America. Cornell Agronomy Mimeo 69-2. 109 pages.*

[3]*Puleston, D. E. 1968. Brosimum alicastrum as a subsistence alternative for the classic Maya of the central southern lowlands. MA thesis. University of Pennsylvania. 141 pages.*

[4]*Judson, S. 1968. Erosion of the land, or what's happening to our continents? American Scientist 56:356–374.*

[5]*Carr, R. F. and J. E. Hazard. 1961. Map of the ruins of Tikal, El Peten, Guatemala. Tikal Report No. 11. University of Pennsylvania. 26 pages + 10 map sheets.*

Figure 1. *Aircraft with left wheel mired in soft runway established on soils with poor trafficability at Tikal.*

Figure 2. *Road subject to frost heaving on soils with poor trafficability in a New York State suburban area.*

Figure 4. *Quarry in soft limestone bedrock at Tikal, with exhumed old soils and recent soils exposed in the background.*

Figure 5. *Road excavations in hard limestone bedrock in New York State.*

Some Implications of Soils for Civilizations

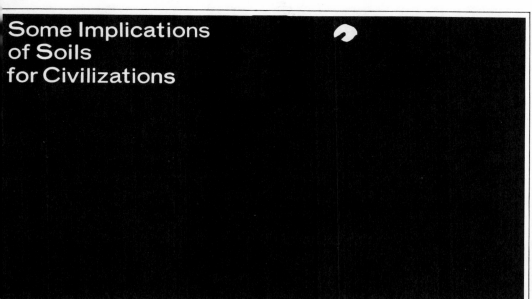

y G.W. Olson, *Department of Agronomy, Ithaca, and* ;.M.A. Hanfmann, *Harvard University*

mportant soil properties and their influences upon vilizations have too often been ignored. Soil studies ow are being used with other resource inventories in lanning for the future (1,2,3), but historical events, too, an help predict more accurately and efficiently the future onsequences of present-day decisions. For example, past nd uses and soil management practices, particularly tose that affect the ecology and environmental quality, tould be examined to avoid repeating past abuses (4). 1 areas where massive investments are to be made, or rge numbers of people are to be served, the oppor- inities for improving environmental quality and man- ging ecological balances are especially attractive (5,6).

Because sites in New York State and the United States enerally lack long histories of extensive development, is sometimes more helpful to look elsewhere. In the se history described here, our exploration was at the uins of Sardis, Turkey—not only because of its long istory of people working with a soils environment, but ecause of that city's role in early Western traditions nd movements.

Sardis is a ruined city about 75 kilometers (47 miles) ast of Izmir in western Turkey, probably first settled in te third millennium B.C. The city has experienced rought, earthquakes, famine, fire, flood, invasion, land-

slides, and sieges. It was the capital of the ancient kingdom of Lydia, the western terminus of the Persian royal road described by Herodotus, a center for adminis- tration under the Roman empire, and the metropolis of the province of Lydia in later Byzantine times. A stra- tegic military location, its position on a main highway between the Anatolian plateau and the Aegean coast, and its access to the wide, fertile plain of the Gediz river valley, all contributed to Sardis' importance.

Sardis was referred to in the *Iliad* (as Hyde), mentioned by the Greek poet Alcman about 650 B.C., and also in the Book of Revelation in the Bible. It was captured by the Cimmerians in the seventh century B.C., by the Per- sians in the sixth century B.C., by the Athenians in the fifth century B.C., and by Antiochus the Great in the third century B.C. It was destroyed by an earthquake in 17 A.D., but rebuilt under Tiberius. The fort on the acropolis was handed over to the Turks in 1306. It was captured by Timur in 1402. The latest conflicts at Sardis were battles of the Greco-Turkish war in the first quarter of the twentieth century. Ruins at Sardis have been excavated since 1958 by a Cornell-Harvard expedition.

Soils of Sardis were of special interest in efforts "to reconstruct the evolution of this urban community in relation to its environment" (7). We collected 107 soil samples, along with soil profile descriptions, from about 55 points to characterize the soils and their archaeological and historical significance (8). A soil map of the central city area was made and the samples were analyzed by

11

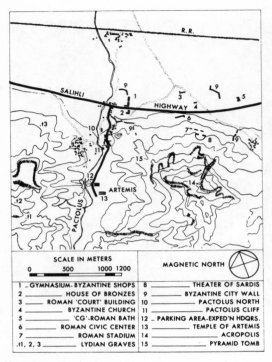

Figure 1. *Plan of Sardis excavations.*

1	GYMNASIUM- BYZANTINE SHOPS	8	THEATER OF SARDIS
2	HOUSE OF BRONZES	9	BYZANTINE CITY WALL
3	ROMAN 'COURT' BUILDING	10	PACTOLUS NORTH
4	BYZANTINE CHURCH	11	PACTOLUS CLIFF
5	'CG'-ROMAN BATH	12	PARKING AREA-EXPED'N HDQRS.
6	ROMAN CIVIC CENTER	13	TEMPLE OF ARTEMIS
7	ROMAN STADIUM	14	ACROPOLIS
11, 2, 3	LYDIAN GRAVES	15	PYRAMID TOMB

SCALE IN METERS
0 500 1000 1200

MAGNETIC NORTH

our laboratory at Cornell University and by that at the Soil and Fertilizer Research Institute in Ankara.

Figure 1 depicts the archaeological ruins and excavations at Sardis in relation to the topography (contour interval about 30 meters). The ancient city spread around the base of the acropolis (point 14) in a huge arc, its population probably as high as 100,000 in Roman times. Prominent archaeological ruins include a Greek theater that seated about 20,000 persons (point 8), a synagogue with a floor plan about 100 meters long incorporated into an even larger Roman gymnasium complex (point 1), and one of the largest known Greek marble temples (point 13). A row of imposing mounds, more than one kilometer long, stretches from point 1 eastward, marking the remains of sizeable buildings yet unexcavated. The building complex at point 1 included a row of 30 shops— an ancient shopping center! The core of this complex has a floor plan about 175 meters by 125 meters. The debris mound at point 1 has an area exceeding two hectares (five acres).

Figure 2 is a view of the soil landscape of Sardis. Soils in the valley are irrigated, and produce generally high yields except in a few spots of saline or alkaline condi-

tions. Soils on upper slopes have been overgrazed ▌ goats and sheep for centuries. South of point 2 (figure ▌ archaeologists dug a trench 12 meters deep through Roman dump containing thousands of animal bon▐ Because of the overgrazing and subsequent soil erosio▐ Roman engineers were forced to design settling pots close intervals in certain water lines at Sardis, so th silt and other solids could be periodically cleaned o▐ Soil erosion has also caused problems in places whe▐ sediments were finally deposited; the Roman building point 5 in figure 1 was almost covered by more than s meters of sediments deposited above its original ba▐ The sediments eventually forced abandonment of t▐ building.

On the other side of the city arc, the soils in the narr▐ alluvial floodplain of the Pactolus river (lower part *figure 3*) contain considerable amounts of gold flakes, a▐ were a source of wealth for the Lydian king Croes▐ reputed to be the world's richest king (9). A Lydian alt▐ between the Temple of Artemis and the Pactolus riv▐ was apparently built on an Al soil horizon more th▐ 2,000 years ago. Traces of the original surface soil st▐ remain beneath the foundation stones.

Upland soils shown in figure 3 have been sever▐ eroded, most containing about two percent orga▐ matter in their surface horizons. A few places, in t ravines below the ridge spur in the right-hand secti▐ of the photograph, have surface horizons under pi▐ trees with as much as 10 percent organic matter. Son▐ how protected from the goats, pines in these places ha▐ grown to fairly large size. The climax vegetation of t▐ area was forest before the trees were cut by the Roma▐ trees in the compound of the expedition headquart▐ have grown to the height shown in about 10 years.

A few soils on the acropolis have formed in aeoli▐ deposits where sparse vegetation caught sand partic▐ Some of the Byzantine walls are covered with shall▐ soils formed from construction materials; other ruins covered with deeper soils developed in fill materials. S horizons just above the conglomerate on the acrop▐ were found to contain artifacts from the siege of !▐ B.C., when the Persians captured the fortifications (1▐

Much of Sardis was subjected to floods and landsli▐ particularly at points 2, 10, and 13 (figure 1). The Lyd▐ occupation seems to have been most affected by floodi▐ and the most conspicuous landslides followed in Greek and Roman periods. A stratum near point 2 ▌ artifacts from 1300 B.C. buried more than 12 me▐ below the modern soil surface. Although the floods ▐ landslides were disastrous for the inhabitants of Sa▐ at the time, the deposits of soil materials were a b▐ to archaeologists because they preserved the ruins fr▐ further destruction by nature and by man.

Some places on ridges radiating out from the acrop▐

have soils with well developed platy structures resulting from soil movement and landslides *(figure 4)*. Many of these soils have large contents of mica flakes, which contribute to sliding, especially when they are wet. The soil structure in these places not only records past soil movements, but also indicates possible directions and magnitudes of future landslides likely to follow major earthquakes.

Valleys between the ridges below the acropolis have gravelly soils formed in torrent deposits; in many places they contain considerable amounts of cut marble stones, pieces of brick, pottery shards, tile fragments, and other artifacts fallen from the acropolis. Many such fragments are still being exposed by soil erosion.

Some of the splendor of ancient Sardis is still evident. *Figure 5* is a view of the partially excavated mound that concealed the Roman gymnasium now being reconstructed. Obviously, when the Romans built this huge gymnasium and bath complex, they did not consider the ecology or sustained yield factors for the forests cut to provide heat for their water baths. Nor did the Greeks fully comprehend the effects of their goat herds on soil erosion. For their part, the Lydians overlooked the

Figure 2. *View of acropolis of Sardis from the north. Piers in foreground are remains of Roman building (point 3 in figure 1); wall in background was part of Roman civic center (point 6). First fortified in eighth century B.C., the hill at one time had a triple defense system admired by Alexander the Great. Present-day soil uses around Sardis include sheep and goat grazing and cropping (cotton, eggplants, figs, grapes, melons, olives, peppers, tomatoes, sesame, and wheat).*

Figure 3. *Western slope of acropolis viewed from hill used as Lydian burial ground; about 1,100 chamber tombs have been excavated here. Ruins at lower right are Temple of Artemis (point 13), built in third century B.C. In ninth century A.D., temple was covered by a landslide to depth shown by marks on pillars; it was excavated in 1910–14 by a Princeton University expedition. About 300 meters upslope from temple is one of anthropically shaped conical mounds of Sardis. Walled compound with trees is Cornell-Harvard expedition headquarters.*

hazards of building on an alluvial floodplain.

What benefits can be obtained from evaluation of past civilizations on the soils of Sardis? Experiences at Sardis should emphasize to future generations that construction on floodplains is likely to be damaged by floodwaters and alluvial deposits. Landslides, common to Sardis and many other parts of the world, can be predicted by internal and external soil characteristics. Soil erosion, whether at ancient Sardis or in modern urban construction areas, cannot extend over large areas for long periods without causing severe damage to structures and watersheds. The

Figure 4. *Exposed soil profile at edge of recent landslide scar in Sardis (about 150 meters upslope from point 15, figure 1). Note platy structure (at left, near spade) typical of landslide-prone soils. In undisturbed soils, this structure is usually parallel with soil surface, but that at right has been severely disrupted from its bedding planes by recent slide.*

Figure 5. *Partially excavated gymnasium complex at Sardis (point 1, figure 1), looking east. From here eastward for more than a kilometer, a complex system of buildings has so deteriorated that the debris mounds are now generally used for grazing and cropping. Partially restored gymnasium building stands more than 15 meters high.*

silting of water systems at Sardis was remarkably similar to some of our siltation problems in municipal water reservoirs. Erosion control is particularly critical for maintenance of soil fertility for food production as well as in environmental quality considerations.

Guiding human activities toward consideration of ecology and natural soil landscape variations would be a positive step toward insuring that future civilizations will enjoy greater success and persist longer than did past civilizations. Interdisciplinary efforts to better understand the environment and its relationships to the welfare of inhabitants would contribute toward a more optimistic view of the future.

We are grateful to M. Ozuygur of the Soil and Fertilizer Research Institute in Ankara, K.W. Flach and G. Holmgren of the Soil Conservation Service of the U.S. Department of Agriculture, R.S. Thomas of Harvard University, and R.E. Bentley, M.G. Cline, T. Greweling, S.W. Jacobs, and L.L. Stewart of Cornell University, for their assistance. Travel expenses were met under the Humanities Grant No. 111–70–3966 for Archaeological Exploration of Sardis (through Harvard University); other contributions came from the Department of Agronomy of Cornell University and the Sardis Expedition Fund of Harvard University. Part of this material was presented in the report of Committee XIV on Environmental Soil Science to the National Technical Work-Planning Conference of the Cooperative Soil Survey, Charleston, South Carolina, January 25–28, 1971.

REFERENCES

1. Jorquera, M. (Editor). 1969. Physical resource investigations for economic development: a casebook of OAS field experience in Latin America. Gen. Secr., OAS, Washington, D.C. 439 pp.
2. Tyson, W.E. and F.M. Bennett (Monitors). 1969. The Appalachian region of New York State: an atlas of natural and cultural resources. Off. Plan. Coord., Albany, N.Y. 42 pp.
3. Olson, G.W. (Project Director). 1969. New York State Appalachian resource studies: soils—phase I (inventory). A volume describing soils in a set of volumes also including agriculture, climate, community facilities, forestry, manpower and industry, mineral resources, recreation and culture, transportation, and water resources. Off. Plan. Coord., Albany, N.Y. 56 pp. and maps.
4. Olson, G.W. and D.E. Puleston. 1970. Examples of ancient and modern use and abuse of soils. N.Y. State Coll. of Agr., Ithaca, N.Y. *New York's Food and Life Sciences Quarterly* 3:27–29.
5. Ciborowski, A. (Project Manager). 1971. Skopje resurgent: the story of a United Nations special fund town planning project. U.N. Devel. Prog., United Nations, N.Y. 383 pp.
6. Hoppenfeld, M. 1967. A sketch of the planning-building process for Columbia, Maryland. *J. Amer. Inst. Plan.* 33:398–409.
7. Hanfmann, G.M.A. 1961. Excavations at Sardis. *Sci. Amer.* 204:124–135.
8. Olson, G.W. 1971. Descriptions, notes, maps, and data on soils of Sardis, Turkey: a collection of materials for relating the soils environment to the Lydian, Greek, Roman, and Byzantine ruins and to the ancient civilizations at Sardis. Cornell University, Ithaca, N.Y. *Agron. Mimeo* 71–1. 155 pp.
9. Pedley, J.G. 1968. Sardis in the age of Croesus. Univ. Okla. Press, Norman. 146 pp.
10. Mitten, D.G. 1966. A new look at ancient Sardis. *Biblical Archaeol.* 29:37–68.

14

The Fall of Rome is a very complex problem and its collapse should probably not be considered the result of any single factor. Many ideas have been advanced for its demise including exterior pressures of Franco-Germanic tribes, and interior decay induced by excessive taxes, loss of spirit and identity, reliance upon mercenary forces, political graft corruption, and deterioration of its economic-political power base. The next two reproductions explore environmental factors that may have contributed or caused the decay of empire. These articles provide an interesting comparison of man-induced changes on the soil and of climatic changes that may have triggered his inability to keep pace with a changing hydrology pattern (see also Bell, 1971). Both presentations agree that economic and political forces are also involved and play important roles in the entire kaleidoscope of events, but disagree on the physical processes that accentuated weaknesses in the Roman agrarian structure. Each article provides some of the earliest and most eloquent appraisal of its theme, but owing to length each has had to be severely abridged. Simkhovitch traces step by step the chain reaction of processes that set the stage for collapse. The agrarian class became indebtors in the Roman society, and so had less money to put into tillage and soil maintenance. Farm population dwindled, farmers had smaller families and with less people the soils received less care. Thus with poorer soils and lower yields it became cheaper for the Roman government to obtain foodstuffs from foreign colonies, but this even increased local tax pressures. After detailing with these interlocking events, Simkhovitch still concludes, ". . . the exhaustion of Roman soil and the devastation of the Roman provinces sheds enough light for us to behold the dread outlines of its doom."

Huntington takes a different approach to the problem, and this work on the importance of climate in determining the destiny of man is typical of much of his writing, since he believed that climate was nearly all-important in the evolution and history of civilization. In his article Huntington examines four different climatic hypotheses, uniformity, local changes, one-way changes on a world scale, and pulsatory-irregular changes and concludes that in ". . . both the Old and New World having Mediterranean type of climate there is evidence of the same kind of irregular change." He cites the Palmyra case history as an example. Thus he believed there was climatic deterioration in Rome and adjacent lands, giving added incentive for restiveness and set in motion the need by barbarians to plunder and expand from their land. He argued that such a chain of events would not have occurred from localization of soil exhaustion in Rome. Huntington also believed that an increased incidence of malaria, brought about by climate change, and a lowering of human efficiency were contributory causes since ". . . power of achievement can remain at a high level for generation after generation except in a climate where there is the stimulus of constant change." Sears (1953, p. 44) responded to Huntington's thesis and stated: "It is a weakness of Huntington's argument that he did not reckon with man-accelerated erosion and other cultural influences." The climate issue and its place in the decline of other societies will also be examined in the articles by Bell (1971), Cooke (1931), and Cowgill and Hutchinson (1963).

Vladimir G. Simkhovitch (1874–1959) was born in Russia and received his Ph.D. (1898) from the University of Halle. He spent his academic life at Columbia University, starting in 1904 where he became Professor of Economic History. He has published widely and two of his books are *Marxism Versus Socialism* (1913) and *Toward Understanding of Jesus and Other Historical Essays* (1921).

Ellsworth Huntington (1876–1947) was born in Galesburg, Illinois, and received his Ph.D. (1909) from Yale University. He taught several years at Euphrates College in Turkey and came to Harvard University in 1907 where he spent the remainder of his professional life as Research Associate and Professor. He has an extensive bibliography and some of his books are *Principles of Economic Geography* (1904), *The Pulse of Asia* (1907), *Civilization and Climate* (1915), and *The Character of Races* (1924).

Copyright 1916 by The Academy of Political Science

Political Science Quarterly, 1916, Vol. 31, pp. 201–243

16

Rome's Fall Reconsidered

VLADIMIR G. SIMKHOVITCH

Volume XXXI]   *June, 1916*   [*Number 2*

POLITICAL SCIENCE

QUARTERLY

ROME'S FALL RECONSIDERED

THE great Roman writers with whom we are familiar seem to have been quite conscious of Rome's progressive disintegration. The testimony of the eyewitnesses of the process is of course of the utmost importance. Let us hear to what fundamental factors they themselves attributed the decline of their commonwealth.

Probably no handy quotation has pursued us through our school years with such perseverance as Pliny's "*Latifundia perdidere Italiam, jam vero et provincias.*"[1] The elder Pliny was not merely a man of great learning, but a much traveled statesman of large and varied experience. Is it not interesting that he is not presenting us with a catalogue of factors that were leading Rome to its destruction? On the contrary, without any apology he is crisply pointing to one predominating factor, which he names. The large estates, the *latifundia*, were ruining Rome as well as its provinces.

More rhetorical in form, but similar in its meaning, is the arraignment of the vast latifundia and their owners in Seneca's letters.[2] Seneca himself was one of the richest land owners of Rome, but as a statesman he gave warning, in public, of what the wealthy landowners did not care to hear in private. Seneca asks: "How far will you extend the bounds of your possessions? A large tract of land, sufficient heretofore for a whole nation, is scarce wide enough for a single lord."[3] In fact, Cicero had already reported the statement of the tribune Philippus that the

[1] Plin. H. N. xviii, 7.
[2] Seneca, Ep. 89.
[3] *Ibid.*

201

entire commonwealth could not muster two thousand property owners.[1]   The concentration of landed property must have been amazing.

The latifundia, according to one view, therefore, were the cause of ruin; but there was a more popular version of the decline, namely, *corruptio*, the corruption of morals, the corruption brought by wealth, the corruption brought by poverty, the all-pervading moral corruption of Rome. Livy invites us to follow first the gradual sinking of the national character, later on the more rapid tempo of its downward course until the days are reached when "we cannot bear our diseases nor their remedies."[2]   And what great Roman of that period did not complain of corruption?   Read Tiberius's famous letter to the Senate, which Tacitus has transmitted to us.   The Senate complained of luxury and corruption and called on the emperor for action and Tiberius answered:

That these abuses are the subject of discussion at every table and the topic of conversation in all private circles, I know quite well.   And yet, let a law be made with proper sanctions, and the very men who call for a reform will be the first to make objections.   The public peace, they will say, is disturbed; illustrious families are in danger of ruin. . . .[3]

Perhaps the most striking expression[4] of the progressive moral deterioration of the Romans is in Horace's ode " Ad Romanos "[5]: " Quid non damnosa dies imminuit? Aetas parentum pejor avis tulit nos nequiores, mox daturos vitiosiorem progeniem "—What does ruinous time not impair?   The age of our parents, more degenerate than that of our grandfathers, made us even more worthless and we will give birth to a still more vicious progeny!   Cheerful prospect!   But why such a

[1] "Non esse in civitate duo millia hominum qui rem haberent."   Cicero, De Officiis ii, 73.

[2] Livius, i.   [3] Tacitus, Ann., iii, 54.

[4] Among the picturesque characterizations of Roman degeneracy Columella deserves a very high place with his " Nam sic juvenum corpora fluxa et resoluta sunt, ut nihil mors mutatura videatur."   For so limp and dissolute are bodies of the young men, that death seems to make no change in them!   Columella, i, 1.

[5] Horatius, Odae, iii, 6.

note of despair?   What is the cause of this moral corruption and degeneracy of which all Roman writers of the period complain?

In that very same ode Horace tells us why he takes so desperate a view of things.   The great deeds of the Romans were the deeds of a sturdy farmer race, of the " mascula proles rusticorum militium, docta versare glebas Sabellis ligonibus "[1]—and these farmers' sons existed no longer.   If they could not maintain themselves on their farms, still worse were the chances for a respectable existence in Rome ; there they lost what little they had and became demoralized, dependent paupers.[2]

The two complaints, the two Roman explanations of their own decline and disintegration *reduce themselves, therefore, to one single explanation*.   For it is clear that the latifundia and corruption are but different aspects of the same social phenomenon.   If the moral disintegration was due to the disappearance of the self-supporting, self-respecting farmer class, and the inordinate wealth and fantastic luxury of the small upper class, *the latifundia were but a real-estate expression of the same phenomenon*.   The place of innumerable small farms was taken by extraordinarily large estates—the latifundia.

I do not doubt for a moment that the Romans were quite conscious that the latifundia and corruption were but different aspects of the same phenomenon.   Take, for instance, Sallust, who states it very clearly in his so-called epistles to Cæsar :

When the people were gradually deprived of their lands, and idleness and want left them without a place to live on, they began to covet other men's property and to regard their liberty and the interests of their country as objects for sale.   Thus the people who had been sovereign and who had governed all nations, became gradually degenerate ; and instead of maintaining their common dominion brought upon themselves individual servitude.[3]

We are therefore justified, I believe, in stating that the con-

[1] Horatius, Odae, iii, 6.

[2] Juvenalis, iii, 21 ff. ; Martialis, iv, 5.

[3] Sallust, i, 5.

temporary witnesses of the decline of Rome had but one explanation of its cause; but while some emphasized its moral
aspect and others its economic, still others, like Sallust or
Pseudo-Sallust, have emphasized the political effect of the
economic and moral disintegration of Rome.

So it happens that the true causes of things are hardly discussed in the markets and meeting-places. It is the future, not
the past, that worries politicians. Remedies, not causes, are
what they are bound to discuss. For life is purposeful, and
only to its dissector is it a chain of causes. But Rome was
not without dissecting scholars.

Let us therefore go and see how the great agricultural scholars
of the time analyzed the situation. Let us read thoughtfully
the writings of Columella. He was writing under the Principate, about 60 A. D. How does he begin his work? The
preface begins:

I frequently hear the most illustrious men of our country complaining
that the sterility of our soil and intemperate weather have now for many
ages past been diminishing the productivity of the land. Others give
a rational background to their complaints, claiming that the land became
tired and exhausted from its productivity in the former ages, and hence
the soil is no longer able to furnish sustenance to mortals with its former
liberality.

Columella does not agree with such a point of view. He
ascribes the lack of productivity to poor farming and hence he
gives us instructions how to farm well. But is it not of the
utmost significance that he published a voluminous treatise
distinctly directed against a prevailing exhaustion-of-the-soil
theory? These opening lines of Columella are far from accidental. Furthermore we learn from him a very important
thing, and that is, *that nearly all agricultural writers of antiquity* (whose writings are lost to us) *viewed their contemporary
agricultural situation as due to the exhaustion of the soil;* or,
as they put it, as the result of the soil's old age.

Attention is called to the opening paragraph of Columella's
second book, chapter i:

You ask me, Publius Silvinus—and I hasten to reply to you—why I began my former book *by refuting the ancient opinion of nearly all agricultural writers, and by rejecting as false their idea that the soil, worn out by long cultivation and exhausted, is suffering from old age.*

Hence we learn that the ideas of Lucretius were not peculiar to him alone, but if we accept the testimony of Columella they were the common conception of nearly all who seriously thought about and scientifically discussed the agricultural affairs of antiquity. If the works to which Columella is referring had survived and had been preserved to us, there would have been little left for us to discuss.

Columella refuted the exhaustion-of-soil conception. Let us see how he did it. We find in his book three arguments. First of all, the Creator has bestowed upon soil perpetual fecundity; hence it is impious to regard the soil as affected with sterility as with a disease. Divine and everlasting youth was allotted to our common parent, mother-earth; hence it is silly to assume that she is ageing like a human being.

His second argument is particularly directed against Tremellius, whose writings (lost to us) he especially esteems. Tremellius is of the opinion that mother-earth has, like a woman, reached that point of her life when sterility takes the place of her former fecundity. To this Columella replies that he would have accepted Tremellius's view had the soil been completely unproductive. But he argues that we do not regard a woman as having reached the barren age, simply because she no longer gives birth to triplets and twins. Furthermore, when a woman has reached that age, the bearing of children cannot be restored to her, while the land, if abandoned for a time, will be found upon the return of the cultivator more fertile.

And, finally, Columella is therefore of the opinion that the soil would never diminish in its productivity if properly taken care of and frequently manured.

When Columella wrote in A. D. 60, Italy certainly was enjoying a long protracted peace. Furthermore, one must remember that war as such, even if it should drive the farmers away from the land and keep them from cultivation for years, does not in any way exhaust the soil. For if the soil is not exhausted it will grow over with weeds and bushes, which will prevent the washing-away of the top soil, and when again put under the plough, the farmer will find his soil improved, because of the decayed weeds and other vegetable matter. If, on the other hand, the soil was abandoned when substantially so exhausted that it would not readily cover with weeds, then the top soil would gradually wash off and make its reclaiming difficult and costly.

The writers of the Principate look back to the sturdy past of the days of Cato the Censor. They were mistaken. For even in Cato's day agriculture had already declined in the greater part of Italy. His *Husbandry*, the earliest Roman agricultural book that has come down to us, practically disregards the cultivation of grain crops. His attention is devoted to the cultivation of the vine and olive.

Here is the story in a nut-shell. An undrained marsh has never been tilled, and therefore never robbed of its fertility. Since one would hardly select low flats for vineyards, which require at least a slope, it is obvious that Cato drained the marshes for purposes of tillage. The initial expenses of drainage are heavy, yet Cato regarded the results as very remunerative, and that, in spite of Sicilian corn on the Roman market. To drain a rich marsh was obviously easier for the Romans than to reclaim large tracts of ordinary exhausted soil.

It is interesting that the lands that were first taken up by Roman cultivators were also, judging from our sources, the first to be exhausted. It was in Latium, where once seven jugera were ample to support a family, that Varro finds an example of notoriously sterile soil. He mentions Pupinia in Latium: "Witness Pupinia, where the foliage is meagre, the vines looked starved, where the scant straw never stools, nor the fig tree blooms, and trees and parched meadows are largely covered with moss."

As the productivity of the soil diminished, and the crops could no longer repay the laborer, then the same process that occurred in England in the 15th and 16th centuries, the turning of arable land into pasturage, began in Italy, about two centuries before Christ. In Rome, too, this process was met by hostile legislation, as was the case in England, but without avail. As in England, so in Rome, it became a matter not of choice but of necessity, although even the thinking heads of both nations refused to admit it at the time, and preferred to ascribe the change to greed and corruption. In England they blamed the poor sheep; in Rome they blamed the attractions of city life. So we hear Varro lamenting:

Our very corn that is to feed us has to be hauled for us from Africa and Sardinia, while our vintages come in ships from the islands of Cos and Chios. And so it happened that those lands which the shepherds who founded the city taught their children to cultivate are now by their descendants converted out of greed from cornfields back into pastures, violating even the law, since they fail to distinguish between agriculture and pasturage, for a shepherd is one thing and a ploughman another.

It seems to me that the progressive exhaustion of Roman soil is, judging by all the sources at our disposal, completely established; but there prevails in literature a diametrically contrary version of the story—that of Rodbertus, who is regarded by economists as their authority. Rodbertus, too, quotes Columella's statement about crops not producing in Italy the fourth grain. He also refers to Varro's statement quoted above, but he explains it all " propter avaritiam." It is through avarice that all good soil was put under pasturage, because cattle-raising paid better. The fact that soil produced next to nothing when cultivated is explained by him thus: only the very poorest soil was under the plow, because wine, oil, and fruits were so much more profitable. The type of production changed, but became by no means worse, and agriculture was certainly not to blame, if Italy was not producing its own grain.

The statement of Rodbertus's can with difficulty be taken seriously. First of all, the Romans not only failed to produce their grain; they failed to produce their vintage as well, in spite of the premium put on Italian wine by prohibiting the planting of vines in Gaul.   Secondly, as a farmer, Rodbertus must have realized that if they practiced rotation of crops, which he assumes, the fact that the Romans of Columella's time could not produce a fourth grain would indicate sterility, not of their poorest field, but of all their arable fields.   Thirdly, to assume that the Romans would select their very worst fields, not out of necessity but out of choice, that they would be satisfied to plough and work and harvest those fields for a gain of one or two bushels over and above the bushel of seed, is to assume that the Romans had become insane.

The soil of Italy did not get exhausted over night.   It was a long process and many were its stages.   Besides, exhaustion is a very relative term; not only relative from an agro-technical point of view, but also relative to the physical needs as well as the economic capacities of the owner.

The expropriation of the Roman peasantry, the concentration of ownership of land in the hands of the few, to which the Romans ascribed the ruin of the Empire, is also a very gradual process and runs parallel with the process of soil exhaustion. Compared with the seven-jugera holdings of the early Republic, the hundred or hundred and fifty acre plantations to which Cato refers are large estates.   These " estates " of Cato, which in size correspond to an average American farm, gradually disappear and their place is taken toward the end of the Republic and under the Principate by vast domains measuring thousands and thousands of acres.   The process of transformation was slow but constant.   If this process was agonizing to the people, it was sapping the very life of Rome as a nation, decreasing its population, undermining its morale and convulsing its political fabric.   The beginnings of this process are almost lost in the darkness of Rome's legendary period.

Still do not let us simplify the process of concentration too much.   It undoubtedly had as an underlying cause the relative unproductivity of the soil.   The process of concentration followed many parallel routes.   Indebtedness was undoubtedly the greatest factor in abolishing small holdings.   Unproductivity of agriculture naturally led to cattle-ranches which required much larger holdings. Wealthy men acquired and accumulated vast domains rather for the pleasure of possession than as a paying investment. But the process of deterioration went on, and legislative interferences could neither stop the robbing of the soil nor the depreciation of land values. Negligent cultivation of one's own land was punishable, so was conversion of arable land into pasturage; but neither law proved effective. To maintain land values, as early as 218 B. C., the Claudian law excluded senatorial houses from mercantile occupations and compelled them to invest in Italian land. Since Trajan's time, one-third of their wealth had had to be invested in land. Tiberius, in A. D. 33, put in force an old law and compelled all bankers to invest, so far as can be made out, two-thirds of their working capital in Italian lands.[1] Such measures maintained for a time the land values but they could not touch the underlying cause—the process of spoliation and exhaustion of the fields as well as the process of proletarisation, corruption and depopulation of the nation.

Some questions suggest themselves in this connection. First of all, did not the Romans know how to conserve or improve their soil and thereby make their agricultural labor more productive? The answer to this can only be that nothing could be more startling than the Roman knowledge of rational and intensive agriculture. The knowledge of the Roman Scriptores Rei Rusticae is superior to any agricultural practice of the Middle Ages or even of modern Europe at the beginning of the 19th century.

Why then did the Roman farmers fail to improve their methods of agriculture even when pressed by necessity to do so, even when threatened with extermination? It was easier said than done. Behind our abstract agricultural reflections are concrete individual farms. The owners of the rundown farms are impoverished, and when a farmer is economically sinking he is not in a position to improve his land.

[1] See Mommsen, Boden-und Geldwirtschaft der Römischen Kaiserzeit. Historische Schriften, Bd. ii, p. 595.

Only one with sufficient resources can improve his land. By improving land we add to our capital, while by robbing land we add immediately to our income; in doing so, however, we diminish out of all proportion our capital as farmers, the productive value of our farm land. The individual farmer can therefore improve his land only when in an economically strong position. A farmer who is failing to make a living on his farm is more likely to exploit his farm to the utmost; and when there is no room for further exploitation he is likely to meet the deficit by borrowing, and thus pledging the future productivity of his farm. Such is the process that as a rule leads to his losing possession of his homestead and his fields, and to his complete proletarisation.

Already in Cato's time the growing of grain crops was so utterly unprofitable that he did not even take the trouble to instruct us on this point. All he could tell us was that ploughing was less profitable than the worst pasture. In the case of Varro, instruction on intensive grain-raising is a tradition of earlier times. His preface to the second book frankly admits that there is no use talking of crop-raising, when agriculture has been abandoned for grazing.

In her early days Italy was famous for her wheat, which provided not only her own population but also that of Greece. The fertility of Italian soil was probably the reason for the establishment of Greek colonies in southern Italy. The importation of Italian wheat into Greece in Sophocles's time is still famous. But in Cato's time Italy was already dependent upon Sicily, which Rome's great old man called the provider for the Roman people. In all probability this dependence upon Sicily as its granary was the paramount reason for Rome's conflict with Carthage. Province after province was turned by Rome into a desert, for Rome's exactions naturally compelled greater exploitation of the conquered soil and its more rapid exhaustion. Province after province was conquered by Rome to feed the growing proletariat with its corn and to enrich the prosperous with the loot. The devastations of war abroad and at home helped the process along. The only exception to the rule of spoliation and exhaustion was Egypt, because of the overflow of the Nile. For this reason Egypt played a unique rôle in the Empire.

Misleading as well is the talk about economic differentiation: Italy producing this or that, while Africa or Spain or Sicily produced grain. The truth is that the granaries of Rome, with the exception of Egypt, were undergoing the same process of exhaustion and devastation. Recall Sicily, Sardinia, northwestern Africa and Spain, not to mention Greece which antedated even Italy in her exhaustion. Neither can the opinion be taken under serious consideration which regards the growing insalubrity of Italian lowlands as the cause of depopulation, which led to undermined national strength, a diminishing agricultural area etc. For those who hold such an opinion seem to forget that many other provinces of the Empire underwent the same process of rapid depopulation without turning into swamps, but rather that many parts of them, like Libya for instance, were turning into arid deserts. As a matter of fact, the same fundamental causes that were increasing the swampiness of Latium and Campania were turning northwestern Africa and portions of Asia into deserts. These causes were, or this cause was: *agri deserti*—abandoned fields.

It is therefore only reasonable to assume, so far as Campania and Latium are concerned, that the population was not driven out by malarial mosquitoes, but that mosquitoes took peaceable possession of the lands already abandoned by their cultivators. Thus in the year 395 the abandoned fields of Campania alone amounted to something over 528,000 jugera.

In proportion as the Roman fields were becoming exhausted, Rome had to rely upon grain from other lands. The conquest of grain-producing countries opened new rich fields of exploitation to the Roman money-men and to its statesmen with an eye on plunder. But to keep the people alive on the bread and to satisfy the appetite of the wealthy with the loot of foreign lands, great armies and a manhood superior to that of the barbarians was required.

Let us now see what effect the exhaustion of the soil and the desertion of the fields had upon the body politic. For a farmer, children are a blessing. For, if a laborer is worth his hire, children are certainly worth more than their keep. In fact, lack of children is even now a hardship to a farmer; but in olden days with the much more primitive instruments of production it was a calamity. The less the productivity of labor, the greater is the effort, the greater the mass of human labor, the larger the coöperation required by a farming unit. For such a coöperation, if children were lacking, men had to be bought or hired. Under certain conditions several families had to coöperate and live in a relatively large group to meet the exigencies of farming. You will find it in Greece, in the five generation groups of the Welsh, in Slavonic Zadurgas etc.

If this actual situation is kept in mind, the agrarian legislation as embodied in the Theodosian and Justinian codes begins to have a stern meaning. Decrees of that type must have been issued by both Hadrian and Trajan, judging from the inscriptions of Ara legis Hadrianae and Henschir Mettich. It goes without saying that the situation did not improve in the following period. Whosoever wants land, waste deserted land, is cordially welcome to it. " Quicunque possidere loca et desertis voluerint, triennii immunitate potiantur." Still more explicit is the law of Valentinian, Arcadius and Theodosius which first of all encourages everyone to cultivate abandoned fields or fields that have been without cultivation for a long time. The original rightful owner of such fields is to have but two years in which he may claim back his property, fully compensating the new occupier for all his outlays. After a period of two years all the property rights of the former owner are to be extinguished in favor of the new occupier.

Such legislation is conceivable only with a background of endless stretches of abandoned and untilled land. But the law was not successful, since the encouragement was not sufficient to induce voluntary reclamation of abandoned farm-land. The reclamation of barren land is thereupon ordered as an obligation upon every possessor of estates under cultivation. He is to cultivate the barren and waste land within his estate. Nor can the possessors of estates sell their land under cultivation without at the same time disposing of the barren and unprofitable parts of their estate which the purchaser is to cultivate. The legislation was known as the 'ἐπιβολὴ or "*iunctio*," the "imposition of desert to fertile land."

It is claimed that there is but one understanding; the misunderstandings are legion. To guard against misunderstandings is impossible. Yet I know that many a charitable reader will sympathetically suggest that while the exhaustion of Roman soil was an important factor I can hardly mean to insist that it was *the* sole factor responsible for Roman decline and fall. For it is not credible that so rich and so complex a texture of life should depend upon one single and solitary factor.

Such would not be my assertion, nor is it my attempt. I have not undertaken to explain the complex fabric of Roman life; we are dealing here with the relatively simple problem of its disintegration. All that this study shows is that the progressive exhaustion of the soil was quite sufficient to doom Rome, as lack of oxygen in the air would doom the strongest living being. His moral or immoral character, his strength or his weakness, his genius or his mental defects, would not affect the circumstances of his death: he would have lived had he had oxygen; he died because he had none. But it must be remembered that while the presence of oxygen *does not explain his life*, the absence of it is sufficient to explain his death.

There is one other misunderstanding which I should like to guard against. So far as argumentation is concerned, this essay might be considered a continuation to the study published some time ago, dealing with the medieval village community.[2] The reader will find there this statement:

[2] Simkhovitch; "Hay and History." POLITICAL SCIENCE QUARTERLY, vol. xxviii, pp. 385-403, September, 1913.

Go to the ruins of ancient and rich civilizations in Asia Minor, Northern Africa or elsewhere. Look at the unpeopled valleys, at the dead and buried cities, and you can decipher there the promise and the prophecy that the law of soil exhaustion held in store for all of us. It is but the story of an abandoned farm on a gigantic scale. Depleted of humus by constant cropping, land could no longer reward labor and support life; so the people abandoned it. Deserted, it became a desert; the light soil was washed by the rain and blown around by shifting winds.

I should hate to be responsible for a new fetish, an interpretation of historical life through exhaustion of soil. It is silly.

First of all deeply and gratefully is it felt that life with all its pain and its glory can be lived; word or brush may aspire its all too inadequate expression, but never will the scholar methodically and mechanically figure it out and interpret it.

But it is a mistake to think that social science is dealing with life. It is not. It deals with the *background* of life. It deals with common things, with what lives had in common, common conditions of existence, common purposes that these conditions suggest. *They* can and must be scientifically explained and determined, if social science is to be taken seriously. Scientific determination is accurate determination. What forces that circumscribe and govern our life must we unquestionably accept? Obviously, the physical forces. Under certain conditions we are born, we live and die. The limits of our mortal existence we cannot transgress. Nor can we change the heavenly course of suns and planets; we do not govern the seasons of the year; they regulate our life.

Within the laws of nature our lives begin and end. They limit and compass our existence. But the laws of nature without our active participation do neither feed nor clothe us. This active participation we call our work, our labor. Social labor varies in its productivity. At all times this productivity had and has its limits. *These limits of the productivity of our labor become, for society, physical conditions of existence.* Within these limits our entire social life must move. These limits life must accept as mandatory and implacable; to them it must adjust itself.

The history of the productivity of our labor is the foundation of a scientific economic history, and the backbone of any and all history. Every law, every statute, every institution has obviously some purpose. But how are we to understand the purposes of the past if we know not the conditions which those purposes were to meet? The accurate knowledge of the productivity of our labor can explain to us why things were as they were, why they became what they are and what one may expect from the future.

In this study, however, which is not concerned with the details of Rome's life, one single, major and strikingly variable productivity factor suffices to solve the problem. That factor—the exhaustion of Roman soil and the devastation of Roman provinces—sheds enough light for us to behold the dread outlines of its doom.

VLADIMIR G. SIMKHOVITCH.

COLUMBIA UNIVERSITY.

The Quarterly Journal of Economics, 1917, Vol. 31, pp. 173–208

17

Climatic Change and Agricultural Exhaustion As Elements in the Fall of Rome

ELLSWORTH HUNTINGTON

The difference between Roman agriculture in early and in later times has given rise to a warm debate. One side is represented by Durneau de la Malle.[1] As he put it: "A vicious system of agriculture, a biennial rotation, the ignorance of the methods of alternation of crops, the too frequent rotation of wheat on the same land, the insufficient and poor preparation of manure, the slight extent of artificial grasslands, the small number of animals supported on cultivated crops, the imperfection of the methods and instruments of culture, the vicious practice of burning the straw in place of converting it into manure — these and a hundred other deadly practices which it would be too long to enumerate form the conflicting but true picture which Greek and Roman agriculture on the whole present to us." Rodbertus [2] strongly contested this view. He attempted to show that the Romans had a most admirable system of agriculture, being familiar with the rotation of crops and the use of fertilizers, and that more labor was expended per acre than is now spent on the best fields of Germany. That there was agricultural decline he admitted, but he ascribed it to social causes. In the writings of such men as Varro, Cato, Pliny, and Columella he accepts the parts which indicate that the science of agriculture was highly developed, but says that other portions must be taken "cum grano sallis." He thinks the Latin writers have been misunderstood or that their statements can be explained by other circumstances. For instance, he supposes that when Rome was able to reach out and obtain grain from other lands the Italian farmers turned their attention to

[1] Quoted by Rodbertus in the paper cited below.

[2] Rodbertus, "Zur Geschichte der agrarischen Entwicklung Roms unter den Kaisern," Jahrbücher für Nat. Oek., vol. ii, (1864) pp. 213–19,

vineyards, olive orchards, and cattle raising, and only the worst fields in Italy were devoted to wheat. Hence it was not surprising that the farmers reaped only four times what they had sowed.

Professor Simkhovitch ably shows that these two views are not really contradictory. The picture painted by Rodbertus indicates the condition in the early days, when Rome was in her prime. The other presents the conditions of later times. Simkhovitch ascribes the difference to exhaustion of the soil. Such exhaustion, as he says, is not a necessary consequence of wrong cultivation, but arises only when unwise methods are pursued. As Van Hise[1] points out, the most crucial element in the exhaustion of the soil is the depletion of the phosphorus, which can be prevented only by abundant fertilization.

The idea that such depletion plays an important part in the decline of nations finds frequent expression. Fetter,[2] for example, expresses a not uncommon view when he says that in Asia " the effects of bad husbandry " have caused " lands that once supported millions of people, perhaps tens of millions " to become deserts. He even goes so far as to imply that the decline of Egypt as well as of Rome was due largely to this cause. No one, however, has stated this view more authoritatively than Liebig.

The opponents of Liebig's hypothesis fall into two classes: these who, like Rodbertus, ascribe the fall of Rome to social and political causes, and those who believe that altho it was due to physical causes, exhaustion of the soil was only a minor factor. One of the

[1] C. R. Van Hise, The Conservation of Natural Resources in the United States, 1912, pp. 322 and 338.

[2] F. A. Fetter, Economic Principles, 1915, p. 445.

first to expound this latter view was Conrad.[1] He was ready perhaps to accept Liebig's statement that " the productivity of the soil alone has caused the rise and fall of nations, and, in a word has made history," but not as it was meant. Speaking of Mesopotamia and the accounts given by Herodotus and Pliny of the marvelous grain crops in ancient times compared with the present sterility of the country, he says: " If we put with this fact the observation of Herodotus that the climate of Assyria was too moist for vineyards, one is led to the conclusion that a decrease of precipitation has taken place, that the present water supply and the present aridity did not prevail in antiquity — a conclusion which alone is enough to explain the present desert condition of the country." He also showed that there is similar evidence of a diminution of the water supply in Greece and elsewhere, while he thought that in Italy volcanic disasters and deforestation were great factors in causing historic decay.

In the half century since Conrad challenged Liebig's interpretation, our knowledge of the climate of the past has increased. Today there is a large body of evidence which seems to indicate that climatic changes have occurred during the last two or three thousand years, and that they may have caused many of the results which Liebig and Simkhovitch have ascribed to exhaustion of the soil. The fact of a ruinous decline of agriculture not only in Italy, but in many other lands, can scarcely be denied. Its consequences were clearly disastrous. If climatic changes may have been responsible for the decline, it is well to discuss the general problem of changes of climate before proceeding to a consideration of Rome specifically.

[1] J. Conrad, Liebig's Ansicht von der Bodenerschöpfung, Jena, 1864.

A single concrete example will illustrate some of the ways in which such changes may have influenced the drier regions of the Roman Empire. About the time of Christ the oasis of Palmyra in the Syrian Desert was famous for the sweetness, purity, and abundance of its waters. Today no one in his right mind would praise it for any of these qualities. The brackish water smells strongly of sulphur, and the natives are always disturbed by its scarcity. The gardens, tho pleasant in themselves, seem sadly forlorn and insignificant in their setting of vast ruins. In its prime Palmyra covered at least as much ground as modern Damascus, and probably had 150,000 inhabitants. Today it has only 1500 at the most. The city reached its greatest prosperity in the third century of our era, when the water supply was apparently diminishing rapidly. This is what might be expected according to the climatic hypothesis. Written records and ruins show that important roads once crossed the Syrian Desert from Petra in the south and from the western Bosra in the latitude of the Sea of Galilee. These roads are today impractical for caravans because of the absence of water and grass. They appear to have been finally abandoned in the second century because of increasing aridity. This naturally threw all the trade between Egypt, Syria, and Damascus on the one hand, and Mesopotamia and Persia on the other, to the route through Palmyra, and thus greatly stimulated that city. By the seventh century, however, when the Mediterranean lands and western Asia apparently became more arid than at any other known period, Palmyra was practically abandoned. In the tenth century, when the water supply for a while became more abundant, it enjoyed a partial recovery, only to decay once more during the next dry epoch. Today the water supply varies directly in harmony with the rainfall of the past few years, and the size of the village changes correspondingly.

Before applying our climatic hypothesis to the fall of Rome, let us gain a clearer idea of the precise changes that have probably taken place in Italy. It does not seem that at any time within the last three thousand years the country had a climate like that of either central Europe or northern Africa. At all times the general character of the seasons has presumably been the same as now. There have been abundant rains in winter and a diminished rainfall in summer. The temperature, as already pointed out, has apparently not been essentially different from what it is today. The change appears to have been primarily in storminess. As nearly as can yet be determined, tho the winters two thousand to three thousand years ago were not essentially different from those of today, the storms may have been more numerous and more severe. On an average the winds were probably stronger than at present. Therefore, the warm wave which precedes a winter storm was warmer than now, and the cold wave which follows was correspondingly colder. Such conditions would have little effect except upon the sturdiness of the people; but this, as we shall see, may be of far-reaching import.

In the autumn, and especially the spring, the difference between the past and present was apparently greater than in the winter. In the autumn the stormy period probably began somewhat earlier than at present, while in the spring it lasted later. Judging by present conditions in years which go to one extreme or the other, the greatest difference was in the spring. At

192

that time not only were the storms apparently more
severe than they are today, but they continued so much
later in the season that the total spring rainfall, which
is the most essential for agriculture, increased in a
greater ratio than did the rainfall at other seasons.
Finally, the summers two or three thousand years ago
apparently had about the same average temperature as
today. Then as now they were decidedly less stormy
than the spring. Nevertheless, in summer, as well as
at other seasons, the storms of that time seem to have
exceeded those of the present both in number and in
severity. Hence while the summers were warm, sunny,
and comparatively dry, they seem to have had more
rainfall than now and to have been more subject to the
pleasant changes which mitigate the effects of long
steady heat.

In order to assign to climatic changes their due
importance in history it is necessary to understand not
only the nature of the changes, but their periodicity.
This can best be done by means of diagrams such
as I have published in my book *Civilization and
Climate*. Figure 33 in that volume (p. 228) shows the
variations in the rainfall of western and central Asia as
inferred from ruins, lakes, famines, old roads, and other
evidence available previous to 1910. The solid line
shows changes of climate in California on the basis of
the growth of the Big Trees measured in 1911 and 1912.
Later studies indicate that the dotted line should be
modified as indicated by the dashes and also in certain
other respects — for example, about 400 B.C., where it
should rise higher. The original curve, however, is
reproduced in order to show the resemblance between
the conclusions reached in two continents by wholly

diverse methods.   In general, the two lines of Figure 33
indicate that approximately the same changes have
taken place in similar climates in the two hemispheres.
It would not be justifiable, however, to assume complete similarity in all the details.   Moreover, according
to conclusions reached simultaneously and independently by Penck in Europe and by the writer in
America, climatic changes seem to consist of a shifting
of the various zones first toward the equator and then
away from it.   Accordingly, a change may occur in one
place somewhat later than in another.

Altho the results presented in *Civilization and
Climate* are by no means final it seems allowable
to use them as the basis of a study of the fall of
Rome.   While not applying directly to Italy, the curve
of the Big Trees seems to show the main trend of
events in that country as well as in California.   Omit-
ting the earlier and more doubtful centuries, it appears
that from 450 to 250 B.C., Italy probably enjoyed a
highly favorable climate.   During the next fifty years
there was marked deterioration.   Throughout the
second century, conditions were less favorable than
before, altho on the whole they were improving.   Even
at the worst, however, they were distinctly better than
today.   From 100 B.C. to 50 A.D. more favorable conditions ensued, altho not equal to those during the
pristine days of the Roman Republic.   Next came a
sudden deterioration so that the second century of our
era was unfavorable, altho possibly not so much so as
the second century before Christ.   After a slight
recovery at the end of the second century and the
beginning of the third, there began a long and steady
decline in climate until the final fall of the Western

Empire. The next century and a half saw a slight improvement until the beginning of the seventh century. Then followed the two worst centuries of the historic period, altho possibly the thirteenth century B.C. may have been almost as bad.

Turning now from the physical side of our problem, let us consider the probable historic results of the adverse climatic changes that appear to have taken place between 250 B.C. and 650 A.D. It will be understood that the reverse of what is here described is supposed to characterize favorable changes.

We may divide the results of climatic changes into three groups: economical, political, and biological. For a statement of the economic conditions I cannot do better than refer to Professor Simkhovitch's article already quoted. I do not agree with him in thinking that exhaustion of the soil was the primary cause of the conditions which he describes, for in countries like Syria cultivation by the methods which he deplores has continued for thousands of years, and people are still fairly prosperous wherever water is abundant.

In view of this we must apparently assume either a most profound and astonishing change in Roman character, or else a change of climate. If the Romans knew how to farm like the Chinese and Japanese and thus indefinitely to ward off the effects of the exhaustion of the soil, but failed to do it when they found themselves falling into dire distress, they surely had suffered an " inner decay " that is scarcely conceivable. On the other hand, if they had not rain enough in the late spring, no amount of care and cultivation would make it possible to carry on intensive agriculture.

In the later days of Rome, *pari passu* with the deterioration of the climate, agriculture progressively declined. Thus by 395 A.D. " the abandoned fields of Campania alone amounted to something over 528,000 jugera." Doubtless much of the land thus abandoned was capable of being restored, for even then the climate was apparently better than at present. That it was not restored seems merely to mean that when people are waging a losing fight against nature they become discouraged. The change is what counts.

So it is with countries. In the fourth century B.C., Italy appears to have been favored with so fine a climate that less than five acres was enough to support an average family. Cultivation was highly intensive so that the most advanced methods of agriculture were developed. Failures of the crops were rare, and general prosperity prevailed. The farmers lived in comfort on their little farms and asked nothing of anyone, and the towns reflected their condition. Then when the spring and summer rains diminished — to speak by hypothesis — a small tract of land was not enough to furnish a living for the farmer and his family. Crops that had previously been profitable ceased to be worth while, the farmers ran into debt, and their lands gradually fell into the hands of large landowners. Since crops were no longer profitable the land was used for grazing purposes, as classical writers often point out. This was bad in two respects. In the first place, sheep and goats eat not only grass, but seedling trees, and thus prevent the growth of new forests. Where they pasture in abundance the soil is badly trampled, and is no longer held in place by roots. Hence it is washed away by the winter rain, leaving the hillsides barren and ruining the fields in the lowlands. In the second place, sheep-raising and cattle-raising demand large areas. Hence they increase the tendency toward the concentration of land in the hands of a few individuals. During the Augustan Age the farmers apparently recovered somewhat, and presumably were better off than in the second century B.C. Then came renewed climatic stress at the end of the first century A.D., and later the long deadening decline that culminated in the seventh century. In those days the Roman farmer was in circumstances as discouraging as those of the banker with a mechanic's income.

Such economic changes must inevitably produce political results. One of the first and most obvious is a disturbance of the system of taxation. Theoretically, taxes ought to be proportioned to the income of the people who pay them. Practically the adjustment is most imperfect, and has a disagreeable way of remaining fixed when other conditions change. When crops are bad the expenses of the government do not diminish. A tax which was easily paid from a full grain bin becomes oppressive when the grain bin is half empty. It is not surprising that the people were discontented and agrarian reforms were needed in the days of the Gracchi. At that time Rome apparently suffered from climatic conditions more unfavorable than at any other period previous to about 300 A.D. Under such circumstances the poverty and discouragement of the many almost inevitably favor the concentration of power in the hands of a few. Hence democracy suffers, and a plutocratic form of government is superimposed upon the old framework. It would be useless to illustrate the matter here, for I should merely be repeating the arguments of Professor Simkhovitch — the only difference between his view and mine being in the interpretation of the cause of the agricultural decline. Not only Rome itself, but the provinces were suffering, and it is not strange that their discontent was finally an important element in the break-up of the Rome Empire.

The theory that agriculture declined because of exhaustion of the soil seems to have little bearing on barbarian invasions. In this respect it is diametrically opposed to the theory of a decline due to climatic changes. Nomads such as those of central Asia are the first to feel the effect of increased aridity. The springs that they have been wont to frequent on the edge of the desert dry up, grass for pasturage is scanty, and therefore they begin to seek new pastures. At first they may meet with no special difficulty, provided the country is not too densely populated. Soon, however, they come into conflict with neighbors who also press into the well-watered regions where there is abundant grass. When tribe meets tribe and there is not enough grass for all, conflict is bound to ensue. Then the tribe which is obliged to content itself with the less favorable locations is practically certain to take to plundering. It may plunder its nomad neighbors, or it may make raids on the settled villages in the oases or in the better-watered tracts on the desert border.

Such movements begin in the driest regions, such as the great deserts of Transcaspia or Arabia. Where the nomads were met by a solid bulwark like that of the Roman Empire in Syria and North Africa, they could not achieve much; but in eastern Europe, where there was nothing to hold them back, one can scarcely doubt that they must have pressed forward. Thus one tribe would upset another, and a whole continent may have been put in commotion. This, I believe, explains to a large degree the barbarian invasions of Europe during the early centuries of the Christian era. Men do not take their wives and children and move in great masses except under some strong compulsion. I do not need to go into details on the barbarian invasions of Rome. It is enough to point out that they were numerous as long as the climate of Asia grew worse. They spread into each of the southern peninsulas of Europe. They spilled over into Africa. Finally, in the seventh century there came the culminating migration from the desert. The power of the Roman Empire had vanished, and the Arabs surged out under Mohammed. The religious impulse doubtless was of the greatest importance as a unifying factor, but hunger may have been the chief impelling force. So too, in later days, Genghis Khan may have been the unifying factor, but hunger due to a second great period of aridity was perhaps the underlying force that impelled his hordes to surge out of Central Asia.

During the period of favorable climate which apparently prevailed in Italy three or four hundred years before Christ, the mountains were probably well wooded, and springs abundant. The streams must have been for the most part perennial, and were presumably well adjusted to their valleys so that they flowed in clearly defined channels. Increasing aridity, as we have already seen, would cause the mountains to become more barren. Consequently the streams would become heavily loaded with mud and gravel. This would be an important element not only in ruining the farms, but in increasing malaria. As physiographers well know, when streams that are heavily loaded with silt emerge from the mountains and enter the plains, they deposit part of their load. Thus they fill their channels, divert themselves into new courses, and gradually spread out into many branches which wander here and there over wide areas, and often produce swamps. When such streams dwindle during the dry summer, most of the channels are converted into mere strings of stagnant pools, ideal places for mosquitoes. Moreover, the drier the summers, the greater the need of irrigation, and this also causes stagnant pools. Thus the supposed climatic changes in Italy were mainly of a kind to induce a great increase in the area where the mosquito was able to thrive. Hence the ravages of malaria were presumably increased, and played a part in destroying the self-control and energy of the Romans.

On the basis of the actual achievements of thousands of people under different conditions of climate, it is possible to make a map showing the amount of energy which different races would have in different parts of the world on the basis of climate alone.[1] This map is strikingly like a map of civilization. The resemblance of the two indicates that today the active and progressive races, those that dominate the world, are all located in climates which possess a highly stimulating quality. If we are right in thinking that the response to climate is almost the same among all races, the matter is highly significant in our interpretation of the fall of Rome. As we have already seen, the climatic changes which have apparently taken place in Italy appear to have been characterized by a decline in the variability of the weather from day to day, especially in the spring and summer. This means that three or four centuries B.C., Rome was blessed with a climate whose mean temperature was as good as that of today,

[1] Such a map is published in my Civilization and Climate, p. 200. The volume contains a full discussion of the relation of climate to civilization. Since it was published new facts have been discovered which show that the response of different races to climate is more uniform than was supposed when the book was written.

and which at the same time was better than that of the present, not only for agriculture, but in its stimulating effect on human activity. It apparently possessed the sparkle and tang which our own climate in the northern United States possesses to so marked a degree. If this is so, the change which took place between 300 and 200 B.C. and still more the gradual change between the time of Christ and the seventh century probably had an appreciable effect upon the energy and ability of the Roman people. Even if there had been no change in the racial composition of the inhabitants, no malaria, no agricultural distress, and no invasions of barbarians, there still would apparently have been a decline in ability. Such a decline would work particular harm at times when other conditions were becoming adverse. For instance, when irrigation was needed to overcome the difficulties of aridity, it would be particularly necessary that people should have abundant energy and initiative. These qualities would be equally needed to overcome malaria, and to prevent the streams from flooding the fields and creating swamps. Energy too would be especially valuable when the barbarians were threatening invasion, or when political questions were becoming difficult because of agricultural adversity, poverty, burdensome taxes, and consequent general discontent.

The lessons of history cannot rightly be understood until the combined work of men in many lines gives us a clear idea of each one of the complex factors leading to such great events as the fall of Rome.

ELLSWORTH HUNTINGTON.

The next four articles all deal with water, climatic components, and man's environmental reactions when he imperfectly understands all elements of the hydrologic cycle. The Bryson and Baerreis article provides an entirely new variation on the theme of climate and its relation to human history. Whereas other articles in this series present implications that climate should be considered in the degradational process, Bryson and Baerreis switch the tune and show the possibility that man can become the creator of his own climate on a massive scale. Of course, recent studies indicate man *does* influence climate on a small scale, such as in cities where temperatures are warmer and rainfall patterns different from those in adjacent areas. These and other studies show his impact on certain "micro-climates." The Bryson–Baerreis thesis is interesting from another viewpoint, because it is opposite to the dogma prevalent in the United States during the 19th century that the "rains follow the plow." Instead they state, "History suggests that the role of man has been important in the making of the desert." A somewhat related approach is taken by Sears (1947) in his book *Deserts on the March*. A similar article by Bryson (1967) shows there is as much moisture in the air above the Rajputana desert in India as above Panama, the Amazon Valley, or the Congo. The climate difference is in the amount of dust, 5.5 t/mi^2, in India which increases the sinking rate of air by 50 percent.

> The Harappans flourished and their population grew—the people farmed more area more intensively. They destroyed the grass cover of the land and the wind blew the dust into the air, just as it did in our American Great Plains area during the dust bowl years. The dust changed the rate at which the atmosphere subsided, and with this change the area became more desert-like. As the climate gets drier, any people tries a little harder to grow enough food to supply the population if the population is dense and not very mobile. This means tearing up more of the surface and loosening more dust to blow into it. (Bryson, 1967, p. 53)

Reid A. Bryson and David A. Baerreis are both at the University of Wisconsin, where Bryson is Professor of Meteorology and Baerreis is Professor of Anthropology. Bryson (1920–   ) was born in Detroit, Michigan, and received his Ph.D. (1948) from the University of Chicago. Baerreis (1916–   ) was born in New York City and received his Ph.D. (1949) from Columbia University. They have both published other articles in their respective fields.

In her article Bell examines in detail the first of the two Near East Dark Ages which began about 2200 B.C. This reproduction provides additional insight into the significance of hydrology and man, and is the most carefully documented report of how low rainfall caused drought conditions and abnormally low streamflow in the Nile resulting in wide-spread sand dune encroachment. Her thesis is that the central government collapsed because it was unable to deal effectively with the famine, and powerless to change the agrarian irrigation economy that depended entirely on climate. Thus the inability to conserve in the hydrologic cycle led to the downfall of the dynasty.

Barbara Bell (1922–   ) was born in Evanston, Illinois, and received her Ph.D. (1951) from Radcliff in astronomy. She has remained at Harvard University where she is Assistant to the Director of the Harvard Observatory. Her specialties are solar physics and solar–terrestrial relations. She has written other articles dealing with climatic changes and with flood records of the Nile.

The setting of the Cooke and Cowgill–Hutchinson articles is the New World, and they provide different reasons for decline of Mayan civilization. Cooke suggests that man may have initiated a chain reaction of events that all contributed to the decline. The Cowgill–Hutchinson article indicates climatic changes may have occurred, but that erosion rate increase was not large, and therefore other causes are equally, if not more important. They introduce a range of new techniques in order to provide a different data base for their analysis. Such quantitative and analytical methods show promise in opening new reference frames for problems that have often been approached with more qualitative-type information. Thus the Cooke article is one of the first that provides a strong discussion for self-induced destruction; whereas many earlier theories dealt with the importance of external forces, and Cowgill and Hutchinson apply modern techniques in an attempt for a solution to the problem.

C. Wythe Cooke (1887–   ) was born in Baltimore and received his Ph.D. (1912) from Johns Hopkins University in geology. He has spent his professional life with the U.S. Geological Survey and the Smithsonian Institute. He is well known for his work and publications on terraces of the Coastal Plain Province and on the problem of the Carolina Bays.

Ursula M. Cowgill (1927–   ) was born in Switzerland and received her Ph.D. (1956) in soil chemistry from Iowa State University. She is Professor of Biology, University of Pittsburgh. George E. Hutchinson (1903–   ) was born and educated in England and in 1961 received an honorary Ph.D. from Princeton University. His specialty is zoology and he is Professor of Biology, Yale University.

[Reprinted from BULLETIN OF THE AMERICAN METEOROLOGICAL SOCIETY, Vol. 48, No. 3, March, 1967, pp. 136–142]
Printed in U. S. A.

possibilities of major climatic modification and their implications: Northwest India, a case for study[1]

Reid A. Bryson
and David A. Baerreis
University of Wisconsin, Madison

18

Abstract

On the basis of field observations and theoretical studies it is believed that the dense pall of local dust over northwestern India and West Pakistan is a significant factor in the development of subsidence over the desert. Archeological evidence derived from the northern portion of the desert within India suggests a pattern of intermittent occupation with the role of man being important in making the desert. As man has made the desert, so through surface stabilization can he reduce the dust and consequently modify the subsidence and precipitation patterns in the region. The social consequences of such climatic modification are briefly considered.

The Rajasthan Desert

Nearly half of the Indian sub-continent is arid or semi-arid. By far the larger part of this dry area is located in northwestern India and southeastern West Pakistan, centering on the very dry area (less than 5 inches annual precipitation) known as the Thar Desert (Fig. 1). The larger area of deficient rainfall surrounding and including the Thar Desert is variously known as the Rajputana or Rajasthan Desert, and occupies an area of a quarter to a half million square miles depending on the definition used. In the following discussion the term "Rajputana Desert" will be used loosely to identify the dry area lying between New Delhi and Karachi, between the Rann of Kutch and the Himalayan foothills.

With regard to the climate of this area, Trewartha has said:

"What appears to be a . . . striking peculiarity of the sub-continent's rainfall, considering the fact that almost the entire region is dominated by a surface flow of equatorial-tropical maritime air in summer, and is crossed twice by the Intertropical Convergence, is the widespread deficiency of rainfall." and

"The fact that the northeastern and northwestern extremities of the continent exhibit such impressive contrasts in rainfall amounts, and this in spite of the fact that the two regions have so many similar climatic controls, presents a problem"[1]. To be sure, the Rajputana is in the normal latitude of the sub-tropical anticyclones in winter and the deserts associated with them, but a shallow monsoon flow of humid air does enter the area in summer. One obtains the impression from the literature [2] that if the atmospheric subsidence over the area were less, the moist monsoon layer would be deeper and the slight summer rainfall maximum would be considerably larger. In fact, it appears that the desert coincides with the extent of divergent, sinking air at about 10,000 ft [3].

The magnitude of the subsidence over the desert area has been studied by Das who computed the daily vertical velocity distribution over India using a ten-layer numerical model, then averaged these values to obtain mean vertical motions [4]. Generally speaking, mean vertical motions imply mean diabatic changes and Das converted his computed vertical velocities into the required cooling rates in mid-troposphere in degrees per day. Over the wet areas of India the warming rates associated with ascending motion were found to be quite compatible with the observed release of latent heat. Quite a different situation prevailed over the desert, for the required diabatic cooling to maintain the subsidence amounted to about 2.4C day^{-1}—a figure which did not agree with the radiation divergence calculated for the observed distribution of water vapor and normal carbon dioxide content. This latter figure came to about 1.8C day^{-1}, and the difference between these two figures is too large to be computational error.

Some insight into the possible explanation of the discrepancy is to be found in the work of Bryson et al. who measured the radiation divergence in the troposphere over northern India [5]. They found that the observed rate of cooling in mid-troposphere was very nearly the same as that required to match the subsidence calculated by Das, and that the calculated cooling due to the distribution of water vapor and carbon dioxide was also very nearly the same as his value—but could show that the observed cooling rate differed from the calculated by 50% due to the presence of atmospheric dust over the desert. This suggests that dust over the desert in-

[1] Various aspects of the research leading to the preparation of this paper have been supported by the Atmospheric Sciences Section of the National Science Foundation, GP-444; the Geography Branch of the Office of Naval Research, Nonr 1202(07); the Environmental Science Services Administration; and the Indian Meteorological Department.

creases the mid-tropospheric subsidence rate by perhaps 50%.

They concluded that in the absence of dust there would be less radiation divergence in mid-troposphere. There would thus be less subsidence and a deeper monsoon layer. With less subsidence, the low level divergence would be less and areal extent of the divergent air less as well—with the monsoon rains extending, then, farther into the present Rajputana Desert area.

If the source of the dust is the desert itself, then the desert would appear to be self-sustaining, for the presence of a vegetative cover would inhibit the raising of dust by the wind, and thus the development of the desert climate which is inimical to the vegetative cover.

The atmospheric dust blanket of South Asia

Flights through South Asia in April 1962, 1963 and 1966 (Fig. 2), winter 1963 and 1966 and October 1964 provided a view of the dust distribution which agrees in general with the small amount of previously known information. Deep, dense dust over North Africa and Arabia in the spring appears to thin eastward along the southern coast of Iran and Baluchistan (Mekran and LasBela coasts) but becomes very dense and deep over the Rajasthan Desert. From there it appears to diminish southward and eastward, though present in considerable quantities over northeast India, and observable as layers over Burma, Thailand and Cambodia. There appears to be little dust over Iran proper. Reconnaissance in the spring of 1963 indicated that the top of the dust layer was around 25,000 ft over the northeastern part

of the Arabian Sea, to 30,000 ft and more over the Rajputana Desert, thinning to 17,000 ft over the lower Ganges Valley. The southern edge of the premonsoon dust is thought to be about 8N, and was so observed along the Malayan peninsula. Over Burma and Thailand the dust was thinner and layered, 20,000 ft or so being a common level for the main layer.

In the South Asian area the greatest dust density appears to be in the West Pakistan-Northwest Indian region, vertical visibilities of 1–2 miles being fairly common there.

In May 1963, still within the premonsoon period, Gordon Cooper took several pictures during his 22 orbit flight which give further information about the dust and its origin. His pictures of the Iranian and West Pakistan coasts show the "washed out" aspect characteristic of photographs taken through haze. The degree of contrast reduction in his picture of the Indus Valley appears to be even greater. The most interesting photograph shows the clouds along a trough line over the Rajputana Desert. On this photograph the wind directions are easily discernible in the cloud patterns, and imbedded in the winds behind the trough is a cloud of dust sweeping out of the desert. This dust cloud is dense enough to obscure totally the ground. Recheck of the Indian Meteorological Department charts for 15–16 May 1963 showed that this trough was evident on the standard synoptic reports and analysis, and the data corroborated the analysis of Cooper's photograph, but the dust cloud had been missed. Cooper's photograph of the Calcutta area shows some evidence

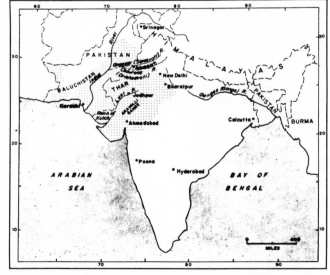

Fig. 1. India and surroundings. The Rajputana Desert is indicated by the stippled area.

137

FIG. 2. Aerial photograph of dust from 28,000 ft over desert surface (April 1966) in southern Asia. Original color photo presents brilliant blue sky at the top, and tan-brown dust beneath. Note emerging surface detail near base of photograph.

of haze (plus complete obscuration of Calcutta by local air pollution), but his photographs of the Burma coast were crisp and clear—apparently free of haze.

These photos agree with the visual observations of April 1963 made from aircraft and lend weight to the suggestion one would get from the dust distribution that the major source of dust for the Indian area is the Rajputana Desert itself.

If the dust is so dense that it drastically reduces visibility, and extends to heights of 30,000 ft, one might expect that it would have a pronounced effect on radiative fluxes in India, and on the climate of the area.

Mani and Chacko have shown that the visible spectrum atmospheric turbidity in northwest India is greatest in March, April, and May, but is high for essentially the whole year. An average yearly Angstrom turbidity coefficient of 0.045 was found for Delhi, and 0.020 for Poona [6].

Bryson, Wilson and Kuhn investigated the infrared radiation fluxes over Northwest India using the Suomi-Kuhn radiation sonde in a series of ascents at Poona, Ahmedabad, Delhi and Srinagar in April 1963 [7]. They found that the dust had a pronounced effect on the

infrared radiation flux divergence, increasing the diabatic cooling rate by 50% over what it would be if the air were free of particulates.

Rough estimates of the dust mass concentration over India were made from the radiation flux measurements on the assumption that dust particles acted as "grey bodies" and were fairly uniformly distributed in height. Both assumptions seem fairly well justified for the layers considered. Estimated particle concentrations ranged from 500 to 7000 per cm³, assuming a diameter of 0.25 μ for the dust particles, in good agreement with the visibilities observed at the time of measurement of the radiation fluxes. In late March and early April of 1961, Junge found Aitken nuclei particle densities of 100 to 1000 per cm³ for comparable levels over Hyderabad [8]. The difference is in the expected direction and magnitude if the dust haze thins southward over India. Direct measurement of the dust concentration was also made in April 1966 using a U. S. Navy Orion aircraft (Fig. 3). Analysis of the data is not complete at the time of this writing but suggests that the magnitudes and distributions arrived at indirectly are correct.

In the preceding discussion a close connection between the desert, a deep, dense, dust layer centered over the desert area, and the desert climate has been indicated. One might then ask whether the region has always been desert, and whether it might not be reclaimed by controlling the dust source and thus modifying the climate. A closely related question is whether the desert is man-made or the result of non-human natural change.

The archeological history of desert occupation

An abundant literature may be found pertaining to what was formerly known as "The Great Indian Desert" but much of it is conflicting. The reasons for this are doubtless similar to those involved in another account attributed to Indian sources in which a group of blind men individually attempt to describe an elephant on the basis of the anatomical part they have grasped. The most adequate archaeological exploration of the desert region within the present limits of India of a systematic survey character is confined to the northern part of the desert between the now dry beds of the Sarasvati and Drishadvati while the southern part of the desert watered by the Luni and its tributaries is less satisfactorily explored. In view of this we may narrow our attention to the northern portion of the Rajputana desert making use of the survey of remains of the protohistoric period carried out by the Archaeological Survey of India with the assumption that it is representative of the area as a whole. The survey was carried out by A. Ghosh, present Director General of Archaeology in India, and represented a further extension of earlier investigations by Sir Aurel Stein [9]. Only a brief preliminary report of this work is available [10]. Extensive excavations in subsequent years have concentrated upon one site, Kalibangan, but again only brief

138

summaries of this work by the School of Archaeology of the Archaeological Survey of India are available [11].

The archeological survey cited was confined to an exploration of desiccated river valleys of northwestern Rajasthan where the river system, now containing water only in its upper reaches, once reached the sea either independently or as a tributary of the Indus. The limited stretch of the valleys of the Sarasvati (modern Ghaggar) and Drishadvati (modern Chautang) explored by Ghosh in presently arid regions contained in excess of a hundred sites representing a considerable chronological and cultural range. Of strategic importance is the site of Kalibangan, located on the left bank of the Ghaggar in the District of Gangan Ganganager, where evidence for the existence of a pre-Harappan culture has been obtained [12]. While this site is primarily an important regional center of the Harappan culture, similar in many architectural features and other details to the great cities of the Indus valley, lower levels contain a distinctive black-on-red ceramic tradition of non-Harappan affiliation. Ceramics of this variety had previously been recognized as more characteristic of the Drishadvati valley where the sites had been designated the Sothi culture and regarded on typological grounds as being later than the Harappan culture. This interpretation, as is indicated above, is now reversed on the basis of stratigraphic evidence. The most detailed study of the ceramics of the pre-Harappan levels available, indicates they ". . . show a generic relationship with the Sind-Baluch sites of pre-Harappan vintage, notably Amri, Kot-Diji, pre-defence levels at Harappa, etc"[12]. Four radiocarbon dates are available for the Kot Diji culture from the type site located some 40 km east of Mohenjo-daro in Pakistan. The dates for Kot Diji range between 2470 ± 141 (P-196) and 2075 ± 134 B.C. (P-195) and while B. B. Lal feels that the latter date may indicate a somewhat late survival of the culture [13], the range is essentially in agreement with recently determined dates for the comparable horizon in the lowest levels at Kalibangan [14]. Five radiocarbon dates for the Sothi culture at Kalibangan range between 2245 ± 115 B.C. (TF-155) and 1660 ± 110 B.C. (TF-240). While the latter date seems young in the light of age determinations of the Harappan culture, present evidence does suggest some contemporaneity of the two cultures and the lag in time as compared with the Pakistan dates is not unreasonable if we are dealing with the expansion of this general culture complex.

At the site of Kalibangan a sterile, sandy layer marks a temporary abandonment of the site prior to the initiation of Harappan occupation but clearly no extended period of time is involved. A. Ghosh reports that more than twenty-five mounds of the Harappan culture have been identified in the desiccated river valleys we have been using to illustrate the early occupation in the desert region. They begin at the Pakistani border while the site of Kalibangan marks the presently-known eastern outpost in the Sarasvati valley. While the data

Fig. 3. Instrument pod on the U. S. Navy Orion aircraft. Light colored round object on pod bottom is radiometer which measured long wave (terrestrial) and short wave (reflected) upward radiation. Within the pod, the sensor and an aluminum parabolic reflector can be seen which measured reflected (collimated) solar radiation. All components of the radiation budget were measured. Atmospheric particulates were captured on slides by means of an impactor, and particulate concentration was measured by a dust photometer on board the aircraft.

reported permit no statement as to the relative density as compared to the earlier Sothi occupation, the fact that one-quarter of the sites located may be attributed to the Harappan culture would seem to indicate that this was a highly favorable period for occupation in the region. Since a total of seventeen radiocarbon dates are now available for the Harappan occupation at Kalibangan [15], the cluster is sufficient to establish a range of 2000–1700 B.C. for the Harappan civilization in the region. While the terminal date for the culture must be held in abeyance, the continuity of occupation with the suggested dates for the earlier Sothi occupation seems confirmed.

The peoples of the Harappan civilization were followed in the area by the Painted Grey Ware culture. A. Ghosh indicates that twenty sites of this culture have been found in the explored region of the Sarasvati valley in Bikaner but only one greyware site was found in the Drishadvati valley. While reports on excavated sites in the region are lacking, Ghosh does comment that the sites are small in extent and present few features. One further bit of evidence which may be derived from the summary accounts is that greyware sites were not superimposed upon the Harappan sites but that new locations were chosen. The Harappan sites were located overlooking the valleys as though the floodplains were farmed, while the later sites are on the river channels proper where the last bit of a dwindling water supply might be used.[2] An estimate of the time of occupancy of the Painted Grey Ware culture is of obvious importance but is handicapped by lack of excavation re-

[2] Ghosh, A., 1964: Personal communication.

139

ports. Ghosh had estimated 600 B.C. as a very rough central date for the culture while Sharma suggested they may have arrived in the region around 1000 B.C. Radiocarbon dates run by the Tata Institute [16] on the site of Hastinapur on the left bank of the Ganga River in Meerut District, Uttar Pradesh, provide one set of absolute dates which can be provisionally extended into the Rajasthan region. Five dates from Period II at this site, the period being characterized by ceramics of the Painted Grey Ware, range in age from 500 to 270 B.C. Dates reported in 1965 [17] on work of a joint expedition by the University of Rajasthan and UCLA at the site of Noh near Bharatpur, Rajasthan, on Painted Grey Ware are 740 ± 220 B.C. (UCLA-703B) and 530 ± 250 B.C. (UCLA-703A). The two sets of dates thus appear to confirm Ghosh's estimate and in turn indicate the possibility of an actual break in regional occupation between Harappan and Painted Grey Ware on the order of a thousand years. Excavations by Ghosh at a site north of Anupgarh, an area where occupation by the Painted Grey Ware culture was in close proximity to a Harappan occupation, revealed that the occupations were separated by sterile layers thus confirming the time break between the cultures.

A final group of sites has been classed by Ghosh as the Rangmahal culture. While actual numbers of sites are not given, they are cited as comprising a "large number" and specific mention is made of their large size, some middens ranging up to 35 and 40 ft in height, while others had mud fortification walls around them. One is given the impression that this is an extensive occupation phase of considerable importance, and thus reflecting again favorable conditions for occupancy of the region. Ghosh states that there is little doubt that the culture flourished in the early centuries A.D., basing this upon similarities in pottery types to excavated sites and on the presence of one or two Kushan coins in the Bikaner sites themselves. A temporal gap between Rangmahal and the Painted Grey Ware phase may be present though it clearly would not be as extensive as the preceding one and indeed may not exist. At least two sites revealed occupation layers of the Rangmahal culture superimposed on the greyware complex but the character of these stratigraphic conditions is not reported. So far as the terminal phase of occupation of this region is concerned, Ghosh indicates that after the decay of the flourishing Rangmahal sites in the seventh or eighth century the population seems to have turned largely to a nomadic existence with campsites as the characteristic archaeological manifestation to be found, though these sites may indeed have been occupied by descendents of the Rangmahal tradition. Medieval ruins in the Drishadvati valley east of Rawatsar suggest, however, some continuity of occupation into more recent times.

Lack of excavation in the region makes a precise evaluation of the pattern of ecological relationships in the region of occupancy impossible. However, at least

beginning with Harappan times an economy based upon both agriculture and domestic animals is present, these being the same plants and animals that characterize the economy of the historic period. In modern India where populations have increased the forests have been destroyed for timber and fuel so that large areas, as in the Indo-Gangetic Plain, are almost completely cleared of trees. Lacking wood, cow dung, which should be used as a manure for fields, is burned as fuel. The consequent loss of fertility can in turn promote overgrazing just as the destruction of the forests, even if these were limited to a gallery strip near the rivers, can also lead to land destruction and sand movement. These factors are mentioned as possible ones that might lead to environmental deterioration which brought the cultural periods enumerated to a close. However, it should be stressed that no archeological evidence has been reported that will permit one to choose between cultural practices as opposed to natural climatic factors as the causative factor in terminating occupation, or at least extensive occupation, in the region. However it is an intriguing feature of the archeological record that a pattern of intermittent, relatively intense occupation within the past four thousand years is indicated. There may have been at least two phases when the occupation was reduced or perhaps eliminated, yet from which the region eventually recovered. While the present desert conditions may well be the most extensive in this recent period, it may be of some significance that the Rangmahal occupation which preceded the recent period was seemingly also the most extensive in the region and consequently may have made the greatest impact on the natural environment. The occurrence of many dust storms in south-western Rajasthan was reported in the seventh century A.D. [18], and the accumulated evidence seems to be that by 1000 A.D. considerable spread of the desert had occurred, becoming accentuated in the recent past [19].

Climate-induced change and man-induced change

There seems to be little doubt that the Rajputana Desert is more hostile to human occupation at the present time than in 2000 B.C. or 400 A.D. It is hard to conceive of the region providing a basis for the Harappan "empire" today. Inevitably one must consider whether the deterioration of the region is due to climatic change as part of the now fairly well-documented worldwide pattern, or whether there has been local climatic change induced by human activities.

It is not necessary to invoke changes of large magnitude. Indeed, the evidence is that the plants that grew in the region during Harappan occupation are largely those found in the fringes of the area today and the same can be said of the animals. At the present time, the desert is said to be advancing into the arable lands at the rate of half a mile a year, indicating that the ecological balance of man, plant, and climate is imperfect. This does not seem to be a recent development, yet the climate around the world has changed within the past hundred years. If one assumes that the advance has averaged a quarter to a half mile per year for some time, and extrapolates backward, the appearance of a widening fringe of desert about the Thar Desert core would date to 400 to 1000 years ago, at the end of Rangmahal time.

The pattern of human occupation in some ways suggests agreement with the pattern of climatic change—occupation during early Sub-Boreal time, abandonment, then occupation during Sub-Atlantic time and somewhat later. At the same time it would appear that the range of climates within the last millennium is such that if only climatic change were involved, there should have been flourishing periods—yet none appear so far. It appears more likely that from Rangmahal times onward there has been a progressive deterioration of the vegetation and perhaps structure of the surface such that deflation has increased. This was the considered opinion of the experts assembled at the New Delhi Symposium on the Rajputana Desert in 1952 according to S. L. Hora, who summarized the consensus, saying:

"One thing which was pointedly brought out in the Symposium, was that the Rajputana Desert is largely a man-made desert . . . by the work of man in cutting down and burning forests . . . (and by) the deterioration of the soils" [20].

Yet, whether the dust over the Rajputana Desert is the result of human activity or climatic change alone, analysis indicates that the climate would be different in the absence of the dust. History suggests that the role of man has been important in the making of the desert. Science suggests that man might have a role in unmaking the desert.

Possible consequences of surface stabilization

Let us consider qualitatively the reasonable consequences of soil surface stabilization in the Rajputana Desert. Let us further assume that ultimately the stabilization would be by use of grasses.

First, with an adequate grass cover there would be little blowing dust, in which case the average subsidence over the desert would be reduced by perhaps one-third, because the infrared cooling rate in mid-troposphere would be reduced.[3] Assuming that the variance of the vertical velocity would be unchanged, moving the mean closer to zero would mean more frequent cases of convergence and upward motion.[4] More summer showers in turn would aid the grass which in turn would hold down the dust, etc.

A second effect of dust control would be an increase of the diurnal radiative forcing function amplitudes. With a smaller turbidity factor, more solar energy

---

[3] The infrared effect of the atmospheric dust blanket is to reduce the infrared radiation divergence at the surface and increase it at upper levels.

[4] The present summer rainfall maximum is apparently associated with a few such changes of direction of the vertical velocity (Trewartha, *op. cit.*, p. 166).

would reach the ground during the day and there would be less direct heating by absorption in mid-troposphere. At night the surface would cool more and the mid-troposphere less. This yields two consequences—more instability during the day (more showers?), and a larger diurnal temperature range at the surface which would appear largely in lower nocturnal minima.[5]

With less subsidence and low-level divergence, the eddy flux of moisture into the area should produce a higher absolute humidity, both because there would be less mass outflow for the eddy flux to run against, and less dry subsident air for admixture. This would make the greater daytime instability more effective. According to preliminary calculations the lower nocturnal minima should result in dew formation on the grass. The grass itself should lower the thermal admittance of the surface, further depressing the nocturnal temperature minima. Lower mean temperatures and dew would make small amounts of precipitation more effective.

How to accomplish the stabilization is a problem in agricultural engineering that will not be treated here beyond saying that discussions with appropriate experts indicate that it is by no means an impossibly large or hopeless task.[6]

Assuming, pending further investigation, that the above qualitative analysis of the effects of dust control by surface stabilization with grass is correct and self-maintaining, what would be the social and economic consequences of such an experiment in regional climatic modification?

Consequences of climatic modification

If we assume that climatic conditions of the desert area can be modified and wish to consider the consequences or implications of such an action, it is necessary to review first some basic facts concerning India's economic and social conditions. One crucial fact is the importance of agriculture to India. Agricultural activities provide employment to 69% of the population and contributed almost 51% of the total national income (1955). Yet despite this prominent role of agriculture, food shortages require the importation of agricultural products. The Indian government, appreciating the seriousness of the problem, allocated 38% of the budget of the First Five Year Plan to agriculture, irrigation, and rural community development projects. But while more efficient methods of production, including mechanization, will undoubtedly increase food production they may also aggravate other problems. It is recognized that agricultural activities disguise unemployment since the number of agricultural workers has increased without a corresponding increase in land cultivated, a factor attributed to the decline of village industries under

---

[5] Lettau, H. H., 1965: Personal communication.

[6] Experiments at the Central Arid Zone Research Institute, Jodhpur, indicate that it is only necessary to exclude animals for a year or two in order for a fine stand of native grass to spring up.

competition with cheap manufactured products. Bound up with all of these factors is India's continued population increase which is occurring despite the fact that there are no empty land spaces capable of absorbing internal migrants and thus relieving population pressures.

Reclamation of desert lands can thus contribute to the improvement of a condition of food shortage and in addition provide desperately needed space for India's large population. Since the Rajputana desert comprises an area of over 250,000 square miles, over 20% of the total land area of India, the very size might seem to indicate that the region is indeed the solution to the problem mentioned. This, however, would be misleading. Portions of the region lying to the southeast of the Aravalli range, are already up to 30% under food grain cultivation though with generally very poor yields. Further, the more profound desert region of the northwest sector is under partial cultivation but even with favorable conditions perhaps should not be expected to be transformed into an area of intensive cultivation, but may be more suitable for limited patterns of land use such as pasturage.

But while the reclamation of the Rajputana desert is not in itself the solution to India's problems, its importance is still great. Partial relief to the food and land problem provides time during which India can achieve further industrialization, population stabilization, and eventual resolution of her economic problems. The availability of reclaimable lands in this area is also of psychological importance to the nation in providing a real means by which the aspirations of the dispossessed farmer, for partition created many landless refugees, or the farmer whose inherited lands have become so fractionated as to be uneconomic, can be resolved. The region also provides a means by which some of India's international problems might be aided. The desert area under discussion is not confined to India but extends across into Pakistan. Problems of desert reclamation or surface stabilization to be effective must cover the entire area and this requires international cooperation. Through such a project as this, paths may be found to ease some of the issues under dispute between these two nations. Finally, as new lands are made available the occupancy of these lands should provide some opportunity for social experimentation. As was suggested above, patterns of inheritance in India have led to fractionization of land holdings beyond efficient levels. Provisions can be made to restrict such procedures in this new area and novel forms of cooperative units can be established to effectively use the new lands made available.

References

1. Trewartha, G., 1961: *The Earth's Problem Climates.* Madison, University of Wisconsin Press, p. 166.
2. Trewartha, G., *op. cit.*, 151–170. Contains a compact review.
3. Sawyer, J. S., 1947: The structure of the intertropical front over NW India during the SW monsoon. *Quart. J. Roy. Meteor. Soc.*, 73, 346–369.
4. Das, P. K., 1962: Mean vertical motion and non-adiabatic heat sources over India during the monsoon. *Tellus*, 14, 212–220.
5. Bryson, R. A., C. A. Wilson, III, and P. M. Kuhn, 1964: Some preliminary results of radiation sonde ascents over India. *Proc. WMO–IUGG Symp. Tropical Meteor., Rotorua, New Zealand, November 1963.* Wellington, New Zealand Meteor. Service, 737 pp.
6. Mani, A., and O. Chacko, 1962: Atmospheric turbidity measurements at Poona and Delhi. India Meteor. Dept., 6 pp. plus tables.
7. Bryson *et al.*, *op. cit.* A radiation sonde network of Poona, Delhi, Jodhpur and Calcutta was operated by the India Meteorological Department as part of this research.
8. Junge, C. E., 1962: Condensation nuclei profiles over India. Joint Indo-United States Balloon Flight Program 1961. GRD Research Report AFCRL-62-1135, 41–50.
9. Stein, Sir Aurel, 1944: A survey of ancient sites along the "lost" Sarasvati River. *Geographical J.*, 99, 173–182.
10. Ghosh, A., 1952: The Rajputana Desert—its archaeological aspect, Proc. Symp. on the Rajputana Desert. *Bull. National Institute Sci. India*, 1, 37–42.
11. *Indian Archaeology 1960–61—A Review (1961)*, pp. 31–32; *Archaeological Remains, Monuments and Museums*, Part I, pp. 4–7 (1963); *Indian Archaeology 1961–62—A Review (1964)*, pp. 39–44; *Indian Archaeology 1962–63 —A Review (1965)*, pp. 20–31. New Delhi.
12. *Indian Archaeology 1962–63—A Review (1965)*, p. 27.
13. Lal, B. B., 1963: A picture emerges: An assessment of the carbon-14 datings of the protohistoric cultures of the Indo-Pakistan subcontinent. *Ancient India*, Nos. 18 and 19, 210–211.
14. Agrawal, D. P., S. Kusumgar and D. Lal, 1965: Tata Institute radiocarbon date list III. *Radiocarbon*, 7, 291–295.
    Agrawal, D. P., and Sheela Kusumgar, 1966: Tata Institute radiocarbon date list IV. *Radiocarbon*, 8, 442–452.
15. Radiocarbon dates in *Radiocarbon*, 1, 6, 7 and 8.
16. *Radiocarbon*, 6, 227–228.
17. *Radiocarbon*, 7, 335.
18. Seth, S. K., 1961: A review of evidence concerning changes of climate in India during the protohistorical and historical periods. *Proc. WMO-UNESCO Symp. on Changes of Climate*, Rome, October, 443–454.
19. Hora, S. L., 1952: The Rajputana Desert: Its value in India's national economy, Proceedings of the Symposium on the Rajputana Desert. *Bull. National Institute Sci. India*, 1, 4.
20. Hora, *op. cit.*, p. 5.

142

19

The Dark Ages in Ancient History

I. The First Dark Age in Egypt[1]

BARBARA BELL

INTRODUCTION

In the history of the ancient Near East two striking Dark Ages have occurred. They occurred more or less simultaneously (within the limits of current dating accuracy) over a wide area extending at least from Greece to Mesopotamia and Elam, from Anatolia to Egypt, and probably beyond. In Egypt, where the chronology is best established, the first Dark Age began around 2200 B.C., when at the end of Dynasty VI Egypt, until then a very stable society, with seeming suddenness fell into anarchy. About the same time the Akkadian Empire disintegrated. Byblos and a number of other sites in Syria and Palestine were destroyed by fire and some were abandoned for a time. Troy II, the wealthy citadel of Schliemann's gold treasure, was destroyed by fire and rebuilt on only a very shabby scale. Lerna and other prosperous Argolid centers were burned and their destruction was followed by greatly lessened prosperity. In western and southern Anatolia "the end of the E.B. [Early Bronze] 2 period is marked . . . by a catastrophe of such magnitude as to remain unparalleled until the very end of the Bronze Age" (Mellaart, 1962); widespread destruction is followed by a general decline in material culture and a decrease by about 75 percent in the number of known settlements. We

may probably include also the decline of the Indus Valley civilization. The radiocarbon dates of Phase F (mature Harappan) lie between 2100 and 1900 B.C. (Dales 1965; half-life 5730), with an average of 1975 B.C. from 12 measurements. But when these dates are corrected for the systematic error in C-14 dates of this period, as determined by Suess (1967) and by Ralph and Michael (1969), the dates fall between about 2500 and 2250 B.C.

The second Dark Age began around 1200 B.C. It was marked by the disappearance of the Hittite Empire of Anatolia and the collapse of the Mycenaean civilization of Greece. About the same time, or a little later, Egypt went into a prolonged decline, while Babylonia and Assyria were also weak for most of the 1100's and 1000's.

When we turn to the revised *Cambridge Ancient History (CAH)* or other modern studies for explanation, we find numerous references to evidence of destruction by fire. The destruction is often attributed to invasions by barbarians about whom little is known, however, and for whose activities the archaeological evidence is often meager or nonexistent. Moreover Adams (1968) has pointed out that the interpretation of seemingly violent destruction and discontinuous layering in a habitation site is more complex and ambiguous

[1] I wish to take this opportunity to thank Dr. Nicholas B. Millet (Harvard University) for his interest, encouragement, and numerous helpful discussions throughout the course of this study; his critical reading of the semi-final draft and advice on the various translations was an aid of particular value because I do not myself have a reading knowledge of ancient Egyptian. The various theories set forth herein are, however, solely my responsibility.

I wish to thank also Professors Sterling Dow (Harvard University), Karl W. Butzer (University of Chicago), and Rhys Carpenter, each of whom kindly read the semi-final draft and made suggestions and comments which enabled me to improve the manuscript.

The chronology followed in this paper is that of the revised *Cambridge Ancient History*, particularly Smith (1962) and Hayes (1961). References (with a few exceptions in the text) will be found at the end of the paper, alphabetically by author, and by date.

than previously recognized, and cannot be considered clear evidence of either intermittent occupation or enemy attack. He thus urges more caution in inferring invasions when there is no clear positive evidence for the presence of invaders. But even where it is clear that barbarian invasions did occur, we are left with the question of whether they are a sufficient cause or explanation for the destruction of a number of apparently powerful and prosperous states, and why so many different barbarian tribes were stirred to attack centers of civilization at about the same time. Any one or two of the above disasters, standing alone, might be sufficiently explained by political factors. But the concentration in time of so many disasters and the universal absence of prosperity throughout the area strongly suggest a common underlying cause.

Of "historical truth," Frankfort (1951) wrote that a concept whereby "many seemingly unrelated facts are seen to acquire meaning and coherence is likely to represent a historical reality." It is the thesis of this study that the two Dark Ages, and the numerous disasters in the periods c. 2200-2000 and c. 1200-900 B.C., can be given coherence and can all be explained at once by a single primary cause. The cause I postulate as "historical reality" is drought—widespread, severe, and prolonged—lasting for several decades and occurring more or less simultaneously over the entire eastern Mediterranean and adjacent lands. This is not to deny the significance of contemporary political and social factors; it is, however, to assert that a climatic-economic deterioration of sufficient magnitude can set in motion forces beyond the strength of any society to withstand.

Such an hypothesis has indeed already been advanced by Rhys Carpenter (1966) for the Second Dark Age, c. 1200-900 B.C.; his argument is based primarily on study of the decline of Mycenaean Greece and the Hittite Empire. And in a subsequent paper I plan to discuss this period with primary reference to Egypt.

The present paper will examine the evidence for the hypothesis that the First Dark Age of Egypt, the so-called First Intermediate Period, was brought on by a similar prolonged and intense drought. Later papers will examine the evidence from other lands, but there are several advantages in beginning with Egypt:

First, Egypt was in ancient times a relatively isolated civilization, generally unified and free of civil war and, because of its formidable and well-defined natural frontiers, of foreign invasions. Thus we have here the best chance of tracing the interaction of man and his natural environment, and making plausible inferences from the level of economic prosperity about fluctuations in the resources provided by the natural environment.

Second, the chronology of Egypt, in the historical period from c. 3100 B.C. onward, is known with greater precision than that of any other ancient land. Thus whatever climatic fluctuations we deduce from Egyptian history will be relatively well dated. Moreover we can test them by looking for contemporaneous patterns, that is for fluctuations in the direction of greater aridity or of greater moisture, in other lands; and if similar sequences can be found, there is a possibility of improving the chronology of other lands.

Third, Egypt was a literate society, so that we may hope to find texts bearing on the conditions of the times, and it is in fact the discussion of such texts which forms the main section of this paper. Mesopotamia also offers the advantage of literacy, but its chronology is less certain; more importantly, the picture there is obscured by frequent warfare between the cities, the lack of natural frontiers, recurrent invasions on a large scale, and a greater complexity in climatic factors. In Egypt we have to do essentially with the volume of the Nile, and particularly of its annual flood; that is, we have a single climatic factor to consider, rather than the combination of river-floods and rainfall characteristic of Mesopotamia.

It may appear a bizarre hypothesis, even to those sympathetic to the concept of climate fluctuations as a factor in history, to link drought in the lands of the eastern Mediterranean, which derive their moisture mainly from winter rainfall, with Egypt which depends for its water on the Nile River—that is on the rainfall over central Africa (White Nile) and on the summer monsoon rains over the East African highlands (Blue Nile). Nevertheless there is a growing body of evidence that such a correlation does at times occur, and indeed that it has occurred over the past century. Studies by Kraus (1954; 1955a,b; 1956) and by Butzer (1961) indicate that the average rainfall was less in many regions in the first four decades of this century than in the late decades of the nineteenth century. This decline occurred over a wide area of the Near East and North Africa, including both the northern and southern fringes of the Sahara, northwest India (Jaipur) and Pakistan (Quetta), and the drainage basin of the Nile. The decrease in average rainfall occurred also in a number of other lands far beyond our present interest, such as parts of Australia (Kraus 1954) and the Dust Bowl of the United States (Butzer 1961). The change over from the moister to the drier climate regime occurred quite abruptly in many places between 1893 and 1908, with the exact date depending upon the region concerned. For the Nile, the annual average volume of water passing Aswan was about 25 percent less for the years 1899-1957 than for the years 1871-1898, with a clear and abrupt shift to the drier regime in 1899 (see Kraus 1956). "Without the tempering effect of dams and barrages, agriculture in the Nile Valley would have suffered badly" (Butzer 1961:50); and as a consequence of the widespread decline in rainfall, "Droughts of economic importance plagued the Levantine area in the 1920s and the entire Near East in the 1930s. Lake Aksehir in Central Anatolia dried out entirely in 1933. Similar conditions can be noted for the peripheries of the Sahara." And similarly in the Red Sea Hills of eastern Egypt, "vegetation was . . . more common prior to the desiccation that has taken place during the present century" (Trigger 1965:11).

This evidence from the past century makes it more plausible that most of the Near East and the Nile catchment basin were afflicted more or less simultaneously by some decades of severe drought at certain times in the past.

It is the prime thesis of my investigation, indeed, that a widespread drought, considerably more severe than the present one, occurred at intervals in the past and that it was precisely these droughts which precipitated the Dark Ages of Ancient History. Even a moderate drought can bring famine to the marginally productive lands on the edges of the deserts and can thereby motivate tribal migrations and invasions of the better-watered river valleys, a phenomenon discussed by numerous scholars (e.g. Brooks 1949). But a severe drought, such as postulated in this paper, and by Carpenter (1966), will bring crop failures and famine and varying degrees of civil disorder even to the richer lands. If sufficiently severe, a drought may not only incite invasions from marginal lands but may weaken the power of the major states to resist invasion, and in

some cases may even plunge them into a Dark Age without any serious foreign threat. In the case of Egypt the evidence which we shall consider presently favors the latter condition.

The first of the postulated Great Droughts in the Ancient Near East occurred from about 2200 to 2000 B.C. More precisely, as we shall see from a detailed consideration of the historical evidence, it occurred in two parts, at least in Egypt—and almost certainly in Iraq—the first around 2180 to 2150, and the second for a few years around 2000 B.C. In Egypt the crisis was not a failure of local rainfall, which was already at a very low level, but a severe failure of the annual floods of the Nile. It is as if Nature set two great exclamation points to emphasize the end of the Neolithic Wet Phase (NWP); or, to reverse Eliot, the NWP ended not with a whimper but with a bang.

Prehistoric Climate. A brief review of the earlier climate fluctuations may be useful before we take up the Dark Age itself, to put our central event in its paleoclimatic setting. It is now a fact beyond dispute that climate has been subject to change since the earliest times known to geologists. Because geology is a relatively young science, however, this fact has been recognized for only about a century; and at first only the larger fluctuations, the extremes of Ice Age and Interglacial, were recognized. But soon geologists found evidence that ice sheets, both in their expansion and their recession, were subject to interruption—that is, neither advances nor recessions proceeded smoothly and linearly, but each was from time to time interrupted by a reversal of the primary trend, a reversal lasting some hundreds to thousands of years. The Pleistocene Ice Age, now thought to cover some two to three million years, has been studied extensively in northern and central Europe and in North America, and much attention in Europe particularly has been given to the larger fluctuations that accompanied the retreat of the latest (Würm) ice sheet. We obtain an impression of damped oscillations, of gradually diminishing amplitude and duration, over the past ten to fifteen thousand years.

Although many details and dates remain to be fixed, it has been established beyond any reasonable doubt that significant fluctuations in climate have occurred in post-glacial times in northern and central Europe (see Brooks 1949, for a convenient[2]

---

[2] But unfortunately in some respects obsolete.

semi-popular summary; for more recent, and more technical, reviews, see Starkel 1966 and Frenzel 1966). It is, to me at least, *a priori* incredible that the climate should not also have fluctuated over all other areas of the earth. This, of course, is not to claim that there is anything *a priori* obvious about the direction and amplitude, or even the timing, of such fluctuations, which cannot be inferred by analogy, but must be determined from paleo-ecological, geological, and archaeological evidence.

The Mediterranean Basin, the Near East, and northern and central Africa, which are the regions of concern to us here, have received much less attention from natural scientists, primarily, it would seem, because the evidence is more subtle and difficult to detect. A number of isolated studies of particular areas were made, but only within the past decade have the relatively meager available facts been synthesized into a coherent picture for the area as a whole. This synthesis was made by Karl W. Butzer (1958, etc.), on whose work most of the following summary of climate variation is based. One of Butzer's most important and interesting contributions is his clarification of the relation in time between the larger subtropical and European climate changes.

For some time it has been recognized that central Africa and the margins of the deserts had a number of pluvial periods, but the relation in time of these tropical and subtropical wet periods to the northern ice sheets was much disputed. The probably most popular view held the two to be contemporaneous, and considered that the increased wetness in lower latitudes, particularly in Africa, was a simple and direct consequence of mid-latitude storm tracks being deflected southward by the presence of the ice sheets. Thus the maximum subtropical wetness would coincide with the maximal extent of the ice sheets. And indeed a number of scholars, beginning with Childe (1929:42, 46) and Toynbee (1934:304f), have linked the development of the great river-valley civilizations to the challenge of a gradually increasing desiccation following upon the recession of the ice sheets.

However this view is no longer tenable. After the work of Büdel and of Schaefer, it now appears that only the expansion phase had heavy rainfall, while the full and late glacial phases were relatively dry in middle-latitude Eurasia. Recent work also indicates that the last major pluvial in Africa is to be dated to the early Würm period, and that this

was a period of advance and growth for the central-east African mountain glaciers (Butzer 1963), although the most recent work (Butzer and Hansen 1968) indicates that the actual situation has many complexities. And finally, Butzer (1963) found that the period of glacial advance was the pluvial period in the Mediterranean Basin as well, whereas the terminal phases of the Pleistocene were quite dry. Thus he concluded (ibid. p. 212) that "subtropical pluvials cannot be genetically interpreted as secondary effects of the presence of continental ice sheets in higher latitudes . . . [but] . . . must be attributed to a primary change of the general circulation, presumably in immediate association with glacial advance in higher latitudes."

Contrary to the views of Childe (1929), Toynbee (1934), and most subsequent scholars who have mentioned prehistoric climate, including Carpenter (1966)—but excluding Hayes (1964), Trigger (1965), and the revised *CAH* (Butzer 1965)—the lands of the Near East and northern Africa were already as dry or drier 15,000 years ago than they are today. Recent evidence from Lake Zeribar in Iran, from the lowlands of Macedonia, and from the mountains of northwestern Greece, indicates that much of this region was then apparently a treeless landscape, perhaps resembling the semi-arid steppe of modern Anatolia (Wright 1968).

Since that time numerous fluctuations have occurred between relatively wetter and drier conditions, on a time scale of hundreds to thousands of years. In amplitude, and hence in terms of geological effects, these fluctuations are small and difficult to detect in the arid and semi-arid lands of interest to us here. However fluctuations that are too small to leave clear geological evidence can still be large enough to produce highly significant ecological effects, which may be reflected in archaeological evidence.

Early in his studies Butzer (1958) noted a curious parallelism between moisture trends in Europe and in the Near East. Every fluctuation to greater or lesser precipitation, the duration of which is measured in millennia, has been more or less parallel in Europe and in lower latitudes. In addition to the parallelism between Europe and the Near East, Butzer (1961) emphasizes that the major paleoclimatic shifts north and south of the Sahara have been, insofar as evidence is available, synchronous and not alternative. That is, the evidence (see also Kraus 1955a:202-204) supports an expanding and contracting Sahara Desert. Thus the ultimate meteorological explanation, Butzer points out, must be sought in terms of a mechanism that will enlarge or shrink the extension of the dry trade-wind circulation zone, which is responsible for the subtropical deserts, in both latitudinal directions at once.

The existence of a Neolithic Wet Phase, and a preceding very dry period, has been suspected in Egypt for several decades by various scholars, including Caton-Thompson and Gardner, Huzayyin, and Murray (1951), but in the absence of any systematic study of the overall evidence, there was little agreement on the duration, extent, and character of the NWP (Butzer 1958). It is outside the scope of the present study to review in any detail the evidence for the NWP in the Near East (see Butzer 1958; 1959b,c; 1965), a period which corresponds approximately to the relatively warm and wet Climatic Optimum or Atlantic Period (see Brooks 1949; Starkel 1966) in northern Europe. For northern Africa much of the evidence is archaeological, such as neolithic artifacts found in desert areas where man cannot now live, rock drawings of animal species that require at least a savanna type of vegetation, and fossil roots and tree stumps in wadi bottoms and the low desert where no trees grow today.

Decline of the Neolithic Wet Phase. "Overall, the Nubian and Egyptian evidence indicates a complex moist interval beginning before c. 7000 B.C., interrupted by some drier spells and terminating in stages between 2900 and 2350 B.C." (Butzer 1966:75). These stages have been documented (Butzer 1959c) by indirect archaeological evidence, including a study of the relative frequencies of various species of animals appearing in rock drawings, tomb and temple wall reliefs, and other art forms. At this time in northern Europe we have a transition to the Sub-Boreal period, which "may be characterized as warm but rather dry, with considerable variations in humidity. . . ." The study of lake levels gives evidence for "the occurrence of great oscillations in precipitation," as does also the periodic desiccation of peat bogs (Starkel 1966:27).

An interesting point for the present study is the extent to which the time-synchronism of wet and dry periods holds, or held in earlier times, over shorter time periods—periods of decades to centuries. The data on these smaller fluctuations are obscure and will remain so at least until the systematic errors (Suess 1967; Ralph and Michael 1969) have been fully determined and corrected for, or other more accurate methods of dating can be developed. We should nonetheless regard it as encouraging if a severe dry spell were found to occur in Europe in the same century as that for which we are postulating one in the Near East. Such may well be the case, for Brooks (1949:296f) cites evidence, from lake levels and peat bogs, for unusually dry conditions in central Europe around 2300-2000 and 1200-1000 B.C., although modern pollen studies (Frenzel 1966) cast doubt upon this picture. However this may eventually be resolved, conditions in Europe have no *necessary* bearing on the validity of our conclusions about conditions in Egypt.

Butzer considers that the NWP rains over Egypt had pretty well declined to their modern low level by the beginning of Dynasty VI, c. 2350 B.C. This conclusion is based in part on a change at this time in the character of hunting and desert scenes depicted on tomb and temple reliefs, a change both in the game hunted and in the background landscape. There appears also to have been a general exodus from the Libyan Desert in Dynasty VI times, evidenced by the cessation of rock paintings and the abandonment of Neolithic sites, together with the appearance, according to O. H. Myers, of Tehenu Libyans in the Nile Valley (Butzer 1958).

The specter of famine first clearly appears towards the end of Dynasty V, when a well-known relief from the causeway of the Pyramid of Unis depicts a group of severely emaciated people, evidently dying of hunger (Drioton 1942; Smith 1965:pl. 48B). Unfortunately no inscriptions have survived to reveal the circumstances of this scene, and nothing is known of either the nationality of the starving people or the cause of their plight—whether a failure of the Nile floods (an unlikely event for the King to wish to commemorate) or the ending of the NWP rains, which drove starving desert-dwellers to seek refuge in the Nile Valley.

It is not unlikely that the decline of the Early Bronze 2 culture in Greece and in Anatolia set in with the ending of the NWP, particularly in regions where many settlements were permanently abandoned, as in western and southern Anatolia (Mellaart 1962). To support more than speculation, of course, much additional study is needed. We may note, however, that four pieces of charcoal from the House of Tiles at Lerna (late EH II) give an average radiocarbon date of 2126 B.C. (from Weinberg 1965; half-life 5730); but this becomes c. 2500 B.C. when corrected for systematic error (see Suess 1967; and Ralph and Michael 1969). Also possibly relevant is the evidence (Wright 1968) for a reduction in percentage of pine pollen around Pylos shortly after 2000 B.C., and evidence for a reduction in the beech-fir forest of northwestern Turkey, dated to around 2000 B.C., changes which might "reflect either a change to a drier climate or deforestation." The dates here are a little late, but they are also quite uncertain (Wright, personal communication), so that the changes could well reflect the ending of the NWP.

But in Egypt the Old Kingdom civilization continued, under Dynasty VI, to flourish for some 150 years after the ending of the NWP. Most Egyptologists agree that the Pyramid complex of King Neferkare Pepi II, the last major monument of the Old Kingdom, exhibits the same high quality of craftsmanship as its predecessors and gives no hint of the Dark Age soon to engulf all aspects of Egyptian civilization. Moreover it appears that the climate of northeastern Africa remained severely arid, probably averaging slightly less rainfall than today, for at least some fifteen centuries, during which time Egypt had two periods of high civilization and three ages of decline.

This serves only to emphasize once again the well-known dependence of Egypt upon the Nile. Without a failure of the floods, it seems unlikely that the ending of the NWP would have caused Egypt more than some inconvenience and local disturbances, when desert nomads of necessity sought to settle in the Valley. Inscriptions indicate that many of them did settle in the Valley, finding employment with the army as mercenaries (Breasted 1906:311; Borchardt 1905), increasing the population and adding to the potential for trouble in any famine that might occur.

The Nile. A few words on the annual Nile floods may be useful here. Because rainfall over all but the northern Delta has long been rare and irregular, Egyptian farmers have depended for at least some 5000 years upon the annual flood of the Nile River to water their fields and prepare the soil for cultivation. The amount of any particular inundation—at least before the building of the modern system of dams and barrages—determined whether that year would bring plenty or famine or something intermediate. These annual floods are the direct consequence of the summer monsoon rainfall over the catchment basin of the Blue Nile and the Atbara in the highlands of Ethiopia. The maximum level of the flood waters in Egypt thus provides a measure of the amount of this rainfall.

According to Hayes (1964), in Middle Egypt the average difference between high and low water is 22′ (6.7 m.), with a yearly variation that depends on the volume of the equatorial rains; 4-5′ (1.2-1.5 m.) below average is a "bad Nile" and in antiquity a succession of these usually resulted in crop failures and famine, while a flood of 30′ (9 m.) or more would cause widespread destruction.

Deposits south of Wadi Halfa suggest that flood levels in early predynastic times were about 10 m. higher than today, that they declined in an oscillatory way to about 5 m. above today in early dynastic times, and to the present level by the time of the New Kingdom (Trigger 1965:31). It is hoped that the present study, in this and subsequent papers (now including Bell 1970), will provide additional details on the flood levels in historical times.

Fluctuations in climate during the past 4000 years have generally been either too small in amplitude or too short in duration to leave behind much geological evidence, as Butzer (1958, 1961) points out, so that it becomes increasingly necessary to resort to archaeological and literary sources, as we shall do in the main section of this paper. But on the fringelands of deserts the drifting of sand is a particularly sensitive indicator of changes in aridity and in aeolian activity. In Middle Egypt, Butzer (1959a,c) found evidence that a chain of dunes from the western desert invaded the valley and covered the alluvium with several meters of sand over a stretch about 175 km. in length and 0.5 to 3.5 km. in width. These fossil dunes are now covered by a few meters of mud, deposited mainly between about 500 B.C. and A.D. 300. The dune invasion was facilitated by weaker Nile floods and consequent shrinkage of the floodplain, as well as by increased aeolian activity and by an eastward retreat of the Bahr Yusef, a secondary branch of the Nile in Middle Egypt which drains into the Fayum lake. The dunes cannot be dated precisely, but a number of passages in the literary evidence to be examined presently, indicate that they were actively invading during the First Intermediate Period. A knowledge of their existence clarifies the meaning of a number of otherwise rather enigmatic passages.

Although the adequacy of the Nile flood is the main determinant of Egypt's prosperity, there are also phrases in the ancient texts, as we shall see, which seem to indicate that the low-water level was at times abnormally low, which in turn implies a deficiency of rainfall over sources of the White Nile in east-central Africa. This is not unlikely, for Brooks (1949) points out that in the records of the Nile floods available from A.D. 641 to 1800 there is a fair correlation between low-water level and flood height, although the low-water levels show the more violent fluctuations. Brooks' conclusion derives from his analysis of the tables of low- and high-water levels published by Toussoun (1925). Toussoun's volume also contains a chronological list of quotations on the level of the Nile and related events, compiled from Arab authors. Several times in years of abnormally low floods there is mention also of a remarkably low level of the "old waters" or pre-flood Nile. And conversely there is a tendency for the old waters to be high before a very large flood. More important, one obtains from these quotations also an impression that the total volume of flood water fluctuates more than the height of the flood. One frequently reads that the flood attained a normal height, then declined at once and there was famine, or at least scarcity, in Egypt.

THE FIRST DARK AGE IN EGYPT

It is now widely believed (Hayes 1961, 1962b; Wilson 1956; Gardiner 1961) that the real Dark Age lasted only some 20-25 years, from the end of Dynasty VI to the start of Dynasty IX, or from about 2180 to 2160. Although the details remain obscure and the primary cause open to dispute, some aspects of the trouble which occurred at the end of Dynasty VI seem clear: texts from the period indicate that hardly any form of civil disorder was absent, ranging from strife between districts, to looting and killing by infiltrating Asiatics in the Delta, to individual crime run riot, to revolution and social anarchy. Reference to famine occurs in several texts. This fact has of course been noted by a number of Egyptologists, including those cited immediately above, and the texts themselves have been intensively studied by Vandier (1936). But none of these scholars gives to famine the importance which I hope to show it

deserves as an explanation of the collapse of the Old Kingdom. Butzer (1959c:68; 1965) points out that a number of these documents refer to "famine resulting from low Niles rather than from human negligence," but analysis of the historical implications lay outside the scope of his investigation.

Although the real Dark Age was short, it had a severely traumatic effect on the psyche of the Egyptian educated classes; it produced a radical change in values and outlook that can only reflect severe shock and disillusionment. In the words of W. S. Smith (1965:87), "The earlier complacent sense of stability had been rudely shaken, and Egypt never regained that simple confidence in an enduring continuity." The collapse of the Old Kingdom was reflected in a new pessimistic literature "foreign to the spirit and thought of earlier times" (Smith 1962:55). This pessimistic literature, Černý (1952: 79) emphasizes, "was not the result of philosophical meditation but a reflection of historical events . . . and is in direct contradiction to the habitual optimistic attitude of the Egyptians to life."

In the absence of unambiguous evidence, various nonclimatic causes have been suggested for this time of trouble; none of them however seem sufficient to explain the magnitude of the effect.

The evidence for famine in ancient Egypt, given by written texts, has been studied by Vandier (1936), who points out that such evidence is scarce because the Egyptians had not the habit of recording their misfortunes for posterity. The principal data for his study are the autobiographical inscriptions of nomarchs (rulers of nomes or districts) who, their personal vanity having overcome national pride, boasted of having fed their towns and districts during the years of famine. Vandier found very few documents on famine during the Old Kingdom, and he attributed this to the strength of the central government—which made it relatively easy to store up large surpluses in years of good Niles and dispense them in years of poor Niles. I do not question the essential soundness of this point, but would add two qualifications. First, in these earlier times the provincial officials were neither as independent in the content of their inscriptions nor as firmly attached to a particular district. And second, as we have seen above, the Neolithic Wet Phase was ending gradually during the time of Dynasties V and VI. Thus while famine probably did threaten from time to time in the earlier years, the danger was unlikely to have

217

been as prolonged or severe, and was less likely
to have exhausted the stores of surplus grain.

Vandier lays great stress on the correlation between weakening of the authority of the central
government and the disastrous consequences of
insufficient floods. His study shows clearly that
such a correlation exists. The problem then is to
distinguish the symptoms of the disease from its
cause. Because of the meager evidence from these
troubled times, the question cannot be answered
with absolute certainty, but I hope to show that a
more consistent picture of "historical truth" results
from the hypothesis that prolonged insufficiency
of the floods destroyed a somewhat weakened central government than vice versa. The claim can
indeed be made that there is no other adequate
explanation for the complete and seemingly sudden
disintegration of both the government and Egyptian society that occurred at the end of the reign
of Pepi II of Dynasty VI, about 2180 b.c. In considering the ancient texts, I follow the viewpoint
of Gardiner (*JEA* 1:36) that one should avoid
undue skepticism about ancient documents, and
should rather "use their statements, in the absence
of conflicting testimony, as the best available evidence with regard to the periods of history to which
they relate."

*Texts relating to the first great famine, c. 2180-
2130 b.c.* Turning now to the written evidence
itself, we may first consider ANKHTIFI, who is
known from the inscriptions in his tomb at Moʻalla,
some 20 miles south of Luxor. This tomb has been
thoroughly studied by Vandier (1950) who is the
source for the quotations[3] which follow. Ankhtifi's
claim to his position is obscure—whether he held
it by birth or simply by his effective leadership in
troubled times—but he was nomarch of Hierakonpolis and of Edfu, two of the southernmost nomes
of Upper Egypt. It is generally agreed that he lived
early in the First Intermediate Period (First Dark
Age), before Inyotef I of Thebes unified the South
and proclaimed himself King of Upper Egypt
about 2134 b.c. Inyotef would surely not have tolerated a hostile prince so near at hand, and Ankhtifi's
inscriptions describe a war he initiated against the
Theban nome, although the outcome is obscure.
Beckerath (1962, *JNES* 21:140) points out that
Ankhtifi must have lived at the virtual start of the

first Intermediate Period, because his inscriptions
give evidence that when he was young Abydos
was still the residence of an "Overseer of Upper
Egypt" who was recognized by the nomarchs.
Toward the end of Dynasty VIII that office had
lost all importance. Thus we may consider that
Ankhtifi's inscriptions provide a picture—probably
the best available—of conditions in the darkest part
of the Dark Age.

Most significant for our purpose is his vivid description of the famine that afflicted Upper Egypt:
*...I fed/kept alive Hefat (Moʻalla), Hormer, and
(?)...at a time when the sky was (in) clouds/
storm (igp) (was a tumult?) and the land was in
the wind* (probably the clouds of a memorably severe season or seasons of dust storms), *(and when
everyone was dying) of hunger (hkr,* the common
word for hunger) *on this sandbank of Hell (tzw
of Apophis,* a place in the underworld where the
dragon-serpent, Apophis, nightly threatened to de-
vour the sun god, Re).

As supporting evidence for the dust-storm interpretation, we note Butzer's (1959b:66) finding that
at Hierakonpolis, nearby, a predynastic cemetery
was denuded by wind action, which removed up
to 2 m. of fairly resistant silt and exposed the burials, probably some time after the end of Dynasty
VI. At Abydos, some 100 km. to the north, the
"funerary palace" of Queen Merneith of Dynasty I
suffered such intense denudation (and perhaps also
deliberate destruction) that its walls were reduced
to only a few courses of bricks, partly buried beneath a layer of sand by the time of Dynasty XII,
when a few small mastabas were constructed over
the ruins (B. J. Kemp 1966, *JEA* 52).

Vandier considers the above-quoted sentence of
Ankhtifi's to be a particularly inspired masterpiece
of erudition, made up essentially of phrases from
the Pyramid Texts, aptly selected to describe the
current local troubles. The reference to the *tzw* of
Apophis is useful in helping to give us a clearer
idea of a key word, *tzw*,[4] which occurs in several of
the famine texts of this period and merits some discussion. The word *tzw* is generally translated *sand-
banks* by Egyptologists. For the famine texts, Vandier (1936:75) considers two hypotheses: either the
tzw are the sandbanks of the Nile that men cultivate at low waters and that are submerged through

---

[3] All quotations attributed to Vandier are my translations
from his French.
[4] The correct printing of this term, I understand, is *tzw*

with the t underlined. The line under the t, however, would
have to be set by hand and because the word occurs so frequently it proved impractical to include the hand-set underline.

ost of the inundation; or they are the higher
nds on each bank of the Nile susceptible to being
ooded for some weeks at the time of the inunda-
on. If the flood is weak, the *tzw* in the first hy-
othesis (lower sandbanks) do not remain long
overed by water, and in the second (upper sand-
anks) they are not covered at all. Although pre-
erring the "upper" hypothesis, Vandier translates
zw as *year(s) of low Nile*, and thus of famine by
etonymy. However, the texts in which *tzw* ap-
ears seem to describe quite dire conditions of
amine, so that I find the first of Vandier's hypothe-
es, the lower sandbanks, the one more probably
orrect. Also for this reason, I do not accept Van-
ier's suggestion that *tzw* was already at this time
 stale over-used image meaning simply famine
om whatever cause, but consider it highly proba-
le that *tzw* was an image meaning *poor Nile* by
etonymy, and famine by consequence.

Moreover it is not clear, either from the exam-
les we shall encounter below or from those cited
y Vandier without a context of famine, that the
zw have to do with any sort of cultivated land.
hey may be simply sandbars in the river, which
re exposed in the season of low water, and remain
xposed, more or less, according to the degree of
eficiency in the flood. This interpretation would
till leave *tzw* as an appropriate figure of speech
 mean famine due to insufficient flood, but not
or famine from other causes. This view is sup-
orted also by the phrase from the Book of the
Dead from whose prototype Vandier (1950) be-
eves that Ankhtifi's scribe derived the terms of
e tomb inscription: *O master of the stormclouds
gp) . . . O thou who sailest the bark (of Re) by
his sandbar (tzw) of Apophis. . . .* Thus the ap-
earance of *tzw* in a context of famine may, and
deed should be taken as evidence of a very low
ood, quite sufficient in itself to cause severe famine
ithout any political complications.

Returning now to the inscription of Ankhtifi,
ve find a very severe famine indeed: . . . *All of
Upper Egypt was dying of hunger (ḥḳr), to such a
egree that everyone had come to eating his chil-
ren, but I managed that no one died of hunger
n this nome. I made a loan of grain to Upper
Egypt. . . . I kept alive the house of Elephantine
uring these years, after the towns of Hefat and
Hormer had been satisfied. . . . The entire country
ad become like a starved (?) grasshopper, with
eople going to the north and to the south (in*

*search of grain), but I never permitted it to happen
that anyone had to embark from this to another
nome. . . .*

Vandier (1936:8) points out that this is one of
only two known references to cannibalism in Ancient Egypt, an act of desperation that also occurred during famines in mediaeval Arab Egypt
(see Toussoun 1925:458-474, for details). Vandier,
and Gardiner too (1961:111), are inclined to doubt
that we should take this part literally, in spite of
the numerous other contemporary references to a
lack of grain. I suggest that while the "everyone"
is surely an exaggeration, instances of cannibalism
did occur, else why should it even occur to Ankhtifi's scribe to record such an atrocity? The rarity of
the practice, and the probability that it occurred at
all, only serve to make more vivid the desperation
of the people in these years of low Niles (*tzw*).

It is noteworthy that virtually none of the famine
inscriptions from the Dark Age mention the name
of any king, a drastic change from the style of Old
Kingdom inscriptions. Ankhtifi, indeed, does make
passing mention of a king in the isolated inscription: *Horus brings/brought (or, May Horus bring)
a (good) inundation for his son Ka-nefer-Re.* The
identity of this king (Nefer-ka-Re?) is quite uncertain and useless for dating the tomb more precisely.
But I suggest that Ankhtifi probably had no faith
in any king for whom Horus sent no good inundation; but when a good flood did finally come he may
have thought it prudent preparation for the afterlife
to offer a phrase of recognition. Or, if we translate
the verb in the past tense, the king could be Neferkare Pepi II of Dynasty VI, who ruled in Ankhtifi's
youth, before the bad times, and the phrase intended
as a criticism of present kings. Or it may be simply
a magic wish.

For vividness of phrasing and interest in natural
conditions (sandstorms), no one equals the author
of the tomb inscriptions of Ankhtifi. Another famine text, however, that Vandier (1950) considers
to be contemporary with it or only slightly later is
the stele of Iti (Cairo 20.001) of Gebelein: . . . *I
made Gebelein live during the years of misery
(ḳsnt), at a time when 400 men found themselves
in . . (?). . I gave wheat from Upper Egypt to
Iuni and to Hefat (Ankhtifi's town) after Gebelein
had been sustained; at a time when Thebes descended and ascended the stream to search for grain
. . . I never let men of Gebelein go up and down*

the stream to another nome to look for grain . . .
(Vandier 1936).

Also probably from this period is the stele of
MERER (Černý 1961) in the Cracow Museum and
of unknown provenance. Merer calls himself . . .
overseer of the slaughterers of the House of Khuu
(probably nomarchs of Edfu, according to Fischer
1962, *Kush* 10:333) and recounts how he took care
of his family during the famine, and offered for
thirteen rulers: . . . *I was a pure one to slaughter
and to offer in two temples on behalf of the ruler;
I offered for thirteen rulers . . . I acquired (property) . . . I fed my brothers and sisters, I buried him
who was dead and fed him who was alive wherever I alighted in this famine (on this sandbar,
tzw) which occurred. I shut off all their fields and
their mounds in town and in the country, I did not
allow their water to inundate for someone else . . .
I caused Upper Egyptian barley to be given to the
town and I transported for it a great number of
times.* . . . Here we have one of the clearer linkings
of *tzw*, a shortage of irrigation water, and famine.

The stelae of Iti and of Merer contain clues that
may explain much of the fighting which occurred
early in this Dark Age, in the references to Thebes
searching upstream and downstream for grain, and
to Merer's efforts to increase his family's supply of
the meager floods at the expense of others. Raids
on the granaries of neighboring districts probably
occurred, as well as violent disputes over water
rights.

Another interesting text comes from Middle
Egypt, where the nomarch of Assiut, KHETY, refers to building new irrigation works and to providing for his people in a time of famine (*tzw*)
in his tomb inscriptions. His date has not been
fixed with certainty, but he evidently grew up at
the royal court in a time of relative calm, if we may
judge from the inscription stating that he learned
swimming with the royal children. There is no
mention of war with Thebes, and Breasted (1906:
405) accordingly suggests that he lived before the
nomarch Tefibi and the latter's son Khety, each of
whom mention war with the south in which they
played an active role on behalf of the Herakleopoli-
tan king of Lower Egypt. Vandier (1936) and
Hayes (1961) also agree in placing this Khety
before Tefibi. Thus we may tentatively consider
that he grew up in the late years of Pepi II, spent
his adult life in the Dark Age, and was able to
maintain a degree of order in his nome and pre-

serve his people from the worst suffering of the
famine. The relevant passages, as kindly translated
for me by N. B. Millet, read:

. . . *I made a monument* (probably, a canal) *in
-- a substitute for the river, of 10 cubits; I excavated for it upon the ploughlands; I provided a
gate . . . in brick . . . in one (act of) building, without dispossessing anyone of any house/property.* . . .

*I nourished my town, I acted as (my own) ac-
countant in regard to food (?) and as giver of water
in the middle of the day, in order to be very wary
of ??? . . in the island(?) I made a dam for this
town, when Upper Egypt was a desert (?), when
no water could be seen. I closed my (?) frontiers
. . . (to outsiders) . . . I made (agricultural) highlands out of swamp and caused the inundation to
flood over old ruined sites. I made ploughlands
out of -- ? -- all people who were in thirst drank.
. . . I was rich in grain when the land was as a
sandbank (tzw), and nourished my town by measuring grain.* . . .

We have in this inscription two of the clearer
references to a low Nile: . . . *when no water could
be seen* . . . suggesting that the White Nile too
was very low at times; and . . . *when the land was
as a sandbank (tzw)* . . . which suggests that Khety
was a contemporary of those others above who
lived in the time of the *tzw*. Khety's dam was most
probably a barrier on the alluvial flats designed to
retain on his fields as much water as possible in the
event of a too-brief flood, a not uncommon cause
of scarcity or semi-famine in the Islamic era (see
Toussoun 1925:455ff; and above, under Ankhtifi).

The word *tzw* appears in four additional texts
collected by Vandier (1936), three of which are
graffiti from Hat-Nub, a quarry in the Hare Nome
in Middle Egypt. (The fourth is Turin 1310, discussed in the following section.) Graffito 20,
from the 6th year of the nomarch NEHERI, reads
in its relevant part: (*I was a man) who . . . kept
alive (nourished) his town during the years of low
Niles (tzw), who supplied it when there was nothing, who gave aid to it without making any distinction between the great and the small.* . . . Graffiti
23 and 24, by two different sons of Neheri, and
within a year or two of 20 in date, state in almost
identical words: . . . *I nourished my town, so that
it was supplied wholly during the low Niles (tzw)
of the country, when there was nothing.* . . .

References to warfare form another major topic
of these same graffiti from Hat-Nub. Egyptologists

have not agreed on the identity of the primary com-
batants nor on the dates of Neheri and his sons,
for one depends upon the other. Faulkner (1944)
gives reasons to interpret the war as a rebellion by
Neheri and his sons against an early Herakleopoli-
tan King (of Dynasty IX ?), that is, before c. 2133
when the nomarch of Thebes established an independent kingdom in Upper Egypt. Hayes (1961),
however, believes that the texts refer to a battle
in the final war by which, c. 2050, the Theban King
Nebhepetre Mentuhotep brought about the forcible
reunification of Upper and Lower Egypt and established the Middle Kingdom. If we accept the
interpretation of Faulkner, we have all known *tzw*-
famines together within a period of 50 years or
less, between c. 2180 and c. 2130. The interpretation
of Hayes (1961) would give us a second, presumably brief, *tzw*-famine around 2050. While this is
not impossible, it is not substantiated by any other
evidence. Moreover, the word *tzw* has not been
found in famine texts (Vandier 1936: 158) outside
the First Intermediate Period. The appearance of
the word in these Hat-Nub graffiti thus lends support to the early dating and to Faulkner's interpretation of the warfare as a revolt by Neheri
against the king. It is natural then to wonder if the
revolt may not have been motivated, at least in part,
by Neheri's unwillingness to pay taxes, that is, to
send any of his nome's scarce grain to the capital.

A tantalizing reference to another sort of violence appears in the tomb stele of NEFER-YU,
from Dendera, probably early in the Dark Age
(Hayes 1953:139), who calls himself *Chancellor
of the King of Lower Egypt*, in this period often
a purely honorary title. Nefer-yu recounts, in addition to his acts of conventional charity, that he
aided his superiors during the troubled times. Unfortunately the translation of the critical line, and
thus the exact nature of the trouble, are not agreed
upon. As translated by Hayes (1953), Nefer-yu
claims: . . . *I gave bread to the hungry (ḥḳr) and
clothes to the naked . . . I succored the great ones
until the year when slaughter was ended. I wrought
mightily with my oxlike arm in order to be established. . . .* But according to Fischer (1968:207):
. . . *I nourished the great in the year of famine. I
wrought greatly with my arm that I might endure
with my children . . .*

However, the slaughter referred to in Hayes'

translation is depicted in several verses (e.g.: *Nay
but the children of princes, men dash them against
walls. . . . The highborn are full of lamentations,
and the poor are full of joy. Every town saith: "Let
us drive out the powerful from our midst. . . ."*)
in the lament of IPUWER, more commonly known
as the Admonitions of an Egyptian Sage. Since
both the beginning and the ending of the manuscript are lost, the circumstances evoking the poet's
lament are unknown. Although van Seter (1964,
JEA 50) presents arguments for assigning the work
to the Second Intermediate Period, most Egyptologists consider it more probably belongs to the
First. The most compelling argument is given by
Erman (1927), who points out that 'the work is
undoubtedly older than the "Instruction of Amenemhet," since the latter quotes a passage, interpo-
lated in corrupt form where it makes no sense, from
the "Admonitions" where, on external grounds,
the passage certainly belongs.

Gardiner, Posener, Hayes, and others consider
that Ipuwer was most probably an eye witness of
the anarchy he laments—civil strife and social
revolution (of a people made desperate by famine),
lawlessness of every sort, including tomb robbery,
and infiltration of the Delta by Asiatics. To the
modern Western mind, the text gives an impression
of disorganization as great as that existing in Egypt
itself at the time. It illustrates what W. S. Smith
(1962:61), in speaking of the Pyramid Texts, called
the Egyptian "tendency to assemble an accumulated
mass of material without synthesis. Contradictions
are not resolved but presented side by side." The
Lament of Ipuwer contains a number of such contradictions; one of the more glaring appears when
we read in one verse that everyone is starving, and
in another that he who formerly had nothing now
has many good things.

I quote below at some length from this important
account probably by an eye-witness. I have aimed
to include every verse that seems to pertain to natural, as opposed to purely social, conditions, but
have included a few of the latter also to give a
more representative impression. The translation is
taken primarily from Faulkner (1964, 1965), with
some phrases and notes from Erman (1927) and
Wilson (1955).[5] Explanatory notes in parentheses
are identified by the initial of the translator (F, E,

---

[5] My choice of which translation to use for each line was
determined by my general concept of environmental conditions, a concept which is supported by the less ambiguous texts
that we have already discussed.

and W); in the absence of any initial, the comments are my own.

But first, to stimulate imaginations that have never witnessed severe famine, we requote from Carpenter (1966:69) part of a description of an actual famine that occurred not so long ago in northeast Brazil: "In 1953, following three preceding years of unremitting drought, the people of the burnt-out countryside descended en masse, armed with every available weapon, to sack and pillage the settlements where any food had been stored. Always . . . there comes a time, a homicidal moment, when the famished cannot longer endure the sight of the well-nourished. Kinsman and friend alike must succumb to their desperation."

We turn now to Ipuwer and his lament over the state of Egypt in this Dark Age: . . . *The inhabitants of the Delta carry shields . . . the tribes of the desert have become Egyptians everywhere. . . . Indeed, the plunderer is everywhere and the servant takes what he finds. . . .*

Indeed, the Nile overflows, yet none plough for it. Everyone says: "We do not know what will happen throughout the land." (E: No one has enough confidence in these times of uncertainty to till the fields.) Perhaps this was the year that Ankhtifi took over Edfu, and found certain areas flooded due to the incompetence of his predecessor. Even in a period of prolonged drought a more or less adequate flood will surely occur from time to time, as an occasional deficient flood will occur in a period of generally liberal ones. A general comment by Frankfort (1951:105) may be illuminating here: "Agriculturalists are inevitably the prey of occasional calamities because they are dependent on weather and water. But if disasters follow one another frequently without relief . . . there is no inducement for the peasant to continue his labours at all."

Indeed, women are barren and none conceive.[6] *Khnum fashions (men) no more because of the condition of the land . . . hearts are violent, plague is throughout the land, blood is everywhere . . . many dead are buried in the river; the stream is a sepulchre and the place of embalmment has become a stream* (E: the corpses are too numerous to be buried; they are thrown into the water like dead cattle). . . . *Squalor is throughout the land, and*

there is no one whose clothes are white in these times. . . .

Indeed, the land turns round as does a potter's wheel. The robber possesses riches. . . . (Considering the second sentence, the first would seem to refer to the social order; but I wonder whether it might not refer also to the land itself, keeping in mind Ankhtifi's sandstorms, and Butzer's invading dunes, and possible shiftings in the course of the Nile.)

Indeed, the river is blood, yet men drink of it. Men shrink from human beings and thirst after water . . . (Perhaps, the river is full of corpses, but men are so desperate for water that they drink anyway).

Indeed, the ship of (the Southerners) has broken up; towns are destroyed and Upper Egypt has become an empty/dry waste . . . ("dying of hunger on the sandbanks of Apophis"; Butzer [1959b] himself suggests this passage may refer to invading sand dunes).

Why really, crocodiles (sink) down because of what they have carried off, for men go to them of their own accord (W: suicide in the river). *It is the destruction of the land. . . . Men are few. He that lays his brother in the ground is everywhere* (E: gravediggers are everywhere).

Indeed, the desert is throughout the land, the nomes are laid waste (probably another reference to the invading dunes, although previously [E, W] interpreted as "desert dwellers"). *Barbarians from outside have come to Egypt, there are really no Egyptians anywhere. . . . Good things are throughout the land, yet house-wives say: "Oh that we had something to eat!"*

None sail north to Byblos today (due no doubt largely to the chaotic conditions in Egypt; however Byblos itself was destroyed by fire about this time [Wilson 1956:100; R. de Vaux 1966, *CAH* fasc. 46]).

Nay, but the entire Delta marshland is no (longer) hidden. The confidence (trusted defense?) *of the Northland is now a trodden road* (E: the natural protection of the Delta afforded by its swamps is no longer of avail). *The inaccessible place . . . belongs now as much to them that knew it not, as to them that knew it, and strangers are versed in the crafts of the Delta.* (Probably, because of low waters, including the White or non-flood Nile,

---

[6] "In times of famine . . . the birth rate is greatly reduced, largely, it seems, because of the actual physiological effect of food shortage in its various aspects . . . ," India *Famine Inquiry Commission, Final Report* (Delhi 1945) 86.

strangers can get about easily in the Delta which is no longer protected by being islands and marsh-lands; cf. Neferty, Texts from c. 2002 . . . below, *The river of Egypt is empty, men cross over the water on foot.*)

. . . *"Cakes are lacking for most children; there is no food. . . . What is the taste of it like today?"* Indeed, magnates are hungry and perishing . . . cattle moan because of the state of the land . . . the children of princes are dashed against walls, and the children of prayer are laid out on the high ground* (E: want drives people to expose them). (More likely, many young children, who are always particularly susceptible to famine, are dying and people cannot afford proper burials for them.)

Indeed, the ways are watched; men sit in the bushes until the benighted traveller comes in order to plunder his burden. . . . He is belabored with blows of a stick and murdered. . . . Indeed, that has perished which yesterday was seen . . . commoners coming and going in dissolution (F: at the point of death).

Nay, but men feed on herbs and drink water; neither fruit nor herbage can be found any longer for the birds and . . . (?) . . . is taken away from the mouth of the swine, without it being said (as aforetime): "This is better for thee than for me," for men are so hungry.* (E: men are now them-selves eating that which they used to feed to the poultry and the pigs.)

Indeed, everywhere barley has perished and men are stripped of clothes, spice, and oil; everyone says: "There is none." The storehouse is empty and its keeper lies stretched on the ground (dead). . . . *The writings of the scribes of the cadaster (?) are destroyed, and the grain of Egypt is common prop-erty* (F: looted). (The granaries have been at-tacked and looted by the starving people.)

Behold, things have been done which have not happened for a long time; the king has been de-posed by the rabble. . . . He who was buried as a falcon (is devoid?) of biers, and what the pyramid concealed has become empty (F: the living king is deposed and the dead one is disinterred). (The ingenuity expended by the kings of Dynasty XII to build robber-proof burial chambers lends further support to the idea that the royal tombs of the Old Kingdom were vandalized during this Dark Age [Edwards 1961]). . . . *The land has been de-prived of the kingship by a few lawless men. . . . The Residence is afraid because of want, and (men*

go about?) *unopposed to stir up strife. . . . The possessor of wealth now spends the night thirsty . . . he who had no shade is now the possessor of shade, while the erstwhile possessors of shade are now in the full blast (?) of the storm. . . . The statues are burnt and their tombs destroyed* (a fur-ther reference to vandalism in the cemeteries).

. . . *Authority, Knowledge, and Truth are with you* (the King), *yet confusion is what you set throughout the land, also the noise of tumult. . . . You have acted so as to bring those things to pass. . . . You have told lies* (E: lies are told thee), *and the land is brushwood* (E: kaka, elsewhere a plant that easily catches fire). (Thus the vegetation is so dry it easily catches fire.) *All these years are strife, and a man is murdered on his house-top even though he was vigilant in his gate-house. . . .* The King is here blamed for the condition of the coun-try, presumably before he was deposed, but in such general terms that his sins of omission or commis-sion remain altogether obscure. However, see be-low, Discussion.

. . . *The troops whom we marshalled for our-selves have turned into foreigners and have taken to ravaging.* (The native recruits, or the merce-naries [Decline of the Neolithic Wet Phase, above] are quite out of control.) . . . *What has come to pass through it is informing the Asiatics of the state of the land* (that they can invade it with impunity). (This suggests that the collapse or revolt of the Egyptian army preceded any invasion or infiltra-tion by Asiatics that added to the woes of the Egyptians.)

The basic cause of all the troubles lamented by Ipuwer is singularly obscure if we consider this text alone. There are several references to famine, to the land becoming as desert, and one to plague, but we look in vain for a direct lament about the level of the floods or even a reference to *tzw*. In the light of other inscriptions, indeed, we wonder if the Egyptians had some religious taboo, or at least a superstitious disinclination, about speaking critically of the Nile. Or one might agree with Van-dier (1936) that civil disorder was the primary cause of the famine, but then one is left with no adequate explanation for the civil disorder. Ipuwer's reproaches to the King are in the most general terms; he gives no clue to the grievances which may have transformed the normally peaceful and docile Egyptian peasants into a violently rebellious rabble. Nor does he reproach any nomarch in particular (or nomarchs in general) with carrying on civil war, for destroying the state with his selfish ambitions. The traditionally unwarlike, unmilitary character of the Egyptian peasant (Kees 1961:141) provides an additional plausibility-argument that famine was originally the cause of civil disorder rather than the result of it, although then civil disorder may well have delayed recovery from the famine. Spontaneous combustion into civil war of such extreme destructiveness as must be assumed if we are to account for so major a famine, seems to me decidedly un-Egyptian, and not to be accepted without more clear and compelling evidence. On the other hand, some of the other texts, especially those designating famine as the time of the *tzw*, seem to indicate clearly a link between very low floods (*tzw*) and severe famine.

Although I have emphasized the word *tzw* because of its clear implication of "low Nile" and its appearance in texts describing the most severe conditions of famine, *tzw* is not the only word that has been interpreted to mean famine in ancient Egypt. Vandier (1936:59-93) identifies and discusses a number of other words, some of which are even more indirect. One of the more interesting (kindly called to my attention by Dr. Millet) which is found in famine contexts of this period is *snb-ib*, literally *the heart is healthy*. The use of this euphemism or "antiphrase" translated by Vandier (1936:90) as *years of courage*—and which could well be imagined, although we have no evidence, as a condensed reference to some currently popular phrase such as "The heart is healthy, though the body is weak"—may be taken as further evidence of the reluctance of the ancient Egyptians to speak plainly of a failure of the Nile floods.

It is noteworthy that not only do our texts fail to speak directly of the Nile, but also they never indicate that any deity is in any way concerned with the disaster. In Egyptian disaster-literature, the gods are neither held responsible for the disaster nor prayed to for relief. Their absence may easily pass unnoticed by the modern western mind. Yet it is quite otherwise in Mesopotamian disaster-literature, where the disaster may be explicitly described as an affliction sent by a god, particularly by the chief god, Enlil—for no evident reason as in the Lament over the Destruction of Ur, or to reduce the human population which had become so numerous and noisy that they interfered with the

sleep of the gods as in Atrahasis (*ANET*, pp. 455-463 and 104, respectively).

There are a few additional texts which may throw an indirect light on the condition of the Nile and on related social conditions. One of these is a Hymn to the Nile (Wilson 1955:372) which was originally composed, most probably, in the Middle Kingdom. Although not strictly an historical document, it is worth quoting for an impression of the conditions which the Egyptians, not long after the Dark Age, associated with a low Nile:

. . . *If he is sluggish, the nostrils are stopped up* (because it is so dry and dusty?), *and everybody is poor. If there be (thus) a cutting down in the food-offerings of the gods, then a million men perish among mortals, covetousness is practiced, the entire land is in a fury, and great and small are on the execution-block. . . . (But) when he rises, then the land is in jubilation. . . .*

. . . *If thou are (too) heavy (to rise), the people are few, and one begs for the water of the year. (Then) the rich man looks like him who is worried, and every man is seen (to be) carrying his weapons. There is no companion backing up a companion. There are no garments for clothing; there are no ornaments for the children of nobles. . . . He* (the Nile) *who establishes truth in the heart of men, for it is said: "Deceit comes after poverty"* (W: poverty from a low Nile brings lawlessness). . . .

Some of the consequences of a low Nile cited here seem reminiscent of Ipuwer's laments and quite excessive for one year under a strong government, and it is natural to infer that the Hymn reflects memories of the many years of very low Niles of the First Intermediate Period.

Texts from the years c. 2150-2000 B.C. By 2130 or a little earlier there were signs of improvement in natural conditions and in political stability. In the north, Dynasty X came to power, with a King Neferkare and his two strong and long-lived successors, Wahkare Khety and Merikare ruling from Herakleopolis over Lower Egypt. In the south, the nomarch of Thebes, Inyotef, established a rival dynasty (XI), declaring himself King of Upper Egypt, c. 2133, as the Horus Sehertowy; he was followed by Inyotef II, Horus Wahankh, who reigned for some 50 years (c. 2117-2069), and by Inyotef III, Horus Nakhtnebtepnefer for 8 years (c. 2068-2061) according to the chronology of Hayes (1961).

Although political stability had clearly improved

Vandier (1936:12) points out nine funerary stelae which he dates to the period of the Inyotef (Antef) kings and which contain an assertion that the owner saved his district or town by distribution of grain in a time of famine (most commonly, *burdensome years, or years of misery, ḳsnt*). Hayes (1961) also discusses a number of these Upper Egyptian stelae.

The word *tzw* appears in only one (Turin 1310) of these inscriptions, in an enigmatic passage which reads (Vandier 1936): *He* (the king?) *repelled (?) the years of famine (tzw) from the land. He*, Vandier suggests, is most probably the founder of the dynasty, Inyotef I. In the light of my general thesis, this may be interpreted to mean that the years of very low Niles (*tzw*) and of severe famines came to an end under his rule, as it is reasonable to believe on other grounds, and King Inyotef, as a true Horus King, is claiming credit for the improvement (see Discussion, below).

This group of inscriptions seem to describe conditions less severe than the time of the *tzw*, and apparently we should imagine that climate conditions improved in a fluctuating manner, with years of good inundation becoming more frequent and deficient years less frequent and less severely deficient. For completeness I include the most relevant passages, translated from Vandier (1936), although because of uncertainties in dating they contribute no great amount of additional information. The first seven (following Vandier's numbering) come from the time of Inyotef I, or slightly earlier, that is, to the later years of the first great drought.

1) Stele of Djari, of Qurneh: . . . *I was a great provider for their houses, in the year of famine (rnpt snb-ib), I gave to those whom I did not know as well as to those whom I did know. . . .*

2) The stele of Iti of Gebelein, already quoted above, is considered by Hayes to be somewhat later than the inscriptions of Ankhtifi, but not necessarily as late as Inyotef I.

3) Stele of Heka-ib (BM 1671), also of Gebelein, and according to Vandier (1936, 1950), contemporary with Iti: . . . *I have provided this entire town with Upper Egyptian grain for several years, without counting (?). . . . I gave oil to Hierakonpolis after my town had been provided for. . . .*

4) Stele of Djehouti of Qurneh: . . . *I supplied the temple of Amun during the years of misery (ḳsnt). . . .*

5) Turin 1310: *He* (the king?) *repelled the years of low Niles (tzw) from the land.*

6) Stele of Antefoker (BM 1628): . . . *I possessed barley and wheat; I gave barley and wheat to the hungry, and I supported everyone in my vicinity during the famine (hḳrw), acting in such a way that no one died. . . .*

7) Stele of Senni (Cairo 20500): . . . *I measured out life-giving grain of Upper Egypt for this entire town in the palace of the count . . . during the miserable years of famine (ḳsnt nt snb-ib).*

The last two of the nine stelae are several decades later; one of them is clearly dated by the name of King Inyotef III. This one (8), the stele of Ideni of Abydos (Cairo 20502), reads in part: . . . *I was a man who gathered his energy in the day of misery (hrw n ḳsnt) . . . a man of whom the Horus Nakhtnebtepnefer, King of Upper and Lower Egypt, son of Re, Inyotef (III), living forever, (said?) on the subject of the plan to keep alive (nourish) this town: "He has done all that I ordered throughout the entire country."*

And finally (9) the stele of . . (?) . . . (Cairo 20503): . . . *I kept alive (nourished) my town, in the year of misery (ḳsnt), so that my name would be good. . . .*

These two stelae indicate a year of scarcity, although not necessarily of severe famine, during the reign of Inyotef III.

Turning now to Lower Egypt, we find that this period remains a Dark Age in terms of available information, in spite of the improvement in political stability. But around 2080 the father of King Merikare, probably Wahkare Khety, is able to say in his Instructions to his son (Wilson 1955): . . . *There is no enemy within the compass of thy frontier. . . . I pacified the entire west, as far as the coast of the sea. . . . But the east is rich in bowmen . . . turned about are the islands in the midst* (later, under Dynasties XVIII-XX, this would mean the islands of the Aegean but whether the phrase had this meaning already c. 2100 is uncertain). . . . *Lo, the wretched Asiatic . . . he has been fighting since the time of Horus, he does not conquer nor yet can he be conquered. He does not announce a day in fighting, like a thief. . . . I made the Northland smite them, I captured their inhabitants, and I took their cattle, to the disgust of the Asiatics against Egypt. Do not trouble thyself about him: he is only an Asiatic. . . . He may rob a single person, but he does not lead against a town of many citizens.* . . . Somewhat puzzling is his description of the land of the Asiatics as both *afflicted with water, difficult from many trees,* unless "water" here means "rain," which the Egyptians may have considered an inferior and unreliable source of water.

Merikare is advised to deal firmly with agitators: *A talker is an exciter of a city* . . . , and traitors, to liquidate them before they can stir up trouble (Wilson 1955; Erman 1927); to be skillful in speech; and to rule benevolently and justly, . . . *but keep thine eyes open, one that is trusting will become one that is afflicted.* . . .

More directly relevant to our main theme: *Thou sufferest not from the Nile, that it cometh not, and thou hast the products* (taxes) *of the Delta* . . . (Erman 1927). This I take as evidence that some of his predecessors, within vivid memory, had suffered from the Nile, that its flood had failed to come.

Another interesting verse seems to refer to the large number of young people among the population: *Behold thy commonalty is full of those newly grown up, of such as are 20 years old. The young generation is happy in following its heart.* . . . *Increase the younger generation of thy followers, that it may be provided with property, endowed with fields and rewarded with cattle* . . . (Erman 1927). While the meaning of this passage is uncertain, it suggests to me that there has been no serious famine for at least twenty years, and that since the end of the famine there has been a great increase in the population.

We should not expect, however, that a return to normal floods would be followed promptly by a full political and cultural revival and the building of fine large monuments. Both the king and his subjects would be too busy reorganizing the kingdom, and repairing and restoring the irrigation system of canals and dikes. Even if the king desired to build a large monument, after a severe and prolonged famine the population would be so much reduced that he would be prevented by a shortage of skilled labor. As for reunification of the Two Lands, of Upper and Lower Egypt, this would have to await the appearance on the throne of a local king who possessed the necessary dynamic qualities.

Merikare was further advised to deal tactfully with the South and not to provoke it. Apparently he disregarded this advice, went to war and recovered the nome of Abydos, with substantial help from another Khety of Assiut. His triumph was shortlived, however, for by 2040 his kingdom had been overthrown, and Upper and Lower Egypt forcibly reunited by King Nebhepetre Mentuhotep of Thebes, who is traditionally regarded as the founder of the Middle Kingdom.

The floods were evidently adequate, or better, during the 50-year reign (2060-2010) of King Mentuhotep II. The large and original funerary monument built by this king at Deir el Bahri near Thebes gives evidence of a high level of prosperity. And Vandier (1936) finds only one possible reference to famine, in the stele of a certain Mentuhotep son of Hepi: *When a little inundation (ḥcpy) happened, in the year 25* (probably of Mentuhotep II although Griffith favors Senwosret I of Dynasty XII, and Goedicke [*JEA* 1962] favors Inyotef II) *I did not allow my nome to suffer hunger; I gave it wheat and barley and I did not allow a famine to occur in it before the years of big inundation returned.* Whatever its date, this does not suggest anything as serious as those we have considered above, but only a poor year in the midst of a series of good floods. It is also more forthright in speaking openly of a *little inundation.*

Texts from the years c. 2002-c. 1950 B.C. With the death of King Seankhkare Mentuhotep II about 1998, Dynasty XI came to an end in a second period of disorder, brought on, I suggest, by another period of low Niles, drought and sandstorms, a second "exclamation point" emphasizing the end of the Neolithic Wet Phase. It is generally considered that the twelve-year reign of Mentuhotep III was peaceful and prosperous, but there is one document that, in retrospect, may be considered an omen of trouble to come. This is a letter written to his family by a certain Hekanakht when he was on a business journey during a famine caused by a low Nile. This document, recently translated by James (1962) and by Baer (1963), states that . . . *the whole land is perished, but you have not been hungry.* . . . *When I came hither southwards I fixed your rations properly. (Now) is the inundation very high? Now our food is fixed for us in proportion to the inundation. So be patient, all you who are listed here.* . . . *I have managed to keep you alive until today.* . . . *Take heed lest you be angry* . . . *everything is mine. It must be said "Being half alive is better than dying altogether.*

Now one should say hunger only in regard to real hunger. They have begun to eat people here. . . .

This last, Vandier (1936) and others consider to be an exaggeration intended to impress those to whom Hekanakht is writing; in absence of other evidence for very bad times, and considering the general tone of Hekanakht's letters, I must agree. But I would also suggest that the statement derives from a memory of the earlier time of more terrible famine, when Ankhtifi speaks of cannibalism.

These terrible times were soon to come again, although more briefly. Following the death of Mentuhotep III come five to seven years of darkness, about which very little is known. A King Nebtowyre Mentuhotep IV apparently occupied the throne for at least two years of this period, but he is known only from the inscriptions in Wadi Hammamat by his Vizier Amenemhet, and seems subsequently not to have been considered a legitimate ruler. Following Seankhkare, the Turin Papyrus mentions seven kingless years. During the period a fresh outbreak of raids by the Libyans of the western desert and by the Asiatics from the northeast apparently occurred.

The primary document on the confused and obscure period between the end of Dynasty XI and the start of Dynasty XII is the so-called Prophecy of NEFERTY, composed during the reign of Amenemhet I. In the words of Posener (*CAH* fasc. 29, p. 8) this document "combines in one sinister picture these recent memories with older memories of the depredations of the Asiatics during the First Intermediate Period." And not only of the Asiatics, but also of the chaotic social and natural conditions in both periods, for Neferty has a good deal to say about the natural conditions of the land, and gives a rather clearer picture than did Ipuwer. The quotes are mainly from Erman (1927), with occasional phrases from Wilson (1955). The invading sand dunes should be kept in mind while reading the words of Neferty.

. . . *That which was made is as if it were never made, and Re must begin to found anew* (E: begin creation over again). *The whole land has perished, there is none left, not the black of the nail survives of what should be there* (W: Not so much of the Black Land of Egypt survives as might be under

a fingernail). Probably it was buried under blowing sand and invading dunes.

This land is ruined; no one concerns himself about it any more, no one speaks, and no eye weeps (E: That is no longer worthwhile). . . . *The sun is veiled and will not shine that men may see. None can live when the storm veils it* (the sun), *all men are dulled (?) through want of it.* (E: By this obscuring of the sun, of which he also speaks below, not a single eclipse is intended, but dust- and sand-storms, suiting, as they do, the following descriptions of the drought.) (Cf. also the dust storms of Ankhtifi, above.)

The river of Egypt is empty, men cross over the water on foot. (This implies a failure of the White Nile, thus of the rains over east-central Africa.)[7] *Men search for water upon which the ships may sail; its road is become a bank, and the bank is become water.* Probably this refers to shiftings in the location of the river bed, accompanying the erratic and abnormal fluctuations in the volume of water, and the drifting sands; it is well established (Butzer 1959a, 1960) that shiftings did occur from time to time.

The south wind drives away the north wind (E: which brings coolness and humidity), *and the sky has still only the one wind* (meaning, the north wind failed to come at its normal season?). *The birds no longer hatch their eggs in the swamps of the Delta, but the bird hath made her a nest nigh unto men* (E: The birds migrate from the dried-up swamps to inhabited regions, where water still exists). . . .

Foes are in the East, Asiatics are come down into Egypt. . . . By night one will suddenly be fallen upon (?). . . .

. . . *This land is taken away and added to* (W: is brought-and-taken) (by the varying course of the river and the drifting dunes?), *and no one knows what the issue will be. . . .*

. . . *Men take up weapons of war, the land lives in confusion* (E: In the prevailing distress all live on robbery). . . . *They beg for bread with blood. Men laugh with a laughter of disease . . . and one slayeth another. . . . Men take the goods of a man of high estate from him and give them to one from without. . . . The possessor is in deprivation and him from without is contented.*

. . . *The land is diminished and its governors are*

---

[7] In the modern fluctuation to greater aridity that set in around 1900, the flow diminished from both the Blue and the White Nile; see H. H. Lamb, *Geogrl* 132 (1966) 188.

many. The field is bare, and its taxes are great; little is the grain and great the grain measure (of taxes), *and it is measured to overflowing.*

The sun separates himself from men (E: by sandstorms); *he arises when it is the hour. No one knows when it is midday, for his shadow cannot be distinguished* (E: on the sundial). . . . *He is in the sky like the moon, and yet he does not deviate from his accustomed time.* . . .

But finally, *a king shall come from the south, called Ameni,* and he put the country to rights again, particularly by driving out the Asiatics, and building the "Wall of the Prince" to keep them out. Fortunately, Nature cooperated and the Nile floods returned more or less to normal, and King Amenemhet I was able to launch his country into one of the most glorious periods of its long history, known as the Middle Kingdom.

Since virtually nothing is known of this brief Dark Age at the end of Dynasty XI, we may speculate briefly in the light of the climatological hypothesis. It is generally agreed that the future King Amenemhet I was the same man as the Vizier Amenemhet who led an expedition to the Wadi Hammamat in year two of King Mentuhotep IV. Hayes (1961) has noted that the tone of the inscriptions of Amenemhet suggest a loyal servant of his king, not a man plotting imminent revolt. I suggest that Amenemhet may have been driven to reconsider whether this Mentuhotep was in truth a proper and legitimate king, approved by the gods, when the floods failed so severely. Or perhaps Mentuhotep himself developed such doubts of his own legitimacy that he abdicated or died (see Discussion, below), since his claim to the throne is anyway obscure.

Further support to the idea of a serious failure of the Nile preceding the reign of Amenemhet I is provided by the quotation from his Instructions to his son: . . . *I was the one who made barley, the beloved of the grain-god. The Nile honored me on every broad expanse* (the inundations were good). *No one hungered in my years; no one thirsted therein.* . . . *Everything which I had commanded was in the proper place* (Wilson 1955).

Regarding the relations between the king and the feudal nomarchs in the early years of Amenemhet I, Hayes (1961:35) states that the new king saw to it that "the boundaries of the nomes were rigorously established and regulations were enacted covering each district's share in the supply of Nile

water available for purposes of irrigation" (see also Gardiner 1961:128; and Breasted 1906:628). This again suggests not only that water was not abundant at the very start of his reign, but also that much of the fighting in the times of great trouble may have been over access to the severely limited water supply. We have already seen that Merer shut off certain fields and did not allow his family's water to irrigate for someone else, and that Khety of Assiut built new irrigation works the better to utilize the meager water available. And we may speculate whether Ankhtifi's ability to supply other towns in the time of worst famine, in spite of living in a relatively poor part of the country, may have been related not only to the organizing efficiency and resourcefulness of which he boasts, but to the fact that his nomes had first access to the water. In normal times of course this would not matter, but if the river fell so low that one could walk across it, there could be some advantage in first access.

In this context we may note two items from the "Protestations of Guiltlessness" (Wilson 1955:34) by the soul appearing before a posthumous court: A31: *I have not held up the water in its season* (W: denied the inundation waters to others); and A32: *I have not built a dam against running water.* No doubt there were many who did, including Merer, and Khety of Assiut, as noted above.

With the reign of Amenemhet I, we come to the end of the First Dark Age in Egypt—an age bracketed by two particularly troubled and dark intervals, each associated with a severe drought, about 2180 to 2130, and 2000 to 1990 B.C. Dynasty XII, c. 1991-1786 B.C. was a period of strong government, cultural advance and general prosperity. There was no significant revival of the rains over the desert (Butzer 1958), no return of the Neolithic Wet Phase, but the inundations were evidently adequate. I shall discuss elsewhere what can be known of their levels. Vandier (1936) was able to find only one text referring to famine in these years, an inscription in the tomb of Ameny, Nomarch of Beni Hasan, during the reign of Senwosret I. The Nomarch Ameny states (Breasted 1906:523): . . . *When years of famine came, I plowed all the fields of the Oryx Nome, as far as its southern and northern boundaries, preserving its people alive, and furnishing its food so that there was none hungry therein.* . . . *Then came great Niles, producers of grain and of all things, (but)*

did not collect the arrears of the field (taxes). . . .
This inscription no doubt gives a picture of the
normal situation in years of low Nile, which must
have occurred from time to time throughout Egyp-
ian history, though rarely with such severity as in
the Dark Ages at the end of Dynasty VI and
between Dynasties XI and XII. Vandier notes
that Griffith considers that the inscription of Men-
uhotep, son of Hepi, refers to the same famine
as Ameny's inscription.

DISCUSSION

Most Egyptologists who attempt to explain the
collapse of the Old Kingdom stress the declining
power and wealth of the king and the growing
power and independence of the provincial nobility.
Evidence of this trend through Dynasty VI is too
plentiful to be questioned and need be mentioned
here only briefly: from as early as the end of
Dynasty IV, the royal pyramids decrease in size
while the mastabas of the great nobles grow in
size and splendor; in Dynasty VI many a noble
abandoned the earlier custom of a tomb near the
royal pyramid in favor of a tomb in his own province; governorships became hereditary, with "only
a perfunctory nod in the direction of Memphis"
(Hayes 1953). This much is beyond dispute. What
is questionable is whether such a trend is sufficient
explanation for a disaster of the magnitude that
overwhelmed Egypt at the end of Dynasty VI.

I have suggested rather that dire famine, due to
prolonged (on the historic, though very brief on
the geologic, time scale) failure of the rains over
the central and eastern African sources of the Nile
—a sort of "exclamation point" emphasizing the
ending of the Neolithic Wet Phase—was the crisis
that shattered a weakened central government
utterly unable to cope with the problem, and decimated the Egyptian people. We have considered a
number of ancient texts that support this point of
view, and the meaning of which becomes clearer
when read in this light. Moreover, the literature
"voicing the bewilderment and despair with which
Egyptians faced the overturn of their once stable
world" (Wilson 1956) is more readily understood
if we conceive of a cause that they were essentially
helpless to remedy.

Let us explore some further political aspects of
this hypothesis. Of the time of Dynasty VI, the
decades before the disaster, Hayes (1953:131)
writes: ". . . One cannot help but feel that it was

only through personal loyalty that the great rulers
of Upper Egypt [served] the crown. Once the
king, incapable of controlling his provincial governors by force, found himself unable to win their
loyalty through favors and wisely chosen conces-
sions, the whole fabric of the pharaonic government fell to pieces."

We consider this situation against the background of the Egyptian concept of Kingship, particularly as described by Frankfort, Wilson and
Aldred. In the words of Frankfort (1951:120):
"The Egyptian system . . . [in which] . . . a god
had consented to guide the nation . . . gave a sense
of security which the Asiatic contemporaries of the
ancient Egyptians totally lacked . . . a pledge that
the forces of nature would be well disposed and
bring prosperity and peace." "That Pharaoh was
of divine essence, a god incarnate" is fundamental
to the Egyptian concept of Kingship, "and this
view can be traced back as far as texts and symbols
take us" (Frankfort 1948:5); the attitude can be
seen most readily in art—in war scenes, hunting
scenes, and scenes involving the other gods—from
the time of Narmer.

Introducing a text from Dynasty XII, Wilson
(1955:431) writes: "The king of Egypt ruled the
land as a god, as the Son of Re, or as the Horus,
or as the incorporation of the deities of Upper
and Lower Egypt. He was also a synthesis of other
gods who represented forces of proper rule, a blend
of force and intelligence, of terror and nurture, or
of sustenance and punishment. . . . Some of the
divine elements which went into the composition
of a pharaoh" are set forth in a poem of instruction addressed to his children by Sehetepibre,
Chief Treasurer under King Ni-maat-Re Amenemhet III: *Worship King Ni-maat-Re, living forever,
within your bodies, and associate with his majesty
in your hearts. He is Perception* (W: cognitive intelligence, an attribute of good rule), *which is in
the hearts, and his eyes search out everybody. He is
Re, by whose beams one sees. He illumines the
Two Lands more than the sun. He makes the Two
Lands more verdant than does a high Nile. For
he has filled the Two Lands with strength and life.
. . . He giveth vital force to them that serve him
. . .* (Wilson 1955; Erman 1927).

Under Dynasty XVIII this attitude was expressed in an inscription in the tomb of Rekhmire,
vizier under King Thutmose III (Frankfort
1948:47): *What is the King of Upper and Lower*

Egypt? He is a god by whose dealings one lives, the father and the mother of all men, alone by himself, without an equal. Moreover the King's power and his concern for his realm do not cease with his death, for we read in another inscription (Frankfort 1948:195): *Thutmose III is in heaven like the moon. The Nile is at his service. He opens its cave to give life to Egypt.*

Aldred (1963, 1965) particularly stresses the relation between king and Nile, and writes that the Egyptian concept of the god-king derived from the "prehistoric rainmaker who kept his tribe, their crops, and beasts in good health by exercising a magic control over the weather . . . [who was] . . . transformed into the Pharaoh, able to sustain the entire nation by having command over the Nile flood. . . . The Kingship and the Nile are intimately associated. . . . The earliest kings were associated with the control of the flood waters . . ." (Aldred 1963:157). "The never-failing inundations of the river were more predictable in their occurrences, though not in their volume, and therefore more amenable to control than the weather" (Aldred 1965:50). Indeed, the climatic conditions of Egypt were almost uniquely suited to inspire the confidence of the people in any divine power claimed by their kings, far more so than in western Asia; and the predictability of the Nile probably played no insignificant role in the successful development of the dogma of divine kingship.

In the earliest Pyramid Texts, inscribed on the walls of the tomb chamber of the Pyramid of Unis, the king is poetically identified with the Nile flood (Černý 1952:85): *It is Unis who inundates the land and who has come forth from the lake, it is Unis who plucks the papyrus plant.* Pyr. 388; and in Pyr. 507-8: *Unis came today from the fullness of the flood, he is Subek, with a green feather, watchful face and uplifted fore-part of the body. . . . He came to his pools which are on the shore inundated by the Great Fullness, to the place of satisfaction, with green fields (the place) which is in the realm of light.* Pyr. 509 (transl. N. B. Millet) continues: *Unis causes the plants to become green on the two banks of the realm of light.* Černý points out that in later Pyramid Texts the god Osiris is connected with the flooding of the Nile on several occasions, and from the Middle Kingdom onward is often referred to as the god of floods and vegetation. Since the earliest texts, those of King Unis, refer thus to the king and not to Osiris, Černý suggests

that Osiris received his flood-vegetation attributes from his identification with the dead king.

King Amenemhet I of Dynasty XII includes the occurrence of good floods among the reasons why he deserves the loyalty and gratitude of all his subjects: . . . *I was the one who made barley, the beloved of the grain-god. The Nile honored me on every broad expanse. No one hungered in my years, no one thirsted therein. . . . Everything which I had commanded was in the proper place* (Wilson 1955:419). Frankfort (1948:57) emphasizes that the king here asserts that he "partakes of the essence of these natural phenomena. . . . The king 'produced barley,' not merely in an indirect way, for instance by caring for the farmers or furthering agriculture, but through his own actions—by maintaining Maat, the right order which allowed nature to function unimpaired for the benefit of man. Hence the Nile rose effectively at the inundation so that the arable land reached its maximum extent and the people prospered."

Frankfort instructively compares this Dynasty XII text with a song written for the accession of King Merneptah of Dynasty XIX, more than 700 years later, as translated by Erman: *Rejoice, thou entire land, the goodly time has come. A lord is appointed in all countries . . . great of kingship like Horus . . . Merneptah. . . . Truth has repressed falsehood* (W: The Egyptian concept of *ma'at* "truth, order, right" was of the essential order of the universe, given by the gods at the beginning and maintained and reconfirmed by the god-king). *The sinners are fallen on their faces. . . . The water standeth and faileth not, the Nile carrieth a high flood. The days are long, the nights have hours, the months come aright* (W: Order is found also in the regularity of times and seasons, restored by the new king). *The gods are content and happy of heart, and life is spent in laughter and wonder.*

Frankfort (1948:58) points out that "The comparison of the two texts enhances their significance. The song might be thought to contain merely the hyperboles of a festive mood, were it not that they recur in the grim context of Amenemhet's teaching. There the beneficial influence of the king is stressed only to bring out his utter loneliness, for notwithstanding it he was betrayed. And yet, though the two texts differ in both mood and age, we find them describing regal power with the same attributes, as strong a proof as we are likely to find that the Egyptians really believed these attributes to pertain to their king. This power, then, includes the remarkable capacity to dominate and further natural processes, especially the inundation of the Nile on which the prosperity of Egypt depends. Because the king, who has established Maat, who has defeated falsehood, comes to the throne, there are abundant inundations; and the seasons—that is, the months and days and nights—follow each other in orderly procession. So the song. But the teaching of Amenemhet says practically the same thing: none was hungry, for the king made the corn grow; and the Nile, in obedience, rose to all accessible places so that they could be tilled. Even as late an author as Ammianus Marcellinus knew that the Egyptians ascribed plenty or famine to the quality of their king—not, in a modern sense, to his quality as an administrator, but to his effectiveness as an organ of integration, partaking of the divine and of the human and intrusted with making the mutual dependence of the two a source of 'laughter and wonder.' "

The concept of the king's influence over nature also appears behind the words of flattery addressed by Sinuhe to King Senwosret I: *Whether I am in the Residence or in this place, it is ever thou that obscurest this horizon, and the sun ariseth at thy pleasure; the water in the river is drunk when thou willest, and the air in heaven is breathed when thou biddest* (Erman 1927:25). Probably this is merely an Egyptian way of saying "I recognize and accept you as the legitimate god-king of Egypt, as the true Horus."

Let us now link together the factors described in the preceding pages of this section: the great nobles of Upper Egypt waxing in independent power and bound to the throne by increasingly fragile ties; the fundamental link between the divinity of the king and his control over the floods; and to this combination add the prolonged and severe failure of the floods, to the extent that people throughout Egypt were dying of starvation—the *tzw*-famines of several ancient texts. Imagine an average king on the throne, a man with no outstanding qualities of leadership but adequate to normal conditions. With these ingredients, I suggest, we have a quite sufficient and entirely plausible explanation for the troubles that afflicted Egypt in its First Intermediate Period, or First Dark Age. The central government, unable to deal effectively with so severe a famine and drought, and

undermined at its ideological core by the very existence of this revolt by nature, simply collapsed. The local nobility became as free in spirit as in fact to cope locally with the famine to whatever extent their various individual abilities permitted, and also free to ignore the supposed king in their tomb inscriptions, a practice general in this period and utterly contrary to earlier usage.

There remains one major characteristic of Egyptian Dark Ages in need of explanation, the short reigns and the very large number of kings to be fitted into relatively few years. Here I shall venture a step beyond what seems to me the realm of sound probability, into the realm of speculation, to propose a hypothesis that I believe makes sense of these numerous short reigns, in the context of a Dark Age caused primarily by deficient Nile floods in a land ruled by god-kings.

When we consult the revised *CAH* (Smith 1962; Hayes 1961, 1962) we find at least 31 Kings, and possibly as many as 40, in the interval from the death of Pepi II to the end of Dynasty IX, a period now believed to cover no more than about 60 years, c. 2190 to c. 2130; and this disregards the description by Manetho of Dynasty VII as composed of 70 Kings who reigned for 70 days. From the death of Pepi II to the end of Dynasty VIII, c. 2160, we have at least 18 Kings in some 30 years. Dynasty VI itself ended with several ephemeral reigns following that of Pepi II; the Turin Papyrus appears originally to have listed eight Kings (Gardiner 1961) but the names of only three have survived, and only these three are included in the total of 18. For Dynasty IX, c. 2160-2130, the Turin Papyrus indicates thirteen Kings. With Dynasty X conditions finally became more stable, with five Kings in some 90 years.

In addition to the evidence from the various King Lists, it is of interest to recall the statement of Merer that he *offered for thirteen rulers (ḥk3w)*, in a single adult lifetime, during which *tzw*-famines occurred. Unfortunately the word *ḥk3w* does not enable us to distinguish between kings and nomarchs, nor is it certain that thirteen living rulers are meant (N. B. Millet, private communication); Černý (1961) interprets it, with some unease, as thirteen living nomarchs. But thirteen living kings seems the most plausible interpretation within the historical context.

Almost nothing is known of the genealogy of the Kings of the First Dark Age. The popularity of the praenomen "Neferkare" in Dynasty VII-VIII, and to a lesser extent in Dynasty IX, is often taken as evidence that the Kings of Dynasties VII-IX regarded themselves as legitimate successors of Neferkare Pepi II (Hayes 1961). Since Pepi II had four known Queens, and an unknown number of sons, daughters and grandchildren, and moreover is believed to have lived to be 100, it is quite likely that he outlived most of his children, and it is easy to imagine that the order of the succession became uncertain and controversial at or shortly after his death, or at the end of Dynasty VI. Then Manetho's tradition of 70 Kings who ruled for 70 days might be imagined as a council of royal princes, descendants of Neferkare Pepi II, ruling collectively while they tried to resolve the question of which of them should become king.

The next Dynasty, be it properly called VII or VIII, evidently began with a King Neferkare "the Younger," a son or grandson of Pepi II by Ankhes-en-Pepi, the Queen of his late years; Neferkare the Younger was credited by the Turin Papyrus (Hayes 1953) with a reign of just over four years, leaving only fourteen years for his fourteen successors of Dynasty VII-VIII. It is clear that there can be no question of a succession of generations among these Kings, and it has been suggested (Millet, 1968 lecture) that for some reason in this period the succession passed from brother to brother. While resulting in shorter reigns, even this hardly seems adequate to account for fourteen Kings in fourteen years, nor even some 31+ Kings in no more than 60 years. (A similar difficulty occurs also in the Second Intermediate Period with Dynasty XIII, and in the early part of the Dark Age around 1200 B.C.)

The need to explain these very numerous short reigns invites a radical hypothesis, which however fits well into our general picture of the situation. In brief, I suggest that the reigns of many of the kings in these periods were terminated rather promptly by death, either by suicide or by secret murder, when their performance of all the correct rites failed to produce any significant alleviation of the drought.

Although there is no evidence from ancient Egypt, there is evidence from recent times in various regions of Africa about what happens to a rain-maker king in a time of unusual drought. From C. G. Seligman's *Egypt and Negro Africa, a Study in Divine Kingship*, p. 38, Frankfort (1948:34)

quotes that the African "king of Juken is . . . able to control the rain and winds. A succession of droughts or bad harvests is ascribed to his negligence or to the waning of his strength, and he is accordingly secretly strangled." And there are other tribes, "like the Shilluk [who] will destroy their king when he threatens to become an imperfect link between man and the gods. . . . It has repeatedly been maintained that the Egyptians, too, killed their king and for the same reason; but of this there is no proof at all. The Egyptians, however, did regard their king in the same manner—a bond between nature and man" (Frankfort 1948:47).

Childe (1953) points out that the Pharaoh is a type of divine king, described by Frazer, who "holds his sovereignty by virtue of his magic power," and as its price must submit to ritual death before his body, and hence his magic power, grows feeble with age. In Egypt he was ritually revitalized by the sed-festival from the time of Menes onward. Egyptologists agree that the Egyptians did not as a regular practice kill their king, and that ritual revitalization played at least some role in the sed-festival. In spite of the magic-symbolic renewal of the king's power by the sed-festival, however, Aldred (1963:157) considers it significant that . . . "the tradition that the king should die for his people persisted in folk-lore and in the more primitive spells of *The Pyramid Texts*; and there are anthropologists who believe that the ceremonial killing of the Pharaoh was sometimes revived in moments of crisis."

If ever there was a crisis calling for such extreme measures, the First Dark Age, the period of the *tzw*-famines, was surely such a time. Frankfort (1948) emphasizes that there is no proof that any such thing ever occurred in Egypt. But then, there is little proof for anything—except famine, civil disorder, and too many kings—from the Dark Ages. Moreover, in addition to influencing the powers of Nature, "the king was the personification of ma'at, a word which we translate as 'rightness' or 'truth' or 'justice,' but which also seems to have the meaning of 'the natural cosmic order.' The forces of evil could upset ma'at until restoration had been effected by some appropriate act—a magic rite, or the advent of a new king" (Aldred 1963:161). A prolonged and severe failure of adequate floods, the *tzw*-famines, must have represented to the ancient Egyptians a uniquely profound upset of the natural cosmic order which might well seem to demand a drastic remedy, and might well lead them to try one new king after another, as each conspicuously failed to restore *ma'at*—particularly if the drought should occur at a time when there was an unusual degree of uncertainty about the identity of the prince chosen for the next incarnation of Horus.

We noted above that Ipuwer seems to blame the king for the sorry state of the land, but completely fails to specify what the king was doing wrong. In the light of the above discussion it appears probable that Ipuwer actually had no specific idea what the king was doing wrong. But since maintaining *ma'at*, by some supernatural power, was the primary duty of the king, the occurrence of disorder, of famine, and of failure of the floods, would mean that the god-king had somehow failed in his prime duty.

Without any particular reference to the Dark Ages, Anthes (1959, *JNES* 18:180) considers that "the Pyramid Texts indicate conclusively that there existed a supreme court of sorts who nominated the king. It is hard to imagine that their activity would have been restricted to the mere acclamation of the new king." I am not able to offer an opinion on the validity of this concept. But if it has any validity, we may imagine the indecision and confusion in this council as year after year the floods failed to rise above famine levels—particularly if there was no one prince who by the usual standards had a claim much superior to those of his rivals. Such a condition could easily occur after so long a reign as that of Pepi II, with at least four queens. One can imagine the council approving one prince after another, as to each Horus brought no good inundation, in an increasingly frantic effort to discover the true Son of Horus, and persuading or coercing each prince in turn to kill himself after he had performed the proper rites and received no recognition from the god. Now and then there would be a year or two or three of hope, with at least meagerly adequate flooding, and then again failure. In all probability the prince himself would lose confidence in his right to be king, and only the most irreligious, or cowardly, would resist the pressure to kill himself.

If this picture corresponds in any way to reality —and the reality of the hypothetical council is not essential to the correspondence—we should surmise that the same situation recurred at the end of Dynasty XI, with the seven-year darkness that followed the death of Seankhkare Mentuhotep III. Hayes (1953:167) mentions three names in addition to Nebtowyre Mentuhotep IV who may have reigned briefly in this interval. The practice in Dynasty XII, whereby each king appointed his chosen heir co-regent in his lifetime, may have been motivated in part by a desire to reduce the influence of the council in the naming of a new king. The power of the council would wax and wane, inversely with the prosperity and stability of the country.

A problem meriting fuller discussion than would be appropriate here is the possible influence of climatic crises on the evolution of religious concepts in Egypt. There can be little doubt that the climate of Egypt, with the normally dependable regularity in the seasonal flooding of the Nile, provided conditions uniquely suitable for the development of the concept of divine kingship. The predictability of natural conditions would readily inspire the people to believe any claims to magic powers and divinity that a king might make.

Furthermore, there can be little doubt that the concern expressed by local nomarchs for the material wellbeing of their subjects in the First Intermediate Period, and the later Middle Kingdom idea of the King as a good shepherd watching over his flock, developed naturally out of the crisis of famine that impoverished and killed the industrious as well as the lazy and shiftless, so that poverty could not be blamed on a deficiency of character.

It is tempting also to link the great increase in the popularity of Osiris, "a divinity who had himself suffered death and resurrection in the process of transfiguration" (Lloyd 1961:118) during the first Dark Age to the nature of the crisis through which the Egyptians themselves were passing. This god, "as one of the forces of nature, personified the growth of plants through the stimulus of the life-giving water of the Nile" (Smith 1962), both of which were in critically short supply. Smith further notes that Osirian beliefs began to appear in private tombs about the middle of Dynasty V, while Gardiner (1961) points out that the Pyramid Texts of Dynasty VI emphasize Osiris, in contrast to the Vth Dynasty emphasis on Re. And the Nile floods, first poetically identified with King Unis, came in Dynasty VI to be often identified with Osiris (Černý 1952). This change coincides with

Butzer's dating for the end of the Neolithic Wet Phase.

Another god whose popularity, or in this case unpopularity, may have been influenced by the end of the NWP is Seth. Wainwright (1963, *JEA* 49) states that Seth is to be considered as originally a storm god, and of great antiquity (Nagada I), and thus to have originated well within the NWP, as "a god of the blessed yet dangerous storm." As the rains became rare, his rites became only a nuisance, and he eventually slipped from his high estate and became the personification of evil. With the decline of the NWP, everything from the desert became sinister to the Egyptian peasant. "Out of the southwestern desert come sandstorms and bad weather, sent by Seth, Lord of the Libyan Desert. ... The hot south and west winds in summer bring 'the pestilence of the year' which kills people" (Kees 1961:37).

And finally we may note a legend according to which "Sekhmet, the lioness goddess dwelling in the desert near Memphis, by order of Re, once destroyed nearly all the first race of men when they were beginning to make settlements, until the god saved the remainder by a stratagem" (Kees 1961: 37). It may well be that this legend reflects a dim and distant memory of an earlier fluctuation to aridity, or drought, within the NWP.

We conclude with a brief return to the broader picture of the First Dark Age of Ancient History outlined in the Introduction. We have considered in some detail a number of texts from the First Intermediate Period which clearly establish that Egypt was afflicted by severe famine, and that this famine was caused primarily by failure of the Nile floods rather than by human negligence. Most of these texts, and particularly those relating to the severest drought (*tzw*-famines), can be dated within a period of no more than 50 years, c. 2180 to c. 2130 B.C. A second drought, less prolonged, and perhaps less severe, occurred between 2002 and 1991 B.C.

If the more general thesis of a *widespread* drought, as set forth in the Introduction, is correct, it would be the first of these great droughts which brought an end to EB 2 civilization throughout the eastern Mediterranean Basin. It would be the first drought also which in Mesopotamia contributed to the destruction of the Akkadian Empire, and the second drought which contributed to the downfall of the Third Dynasty of Ur. I plan to investigate the evidence from Mesopotamia in detail in a later paper. The conclusions reached in the present paper should, however, be judged primarily on the internal Egyptian evidence. They do not depend in any necessary way on the correctness of the hypothesis of a widespread drought.

HARVARD COLLEGE OBSERVATORY

REFERENCES

Adams, William Y.
    1968   Invasion, diffusion, evolution?, *Antiquity* 42: 194-215.

Aldred, Cyril
    1963   *The Egyptians*, Praeger, New York.
    1965   *Egypt to the End of the Old Kingdom*, McGraw-Hill, New York.

Baer, Klaus
    1963   An Eleventh Dynasty Farmer's Letters, *JAOS* 83:1-19.

Bell, Barbara
    1970   The oldest records of the Nile floods, *GeogrJ* (in press).

Breasted, James Henry
    1906   *Ancient Records of Egypt*, vol. I, University of Chicago Press.

Brooks, C. E. P.
    1949   *Climate through the Ages*, McGraw-Hill, New York.

Borchardt, Ludwig
    1905   Ein Königserlass aus Dahschur, *ZAeS* 42:1-11.

Butzer, Karl W.
    1958   *Quaternary Stratigraphy and Climate in the Near East*, Bonner Geogr. Abh., Heft 24, Bonn.
    1959a Some recent geological deposits of the Egyptian Nile valley, *GeogrJ* 125:75-79.
    1959b Environment and human ecology in Egypt during predynastic and early dynastic times, *BullSocGeogr.d'Egypte* 32:43-87 (a condensed English transl. of 1959c, q.v. for documentation).
    1959c Die Naturlandschaft Ägyptens während der Vorgeschichte und der Dynastischen Zeit, *AbhAkWissLit* (Mainz) *Math.-naturw.Kl.* No. 1, 80 pp., Wiesbaden.
    1960   Archeology and geology in ancient Egypt, *Science* 132:1617-24.
    1961   Climate change in arid regions since the Pliocene, pp. 31-56 in *A History of Land Use in Arid Regions*, ed. L. D. Stamp, UNESCO Arid Zone Research XVII.
    1963   Changes of climate during the late geological record; and The last "pluvial" phase of the Eurafrican sub-tropics, pp. 203-206, and 211-

218 in *Changes of Climate*, Proc. Rome Symposium, UNESCO Arid Zone Research XX.

1965 Physical conditions in Eastern Europe, Western Asia, and Egypt, *CAH* I, ch. 2 (fasc. 33).

1966 Climate changes in the arid zones of Africa, pp. 72-83 in *World Climate from 8000 to 0 B.C.*, Symposium Proc., Roy. Meteorol. Soc., London.

Butzer, Karl W., and Carl L. Hansen
1968 *Desert and River in Nubia*, University of Wisconsin Press, Madison.

Carpenter, Rhys
1966 *Discontinuity in Greek Civilization*, Cambridge University Press.

Černý, Jaroslav
1952 *Ancient Egyptian Religion*, Hutchinson, London.
1961 The Stele of Merer in Cracow, *JEA* 47:5.

Childe, V. Gordon
1929 *The Most Ancient East*, London.
1953 *New Light on the Most Ancient East*, Praeger, New York.

Dales, George F.
1965 A suggested chronology for Afghanistan, Baluchistan, and the Indus Valley, pp. 257-284 in *Chronologies in Old World Archaeology*, ed. R. W. Ehrich, University of Chicago Press.

Drioton, Etienne
1942 Une représentation de la famine sur un bas-relief égyptien, *BIE* 25:45-53.

Erman, Adolf
1927 *The Ancient Egyptians*: a sourcebook of their writings, Harper Torchbooks, transl. from German by A. M. Blackman.

Faulkner, R. O.
1944 The rebellion in the Hare Nome, *JEA* 30: 61-63.
1964 Notes on "The Admonitions of an Egyptian Sage," *JEA* 50:24-36.
1965 The Admonitions of an Egyptian Sage, *JEA* 51:53ff.

Fischer, Henry G.
1968 *Dendera in the third Millennium B.C.*, New York.

Frankfort, Henri
1948 *Kingship and the Gods*, University of Chicago Press.
1951 *The Birth of Civilization in the Near East*, Bloomington.

Frenzel, B.
1966 Climate change in the Atlantic/sub-Boreal transition on the Northern Hemisphere, pp. 99-123 in *World Climate from 8000 to 0 B.C.*, Symposium Proc., Roy. Meteorol. Soc., London.

Gardiner, Sir Alan
1961 *Egypt of the Pharaohs*, Clarendon Press, Oxford.

Hayes, William C.
1953 *The Scepter of Egypt*, vol. I, Harper, New York.
1961 The Middle Kingdom of Egypt, *CAH* I, ch. 20 (fasc. 3).
1962 Chronology: Egypt; Western Asia; Aegean Bronze Age, *CAH* I, ch. 6 (fasc. 4).
1964 *Most Ancient Egypt*, University of Chicago Press.

James, T. G. H.
1962 *The Hekanakhte Papers and other early Middle Kingdom Documents*, New York.

Kees, Hermann
1961 *Ancient Egypt*, University of Chicago Press.

Kraus, E. B.
1954 Secular changes in the rainfall regime of SE Australia, *Quartl. Roy. Meteorol. Soc.* 80: 591-601.
1955a Secular changes of tropical rainfall regimes, *ibid.* 81:198-210.
1955b Secular changes of east-coast rainfall regimes, *ibid.* 430-439.
1956 Graphs of cumulative residuals, *ibid.* 82:96-98.

Lloyd, Seton
1961 *The Art of the Ancient Near East*, Praeger, New York.

Mellaart, James
1962 Anatolia, c. 4000-2300 B.C., *CAH* I, ch. 18 (fasc. 8).

Murray, G. W.
1951 The Egyptian climate: an historical outline, *Geogrl* 117:424-434.

Ralph, Elizabeth K. and Henry N. Michael
1969 University of Pennsylvania radiocarbon dates XII, *Radiocarbon* 11:469-81.

Smith, William Stevenson
1962 The Old Kingdom in Egypt, *CAH* I, ch. 14 (fasc. 5).
1965 *The Art and Architecture of Ancient Egypt*, Penguin Books, Baltimore.

Starkel, L.
1966 Post-glacial climate and the moulding of European relief, pp. 15-33 in *World Climate from 8000 to 0 B.C.*, Symposium Proc., Roy. Meteorol. Soc., London.

Suess, Hans E.
1967 Zur Chronologie des alten Ägypten, *ZfPhysik* 202:1-7.

Toussoun, Prince Omar
1925 *Memoire sur l'Histoire du Nil*, Cairo.

Toynbee, Arnold J.
1935 *A Study of History*, vol. I, Oxford University Press.

Trigger, Bruce
1965 *History and Settlement in Lower Nubia*, Yale Univ. Publ. in Anthropology, No. 69.

235

Vandier, Jacques
  1936 *La famine dans l'Egypte Ancienne*, Cairo.
  1950 *Mo'alla*, Cairo.
Weinberg, Saul S.
  1965 The Relative Chronology of the Aegean in the Stone and Early Bronze Ages, pp. 285-320 in *Chronologies in Old World Archaeology*, ed. R. W. Ehrich, University of Chicago Press.

Wilson, John A.
  1955 translations from *Ancient Near Eastern Texts* (*ANET*), ed. J. B. Pritchard, Princeton University Press.
  1956 *The Culture of Ancient Egypt*, University of Chicago Press.
Wright, H. E., Jr.
  1968 Climate change in Mycenaean Greece, *Antiquity* 42:123-127.

20

JOURNAL

OF THE

WASHINGTON ACADEMY OF SCIENCES

VOL. 21   JULY 19, 1931   No. 13

PHYSICAL GEOGRAPHY.—*Why the Mayan cities of the Petén District, Guatemala, were abandoned.*[1] C. WYTHE COOKE, U. S. Geological Survey.

Two thousand years ago what is now the Petén District of Guatemala was the seat of a flourishing Mayan empire. Its massive temples and palaces still mark the sites of large cities which endured for many generations but were finally abandoned. Today, that once-populous region is, for the most part, totally uninhabited. The great cornfields which fed its people have reverted to the jungle, and the ruins of its public buildings lie hidden in a dense forest. The few permanent habitations are on the banks of perennial lakes and rivers along the main route of travel across the District. The remainder of the region is accessible only by means of narrow trails kept open by chicleros or cut by exploring archeologists.

My acquaintance with the Petén District was gained in March and April, 1931, when I was sent by the Carnegie Institution of Washington to study the geology of the region accessible from the camp of the Institution's Department of Historical Research at Uaxactún. I entered Guatemala at Yaloche, a customs house on the frontier, a day's ride northwest of Cayo, British Honduras, travelled 3 days westward to Uaxactun, spent 10 days there, and proceeded southward past Tikal to Remate, a settlement at the eastern end of Lake Petén. From this lake I followed a well-travelled road northeastward past Lake Macanxé to Yaxhá, a settlement between two lakes, thence to Tikan Sakan and down the valley of Río San Felipe to Fireburn on the frontier of British Honduras.

[1] Received June 5, 1931. Published by permission of the Acting Director of the U. S. Geological Survey.

283

Travel in the Petén is slow and tedious. The length of a day's journey varies according to the season and is determined in large part by the distance between water holes, for there are few perennial streams and many of the water holes become dry after the end of the rainy season.

Uaxactún lies on or near the divide that separates the drainage systems of the Gulf of Honduras from those of the Gulf of Mexico. Streams east of Uaxactún flow into Río Hondo or into Belize River, which empty into the Gulf of Honduras, but water falling west of Uaxactún finds its way into tributaries of the Usumacinta, which flows into Campeche Bay.

Because of the thick cover of forest which cuts off the view in all directions, it is difficult to visualize the topography of the Petén. The clearings around the camp at Uaxactún, which are on the lowlands, show only a shallow depression containing a plant-covered water hole (*aguada*), a grassy flat, and hillocks about twenty feet high, beyond which the view is stopped by the edge of the forest. Even from the top of the highest temple, nothing can be seen but the enclosing jungle. But from the window of a ruined Mayan building which is perched on a mound at the edge of the upland 150 feet above the aguada, one can look eastward over the tree tops and the clearings, across a wide forested plain to low, broken ridges on the horizon.

There are two very different kinds of topography in this part of the Petén—uplands and lowlands, or *bajos*. The uplands are hills and ridges of limestone which rise to a maximum height of several hundred feet above the bajos. They are barely covered by a thin soil of black clay, and are dotted here and there with sinks. In the neighborhood of Uaxactún, the highest hills stand 650 or 700 feet above sea level, and the bajos about 500 or 550 feet. The bajos are flat plains with almost no perceptible relief. They are underlain by tough black carbonaceous clay. The uplands are clothed with a fairly open forest containing many tall, large trees, such as mahogany, chicle, and ceiba but comparatively little underbrush. The bajos are covered with a tangled mass of low gnarled and twisted trees, such as logwood. Many of the trees in the bajos are small-leaved and thorny, and are festooned with large vines. During the rainy season the bajos are flooded; at the beginning of the dry season they are floored with deep tough mud which, later in the year, drys hard and cracks. At all seasons they are very unpleasant to travel through.

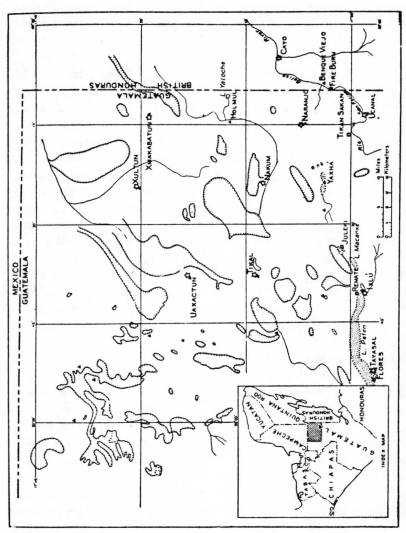

Figure 1. Sketch map of part of Guatemala showing bajos and lakes. Stars indicate places whose geographic position has been determined astronomically by the Department of Terrestrial Magnetism of the Carnegie Institution of Washington. Solid triangles indicate Mayan ruins. Based on a map made by F. Vans-Agnew and Didier Masson for the P. W. Shufeldt Cía.

The bajos evidently once were lakes. They are still lakes during the rainy season, but they have been so nearly filled with silt that a slight depression of water level due to run-off or evaporation reduces them to ponds or drains them completely. The source of the clay that fills them is the soil of the uplands—black, carbonaceous clay formed by the decomposition and solution of limestone and mixed with organic matter.

The bajos are thickly scattered over the Petén (see figure 1), and some of them are very large. If the bajos were restored to their former condition, the Petén would be a region of many beautiful lakes. Travel in it would be easy, for one could go from place to place by boat, with only short journeys overland, from one lake to another, across country that offers little impediment to travel at any season. It is quite likely that many of the bajos are connected by waterways which carry off the surplus water during the rainy season, although others occupy enclosed basins from which the water drains away through underground channels. Some idea of what the country once was like can be gained from views of the beautiful lakes that still remain. Of these Lake Petén, about 18 miles long, is the largest and best known. Flores, the principal town of the district, lies on an island in Lake Petén and there are several smaller settlements on its banks. Many of the smaller lakes, such as the Laguna de Yaloche, are already silted up to such an extent that small fluctuations in water level cause great changes in area.

How long ago these ancient lakes became filled with silt and converted into bajos can not be determined precisely. Doubtless the process was continuous and gradual although there may have been times when silting was more rapid than at others. Silting is still going on but probably very slowly because the uplands from which the silt is derived are thickly forested. It is quite possible that the transition from lake to bajo may have occurred during the time of the Mayan Empire, when much of the uplands must have been under cultivation. The Mayas were an agricultural people and needed much cleared land to raise the great quantities of corn required to feed their large population. The rate of erosion of the soil must have been enormously accelerated when the forest was cut and the cultivated soil was exposed to the full force of the torrential rains. One may imagine the Petén when first occupied by the Mayas to have had a thick fertile black soil. During the many centuries of the Mayan occupation more and more of the soil was washed away until the bare limestone was exposed.

Then the land was abandoned and reverted to the jungle, soil erosion was greatly retarded, and today, after the lapse of several centuries, the ground is covered by a thin but fairly even coating of black clay through which the rock still shows in many places. Soil is probably being formed now more rapidly than it is being washed away.

One can scarcely imagine the Petén, in its present condition, as the home of a large permanent population. One difficulty is the lack of an adequate water supply. There are few permanent water holes in the Petén and some of the old Mayan town sites are without any obvious present source of water. The Mayas may have depended upon stores of rain water to tide them over the dry season, just as Belize today gets its entire water supply from the clouds, but the rainfall is much more seasonal in the interior than at Belize. Another difficulty is the lack of transportation facilities. If the geography during the time of the Mayan occupation had been like the present, all the provisions and merchandise would have had to be carried to or from the cities on the backs of men (for the Mayas had no beasts of burden), and the bajos would have offered almost impassable barriers to transportation during part of the year. If, however, the bajos were permanent lakes during the time of the Mayan occupation, there was plenty of water throughout the whole year and commerce was speeded at all seasons by water transportation.

Another way in which the transition from lakes to bajos may have influenced the occupation of the Petén is its effect upon the health and comfort of the people by the increase of mosquitoes. As long as the water remained deep near shore, mosquitoes probably were not very numerous, for their larvae would have fallen prey to fishes, but when the deep water was converted into swamps and marshes, swarms of mosquitoes must have plagued the people. If, about this time, malaria was introduced into the country, sickness and death may have taken their toll of the population.

Some of the factors, then, that may have caused the decline of the Mayan Empire and the depopulation of the Petén are (1) erosion of the soil and the consequent scarcity of arable land, (2) silting of the lakes and the destruction of water transportation, (3) diminution of the water supply during the dry season, (4) increase in the number of mosquitoes, and (5) introduction or increase of malaria.

ECOLOGICAL AND GEOCHEMICAL ARCHAEOLOGY IN THE SOUTHERN MAYA LOWLANDS[1]

URSULA M. COWGILL AND G. E. HUTCHINSON

21

INTRODUCTION

MAYAN PEOPLES occupied the southernmost portion of the Yucatán Peninsula and developed one of the highest known indigenous cultures of the New World during the first millenium A.D. This culture collapsed before 1000 A.D. and the Petén, as it is now known, never regained either the level of civilization nor the population it once is supposed to have supported. Other Mayan groups living to the north and south of the Petén underwent various types of cultural disturbances but generally there was no permanent depopulation in these areas. It would appear therefore that the population that once lived in the Petén presents a rather special case. It is presently thought that this population virtually disappeared.

A number of hypotheses attempting to explain the cause of the collapse of Classic Maya civilization have been proposed. The purpose of the subsequent discussion is to review such ideas in the light of research that has been carried out in the southern Maya lowlands, namely El Departamento de El Petén, the northernmost state of Guatemala.

STATEMENT OF PROBLEM

The excavation of any large aboriginal site invariably brings forth the problem of attempting to estimate the size of its prehistoric population. One way of arriving at such an estimate is to determine presently the number of people the land can comfortably support and then extrapolate back in time. During the

1 The present contribution, designed to give a summary of such of our results as bear on archaeological problems, is based on a paper presented as part of the symposium, Pollen and Prehistory, held at the Society of American Archaeology, May 3, 1963, Boulder, Colorado. A full account of the study of the Bajo de Santa Fé is in press, while the cores from Laguna de Petenxil will be published in detail shortly.

The initial field work was supported by a fellowship obtained by Dr. George L. Cowgill from the Henry L. and Grace Doherty Charitable Foundation, Inc. All subsequent field work and laboratory studies have been supported by grants from the National Science Foundation (Grant nos. 17831, 15606 and 8916). The lake cores here described were taken by George and Ursula Cowgill. Dr. George L. Cowgill was extremely helpful in many aspects of the agricultural study.

Mr. A. L. Bump of the United Fruit Company materially aided the transportation of equipment and personnel to and from Guatemala and we are also grateful to Mr. Dana Condon,

excavation of Chichén Itzá, a number of people, Emerson (n. d.), Emerson and Kempton (1935), Kempton (1935), Steggerda (1941) and Hester (1951, 1952, 1953, 1954), carried out various types of agronomic studies in an attempt to arrive at some workable estimate of prehistoric population size.

Steggerda (1941) was primarily interested in the problem of yield decline with continuous cultivation. He established four experimental plots, noted their yield and took soil samples yearly from 1933 to 1938. One of these plots was used as a control, allegedly virgin bush; another was a garden plot that was kept free of weeds and allowed to produce two annual crops; a third was a plot that had been cropped and was allowed to revert to bush; and the fourth consisted of a corn field that was planted annually during this period. Chemical analyses were performed yearly on soil samples taken from these plots. The decline in yield with increasing cultivation was not reflected in concurrent decreases in soil nutrient levels, and hence it was presumed that weed competition and possibly factors such as disease and climate were responsible for the noted decline. Steggerda was obviously unable to arrive at any other conclusions from the data given him; unfortunately, however, graphing such data as a function of the year, it was noticed that for some years a given element was low in all plots and other years it was high. This strongly sug-

General Traffic Manager for Central America of the same company, without whose assistance the field work objectives would never have been realized.

Sr. Carlos Samayoa Chinchilla, Director of the Instituto Nacional de Antropologia e Historia in Guatemala City made available the many excellent facilities of the museum.

Sr. Francis Gall of the Dirección General de Cartografia provided access to aerial photographs of the Petén region which proved to be extremely helpful during field work.

Licenciado Jorge Salazar V., acting secretary of the Ministerio de Educación Pública, helped procure authorization to bring field equipment into Guatemala.

The Rev. and Mrs. Stanley Storey of the Nazarene Mission in Santa Elena, El Petén, assisted in taking one of the cores from Lake Petenxil, helped make contact with some milperos in some communities and were kind enough to collect lake, river and rain water samples for analyses.

We are very grateful to Dr. Jaime Litvak of the Instituto de Prehistoria in Mexico City for his assistance in obtaining some of the statistical data reported in the population study, and to the authorities of the Dirección General de Estadística in Mexico City for making available their excellent library and its facilities.

Dr. Francis Kukachka of the Forest Products Laboratory in Madison, Wisconsin was kind enough to examine charred material from both the pit dug in El Bajo de Santa Fé and cores from Laguna de Petenxil. Dr. John Reeder of the Biology Department at Yale University assisted in the identification of some charred plant tissues found in the cores from Laguna de Petenxil. Dr. G. K. Voigt of the School of Forestry at Yale University was kind enough to allow the use of his Kjeldahal apparatus.

During the few weeks stay at Tikal, Dr. William R. Coe and Mrs. Vivian Broman de Morales were always generous with their assistance and equipment.

gests that the study really involved the variations in ability of the technicians employed to perform chemical analyses from year to year rather than a real variation brought about by cultivation.

Emerson was inclined to believe that the decline in yields was brought about by weed competition, while Kempton on the basis of a survey made in northern Yucatán felt that successive cropping caused a notable decline in fertility and hence also in yield. He suggested that the first crop received more fertilizer in the guise of ashes than the second year, and as a consequence the latter would be less productive than the former.

The results of these investigations carried out in the northern portion of the Yucatán Peninsula unfortunately have been extrapolated to all of Middle America to explain population decline and agricultural problems in general, despite the fact that this portion of the Peninsula is rather different from the southern part.

The data presented by early agronomic workers unfortunately do not agree with one another. If the yield decline on successive cropping is due to weed competition, presumably weeding would increase the productivity. If, on the other hand, the decline is due to a decrease in soil fertility, it has been supposed that only fertilizer could alleviate the situation, and as far as is known there was no pre-Columbian source.

Despite the scientific confusion, one hypothesis that has appeared attractive to some archaeologists has remained in the literature, namely that the Classic Maya collapse was due to misuse of the land. Underlying all hypotheses concerned with cultural collapse of the ancient Maya is the attitude that slash and burn agriculture is harmful to the soil, that it makes an inefficient use of the land, and that it is basically incapable of supporting adequately any population of large size.

Cooke (1931, 1933) and Ricketson (1937:11) on the basis of a pit dug in a seasonal swamp near Uaxactún, known as El Bajo de Joventud, concluded that there had been an intensive and excessive use of the land, bringing about denudation, excessive erosion and subsequent filling up of the bajos, which they believed had at one time been large lakes. Had these seasonal swamps once been lakes, they would have provided fish for food and a means of transportation, solved the present day problem of a shortage of dry season water, and perhaps have provided a more salubrious environment than today.

The pit is described as having a 2.05 m. thick black layer of clay containing, at Uaxactún, a smaller proportion of calcite crystals than the underlying layer, which consisted of equal parts of paler clay and calcite. The presence of the black layer is interpreted as evidence for a period of intensive erosion brought about by overuse of the land. Cooke states that this black layer is similar to the soils found in the upland regions.

Bullard (1960) accepts the hypothesis that the *bajos* were once lakes and also thinks that some portions of the larger ones were still open water at the beginning of the Classic Period. He doubts that their silting up was the principal reason for the collapse of the civilization, since sites along streams, rivers and modern lakes which could not have suffered from water shortages and other effects of silting also suffered decline.

A somewhat different hypothesis, also involving the idea of the misuse of land, had been put forward by O. F. Cook (1909, 1921) somewhat earlier. He concluded that the agricultural system in Yucatán was adapted only to the support of sparse populations. He presumed that, once the population reached a certain density, the resting period of the forest would become too short and that as a result frequent overburning of forested areas would destroy the forest, encourage the encroachment of perennial grasses, and hence make the land impossible to plant and crop in view of the primitive system then used.

Bartlett (1956) among others suggested correctly that burned-over forest land is soft, easy to plant, and as a result of the burnt material is almost self fertilizing. Initially, the burnt area is free of weeds. He further concluded that perennial grasses have a rather tough root system which makes penetration with a dibble stick, for example, not feasible, and that the breaking of such sod involves a great deal of labor. Occasional fires during the dry season when the grasses are dormant do not destroy them, and they quickly regenerate.

There are thus two hypotheses relative to inefficient land use. The Cook-Bartlett hypothesis is that the population increased to such an extent that it no longer became feasible to allow the forest its normal resting time; the length of the entire growing-fallow cycle became too short, with the result that the forest was entirely destroyed and replaced by grasslands which were too difficult to plant. The Cooke-Ricketson hypothesis presumes that the population increased to such an extent that intensive agriculture became necessary, which in turn brought about extensive erosion that silted up the lakes, decreased the water supply, removed soil and hence a chance of cropping it, and generally denuded the area. Neither hypothesis logically excludes the other; both might be correct or incorrect.

Meggers (1954, 1957) suggested that the high civilization apparent among the ancient Maya had been developed elsewhere, for tropical forests are not blessed with an adequate environmental potential. Her opinion is that civilizations unfortunate enough to begin in a tropical area are doomed from the beginning to decline and eventual collapse. As Coe (1957) has aptly commented, there is no archaeological evidence that Classic Period culture did not develop in the Petén, and the record indicates that there was a constant growth toward the height of the Classic rather than a slow continuous decline from the time man is known to have lived in the region. More recently Ferdon (1959) has stated that the southern Maya lowlands are indeed an area of high subsistence potential.

Huntington (1951:411-412) was of the opinion that all of Central America suffered from what he calls a low climatic energy, giving as a rule of thumb the relationship that the higher the civilization, the cooler the climate. During the past five millenia civilizations have been steadily moving toward cooler climates. Those unfortunate groups who have returned to warmer climates during this gradual movement have suffered declines in the degree of their civilization. Huntington implied that the climate was at first drier in Central America than it is now or has been since the major population became established. Russell (1956:458) likewise implied that possibly the disappearance of advanced civilizations from various portions of Middle America may have been due to an increase in precipitation which would have brought about flourishing vegetation, insect populations and pathogenic organisms.

Thus, as distinct from the poor use of the land, another reason for the cultural decline of the ancient Maya is presented, some students believing that the area was doomed from the beginning because regions of this type are allegedly incapable of supporting advanced civilizations.

AGRICULTURE

As a result of the many conflicting hypotheses concerning the decline and collapse of Classic Maya civilization, many without pertinent regional data to substantiate them, a field study was made in 1959 to determine, if possible, what the situation had been in Classic times. The problem was approached from various viewpoints.

An agricultural study of modern methods (Cowgill 1961; 1962), it was hoped, would answer some questions concerning subsistence levels, efficiency of present land use systems, and possibly the maximum population which the land could support with primitive methods of farming. It is realized that now the *milperos* or corn farmers have machetes, though the ancient Maya did not have steel implements. Hester (1952) presumed that they felled the forest with limestone chips and that this initial method of clearing took twice as long as steel tools. Evidence of the efficacy of stone tools in clearing land unfortunately mainly comes from Europe.

Evans (1897:162) presents some discussion on the problem of felling trees. He mentions that some years earlier Vicomte Lepic felled a small oak eight inches in diameter with a polished Danish flint hatchet eight inches long. Jacob-Friesen compared the effectiveness of chipped and polished flint axes (Nietsch 1939:70). He needed seven minutes to cut a pine tree whose diameter was 17 cm. using a chipped ax; but it took him only five minutes to fell a similar sized tree with a polished ax. It is reasonably certain that in any well developed swidden agriculture, the time spent in clearing is only a small fraction of the total time required to prepare the ground, plant, mature and harvest a crop. Even if the Maya took twice or three times as long to fell a tree with a stone tool as with a metal one, this would not increase the total time spent by a like factor. Diaz (1956:12) wrote ". . . and they attacked our men with their two-handed knife-like swords." The statement is footnoted "macanas or maquahuitls—a wooded sword edged with flint or obsidian." It is most unlikely that any people who could make weapons of this nature would not have used more effective tools in clearing than limestone chips. Flint or obsidian tools in the hands of the experienced might prove almost as fast as steel implements. There is clearly need for a more detailed study of the possible uses of the stone tools found in Maya sites. It is believed that except for the introduction of steel tools, agricultural methods have remained largely the same.

In the central Petén region, it is possible to sow four crops of corn annually; first year milpa, second year milpa, San José (the dry season crop normally planted in low lying areas) and Yaxkín (the wet season crop usually found on slopes and steep places). Yaxkín is a Maya word which roughly corresponds to the month of November, at which time of year this crop is planted. Usually the land utilized for the Yaxkín and San José crops, both emergency plantings, is less than that of the regular crop. As a result of the types of crops planted the majority of the land in the region is usable, save that occupied by rivers, lakes and towns.

On the basis of food consumption and production as related to modern land use, population density of 100 to 200 people per square mile is possible. Hester (1954) estimates for the northern portion of the Yucatán Peninsula a population of 60 per square mile. The reason for the discrepancy is the longer rest period needed for the land in the north. Because of this difference the two estimates are by no means discordant. At present one *milpero* can supply the food requirements of 12.6 persons.

Slash and burn agriculture employing non-metallic tools would still leave close to half the total labor supply available for other tasks. Such a labor supply is believed to be adequate for the construction of the monumental ruins of the Classic

Period. Without independent evidence of the size of the Classic Period population, it is not possible to state categorically that it did not exceed the limit set by slash and burn agriculture. The data on recent settlement patterns, however, make such a possibility unlikely.

The supply of nutrients in the soil decreases when successive crops are grown on a plot and increases when plots are left to fallow. Chemical analyses of soil samples from plots with various agricultural histories were performed to determine nitrogen, organic matter, plant available phosphorus, exchangeable sodium, potassium, calcium and magnesium and pH. Burning the land has no effect on exchangeable sodium or pH, brings about an increase in exchangeable potassium and magnesium, and causes all other items measured to decrease. Organic matter and all the elements determined increase with rest. It is believed that the observed declines when successive crops are grown are sufficiently great to explain the observed decline in yield.

Invasion of agricultural land by grasses is not a problem at the present time. Data from pollen analysis (to be discussed later) clearly shows that such an invasion did not play a part in the overall agricultural decline at the end of Classic times.

It is felt that a material decrease in food supply can, for this region, be ignored as a possible cause for the collapse of Classic Maya culture.

The present system is by far the most efficient use of the land possible with the means available, and there is no evidence that the modern indigenous population is making any misuse of the land.

EROSION AND THE COOKE-RICKETSON HYPOTHESIS

The system of *bajos* appears to be a series of valleys that have been elevated at their lower ends by tectonic movements, thus bringing about the development of flood plains. The tilting may have been sufficient to form shallow lake basins, which were silted by the process of mass wasting. The wasting must have been even more intense initially, prior to the solution of limestone, when differences in level between the bottom of the *bajos* and the top of the scarp surrounding them must have been greater than today.

In order to investigate this matter, a pit (339 cm. long, 122 cm. wide, 511 cm. deep) was dug in the Bajo de Santa Fé, a large seasonal swamp east of the ancient Maya city of Tikal, El Petén, Guatemala. The results of the digging and subsequent laboratory studies on the samples are given in detail by Cowgill and Hutchinson (MS).

The section in the Bajo de Santa Fé shows 5.11 m. of sediment below which it was not possible to dig, though it is quite likely that the Bajo filling extends downward very much further. At 5.11 m. structureless carbonized organic matter of unknown nature gave a C^{14} date of 11,560 ± 360 years B. P. (Stuiver and Deevey 1962). The greater part of the observed deposit consists of a rather pure clay, mainly montmorillonite. In the upper and lower parts of this profile there are numerous flint nodules, but they are absent from the middle section. At the top, the deposit is much darker and browner; analysis shows an increased but still very small amount of organic matter.

The clay found in the *bajos* today was formed by the decomposition of limestone from the scarp. The decomposition could not have occurred *in situ* since datable organic carbon was found at 5 m., and root casts were encountered throughout the extent of the pit. The limestone at the top of the scarp contains 1.107 percent residue on treatment with acid. This residue is largely montmorillonitic clay and is extremely similar to the clay found in the Bajo pit. About 200 m. of limestone per unit area must have dissolved to produce the clay deposited per unit area in the past 11 millenia.

On the basis of evidence obtained from this study it is concluded that the Bajo deposit during the past 11,560 years was laid down in a seasonal swamp and not in an open water lake. The irregular occurrence of isolated unwater-worn flints embedded in the clay without any indication of sorting or the formation of littoral deposits is the most critical evidence. The petrology of the flints (Sanders, Appendix I in Cowgill and Hutchinson MS) shows them to have been formed by replacement in partially dolomatized marine limestone. They must have arrived at the site of the pit by a process of mass wasting. When the scarp was higher, the process was somewhat faster. The middle section is void of flint nodules, but they are present in the upper part.

The presence of live roots at the top of the profile, of dead roots underneath this layer followed by fossilized roots beneath the dead ones, the latter filled with gypsum and haematite in the middle and lower sections of the core, would suggest that the region of the pit has been covered with a forest for the past 11 millenia. The absence of pollen and the presence of haematite throughout the sediment imply oxidizing conditions, and the absence of diatoms would all point toward the absence of a lacustrine deposit.

Conditions of sedimentation must have been fairly uniform, for below the live root zone the clay, except for a slight change in color, is amazingly uniform. The distribution of flint nodules does suggest some changes in the rate of sedimentation. With the exception of 235 to 290 cm. and 345 to 410 cm. they are present throughout the extent of the pit. The lower flint zone represents more active mass wasting when the scarps around the *bajos* were steeper. The renewed appearance of flint above 235 cm. indicates disturbances of the slopes by man's activities.

The over-all rate of sedimentation based on the date obtained from the carbon found at 5 m. below the datum point is 460 cm. per 11,560 years or about 40 cm. per millenium. If it is assumed that man has been in the region 3000 to 4000 years and his entry is marked by the renewal of flint deposits, the latter would be expected to begin in the 120 to 160 cm. region below the surface or 170 to 210 cm. below the datum line. The higher figure is not far from the observed base of the upper flint at 235 cm. There may well have been some acceleration in erosion on account of human activity but the over-all rate is unlikely to have increased by more than a factor of 1.5.

Ricketson (1937) reports the presence of a 2.05 m. layer of decomposed vegetable matter, which he compares to upland soil. The top layers of the Bajo de Santa Fé are indeed somewhat organic, though chemical analyses show the organic content to be lower than that of the upland soils which also contain much calcium carbonate, a mineral that is entirely lacking in our section. Samples of soil were taken from the top of the scarp, the slopes of the scarp and the bottom of the scarp, all of which erode into the Bajo. At the bottom of the scarp, the deposit is void of calcite crystals, and the upper portion is dark and does show a higher ignition loss. It is possible that Ricketson's pit in the Bajo de Joventud near Uaxactún was dug in such a marginal area, though one in which calcite was apparently present, since he records the presence of the mineral. It is possible that his pit lay in an old stream bed, since he mentions finding gravel and water-worn pebbles, totally lacking in the excavation near Tikal.

There thus seems to be considerable difference between the two pits dug in the two *bajos*. It is certain that there can have been no lake or lake shore at the site of our pit during the past 11 millenia. The section in the Bajo de Santa Fé, however, shows stratigraphy that is remarkably similar to that described by Simmons *et al.* (n. d.) for all *bajo* soils; there is a little further evidence for the existence of a great thickness of such deposits in other *bajos*. It is possible that Ricketson's pit, dug much nearer to the edge of the *bajo* than was ours, shows a section in a marginal deposit that does not bear very much on the general history of the area; it clearly cannot be used as evidence of widespread destructive erosion and filling of lakes.

Further information on erosion rates as well as an extremely important body

THE SEDIMENTARY HISTORY OF LAKE PETENXIL

of data on pollen sequences and other microfossils have been obtained from a study of two cores from Laguna de Petenxil, to the east of Lake Petén Itzá. The cores studied are not more than 2.5 m. long, covering about four millenia of the history of the lake. The sediment consists primarily of halloysite with a moderate organic carbon content of about 5 percent throughout most of the section. At the bottom of the longer core the organic content is much higher, but at the top of both cores it is much lower. The fall in the organic content at the top clearly implies increased erosion. The effect is most noticeable in the shorter core P_3, taken nearer to the southern shore of the lake than the central core P_2.

In P_3 from which we have a number of C^{14} dates covering the period from 2180 B. P. to the present, the rate of sedimentation rises very slowly and probably not significantly from 0.7 mm. per year to 0.9 mm. per year until 635 B. P. (Stuiver and Deevey 1961). Above this level the rate is 1.4 mm. per year. The bottom section of the longer core P_2 shows a sedimentation rate of 0.5 mm. per year between 3990 B. P. and 2050 B. P. (Stuiver, Deevey, and Rouse 1963).

It is clear that the major increase in erosion in the Petenxil basin occurred in Post-Classic and probably Post-Columbian times. It is clearly associated with the events on the south side of the lake, though as far as is known the important Pre-Columbian sites in the area are likely to have been north of the lake. The area is sparsely inhabited today and no evidence of striking erosion due to agriculture is evident. We suspect that the change was due to a shift in human settlement and agricultural patterns, possibly as a result of rumors circulating as to Spanish penetration in the 16th century. The change, whatever its nature, is too late to bear on the problem of the collapse of the Classic civilization. The increase in inorganic sediment may be compared with that of Linsley Pond, where clearing the land in the 18th century caused the organic matter content of the lake mud to drop from 50 percent to 25 percent (Hutchinson and Wollack 1940).

VEGETATIONAL CHANGES IN THE PETENXIL BASIN

Tsukada prepared a remarkable account of the illuminating and in some ways surprising results of his studies of the pollen sequence in our cores (Tsukada et al. 1962). He divides the sequence into three periods. G_1, anterior to about 2800 B. P. or perhaps rather earlier (gap in core), corresponds to savanna vegetation with *Quercus* and *Pinus* and some *Moraceae*. Grass pollen is very abundant, composites less so. A very few *Zea* grains indicate the presence of agricultural man, but clearly no great human occupation.

In G₂, which lasted until about 1300 B. P., the vegetation was in general similar to that of G₁, save that a large quantity of an *Ambrosia*-like pollen is present along with a notable quantity of *Zea*. The *Ambrosia*-like grains presumably belong to a cultivation weed. After 1300 B. P. in G₃, *Zea* slowly declines and the vegetation becomes dominated by tropical forest genera, members of the *Moraceae*, *Terminalia* and *Zanthoxylon* being important while the grasses decline. The pollen of G₃ is similar to that produced by modern vegetation, while that of G₂ represents a period of intensive agriculture, and G₁ is clearly a savanna period.

These findings clearly imply that in the vicinity of Petenxil agriculture developed, even though we cannot say categorically that it originated, in an area that was largely grassland; the tropical forest took over from the Mayan agriculturalists as their planting declined.

Welcome confirmation of the sequence was provided by the discovery in the Petenxil sediments of numerous small fragments of epidermis of grasses. These fragments were for the most part, though not entirely, carbonized and must have been produced by grass fires, from which the smallest fragments were blown into the lake. At present milpas are normally burned before planting, when a high wind heralds the advent of a rainstorm. The carbonized grass fragments were most abundant in the deepest layers of the core, in G₁ and the beginning of G₂. They become less abundant in G₂ at the time of the *Zea* maximum, and least abundant late in G₃ when the rate of sedimentation had increased. Even allowing for the more rapid sedimentation, the abundance declines somewhat at the top. The record suggests that originally much more burning took place than would be necessary for optimal cultivation, in a landscape covered largely with grasses. During the agricultural peak perhaps more systematic planning and control of burning took place. Whatever the detailed interpretation, these findings are clearly concordant with the hypothesis that the early phases of agriculture involved the cultivation of a grassland rather than a forest.

Today, it is not unusual to find people planting in the savanna. Some *milperos* clear the land of grass by burning. In the shorter grass regions a hoe-like stick may then be used to break the sod, after which planting is easily possible.

POSSIBLE EVIDENCE OF VEGETATIONAL CHANGE IN THE BAJO DE SANTA FÉ

In contrast to the vegetation surrounding Petenxil, the Bajo de Santa Fé appears to have been occupied by swamp forest vegetation for the past 11,560 years. No fossils other than replaced roots, which occur throughout the section, have been found, but one hint of a possible change in plant cover has been observed. Between 293 and 307 cm. and at 330 cm. a rare earth bearing calcium, strontium, lead, aluminum phosphate, apparently a variety of crandallite, was found (Cowgill, Hutchinson and Joensuu MS). At 330 cm. it is dispersed in the clay; in the other 14 cm. it is associated with gypsum or found in root cavities. On the basis of the assumption of uniform sedimentation, this mineral was formed about the fifth millenium B. C. Where the mineral occurred with gypsum, it was always found deposited on the surfaces or between gypsum crystals; hence the gypsum was formed prior to the phosphate. The only conceivable method of formation of the latter is by the biogeochemical activity of plants.

A composite of the leaves of twenty species growing in the vicinity of the pit at the time of excavation was analyzed, and no remarkable enrichment of any element was found.

In order to develop such a mineral, plants that accumulated strontium, aluminum, and perhaps lead and the rare earths would be necessary. The Melastomaceae as a group accumulate aluminum (Hutchinson and Wollack 1943). At the present time no members of the family grow in the part of the Bajo where the pit was dug, but species of *Miconia* and of other genera occur in other parts of the region (Lundell 1961). Samples of *Miconia ciliata* from British Honduras were found to accumulate both aluminum and strontium but no rare earths. Indeed the only rare earth accumulators at present known are species of *Carya* (Robinson *et al.* 1958), a genus which does not occur in the Petén.

It would be reasonable to assume that the crandallite was formed by the decomposition of roots of the Melastomaceae, in which process an aluminum alkaline earth phosphate gel was produced that sorbed other elements and precipitated on gypsum crystals, formed in root cavities. Throughout the part of the section in which the mineral occurs, the phosphate is somewhat higher than above or below, being specially enriched at 330 cm. It is therefore possible that because of the increased phosphate a change in vegetation occurred, characterized by an increase in the number of the Melastomaceae, or possibly some other accumulator plant. The cause of the higher phosphate content may be that at the period in question a rather more phosphatic limestone was eroding than at other times. This explanation must remain hypothetical since the postulated limestone would have disappeared by now. Whatever vegetational or other change was responsible for the formation of the curious phosphate, climatic changes did not appear to have been involved.

EVIDENCE OF CLIMATIC STABILITY AND CHANGE

The changes in erosion rate in the Bajo section can be explained formally by the reduction in slope as limestone dissolved and by the advent of man. In neither case is the change impressive. At least the later change in Lake Petenxil is also likely to involve human settlement, though perhaps neither of the two changes here appear to be associated with the development of a high agricultural civilization. It remains to be considered whether there is any independent evidence of climatic change that might be correlated with erosional changes, archaeological events or other phenomena in the region.

The only geochemical indicator of climatic change likely to be available in the region is chloride. This ion is presumably supplied to the region almost exclusively in rain, the chloride content of calcareous sediments being ordinarily very low. The chloride delivered per unit area of land surface is likely to depend largely on the rainfall. What happens to the chloride will also depend on evaporation.

In a lake sediment which has been permanently wet, it is probably legitimate to consider the chloride content of any layer, referred to the water content of that layer, as an indication of the chloride concentration of the lake water when the sediment was formed. Applying this concept to the Laguna de Petenxil we find that in the deepest layers accessible, corresponding to the bottom of G_1, the chloride content was rather high, and fell throughout the period. During G_2 the chloride is relatively low. Sometime after the beginning of G_3, there is an irregular rise in chloride. During the period of rapid sedimentation a clear fall occurs in both cores; there appears to be a secondary maximum near the surface in P_2, not found in P_3. We may reasonably conclude that at times of high chloride the lake level was lower and the balance of evaporation and precipitation more in favor of the former; when the chloride content was low, the lake level was high and the precipitation had increased relative to evaporation. We conclude, therefore, that in G_1 the lake level was rising, and during most of G_2 was relatively high, though falling in the second half of the period. This fall is continued into G_3, with a minimum level somewhat before the sudden rise in sedimentation rate. During the period of increased sedimentation the record from the two cores is inconsistent and ambiguous, but there was probably a high water level at about the time of the beginning of the process, then a lower one, and at the present time again a high level. A rise of 1 m. occurred between 1959 and 1961, according to the Rev. S. Storey who visited the lake in the latter year.

Confirmatory evidence of higher lake levels during G_2 is obtained from Dr. Clyde Goulden's study of the Cladoceran remains. In interpreting this data it must, however, be remembered that when the sediment at about 150 cm. was formed, if the lake level was at the modern position, the water would inevitably be 1.5 m. deeper. The ratio of planktonic to benthic-littoral species should be a good indication of the amount of open water in a shallow lake undergoing fluctuations in level. It is clear from Dr. Goulden's work that this ratio was much greater in G_2 than in G_3. Since the lake is still largely open water, the meaning of the low planktonic figures at the present day is not clear. The much greater ratio of planktonic to littoral-benthic forms in G_2 is, however, in accord with our belief that the water level was rather higher during the latter period. This would imply a somewhat wetter period during the height of Maya civilization than during the subsequent decline when tropical forest was establishing itself. It is clear that the latter process was not accompanied by an increase in rainfall but rather the reverse.

A longer historical record is represented by the continuous column of samples taken from the pit dug in El Bajo de Santa Fé. The distribution of chloride in the profile is very different from that presented by Lake Petenxil. Throughout the lower portion of the column the chloride content is high, about 0.1 percent in the dry sediment or about 0.5 percent when referred to the water in the wet sediment. At 260 cm. it rises abruptly, reaching a striking maximum at 250 cm. followed by a minimum at 235 cm. Above the latter level it returns to almost the same values as that found in the lower portion of the section, and then declines rather irregularly to a low content at the surface. With the exception of the uppermost portions of the Bajo profile the chloride content found is considerably higher than that encountered in any of the samples studied from the two cores of Petenxil.

A series of rainwater samples were collected in the Petén and analyzed; the mean chloride content is 1.57 mg. per liter. If we assume a mean annual rainfall for the region of 1800 mm. per year, the annual delivery of chloride would be 0.28 mg. cm.$^{-2}$. Taking into account the mean density of the sediments (1.79) and integrating over the entire profile, we find 675 mg. cm.$^{-2}$, which for a period of 11,560 years corresponds to an accession of 0.0584 mg. cm.$^{-2}$ per year. The chloride that is found to have remained in the Bajo during this period could therefore have been supplied by 20.8 percent of that in modern rainfall, assuming a constant rainfall and a constant amount of chloride over this period. This implies that the runoff from the Bajo is 79.2 percent of the rainfall. Actually this would be an underestimate since a good deal of water must flow from the high forest and through the Bajo during the wet season.

Were the Bajo a lake, one could assume that the chloride content of any given layer represents that of the water retained in that layer as it formed and was covered by a new layer. However, the Bajo is not a lake and supports a rather short but nevertheless luxuriant forest. In the lower portion of the section the chloride content is rather uniform. As rainwater percolates through the live root portion of the section, nearly all the water, but only some of the chloride, will be taken up by trees. During the time that transpiration proceeds, the chloride will accumulate in the deeper part of the root zone. As the sediment accumulates and the live root zone moves upwards, the chloride in the layer below will remain in relatively stable concentrations.

The chloride maximum therefore probably represents an intensification of the concentration-transpiration process just described, reflecting a period of longer wet seasons. The minimum, though less well developed, may represent excessive removal of partially concentrated chloride moving downward during the wet period or alternatively a period of short rainy seasons.

Because the postulated effect of the supposed climatic oscillation did not occur at the surface, the time at which the change occurred is later than the time when the sediment was laid down. The rapid fall in chloride at the top begins at 150 cm. or just below the live root zone. The chloride maximum at 250 cm. probably was generated when that layer was covered by 100 cm. of sediment less than today. Assuming a constant rate of sedimentation of 40 cm. per millenia, we calculate that the date of the chloride maximum would be about 2500 B. P. Since there is some evidence that the top 100 cm. have accumulated somewhat faster than the middle section, this date is probably too great. It is therefore possible that the high chloride in the Bajo corresponds to the minimum in chloride and maximum in rainfall in the Petenxil Basin, probably about 2000 B. P.

MISCELLANEOUS FIELD OBSERVATIONS

During the course of field work certain peripheral observations were made which throw some light on structures which have been believed to have archaeological significance. These observations relate to the *aguadas,* water holes or ponds supposed to have been constructed or enlarged to conserve water, and the smaller deeper holes in the bed rock, locally called *chultunes,* and supposedly used as storage pits. At least the existence of *aguadas* has been used by Bullard (1960) as an argument for water shortage being a significant factor in Maya economy. He feels that the supposed construction or enlargement of the *aguadas* occurred about the time the *bajos* were allegedly being silted, as the result of an excessive agricultural use of land during the height of the Classic Period. As far as we are aware, no way of dating the *aguadas* has been discovered. In almost every case, the Aguada Términos at Tikal being an exception, these basins are dry during part of the year. Any core taken in such a locality would be valueless, for pollen and other micro-fossils as well as datable organic matter would have been oxidized during the dry season.

During a visit to Tikal in the spring of 1962 while sampling an *aguada* for water and plankton, it was noticed that peccaries were wallowing in it. Close observation indicated that at least part of the *aguada* had been enlarged by the process. It would therefore be difficult to determine whether some types of enlargement have been the result of zoogenous erosion or of man's activities. Comparable cases of this type of erosion are known elsewhere (Hutchinson 1957:130, 132).

The present consensus in archaeological circles concerning the origin of the pits or *chultunes* frequently found in limestone regions throughout the world is that at least in the Maya region they are artificial. In the Yucatán Peninsula there is, however, a palm tree locally called *botan* (*Sabal* sp.) which has an extremely fibrous root system. After this palm has achieved a certain height any violent storm is able to uproot it. During the last visit to the Tikal region, it was noticed that several of these trees had collapsed, leaving deep holes not unlike those that would be called *chultunes* by archaeologists. It would appear therefore that these trees are initially responsible for forming *chultunes*, though in some cases the ancient Maya have modified them for use as storage pits or for waste disposal. Comparable observations have been made elsewhere (Romney 1959:302; Scott 1910).

CONCLUDING REMARKS

Our studies would therefore lead us to conclude, contrary to the opinion of so many of our predecessors, that the central Petén can under current conditions support a very much larger agricultural population, using indigenous methods, than it does at present; that a high agricultural civilization developed, even if it did not originate, when the vegetation of the area was largely grassland, which was later invaded by tropical forest after agricultural abandonment; that the increase in erosion rate has been small and, in the one locality where it can be measured, series of vast open lakes in the region is not founded on adequate evidence and, at least in the vicinity of Tikal, is erroneous; and that insofar as there have been significant climatic changes, around 2000 years ago the region was slightly wetter than previously or subsequently. There may thus have been a reduction in rainfall in the later Classic and Post Classic, but the evidence does not suggest anything catastrophic. We feel that the present studies tend to invalidate practically **every** idea of external ecological change that has been put forward to explain the Maya collapse in the so-called "Old Empire."

The problem may well be resolved only in terms of a multiplicity of causes, not all acting in the same way over the entire area. In other papers (Cowgill and Hutchinson 1963a, 1963b) we have pointed out that a very peculiar demographic situation exists in the present Indian population of the Petén. Compared with Ladino families in the same region, female children of Indian families appear to suffer an extraordinary mortality, leading to a sex ratio in early adolescence of about 180 males per 100 females. This ratio is probably established as the result of less careful nurture of female children in Indian families. Existing data indicate that this effect could not be the result of an abnormal new-born sex ratio. There is in fact a suggestion of less than 100 males per 100 females at birth among the Indian population of the Petén, though the numbers are too small to carry much statistical significance. We have suggested that if practices resulting in the observed sex ratios at the onset of adolescence evolved in a population which was initially static or expanding slowly, such a sex ratio could lead to a rapid decline. Obscure demographic phenomena may therefore have contributed to the observed depopulation of the area.

BIBLIOGRAPHY

BARTLETT, H. H.
  1956 "Fire, Primitive Agriculture and Grazing in the Tropics," in *Man's Role in Changing the Face of the Earth,* pp. 692-721. Chicago: University of Chicago Press.

BULLARD, W. R.
  1960 Maya Settlement Pattern in Northeastern Petén, Guatemala. *American Antiquity* 25:355-372.

COE, W. R.
  1957 Environmental Limitation on Maya Culture: a Re-examination. *American Anthropologist* 59:328-335.

COOK, O. F.
  1909 *Vegetation Effected by Agriculture in Central America.* U. S. Department of Agriculture, Bureau of Plant Industry, bulletin 145, Washington, D. C.
  1921 Milpa Agriculture, a Primitive Tropical System. *Annual Report of the Smithsonian Institution for 1919,* pp. 307-326. Washington, D. C.

COOKE, C. W.
  1931 Why the Maya Cities of the Petén District, Guatemala Were Abandoned. *Journal of the Washington Academy of Science* 21:283-287.
  1933 A Possible Solution of a Maya Mystery. Science Service Radio Talks, presented over CBS, pp. 362-365.

COWGILL, U. M.

1961 Soil Fertility and the Ancient Maya. *Transactions of the Connecticut Academy of Arts and Sciences* 42:1-56.

1962 An Agricultural Study of the Southern Maya Lowlands. *American Anthropologist* 64:273-286.

COWGILL, U. M., AND G. E. HUTCHINSON

1963a Sex Ratio in Childhood and the Depopulation of the Petén, Guatemala. *Human Biology* 35:90-103.

1963b Differential Mortality Among the Sexes in Childhood and Its Possible Significance in Human Evolution. *Proceedings of the National Academy of Sciences* 49:425-429.

MS El Bajo de Santa Fé. *Transactions of the American Philosophical Society* (in press).

COWGILL, U. M., G. E. HUTCHINSON AND O. JOENSUU

MS An Apparently Triclinic Dimorph of Crandallite From a Tropical Swamp in El Petén, Guatemala. *American Mineralogist* (in press).

DIAZ DEL CASTILLO, BERNAL

1956 *The True History of the Conquest of New Spain.* Translated A. P. Maudslay. Hakluyt Society.

EMERSON, R. A.

n.d. A Preliminary Study of the Milpa System of Maize Culture as Practiced by the Maya Indians of the Northern Part of the Yucatán Peninsula. Cornell University, New York. Unpublished manuscript.

EMERSON, R. A., AND J. H. KEMPTON

1935 Agronomic Investigations in Yucatán. *Carnegie Institution of Washington Yearbook* 34:138-142.

EVANS, SIR J.

1897 *Ancient Stone Implements, Weapons and Ornaments of Great Britain.* 2nd. ed. rev. London and Bombay: Longmans, Green, and Co.

FERDON, E. N., JR.

1959 Agricultural Potential and the Development of Cultures. *Southwestern Journal of Anthropology* 15:1-19.

HESTER, J. A., JR.

1951 Agriculture, Economy and Population Density. *Carnegie Institution of Washington Yearbook* 51:266-271.

1952 Agriculture, Economy and Population Density. *Carnegie Institution of Washington Yearbook* 52:288-292.

1953 Maya Agriculture. *Carnegie Institution of Washington Yearbook* 53:297-298.

1954 Natural and Cultural Bases of Ancient Maya Subsistence Economy. Unpublished Ph. D. dissertation, University of California, Los Angeles.

HUNTINGTON, ELLSWORTH

1951 *Principles of Human Geography.* 6th ed. (ed. by E. B. Shaw). New York: John Wiley & Sons, Inc.

HUTCHINSON, G. E.
  1957   A Treatise on Limnology, vol. 1. New York: John Wiley & Sons, Inc.
HUTCHINSON, G. E., AND A. WOLLACK
  1940   Studies on Connecticut Lake Sediments II. Chemical Analyses of a Core from Linsley Pond, North Branford. American Journal of Science 238: 499-517.
  1943   Biological Accumulators of Aluminum. Transactions of the Connecticut Academy of Arts and Sciences 35:73-128.
KEMPTON, J. H.
  1935   Report on Agricultural Survey. Carnegie Institution of Washington, Report to the Government of Mexico, 12th year of Chichén Itzá Project and Allied Investigations.
LUNDELL, C. L.
  1961   Plantae Mayanae II, Collections from Peten and Belice. Wrightia 2: 111-126.
MEGGERS, B. J.
  1954   Environmental Limitations on the Development of Culture. American Anthropologist 56:801-823.
  1957   Environmental Limitations on Maya Culture: a Reply to Coe. American Anthropologist 59:888-890.
NIETSCH, H.
  1939   Wald und Siedlung im Vorgeschichtlichen Mitteleuropa. Leipzig: Curt Kabitzsch.
RICKETSON, O. G., AND E. B. RICKETSON
  1937   Uaxactún, Guatemala, Group E, 1926-31. Carnegie Institution of Washington Publication 477.
ROBINSON, W. O., H. BASTRON AND K. J. MURATA
  1958   Biogeochemistry of the Rare-earth Elements with Particular Reference to Hickory Trees. Geochmica et Cosmochimica Acta: 14:55-67.
ROMNEY, D. H. (ED.)
  1959   Land in British Honduras. Colonial Research Publication 24. H. M. S. O., London.
RUSSELL, R. J.
  1956   "Environmental Changes Through Forces Independent of Man," in Man's Role in Changing the Face of the Earth, pp. 453-471. Chicago: University of Chicago Press.
SCOTT, W.
  1910   The Fauna of a Solution Pond. Proceedings of the Indiana Academy of Science 26:395.
SIMMONS, C. S., J. M. TÁRANO AND H. PINTO
  n.d.   Informe Sobre la Clasificación de Reconocimiento de los Suelas del Departamento de Petén. Ministerio de Agricultura, Servicio Cooperativo Interamericano de Agricultura. Guatemala. Unpublished manuscript.

STEGGERDA, M.
    1941   *Maya Indians of Yucatán.* Carnegie Institution of Washington Publication 531.
STUIVER, M., AND E. S. DEEVEY
    1961   Yale Natural Radiocarbon Measurements VI. *Radiocarbon* 3:126-140.
    1962   Yale Natural Radiocarbon Measurements VII. *Radiocarbon* 4:250-262.
STUIVER, M., E. S. DEEVEY, AND I. ROUSE
    1963   Yale Natural Radiocarbon Measurements VIII. *Radiocarbon* 5:312-341.
TSUKADA, M., U. M. COWGILL AND G. E. HUTCHINSON
    1962   The History of Lake Petenxil, Departamento de El Petén, Guatemala. (Abstract.) *Science* 136:329.

YALE UNIVERSITY
NEW HAVEN, CONNECTICUT

A problem that has caused much controversy in the past and according to recent literature is still unresolved, concerns the cause of late 19th century arroyo cycles in the American Southwest. The Rich article is reproduced here to introduce one view in this debate. His work represents some of the first by a well-qualified geologist to unequivocally state that the stream trenching was started by man-induced measures. The lack of references in his article suggests that he believed his theory was original. His thesis is that man by introducing the open range along with millions of livestock (New Mexico had 4,000,000 sheep by 1880, Denevan, 1967) brought about overgrazing which caused ruination of the vegetative cover, and pulverization of the topsoil which then initiated a new cycle of erosion. His ideas are supported by those of Bailey (1935) and by Gregory and Moore (1931) who state:

> ... the effect of grazing, especially overgrazing, on run-off and stream trenching is obvious. The net result of the interference by man with the delicately adjusted streams is an increase in the amount of surface water and number of intermittent springs accompanied by a destruction of forage and arable land.

Bryan (1925) provides some support for Rich's overgrazing hypothesis but believed there may also have been multiple causes that could have included such factors as regional uplift with increased gradients, a drier climate causing more runoff because of less vegetative cover, disrepair of ancient man's check dams, and incisement of main channels because of less water in tributaries.

A contrasting view is advanced by Leopold (1951) who rejects the usual climate-change hypothesis of different amounts of annual precipitation in favor of a change in storm patterns causing different frequency and intensity of rainfall. Hack (1942) provides additional information on past climates of the Southwest. Review articles concerning arroyo cycles have been written by Peterson (1950) and Tuan (1966) who conclude the problem is unresolved but probably due to multiple causes. Denevan (1967, p. 691) summarizes his views, after review of different ideas, and states: "The incomplete record of livestock numbers in relation to climate and gullying backs up the climatic argument but also gives some new support to the older view that overgrazing was a major contributive factor causing severe modern gullying."

John L. Rich (1884–1956) was born in Hobart, New York, and received his Ph.D. (1911) from Cornell University. For three years he was a petroleum geologist and he taught at the universities of Cornell, Illinois, and Cincinnati. He has written several articles and two of his books are *Glacial Geology of the Catskill Mountains* (1935) and *The Face of South America: An Aerial Traverse* (1942).

22

THE

AMERICAN JOURNAL OF SCIENCE

[FOURTH SERIES.]

—◆◆◆—

ART. XXVII.—*Recent Stream Trenching in the Semi-arid Portion of Southwestern New Mexico, a Result of Removal of Vegetation Cover ;** by JOHN LYON RICH.

A CONSPICUOUS development of recent stream trenches in the valleys of many of the temporary streams of the western states is a feature of such widespread and common occurrence that it cannot be assigned to accidental causes, but calls for an explanation which shall have more than a local application. This trenching is particularly well developed in portions of southwestern New Mexico. Here it is apparently an effect of the removal of vegetation cover by excessive grazing. A brief description of the nature of the trenching and a statement of the evidence on which the above explanation of the phenomenon is based is the purpose of the following discussion.

The portion of New Mexico on which our study is particularly based is included within the Silver City quadrangle in the southwestern part of the state. The quadrangle may be roughly divided into two physiographic units, a mountainous portion and a desert plain formed by the accumulation of gravels derived from the mountains. Of the whole area of the quadrangle, about one-third is covered by these desert accumulations.

The climate is semi-arid, with an average rainfall in the neighborhood of 18 inches in the mountainous parts, and considerably less in the lower, desert portions. The precipitation comes mostly in the form of showers during the hot summer months, from about the middle of June until the latter part of September. General rains are not of common occurrence. As a result of these climatic conditions there are no permanent streams in the area outside the higher mountains, and even in

* Published by permission of the Director of the U. S. Geological Survey.

AM. JOUR. SCI.—FOURTH SERIES, VOL. XXXII, No. 190.—OCTOBER, 1911.
18

the mountains, the permanent streams are of small consequence except when swollen by the summer rains.

In the following discussion when we speak of streams we would be understood as referring to the temporary streams which carry water only during, or immediately after, a storm.

A conspicuous feature of the topography of the Silver City quadrangle, outside the more rugged mountains, is a pronounced stream trenching in all the valleys; a trenching of recent date which is evidently still in progress. Along the steep-walled mountain gorges this feature is, of course, not evident, but outside of the higher mountains it would be difficult

FIG. 1.

FIG. 1. View showing typical features along the course of the Cane Spring Canyon stream across the piedmont fan. The photograph shows recent trench in the foreground cut into alluvial valley filling, piedmont gravels in the middle distance along the sides of the valley, and mountains at source of the stream in background. Note the bowlders and flood débris spread out over the surface of the alluvial flat.

to name a valley in which it is not conspicuous. The features shown in different parts of the quadrangle are so similar that a description of one of the most typical valleys will serve as a characterization of the general conditions throughout the area, and as a basis for a discussion of the causes of the trenching. For such a description the valley called Cane Spring Canyon, along which some of the accompanying photographs were taken, will admirably serve our purpose.

The stream, which is a temporary one, flowing only in times of flood, heads with several branches in a region of rocky hills of moderate height. Within the hills it has a drainage area of about seven square miles. After leaving the hills the stream flows with an average slope of 120 feet per mile for about 5 miles across a dissected piedmont gravel accumulation to the Mangas, a larger temporary stream which, about 15 miles below, empties into the Gila, a good-sized permanent stream.

The salient features of the Cane Spring valley in its course across the piedmont gravels are well shown in the accompanying photograph (fig. 1). There are first the steep-sided valley walls of partly cemented desert conglomerate from 50 to 150 feet high; then, forming the valley floor, comes an alluvial flat, nearly level in cross section; and finally, cutting sharply

FIG. 2.

FIG. 2. Recent stream trench working back into the still undissected flat of a small tributary of Cane Spring Canyon. This picture was taken near the site of fig. 1.

into the material of this flat, is the recent stream trench from 50 to 200 feet in width and from 2 to 15 feet in depth, and bounded, as a rule, by vertical walls of alluvium.

The history of the valley as revealed by its cross section may be briefly summarized as follows: The valley was initiated on the surface of the piedmont desert fan. For some reason—an uplift of the land or a change in climatic conditions—the stream began cutting through the fan. This cutting continued until a valley from one-eighth to one-fourth mile in width and locally over 150 feet in depth had been formed. Following this period of cutting came one of filling, during which the alluvial flats in the valley were formed. Lastly, the streams began cutting again, forming the trenches whose origin we are seeking. These trenches are still working their way up the tributary valleys by headwater recession and sapping. This is well illustrated by fig. 2, which shows the trench working back into the still undissected flat of a small tributary.

The alluvial flats are composed of fine sandy loam and gravel. The latter occurs in the form of irregular lenses interspersed through the loam. Its component pebbles range in size up to 5, 6, or 8 inches in diameter, but seldom larger, and even these sizes are uncommon. Two or three inches in diameter would represent a fair average for the coarser gravel. From this there is every gradation down to fine sand. The stratification is indistinct, but may usually be made out. In characteristic exposure the material stands up in vertical bluffs. From its general make-up and composition there can be no doubt that it is a stream deposit of the type formed by aggrading temporary streams.

Fairly uniform conditions of deposition are shown by the nature of the sediment. That heavy floods were not common during the time of deposition is indicated by the lack of heavy bowlders in the deposit. The valley filling is not an ordinary flood plain such as may be formed along permanent streams, for, in the first place, the slope of the valley bottom, 120 feet per mile, is too great for the formation of a flood plain so wide and flat as the one we are considering; and in the second place, the surface of the flat is not a graded slope along the stream course. Alluvial fans from the valley sides form an integral part of the valley filling. Their prominence, and their effect in breaking the normal valley profile, indicate that a large proportion of the filling came from the sides down the short steep tributaries rather than down the main valley.

On the whole, then, the character of the valley filling indicates accumulation under conditions such that there was no permanent stream in the main valley, and such that accumulations from the sides were as important as those from the main stream. These conditions would be realized under an arid or semi-arid climate during the time of filling.

In the bottoms of the trenches and sometimes spread out over the surface of the flats above, there is *coarse* stream gravel with bowlders ranging up to two feet in diameter, and much of it evidently of very recent deposition. This coarse material presents a marked and significant contrast to the fine textured alluvial valley filling revealed in the side walls of the trenches. The significance lies in the fact that its transportation must have required a volume of water much greater than that of the finer alluvial material on which it rests. Its presence overlying the finer material and the fact that it is associated with flood débris in such a manner as to prove its deposition within a very few years at most, clearly indicates that, in recent times, the maximum volume of water coming down the valley in times of flood has been greater than while the alluvium was accumulating.

On the basis of such evidence of the increased volume of flood waters, we are justified in suspecting that the waters of these floods may have been responsible for the cutting of the stream trenches in question. In an endeavor to explain the trenching it is, therefore, necessary to look for the cause of the increased volume of the flood waters.

Such an increase may be the result of one or the other of two conditions or a combination of both. These conditions are: either an increase in the amount of water by increased precipitation, or a more rapid run-off with no increase in precipitation. An analysis of the results of each of these two conditions taken separately may serve to indicate which is most probably the responsible one in the case at hand.

Taking first the condition of increased precipitation, we will start with a semi-arid climate, such that the streams are not permanent and are silting up their valleys—in other words, with conditions as we conceive them to have been at the time of the formation of the valley fill of Cane Spring Canyon and other valleys of the region. There would undoubtedly be some vegetation which might serve as a fairly efficient cover and constitute an important factor in the absence of heavy floods. With an increase in precipitation we should expect the vegetation to become more luxuriant and more effective as a protective covering; in this way perhaps equaling or over-balancing the tendency of the stream toward cutting, resulting from the increased volume of water. Even though the storms became heavier, the run-off would be slower, so that it is likely that, until the time that the precipitation became so great that the streams became permanent, there would be little, if any, increased tendency toward cutting.

Considering next the second factor; if we have a semi-arid climate favorable to the formation of a fairly efficient vegetation cover, and the balance between erosion and deposition is so adjusted that the streams are silting up with fine material; with considerable rainfall at certain times of the year, prevented, however, by the vegetation cover from forming heavy floods, and if by some means we remove the vegetation cover without changing the amount or distribution of the rainfall, marked results of a different nature will follow. The rain, still as heavy as before, will fall on a bare surface unprotected by vegetation and with little capacity to hold in reserve the excess precipitation. A rapid run-off in the form of floods must result. These floods, rushing down the valleys, will have power to cut where before deposition was in progress. Good sized bowlders will be carried down and strewn along the stream courses and over the flats. The result of such floods would be manifest in the trenching of the valley bottoms and the spreading out over the flats of bowlders larger than those in the valley fill itself. They would produce conditions exactly the same as those we have described as characteristic of the valleys of the Silver City quadrangle.

Having been led to the belief that a removal of the vegetation cover would be competent to cause stream trenching, it becomes pertinent that we inquire whether there is evidence of such a removal of cover in the region under discussion. The answer is in the affirmative.

An efficient cause for the removal of such a vegetation cover is the excessive grazing to which the country has been subjected during the past few years. A good account of the former conditions of the region was given me by Mr. Mac-Millan, a rancher living in the Mangas valley, who has been a resident of the region since 1876. His statement of the early conditions is substantiated by that of all the old residents of the neighborhood with whom I had occasion to talk. According to him there was formerly much more timber than at present along the Mangas valley and on the piedmont desert fans, but probably never enough to modify materially the run-off of the water. More important than the timber, there was, along the valley bottoms, as well as on the hills and desert fans, a thick carpet of grass. This is reported to have been about knee high and quite thick. Along the valley bottoms it was thick enough to be cut for hay by the ranchers.

Such were the conditions in places where now scarcely a spear of grass can be found. The cattle, often forced to extremes of hunger so great that, sometimes, in a single season, as during the past year, they die by the hundreds of starvation alone, have kept the grass eaten so closely that there has been little opportunity for natural maturing and seeding, with the result that not only has the grass been kept closely cropped, but it has been to a large extent exterminated. The vegetation cover has been reduced from one of relatively high efficiency to almost nothing.

Coincident with the removal of the vegetation has come an increase in the violence of the floods. In the early days, according to MacMillan and others, heavy floods were rare. The storms were just as severe as now, but the run-off was slower. For instance, when a heavy storm occurred in the Burro Mountains, at the head waters of the Mangas, the water would continue to come down the valley for two or three days, whereas now it all comes at once in a single flood. When overstocking had reduced the vegetation cover the first floods began to come, and have been coming with increased frequency and violence every year since.

Having found from an inductive study that the trenching and other conditions of the valleys might be explained by a removal of vegetation cover, and having found from the his-

FIG. 3.

FIG. 3. Typical recent stream trench in the Mangas valley. Note the flat alluvial valley filling in which the trench is cut.

FIG. 4.

FIG. 4. Another view showing characteristic recent stream trenching. This is near the head of a small valley, but the trench is well developed.

torical evidence that such a reduction has actually taken place, with an accompaniment of increased floods, we may further test the theory by inquiring whether the formation of the trenches corresponds in time with the removal of the vegetation. On this point the testimony of the settlers is unanimous that, in the early days, there were few, if any, trenches in the valley bottoms, and that trenching has followed the appearance of the heavy floods. The deep trenches in the Mangas, one of which is shown in the photograph (fig. 3), have practically all been formed within the past 20 or 30 years, and are still deepening. The town of Silver City is built partly on an alluvial flat, such as those we have described. Running through the town is a trench or gulley cut through the alluvial valley filling to a depth of at least 20 feet and with a width of about 100 feet. A little over 15 years ago the site of this trench was one of the main streets of the town. During a severe storm the street was partly washed out and the trench begun. This trench has been cut deeper every year until the present condition has been reached.

From physiographic evidence of this sort, and from the testimony of the early settlers, there is good proof that the trenching is of recent date, corresponding in time with the removal of the grass by too close pasturing.

Our own observations, in so far as we had opportunity to make them in the short space of one summer, bear out the statements of Mr. MacMillan and others as to the normal vegetation conditions. In certain portions of the Silver City quadrangle, which were so far removed from water that the cattle seldom visited them, we found a fairly good cover of grass. These portions were on rocky hills of lava, never, at the best, fitted to maintain a great amount of vegetation, so that in the more fertile valley bottoms and on the gravel plains one would expect a good growth of grass. Within the Fort Bayard military reservation there is a tract of land which has been kept fenced for several years, and has been subjected to very slight grazing. Within this area the grass grows thick and often knee high. There can be no doubt that this grass as a covering is efficient, both in preventing a rapid run-off, and, on account of the sod which is formed, directly hindering stream cutting. Mr. MacMillan reports that in a watershed which he has kept fenced for several years and has not allowed to be closely pastured, the stream trenches which had begun to form before the fencing are gradually filling up.

The conspicuous nature of the physiographic results of overstocking of a region, and the rapidity with which they are brought about are surprising, and afford a striking illustration of the influence of man on geologic processes. If the grazing of a region for a period of 40 years, more or less, has produced so great results, it requires no great stretch of the imagination to picture the conditions in this section a few centuries hence if the same processes continue, as there is every reason to believe they will.

It is not alone within the area of the Silver City quadrangle that stream trenching is a conspicuous feature, for it is common in many parts of the west. In traveling through the states of New Mexico, Colorado and Wyoming, one finds that this trenched condition is widespread. The recency of the trenching is indicated by the fact that it is still in progress, and the gulleys are still working back towards the heads of the smaller tributaries.

In making a wider application of the principles of stream trenching which we have outlined, it is evident that, since the trenching is the result of the removal of vegetation cover, we will be likely to find it only in those regions whose normal climate is such that the normal vegetation would be luxuriant enough to become an important factor in the conservation of the rainfall, and in the protection of the valley bottoms from direct erosion. In such regions the overstocking, to which the west has been subjected, will have so reduced the cover as to cause increased floods with accompanying stream trenching. In regions normally too arid for the formation of an efficient vegetation cover the trenching should not be apparent.

Within the area of the Silver City quadrangle alone there is some evidence bearing on this point. The extreme southeastern corner of the sheet is lower and much more arid than the rest of the area, and it was noted that here the trenching is not so well developed as in the portions of the quadrangle which receive a greater precipitation. In order to thoroughly test the principle, comparison should be made between portions of the state, or of other states, which have climatic conditions similar to those of the Silver City region and other portions where climate is distinctly more arid, as, for instance, portions of southern New Mexico and Arizona.

The last selection in this part is aptly concluded with both an outstanding article by an unusually gifted scientist, and a new dimension of man's interference with the landscape. Grove Karl Gilbert is the greatest geomorphologist that has lived in the history of American science. His long list of publications, and especially his outstanding governmental monographs, all best sellers, became models in geology and are recognized as representing American science at its best. For example, his geology of the Henry Mountains provided a new baseline in the dynamics of fluvial processes and the type of implacement of igneous bodies. His Lake Bonneville work gave new insight into shoreline development, pluvial history, and confirmed the concept of isostasy. His hydraulic studies of running water paved the way with mathematics, models, and experimentation procedures that remain valid today. His paper on the Great Basin was the first to document carefully the supporting proof from geomorphic evidence of the large-scale faulting in the region. The originality of Gilbert is clearly evident as he traces the changes by man in the rivers and bays west of the Sierras. This article shows a different mood and class of man-made disturbances (see also Kedar, 1957) when he deliberately causes massive erosion in order to produce economic gain. This theme will be continued in Volume 2 with such examples as strip mining. Gilbert shows how the stupendous amounts of sediment that were removed from upstream hillslopes and channels in the mountains in man's quest for gold produced major upsets in stream regimes with sedimentation throughout the valleys and in coastal bays. Of course this phenomenon is not only restricted to the United States. McCaskall (in Eyre and Jones, 1966) describes hydraulic gold mining in New Zealand and how by 1885 there were 1,200 miles of water races and the ". . . water jets cut ragged swathes into the terrace edges. The gravels were undermined and dislodged and passed in muddy streams down lines of wooden tailraces . . . The tailings accumulated in artificial alluvial fans or were swept into stream beds. The bed of Waimea Creek was reported in 1891 as having been raised 20 ft . . ." (p. 278).

G.K. Gilbert (1843–1918) was born in Rochester, New York, and graduated from Rochester University in 1862. He was a geologic assistant at Ward's Museum 1863–1868, a geologist with the Ohio Survey 1868–1870, and with the Wheeler Survey 1871–1874, and Powell Survey 1875–1879. From its beginning in 1879 till his death he was a geologist with the U.S. Geological Survey. His monumental works still stand as lofty ideals for all aspiring young geomorphologists.

23

HYDRAULIC-MINING DÉBRIS IN THE SIERRA NEVADA.

By Grove Karl Gilbert.

Chapter I.—INTRODUCTION.

In the early days of gold mining in the Sierra Nevada only a moderate amount of earth was disturbed. An army of men were engaged, but they worked as laborers, with pick, shovel, and rocker. It was only gradually that more efficient methods were developed; but finally the resources of the engineer were brought to bear, water power was substituted for man power, and vast quantities of earth were handled. At the height of hydraulic mining, when hundreds of large jets of water were turned on the auriferous deposits, the material annually overturned was reckoned in scores of millions of cubic yards.

The material thus washed from the hillsides consisted chiefly of sand and the finer detritus called "slickens," but included also much gravel and many cobbles and boulders. The slickens was taken in suspension by the water used in mining and went with it to the creeks and rivers. Much of it escaped from the mountains altogether and found eventual lodgment in the Great Valley of California or in the tidal waters of San Francisco Bay and its dependencies. The coarser stuff tarried by the way, building up alluvial deposits on the lower hill slopes, in the flatter creek valleys, and in the river canyons. (See Pls. I, VI, and VII.) When rains and floods came the sands and gravels were moved forward toward the lowlands, and in 1862 a great flood washed so large a quantity into the lower reaches of the Sierra rivers and into the rivers of the Great Valley that the holders of riparian lands became alarmed. The mining-débris question, then for the first time generally recognized, assumed greater and greater importance and prominence in subsequent years and led to protest and litigation which in 1884 culminated in a series of injunctions whereby the miners were restrained from casting their tailings into the streams. The petitioners were valley dwellers, and the evils cited by them included the burial of alluvial farming lands by the flood of débris, the obstruction to navigation from shoaling of Sacramento and Feather rivers, and the raising of the flood levels of the valley streams whereby the area of periodic inundation was increased and protection against inundation became more difficult and expensive.

In connection with the litigation the subject was elaborately discussed, and the testimony included the evidence of a number of engineers who differed as widely in opinion as in point of view. Impartial and valuable investigations and reports were made by a series of officials and commissions at the instance of National and State governments. In 1880 the State engineer of California, William Ham. Hall, reported on the flow of mining detritus.[1] In the same year Lieut. Col. George H. Mendell, Corps of Engineers, United States Army, was designated to conduct a general investigation authorized by Congress, and his preliminary and final reports were printed in 1881 and 1882.[2] In 1888 a commission constituted of three Army engineers, Lieut. Col. W. H. H. Benyaurd, Maj. W. H. Heuer, and Maj. Thomas H. Handbury, began a still more extensive study, the report on which was printed in 1891.[3]

---

[1] California State Eng. Rept. to Legislature, sess. 1880, pt. 3, Sacramento, 1880.

[2] Mendell, G. H., Protection of the navigable waters of California from injury from the débris of mines: Chief Eng. U. S. Army Ann. Rept. for 1882, pt. 3, pp. 2543–2640; also in 47th Cong., 1st sess., Ex. Doc. 98.

[3] Report of board of engineers on mining débris in the State of California: Chief Eng. U. S. Army Ann. Rept. for 1891, pt. 5, pp. 2996–3118; also in 51st Cong., 2d sess., Ex. Doc. 267.

11

Chapter IV.—CHANGES IN THE CONDITION OF RIVERS FROM ARTIFICIAL CAUSES.

The changes in streams brought about by the activities of white men, practically dating from the discovery of gold in 1848, have arisen (1) from the overloading of the streams with detritus and (2) from the surrounding of parts of the inundated area by levees so as to restrict the freedom of the valley rivers to expand in time of flood. The overloading was caused chiefly by hydraulic mining. Agriculture and other industries which disturb the soil and expose it to wash by rain contributed to the effect, but their influence was relatively small.

CHANGES DUE TO MINING.

Some of the hydraulic mines discharged their tailings directly into streams, others upon gentle slopes of the land, where the coarser material accumulated in fan-shaped heaps or dumps. Usually the coarser material accumulated also in the streams, forming local deposits which were gradually swept forward. Examples of mine dump and coarse stream deposit are shown in Plate V.

Initially, as the tailings issued from the mining sluices, there was a division of the débris, the coarser part being swept along the bed and constituting the bed load of the stream, the finer being borne in the body of the current and constituting the suspended load. The partition of débris into bed load and suspended load continued throughout its journey, but the nature of the partition varied, because sluggish currents could suspend only the finest clay, whereas swift currents might suspend fine or coarse sand.

Some of the creeks flowing through the uplands that stand between river canyons acquired very heavy deposits, and there were large accumulations also in the mountain canyons of some of the rivers. (See Pl. VI, B.) After the checking of the mining operations these deposits were attacked by the streams, those of the upland creeks being trenched and those of the river canyons largely removed.

Where the rivers leave the mountain gorges and enter the Great Valley there was an abrupt reduction of slope and of velocity. Consequently in each river the capacity for transportation was reduced at this point, and part of the load of débris was arrested. The resulting deposit extended toward the valley from the foot of the range, and usually reached quite to the mid-valley trunk stream. It may conveniently be called a piedmont deposit. Its material was very coarse near the head and finer below.

Continuous with the piedmont deposits were deposits in Sacramento and Feather rivers, the trunk streams of the Sacramento Valley. Their characteristic material was at first mud, or "slickens," and afterward sand.

Each mining dump had a somewhat conical form, its slopes radiating from a vertex. The deposits of the upland creeks made broad gravelly plains on which channels shifted with every flood, and later they were carved into terraces. The same description applies to the piedmont deposits, except that not all of them have been excavated to such an extent as to develop terraces. The deposits of the trunk rivers are little wider than the original channel beds.

With the building up of stream beds the planes of high water were raised and the area of inundation was increased. In the mountain and piedmont districts this has been accompanied by a decreased flood depth, a change tending to reduce velocities and limit the ability of the streams to transport débris. Along the trunk streams it has turned a larger share of the flood water into the lateral basins, thus reducing the discharge in the channels and tending to reduce the ability of the streams to transport. On each stream, however, the tendency to reduce transportation was a tendency only, being opposed and overpowered by the influence of increased slope.

CHANGES DUE TO RECLAMATION.

During the entire period of the invasion of the Sacramento Valley by mining débris, the regimen of the rivers has been modified also

25

by the construction of levees. Tract after tract belonging to lateral basins or to the deltas has been surrounded by embankments so as to shut out the flood waters, and eventually the entire area of natural inundation will be reclaimed in the interest of agriculture. Restricted in area, the flood waters have increased in depth, and each great flood has risen higher than its predecessor. As the waters have been more and more confined to the channels the channel velocities have increased, and with them the ability to transport débris. If these changes had been independent of those wrought by mining débris they would have resulted in the automatic deepening and widening of the channels.

Mining débris and reclamation by levees work together in producing high floods, and their flood effects can not be fully discriminated. They work in opposed ways on depth of channel, the mining débris tending to build up the bed and reclamation to scour the channel deeper.

TRANSPORTATION OF DÉBRIS.

The series of changes thus outlined have been effected under the natural laws controlling the work of streams. Changes are still in progress and their results may be forecast, provided the stream laws are known. The following paragraphs summarize such of the laws as are specially involved in the movement of mining débris and the associated problems of flood control.

The quantity of débris which a given stream transports is its load; the quantity it can transport may be called its capacity. The load may be less than the capacity but not greater.

Capacity varies with slope. The greater the slope the greater the capacity; and the change in capacity is always larger than the change in slope.

Capacity varies with discharge. When discharge is increased the resulting increase in capacity is greater than the increase in discharge; the capacity per unit of discharge is increased. But an increase in discharge does not enhance capacity so much as the same ratio of increase in slope.

Capacity varies with the character of the débris transported. The lower the specific gravity of the débris the greater the capacity— that is, the greater the weight of load which

may be transported. The finer the débris the greater the capacity. Capacity is affected also by the shapes of the particles of débris. The range of variation in respect to size is so much greater than the range in respect to density and shape that only the size factor is usually considered in relation to capacity. Size may be measured by diameter or by volume. In whichever way it is measured, an increase in fineness causes a somewhat greater increase in capacity.

Capacity varies with the ratio of depth of water to width of stream. In the main, capacity increases with increase of the ratio (and this is true of the streams of Sacramento Valley), but the opposite rule applies to very small values of the ratio.

The fact that there is a limiting condition below which transportation does not take place finds expression in the word competent. For a stream of given discharge, flowing in a given channel and dealing with débris of a given fineness, there is a competent slope; in a channel of given form and slope and with débris of given fineness there is a competent discharge; and for a given discharge in a given channel there is a competent fineness.

The ratio in which capacity is modified by a change in slope, discharge, fineness of débris, or depth of current is greater when the conditions are near competence than when they are far above competence. In other words, capacity is most sensitive to changes in the conditions which control it when near its lower limit.

These laws have been experimentally determined for the bed load [1] treated by itself, and they are believed to be approximately true for the suspended load by itself. Nevertheless they can not be affirmed of the total load, because of certain complications growing out of the shifting of material from one load to the other. For most of the purposes of this report their important application is to capacity for the transportation of bed load.

If a stream which is loaded to its full capacity reaches a point where the slope is less, it becomes overloaded with reference to the gentler slope and part of the load is dropped, making a deposit. If a fully loaded stream reaches a point where the slope is steeper, its enlarged capacity causes it to take more load, and the taking of load erodes the bed. If the slope of

---

[1] See U. S. Geol. Survey Prof. Paper 86, 1914.

a stream's bed is not adjusted to the stream's discharge and to the load it has to carry, then the stream continues to erode or deposit, or both, until an adjustment has been effected and the slope is just adequate for the work.

Any change of conditions which destroys the adjustment between slope, discharge, fineness, and load imposes on the stream the task of readjustment and thus initiates a system of changes which may extend to all parts of the stream profile. The mining débris disturbed the adjustment of streams by adding to their load. Reclamation by levees disturbs it by increasing the flood discharge in certain parts of the river channels.

The law of adjusted profiles applies to streams with mobile beds—alluvial streams. Streams with fixed beds are normally underloaded, and their beds are modified only by abrasion. This process works toward an adjustment of slopes but with exceeding slowness, and the factors involved are different from those of alluvial streams.

The channel of an alluvial stream is composed of an alternation of deeps and shoals. The dimensions of these are related to the discharge. With variable discharge they are continually modified, each particular discharge tending to adjust them to its needs. Because of the greater power of streams during flood, the pattern of the bed is more nearly adjusted to flood conditions than to any other.

An alluvial stream which is not confined by rigid banks shapes for itself a course made up of curves. The curves are not stationary but undergo continual changes. The curve pattern is large for a large stream and small for a small one. In a variable stream the pattern is adjusted to the needs of the flood discharge. The general slope of a stream bed is determined chiefly by the magnitude of the load that travels at time of the larger floods.

The laws thus far stated apply to the transportation of débris along a bed composed of similar débris. When a stream is made to sweep débris along the unyielding bed of a sluice or flume other laws apply. Capacity is greater for smooth beds than for rough. It is greater for coarse débris (up to the limit of competence) than for fine. It is in general greater for a flume than for a natural stream of the same size.

ACCUMULATIONS OF DÉBRIS IN THE MOUNTAINS.

The stream of water by which tailings were delivered to a mining dump was artificially guided and usually ceased to flow after cessation of mining. If the dump lay wholly on a hillside it was afterward washed only by rain, and no important fraction of it was removed. Many of the smaller dumps thus became essentially permanent deposits. The larger hillside dumps extended to waterways, and these were excavated by the streams on whose courses they encroached. Other dumps were built wholly in stream valleys and were subject to excavation from their beginning. As a whole the dumps have yielded and are still yielding a large annual tribute to the streams. Their contribution will continue, with gradual diminution, for an indefinite period; but a portion of their store of débris may be regarded as permanently placed.

Drifting forward from the dumps, during the mining and afterward, a large amount of débris gathered in the valleys of the upland creeks. This material is being fed to the rivers gradually and is perhaps at present the chief source of the rivers' supply of débris. (See Pl. VIII.) The excavation of such deposits leaves a terraced valley, and as the stream works down toward its original channel patches of terrace are here and there stranded on the slope in such positions as to be exempt from further attack.

Some mines discharged their tailings directly into the canyons of rivers, and the mountain rivers have received also the outwash from dumps and creek valley deposits. Before the hydraulic mining the river beds were made up largely of bedrock and great boulders, with only a few reaches of coarse gravel. (See Pl. VI, A.) Their normal load of débris was less than their capacity. In the period of most active mining they received more débris than they could carry, and the overload was deposited. When mining was checked they again became underloaded and the new deposits were excavated. (See Pl. VII, A.) Little débris now remains in their beds, and the rivers deliver promptly to the piedmont deposits all that they receive from the dumps and upland creek deposits.

PIEDMONT DEPOSITS.

The piedmont deposits began with the beginning of hydraulic mining and grew not only during the mining period but for years afterward. The coarse gravel of the canyon deposits was all caught by them, and their growth probably continued until the canyons were emptied. They received also both gravel and sand from the upland creeks. Their building was accompanied by a sorting of the débris, the coarser portion lodging high on the slope and the finer farther down. Their growth continued long after the culmination of the upland deposits but eventually ceased and was followed by excavation. In the piedmont deposit of American River the stream is well intrenched, and stages of its erosional work are recorded by terraces. Low terraces have appeared also along Bear River. On Yuba River the main channel has been deepened near the head of the deposit, and farther down the natural development of excavation has been modified by a dam.

At Parks Bar Bridge, which crosses the Yuba where its bed begins to broaden outside the mountain canyon, the summit plain of the deposit was well recorded by a photograph in 1905 (see Pl. IX, A), and in 1913 it was observed to retain the same height, but the depth of the channel dividing it had increased in the interval from 11 to 21 feet, showing a scour of 10 feet in the eight years. Three miles above, in the mouth of the canyon (see Pl. IX, B), where the passage is too narrow for the development of terraces, is a gaging station of the Geological Survey, and the changes in the channel bed are well shown by the records of low-water stages in successive autumns. The gage readings corresponding to a discharge of 500 cubic feet per second are as follows:[1]

	Feet.		Feet.
1903	13.6	1909	5.0
1904	13.5	1910	4.8
1905	11.6	1911	4.4
1906	9.3	1912	4.0
1907	8.3	1913	4.0
1908	7.1		

These readings not only confirm the record at Parks Bar Bridge, by indicating a total scour of 9.6 feet in 10 years, but show that the deepening of the channel has been progressive.

[1] Based mainly on data published in U. S. Geol. Survey Water-Supply Paper 298, pp. 254–255, 1912.

At Marysville, where the Yuba joins the Feather, the record of low-water stages for the same period (see p. 29) shows a total lowering of 2.9 feet. The sequence of levels is here less orderly than at the upper gaging station, partly because the low-water stages for different years correspond to different discharges and partly because the local conditions have been modified by engineering works for the control of the rivers, but the two records are of the same general tenor. The maximum phase of the piedmont deposit has been passed, and the work of excavation has begun. The maximum came earlier at the head of the deposit, having already been passed when the definite record began in 1903; at the river mouth it occurred between 1903 and 1906. But for artificial interference with the work of the river the rate of scour at the head of the deposit would have been considerably greater and the scour at its foot less.

The excavation of the deposit is accompanied by further sorting of the débris. That which is swept out at Parks Bar Bridge consists of coarse and fine gravel, with a generous filling of coarse sand, but that which reaches the mouth of the river at Marysville consists of fine and coarse sand, with a small amount of fine gravel. The coarse gravel is arrested on the way,[2] doubtless in company with other gravel brought from the upper river, while part of the sand which had been incorporated with the gravel at the head of the deposit joins with the finer débris in transit from above. It is not to be assumed that the coarse débris is permanently arrested, but only that its forwarding is delayed until the upper river shall cease to send down a heavy load of sand. On the exhaustion of the mining débris stored above, the transportation of the coarse débris of the piedmont deposit will become more active, and gravel will largely replace the sand in the lower Yuba and lower Feather. A return toward the normal profile will tend to restore the "gravelly ford" of the Yuba by which travel is said to have approached Marysville in early days.

The piedmont deposits of Yuba and Bear rivers extend to their mouths in Feather River and are there continuous with deposits in the Feather. That of American River is continuous with a deposit in Sacramento River.

[2] These statements as to the movements of gravel at the mouth of Yuba River were written several years ago and were then accurate. The present condition is described in the closing paragraphs of this chapter.

Other piedmont deposits clog only the streams from which they originate. The largest is that of the Feather, which has a visible length of about 30 miles and then passes under a slack-water pool occasioned by the deposit from the Yuba, which acts as a dam.

DEPOSITS IN THE VALLEY RIVERS.

The débris delivered by the piedmont streams to the trunk rivers of the valley imposed a load which those rivers could not transport without increase of slope, and the necessary increase was made by depositing part of the load on the channel beds and building them up. The depth of the deposit was thus related to the magnitude of the load transported on its slope. The deposit grew through the period of active mining and afterward until the piedmont deposits had passed their maximum, and then it began to decline. The depth of the deposit was also affected by the quantity of water flowing through the channel in time of flood, a quantity which tended to increase as access to lateral basins was restricted by levees.

The history of change is most definitely known through records of low-water level at Marysville and Sacramento, the variations of lowest water surface from autumn to autumn corresponding approximately to variations of the general level of the channel bed. At Marysville the observations were made on a gage established in Yuba River about 0.7 mile from its junction with the Feather, and a daily series has been kept since 1893 under the direction of the levee commissioners of the city, to whom I am indebted for data contained in Table 2. The gage was established in 1873, and the low-water record is continuous from 1883. For years earlier than 1873 there are no exact data, but estimates of different observers indicate an original low-water level at least 10 feet below that of 1873.

At Sacramento gagings of Sacramento River were made, and continuous readings have been reported by the United States Weather Bureau since 1896.[1] For certain earlier years records of low-water are reported or cited by Mendell[2] and by Rose.[3] In the original condition of the river there was a tide at Sacramento with a range of about 3 feet. In 1871, when the low-

stage level had been raised 4 or 5 feet, there was still a tide of 9 inches,[4] and Hall records 2 inches in 1879.[5] Rose also gives the range for years earlier than 1860 as "about 2 feet." The United States Coast and Geodetic Survey tide tables give 1.5 feet as the mean range and 3.2 feet as the great tropic range, the figures being based on observations made in 1857. As the bed continued to rise the tide disappeared, but it was again observable when the bed was afterward reduced. In 1913 the range was reported as 1.5 feet. The freedom of tide transmission from Suisun Bay to Sacramento is related to depth of water in the lower river, and the periods of larger tide at Sacramento are also periods of greater depth of water. During such periods the deposits in the channel were relatively shallow, and because of these correlations the range of variation of the annual low-stage levels is less than the range of variation in the depth of the river deposit. The raising of the low-stage plane from the vicinity of mean tide level to a position 13 feet higher was associated with more than 13 feet of deposit in the channel.

TABLE 2.—*Low-water records of Yuba River at Marysville and of Sacramento River at Sacramento.*

[Feet above mean sea level.]

Year.	Marysville.	Sacramento.
1849	[36. 8]	0
1856		0
1869		2. 9
1873	46. 8	
1874	47. 8	4. 9
1875		4. 5
1876		7. 1
1877		5. 3
1878		5. 5
1879		5. 8
1880	52. 8	7. 4
1881		6. 5
1883	52. 0	
1884	52. 8	
1885	51. 1	
1886	52. 6	
1887	51. 3	
1888	52. 0	
1889	52. 3	
1890	52. 4	10. 5
1891	52. 7	
1892	53. 6	
1893	53. 0	
1894	53. 0	7. 5
1895	53. 0	
1896	53. 4	10. 0
1897	54. 5	10. 8
1898	54. 0	9. 6
1899	53. 8	9. 9
1900	54. 1	7. 6
1901	54. 5	7. 2

---

[1] Daily river stages at river gage stations on the principal rivers of the United States, 1896–1910, pts. 6–10, U. S. Weather Bur.

[2] Mendell, G. H., Chief Eng. U. S. Army Ann. Rept. for 1882, p. 2507.

[3] Rose, A. H., California Comm. Pub. Works Rept. for 1894, p. 33.

[4] Rose, A. H., op. cit., p. 33.

[5] Hall, W. H., California State Eng. Rept. for 1880, p. 68.

TABLE 2.—*Low-water records of Yuba River at Marysville and of Sacramento River at Sacramento*—Continued.

Year.	Marysville.	Sacramento.
1902	55. 0	6. 9
1903	55. 3	7. 0
1904	55. 8	8. 2
1905	55. 9	6. 3
1906	55. 7	6. 8
1907	55. 3	7. 3
1908	55. 1	5. 3
1909	53. 0	5. 5
1910	52. 5	5. 1
1911	52. 9	5. 5
1912	52. 2	4. 1
1913	52. 4	3. 0

Table 2 contains the low-stage gage readings at Marysville and Sacramento, together with water-level records of less precision for earlier years; and the same data are plotted in figure 4. The zero of the Marysville gage was placed

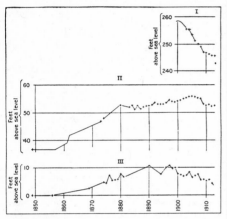

FIGURE 4.—Fluctuations of low-water level due mainly to the deposition of mining débris on river beds and its subsequent erosion. I, Yuba River in narrows near Smartsville; II, Yuba River at Marysville; III, Sacramento River at Sacramento.

at the low-water level of 1873. At Sacramento there were two gages. The zero of one is reported to correspond to the low water of 1856, and the readings from the other, as tabulated, are reduced to the same zero. A certain amount of ambiguity is occasioned by the tides, but it is probable that the lower low-water records at Sacramento all represent the combination of low tide with the autumnal low-river stage; and the graphic record has been adjusted under this assumption.

The irregularities of the plotted curves are connected largely with inequalities of maximum and minimum discharges from year to year. Exceptional flood discharges leave exceptional configurations of channel bed, which affect local details of low-water plane, and the low-water plane also varies in position with the magnitude of the low-stage discharge. Minor details of the curves may therefore be ignored in reading from them the general history of the building up and paring down of the channel deposits.

The bed of Feather River at Marysville was built up rapidly during the period of increasing output of débris from the hydraulic mines of the Yuba River basin. It continued to be up-built, but more slowly, after the checking of mining and during the chief excavation of the débris banks in the mountains, and accretion was not exchanged for reduction until five or six years after the excavation of the head of the Yuba piedmont deposit had begun. The downstream movement of the great body of débris is thus analogous to the downstream movement of a great body of storm water, the apex of the flood traveling in the direction of the current. The apex of the débris flood, leaving the mines in 1883, passed the mouth of the mountain canyon in about the year 1900 and the mouth of Yuba River in about 1905.

The stream of débris from the Yuba is joined in the Feather by a smaller stream from the Bear and in the Sacramento by a stream from the American. Water levels at the Sacramento gaging station are affected by all these streams. The débris wave from the Yuba may be assumed to be flattened and greatly extended during its long journey from Marysville, so that its influence on the water plane at Sacramento is gradual and of moderate amount. Its apex has perhaps not yet arrived, and if it has arrived it can not be discriminated in the composite effect. The wave from the American, having a much shorter course, reached the station while less expanded and has been the dominant factor in the determination of the low-water curve. Its apex seems to have passed in about the year 1896; and the reduction of the river deposit began here a decade earlier than at the mouth of the Yuba.

So far as the flow of débris from the hydraulic mining of the past is concerned, the future history of the channel deposits will be one of continual diminution, a progress toward the restoration of the river conditions of the early fifties. That progress might be arrested by the resumption of hydraulic mining. It will be promoted by the reclamation of the lands now subject to overflow. The confinement of flood waters of the Sacramento and Feather to the channels of those streams would greatly increase their capacity for transporting débris and would eventually reduce the channel beds to lower levels than have been known. The partial confinement contemplated in the engineering plans for flood control will probably obliterate the effect of the invasion by mining débris.

The deposit built in the Feather River channel by débris from the Yuba has the effect of a dam, causing slack water in the Feather just above. The pool had at one time a length of 10 miles or more, being limited upstream by the piedmont deposit of the Feather. Afterward it was diminished by the encroachment of that deposit and in recent years by the lowering of the low-water plane at Marysville. Its length in 1913 was said to be about 6 miles. There is a similar ponding of Sacramento River by débris brought to its channel by Feather River.

The piedmont deposits in the basin of San Joaquin River are reported to be of moderate extent, and so little mining débris has reached the trunk stream that the river has remained tidal and navigable.

As already stated, the flood of mining débris is analogous to a flood of water in its mode of progression through a river channel. It travels in a wave, and the wave grows longer and flatter as it goes. Where the channel is too small to contain it, the water wave spreads out over adjacent lands, and the volume thus escaping from the channel is temporarily stored, so as to regulate the flow at points below. The débris wave differs from the water wave in the fact that part of its overflow volume is permanently lodged outside the river channel, and in the additional fact that the material of the wave is not homogeneous. From the start there is a sorting of the débris, and the finer parts travel faster than the coarser, except that

71139°—17——3

some of the finer material is held in the interstices of the coarser. The visible part of the wave, that which at any time is exposed to the action of the current, exhibits a gradation from fine at the front to coarse at the rear. The débris in transit at any point is first silt— the "slickens" of the miners—and then in succession sand, fine gravel, coarse gravel. At the mouth of Yuba River all these phases have been observed, the sequence being automatic or normal as far as fine gravel. The appearance of coarse gravel, recently observed, has been hastened by engineering works that have narrowed, and thereby strengthened, the flood current a few miles upstream. In the lower Sacramento silt has been succeeded by fine sand and coarser sand.

The progress of such a wave and its manifestation in the texture of bed material are complicated by two other factors—progressive comminution of débris and variation of flood discharge. The débris in transit is continually ground upon itself, and its particles are worn to smaller size, so that the coarser débris characteristic of the upper reaches of a stream does not appear in the lower reaches, and the load of fine débris is greater.

A great flood, as compared to a small flood, is able to carry coarser débris, or to carry more débris, or to do its work on a gentler slope. Which of these phases of its comparative activity shall be manifested in a particular division of the stream's course will depend on the character and quantity of the load brought from above. It may reduce the slope of its channel by scouring and leave behind a low-level channel bed of coarser débris, and in that event the minor floods of succeeding years will tend to steepen the slope by depositing débris, and the deposited débris will be finer than that on which it rests. As the closing work of each flood is performed by a discharge less than its maximum, it often happens, especially in the lower part of a river's course, that the coarsest part of a flood's load is so buried by fine material as not to be visible when the bed is exposed at low stage.

280

Chapter V.—CHANGES IN THE CONDITION OF BAYS.

The streams that discharge to the chain of bays (Suisun, San Pablo, and San Francisco) deliver along with the water a quantity of fine detritus, consisting of mud and sand. Lodging on the bottom the detritus tends to shoal the bays, and combining with vegetation along the margins it tends to contract them. These tendencies are opposed by the slow subsidence of the land, and in the natural condition of the region there may have been an approximate balance between the opposed factors. If such a balance existed, it has been overthrown by the activities of the white man, which have so increased the detrital loads of the streams that the bays are now losing in depth and area.

The water of Sacramento and San Joaquin rivers reaches first Suisun Bay, then San Pablo and San Francisco bays, and then escapes through the Golden Gate to the ocean. The forward movement is not continuous but is reversed twice a day by the tides, with the result that many eddies are formed and the river water is gradually mingled with ocean water. The river water is also carried to all the remoter reaches of the bays. The sediment is widely spread within the bays, mingling with smaller quotas from minor streams. It is evident also that a part of it reaches the ocean, for in times of flood, while the rivers are turbid and opaque, the outgoing tide through the Golden Gate shows a tinge of yellow.

Some information as to the extent and distribution of the recent deposits is afforded by the charts of the United States Coast and Geodetic Survey, which give soundings in all parts of the bays and at different dates. Complete surveys of Suisun Bay were made in 1867–68 and in 1887–88. A complete survey of San Pablo Bay was made in 1856, a small part was resurveyed in 1887, and the remainder was resurveyed in 1896. The northern part of San Francisco Bay was surveyed in 1855 and again in 1895–1901; its southern part in 1857–58 and in 1895–1899.

The interval of 20 years between the two surveys of Suisun Bay included 16 years of the most active hydraulic mining, together with the 4 years immediately following, when the temporary deposits of débris in the mountains

32

presumably yielded their maximum quantity of waste. The interval between surveys of San Pablo and San Francisco bays, averaging for all parts about 41 years, covered the same time as the Suisun Bay interval, with the addition of an earlier decade during which hydraulic mining was advancing toward its maximum and a later decade during which the flow of mining débris was slowly diminishing.

Suisun Bay is relatively deep in the southern and middle parts, where it is traversed by a group of channels from the river mouths to Carquinez Strait. Among the channels are islands and a broad, irregular shoal, to part of which the name Middle Ground is given. At the north are two arms, broad and shallow, known as Grizzly Bay and Honker Bay. In the period of 20 years the shoals, having a total area of about 30 square miles, received an average deposit of 1.63 feet, the quantity of sediment being 51,000,000 cubic yards. The depth of fill was greatest in ˙Honker Bay (2.17 feet) and least on the Middle Ground (1.25 feet). The channels are so irregular in form that it is not practicable to compute their changes with close approximation by means of the published soundings, but the general nature of their modifications is quite clear. Almost without exception they became narrower and deeper; almost without exception, also, the quantity of material added at the sides was notably greater than the quantity scoured out between, so that a net fill resulted. A rough estimate places the net fill of channels at 13,000,000 cubic yards, and makes the total deposit in the bay 64,000,000 cubic yards.

In Carquinez Strait, which connects Suisun and San Pablo bays, the bottom is irregular. The depth changes so greatly within short distances that the magnitude of each recorded sounding may be assumed to depend in part on an accident of location, and computations of average depth are subject to considerable uncertainty. Moreover, the surveys on which the earliest and latest maps are based were made at uneven dates, so that the intervals between dates contrasted in different parts of the maps range from 20 to 41 years. A comparison was made by dividing the area into 14 parts and studying each part separately, and it was found that the depth had apparently increased in 3 divisions and diminished in 11. The average apparent loss of depth in the 11 divisions was much greater than the average gain in the other 3. From the data thus obtained it was estimated that the total amount of material deposited in the strait from the beginning of hydraulic mining to the year 1890 was 40,000,000 cubic yards.

San Pablo Bay is traversed, from Carquinez Strait to the constriction separating it from San Francisco Bay, by a broad channel of simple contour. North of this is a great shoal occupying more than half the total area, and south of it are minor shoals. In the 41 years between surveys the channel was much reduced in width and was also reduced in depth. The filling along the middle line was small compared to the marginal filling. The great northern shoal received a large deposit, and the eastern division of the southern shoal an important though small deposit, but the western division of the southern shoal suffered a loss. To give quantitative expression to some of these facts the computations were made by divisions, the channel being arbitrarily limited by the position of the 3-fathom contour in 1856, and the northern shoal being separated into two parts, distinguished by different dates of resurvey. The data are exhibited in Table 3. It is worthy of note also that the eastern part of the northern shoal received a much heavier deposit than the western part.

TABLE 3.—*Data on sedimentary deposits in San Pablo Bay between the survey of 1856 and later surveys.*

Part of bay.	Period (years).	Area (square miles).	Depth of deposit (feet).	Volume of deposit (million cubic yards).
Channel	42	29.4	4.86	147.2
North part of north shoal	31	8.4	2.11	18.3
Main part of north shoal	41	60.9	2.97	186.3
Southeast shoal	42	7.3	2.84	21.4
Southwest shoal	42	7.2	−1.25	− 9.3
Means and totals	41	113.2	a 3.13	a 366.0

a The mean depth and total volume of the deposits are adjusted to the mean period of 41 years.

San Francisco Bay is divided by a moderate constriction at Goat Island into a northern third and a southern two-thirds. The northern division is traversed by the Sierra waters on their way to the sea. The southern receives drainage from valley plains and coastal hills. The deposits in the southern division must be derived chiefly from soil waste, but they may include also a small tribute of mining débris, for the tidal currents tend to mingle the waters of the two divisions, and the strong day winds of summer promote the mingling by driving the surface waters southward.

Table 4 contains estimates of the mean depth of deposits not only for the entire bay but for certain subdivisions. It fails to include, however, any estimate for Raccoon Strait or for deep-water tracts south and west of Angel Island. In those regions the bed is so uneven that soundings made at different dates and at slightly different places are not comparable. The omission is thought to be unimportant, because the currents there are so strong that the formation of deposits is not probable.

TABLE 4.—*Data on sedimentary deposits in San Francisco Bay between the survey of 1855–1858 and the survey of 1895–1901.*

Part of bay.	Period (years).	Area (square miles).	Depth of deposit (feet).	Volume of deposit (million cubic yards).
Channels:				
North of Goat Island	43	36	2.7	100
Goat Island to San Bruno Point	41	36	−1.8	− 67
San Bruno Point to Dumbarton Point	40	15	1.9	29
Shoals:				
North of Goat Island	43	37	1.0	38
Goat Island to San Bruno Point	41	53	.5	27
South of San Bruno Point	40	95	.7	69
Means and totals	41	272	.70	196

In two of the tracts separately recorded in the tables there is indication of negative deposition—that is, the charts show for those tracts increase of depth of water instead of decrease. One tract is a shoal in San Pablo Bay lying south of the channel and east of Pinole Point; the other is the deeper water south of Goat Island. For each tract the mean increase in depth is more than 1 foot. There are at least three possible modes of explaining these exceptional indications—by local scouring of the bottom, by local subsidence, and by errors in the charting. As to the first-mentioned possibility, the shifting of deposits on the beds of channels is a common occurrence, but the scouring of muddy shoals is less common. Usually such a shoal presents at its surface a layer of soft mud resting on firm tenacious clay, the one being easily disturbed and the other opposing a strong resistance to current action. Ordinarily the mobile layer is thin, and for this reason the scouring of a foot or more from the general surface of one of the lateral shoals is improbable.

The evidence adduced in Chapter II leads to the belief that the general region is affected by slow subsidence and that some changes are more or less localized. The two tracts under consideration both lie in the district west of the Haywards fault, where prehistoric subsidence has been most pronounced. The hypothesis of present subsidence is therefore worthy of consideration, but neither of the two localities affords corroborative evidence. If subsidence had occurred in the tract between Pinole Point and San Pablo Point the level of the adjacent marsh would have been lowered and its margin would have retreated landward; but instead of that its margin was somewhat advanced so as to encroach on the open water of San Pablo Bay. If subsidence had affected the channel between Goat Island and San Bruno Point it presumably would have affected also the adjacent shoals, but the shoals were found to stand higher at the time of the second survey.

As to the possibility that the exceptional indications arise from errors of survey it is safe to say that the later survey is not at fault Its methods, which are fully recorded in the archives of the Coast and Geodetic Survey, were thorough and adequate. The records of the earlier work are less complete and leave doubt as to some matters of method. A comparative study of earlier and later charts, undertaken with reference to encroachments on the tidal prism (see pp. 86–88), revealed discrepancies which may be significant. In localities where a tidal marsh adjoins a shoal of gentle slope one would expect the high-water line (represented by the marsh margin) and the low-water line to advance or recede together, whether their positions are modified by deposition, by scour, or by subsidence. There are three such localities near the junction of San Pablo and San Francisco bays, one just east of San Pablo Point, the second north of San Quentin Point, and the third south of San Quentin Point. In each locality the recorded change in the high-water line between 1855–56 and 1899–1901 has been slight, but the recorded change in the low-water line has been great. If it is assumed that the actual change in the position of the low-water line was small, and that the line is correctly placed on the later charts, its position as given on the earlier charts is on the average nearly half a mile too far out. This is such a discrepancy as would be occasioned if the "plane of reference" for the earlier soundings were 1.5 to 2.0 feet lower than the plane of reference for the later soundings. Planes of reference are determined by the discussion of tidal observations, but the records discovered fail to show what observations were used for the reduction of soundings in these localities in 1855 and 1856. Negative evidence indicates that the plane of reference and tidal corrections in 1855 were based on tidal observations at Fort Point, and the Fort Point plane of reference used in 1855 was 1.0 foot too low. In computing the averages assembled in Table 4 I have applied a correction for this recognized error.

Because the Coast and Geodetic Survey charts are prepared for the use of navigators, and because an overestimate of depth involves danger to vessels, the general principle is recognized that such errors as affect the charted soundings should be on the side of safety. The application of this principle has affected observations of depth and their reduction and also the selection of "characteristic" soundings for the charts and has been embodied in rules for the rejection of fractions, etc. The result is, first, that the charted depths are on the average less than the actual depths and, second, that the average difference between the charted and actual depths is greater for rough surveying than for refined surveying. As the earlier work was relatively rough and the later was refined, the charted depths are likely to be less on the old charts than on the new in localities where the actual depth was unchanged.

In view of these considerations I think it probable that the indication of increased depth on the shoal west of Pinole Point is due to error connected with planes of reference and possible that the apparent increase of depth south of Goat Island is due also to some difference in method between earlier and later surveys. If this opinion is correct it follows that other results based on surveys of the same dates are questionable and that generalizations from them must be regarded as of low precision. This qualification applies to the results for the northern half of San Francisco Bay, where the earlier soundings were made in 1855, and to the results for the whole of San Pablo Bay, where the earlier surveys were made in the first half of the year 1856. For these dates there is no record of tide stations in close association with the field work, but there was a permanent station at Fort Point. The southern part of San Francisco Bay was surveyed in 1857–58, and in connection with that work the tide observations at Fort Point were supplemented by observations at local stations. The first comprehensive survey of Suisun Bay was made 10 years later and had the advantage of progress in the development of methods. Not only were there local tide stations, but provision for the stability of the plane of reference was made by connecting some of the tide gages with bench marks. So far as I am able to judge, the estimates of deposition in Suisun Bay are well founded, and the estimates for the southern part of San Francisco Bay rank next in credibility.

No attempt is made to improve the estimates by applying corrections for the inferred inaccuracy of the plane of reference; the general averages may have been affected by compensatory inaccuracies in the planes used for other tracts. On the other hand, the least trusted estimates of average deposition are not discarded, because there is independent evidence accordant with their general tenor.

A corroborative fact is found in the contraction of the channel through San Pablo Bay, which has been brought about by the extension of the banks or shoals that border it. The deposits involved in that extension have in some places a recorded depth of 8 feet and over considerable areas a recorded depth of 5 feet; and these quantities are much too large to be charged to errors of survey.

Other corroboration is found when the estimates for the three bays are compared. Limiting attention to the deposits on shoals, and expanding the Suisun estimate, which is based on surveys only 20 years apart, so as to make it properly comparable with the San Pablo and San Francisco estimates, I obtain:

Estimates of average deposition on shoals in a period of 41 years.

	Feet.
Suisun Bay	3.3
San Pablo Bay	2.5
San Francisco Bay	.7

The general aspect of this sequence, which places the heaviest deposit in the bay that is nearest the river mouths and the lightest in the bay that is most remote, is such as might have been anticipated, but my first impression in making the comparison was that a greater difference should be expected between the first and second terms and a less difference between the second and third. There is, however, a modifying condition of which account should be taken. The material deposited on the shoals is fine mud that is brought by the rivers in suspension. Deposition is determined in part by the slackening of current as the muddy water enters a bay and in part by flocculation as it is mingled with salt water. Deposition from slackening would be much heavier in the first settling reservoir than in the second, but deposition from flocculation would begin wherever the salt water was met. At low stages of the rivers the principal meeting occurs in Suisun Bay, but at low stages there is little mud in suspension. In times of great flood, when the largest load of mud is brought down, the river current dominates over tidal currents in Suisun Bay, and the principal meeting with brine takes place in the larger water body beyond Carquinez Strait. (See Chapter IX.) When account is taken of this factor there appears no improbability in the relative magnitudes of the estimates of deposition for Suisun and San Pablo bays.

If the figures are taken at their face value it appears that heavy deposits have been made in Suisun and San Pablo bays and the connecting strait, and a moderate deposit in San Francisco Bay. These deposits have been caused primarily by the surcharging of the valley rivers by mining débris and the detritus contributed by other industries, and secondarily by the outwash of soil waste from the country immediately surrounding the bays.

As the periods covered by the comparison of charts do not in any case represent the entire period of augmented detrital load, considerable allowances are necessary in order to pass from the measured volume of deposit to the total volume accrued since the beginning of

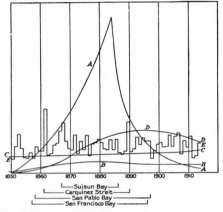

FIGURE 5.—Graphic statement of factors controlling estimation of deposition in bays and strait for periods not covered by measurements. The periods covered by measurement are indicated for the several units. *A*, Output of mining débris; *B*, soil waste; *C*, percentage of fine débris not deposited on inundated lands; *D*, delivery of débris to bays; *E*, relative precipitation.

placer mining in the Sierra. In estimating these allowances account has been taken of variation in the activities which have contributed débris to the streams, of variation in the transporting power of the streams, and of variation in certain conditions that have tended to retard or prevent the delivery of débris in the bays. As most of these factors are to be discussed in following chapters they will be only briefly considered here.

The output of mining débris increased in geometric ratio until the year 1884, when it was suddenly checked, and since that time it has diminished, at first rapidly and then slowly. These facts are expressed in curve *A* of figure 5.

The waste of the soil by rains, which under natural conditions was slow, has been greatly hastened by agriculture, by grazing, and by traffic over roads and trails. Its supposed history of variation is expressed by curve *B*.

The débris brought to the bays is dominantly fine. Fine débris is also deposited on inundated lands, including the lateral basins of the Sacramento Valley, the delta marshes, and marshes bordering the bays. Therefore the bays receive only a fraction of the entire suspended load of the streams. The fraction has been varied by the construction of levees, the direct effect of which is to reduce the inundated area. In the Sacramento Valley the protection of tracts from inundation has raised the flood plane, and this has caused floods to spread over other tracts, so that the construction of levees has indirectly enlarged the inundated area. Clogging of stream channels by mining débris has also tended to increase the inundated area. The supposed history of the variation of the percentage of the fine débris carried to the bays is expressed by curve *C*.

Up to and somewhat beyond the epoch of most active hydraulic mining a part of the mining débris was temporarily deposited along the lines of stream conveyance, and the stores thus created were afterward drawn upon. The general effect of such stores was to delay and equalize transmission, causing the crest of the great wave of mining débris to reach the bays some years after it left the mountains, and giving the wave a broader and flatter profile. With the addition of this consideration to those involved in curves *A*, *B*, and *C*, curve *D* was constructed to represent in general terms the history of the delivery of débris to the bays.

The remaining factor of recognized importance is the variation in the carrying power of the streams. The work of transportation has been performed chiefly by floods, and the efficiency of great floods is much higher than that of small floods. The greater floods of the rivers are associated with heavy rainfall, and it is during heavy rain that soil waste occurs. Because the records of floods are imperfect except for recent years, and because data as to heavy rains are not readily accessible, I have made use, instead, of precipitation records, which are published by the United States Weather Bureau in convenient form. Curve *E* in figure 5 shows for each rainy season

(July 1 to June 30) the relative precipitation (in rain and snow) from 1850 to 1914.

The transporting capacity of the streams depends largely on the concentration of rainfall into short periods, and the printed record tells little about such concentrations, but the relation of precipitation in the Sierra to cyclonic disturbances tends toward a sort of rhythmic concentration, and there is a rough correlation between seasonal floods and seasonal precipitation. In a general way transporting capacity varies with precipitation, and it varies in greater ratio than precipitation. On the basis of this law a set of factors of relative stream efficiency were derived from the data of relative precipitation, and these were multiplied, for the several annual seasons, by the ordinates of curve D. The products were then assumed to be proportional to the delivery of débris to the bays in the corresponding seasons.

To the results of the computations thus made a further qualification was applied, to take account of special conditions affecting channel portions of the bay system. Carquinez Strait is essentially a channel for the flow of waters, and its depth is determined automatically, being so adjusted that the traversing currents may be able to transport sand along the bed. It is probable that the strait received its principal deposit rather early in the history of the mining-débris invasion and that later additions have been small. A similar statement applies to the central portions of the channels through Suisun and San Pablo bays.

The estimates of the total deposition in the bays for the period 1849–1914 are contained in Table 5

TABLE 5.—*Estimates of the volumes of débris deposited in the San Francisco Bay system from 1849 to 1914, inclusive.*

Body of water.	Dates of surveys.	Volume of deposits between dates of survey.	Volume of deposits, 1849–1914.
		Cu. yds.	*Cu. yds.*
Suisun Bay........	1867–1886	64,000,000	200,000,000
Carquinez Strait...	1861–1890	40,000,000	50,000,000
San Pablo Bay....	1857–1897	366,000,000	570,000,000
San Francisco Bay.	1856–1896	196,000,000	326,000,000
Bay system.	....	....	1,146,000,000

These estimates take no account of subsidence, although it is probable that the period to which they pertain witnessed subsidence, especially of the crustal block west of the Haywards fault. If it were possible to make the proper allowance the estimates would be somewhat larger.

The shoaling of the bays has been accompanied by a lessening of their areas. The salt marshes, whose margins are intimately associated with the lines of high tide, have steadily encroached on the muddy shoals, and the lines of low tide have as steadily encroached on the areas of continuous open water. Such encroachments diminish the tidal prism, on the magnitude of which depends the depth of entrance to the Golden Gate, and their relations to foreign commerce give them special importance, but it is convenient to defer their consideration until estimates have been made of the total volume of the mining débris.

CHAPTER VI.—QUANTITY AND DISTRIBUTION OF DETRITUS.

DATA TO BE DETERMINED.

Nearly all phases of the economic questions connected with the débris from hydraulic mining are concerned with quantities. It is desirable to know (1) how much detritus—gravel, sand, and clay—was excavated by the miners and started toward or down the streams; (2) how much detritus the streams received from other sources; (3) what is the present distribution of this material; and (4) what changes are in progress and toward what results do they tend. The present chapter will consider the first three of these subjects. With reference to each of them there is a certain amount of definite information, but this falls so far short of complete knowledge that the field remaining for conjecture is regrettably large. The lack of satisfactory data has been shown by the wide diversity in the earlier estimates, and the task of adding to a series of ill-supported and conflicting conjectures is not attractive. Nevertheless it is undertaken, first, because the contribution of a body of new measurements gives presumptive advantage to a new system of estimates, and second, because the importance of the question of quantities gives value to a demonstration of their order of magnitude, even where actual magnitudes may be only roughly approximated. I shall not hesitate, in the pages that follow, to base estimates on personal judgment when no better foundation is available.

QUANTITY OF MINING DÉBRIS.[1]

The belt of hydraulic mining in the Sierra Nevada traverses the drainage basins of a series of streams tributary to the Sacramento and the San Joaquin. On the tributaries of the San Joaquin the quantities of mining débris were relatively small—so small as to produce little or no effect on the navigability of the rivers. On Feather River proper the mining operations were more extensive but still small

as compared to those on the Yuba, the Bear, and the American. Of the quantity of material excavated in the basins of those three rivers a number of estimates have been made, and the estimated amounts vary through a wide range. The latest estimate that makes use of first-hand data is given in the report of a board of Army engineers headed by Lieut. Col. W. H. H. Benyaurd.[2] The data were collected and discussed chiefly by F. C. Turner,[3] assistant engineer, and apply to the year 1890. For the present purpose this estimate is the most available, especially as it was made some years after the stoppage of general hydraulic mining, whereas a number of the earlier estimates were made during the progress of the mining. It constitutes part of the report of a detailed reconnaissance of the region of hydraulic mining, in which a large body of valuable data was accumulated. The method of making the estimate is not stated by Turner, but may be assumed to have been indicated in general terms in the following passage from the report of the board:

The usual manner of estimating the amount of material moved is to determine the amount of water used, in miner's inches, and assign a duty to the inch. This, however, varies in different localities, in some places being as low as 2,000 and in others as high as 2,600 cubic feet in 24 hours. In the usual determination the quantity is taken at 2,230 cubic feet in that time. The duty depends upon the quantity of water used, the pressure, the character of the material washed, and the grade and size of the sluices; character of material and grade are the ruling elements. With heavy material the duty may be as low as 1.5 to 2 cubic yards, and with light material as high as 10 cubic yards per inch. Instances are quoted in the report of the State mineralogist for 1889 where, with increased grade of sluices (12 and 18 inch grades), the duty attained was 24 and 36 yards, respectively. The usual calculations are upon a basis of 3½ cubic yards. It will therefore be seen that great variations must exist in the estimates of amount of material that has already been mined out.

Impressed by the uncertainty of this mode of estimation, in which no engineer appears to have reposed great confidence, I undertook to check it by an independent estimate based on

---

[1] A part of this text has already been printed, with small verbal differences, as pp. 18-21 of U. S. Geol. Survey Prof. Paper 73, 1911, The Tertiary gravels of the Sierra Nevada of California, by Waldemar Lindgren.

38

[2] Chief Eng. U. S. Army Ann. Rept. for 1891, pp. 2996-3118.
[3] Idem, pp. 3041-3087.

an entirely different procedure, namely, the measurement of the cubic contents of the cavities produced by the excavation. This work was carried on in the spring and autumn of 1908, and after a few preliminary experiments the following method was adopted and followed:

The surveying instruments were a plane table and a stadia rod. With these a traverse was run through the bottom of each cavity or along its edge, and where the area was large a traverse circuit was completed. From the stations of the traverse numerous points were determined by stadia and others by angulation, the position and altitude of each being fixed. A complete sketch was made of the rim or outer margin of the excavation, and for a short distance outside the rim the ground was contoured. The scale adopted was 200 feet to 1 inch, and the contour interval was 20 feet. After the completion of the field work the contours of the ground previous to the excavation were restored by estimate, use being made of the determined contours outside the rim and of the determined courses of drainage lines outside the rim. With the aid of these restored contours and the determined points within the area of excavation a series of cross sections were constructed, and from these the volume of the excavation was computed. Some of the features of the excavated cavities are illustrated by Plate X.

The precision of this method can not be definitely stated, as there were no absolute checks on the accuracy of the restored contours; and the data controlling the restoration varied in cogency through a considerable range. In the opinion of the writer, who was also the surveyor, the general accuracy is such that the grand totals are true within 10 per cent, although many individual measurements have a lower precision.

The work was not carried on through the entire hydraulic district, but comparison with the Turner estimate indicates that it covered about four-fifths of the excavation in the basin of Yuba River and three-sevenths of the total excavation of Yuba, Bear, and American rivers. The table on page 40 gives the results in some detail and also compares them, so far as practicable, with the items of the Turner estimate. The difference in method of estimate led to a difference in the classification of the excavations, so that the comparison can not be refined, but it serves nevertheless as an effective check on the Turner estimate.

Examination of the table shows that a few of the earlier estimates are higher than the later, but the majority fall below and the new general totals exceed the earlier by 51 per cent. The difference is in part explained by the fact that some mining took place in the interval between 1890 and 1908. A number of mines were worked for short periods or in a small way under permits from the Débris Commission, and there was some surreptitious work without permits. During the surveys in 1908 it was easy to see that certain parts of the excavations, on which a young forest growth had sprung up, were of early date, and that other parts, still bare of vegetation, were relatively recent; but it was not practicable either to infer dates with approximate accuracy or to estimate separately the more recent work. It is believed, however, that the work subsequent to 1890 can account for only a small part of the discrepancy between the two estimates, and that the greater part of the 51 per cent of difference inheres in the methods of estimation and the data employed. Assuming the substantial accuracy of the later estimate, and assuming further that the ratio of difference derived from the totals of the table may be applied as a correction to the other parts of the Turner estimate, I have deduced revised estimates for the total hydraulic excavation in the combined Yuba, Bear, and American basins. Turner's summary is as follows:[1]

Material excavated by hydraulic mining in the basin of—

	Cubic yards.
Yuba River	452, 690, 000
Bear River	234, 650, 000
American River	170, 330, 000
	857, 670, 000

The application of the ratio 1.51 to these quantities yields for the Yuba basin 684,000,000 cubic yards, for the Bear basin 354,000,000 yards, and for the American basin 257,000,000 yards. The values thus derived have been adopted for the Yuba and American basins but have not proved satisfactory for the Bear basin. The quantity of mining débris accumulated in the canyons of the Bear and its tributaries has twice been estimated with more

---

[1] Chief Eng. U. S. Army Ann. Rept. for 1891, pt. 5, p. 3080.

care than was bestowed on similar deposits along the other rivers, and something is known also of the volume of the river's piedmont deposit. (See p. 48.) When these estimates are considered in connection with the small discharge of the Bear and other factors affecting the ratio of the local arrest of débris to the total output of the mines, good reason is found

The only other stream to receive mining débris and convey it eventually to the Sacramento is the main branch of the Feather. Turner's estimates do not include the mines of its basin, and my own observations covered but a small area. W. H. Hall,[1] in 1880, estimated the "water used and material washed out per annum" for the several river basins of the

TABLE 6.—*Volume of hydraulic excavation in part of the Yuba River basin as estimated by G. K. Gilbert in 1908 and by F. C. Turner in 1889–90.*

[Excavation expressed in thousands of cubic yards.]

District, mine, or locality and excavation therein.		Total excavation.	
1908	1889–90	1908	1889–90
Camptonville (7,100), Youngs Hill (7,500), Galena Hill (4,400), Weeds Point (3,000).	Willow Creek and Camptonville (5,800+1,500).	22,000	7,300
Indian Hill.	Indian Hill.	7,800	4,500
Moores Flat (21,000), Orleans Flat (3,400), Snow Point (3,900).	Moores Flat, Orleans Flat, and Snow Point.	28,300	26,000
Woolsey Flat.	Woolsey Flat.	20,700	4,100
Badger Hill and English Co.	Badger Hill and Cherokee (10,000), English Co. (7,000).	22,600	17,000
North Bloomfield (main pit, 64,400; minor pits, 13,600).	North Bloomfield (29,000) Last Chance, Porter, etc. (3,000).	78,000	32,000
North Columbia (main pit, 89,500); Howleys, Ohio, Neversweat, etc. (2,560).	Columbia Hill (20,000+20,000).	92,060	40,000
Union Gravel.	Union Gravel.	9,100	10,000
Yuba (Grizzly).	Grizzly Hill.	1,400	1,000
Paterson and vicinity.	Paterson claims (5,000), Montezuma Hill (500).	7,800	5,500
North San Juan (25,350), Manzanita and American (47,900), Bed Rock (10,050), Buck Eye (12,650).	North San Juan and part American (20,000+500), Sweetland Creek, Birchville, Manzanita and part American (60,000).	95,950	80,500
Esperance (and Kinney).	Esperance.	3,500	1,500
French Corral.	French Corral.	16,050	31,000
Omega.	Omega.	22,700	12,000
Alpha and vicinity.	Alpha (5,000), Place, Merrill, etc.	9,000	7,000
Sailor Flat and Blue Tent.	Sailor Flat and Blue Tent.	46,200	15,000
Cement Hill (?).	Nevada City, Cement Hill.	1,800	2,550
Rough and Ready, Randolph Hill and vicinity.	Rough and Ready, Randolph Hill.	910	3,000
Nevada City (Manzanita or Sugar Loaf, 6,000; Hirschman, etc., 6,400).	Nevada City, Sugar Loaf.	12,400	10,000
Murchies, McCutcheon, Charonnat, etc.	Murchies, Gold Flat, etc.	2,100	500
Scotts Flat.	Scotts Flat.	18,600	12,000
Smartsville and Timbuctoo (24,460), Mooney Flat (3,800).	Smartsville, Timbuctoo, and Mooney Flat.	28,260	44,800
Sicard Flat.	Sicard Flat.	3,030	1,700
Depot Hill.	No record.	3,900	....
Railroad Hill.	....do.	2,700	....
Two miles west of Parks Bar Bridge.	....do.	320	....
Dry Creek.	....do.	40	....
Two miles west of Grass Valley.	....do.	30	....
		557,250	368,950
Percentage.		151	100

for regarding the estimate of 354,000,000 cubic yards as excessive. As all the quantities involved in the discrepancy were subject to considerable uncertainty, the adjustment was of the nature of a compromise, and the correction assigned to the estimate of output of débris was a deduction of 100,000,000 cubic yards, reducing the estimate to 254,000,000 cubic yards.

Sierra from the American northward. For the basin of the Feather the estimate of material washed is 12,687,500 cubic yards, and the sum of the estimates for the Yuba, Bear, and American is 36,480,500 cubic yards. Lieut. Col. Mendell[2] makes a similar estimate for the

---

[1] California State Eng. Rept. for 1880, pp. 23–24.
[2] Chief Eng. U. S. Army Ann. Rept. for 1881, pp. 2486–2487, 2494–2501..

year 1880 in which the corresponding figures are 4,407,770 and 31,070,094. Mendell also gives with full detail the assessors' returns of the water used in mining. Hall and Mendell both qualify their estimates—Hall because his data were incomplete and Mendell because the method was unsatisfactory. In 1881 the canyons and mining regions of the Feather and the Yuba were inspected by Marsden Manson, and his report[1] tends to discredit the estimates based on assessors' returns. He found that much of the water ascribed to hydraulic mining was actually used in drifting and quartz mining and in other ways not involving the handling of large quantities of earth.

Disregarding for the moment Manson's implied criticism, accepting the estimates of Hall and Mendell, and assuming further that the total output of débris for the several basins for the whole period of hydraulic mining was proportional to the annual output, I have made two computations of the total output of the Feather. The figures quoted from Hall's table give 366,200,000 cubic yards, and the figures from Mendell's table 186,600,000 cubic yards. The details reported by Manson and Turner, as well as data from other sources, indicate the probability that both these figures are excessive. On the other hand, a minimum estimate is suggested by the volume of the piedmont deposit of the Feather, which occupies the river bed between Oroville and Marysville. Hall estimated this, from surveys probably made in 1879, at 18,257,000 yards,[2] and the observations of Turner indicate that only moderate additions were made in the following decade. The suggested minimum is 40,000,000 cubic yards, and this might serve as a practical estimate, so far as conditions of the lower river are concerned; but it would probably not be coordinate with the estimates for the other basins, which aim to show the full extent of the exploitation of the auriferous deposits. According to Manson, most of the tailings from the greatest operations were lodged in a permanent way in the American Valley, an opening in the heart of the mountains. Between the limits 40,000,000 and 186,000,000 cubic yards, the value of 100,000,000 cubic yards is arbitrarily chosen. Adding the estimate for the Feather basin to that for the

three basins farther south gives a total of 1,295,000,000 cubic yards as the output of the hydraulic mines on streams whose waters join the Sacramento.

With reference to problems connected with the flow of mining débris there is no occasion to discriminate between the tailings of the hydraulic mines and the waste from three other sources—ordinary placer mining, placer drifting, and quartz mining. All through the auriferous belt the initial mining was done with pick, shovel, and cradle, and only a small quantity of tailings resulted from the work of each miner, but the miners were an army. They attacked first the gravel bars of creeks and rivers and the associated low-lying alluvial terraces (see Pl. XI), and gradually extended their activities to the unconsolidated formations that sheathed or composed the hills. The material was worked over with the aid of water, the pebbles and boulders were left on the ground, and the finer particles were washed away, for the most part quickly reaching the river. So far as the deposits were stream bars, the fine stuff that floated off was soon afterward replaced by the streams, so that there was no permanent local loss of material, and there seems to be no occasion to take account of such washings in this connection. It was different, however, with the washings on the hillsides. The pits thus excavated still remain, and the material removed has been added to the detrital load of the streams. The cradle was soon supplemented by appliances that used water to better advantage, and the system of work in which excavation is accomplished by a powerful jet of water—the system that has appropriated as its title the comprehensive adjective hydraulic—was gradually developed. Where the hill deposits were deep the earlier work was superficial or marginal, and the rims of its shallow pits were effaced by the greater operations that followed. In this way a portion of the volume of pre-hydraulic work came to be included in the measurement of hydraulic pits and is thus covered by the revision of the Turner estimate. To complement that estimate allowance should be made only for the shallow excavations remaining outside the areas of the hydraulic work.

The data are vague. In traversing the Yuba mining region on various errands and especially in the search for outlying hydraulic pits hidden

[1] Chief Eng. U. S. Army Ann. Rept. for 1882, pp. 2604-2612.
[2] California State Eng. Rept. for 1880, p. 11.

in the forest, I often came across shallow work-ings. At half a dozen localities the evidence of placer work was almost continuously visible for a mile or more; at numerous localities it was seen for only a few rods. Usually the view was obstructed by forest or chaparral, so that casual observation gave little information as to areal extent. An arbitrary estimate of 10 square miles for the entire Yuba area includes not only tracts that were imperfectly seen but many other tracts assumed to be distri-buted through the hillsides of the basin. It is estimated that earth was removed from this area to an average depth of 3 feet; and these assumed dimensions give as the estimated total volume of the débris 30,000,000 cubic yards. As the basins of the Bear and American together nearly equaled that of the Yuba in hydraulic output, the same volume of placer débris is ascribed to them.

The large expense of drifting, as compared to surface washing, tends to limit the extent of operations, but its waste is of the same char-acter as that from hydraulic washings except that it includes more boulders. The mining of quartz veins, however, produces much waste of a type unsuited for transportation unless it is dumped directly into the streams. Ordi-narily the mine refuse is so coarse and angular that it lies permanently where it is originally thrown; and only the ore that is milled goes to swell the load of the streams. An estimate of the débris from drifting might therefore be based on the volume of the mine openings, and an estimate for quartz mining on the work of the stamp mills. The statistics of the stamp mills, though irregular and discontinuous, give the amount of ore crushed for a number of individual years and yield, with generous interpolation, an estimate of 35,000,000 cubic yards for the whole mining belt from the Feather to the Tuolumne. To this I add 15,000,000 yards as an allowance for unmilled mine waste dumped directly into streams or otherwise finding its way to them, thus raising the estimate for quartz-mining débris to 50,000,000 yards. There are practically no statistics of the output of débris from drifting, and the allowance of 30,000,000 cubic yards which I make is a mere guess. It does not include the output for the basin of the Feather, which was practically covered in estimating the débris from hydraulic mining.

Two other bodies of débris remain to be con-sidered. A few of the hydraulic mines of the Sierra are on streams which belong to the general hydrographic basin of the Sacramento but do not send their detrital loads either directly or in any considerable share to that river, because they discharge directly to one or another of the lateral overflow basins of the Sacramento Valley. Their débris belongs to the general total for the mining industry of the Sacramento River basin but has little if any connection with the "débris problem." A greater number of mines are associated with rivers south of the American that are not tributary to the Sacramento but send their waters either to the San Joaquin or to the délta plexus east of the mouths of the Sacramento and San Joaquin. The débris from these rivers has no recognized connection with the problem of the economic treatment of the Sacramento but may affect economic problems in the tidal waters of the bays.

The only important group of mines sending débris to the lateral basins of the Sacramento Valley are on Table Mountain Creek, north of Feather River, and their output is estimated at 25,000,000 cubic yards. An allowance of 5,000,000 cubic yards is added for mines on Butte Creek, north of Table Mountain, and creeks between Bear and American rivers.

The hydraulic mines south of the American, discharging tailings to Cosumnes, Mokel-umne, Calaveras, Stanislaus, and Tuolumne rivers and to a group of creeks between the Cosumnes and Mokelumne, were the subject of a critical examination by Lieut. A. H. Payson [1] in 1880. He reported that profitable hydraulicking was limited by natural condi-tions in much of the region, that local storage of tailings was practicable at many points, that the damage to farming lands, although noteworthy, was far less than in the Sacramento River basin, and that the injury to navigation was very small. He made a detailed estimate of the annual output of the mines, placing the total at 7,352,465 cubic yards. In 1889 or 1890 C. L. Higgins [2] examined the same district for the Benyaurd commission. He found that only minor changes had taken place in the condi-tion of farming lands affected by the débris,

[1] Chief Eng. U. S. Army Ann. Rept. for 1881, pp. 2501-2514; idem for 1882, pp. 2584-2604.
[2] Idem for 1891, pp. 3114-3118.

and he estimated the annual output of the hydraulic mines at 4,348,600 cubic yards. One of these estimates preceded and the other followed the great restriction of mining by injunctions, but the restriction appears to have been much less in the southern field than in the northern. Taking these estimates at their face value and applying them, with what appears reasonable qualification, to the whole period of placer and hydraulic mining, I deduce 230,000,000 cubic yards as an estimate of the entire body of earth moved from its original place to the present time in the region from Mokelumne River to Tuolumne River, inclusive.

The estimates brought together in Table 7 cover a period closing with the year 1909, which was the last year of my personal observation in the region of the mines. No definite data are available for the five years that have followed, but it is believed that a proper allowance would increase the totals by less than 10,000,000 and possibly by less than 5,000,000 cubic yards.

TABLE 7.—*Summary of mining débris, 1849–1909.*

Million cubic yards.

From hydraulic mining in basin of—	
Upper Feather River	100
Yuba River	684
Bear River	254
American River	257
Streams tributary to lateral basins of Sacramento River	30
Mokelumne River to Tuolumne River, inclusive	230
From ordinary placer mining	60
From quartz mining (one-fourth in Sacramento basin)	50
From drifting (three-fourths in Sacramento basin)	30
Total mining débris:	
From hydraulic mining	1,555
From all mining tributary to Sacramento River	1,390
From all mining tributary to Suisun Bay	1,665

To most laymen, and possibly to some engineers not concerned with great movements of earth, the term 1,000,000 cubic yards conveys no definite meaning. It helps us to a conception of the actual magnitude of the hydraulic-mining operations of the Sierra to know that the volume of earth thus moved was nearly eight times as great as the volume moved in making the Panama Canal.

292

CHAPTER X.—THE OUTLOOK FOR HYDRAULIC MINING.

The interests that suffered most acutely and consciously by reason of the great wave of mining débris from the Sierra were those of lowland farm lands and lowland towns. Some farms were buried, and for others the cost of protection from inundation was increased. Towns had to levee against sands and rising floods and were deprived of the advantages of river transportation. In respect to these interests the period of tension is now past. The piedmont rivers have intrenched themselves in the piedmont deposits, and their sands have ceased to spread. The valley rivers are lowering their beds, and the full resumption of river traffic is in sight. The débris in the river beds has lost prominence as a factor in the aggravation of floods, being now clearly subordinate to the reclamation factor.

The remoter effects of the débris invasion, though not neglected by the Government engineers in charge of rivers and harbors, received little attention from the general public, despite the fact that the integrity of the harbor is of higher importance to the community as a whole than the navigability of the rivers.

The building of the piedmont deposits gave to the channels of the piedmont rivers such slopes that they are now able to carry forward a much larger annual load of débris than in pre-mining years. The system of levees by which the valley floods are being controlled is giving to the valley rivers also an ability to transport a greater annual load. So far as riparian interests are concerned it would soon be possible to admit to the rivers a considerable annual load of mining tailings without a recurrence of the old-time tension. Such a modification of the existing system of regulation is inadmissible chiefly or wholly because the consequence would be prejudicial to navigation—because it would tend to diminish the depth of water in the rivers, on Pinole Shoal, and on the Golden Gate bar.

Back of this proposition lie certain postulates as to relative values. It is true that the present restrictions on mining were determined in chief

104

part by considerations of justice between two local interests—the miners should not continue their work in a manner injurious to property in the valley—but San Francisco Harbor belongs to the whole community, and it is proper for the community to weigh its impairment, in such measure as it might be impaired, against the advantage to the community of having the gold extracted from the Sierra gravels. So too the community—or the custodians of its interests—may weigh the embarrassment of navigation in bays and rivers against the advantages from gold extraction. The regulations that restrain hydraulic mining should not be made less stringent unless the advantage from the mining is of greater moment to the community than the disadvantage to navigation that a change of policy might entail.

In this connection it is to be observed that the public and its representatives may properly consider to what extent the interests of agriculture and commerce are brought into antagonism by existing conditions in the bays. Now that the flow of mining débris is waning the flow of soil waste, whose effects are of the same character, is acquiring relative importance. Soil waste is mainly the tailings of agriculture, and through it agriculture is obstructive to navigation and commerce. Coordinate with the weakening of the Golden Gate currents by deposits of mining débris and soil waste is the weakening caused by the reclamation of tidal marshes, and nearly all that reclamation is for the purposes of agriculture. That agriculture in its entirety is the industry of first importance is recognized by all, but it does not follow that commerce should yield to it at every point of interference. Each particular case of conflicting interest involves an economic problem in relative values and should be adjudged on that basis.

As to soil waste there is no essential conflict of interest, for the conservation of soil is more important to agriculture than to commerce. The injury to commerce is occasioned only by the improvident and profligate methods of frontier farming. In time the methods will be reformed without regulative compulsion, and it is possible that this result may be achieved somewhat quickly through education, but if it must await for its motive a strong pressure of population on agricultural area much harm to navigation may first be caused.

In respect to reclamation the interests of agriculture and commerce are directly antagonistic. Every acre of reclaimed tide marsh (except in the upstream parts of the river deltas) implies a fractional reduction of the tidal current in the Golden Gate. For any individual acre the fraction is minute, but the acres of tide marsh are many, and if all shall be reclaimed the effect at the Golden Gate will not be minute. The question whether the community should make a large addition to its permanent agricultural wealth at the cost of a small permanent injury to its great harbor is a question of relative values.

Returning to the consideration of hydraulic mining, I shall assume that, in the future as now, the working of the auriferous gravels will be permitted only on condition that the tailings, coarse and fine, are kept from the rivers.

The history of mining under permit has served to bring out certain economic limitations. When the system of regulation was first established its rules were framed especially for the immediate arrest of the coarser débris. Much of the finer material was allowed to escape, and the types of impounding dams prescribed were not such as to make the débris storage permanent. Rules formulated later were more stringent, and the expense to the miner was increased, especially by the requirement that his dams have the quality of permanence. Partly because of the increasing stringency of regulation, and partly because of the exhaustion of the richer gravels and of the more available storage sites, the industry has slackened, and its magnitude is now relatively small. With minor exceptions, the gravels that remain in the Sierra can not be worked profitably so long as the cost of storage is added to the cost of washing.

With the lapse of time, also, the money value of water power has risen. Hydraulic mining must now compete with those valley industries which obtain power from the Sierra through electric transmission, and the restric-

tions thus imposed on mining increase with the development of the power-using industries. In the near future agriculture, which has postponed the full utilization of Sierra waters for irrigation, will be imperative in demanding a large share in the control of the streams, and the arrangements to meet the joint needs of irrigation and electric power are likely to so increase the storage of water in reservoirs that mining will have comparatively little opportunity for that use of surplus or otherwise unappropriated water which it now finds a resource.

As a result of the enlarged and growing cost of hydraulic mining the quantity of auriferous gravel that can be worked at a profit is less than it was 25 years ago. If the estimates made at that time were to be shorn of all exaggeration they would still need much paring to bring them into accord with present conditions.

In the memorial of the California Miners' Association (p. 12) asking for an investigation by the Geological Survey it was suggested that waste lands might be found in the foothills on which the mining débris could be deposited. The lands that are waste in the sense of having little or no value for agriculture are lands of steep slope, on which the débris could not be deposited without expensive dams. Deposition in the foothills could not in any case be accomplished without local control of the rivers, and such control would be more expensive than the control of streams near the mines.

Various schemes have been broached for the storage of mining débris in one of the lateral basins of the Sacramento. The cost would include engineering works for the control of large streams and also the purchase of the lands to be covered by the deposit, and such cost would be greater than the benefited mining industry could afford. Nevertheless, such projects are not necessarily visionary, because the mining interest is not necessarily the only one to receive benefit. A project of that kind might include the complete protection of a piedmont deposit of mining débris from further erosion and thus deserve consideration by the State as a measure for the conservation of San Francisco Harbor.

The reasons that have been given by engineers for the rejection of such schemes have included interference with vested rights, prohibitive cost, and inadequate fall or slope. While I do not question that the second reason is adequate, it seems to me desirable to point out that the third is fallacious. It is indeed true that a stream which carries a load of débris can not carry its load on a route giving less slope if other conditions remain the same, but it is also true that on most streams the ability to carry load may be greatly increased by reducing the width of channel. An unrestrained stream that has a load to carry shapes for itself a wide, shallow channel, whereas the channel form most efficient for the transportation of débris is narrow and deep. It results that a stream with a fixed load which has adjusted its slope to a wide channel can be made to do its work on a gentler slope by narrowing its channel.

As already mentioned (p. 63), this principle is illustrated by results from the training walls at Daguerre Point; and it is further illustrated at the narrows of Yuba River near Smartsville. In the narrows, where rock walls determine a width of 300 to 400 feet, the Yuba established a slope of 5 feet to the mile as appropriate to the transportation of its load of coarse gravel at a time when the movement of mining débris was near its maximum. Outside the narrows, where the width of the flood channel was 1,000 to 1,500 feet, the slope adjusted to the same load was about 18 feet to the mile. Had the rock walls at the narrows been smooth instead of uneven, a slope of less than 5 feet to the mile would have been established there. If the river were to be constrained by smooth training walls 400 feet apart all the way from the narrows to its mouth, 20 miles away, and if the height of the bed at the river mouth were to be so determined by a sill that the slope from narrows to sill would serve for the transportation of a maximum load of débris, the height of the sill would be more than 100 feet above the highest flood level of Feather River. It would be feasible, therefore, as a project in hydraulic engineering and without reference to cost, to carry Yuba River by an aqueduct across Feather River, taking with it the largest load of débris ever imposed on it by mining and delivering the load in Sutter Basin.

If it is true, as I believe, that the community can not afford to permit more mining débris to be sent to the bays and that the chief parts of the unworked auriferous gravels are not rich enough to meet the expense of permanent storage of tailings, whether in the mountains, in the foothills, or in the valley, the outlook for any important enlargement of the hydraulic mining operations is certainly not assuring. There remains, however, a possibility that something may be accomplished through cooperation with other industries. Cooperation between the great users of the Sierra water, the irrigator and the distributor of power, has probably already begun; if not, then it impends, for it is the logical relation; and there may be places where to the interests of these two the interests of the miner can be joined, so that a single plant for water control may serve three purposes.

In a tentative way I have developed such a project for the control of Yuba River at the edge of the Great Valley, and the scheme will be presented in brief outline, notwithstanding the fact that I have been informed by a competent engineer that the cost of the projected works would be prohibitive. The project will serve to illustrate my idea as to the general character of possible cooperative undertakings, and it may contain suggestions toward a better-considered scheme.

South of the Yuba near Hammonton is an outlying foothill of which the north base is called Hallett Point. It is connected with the main line of foothills by a ridge, which is notched at several points by cols. The project includes a dam running straight northward from this hill and of such height as to divert the river across one of these cols. The diverted river would follow the line of Reed Creek to Feather River, being guided by training walls. The reservoir created by the dam would have an initial capacity of 560,000,000 cubic yards, or 350,000 acre-feet. It would catch and store all débris delivered by the river, except the very finest. If the old mining débris and the soil waste for 50 years are estimated at 100,000,000 cubic yards the reservoir could still receive 250,000,000 cubic yards of new mining débris before its serviceability for irrigation and power development would begin to be impaired. In computing power development I assumed that the head would vary from 175 to 95 feet, the daily requirement in discharge being inversely as the head, and I computed only the theoretic power, without allowance for the coefficient of efficiency. I assumed that the development of power would be uniform through the year, so that during the height of the irrigation season a certain portion of the discharged water would not be utilized for power but only for irrigation. In computing the acreage for irrigation, I allowed a duty of one-third acre per acre-foot and estimated the quotas of water for different months on the basis of the experience at Orland. The run-off of the Yuba River basin was taken month by month from gaging records at the narrows, and the monthly requirements for power and irrigation were treated in combination with the monthly run-off, so as to take continuous account of the water level in the reservoir. An allowance of 10 per cent was made for evaporation and seepage. Independent computations were made (1) for the average annual run-off and (2) for the smallest recorded run-off, that of the year 1910. The resulting figures are as follows:

TABLE 29.—*Irrigation and power from Yuba River project.*

	With average run-off.	With run-off of 1910.
Area furnished with water for irrigation..................acres..	159,000	133,000
Continuous (theoretic) power developed...........horsepower..	27,600	20,400

The intake of the irrigation canals, being below the outfall of the projected power house, was placed at the 100-foot contour above sea level, and the lands to be served all lie east of Feather and Sacramento rivers and north of American River. The tracts under the lines of canal, after deducting lands already irrigated in 1912 and after deducting 10 per cent for roads, etc., contain 191,000 acres.

If such a reservoir were to be used only for the storage of débris, its capacity would be about 750,000,000 cubic yards, and the provision for new hydraulic tailings would be 650,000,000 yards, instead of the 250,000,000 admitted in the cooperative scheme. If it were to be used for power development alone the output estimated, for a year like 1910, is 26,700 horsepower, instead of 20,400. If it were to be used for irrigation alone, high-level as well as low-level canals could be employed, increasing the available area east of Feather and Sacramento rivers to about 350,000 acres; and the water supply in a year like 1910 would suffice for about 300,000 acres.

In addition to its service in power development and its service to agriculture and mining, the project would benefit commerce by increasing or conserving the depth of water at points of critical importance to navigation. Not only would it arrest a large body of soil waste and old mining débris at its point of issue from the mountains, but it would fix beyond possibility of future erosion all that remains of the Yuba piedmont deposit. The Yuba, which now brings more débris to clog the navigable channels below Marysville than all other streams combined, would be loaded only with fine mud in suspension, and its water would help to scour channels deeper; while the regulation of its flow would increase the low-water discharge and the low-water depth on river bars. The trouble at Pinole Shoal would be slightly reduced, and the contraction of the bays which is slackening the tidal current at the Golden Gate would be retarded. The project would thus serve the interests of the community as a whole, and because of this service the State might assume, without injustice to its taxpayers, a share of the cost.

A. A MINING DUMP ON THE SIDE OF A SMALL CREEK VALLEY.

The mine (not shown) is at the right.   The tailings, discharged from the mining sluice, have built a fan-shaped deposit, but this deposit contains only the coarser part of the tailings.   At its lower edge the dump is attacked by the creek, and some of it is washed away whenever the creek is in flood.   Photographed in 1905.

B. ONE OF THE LARGER CREEKS OF THE UPLAND, WITH ITS DEPOSIT OF MINING DÉBRIS.

At the right is a partly eroded mining dump.   The photograph was made in 1908, and at that time the mining dumps were furnishing so much débris to the creek that the erosion of its deposit had scarcely begun.

MINING DÉBRIS NEAR ITS SOURCE.

A. A SIERRA CANYON BED IN ITS NATURAL CONDITION.

The water channel occupies the entire width.

B. A SIERRA CANYON CLOGGED BY MINING DÉBRIS.

The surface of the débris constitutes a broad plain that is covered by water only when the stream is in flood. The low-water channels traverse this plain. The photograph was made in 1908. At that time most of the canyon deposits had been removed. (See Pl. VII, *A*.) This one is the head of a piedmont deposit. (See pp. 28, 52.)

CHANGE OF CONDITION CAUSED BY MINING DÉBRIS.

A. AN UPLAND-CREEK DEPOSIT IN A REGION OF MANY MINING DUMPS.

During the growth of the deposit a forest was overwhelmed, and its stumps and logs are now being disentombed.   New vegetation takes possession of parts of the valley where erosion is least active and helps to restrain the erosive work.   Photographed in 1905.

B. A HEAVY CREEK DEPOSIT OF THE UPLAND, NOW SUFFERING EROSION.

Photographed in 1905.

MINING-DÉBRIS DEPOSITS OF UPLAND CREEKS.

299

A. MANZANITA MINE, NEAR SWEETLAND.

Beyond the buildings is a ridge bearing trees on its crest. The camera stood on a similar ridge. The outer slopes
of the ridges and the tabular top of the intervening hill are parts of the original surface before the mining. In
the survey to measure the quantity of earth removed they helped to indicate the original configuration of the land.
The greatest depth of excavation within the field of view was 180 feet, and the volume of the visible part of the
opening is about 13,000,000 cubic yards. The estimated volume of the entire excavation at this point, including
the Manzanita and American mines, is 47,900,000 cubic yards.

B. NORTH WALL OF THE WEST ARM OF THE NORTH BLOOMFIELD MINE.

The height of the wall is 250 feet. The photograph was made in 1908, about 20 years after the last mining in this part
of the opening. Storm waters have continued the work of excavation, sculpturing the cliff into alcoves and
buttresses. Part of the excavated earth has lodged in a lower part of the mine and part has escaped to a neighboring creek. On the cliff the surface wash has been so active that vegetation has found no foothold, but elsewhere
the work of reforestation has begun. The trees in the foreground all stand within the mine.

HYDRAULIC PLACER MINES.

Landscape Conservation

V

The purpose of this section is to place in perspective the total range of man's activities for dealing with the earth's surface. Part IV emphasized his destructive tendencies and it is now appropriate to attempt some balancing of the human attitude. Man's full awareness of the necessity for environmental protection was not reached prior to 1900, so future volumes will show new avenues of his involvement in attempts to correct old wounds and to prevent aggravation of the earth by more comprehensive planning and management of the landscape. The term "landscape" is not meant to pertain only to the dry earth, but includes the entire framework and setting of the earth's surface. Thus additional hydrographic terms such as "seascape" and "riverscape" become redundant with such usage. The land and waters associated with terrain are difficult to separate because they are intricately united in so many ways—the slope of the land, the porosity and permeability of soils, the ground–surface water interface, the changing areal extent of water bodies during wet and dry seasons, in times of flood or of low streamflow. In such context the new flashy jargon of the "land–water ecosystem" does have validity and can be conveniently used.

In similar manner the term "conservation" is being used in a broad sense in order to prevent a semantical debate. Conservation in these volumes, therefore, implies management of the earth's surface resources and features such as its soil, its land, its water, and includes the companion concepts of preservation and reclamation. The combination of terms "landscape conservation" provides an eclectic approach that has the advantage of including a closely related network of topics which should not be arbitrarily separated in an artificial way. Only through an integrative approach can environmental management for man's benefit and nature's balance be consummated.

301

A. Water Management

Although some aspects of water use were mentioned in Part I, the focus of this section is on the conservation and reclamation activities of man. The articles by Evenari and others and by Kedar illustrate how divergent views can result from a common set of observations. The locale is the Negev desert in Israel, the observational data were obtained from the ancient fields and hillslopes of the region, and the problem concerns the conservational practices of the early agrarian society that inhabited the area. Very ingenious methods, devices, and terrain modifications were used (although less well-known constructions occur in other deserts) that permitted farming in an exceptionally dry climate. Evenari and Kedar are in agreement concerning the many flat fields with associated check dams (Kedar found 17,000 in a 130 km² area), and the presence of artificial stone heaps and stripes on many hillslopes (up to 80 mounds per hectare). The main disagreement concerns reasons for removal of stones into the heaps and stripes, although the result was the same, namely, exposure of the loess soil to the elements. Evenari proposes it was for the purpose of increasing surface runoff which then flowed into the check dams where water could be diverted to the fields. Kedar, however, interpreted the removal of stones as a deliberate attempt by man to increase upland erosion so that the silt particles could then be washed into the check dams and produce new soil on flat lands (see Fig. 1). Thus, the question whether water or whether soil is the limiting factor for agriculture in the Negev environment remains. Kedar (1967) in a book elaborates his position and the following diagram from that book illustrates his ideas concerning the evolution of the man-created features. Also in a new book (1971) Evenari and others provide further expansion for their thesis.

Michael Evenari (1904–   ) received his Ph.D. (1926) from Frankfurt in botany. He has taught at the University of Frankfurt, German University in Prague, and California Institute of Technology. Since 1934 he has been at Hebrew University where he is Professor of Botany.

Yehuda Kedar (1925–   ) was born in Hungary and received his Ph.D. (1959) in geography at Hebrew University. He taught at Hebrew University from 1961–1967 and became Chairman, Department of Geography. From 1967–1968 he was Visiting Professor at the University of California at Santa Barbara, and from 1968–1970 he was Research Associate at NASA, Washington, D.C. Since 1970 he has been Professor of Geography, State University of New York at Binghamton.

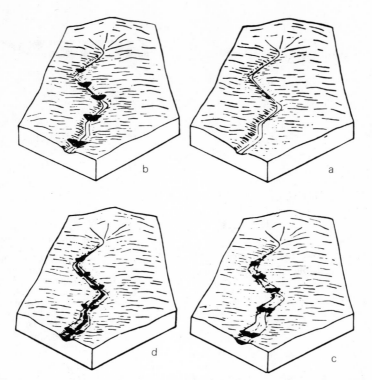

Figure 1, Stages in check-dam farming (Kedar, 1967.) a. Initial stage; b. installation of series of check dams; c. siltation behind dams for location of farms; d. after abandonment of dams, structures are breached and new erosion cycle and entrenchment occurs.

31 March 1961, Volume 133, Number 3457

SCIENCE

24

Ancient Agriculture in the Negev

Archeological studies and experimental farms show how agriculture was possible in Israel's famous desert.

M. Evenari, L. Shanan, N. Tadmor, Y. Aharoni

The Negev desert of Israel, with its numerous, clearly visible traces of ancient civilizations dating back at least four to five thousand years, has attracted the attention of many scientists. Since Palmer (*1*) in 1871 described the general character of these civilizations as well as the intriguing agricultural remnants that he observed in the area, the Negev has become a field of research for many phases of science.

We have been working as a team in the Negev desert for five years with the specific aim of solving the enigma of the once flourishing agricultural civilizations in a now barren desert. This team covers the fields of botany, archeology, ecology, hydrology, and water engineering, and this combination of experience and interests enabled us to correlate widely differing fields of observation. In this article we present some of our conclusions as to how the ancient civilizations maintained a thriving agriculture in the desert and also indicate their possible application in the future.

Description of the area. The Negev

Dr. Evenari is professor of botany at the Hebrew University, Jerusalem, Israel; Mr. Shanan is a hydrological engineer in Tel Aviv; Dr. Tadmor is a plant ecologist with the Ministry of Agriculture of Israel; and Dr. Aharoni is an instructor in the department of archeology of the Hebrew University, Jerusalem.

is shaped like a triangle (Fig. 1). Its base line stretches in the north from an imaginary line drawn from Gaza on the Mediterranean Sea, through Beer Sheva, to Ein Gedi on the Dead Sea. Its two sides stretch from Gaza and from Ein Gedi down to Eilat on the Gulf of Aqaba. The 12,500 square kilometers of the Negev can be divided into the six following subregions: (i) the coastal strip; (ii) the lowlands and foothills; (iii) the central highlands; (iv) the sedimentary southern Negev, mostly consisting of rolling gravel plains; (v) the crystalline southern Negev representing the northeast corner of crystalline Sinai; and (vi) the Wadi Araba depression.

The physiographic and climatic conditions vary from subregion to subregion, and the various civilizations naturally adapted their agricultural projects to these differing features. The densest settled areas have been discovered in the lowlands and the highlands, and since most of our investigations have been concentrated in these subregions, we will describe them briefly.

The lowlands and foothills. This subregion is a strip about 10 to 25 kilometers wide, bounded by the coastal region on the west and the central highlands on the east and covering about 150,000 hectares. The morpho-

logical structure is made up mostly of Eocene limestone hills separating wide rolling plains, with the elevations ranging from 200 to 450 meters above sea level. This area contains the ancient towns of Nessanah, Sbeita, Ruheibeh, and Khalassah. A number of large wadis, whose sources are in the highlands, cut through the plains and drain towards the Mediterranean Sea. The hillsides are generally covered with a very shallow, gravelly, saline soil possessing an immature profile. The flora is dominated by the Zygophylletum dumosi association (*2*).

On the other hand, the Quaternary aeolian-fluviatile loess soils of the plains are relatively deep (2 to 3 meters) and only slightly saline. The Haloxylonetum articulati association is typical for these areas.

The highlands. This subregion covers some 200,000 hectares and contains the ancient towns of Mamshit (Kurnub) and Avdat (Abde). It is composed of a series of parallel anticlines, and the elevations vary between 450 and 1,000 meters above sea level. The anticlines are composed of Cenomanian Turonian limestones and cherts.

Between the high ridges, the main wadis drain to the Mediterranean and Dead seas. Adjacent to the wadis lie relatively narrow alluvial plains, and near the watershed divides where the wadis have not cut down to a stable base level, there are a number of expansive plains.

There are two principal plant habitats common to the area. On the rocky slopes (80 to 90 percent of the area) where the soil cover is shallow, gravelly, and saline, the Artemisietum herbae albae association prevails with transitions to the Zygophylletum dumosi.

On the loessian plains and in the wadi bottoms where loess has accumulated, the vegetation consists of sparsely distributed low shrubs of the Haloxylonetum articulati association.

Rainfall conditions. The rainfall records of our area have not been kept systematically for any long period of time. But even the few short records

979

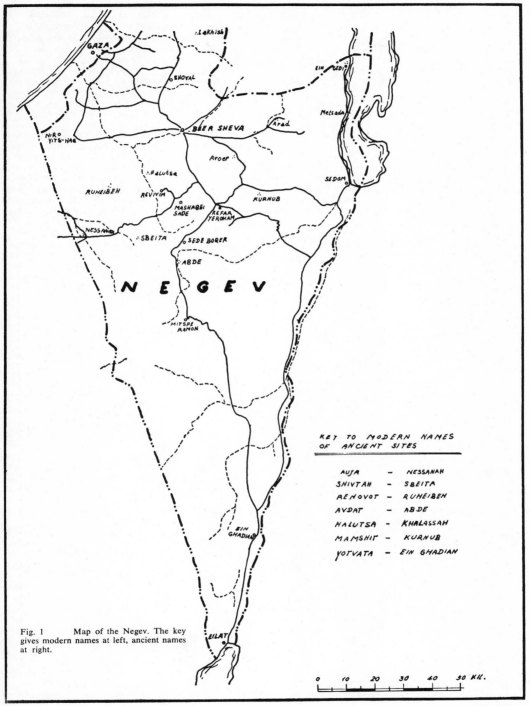

Fig. 1   Map of the Negev. The key
gives modern names at left, ancient names
at right.

KEY TO MODERN NAMES
OF ANCIENT SITES

AUJA   — NESSANAH
SHIVTAH   — SBEITA
REHOVOT   — RUHEIBEH
AVDAT   — ABDE
HALUTSA   — KHALASSAH
MAMSHIT   — KURNUB
YOTVATA   — EIN GHADIAN

0   10   20   30   40   50 KIL.

that have been published show that we deal here with that typical pattern of rainfall which is so characteristic for all deserts.

A study of Table 1 shows that the variations between maximum and minimum annual amounts of precipitation are large and that most of the rain falls in quick short showers of less than 10 millimeters. The difference between the average and median annual values should be noted, as, for agriculture, the median and not the average is significant.

The average number of rainy days with daily totals of precipitation of 0 to 3, 3 to 10, and more than 10 millimeters is another important figure, as it touches on the problem of the minimum "effective" rainfall (3).

Agricultural history of the Negev. The Northern Negev was, in historical times, first settled during the chalcolithic period (4th millennium B.C.). But up to now, no trace of this period has been found in the Central and Southern Negev (4).

During Middle Bronze I (21 to 19th century B.C.), the Negev was quite densely populated. The next period of sedentary settlement dates from the end of the 10th century B.C. to the beginning of the 6th—that is, the period of the Judaean Kingdom (Israelite periods II–III, or Iron Age II). However, the time between about 200 B.C. and A.D. 630 represents the longest and most flourishing period of almost continuous settlement in the Negev. During this time, the Nabataeans and Romans (about 200 B.C. to A.D. 330) and the Byzantines (A.D. 330 to 630) ruled the area (5). After the Arab conquest, from the 7th century A.D. up to our time, the Negev was occupied only by nomadic Bedouins (6).

As far as the *agricultural* history of the Negev is concerned, our own surveys and excavations of Israelite farms and settlements (7) and the surveys of Glueck (8) have shown that the Israelite period III settlers already carried out desert agriculture based on flood-water irrigation. We may men-

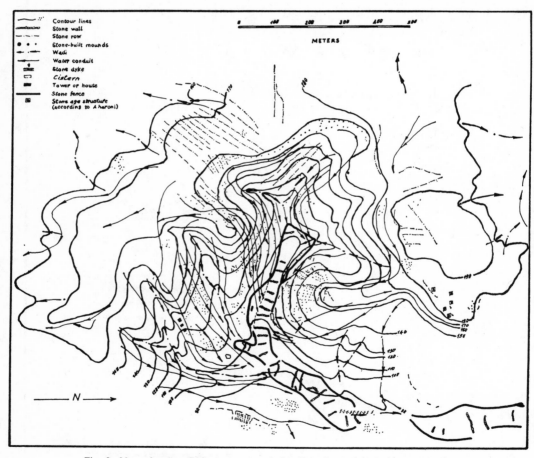

Fig. 2. Map of a runoff farm area near Avdat. Note the conduits and stone mounds.

Fig. 3. An oblique aerial photograph showing a number of ancient runoff farms near Shivtah.

The exploitation of runoff from small watersheds (20) is by far the most interesting of all the methods utilized by the ancients, since it made possible the very intensive development of the area.

The basic principle of the method was simple but nevertheless required a good understanding of the sciences of hydrology, soils, and meteorology. Table 1 shows that most of the rainfall in the desert falls in relatively light showers—3 to 10 millimeters at a time. These meager amounts of rainfall are generally regarded as ineffective—that is, they wet a very shallow depth of soil, which dries by evaporation before plants can utilize the moisture. However, the loess soils of the area have a characteristic of forming a crust when wet. This crustal formation was studied by D. Hillel (21), who has shown it to be an intrinsic feature of the Negev loess soil: the aggregated structure of the soil surface is destroyed by a wetting or slaking process. The crust decreases the water-intake rate of the soil and so increases the rate of runoff.

This phenomenon was observed by the ancients and exploited to the maximum. The loessial hillsides, which became more or less impermeable after wetting, were utilized as catchment basins to produce runoff for subsequent utilization in nearby fields. The desert farmer's aim was to prevent a penetration of rain on the slopes and so produce maximum runoff, whereas the farmer in more humid lands aims to soak all of the rain into the soil and so minimize runoff. The desert farmer directed the runoff from a large area on the slope to a small cultivated area in the bottomlands, and in this way he was able to collect sufficient water to ensure a crop even under adverse desert conditions.

This ingenious type of runoff agriculture we define as runoff farming, and the cultivated units to which it was related we call runoff farms.

Each runoff farm consisted of the farm area proper, containing the cultivated fields, and the surrounding catchment basin. The cultivated area

tion that this is corroborated by the Bible (II Chron. 26:10), where it says of King Uzziah, who ruled the Negev down to Elath, "also he built towers in the desert, and hewed out many cisterns . . . for he loved the land." But it may even be that the Middle Bronze I people practiced run-off desert agriculture, as the Negev is full of their settlements (9). During the Nabataean-Roman-Byzantine period, desert agriculture reached its peak of development. After the Arab conquest, the ancient desert agriculture slowly disintegrated, and the Bedouins of the area at best merely utilize dilapidating old systems for patch cultivation.

Outside of the Negev of Israel, ancient desert agriculture is known from the following areas: (i) North Africa [Algeria, Tunisia, Lybia (10–14)], Syria (15), and Transjordan (16), where it flourished under Roman domination; (ii) Southern Arabia (17); (iii) North America, where it was practiced and is being practiced by the Indians (18); and (iv) South America, where it was carried out by the pre-Hispanic civilizations (19).

Ancient desert techniques of water utilization for agriculture. There are relatively large areas in the desert where the soils are suitable for cultivation and the only requirement is water. This is true for most of the not too steep wadis, the flood plains, and the depressions where loess soils have accumulated to a depth of 1 to 2 meters. The key to establishing sedentary agriculture in a desert is, therefore, maximum utilization of the meager rainfall.

For this reason, our work has been concentrated on studying the techniques used by the ancient civilizations to collect and exploit the meager water resources of the area. The techniques that we have so far studied in detail, and that are presented in this article, can be divided into the three following main categories: (i) exploitation of runoff from small watersheds (up to 100 hectares in size); (ii) exploitation of runoff from large watersheds (up to 10,000 hectares in size); and (iii) chain-well systems.

Table 1. Rainfall data (in millimeters).

Item	Station		
	Aslug	Auja	Mam-shit
No. of years of record	13	14	9
Highest total annual recorded	170	285	171
Lowest total annual recorded	52	25	58
Average annual	100	89	98
Median annual	86	65	80
Av. No. of days per year with total of 0–3 mm	9	5	5
Av. No. of days per year with total of 3–10 mm	7	3	6
Av. No. of days per year with total of more than 10 mm	2	2	2

Fig. 4 (right). A vertical aerial photograph of a gravel mound and strip area near Shivtah.

982

Fig. 5. A field of gravel mounds near Shivtah.

was subdivided into terraces by low terrace walls. The function of the terrace walls was to retain the flood water on the field, where it could soak into the soil and be stored for subsequent use by the crops. A number of terraced fields were surrounded by a stone wall, constituting a distinct unit (22). Within the area bounded by the wall there is very often a farmhouse or a watchtower. The hillsides surrounding the farm served as a catchment area from which water conduits channeled the runoff water onto the fields. Once the water was inside the farm, drop structures, ditches, and dividing boxes gave the farmer complete mastery over the distribution of the water. Figures 2 and 3 illustrate this very well. Figure

2 represents a system near Avdat. The whole catchment area comprises about 70 hectares and is artificially divided into a number of smaller catchment basins by several conduits, each leading to a specific terraced field in the narrow valley. Some of the conduits begin high on the plateau and collect runoff from there.

The 70 hectares of watershed of this system supplied water to about 2.2 hectares of cultivated land.

Figure 3 represents a number of runoff farms in the Shivtah area. Each farm received its runoff water from its own small wadi and from the many conduits which collected water from the small catchment basins on the hillside adjoining each farm.

About 100 runoff farms, together with their catchment basins, have been studied in detail.

Each farm unit formed an entity comprising a catchment basin and cultivated land. The larger the catchment basin, the more the water yield and the greater the corresponding area that could be irrigated. The ancient farmers often extended their water-collecting conduits to the plateaus high above their fields in order to increase the available water supply, and sometimes conduits were led around the hillsides so as to increase artificially the natural drainage area of the runoff farm. These catchments were therefore "water rights," and each runoff farm possessed a water right on a definite portion of the slope. These water rights, which generally vary in size from 10 to 100 hectares, were no less important a part of the runoff farm than the cultivated land itself. The man who owned water rights on the slopes could always build himself a farm, but not vice versa.

The farm land and its catchment on the slope are thus a mutually balanced system of land and water. All the precious water collected from the slope was used. If there was any surplus water on the farm, the cultivated area was extended by adding a new terrace downstream. It was probably only in exceptionally rainy years that surplus water passed over the lowest spillway of a runoff farm and flowed to the next terrace. On the other hand, permanently "dry" terraces were of no avail, and the farmer only built a new terrace if his expectations of getting it wet were reasonably good. Catchment and cultivated area are thus seen as a clearly defined unit—an integral part of an over-all plan of watershed subdivision.

The conduits generally collected water from a relatively small area, sometimes as small as 0.1 to 0.3 hectare and generally not larger than 1.0 to 1.5 hectares. The result was that the overall runoff was always divided into small streams of water, preventing the occurrence of large flash floods. Such controlled flows are suited to the dry stone structures of the ancients; moreover, only such small flows could be handled by a farmer and allow him to control the flow during the flood period. Flows from even 1 hectare of catchment might reach a high peak intensity for short periods. For example, with a peak rain intensity of 30 millimeters per

Fig. 6. A field of gravel strips near Shivtah.

hour and a 60-percent (an extreme figure) runoff for a short period during a single rain storm, 1 hectare of slope might yield a peak flow of 180 cubic meters per hour, if only for a few minutes. This requires a ditch with a cross section of 0.05 to 0.10 square meter (depending on gradient), a requirement which readily fits observed ditch dimensions.

The farmer could therefore not allow the waters to collect from a larger area, as the resulting peak flow would have been unmanageable and would have destroyed his terrace structures. The over-all runoff was thus effectively broken up into small streams.

The crucial question that arises is the amount of runoff the ancient farmers received per unit area. Actual field measurements of runoff already initiated on our two reconstructed farms, discussed below, will have to be made for at least 10 years before a reliable estimate can be made. We approached this question indirectly by analyzing the ratio

$$R = \frac{\text{area of catchment basin of ancient farm}}{\text{area of cultivated area of ancient farm}}$$

About 100 farms in the Avdat, Shivtah, and Auja areas show that this ratio varies between 17:1 and 30:1, with an average value of about 20:1. This means that between 20 and 30 hectares of catchment area were needed to irrigate 1 hectare of cultivated field. Present-day agricultural experience has shown that flow of at least 3000 to 4000 cubic meters per hectare has to be applied as supplementary irrigation in order to insure any crop in this desert area. (Each 1000 cubic meters of water per hectare will wet about a meter of soil depth.) Taking these figures as a basis, we calculated that if 20 hectares on the slopes supplied the 3000 to 4000 cubic meters of water, every hectare of catchment supplied 150 to 200 cubic meters of water per year. If each hectare of catchment supplies 150 to 200 cubic meters of water (which is equivalent to 15 to 20 millimeters of rainfall), we can safely conclude that the coefficient of runoff was at least 15 to 20 percent of the total annual precipitation.

These runoff farms formed an important part of the desert settlements throughout the ages, and primitive but

nevertheless well-defined runoff farms have been found dating from the 10th to the 8th centuries B.C. (7). This form of intensive sedentary agriculture was probably continuous throughout all the civilizations, reaching its peak in the Roman-Byzantine era. Interesting and conspicuous features related to the runoff farms are the gravel mounds and gravel strips (see Figs. 4–6) and stone mounds and strips. These man-made structures cover thousands of acres and are common in the vicinity of the ancient cities of Avdat and Shivtah. The gravel mounds are low heaps of gravel artificially arranged in long rows with a more or less uniform distance between the mounds. The strips are of the same material. Mounds and strips are often intermingled and form all kinds of intricate patterns. They are only found on hammadas (23) covered by small gravel and are made by raking together the gravel.

The stone mounds and strips are built of much bigger stone fragments and are typical for those areas where for geological reasons the slopes are covered with big stone fragments and not with gravel. Gravel mounds, gravel strips, stone mounds, and stone strips are found exclusively on slopes leading to farms or cisterns (24, 25).

Since Palmer (1) first discovered these structures, all authors dealing with them agree that they are related to agriculture, and the following theories have been proposed concerning their function.

1) Palmer was told by his Bedouins that the arabic name for these structures is *teleilât el 'anab* or *rujum el Kurum*—that is, "grape mounds" or "vineyard heaps." "These sunny slopes," he concluded, "would have been admirably adapted to the growth of grapes and the black flint surface would radiate the solar heat, while these little mounds would allow vines to trail along them and would still keep the clusters off the ground."

A number of authors (26), and lately Mayerson (27), follow Palmer's theory. In our opinion, the slopes can never have been used for growing grapes because there is either no soil at all or only a very shallow superficial soil cover which is highly saline (2 to 5 percent total soluble salt). The naturally occurring plant associations on these slopes indicate the most difficult growing conditions for plants. As we have shown, the amount of rain

water these slopes receive is insufficient for growing grapes, and since the ancient farmers never used all the good loess soils available, there was no reason for them to cultivate the worst soil to be found in all the desert (28).

2) Some authors (10, 29, 30) believe that the function of the mounds was to condense dew. But experiments have shown that no dew can be collected in the mounds and that the water relations of the soil below the mounds do not differ from those of the surrounding soil (31).

3) Kedar (24, 32) put forward the theory that the main function of the mounds was to increase soil erosion from the slopes in order to accumulate more soil in the wadi bottoms ("accelerated erosion"), as in his opinion the main hindrance to agriculture was lack of suitable soil and not lack of water. There are a number of objections to this theory. First, there is and was plenty of good loess soil in the valley bottoms and flood plains close to the ancient agricultural systems. As today, lack of water and not lack of cultivable soil was the main problem of the ancients. It is hard to believe that the ancients, who knew so much about water spreading, would have endangered their elaborate systems by intentionally introducing silting, the arch enemy of any water-spreading system. Furthermore, some of the gravel-mound areas lead to water cisterns, where the accumulation of silt by erosion is most undesirable. The gradient of some of the collecting ditches varies from 0.5 to 1 percent. If they had been designed to carry silt, a much steeper gradient would have been necessary. But the main objection lies in a simple calculation. According to Kedar's experimental figures (33), an ancient farmer would have had to wait patiently for about 20 to 50 years after building an elaborate structure in the wadi before sufficient soil had accumulated to justify the planting of a crop (34).

4) We have proposed (31) that mounds and strips were established in order to increase the amount of surface runoff and gain more water for the fields below (35). Hillel (21) has shown that the infiltration capacity of the prevailing soil of the region decreases markedly with the formation of a characteristic surface crust through the physical slaking of the upper layer during the wetting-drying cycle. This

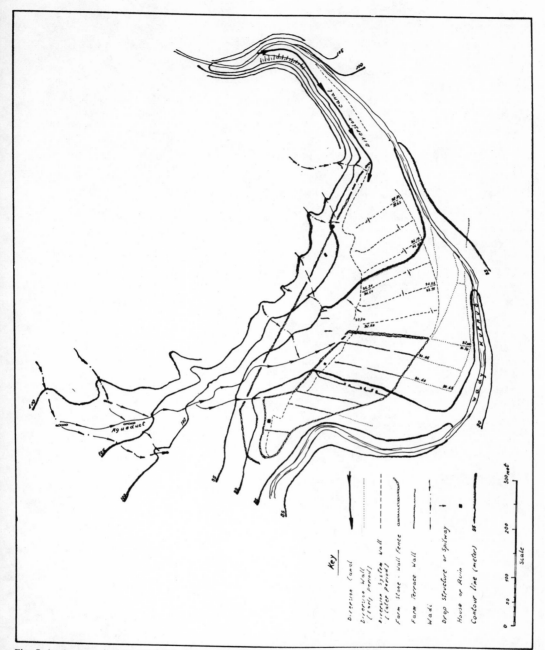

Fig. 7 (top). A map of the Mamshit system, which exploited runoff from a large watershed, showing the various periods of development.

311

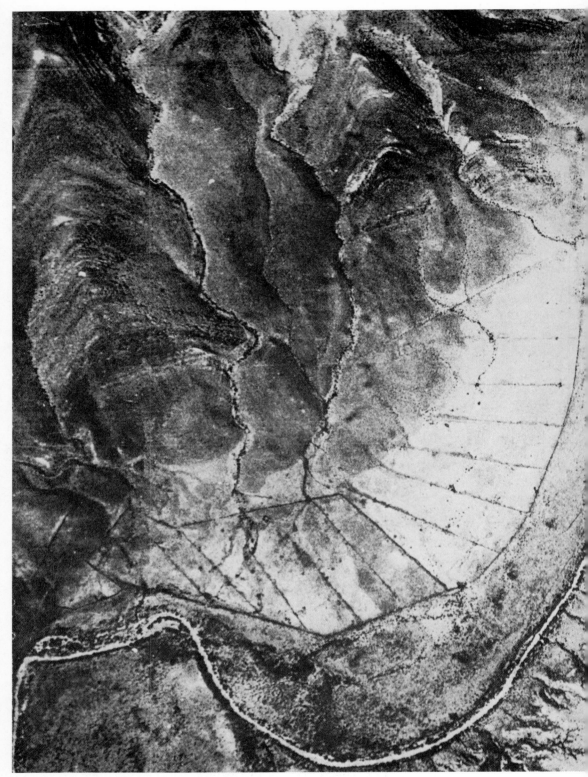

Fig. 8 (right). A vertical aerial photograph of the same system.

increases the runoff. Crust formation is prevented by the presence of a protective surface of gravel. Therefore, by clearing the slopes, the soil surface was exposed, crust formation was enhanced, and runoff was increased. This resulted in greater water yields from the slopes.

Thus, mounds were only a by-product of clearing the surface of stones. Strips sometimes fulfilled an additional function in channeling the water from the slopes to the fields. This is especially obvious in connection with the stone strips and conduits (see Fig. 2).

The fact that the mound and strip areas are always connected to the fields by channels (Fig. 2) is in conformity with this theory. Apparently this ingenious system was not restricted to the ancient desert agriculture of the Negev (36).

Exploitation of Runoff from Large Watersheds

For purposes of our work the term *large watersheds* is taken to mean watersheds greater than about 100 hectares in size. The hydrology of these large watersheds differs from that of small catchment areas. In the small catchment, runoff may begin after a small amount of rain (3 to 6 millimeters) has fallen, while on the other hand, a rainfall of at least 10 to 15 millimeters is required to cause a flow in the wadi of a large watershed (37, 38). Furthermore, the percentage of runoff from a small catchment basin may be as high as 20 to 40 percent of the annual rainfall, but in the larger watershed it would not be greater than 3 to 6 percent. The small watersheds produce relatively small streams that can be handled easily by simple structures, whereas the flash-flood flows of the large wadis can destroy even the strongest of engineering structures. These factors led to the development of systems of water exploitation which differed both in form and extent from those described above for small watersheds. The Mamshit System is one of the best preserved. The ancient town of Mamshit is situated on a range of Turonian Cenomanian hills overlooking the Tureiba plain. Just south of the town, Wadi Kurnub cuts a narrow gorge through the Hatira anticline and enters the Tureiba plain. At the point where the gorge enters the Tureiba plain, the drainage basin has an area of about 27 square kilometers, and it

was below this point that the flood waters from the large watershed were exploited.

Figure 7 is a map of this system and Fig. 8 is an aerial photograph of the area. A large diversion channel, about 400 meters in length, leads the diverted waters of Wadi Kurnub at a 2:1000 gradient to the flood plain. The original diversion dam has been completely destroyed but need only have been a simple rock structure to have raised the water level 30 to 50 centimeters in order to control the lower flood plain. This diversion channel leads the water to a series of broad terraces which are all in good condition. The terraces are more or less level in the transverse direction but have a slight gradient (2:1000 to 4:1000) in the direction of flow of the water. This arrangement made it possible to irrigate the area either in large basins or in small plots. The excess water from each terrace flowed to the next lower terrace through well-built drop structures.

The total area of the cultivated terraces is about 10 to 12 hectares. Agricultural experience has shown that about 3000 to 4000 cubic meters of water per hectare should be applied each year in order to insure an agricultural crop. This means that the watershed supplied about 40,000 to 50,000 cubic meters per year to the cultivated terraces. This represents less than 2 percent of the annual rainfall on the large watershed and could be expected every year as runoff. This quantity of water could have been carried by the diversion canal in 6 to 10 hours, according to the depth of flow (which probably did not exceed 40 to 60 centimeters).

A detailed examination of the area disclosed that the most ancient system was established when the wadi flowed in a shallow depression in the flood plain and before it had cut through the alluvial soils. The first walls were built primarily as stabilizing structures for the shallow depression, and only subsequently were they extended, in order to spread the water across the flood plain. Some of these walls can still be found on the opposite side of the wadi, showing that they predate the gulley stage of Wadi Kurnub. The most ancient potsherds found in the vicinity belong to the Middle Bronze and Iron ages, but there is still no certain evidence that this first system antedates the Nabataean period.

These stabilizing walls assisted in the

deposition of alluvial silt in the terraces, and so their level was gradually raised. At some period, either through natural flood conditions or because the inhabitants abandoned the area for historical reasons, the wadi destroyed the stabilizing walls, and an ever-deepening gulley was cut through the system. The next users of the area were therefore faced with an entirely different problem: the runoff water no longer flowed in a shallow depression but concentrated in a wadi, one or two meters below the flood plain. They therefore had to base their system on a diversion structure which raised the water out of the wadi bottom and directed it to a diversion canal, which in turn led the water to the old terraces. The remains of this system stand out clearly on the aerial photographs and are the easiest to find in the field. Close inspection also revealed a number of diversions in the lower reaches of the wadi. These indicate that the elevations of the terraces were continually rising because of a silting process and that new diversion structures at higher elevations had to be built in order to control these new elevations.

Chronologically, the next system that is clearly discernible in the field seems to have been constructed when the diversion channel had become so silted that the whole system based on a diversion channel may have had to be abandoned. This system is based on a completely different principle. The main area with the diversion channel was not used, and only the lower terraces (about 3 to 4 hectares) were irrigated. This area was developed as a runoff farm and received its water from the relatively small watershed (3500 dunams) adjoining the area, not from Wadi Kurnub.

The system in Nahal Lavan (Wadi Abiad) (see Fig. 9) is much more complicated but nevertheless shows similar lines of development. Nahal Lavan is the largest wadi in the vicinity of the ancient town of Shivtah and drains from the high plateau of the Matrada through a large area of barren rocky Eocene hills. The torrential floods which have poured off these hillsides have cut a deep wadi through the alluvial plain. In the upper reaches, the plain is narrow (100 to 200 meters wide), but in the lower reaches the flood plain is more than a kilometer in width. Today the wadi is a gravel-bed watercourse typical of the area. All along these alluvial flood plains are

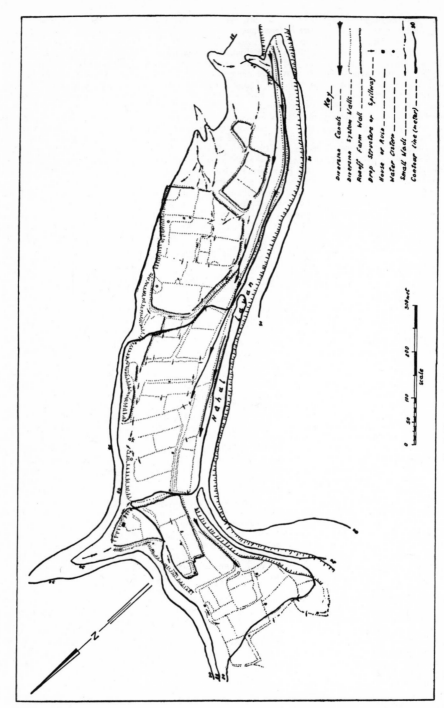

Fig. 9. Map of a section of the Nahal Lavan system.

Fig. 10 (above). A diversion canal wall of the Nahal Lavan system. Note the different stages of construction. The foundations are about 2 meters below the present soil surface. Fig. 11 (bottom of page). A large spillway with a crest length sufficient to allow passage of large floods.

remnants of ancient walls and terraces, some of the walls reaching a height of 4 to 5 meters. These high walls (Fig. 10) attracted our attention, and a specific area covering 200 hectares was studied in detail (*39*). The drainage area of Nahal Lavan at this point is about 53 square kilometers.

A close examination of the area disclosed again the superimposition of many systems. For a long time it was difficult to unravel the intricacies of each period or even to differentiate between the systems. Only toward the end of the survey did we realize that the capacity and size of the spillways, canals, and drop structures give the key to understanding the area. The spillways, which served as drop structures to carry the water from one terrace to the next lower one, can be classified into three distinct categories: (i) spillways with crest lengths of 30 to 60 meters, capable of handling flows in the range of 10 to 30 cubic meters per second (see Fig. 11); (ii) spillways with a crest length of 3 to 8

meters, capable of handling flows in the range of 1 to 5 cubic meters per second; and (iii) small spillways up to 1 meter wide for flows of less than 1 cubic meter per second.

Using this criterion as a starting point, we were able to differentiate between three different types and stages of development.

The earliest use of the area was found in the lower reaches of the area surveyed, where well-constructed stone spillways with a 30- to 60-meter opening are the common form of structure. However, these spillways were not connected to any stone walls, and it seemed as though these structures were all that remained of some ancient system—that is, that the stone walls had been dismantled and only the structures had been left standing. However, a special helicopter reconnaissance flight revealed that these wide stone spillways were connected to faint lines in the fields. Inspection of these lines disclosed them to be the remains of earth embankments which had

stretched across the flood plain. The complete extent of this flood-plain spreading system was not surveyed, but it was clear that it was in use long before Nahal Lavan became a deep gravel-bed watercourse. Some of the spillways are capable of handling a flood flow of up to 100,000 cubic meters an hour (see Fig. 11). The topographic situation of this system indicated that it was in use when Nahal Lavan was a shallow depression and that the earth embankments were built in order to spread the runoff waters across the wide flood plain. The wide stone spillways were used to control or direct the water as it passed from a higher to a lower elevation.

In the upper reaches of the surveyed area, a second system based on diversion canals and structures (capable of handling 1 to 5 cubic meters a second) was discovered. Some of these main diversion canals are more than a kilometer in length and 5 to 10 meters wide, and most possess a gradient of 4 to 5 percent. All lead to diversion

315

structures which served to divide the canal flow into as many as seven secondary canals leading to leveled terraces. Some of these terraces are in good condition, but most of them are badly eroded by gulleys which join Nahal Lavan 5 meters or more below the level of the terraced fields. Each diversion canal serves an area of about 2 to 4 hectares.

Detailed investigation of the walls of the diversion canals and the terraced walls associated with them showed that these systems were also built in stages. Figure 10 shows one of the diversion canal walls and the three distinct periods of construction. Excavation alongside the terraced walls showed similar periods of construction. These observations indicated that the diversion system silted up during its operation and that the settlers were continually faced with the problem of raising the elevations of the terraced walls as well as the diversion structures. Potsherds in the area dated from the Nabataean-early Roman period.

The next use of the area was again as runoff farms connected to adjoining small watersheds (Fig. 9). These farms adapted the existing structures and stone walls of the diversion systems to their needs and did not exploit the runoff from Nahal Lavan. Potsherds in the vicinity of these farm units generally dated to the Byzantine era.

We were originally under the impression that diversion systems of this type were widely used by the ancient civilizations. Although we have traveled widely in the area and have studied hundreds of aerial photographs, we have now come to the conclusion that this method was used only in very special restricted areas, and furthermore no diversion canal has been found that served more than 3 to 5 hectares.

All the systems studied showed a

Fig. 12. An oblique aerial photograph of a chain-well system near Ein Ghadian.

remarkable similarity in their development. This development is characterized by three stages each related to the erosion that was taking place in the flood plains and wadis associated with the large watersheds (40). This development can be divided into three stages, as follows:

Stage 1: Flood-plain development. The major wadis were originally wide shallow depressions meandering in alluvial plains. Cultivation of these depressions necessitated the construction of stone walls in order to stabilize the cultivated fields. These walls were subsequently extended so as to spread the water over larger sections of the flood plain (41).

The main spillways of this system were characterized by wide openings (30 to 60 meters) for handling the whole flood flowing in the depression. The embankments in some cases were built of earth.

This flood-plain development period

dates back at least to the Nabataean period and may be earlier.

Stage 2: Diversion systems. At some stage, these flood-plain spreading systems were abandoned and the system deteriorated through lack of maintenance. During or subsequent to this abandonment, the wadi cut a deep gulley through the flood plain. The next settlers in the area utilized the technique of raising the water from the wadi with the aid of a diversion structure and leading the water by means of a channel to the flood plain. These diversion channels generally served small areas, and in most cases the new settlers utilized the remnants of the previous flood-plain development walls and structures. During this period the wadi continued to erode, and at the same time silt from the large watershed (or from the eroding banks of the wadi itself) was deposited in the terraced fields. This silt raised the level of the fields until a stage was reached

that first necessitated raising the walls and later required the building of a new diversion structure higher up the wadi to raise the diversion canal.

The period of construction of these diversion systems must have been one in which the science of engineering was well developed, since all the structures required sound knowledge of hydrology and hydraulics. Furthermore, this period must have been one in which a central authority controlled the whole system and had the legal authority to distribute the flows during the short flood period that occurred in the ephemeral wadis. In both the Roman and Byzantine periods these conditions existed, and the Roman and Byzantine potsherds found in the area probably relate to this diversion-system period.

Stage 3: Runoff farms. The diversion system may have become unmanageable because of the silting problem, or serious flood conditions may have de-

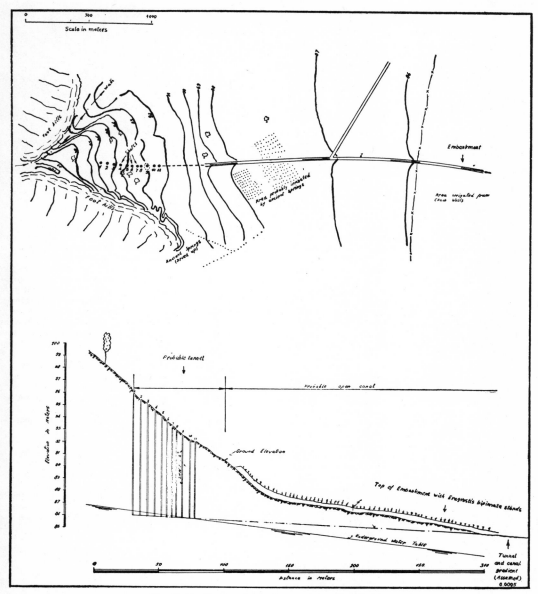

Fig. 13. Details of a chain-well system near Ein Ghadian.

317

stroyed the main diversion features, and the system was abandoned. The next system no longer relied on the main wadis but utilized the small watersheds adjoining the area in order to obtain the required runoff water. These runoff farms adapted existing walls and structures to their new requirements and generally utilized only part of the original diversion-system area (42).

Chain-Well Systems

In the Middle East and Central Asia, chain-well systems ("artificial springs") have been used since ancient Persian times and are still widely used today. Their construction and operation have been fully described in the literature (43).

While well digging was a common method of exploiting shallow groundwater resources in the ancient civilizations in Palestine, the more intricate chain-well systems have only been found in Jordan and the Arava Rift Valley (37, 44). As the mean annual rainfall in the valley is only about 40 millimeters and this amount of rainfall is without agricultural value, the chain-well systems must have been the main source of irrigation water.

Chain-well systems have been located at three oases in the Wadi Arava Rift Valley. The largest and most intricate is near the Ein Ghadian (Yotvata) oasis. Other systems were discovered near Ein Zureib and near Ein Dafieh (Ein Evrona) (45). Since these systems are hardly discernible on aerial photographs and are difficult to discover from the air or even in the field, it is likely that a thorough investigation of the Wadi Arava would disclose many other systems.

A chain-well system is composed of three essential parts: (i) one or more wells (sometimes called "motherwells") dug down to the water table; (ii) an almost horizontal underground tunnel leading the water, at small gradient, to the soil surface and ending in an open ditch; and (iii) vertical shafts connecting the tunnel to the ground surface. These shafts facilitate the construction of the tunnel and the disposal of excavated material in a molelike fashion and also provide access and ventilation to the tunnel for maintenance purposes. The surplus excavated material is deposited near the shafts, forming a circular mound around the shaft opening.

The oasis of Ein Ghadian, which

was examined in detail, is presented as a typical example of a chain-well system of the Arava Valley. The oasis itself is of the playa type, and the central part, where the water table is 1 to 1.5 meters deep, is saline and sterile. It was natural that this oasis, the largest on the western side of the Arava valley floor, was constantly settled. There are several remnants of ancient settlements extending from Middle Bronze to Roman-Byzantine times. Ein Ghadian was also the first station on the Roman road from Eilath to the north of Palestine (46).

Figure 12 shows a part of one chain-well system at Ein Ghadian as seen from the air; Fig. 13 shows details of one of the systems.

The chain-well systems vary in length; some are 3 to 4 kilometers long, others seem to be only a few hundred meters long. The vertical shafts are spaced at distances of about 15 to 25 meters, center to center. In most systems, only relatively few of the original circular mounds and shafts are still intact, owing to the obliterating action of winter flash floods. In those sections where the danger of destruction by floods was greatest, remnants of stone protection walls are found on the upstream side of the line of shafts.

All systems apparently begin in the gravelly wadi-fans on the western edge of the Arava depression and may possibly be connected to a definite fault line. The tunnel part of the system always seems to terminate in an elevated earth ridge on which there is a thick growth of *Eragrostis bipinnata* ("love grass"). These ridges are probably the old irrigation channels.

The systems and their channels lead to the northwestern edge of the Ein Ghadian playa, which is covered with stands of *Eragrostis bipinnata* rooted in the water table. Closer inspection reveals that the individual tussocks of *Eragrostis bipinnata* form regular checkerboard patterns. It is possible that these stands indicate the area of ancient irrigation. Each tussock would then represent an irrigated basin, or possibly the point where a palm tree was rooted. However, if the water level in ancient times was different, the irrigable area would, of course, have changed correspondingly.

Practical application. Many authors (47), investigating the area, have suggested that the ancient and forgotten civilizations of the Negev could teach a practical lesson for the future. We, too, felt that some of the principles

Fig. 14. An aerial photograph of the reconstructed Shivtah farm. Note one branch of one runoff conduit entering the farmhouse. bringing water to an underground cistern.

on which the ancient civilizations developed their desert agriculture could be applied today. The written records of ancient agriculture in the desert are limited principally to the Nessanah documents (48). But even the little information given in these publications encouraged us in this line of thinking.

However, the first question that we had to decide was whether there had been any climatic changes during this period of time. We are of the opinion that there has been no major climatic change in the area—that is, that the Negev has always been a desert with an average annual rainfall of about 100 millimeters. If there had been a more humid climate in ancient times, there would have been no need to develop this ingenious desert agriculture based on maximum water conservation; necessity was the mother of invention. However, we are also of the opinion that there were definite variations in the average annual rainfall. The 20-year moving average may have fluctuated between 70 and 150 millimeters, but these differences would probably have evened out on a 100- to 200-year moving average.

Fig. 15. The reconstructed ancient farm near Avdat. Note the farmhouse on the hill. The reconstructed conduits leading runoff from the small watersheds may be seen in the background.

We then decided to reconstruct two ancient runoff farms, one near Shivtah and one near Avdat. In doing so, our aims were (i) to collect exact data about rainfall and runoff and, if possible, develop an analytical relationship between them, and (ii) to find out what, if any, agricultural crops and fruit trees could be grown by utilizing *only* the runoff from small watersheds.

After a careful survey, both farms were reconstructed with all their terraces, walls, and channels.

The Shivtah farm. The runoff farm shown in Fig. 14 was chosen for reconstruction (*49*). The reconstruction was started in the summer of 1958. Where a channel of the wadi led water into the farm, a weir and an automatic flood-recording gauge were built. A meteorological station was erected near the farm, and nine automatic and simple rain gauges were distributed over the whole catchment area. In February 1959, after the first flood, 250 fruit trees and vines were planted (grape, almond, apricot, peach, plum, carob, olive, pomegranate, and fig). During the summer of 1959 the young trees received small amounts of additional irrigation in order to insure their establishment. From then on, they received only runoff water from the small watersheds. The results by August 1960 were very encouraging, since during this short period the young saplings grew from a height of 40 to 50 centimeters into trees 2 to 2.50 meters high, despite the fact that both years were severe drought years, the season 1959–60 be-

ing the driest one since meteorological measurements were established in Palestine-Israel. During the coming rainy season (1960–61) we will plant another 50 fruit trees.

The Avdat farm. This reconstructed farm lies at the foot of the hill on which the ancient city of Avdat is situated. Its reconstruction was started

in July 1959 after a careful topographic and soil survey.

The soil (as in the case of the Shivtah farm) is the typical aeolian-fluviatile loess of the Negev. It is uniform over the whole farm area with the exception of small strips in the upper part and along the sides of the farm. These parts will not be used for

Fig. 16. Harvesting barley on the Avdat farm in May 1960.

994

our agricultural experiments. The loess is uniformly 1.50 to 2.50 meters deep. A farmhouse (see Fig. 15) containing a laboratory, a kitchen, two sleeping rooms for the staff, and one sleeping room for visiting scientists was built on the hill overlooking the farm (50). Near the house there is a meteorological station more complete than that at the Shivtah farm. Two automatic and 17 simple rain gauges were distributed over the whole area. Eight weirs and automatic runoff recording gauges were set up as described for the Shivtah farm.

After the first rain of 16 to 22 millimeters, in November 1959, a heavy flood wetted the whole farm area down to a depth of 1 to 2.5 meters. Barley of the Beacher variety was sown. It sprouted quickly and was harvested in May 1960. On selected parts of the area, the yield was 125 kilograms per dunam (or 500 kilograms per acre) (Fig. 16). This is a quite astonishing yield for this most severe drought year, with only 40 millimeters of rain, when thousands of dunams of barley in the more northern area of Israel, with 80 millimeters and more of rain (but without additional runoff), failed utterly.

On the basis of the encouraging results of the first year, our agricultural committee has drawn up the following plan, which is now being carried out (51) for the coming rainy season.

1) Field crops: 80 plots (3 by 25 meters) will be established. The water-distribution-system to these plots is so arranged that the plots will get equal, known quantities of runoff water and there will be full control of this distribution of the flood runoff. The plan provides for different field crops to be sown according to the time of year when the first flood occurs and according to the depth of penetration.

2) Pastures: 10 plots will be established as nursery areas. An additional 5 to 7 dunams will be used as observation areas which will receive only partially controlled quantities of runoff water.

3) Orchards: On 10 to 12 dunams, 200 fruit trees and vines will be planted (pistachio, cherry, peach, apricot, and grape).

References and Notes

1. E. H. Palmer, *The Desert of Exodus* (Cambridge, England, 1871).
2. For phytogeographical, phytosociological, and ecological data about the Negev, see H. Boyko, *Palestine J. Botany Rehovot Ser.* **7**, 17 (1949); D. Zohary, *Palestine J. Botany, Jerusalem Ser.*, **6**, 27 (1953); M. Zohary, *ibid.* **4**, 24 (1947); —— and G. Orshan, *Végetatio*

5–6, 341 (1954); M. Zohary, *Geobotany* (Sifriath Hapoalim, 1955) (in Hebrew).
3. The question of the minimum "effective" rainfall is a most important one for all desert areas. N. H. Tadmor and D. Hillel [Israel **Agr.** Research Sta. Rehovot, paper No. 38 (1957)] suggest that rainfall in amounts of less than 10 to 15 mm is "ineffective"—that is, has no or little effect on vegetation and runoff. Y. Kedar [*Econ. Quart.* **5**, 444 (1958) (in Hebrew)] estimates that 50 percent of the average yearly rainfall in the Negev is effective. However, our own first measurements showed that rainfalls much smaller than 10 to 15 mm are effective and start runoff.
4. For the history of the Negev, see the many publications of N. Glueck and especially his book *Rivers in the Desert* (Farrar, Straus, and Cudahy, New York, 1959). As for prehistoric times, there is much evidence of prehistoric settlement in the Negev, perhaps even reaching back to the Palaeolithicum [see N. Glueck, *Bull. Am. Schools Oriental Research* **142**, 17 (1956)]. Concerning the Chalcolithicum, we may have to change our opinion, as N. Glueck [*Biblical Archaeology* **22**, 82 (1959)] reports that he found chalcolithic sites in the Central Negev.
5. An excellent historical sketch on the Nabataeans has lately been written by J. Starcky [*Biblical Archaeologist* **18**, 84 (1955)]; see also M. Evenari and D. Koller, *Sci. Am.* **194**, 39 (1956).
6. N. Glueck [*Biblical Archaeology* **22**, 82 (1959)] writes of this period: "The Byzantine period in the Negev came to an end . . . as a result of the Mohammedan conquest. Darkness and disintegration and reversion to desert have characterized its history since then."
7. M. Evenari, Y. Aharoni, L. Shanan, N. H. Tadmor, *Israel Exploration J.* **8**, 231 (1959); Y. Aharoni, M. Evenari, L. Shanan, N. H. Tadmor, *ibid.* **10**, 23, 97 (1960).
8. N. Glueck has stressed this point in his surveys of the Negev published in many issues of the *Bulletin of the American Schools of Oriental Research;* see also N. Glueck, *Rivers in the Desert.* See also F. M. Cross and J. T. Milik [*Bull. Am. Schools Oriental Research* **142**, 5 (1956)], who reported Iron Age II sites and desert agriculture from the wilderness of Judaea (Wadi Buqeah, near Qumran). According to their description, they found what we call "runoff farms."
9. The Middle Bronze I period presents two main problems. To what ethnic group did the people of this period belong? N. Glueck [*Biblical Archaeology* **18**, 2 (1955); *Bull. Am. Schools Oriental Research* **149**, 8 (1958)] calls this period in the Negev the "Abrahamitic age." But the scholars are not yet agreed on the date of Abraham's wandering through the Negev. Even if Glueck's date is right, the people of this period cannot be identified with Abraham's people. The second question arises in connection with the occupation of the people in the Middle Bronze I period. Were they cattlemen or agriculturists or both? Glueck [*Bull. Am. Schools Oriental Research* **138**, 7 (1955)] calls them "Tillers of the soil" and states in many of his publications that they practiced agriculture. However, no investigator has yet related ancient fields to any of these settlements.
10. R. Calder, *Man Against the Desert* (Allen and Unwin, London, 1951).
11. J. Baradez, *Fossatum Africae* (Arts et Métiers Graphiques, Paris, 1949).
12. Carton, *Rec. notes et mém. soc. archeol. Constantine* **43**, 193 (1909).
13. O. Brogan, *Illustrated London News* (22 Jan. 1955); M. Renaud, *Rev. agr. Afrique du Nord* **56**, 689 (1958).
14. Carton, in his excellent paper, was perhaps the first to recognize clearly the main principles of ancient desert agriculture—that is, the use of runoff from sterile hills and the storing of the runoff water in the soil. He writes: "Il s'agit ici d'ouvrages ayant pour but *non pas l'irrigation proprement dite, mais l'inondation ou la submersion*" (italics ours) The main aim of the system was "de faire pénétrer lentement et profondément l'eau dans le sol." He was the first, too, to point out "l'ingénuité et la prévoyance des Anciens qui, au lieu d'énormes barrages-réservoirs, coûteux et dangereux, destinés à l'irrigation, avaient préféré réserver l'eau dans ces immenses réservoirs-souterrains . . . ." We cite him verbatim because his paper is not easily available. Though this desert agricul-

ture flourished most in Roman times, Carton is of the opinion that it may be older than the times of Carthage and Rome and dates perhaps back to the old Berber population.
15. A. de Poidebard, "La trace de Rome dans le désert de Syrie," (Librairie orientale P. Geuthner, Paris, 1934); S. Mazloum in R. Mouterde and A. de Poidebard, *Le limes de Chalcis* (Librairie orientale P. Geuthner, Paris, 1945).
16. N. Glueck, *Ann. Am. Schools Oriental Research* **14** (1934); **17-19** (1939); **25-28** (1951).
17. F. Stark, *Geograph. J.* **93**, 1 (1939); H. St. J. B. Philby, *Sheba's Daughters* (Methuen. London, 1939); W. Phillips, *Quataban and Sheba* (Harcourt, Brace, New York, (1955); R. L. Bowen, Jr., in *Archaeological Discoveries in South Arabia* (Johns Hopkins Press, Baltimore, 1958). Special mention must be made of the enormous ancient irrigation dam of Marib—probably the biggest ever built in ancient times—constructed in the 8th century B.C., which broke down in the 6th century A.D. [E. Glaser, *Reise nach Marib* (Hölder, Vienna, 1913); A. Grohmann in *Encyclopedia of Islam* (Brill, Leiden, 1913)]. The oldest irrigation dam, which apparently broke immediately after it was finished, was found in Egypt, dating back to the IIIrd or IVth dynasty (about 3000 B.C.) [see B. Hellström, *Houille blanche* **1952**, No. 3, 424 (1952)].
18. E. F. Castetter and H. W. Bell, *Pima and Papago Agriculture* (Univ. of New Mexico Press, Albuquerque, 1942); *Yuman Indian Agriculture* (Univ. of New Mexico Press, Albuquerque, 1951).
19. G. de Reparaz, *El programa de estudios de la zona arida Peruana* (UNESCO, 1958).
20. See L. Shanan, N. Tadmore, M. Evenari, *Ktavim* **9**, 107 (1958); **10**, 23 (1960).
21. D. Hillel, *Bull. Israel Agr. Research Sta. Rehovot* **63**, 1 (1959) (in Hebrew with English summary).
22. These farm fences apparently served two purposes. They are a symbol of property [Y. Kedar, *Israel Exploration J.* **7**, 178 (1957)] and, at the same time, a control structure. Most of them run around the farm at the base of the slopes preventing undesired material from the slopes from being carried into the fields and permitting the runoff water to enter the fields only at the places desired [see also N. Glueck, *Bull. Am. Schools Oriental Research* **149**, 8 (1958); **155**, 2 (1959).
23. In an earlier paper [M. Evenari and G. Orshansky, *Lloydia* **11**, 1 (1948)], hammadas were described as follows: "Hammadas are slightly rolling gravelly desert plains whose surfaces are strewn with vari-sized stone fragments and pebbles. Such fragments are brown or black, encased in the so called 'Schutzrinde' of the German authors, regardless of whether the core itself is composed of chalk, granite, flint, or schist. The brown and black surface of the pebbles shines brightly as it is covered by the 'desert lacquer' . . . . This black lacquer gave rise to the Arab legend that these stones were scorched by heavenly fires."
24. Y. Kedar, *Bull. Israel Exploration Soc.* **20**, 31 (1956) (in Hebrew with English summary).
25. Kedar was the first to point out the difference between stone and gravel mounds, according to the lithological material available.
26. A. Musil, *Arabia Petraea* (Hölder, Vienna, 1907); T. Wiegand, *Sinai* (Gruyter, Berlin and Leipzig, 1920); C. A. Woolley and T. E. Lawrence, "The wilderness of Zim," *Palestine Exploration Fund Annual* (1914–15).
27. P. Mayerson, *Bull. Am. Schools Oriental Research* **153**, 19 (1959).
28. Most of the arguments against this theory are discussed in N. H. Tadmor, M. Evenari, L. Shanan, D. Hillel, *Ktavim* **8**, 127 (1957). N. Glueck [*Bull. Am. Schools Oriental Research* **149**, 8 (1958); **155**, 2 (1959)] and Y. Kedar [*Bull. Israel Exploration Soc.* **20**, (1956); *Geograph. Rev.* **123**, 179 (1957)] also refute Palmer's (and Mayerson's) theory. There are only two points of Mayerson's which merit attention additional to that given by Glueck (1959). First, Mayerson presents a photograph of some stone heaps which were not on a slope but in a wadi bottom and uses this single observation as an argument against Kedar, Glueck, and ourselves. He fell victim to an error, as the rubble piles depicted in his photograph from Wadi Isderiyeh are the leftovers of a relatively recent excavation made by the Mandatory Government of

Palestine for a telephone cable which was laid along Wadi Isderiyeh. Second, Mayerson agrees that the vineyards planted on the slopes could not have existed on the available rainwater, but he believes that they were hand-irrigated from water stored in cisterns. A very simple calculation, already partly made by Kedar, shows that this is an impossibility. Kedar calculates that there are about 80 mounds per hectare (this is an underestimate; Mayerson talks about 600 per hectare) and that about 2300 hectares are covered by these mounds in the vicinity of Avdat. We estimate that each vine planted on or near a mound would require at least 0.5 cubic meter of additional water per year. The ancient farmers would, therefore, have had to supply 92,000 cubic meters as additional irrigation. Kedar has calculated that all the cisterns in the vicinity do not contain more than 4000 cubic meters altogether. The discrepancy between the figures is even more enormous if we assume that the people used some of the water from the cisterns for domestic purposes, and for cattle, as the Bedouins do today.

29. H. Boyko, Proc. UNESCO Symposium on Plant Ecol. (1955), pp. 1–8.
30. A. Reifenberg, The Struggle between the Desert and the Sown (Mossad Bialik, Jerusalem, 1955).
31. N. H. Tadmor, M. Evenari, L. Shanan, D. Hillel, Ktavim 8, 127, 151 (1957).
32. Y. Kedar, Geograph. Rev. 123, 179 (1957).
33. ———, in Study in the Geography of Erets Israel (1959), vol. 1, pp. 122–124 (in Hebrew).
34. D. Sharon, in an excellent experimental study, [see Study in the Geography of Erets Israel (1959), vol. 1, pp. 86–94], came to the following conclusions concerning soil erosion from the slopes: (i) The mounds were made by clearing the slopes of their dense stone cover. (ii) The soil beneath the mounds is undisturbed, but the clearance of ground between the mounds disturbed the natural equilibrium, exposed the slope to erosion, and through differential action on the soil-stone mixture led to the reformation of the stone cover between the mounds and the restoration of equilibrium. This explains why today the slopes between the stones are again covered by a stone pavement. As the difference in height between the old and "new" level of stone pavement is 10 to 15 cm only, only this amount of soil can have been washed down the slopes during the centuries (actually less, as the 10 to 15 cm contained a considerable number of stones, now left on the slopes). (iii) There were originally two types of strips—strips built of stones and strips made of soil. The latter type is the more frequent. As the soil from the soil strips has been eroded, only the original stone cover lying originally beneath the soil strips remains today. In Sharon's opinion, the function of the strips was to direct the water down slope. Therefore they were made of soil, as in this way their impermeability was greatly

increased in comparsion with that of strips built of stone. All this tallies well with our own findings.
35. N. Glueck [Bull. Am. Schools Oriental Research 149, 8 (1958)] came to the same conclusions.
36. G. Caton Thompson and E. W. Gardner [Geograph. J. 93, 32 (1939)] report "evenly spaced stone-rubble heaps" tied up with ancient fields from Hadhramaut, and W. J. H. King [ibid. 39, 133 (1912)] reports similar findings from Lybia. Photographs in the book of Baradez (11) seem to show areas of mounds and strips on the slopes near ancient fields in Algeria. A most interesting observation was made by B. Hellström [Roy. Inst. Technol. Stockholm, Inst. Hydraulics, Bull. No. 46 (1955)]. In the desert between Cairo and Alexandria he found numerous sand walls called today kurum (compare our rujum el kurum), dating from Roman times. His explanation is as follows: "When it was raining, the water ran quickly downwards along the sides of the walls . . . . The walls were constructed for the sole purpose of irrigating surrounding cultivated areas by means of the discharging water . . . . The areas along the walls were used for vineyards."
37. M. G. Jonides, "Report on the water resources of Transjordan and their development," Publ. Govt. Transjordan (London, 1939).
38. A. Schori and D. Krimgold, Internal Rept. Dept. Agr. Israel (1959) (in Hebrew).
39. Kedar [Israel Exploration J. 7, 178 (1957)] studied part of this area. However, he did not differentiate between the various periods of development in the area, and hence he shows the system as having been built and operated all at one time.
40. Kedar (24, 32) indicates a different erosion cycle. We feel that he did not notice the superimposition of earlier structures on later ones.
41. Examples of this flood-plain development were mentioned in our work on the Matrada plain and Sahel-El Hawa (7) and are common in all those flood plains where the main wadi has not eroded down below the flood plain. In these areas the process of active head gulley growth can be seen even today. A deep gulley (2 to 4 m deep) is cutting into the flood plain, progressing at a rate of tens of meters per year and so changing the base level of the area.
42. The cultivation of shallow depressions (stage 1) probably also occurred in the small watersheds, and the simple terraces and cultivation of wadis found in these areas may relate to this stage. But we have not yet studied in detail either the hydrology or the historic development of this type of desert agriculture. Moreover, we have only begun an investigation of the role the numerous water cisterns played in collecting runoff from small watersheds for domestic purposes. It should also be pointed out that, although

the final use of the diversion areas was as runoff farms, the runoff farms occur mainly in areas which were never related to diversion projects.
43. See, for example, M. Cressey [Geograph. Rev. 48, 27 (1958)], A. Smith [Blind White Fish in Persia (Allen and Unwin, London, 1953)], and A. Reifenberg (30).
44. B. Aisenstein, J. Assoc. Engrs. and Architects in Palestine 8, 5 (1947).
45. M. Evenari, L. Shanan, N. Tadmor, Ktavim 9, 223 (1959).
46. Y. Aharoni, Eretz-Israel (1953), vol. 2, p. 112 (in Hebrew); F. Franck, Z. deut. Pal. Ver. 57, 191 (1934).
47. N. Glueck, in many of his papers cited in these notes; Y. Kedar, Econ. Quart. 5, 444 (1958) (in Hebrew); Carton (see 12), who writes: "Il peut être . . . intéressant de montrer que les études archéologiques méritent d'être favorisées en raison des enseignements utiles qu'elles peuvent donner" (italics ours); Woolley and Lawrence [Palestine Exploration Fund Annual (1914–15)], who write: "We believe that today . . . the Negev could be made as fertile as it ever was in Byzantine times."
48. C. J. Kraemer, Jr., Excavations at Nessanah (Princeton Univ. Press, Princeton, N.J., 1958), vol. 3.
49. Jossi Feldmann, then a member of kibbutz Revivim, carried out the reconstruction work at the Shivtah farm. The agricultural planning for both farms is done by an agricultural committee headed by Dr. J. Carmon. Its members are Dr. Samish (fruit trees) and Dr. R. Fraenkel (field crops), both from the National and University Institute of Agriculture; M. Hilb, Government Minister of Agriculture; J. Dekel, Jewish Agency; and M. Eshel, Government Department of Soil Conservation. Joel de Angeles, from Revivim, is responsible for carrying out the agricultural planning.
50. The farmhouse is called "The Lauterman Negev House" and is a gift of Rose Annie Lauterman, Montreal, Canada. We hope that scientists interested in animal or plant ecology of deserts will use this opportunity to study desert fauna and flora in situ. We ourselves, in addition to pursuing the hydrological and agricultural aims of the project, are carrying out an ecological-physiological investigation of the main desert plants, based on fixed observation plots around the two farms.
51. This investigation was supported by the Ford Foundation, the Rockefeller Foundation, and the Irsaeli Government. Our studies of ancient agriculture were supported by a grant from the Ford Foundation; the reconstruction and agricultural work was and is being financed by the Rockefeller Foundation and the office of the Israeli prime minister. Our thanks are due to the Israeli Air Force for the aerial photographs and to Mrs. L. Evenari for the ground photographs.

Reprinted from
The Geographical Journal, Vol CXXIII Part 2, June 1957

WATER AND SOIL FROM THE DESERT: SOME ANCIENT AGRICULTURAL ACHIEVEMENTS IN THE CENTRAL NEGEV

YEHUDA KEDAR

25

IN CONNECTION WITH G. W. Murray's article on water storage and exploitation in ancient Egypt,[1] it may prove useful to record what was achieved in this field in yet another arid region and in a different historical period.[2] The central Negev lies beyond the settled land of Israel, between the steppe to the north, and the desert region of the south (see map).

During the time that elapsed between the second century B.C. and the seventh century A.D., this region, which forms one morphotectonic and climatic unit with

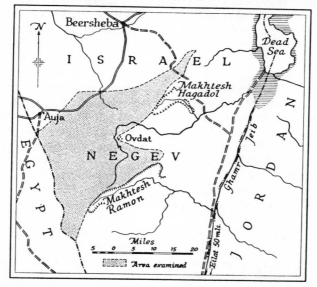

the Sinai Peninsula, was fairly densely inhabited[3–7, 10, 11] The settlements' prime function was, at first, to watch over the Nabatean kingdom's caravan routes and, later on, to protect the boundaries of the Roman and Byzantine Empires from the incursions of desert nomads. This *limes* protected the Negev, the southern part of Palestina *tertia*, from raids coming from the Sinai Peninsula.[8] The settlers were well versed in the wise use of water, and the remains of the agriculture which they engaged in, densely scattered over all parts of the central Negev, afford us an opportunity to judge the extent of their acquaintance with the physio-geographic conditions of the region.

The morphological elements which make up the region under discussion—the mountainous central part of the Negev—are parallel anticlinal ridges trending NE.–SW. Five of these ridges, spaced about 15 kilometres apart, are particularly prominent. As one proceeds southward, their crests grow higher, rising by 600 metres over a distance of 30 kilometres. These anticlines are breached: *makhteshim,* or erosive cirques, have developed in the structural domes of the ridges. Largest of the *makhteshim* is the Ramon, 35 kilometres long, 7·5 kilometres wide and 400 metres deep.[9] There is a definite correspondence between the geological structure and the geomorphological features of this mountain area, built of Cretaceous and Eocene formations, while the "windows" of the *makhteshim* reveal strata going back to Jurassic and Triassic time. The anticlinal ridges are drained by a trellis pattern of streams, with the major valleys occupying the synclines while their tributaries are sometimes resequent and sometimes consequent.

The climate is arid, the maximal isohyet being 100 millimetres at the lower altitudes. It should be noted, however, that climatic maps of the region are based not on actual on-the-spot measurement but on ecological conditions and on interpolation between data collected along its margins. The characteristic vegetation consists of *Artemisietum*, *Herbae albae* and *Zygophyllum dumosi*, with occasional trees occurring in depressions and wadis at altitudes above 600 metres. The region as a whole is an average 650 metres above sea level. The rainfall also spells out true desert conditions, being erratic, unreliable and unstable in its geographical as well as seasonal or annual distribution, but if it rains it rains hard. For the rest, it perfectly fits Murray's description. Since the loessy soil is covered with a hard crust and the relief is strong, within minutes of any shower the wadis are filled with large amounts of water.

Today the central Negev is beyond the borders of the *oecumene*. Although Jewish settlements have succeeded in overcoming a number of obstacles in other parts of Israel, only three have been established here, all of an experimental nature. The only other inhabitants are a few Bedouin families. Yet the entire region is very densely covered with remains that attest to the successful development of the agriculture that was carried on here in Nabatean and Roman times under official sponsorship and with official encouragement.[10] Although physical and climatic conditions then were much the same as today, this arid and mountainous region contains, in addition to a very large number of ruins, individual and in groups, the remains of at least six cities, each of which had a population ranging between 3000 and 6000.

The ancient farmers were able to develop this stretch of desert into a food-producing area through the wise and intensive use of a few simple methods which we shall now describe. The ancient city of Ovdat (Aboda) in the centre of an agricultural district of some 130 square kilometres in the central Negev, will serve as a sample area. It was founded by the Nabateans about the second century B.C., but the traces of the first settlement are largely obliterated by Roman and Byzantine remains.

The only source of water that is available here comes from the episodic showers that fall on a maximum of some fifteen days out of the year, producing run-off that lasts for a seasonal total of twenty hours at best. It is this flow that the canals of the area, as well as its dams, were designed to capture. In this they differ from the canals of non-arid areas, where the water source is either perennial or seasonal, such as a well, a spring, or a rising river. Unlike most agriculture in desert areas, these canals did not distribute water from springs or wells but put the rainfall and flood water of desert downpours to immediate agricultural use. We deal, therefore, here not with farming in an oasis, but farming in the desert.

In order to produce the moisture required for growing crops in this desert area, and to retain the moisture at a depth available to roots, run-off from an area twelve times the size of the cultivated plot is required. In its dimensions, of course, the irrigation network that channelled this flow cannot compete with those of the ancient civilizations of Mesopotamia and the Nile Valley. Considering the limited number of ruined sites in this area, this, however, was quite an ambitious scheme, the largest of the canals being 2 kilometres long, 6 metres wide and 2 metres deep.

Two kinds of canals were used here side by side, the first drawing its water from a barrage in the wadi bed—*i.e.* down in the valley. It is not long and it has a low gradient, but it is sturdily built, for it was generally called upon to deliver flood-water to fields of several hectares. The other type of canal has its starting point at the divide—*i.e.* high up on the valley slopes. Thence it goes down, generally across the slope, to collect the water that comes down the slope and to divert it to a given spot. Its gradient is steeper and in its upper part, where it has to carry less water, the canal is less sturdily built. Its advantage is that its length, its width and its path may be designed to fit any agricultural requirements. A canal of the first type, on the other hand, must be adapted to the local topography, which will govern both its size and its direction.

Within these two broad classifications, we may distinguish six ways in which the ancient farmers of the Negev were able to distribute the last drop of water in accordance with their needs. The canals supplying irrigation water from the bed of the wadi to land on its old fluvial terraces were generally the sturdiest. They were about a kilometre long and 15 square metres in cross-section, and carried water to lands up to 7 hectares in area. The lands, in turn, were divided into plots set stairway-fashion on the wadi banks. The water was fed to the highest plot and flooded it, after which the surplus passed on to the plot below, and so on down the wadi side until the surplus water from the lowest-lying plot had found its way down to the wadi bottom. Sometimes it was necessary to carry water not to the whole system of plots but to one of the plots only, either because it lay higher than the rest and could not be supplied in the same way as the others, or because there was not enough water to irrigate the whole system. The canals discharging this function have been found to be smaller and less sturdy. The same is true of canals serving a third function—supplying cisterns with water, generally collected from surface run-off up on the slopes and not diverted from the wadi itself.

A fourth task that canals had to do was to divert water from the catchment area of one wadi to that of another, where more land was cultivated than the basin's own run-off alone could irrigate. There are also canals built across the slope in order to divert the run-off further upstream than where it would normally drain. Finally, where a wadi had been dammed in so many places that water going through all the reservoirs in succession could not get all the way downstream in sufficient quantities, canals were dug for the very opposite purpose—short-circuiting the wadi's course and carrying the water directly from its higher to its lower reaches.

Most interesting are canals that were meant to supply not only run-off but also soil and silt. Built almost along the slope instead of across it, they collected the run-off which was rich in soil particles. This they deposited lower down to create cultivable fields in the valley behind small check-dams. This subject will be dealt with more fully in connection with the mounds in the area.

Damming was the second means by which the ancient Negev farmer was able to expand his cultivable land. He made extensive use of it in this region, investing far more effort in it than in canal building, both from the point of view of planning and with regard to the physical work involved. No less than 17,000 dams are found in our sample area of 130 square kilometres. In order to appreciate the reason for this great density of dams, it must be remembered that one of the limitations of

farming in this arid region is the lack of soil. The only natural conditions under
which cultivable land is found here are the old fluvial terraces of the larger streams
and the alluvial fans at the mouth of the smaller streams. Together, the cultivable
land in these two categories account for only about 0·4 per cent. of our sample area—
50 hectares (125 acres). So little land could never support the population of
6000 in and around the town of Ovdat, and the land problem must have been as
acute as the water problem. In order to solve it, our ancient farmers dammed the
course of every wadi in the area, except the largest ones, whose flow they were
unable to control.

The Negev dams fall into four functional categories. The first is a barrage,
diverting the run-off that it impounds into those canals that supplied water to
systems of fields on the stream banks (see above). Such dams are found inside the
beds of the larger wadis, and they are of respectable dimensions. In the Wadi
Ovdat, for instance, there are remains of one dam erected out of big stones and
built in the shape of an arc, convex upstream: it is 4·2 metres thick. There are not
very many dams in this category, and they have all deteriorated to the point where
it is difficult indeed to reconstruct them.

Very different was the function of the thousands of smaller dams that were built
inside the small and medium-sized wadis. Here the average structure is 40–50
metres long, 1·8–2 metres high and 2–2·5 metres thick. This structure has two
faces, in which the stones are set in stepped courses, so that the dam is appreciably
less thick at the top than at the bottom. The space between the two faces is filled
in with rubble and earth. These dams are spaced about 40 metres apart, and
upstream of each there is an accumulation of silt that reaches back to the next dam,
so that a continuous strip of alluvium has been created inside the stream bottom.
(See plate facing p. 185.)

The main purposes of the damming, then, were apparently to force the eroded
material carried by the floodwaters in suspense to settle and, at the same time, to
check the flow of the water so that it could seep into this alluvium and be stored in
it. In other words, the ancient farmers of the Negev built these dams in order to
conserve the two fundamental elements of agriculture—soil and water. The 17,000
dams in our sample district brought about the deposition of alluvium on 700
hectares devoid of soil, increasing the amount of cultivable land from 50 hectares to
750—from 0·4 per cent. of the total area to 5·8 per cent. (in some places, the proportion of cultivable land to total basin area even grew from nil to 7 per cent. and 8 per
cent.). In other words, man had expanded the area that could support human life
in this arid region by 1400 per cent. and more.

Thus the ancient Negev farmer, far from surrendering to the physio-geographic
conditions around him or even from adjusting himself to them, managed to gain
control over them. Refashioning the hydrographic net at will, he took a hand himself in the pattern of exogenic forces by converting a denudative zone into an
accumulative one—and, as we shall see later, an area of natural equilibrium into an
area of increased denudation. In effect, this meant writing a new chapter in the
history of the wadis. Ever since Pluvial times, they had been in the erosive stage;
now they entered the stage of deposition. In some places, the wadi floor widened
as much as tenfold. Today, of course, with the region deserted for 1500 years and
the elements allowed to breach the dams, the streams are forsaking the constructive,
leisurely course which was forced on them and have cut themselves once more
deeper and narrower beds.

The achievements of the ancient Negev farmer were won through the intensive use of resources that were severely limited when one considers the magnitude of the natural forces with which he was confronted, and the fact that those forces were working, as it were, at cross-purposes with him. In the valley of a river that regularly floods its banks at the proper season and deposits fertile sediment on them, no special power of observation is required to take advantage of these periodic and predictable inundations in order to start storing soil and have it flooded with water. Here, on the other hand, nature is not an ally but an enemy. The water is scant, the floods can never be counted on, the run-off erodes what little soil there is and its flow grinds the wadi beds ever deeper. To curb the destructive forces of nature and harness them for constructive use, required understanding, skill and extensive powers of observation. The canals, the dams, and, as we shall see later, the mounds in the area all attest to the ancient settlers' ability to realize the size of a wadi's catchment, the potential volume of the stream flow and the area of the land that could be irrigated with it, as well as the amount of soil eroded by the flood-waters. They evidently also knew the best ways of increasing the rate of erosion on the slopes while bringing about depositions in the wadi bed, where the soil could be relied upon to receive the most water, when there was water anywhere about.

The dimensions of each dam, in fact, are strictly allied to topographic conditions in the wadi across which it has been built. The length is governed by the width of the potential stream, *i.e.* the distance between the foot of the slopes. Accordingly, some dams are as much as 200 metres long while others reach barely 5 metres. The width of the dam is proportional to the volume of the water it impounds, but 1 metre seems to be the minimum. The height of the dam, finally, is that of the highest point in the reservoir—*i.e.* the bottom of the next dam up-stream. In fact, the combined height of all the dams in one wadi barely exceeds the difference in altitude between the beginning of the wadi and the dam that lies furthest downstream.

The intervals at which the dams were put up inside the bed of any one wadi are further proof of sound calculation on the part of the builders. Had the dams been twice as high and twice as far apart, for instance, the deposition of alluvium through-out the length of the bed would have required at least four times as much eroded material, and this over a period at least four times as long. In addition, at least three times as much work and material would have had to be invested in the construction of the dams. We did not find it possible accurately to determine the time that elapsed between the damming of the stream bed and the beginnings of agricultural activity. At any rate, the amount of work which the damming entailed was so great that we surmise a man would not want to carry it out unless he expected to reap the results in his lifetime. To create one particular plot of 3 hectares, for instance, the builders had to erect a fence all around it and dam the stream bed in a dozen places. The combined length of these structures is 860 metres, and their combined volume, 3000 cubic metres of stone. The number of workdays all this called for is a matter of conjecture, and we do not have enough data on the social structure of these ancient settlers to come to far-reaching conclusions, but two facts can be established. One is that the creation of cultivable land never stopped until water and soil had been provided for all the potential cultivable space; in other words, in our sample district, the 5·4 per cent. of the area that was actually reclaimed represented the sum total of all space for which soil and water could possibly be secured. The other fact, to which we shall return later, is that canal building and damming could not have been the only process creating agricultural land, as they cannot possibly account in themselves for all the soil that was in fact deposited on the reclaimed land.

327

Complementary to the dams which brought about the accumulation of silt in stream beds were those that were designed to hold up in stepped artificial banks the soil of fluvial terraces. While the former were built on gravelly subsoil in order to create cultivable land, the latter were erected on alluvial subsoil in order to conserve cultivable land that was already there. It is likely that they were the first ones to be put up, since the farmer could immediately proceed to cultivate the land which they protected, while building dams inside the wadi bed meant years of waiting until sufficient silt had accumulated behind them to make cultivation possible. The dams on the banks were not of great moment to this agriculture: the land which they protected made up only 7 per cent. of the total cultivated acreage in our sample area. For the farmer, however, the soil which they held up presented several advantages over the silt in the wadi beds. Being thicker, it stored more water, and was also better suited to the growing of deep-rooted crops; and since it was generally found on the fluvial terraces of the bigger streams, it was assured of a more reliable supply of run-off than land inside the smaller wadis. Rainfall, we must remember, is so erratic in this desert area that the chances of flow in a wadi are directly proportional to the size of its catchment area. Although soil conservation was the prime function of this category of dams, their use incidentally resulted in two equally important by-processes: flooding, the only irrigation method that is practicable here, and the deposition of alluvium, whose fertilizing function also deserves special mention. The last of our four categories of dams are small and have an ancillary function only—to break the erosive force of water streaming down the gullies and threatening to destroy canals, fences, etc.; and to force the sediment to be deposited inside the gullies, behind the dams, in order to save the canals from silting up.

One last remark: every dam has a spillway. None of the dams in the central Negev were designed to impound the run-off entirely, but rather to delay its flow in order to encourage deposition and seepage, and to transfer water from one place to another. There are only isolated instances of storage dams.

While everyone recognizes the various purposes for which the canals and dams in the central Negev were built, opinions are divided on the function of the third class of remains there—rows upon rows of stone mounds on the hill slopes. Investigators are agreed only on the correlation of these mounds with the cultivated valleys, which are never very far below, and on their apparent consequent connection with agriculture. The mounds are small and round, consisting of stones heaped or laid to a height of 70 centimetres and a diameter of 1·5-1·7 metres. The stones are of the same kind as the ones that happen to litter the ground in the immediate vicinity—limestone, flint, or any other rock. There are hundreds of thousands of these mounds in the central Negev. In the Ovdat district they occupy 2500 hectares out of a total area of 130 square kilimetres. This is three times as much space as the 750 hectares that were devoted to cultivated land. They are invariably found on slopes above the cultivated valleys, but never inside the valleys, and they never occur singly but always in groups, their number rarely departing from an average of eighty to the hectare. They are laid out in perfectly straight rows, with shallow canals or raised furrows running down between every row and the next. On an aerial photograph, the pattern resembles a mosaic or a geometrical design. The direction of the rows is almost identical with that of the slope. The canals, which lead down into the cultivated valleys, are the ones that were mentioned at the end of our section on canals as carrying eroded soil as well as run-off.

As has been said above, investigators disagree about the agricultural function of the fields of mounds. Some believe that they were all vineyards, finding support for their view in the Arabic name for these fields, which is *tuleilat el 'anab* or *rujum el kurum* (vine mounds). Others, who share this view, explain that the mounds were meant to exert a microclimatic influence. Others yet believe that the mounds are simply heaps of stones removed from the area in order to prepare it for cultivation.[11] All these views overlook the fact that the average annual rainfall in the entire region where the mounds are found is below 100 millimetres. This is far from sufficient to grow grapes, or any other fruit, without irrigation. Any possibility of irrigating the fields of mounds, on the other hand, must be dismissed in the light of what we know about the water resources of the region then as today. The mystery of the mounds will be solved, however, if we consider it in conjunction with another puzzle—the origin of the prodigious amount of eroded soil that was washed down into the wadis and created cultivable plots behind the dams when man began to modify conditions of natural drainage. The bed of one wadi section, for instance, with a catchment area of 54 hectares, has been found to contain 20,000 cubic metres of alluvium; into another, draining 73 hectares, have been silted 24,500 cubic metres; another yet, with a catchment area of 30 hectares, has accumulated 2600 cubic metres.

It has been calculated that at the yearly erosion rate of approximately 0·8 millimetres which can be taken as average in these regions,[12] the men who dammed the wadi beds would have had to wait for four centuries before the soil on their newly-created fields was deep enough to grow anything on—if they had depended on nature alone. To build a sufficient soil column inside the wadi within ten years of the damming would require a yearly erosion rate of 32·8 millimetres, which would be fantastic indeed under natural circumstances.

This is where the mounds come in. They were created when man decided to speed up the processes of natural erosion. In order that the slopes should supply him with run-off water and soil, he opened the desert pavement and broke the crust that covers the softened soil underneath. He thus created new conditions for the erosive forces which from now on could wash down the soft soil onto the wadi grounds. This process was originated only by active intervention of man.

To lay bare the soil and then allow it to be washed off unhampered into the canals which directed it onto the cultivated plots below, our ancient farmers had to rake together or pick up the stones that formed the *hamada* cover, and the logical thing to do was to heap them into mounds. The mounds, then, had an origin but not a function. They served no purpose in themselves in ancient agriculture, they were simply dumps of material to be cleared from the ground. They were the by-product of man's endeavour to create cultivable land where the probability of run-off would be highest when it rained somewhere in the area—to bring together soil and water, the two fundamental elements of agriculture, at the most favourable spot. This interpretation is borne out by the invariable correlation of fields of mounds above and cultivable plots below.

This study would not be complete without a short summary of what can be learned about the climate of the times from a survey of the remains of agriculture in this area. One way of finding out is to work out the ratio between the size of the cultivated fields and the area of the catchment that fed them with water; another, to determine the relation between the capacity of the cisterns and the area of the catchment whose run-off was channelled into them. Much can also be surmised from the general principles on which this ancient agriculture was based. All of these methods prove conclusively that the climate here was as arid then as it is today, and that from this point of view there is no difference between the central Negev and the Egyptian regions with which G. W. Murray deals in his article. The required ratio of 1 to 12 between the size of any area where deep-rooted perennials can be grown and the extent of the catchment that provides it with run-off, for instance, is based on rainfall and surface flow measurements recently recorded by settlements in this climatic zone. It also happens, however, to be the ratio between every field cultivated by the ancient settlers of the Negev and the size of the catchment that supplied it with water. Where this ratio did not prevail under natural conditions, canals were built to establish it.

The conclusion that both rainfall and the rate of surface flow were much the same then as today is supported by the ratio between the capacity of each cistern in the area and the size of the catchment that fed it with run-off. It averages 1 cubic metre of cistern capacity to 30 square metres of catchment, because the builders were on the conservative side in their calculations in order to make sure that the cisterns would fill up in dry years as well. Finally, if all agriculture here was based on run-off, it must have rained on only a few days out of the season and the showers must have been heavy, resulting in immediate floods. Not only the annual precipitation but also its distribution and character, then, must have been the same as today.

SUMMARY

The central Negev lies beyond the borders of the settled land of Israel. South of it is a desert region, which remained outside the domain of human habitation throughout all the periods of history; north of it are steppes and the Mediterranean lands which have always been inhabited. The central Negev, on the other hand, was settled at times and deserted at others, but at such times as it was inhabited, it was able to support its population, at least to a considerable extent.

It appears, then, that this region is not an absolute *anoecumene* but a "*pseudo-anoecumene*," which lacks neither of the elements essential for agriculture—soil and water. Almost nowhere, however, are soil and water available at the same place. Water, furthermore, is available for very short times only, at highly irregular intervals. When man knew how to bring water and soil together, the region became an *oecumene*. At other times it reverted to desert.

The physical features of the central Negev lead the geographer to expect a nomadic population, the absence of agriculture, and a low level of civilization—and this is just what he finds there today. What remains of the ancient settlers' fields and habitations, however, spells out the very opposite. With the dams and canals to which it owed its existence, there was created here agriculture of a very advanced type by growing crops on a series of absolutely level fields by inundation with flood water.

This, however, is another striking example to show that there is no fixed relationship between man and land and that, furthermore, there is no absolute land use classification, fixed by nature alone, applicable even to desert areas. Here, as in many other similar cases, it depends on man whether a certain stretch of arid land belongs in the category of the desert or the sown.

REFERENCES

[1] Murray, G. W., "Water from the desert: some ancient Egyptian achievements." *Geogr. J.*, 121 (1955), pp. 171–81.

[2] This article is based on research carried out in the arid parts of Israel by the Department of Geography of the Hebrew University, Jerusalem, and directed by the writer under the guidance of Dr. D. H. K. Amiran, head of the department.

3 Lewis, N., "New light on the Negev in ancient times," *Palestine Exploration Quarterly*, **80** (1948), pp. 102–30.

4 Kirk, G. E., "Archaeological exploration in the southern desert," *Palestine Exploration Quarterly*, **70** (1938), pp. 211–35.

5 Kirk, G. E., "The Negev, or the southern desert of Palestine," *Palestine Exploration Quarterly*, **73** (1941), pp. 57–71.

6 Colt, D., "Discoveries at Auja Hafir," *Palestine Exploration Quarterly*, **68** (1936), pp. 216–20.

7 Anati, E., "Ancient rock drawings in the central Negev," *Palestine Exploration Quarterly*, **87** (1955), p. 49.

8 Avi-Yonah, M., "Economic past of the Negev," *Palestine and Middle East Economic Magazine*, No. 9 (1937), pp. 436–40.

9 Amiran, D. H. K., "Geomorphology of the central Negev highlands," *Israel Exploration Journal*, **1** (1950–1), pp. 107–20.

10 Woolley, C. L., and T. E. Lawrence, 'The wilderness of Zin.' London, 1914.

11 Palmer, E. H., 'The desert of the Exodus.' New York, 1872.

12 'The sediment problem.' Flood Control Series No. 5, U.N., 1953, p. 12.

The ancient city of Ovdat (Aboda) from the air: scale approximately 1:10,000

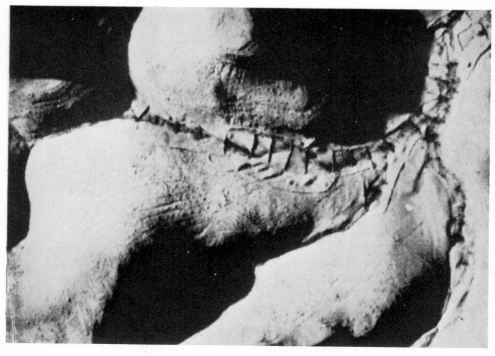

Smaller dams built in wadis: scale approximately 1:4000

Examples of wadi dams, described page 182

333

The next selections from books by Marsh and by Burrows show other aspects of water conservation in a marine setting and the production of new lands from the ocean by reclamation engineering. Of course treatment of any reclamation topic would be incomplete without inclusion of materials that describe the most monumental works that man has produced in changing the landscape, namely, the projects designed to create new land from the North Sea and build the polder country of the Netherlands. Veen (1962) traces the history from the first Dutch farms about 4,000 B.C. until by 1860, using only hand and animal labor, the following had been accomplished: (1) movement of 100 million yd^3 into small hills; (2) movement of 200 million yd^3 to build 1750 miles of working dikes and 50 million yd^3 for dikes later abandoned; (3) digging out 800 million yd^3 for draining of land; (4) digging out 200 million yd^3 for canals; and (5) removal of 10 million yd^3 of peat. Such figures are staggering when compared to the largest pyramid of 3.5 million yd^3 or the Suez Canal of 100 million yd^3 (which had powered machinery). The selection from 'Marsh is one of the early accounts in English of the Netherlands example.

In Great Britain the draining of swamps and reclamation of land in the coastal area also had an early beginning. The selection from the book by M. Burrows provides one of the earliest syntheses of man's alteration of eastern England for his benefit, as at Romney Marsh. A. J. Burrows (1885) also presents additional data for this area, and shows that 24,049 acres in Romney Marsh proper and 23,010 acres in adjacent areas were produced. Cadwell (1929) discusses land reclamation in the coastal area of Scotland and shows that by 1840 1581 acres had been created in the Forth Valley.

Man creates other structures at the seashore, but this topic will be more fully explored in Volume 3. One of the best accounts of preventative measures taken against coastal erosion prior to 1900 occurs in chapter 8 of the book by W. H. Wheeler (1902), where he provides details of works in France, Holland, and Belgium.

Montague Burrows (1819–1905) was born in England and became a Captain in the Royal Navy. He was a very colorful figure, fighting in actions against the Malay pirates and serving on vessels charged with suppressing the slave trade. Upon retirement from service in 1862 he became Professor of Modern History at Oxford University. He has written a number of books that include *Parliament and the Church of England* (1875), *Imperial England* (1880), and *Commentaries on the History of England* (1893).

Scribner, Armstrong & Co., New York, 1877, 674 pp.

26

The Earth as
Modified by Human Action:
A New Edition of
Man and Nature

G. P. MARSH

THE WATERS.

Land artificially won from the Waters.

MAN, as we have seen, has done much to revolutionize the solid surface of the globe, and to change the distribution and proportions, if not the essential character, of the organisms which inhabit the land and even the waters. Besides the influence thus exerted upon the life which peoples the sea, his action upon the land has involved a certain amount of indirect encroachment upon the territorial jurisdiction of the ocean. So far as he has increased the erosion of running waters by the destruction of the forest or by other operations which lessen the cohesion of the soil, he has promoted the deposit of solid matter in the sea, thus reducing the depth of marine estuaries, advancing the coast-line, and diminishing the area covered by the waters. He has gone beyond this, and invaded the realm of the ocean by constructing within its borders wharves, piers, light-houses, breakwaters, fortresses, and other facilities for his commercial and military operations; and in some countries he has permanently rescued from tidal overflow, and even from the very bed of the deep, tracts of ground extensive enough to constitute valuable additions to his agricultural domain. The quantity of soil gained from the sea by these different modes of acquisition is, indeed, too inconsiderable to form an appreciable element in the comparison of the general proportion between the two great forms of terrestrial surface, land and water; but the results of such operations, considered in their physical and their moral bearings, are sufficiently important to entitle them to special notice in every comprehensive view of the relations between man and nature.

There are cases, as on the western shores of the Baltic, where, in consequence of the secular elevation of the coast, the sea appears to be retiring; others, where, from the slow sinking of the land, it seems to be advancing. These movements depend upon geological causes wholly out of our reach, and man can neither advance nor retard them.*

---

* It is possible that the weight of the sediment let fall at the mouths of great rivers, like the Ganges, the Mississippi, and the Po, may cause the depression of the strata on which they are deposited, and hence if man promotes the erosion and transport of earthy material by rivers, he augments the weight of the sediment they convey into their estuaries, and consequently his action tends to accelerate such depression. There are, however, cases where, in spite of great deposits of sediment by rivers, the coast is rising. Further, the manifestation of the internal heat of the earth at any given point is conditioned by the thickness of the crust at such point. The deposits of rivers tend to augment that thickness at their estuaries. The sediment of slowly-flowing rivers emptying into shallow seas is spread over so great a surface that we can hardly imagine the foot or two of slime they let fall over a wide area in a century to form an element among even the infinitesimal quantities which compose the terms of the equations of nature. But some swift rivers, rolling mountains of fine earth, discharge themselves into deeply scooped gulfs or bays, and in such cases the deposit amounts, in the course of a few years, to a mass the transfer of which from the surface of a large basin,

There are also cases where similar apparent effects are produced by local oceanic currents, by river deposit or erosion,
by tidal action, or by the influence of the wind upon the waves
and the sands of the seabeach.   A regular current may drift
suspended earth and seaweed along a coast until they are caught
by an eddy and finally deposited out of the reach of further disturbance, or it may scoop out the bed of the sea and undermine
promontories and headlands ; a powerful river, as the wind
changes the direction of its flow at its outlet, may wash away
shores and sandbanks at one point to deposit their material at
another ; the tide or waves, stirred to unusual depths by the
wind, may gradually wear down the line of coast, or they may
form shoals and coast-dunes by depositing the sand they have
rolled up from the bottom of the ocean.   These latter modes of
action are slow in producing effects sufficiently important to be
noticed in general geography, or even to be visible in the repre-
sentations of coast-line laid down in ordinary maps ; but they
nevertheless form conspicuous features in local topography, and
they are attended with consequences of great moment to the
material and the moral interests of men.   The forces which
produce these limited results are all in a considerable degree

---

and its accumulation at a single point, may be supposed to produce other
effects than those measurable by the sounding-line. Now, almost all the operations of rural life, as I have abundantly shown, increase the liability of the
soil to erosion by water.   Hence, the clearing of the valley of the Ganges, for
example, by man, must have much augmented the quantity of earth transported by that river to the sea, and of course have strengthened the effects,
whatever they may be, of thickening the crust of the earth in the Bay of
Bengal.   In such cases, then, human action must rank among geological influences.

To the geological effects of the thickening of the earth's crust in the Bay of
Bengal, are to be added those of thinning it on the highlands where the Ganges
rises.   The same action may, as a learned friend suggests to me, even have a
cosmical influence.   The great rivers of the earth, taken as a whole, transport
sediment from the polar regions in an equatorial direction, and hence tend to
increase the equatorial diameter, and at the same time, by their inequality of
action, to a continual displacement of the centre of gravity, of the earth.
The motion of the globe, and of all bodies affected by its attraction, is modified
by every change of its form, and in this case we are not authorized to say that
such effects are in any way compensated.

subject to control, or rather to direction and resistance, by human power, and it is in guiding, combating, and compensating them that man has achieved some of his most remarkable and most honorable conquests over nature. The triumphs in question, or what we generally call harbor and coast improvements, whether we estimate their value by the money and labor expended upon them, or by their bearing upon the interests of commerce and the arts of civilization, must take a very high rank among the great works of man, and they are fast assuming a magnitude greatly exceeding their former relative importance. The extension of commerce and of the military marine, and especially the introduction of vessels of increased burden and deeper draught of water, have imposed upon engineers tasks of a character which a century ago would have been pronounced, and, in fact, would have been, impracticable ; but necessity has stimulated an ingenuity which has contrived means of executing them, and which gives promise of yet greater performance in time to come.

Indeed, although man, detached from the solid earth, is almost powerless to struggle against the sea, he is fast becoming invincible by it so long as his foot is planted on the shore, or even on the bottom of the rolling ocean ; and though on some battle-fields between the waters and the land he is obliged slowly to yield his ground, yet he retreats still facing the foe, and will finally be able to say to the sea, "Thus far shalt thou come and no farther, and here shall thy proud waves be stayed ! " *

Origin of Sea-dikes.

It has been conjectured, and not without probability, that the causeways built by the Romans across the marshes of the Low Countries, in their campaigns against the Germanic tribes, gave the natives the first hint of the utility which might be derived from similar constructions applied to a different purpose.* If

---

* It has often been alleged by eminent writers that a part of the fens in Lincolnshire was reclaimed by sea-dikes under the government of the Ro-

this is so, it is one of the most interesting among the many in
stances in which the arts and enginery of war have been so
modified as to be eminently promotive of the blessings of peace,
thereby in some measure compensating the wrongs and suffer-
ings they have inflicted on humanity.* The Lowlanders are

---

mans. I have found no ancient authority in support of this assertion, nor
can I refer to any passage in Roman literature in which sea-dikes are expressly mentioned otherwise than as walls or piers, except that in Pliny (*Hist. Nat.*,
xxxvi. 24), where it is said that the Tyrrhenian Sea was excluded from the
Lucrine Lake by dikes. Dugdale, whose enthusiasm for his subject led him to
believe that recovering from the sea land subject to be flooded by it, was of
divine appointment, because God said : " Let the waters under the heaven
be gathered together unto one place and let the dry land appear," unhesita-
tingly ascribes the reclamation of the Lincolnshire fens to the Romans, though
he is able to cite but one authority, a passage in Tacitus's Life of Agricola,
which certainly has no such meaning, in support of the assertion.—*History of
Embankment and Drainage,* 2d edition, 1772.

* It is worth mentioning, as an illustration of the applicability of military
instrumentalities to pacific art, that the sale of gunpowder in the United
States was smaller during the late rebellion than before, because the war
caused the suspension of many public and private improvements, in the exe-
cution of which great quantities of powder were used for blasting.

The same observation was made in France during the Crimean war, and it
is alleged that, in general, not ten per cent. of the powder manufactured on
either side of the Atlantic is employed for military purposes.

The blasting for the Mount Cenis tunnel consumed gunpowder enough to fill
more than 200,000,000 musket cartridges.

It is a fact not creditable to the moral sense of modern civilization, that
very many of the most important improvements in machinery and the working of metals have originated in the necessities of war, and that man's highest
ingenuity has been shown, and many of his most remarkable triumphs over
natural forces achieved, in the contrivance of engines for the destruction of his
fellow-man. The military material employed by the first Napoleon has become, in less than two generations, nearly as obsolete as the sling and stone of
the shepherd, and attack and defence now begin at distances to which, half a
century ago, military reconnoissances hardly extended. Upon a partial view
of the subject, the human race seems destined to become its own executioner—on the one hand, exhausting the capacity of the earth to furnish sustenance to her taskmaster ; on the other, compensating diminished production
by inventing more efficient methods of exterminating the consumer. At the
present moment, at an epoch of universal peace, the whole civilized world,
with the happy exception of our own country, is devoting its utmost ener-

believed to have secured some coast and bay islands by ring-dikes, and to have embanked some fresh-water channels, as early as the eighth or ninth century; but it does not appear that sea-dikes, important enough to be noticed in historical records, were constructed on the mainland before the thirteenth century. The practice of draining inland accumulations of water, whether fresh or salt, for the purpose of bringing under cultivation the ground they cover, is of later origin, and is said not to have been adopted until after the middle of the fifteenth century.*

Gain and Loss of Land in the Netherlands.

The total amount of surface gained to the agriculture of the Netherlands by diking out the sea and by draining shallow bays and lakes, is estimated by Staring at three hundred and fifty-five thousand *bunder* or hectares, equal to eight hundred and seventy-seven thousand two hundred and forty acres, which is one-tenth of the area of the kingdom.† In very many instances the dikes have been partially, in some particularly exposed localities totally, destroyed by the violence of the sea, and the drained lands again flooded. In some cases the soil thus pain-

gies, applying the highest exercise of inventive genius, to the production of new engines of war; and the late extraordinary rise in the price of iron and copper is in great part due to the consumption of those metals in the fabrication of arms and armed vessels. The simple substitution of sheet-copper for paper and other materials in the manufacture of cartridges has increased the market-price of copper by a large percentage on its former cost.

But war develops great civil virtues, and brings into action a degree and kind of physical energy which seldom fails to awaken a new intellectual life in a people that achieves great moral and political results through great heroism and endurance and perseverance. Domestic corruption has destroyed more nations than foreign invasion, and a people is rarely conquered till it has deserved subjugation.

* STARING, *Voormaals en Thans*, p. 150.

† Idem, p. 163. Much the largest proportion of the lands so reclaimed, though for the most part lying above low-water tidemark, are at a lower level than the Lincolnshire fens, and more subject to inundation from the irruptions of the sea.

fully won from the ocean has been entirely lost; in others it
has been recovered by repairing or rebuilding the dikes and
pumping out the water.   Besides this, the weight of the dikes
gradually sinks them into the soft soil beneath, and this loss of
elevation must be compensated by raising the surface, while the
increased burden thus added tends to sink them still lower.
"Tetens declares," says Kohl, "that in some places the dikes
have gradually sunk to the depth of sixty or even a hundred
feet." *   For these reasons, the processes of dike-building have
been almost everywhere again and again repeated, and thus
the total expenditure of money and of labor upon the works
in question is much greater than would appear from an estimate of the actual cost of diking-in a given extent of coast-
land and draining a given area of water-surface.†

Loss of Land by Incursions of Sea.

On the other hand, by erosion of the coast-line, the drifting
of sand-dunes into the interior, and the drowning of fens and
morasses by incursions of the sea—all caused, or at least
greatly aggravated, by human improvidence—the Netherlands

* *Die Inseln und Marschen der Herzogthümer Schleswig und Holstein*, iii., p.
151.

† The purely agricultural island of Pelworm, off the coast of Schleswig,
containing about 10,000 acres, annually expends for the maintenance of its
dikes not less than £6,000 sterling, or nearly $30,000.—J. G. KOHL, *Insc'n
und Marschen Schleswig's und Holstein's*, ii., p. 394.

The original cost of the dikes of Pelworm is not stated.

" The greatest part of the province of Zeeland is protected by dikes measuring 250 miles in length, the maintenance of which costs, in ordinary years
more than a million guilders [above $400,000]. . . .   The annual expendi
ture for dikes and hydraulic works in Holland is from five to seven million
guilders " [$2,000,000 to $2,800,000].—WILD, *Die Niederlande*, i., p. 62.

One is not sorry to learn that the Spanish tyranny in the Netherlands had
some compensations.   The great chain of ring-dikes which surrounds a large
part of Zeeland is due to the energy of Caspar de Robles, the S[...]ish governor
of that province, who in 1570 ordered the construction of these works at the
public expense, as a substitute for the private embankments which had previously partially served the same purpose.—WILD, *Die Niederlande*, i., p. 62.

have lost a far larger area of land since the commencement of the Christian era than they have gained by diking and draining. Staring despairs of the possibility of calculating the loss from the first-mentioned two causes of destruction, but he estimates that not less than six hundred and forty thousand bunder, or one million five hundred and eighty-one thousand acres, of fen and marsh have been washed away, or rather deprived of their vegetable surface and covered by water; and thirty-seven thousand bunder, or ninety-one thousand four hundred acres, of recovered land, have been lost by the destruction of the dikes which protected them.* The average value of land gained from the sea is estimated at about nineteen pounds sterling, or ninety dollars, per acre; while the lost fen and morass was not worth more than one twenty-fifth part of the same price. The ground buried by the drifting of the dunes appears to have been almost entirely of this latter character, and, upon the whole, there is no doubt that the soil added by human industry to the territory of the Netherlands, within the historical period, greatly exceeds in pecuniary value that which has fallen a prey to the waves and the sands during the same era.

Upon most low and shelving coasts, like those of the Netherlands, the maritime currents are constantly changing, in consequence of the variability of the winds, and the shifting of the sand-banks, which the currents themselves now form and now displace. While, therefore, at one point the sea is advancing landward, and requiring great effort to prevent the undermining and washing away of the dikes, it is shoaling at another by its own deposits, and exposing, at low water, a gradually widening belt of sands and ooze. The coast-lands selected for diking-in are always at points where the sea is depositing productive soil. The Eider, the Elbe, the Weser, the Ems, the Rhine, the Maas, and the Schelde bring down large quantities of fine earth. The prevalence of west winds prevents the waters from carrying this material far out from the coast, and it is at last deposited northward or southward from the mouth

---

* STARING, *Voormaals en Thans*, p. 163.

of the rivers which contribute it, according to the varying drift
of the currents.

Marine Deposits.

The process of natural deposit which prepares the coast for
diking-in is thus described by Staring: " All sea-deposited soil
is composed of the same constituents.   First comes a stratum
of sand, with marine shells, or the shells of mollusks living in
brackish water.   If there be tides, and, of course, flowing and
ebbing currents, mud is let fall upon the sand only after the
latter has been raised above low-water mark ; for then only, at
the change from flood to ebb, is the water still enough to form
a deposit of so light a material.   Where mud is found at great
depths, as, for example, in a large proportion of the Ij, it is a
proof that at this point there was never any considerable tidal
flow or other current.   .   .   .   The powerful tidal currents,
flowing and ebbing twice a day, drift sand with them.   They
scoop out the bottom at one point, raise it at another, and the
sand-banks in the current are continually shifting.   As soon as
a bank raises itself above low-water mark, flags and reeds establish themselves upon it.   The mechanical resistance of these
plants checks the retreat of the high water and favors the
deposit of the earth suspended in it, and the formation of land
goes on with surprising rapidity.   When it has risen to high-
water level, it is soon covered with grasses, and becomes what
is called *schor* in Zeeland, *kwelder* in Friesland.   Such grounds
are the foundation or starting-point of the process of diking.
When they are once elevated to the flood-tide level, no more
mud is deposited upon them except by extraordinary high tides.
Their further rise is, accordingly, very slow, and it is seldom
advantageous to delay longer the operation of diking." *

---

* *Voormaals en Thans*, pp. 150, 151.   According to Reventlov, *confervæ*
first appear at the bottom in shoal water, then, after the deposit has risen
above the surface, *Salicornia herbacea*.   The *Salicornia* is followed by various
sand-plants, and so the ground rises, by *Poa distans* and *Poa maritime*, and
finally common grasses establish themselves. — *Om Markdannelsen paa Vestkys-
ten af Slesvig*, pp. 7, 8.

Sea-dikes of the Netherlands.

The formation of new banks by the sea is constantly going on at points favorable for the deposit of sand and earth, and hence opportunity is continually afforded for enclosure of new land outside of that already diked in, the coast is fast advancing seaward, and every new embankment increases the security of former enclosures. The province of Zeeland consists of islands washed by the sea on their western coasts, and separated by the many channels through which the Schelde and some other rivers find their way to the ocean. In the twelfth century these islands were much smaller and more numerous than at present. They have been gradually enlarged, and, in several instances, at last connected by the extension of their system of dikes. Walcheren is formed of ten islets united into one about the end of the fourteenth century. At the middle of the fifteenth century, Goeree and Overflakkee consisted of separate islands, containing altogether about ten thousand acres; by means of above sixty successive advances of the dikes, they have been brought to compose a single island, whose area is not less than sixty thousand acres.*

In the Netherlands—which the first Napoleon characterized as a deposit of the Rhine, and as, therefore, by natural law, rightfully the property of him who controlled the sources of that great river—and on the adjacent Frisic, Low German, and Danish shores and islands, sea and river dikes have been constructed on a grander and more imposing scale than in any other country. The whole economy of the art has been there most thoroughly studied, and the literature of the subject is very extensive. For my present aim, which is concerned with results rather than with processes, it is not worth while to refer to

---

* STARING, *Voormaals en Thans*, p. 152. Kohl states that the peninsula of Diksand on the coast of Holstein consisted, at the close of the last century, of several islands measuring together less than five thousand acres. In 1837 they had been connected with the mainland, and had nearly doubled in area. —*Inseln u. Marschen Schlesw. Holst.*, iii., p. 262.

professional treatises, and I shall content myself with presenting such information as can be gathered from works of a more popular character.

The superior strata of the lowlands upon and near the coast are, as we have seen, principally composed of soil brought down by the great rivers I have mentioned, and either directly deposited by them upon the sands of the bottom, or carried out to sea by their currents, and then, after a shorter or longer exposure to the chemical and mechanical action of salt-water and marine currents, restored again to the land by tidal overflow and subsidence from the waters in which it was suspended. At a very remote period the coast-flats were, at many points, raised so high by successive alluvious or tidal deposits as to be above ordinary high-water level, but they were still liable to occasional inundation from river-floods, and from the seawater also, when heavy or long-continued west winds drove it landwards. The extraordinary fertility of this soil and its security as a retreat from hostile violence attracted to it a considerable population, while its want of protection against inundation exposed it to the devastations of which the chroniclers of the Middle Ages have left such highly colored pictures. The first permanent dwellings on the coast-flats were erected upon artificial mounds, and many similar precarious habitations still exist on the unwalled islands and shores beyond the chain of dikes. River embankments, which, as is familiarly known, have from the earliest antiquity been employed in many countries where sea-dikes are unknown, were probably the first works of this character constructed in the Low Countries, and when two neighboring streams of fresh water had been embanked, the next step in the process would naturally be to connect the river-walls together by a transverse dike or raised causeway, which would serve as a means of communication between different hamlets and at the same time secure the intermediate ground both against the backwater of river-floods and against overflow by the sea. The oldest true sea-dikes described in historical records, however are those enclosing islands in the estuaries of the great rivers, and it is not impossible that the double character they possess as a security against maritime floods and as a military rampart, led to their adoption upon those islands before similar constructions had been attempted upon the mainland.

At some points of the coast, various contrivances, such as piers, piles, and, in fact, obstructions of all sorts to the ebb of the current, are employed to facilitate the deposit of slime, before a regular enclosure is commenced. Usually, however, the first step is to build low and cheap embankments, extending from an older dike, or from high ground, around the parcel of flat intended to be secured. These are called summer dikes. They are erected when a sufficient extent of ground to repay the cost has been elevated enough to be covered with coarse vegetation fit for pasturage. They serve both to secure the ground from overflow by the ordinary flood-tides of mild weather, and to retain the slime deposited by very high water, which would otherwise be partly carried off by the retreating ebb. The elevation of the soil goes on slowly after this; but when it has at last been sufficiently enriched, and raised high enough to justify the necessary outlay, permanent dikes are constructed by which the water is excluded at all seasons. These embankments are constructed of sand from the coast-dunes or from sand-banks, and of earth from the mainland or from flats outside the dikes, bound and strengthened by fascines, and provided with sluices, which are generally founded on piles and of very expensive construction, for drainage at low water. The outward slope of the sea-dikes is gentle, experience having shown that this form is least exposed to injury both from the waves and from floating ice, and the most modern dikes are even more moderate in the inclination of the seaward scarp than the older ones.* The crown of the dike, however, for the last three or four feet of its height, is much steeper, being intended rather as a protection against the spray

---

* The inclination varies from one foot rise in four of base to one foot in fourteen.—KOHL, iii., p. 210.

than against the waves, and the inner slope is always comparatively abrupt.

The height and thickness of dikes varies according to the elevation of the ground they enclose, the rise of the tides, the direction of the prevailing winds, and other special causes of exposure, but it may be said that they are, in general, raised from fifteen to twenty feet above ordinary high-water mark. The water-slopes of river-dikes are protected by plantations of willows or strong semi-aquatic shrubs or grasses, but as these will not grow upon banks exposed to salt-water, sea-dikes must be faced with stone, fascines, or some other *revêtement*.[*] Upon the coast of Schleswig and Holstein, where the people have less capital at their command, they defend their embankments against ice and the waves by a coating of twisted straw or reeds, which must be renewed as often as once, sometimes twice a year. The inhabitants of these coasts call the chain of dikes "the golden border," a name it well deserves, whether we suppose it to refer to its enormous cost, or, as· is more probable, to its immense value as a protection to their fields and their firesides.

When outlying flats are enclosed by building new embank-

---

[*] The dikes are sometimes founded upon piles, and sometimes protected by one or more rows of piles driven deeply down into the bed of the sea in front of them. "Triple rows of piles of Scandinavian pine," says Wild, "have been driven down along the coast of Friesland, where there are no dunes, for a distance of one hundred and fifty miles. The piles are bound together by strong cross-timbers and iron clamps, and the interstices filled with stones. The ground adjacent to the piling is secured with fascines, and at exposed points heavy blocks of stone are heaped up as an additional protection. The earth-dike is built behind the mighty bulwark of this breakwater, and its foot also is fortified with stones." . . . "The great Helder dike is about five miles long and forty feet wide at the top, along which runs a good road. It slopes down two hundred feet into the sea, at an angle of forty degrees. The highest waves do not reach the summit, the lowest always cover its base. At certain distances, immense buttresses, of a height and width proportioned to those of the dike, and even more strongly built, run several hundred feet out into the rolling sea. This gigantic artificial coast is entirely composed of Norwegian granite."—WILD, *Die Niederlande*, i., pp. 61, 62.

ments, the old interior dikes are suffered to remain, both as an additional security against the waves, and because the removal of them would be expensive. They serve, also, as roads or causeways, a purpose for which the embankments nearest the sea are seldom employed, because the whole structure might be endangered from the breaking of the turf by wheels and the hoofs of horses. Where successive rows of dikes have been thus constructed, it is observed that the ground defended by the more ancient embankments is lower than that embraced within the newer enclosures, and this depression of level has been ascribed to a general subsidence of the coast from geological causes ;* but the better opinion seems to be that it is, in most cases, due merely to the consolidation and settling of the earth from being more effectually dried, from the weight of the dikes, from the tread of men and cattle, and from the movement of the heavy wagons which carry off the crops.†

---

* A similar subsidence of the surface is observed in the diked ground of the Lincolnshire fens, where there is no reason to suspect a general depression from geological causes.

† The shaking of the ground, even when loaded with large buildings, by the passage of heavy carriages or artillery, or by the march of a body of cavalry or even infantry, shows that such causes may produce important mechanical effects on the condition of the soil. The bogs in the Netherlands, as in most other countries, contain large numbers of fallen trees, buried to a certain depth by earth and vegetable mould. When the bogs are dry enough to serve as pastures, it is observed that trunks of these ancient trees rise of themselves to the surface. Staring ascribes this singular phenomenon to the agitation of the ground by the tread of cattle. "When roadbeds," observes he, "are constructed of gravel and pebbles of different sizes, and these latter are placed at the bottom without being broken and rolled hard together, they are soon brought to the top by the effect of travel on the road. Lying loosely, they undergo some motion from the passage of every wagon-wheel and the tread of every horse that passes over them. This motion is an oscillation or partial rolling, and as one side of a pebble is raised, a little fine sand or earth is forced under it, and the frequent repetition of this process by cattle or carriages moving in opposite directions brings it at last to the surface. We may suppose that a similar effect is produced on the stems of trees in the bogs by the tread of animals."—*De Bodem van Nederland*, i., pp. 75, 76.

It is observed in the Northern United States, that when soils containing

Notwithstanding this slow sinking, most of the land enclosed by dikes is still above low-water mark, and can, therefore, be wholly or partially freed from rain-water, and from that received by infiltration from higher ground, by sluices opened at the ebb of the tide. For this purpose the land is carefully ditched, and advantage is taken of every favorable occasion for discharging the water through the sluices. But the ground cannot be effectually drained by this means, unless it is elevated four or five feet, at least, above the level of the ebb-tide, because the ditches would not otherwise have a sufficient descent to carry the water off in the short interval between ebb and flow, and because the moisture of the saturated subsoil is always rising by capillary attraction. Whenever, therefore, the soil has sunk below the level I have mentioned, and in cases where its surface has never been raised above it, pumps, worked by wind or some other mechanical power, must be very frequently employed to keep the land dry enough for pasturage and cultivation.

---

pebbles are cleared and cultivated, and the stones removed from the surface, new pebbles, and even bowlders of many pounds weight, continue to show themselves above the ground, every spring, for a long series of years. In clayey soils the fence-posts are thrown up in a similar way, and it is not uncommon to see the lower rail of a fence thus gradually raised a foot or even two feet above the ground. This rising of stones and fences is popularly ascribed to the action of the severe frosts of that climate. The expansion of the ground, in freezing, it is said, raises its surface, and, with the surface, objects lying near or connected with it. When the soil thaws in the spring, it settles back again to its former level, while the pebbles and posts are prevented from sinking as low as before by loose earth which has fallen under them. The fact that the elevation spoken of is observed only in the spring, gives countenance to this theory, which is perhaps applicable also to the cases stated by Staring, and it is probable that the two causes above assigned concur in producing the effect.

In: *Cinque Ports, London, 1888, 261 pp.*

27

The Cinque Ports

M. BURROWS

CHAPTER II.

PHYSICAL CHANGES AT THE CINQUE PORTS.

The 'Law of Eastward Drift'—Changes on the Hastings coast—at Romney Marsh—on the Wantsum.

THE South-eastern shores of England have been more altered in form, more cut away in projecting parts, and more filled up in the recesses, than any others in the British Isles. This effect has been produced by the constant action of the winds and tides upon the materials within their reach, and with a remarkable uniformity on those portions of the coast which face the South-west. The projecting edges are smoothed away in lines from North-west to South-east as if cut straight by some mighty instrument; and the visitor, following the coast up Channel, will observe masses of shingle lining those shores with a regularity of which the least intelligent cannot but require an explanation. In the embayed portions of coast, and after he has passed the South Foreland, he will find sand instead of shingle. Though he may possess no special knowledge of the geological features of the country, he will see at once that these substances are heaped up by some potent agency of nature upon strata of a different kind from themselves.

351

Even as far west as the coast of Dorsetshire we have a conspicuous instance in Chesil Beach, one of the best known wonders of England; the projecting coast-lines of Sussex, ending with the ever-growing shingle-promontory of Dungeness over the border, possess much the same character as Chesil Beach; and all along the coast of Kent up to the South Foreland, vast accumulations of shingle were heaped up before Dungeness began to stop the process, and gradually became, by appropriating the drift, what it is now. Incessantly travelling from West to East, accelerated every mile by the narrowing space through which they have to make their way, and at length rushing along at full speed as from the neck of a bottle, these masses of shingle and sand, swept along by wind and tide, are the actual agents, conjointly with the deposits of rivers, of the changes which have filled up the Cinque Ports, and affected all the neighbouring coasts.

The wind and tide produce these effects in the Eastern portion of the British Channel in a manner so uniform, that their action may be described as the result of a natural law. Let it be called 'The Law of Eastward Drift.' It may be thus defined. Two forces, one obtained by means of the flood tide, and the other through the strength and prevalence of south-west winds for three-quarters of the year, united and working together at all favourable times, take up the moveable substances in the bed of the Channel, and scatter them upon projecting obstacles from West to East. Change produces change; and in the course of ages the whole coast is transformed. It is possible that this effect is produced by the mere force of the south-west gales, acting during the flood tide, but a further reason may be assigned for the regularity of this Eastward Drift.

The tidal wave from the Atlantic, on its way to traverse the North Sea and the Baltic, finds its progress arrested at each of the south-west points of England and Ireland. It divides into three branches, of which we may here neglect the middle one, since, passing up St. George's Channel, it rejoins and is absorbed in the main stream which has been sweeping round the west coast of Ireland. Part of this united wave, after it has travelled round the coast of Scotland and expanded over the North Sea on its way to the South and East, arrives in 20 hours at the Straits of Dover. There it meets the third stream, which has come directly up Channel, and arrived at the Straits in the course of 12 hours. As water must find its own level, these opposing streams, which have hitherto been running undisturbed, are forced, when they meet, to obtain that level with great rapidity. Hence the extraordinary variety of currents, eddies, and times of high water at different places in the same neighbourhood. Every one of these apparent irregularities is of course attributable to some special action of the general law that the same quantity of water has to pass and repass through the Straits twice in every 24 hours. One such anomaly is that, under certain conditions so frequently occurring that it is generally stated as an acknowledged fact, the flood tide makes from South-west to North-east in a shorter time than the ebb which makes in the opposite direction. To do its allotted work the flood must therefore move just so much faster than the ebb as the allotted time for doing it is shorter.

We can then understand how it is that, under ordinary circumstances, wind and tide work out the 'Law of Eastward Drift.' Twice in every 24 hours the south-west winds, if strong enough, find their opportunity. The swift flood has moved and slightly lifted the substances which pave the bed of the sea; the waves, when sufficiently powerful, take them up and carry them along. On the other hand the more languid ebb tide moves these substances less, and the waves which might drive them to the West are less often raised, and very seldom with anything like the same effect, since the south-west winds blow on, and the opposite winds off, the shore. Hence the formation of the shingle beaches and the shoals of sand, the latter of which substances is held longer in suspension and carried further than the former. The accumulation of shingle is directly due to the violent action above described; that of sand to its more indirect effects. Having been stirred up by storms, the sand settles down in places where eddies are produced by the meeting of tides and the slackening of their pace. This is especially marked at the Goodwin Sands, at Sandwich, and on the coasts of Belgium and Holland.

Whence came these vast stores of material? In this place it is enough to say that they are mainly traceable to two sources, the ancient quaternary formations called 'old sea-beaches,' of which our shores have been denuded in past times by the action of winds and waves upon the softer strata; and secondly, in more modern times, to the washing down of gravel from the Sussex valleys to the sea. From the constant attrition of this gravel great quantities of sand are added to that which covers the bed of the Channel in many places. It is obvious to remark in reference to these coast-changes that they can hardly but vitiate the calculations which have been held to decide the place of Cæsar's landing in the Cinque Port districts. Not only may the depth of the Channel have largely varied, but the space over which the tides travel must be at least two miles wider than it was some 2,000 years ago, and therefore the point of meeting of the North and South tide-streams cannot possibly be exactly the same; yet this is the assumption under which all these calculations have been made.

The operation of the 'Law of Eastward Drift' must be traced first at Hastings and its immediate neighbour-hood; secondly at Winchelsea, Rye, Romney, and Lydd, grouped as they are under the system of Romney Marsh,—with which may be taken Hythe, Folkestone, Dover, Walmer, and Deal; and lastly at Sandwich and the towns affected by the river-system of the estuary which once divided the Isle of Thanet from the rest of Kent. Not one of them has escaped. All have been separated from the element to which they owed their existence, and if not deserted by the routes of commerce quite so completely as the 'Dead Cities of the Zuyder Zee,' some of them have fared worse. Even Dover offers no real exception to the operation of the law, for it has only held its own by the aid of a vast expenditure of the national funds.

Hastings, situated just where the narrowing of the Channel produces a violent current, perceptible enough in the hurry-scurry of the tides along the 'Races' of

Alderney and Portland, was the first of the Ports to feel the effect of the Eastward Drift, cutting away the cliffs each year and filling up the havens. The processes can be traced with something like certainty. The ancient harbour once occupied the site of what is now called ' Priory Valley.' The rocks which line the coast well out to sea mark the old shore-line. The old town which once flourished at the harbour mouth was, like the first Winchelsea, submerged from the effect of storms and the want of sea embankments. Accumulating shingle, left uncontrolled, forced its way across the entrance, choking the flow of the Priory Brook; and then the silting-up process, always going on, became unchecked. The circuitous roads running round the old bed of the harbour indicate its gradual change from water to marsh, and from marsh to dry land; while outside of it, running along the coast-line, is found the shingle beach which wrought the change, and now forms the foundation of parades and terraces. The same fate in time overtook the haven formed by the Bourne between the East and West Hills, as well as the havens of Seaford, Pevensey, and the other Sussex ports which once owned Hastings as mistress. No dates, no records of these changes remain, but history comes to the aid of geography, and in the rise of Winchelsea and Rye, closely bound up with the decline of Hastings, we read that these effects had begun to show themselves in the very century of the Norman Conquest. Even modern records fail to tell us of the disappearance of an island, a mile and a half long, which extended along the coast of St. Leonard's, but which appears in Norden's map of the seventeenth century.

Turning to the more complex phenomena of the Romney Marsh system, it must be observed that there was at one time, we cannot doubt, an almost continuous and even line of beach from Fairlight Point, by way of Lydd, to the high land of Shorncliffe, inside which the sea penetrated, and through which rivers made their way, at points afterwards known as Romney and Hythe,—perhaps also at Rye. Within this line of beach was the great tidal estuary which the Romans found on their arrival and called the 'Limen.' This inland sea extended over the whole of what is now designated in a general way as Romney Marsh, but which is, properly speaking, an aggregate of marshes known by different names. Following the line of high land running round from Shorncliffe to the West, it penetrated into the Rother, Tillington, and Brede valleys. Above it rose on the West the Isle of Oxney, the island-rock on which Rye was afterwards built, and the promontory of Iham, crowned in later days by the second Winchelsea. To the eastward of those sites rose the Isle of Romney and the long low shore of Lydd. The estuary was a shallow basin, not unlike that of Arcachon, near Bordeaux, which had once been deep, but the bed of which had been gradually raised during the course of ages by layer upon layer of muddy deposit washed in by the tides from the soft tertiary strata of the neighbourhood. These layers have been found to extend to a depth of fifty or more feet, and thus account for the extraordinary fertility of the marsh lands. All this time the Eastward Drift had been forming, unimpeded by any such promontory as Dungeness is now, the extensive beaches of Dymchurch, Hythe, Dover,

Walmer, Deal and the rest, which had not however, by the time of the Romans, yet received anything like their full contribution of shingle. The passages into this shallow inland sea were kept clear by the vast mass of water rushing in and out at every tide, much as we may now see on a smaller scale at Portsmouth, and by the scouring outflow of many considerable streams, draining the eastern side of Andred Forest. At the Portus Lemanis formed by the chief of these streams, the Limene, the Romans established the military station Lemanæ, and defended it by the *castrum* the ruins of which are known by the name of Stutfall Castle.

It has been thought that, even before the Roman conquest of Britain, the inland sea had been so much filled up that the Britons had themselves made great progress in what was called by the English settlers 'inning' the marsh, or damming out the tides by embankments. At any rate a great change took place during the Roman occupation of the island. The shingle was driven in by south-east winds upon the north-east part of the marsh, closing up the passage between it and the Portus Lemanis, and it thus excluded the tides from the eastern end of the basin, as well as blocked out the river Limene. This river would seem to have been already diverted from its course to some extent by the erection of the famous Rhee Wall, which stretched from Appledore to Romney, comprising a channel and embankments from 80 to 100 feet wide, and it now altogether took its course through this channel. Though a surface of 22,000 acres was thus completely drained and protected from the tides, it was still a depressed basin, at a level several feet below the sea ; and such of course it has remained. Hence the incessant vigilance, hence the intricate organization of labour, which, under the 'lords of Romney Marsh,' have ever since been found necessary for its preservation. But the work was also the cause of the formation of a new port. The low island on which Romney afterwards stood now became united to the reclaimed land on its north-eastern side, while the flow of the new stream and the narrowing of the estuary deepened its haven, and made it the fine harbour which, if antiquaries are not mistaken, was named *Novus Portus* by the Romans. At any rate it is so marked—Καινὸς Λιμήν—in the earliest edition of Ptolemy's maps. No remains of the Romans have been found at Romney, but abundant evidence of their having settled in great numbers at Dymchurch, halfway between the Old and New Ports, has of late years been discovered in the form of very extensive potteries. This proves how secure a barrier the beach offered at that time against the sea, and suggests that extensive cultivation of the reclaimed marsh had already taken place before the fifth century.

The further 'inning' of marshes was due to Archbishop Thomas. 'St. Thomas' Innings,' adjoining the middle part of Rhee Wall, led the way, and was followed by those of Archbishops Baldwin, Boniface, and Peckham, and by some smaller works : but this process could not have been effective except under the operation of a law affecting inland tidal districts, which is practically almost as definite as that of the 'Eastward Drift,' and of much wider application. Just in proportion as tidal marshes are reclaimed and the area covered by the tide thus diminished, so more and more marsh offers itself for reclamation, and the port by which the tides enter becomes, for want of the former large volume of the scouring element, more and more choked up. The Roman works led to the ' innings ' of the archbishops, and those to the destruction of Romney Harbour. It may be noticed here that when Archbishop Thomas found himself obliged to fly the kingdom he naturally turned to the place with which he had been so much concerned, and embarked from Romney. Twice baffled, he gave up the attempt; and on his second flight crossed the sea from Sandwich.

The immediate result of this progressive inning was to drive the Rother to take a sweep round the new land and enter Romney Port by a circuitous channel as shown (approximately) in the accompanying map. Such was the condition under which the central Cinque Port was working at the time when its prosperity was most marked and as yet unshaken. No further progress was made in reclaiming marshes till the occurrence of that great convulsion of the elements which was remarked by all the chroniclers in 1287. This tremendous incursion of the sea submerged Winchelsea (Gwent-chesel-ey, the shingle isle on the level) and Bromehill, broke up the sandbanks on which they stood, and bringing the full force of the waves to bear upon the interior of the estuary, hurled great masses of débris upon the artificial course of the Rother, thus changing it to the more natural one which it still follows on its passage to the sea by Rye, and damming out the tides from a large portion of the already shrunken lagoon. With the loss of the river, Romney began to lose its fine

harbour; but it was the process of inning the marshes
west of Rhee Wall which gradually reduced the volume
of the tides so much that their scouring power was
no longer available to keep the mouth of the harbour
open.   Capital and labour not being any longer in the
peculiar power of the archbishops, Walland (Wall's end)
and Guildford Marshes were gradually taken in hand by
other landowners; but the process was not absolutely
complete till 1661.   Thus Romney Haven became dry
land.   Rye on the other hand gained a fuller supply of
river-flow by the change; Lydd, saved by Dungeness
as by a breakwater, was rather better off for a time
than it had previously been; and Winchelsea was re-
planted on a better site.   The history we are about
to trace was entirely governed by these physical
changes.

The subsequent history of Rye itself remarkably
illustrates that of Romney Marsh, for the inning of its
surrounding marshes in the eighteenth century has
equally destroyed the tidal backwater which used to
keep its channel open to the sea.   The same thing
had happened long before at the second Winchelsea,
where Edward I. placed the homeless fugitives from the
submerged town in 1287.   The neighbouring marshes
were drained and embanked by Commission after
Commission appointed by the Crown in order to put
an end to periodical inundations.   In that attempt
they were successful; but the town was soon left high
and dry, and so it remains.   In short, however praise-
worthy the effort to prepare tidal marsh-lands for cultivation, the process has hitherto invariably been con-

nected with the destruction of the port through which
the tide has had access, and the impoverishment of the
towns which depended on those harbours. To decide
which of the two evils is the least involves the national
question of the usefulness of particular ports, a question
just as pressing now as it ever was. In the case of the
Cinque Ports no such question was in those early times
understood to require solution. The marshes disappeared first ; people were astonished to find that the
harbours followed ; but, though bitterly distressed, they
were scarcely surprised to discover that the towns
shrivelled up, and they learnt in time to resign themselves to their fate.

The annual march out to sea of Dungeness, which
has been calculated at from 7 to 20 feet, assisted the process of harbour destruction on either side of it. This has
probably not been an equable growth, nor can we say when
it began ; but we can trace its effects. There is no doubt
that it helped to divert the tides from entering Romney
harbour by passing the current across the bay of Dymchurch ; and by checking the Eastward Drift it caused an
accumulation of shingle at Rye which counterbalanced
the advantage gained by the diversion of the Rother.
Further, the increasing projection of the point has interfered in the course of time, as already said, with
the travel of shingle along the coast to the North-east,
and so much denuded Dymchurch beach that in order
to protect Romney Marsh the old wall has had to be
rebuilt and greatly enlarged. It is now three miles
long, 300 feet broad at the base, 20 at the top, and 20
feet high. Something like a return to the condition of
things which obtained 2,000 years ago would be the

result of a serious breach in this wall. The evil genius of Dungeness has, however, a brighter aspect. The beach being composed of heaped-up shingle which is capable of forming itself into a steep wall against the force of the sea, deep water is found close by ; and it thus affords the shelter of a good roadstead on its two faces, north-east and south-west, for hundreds of vessels which may be seen lying securely at anchor when either wind prevails. If it has helped to destroy harbours, it has provided a substitute.

The case of Hythe is more simple than that of the Romney Marsh towns. The harbour, like that of Hastings, has yielded foot by foot to the Eastward Drift of shingle, till what had been water turned to marsh, and then became dry land; while the enemy now, as at Hastings and elsewhere, presents itself in the guise of a benefactor, inviting modern visitors to the sea-side. The long-continued struggle at Dover, to prevent that harbour from sharing the fate of its neighbours, tells the same tale of resistless tides and winds, driving along the materials which grind away the cliffs and choke the outflow of a stream never large enough to offer much resistance to the obstacle. So also with Walmer, Deal, and the rest; all alike losing in recent times some portions of the beaches which accumulated before the growth of Dungeness, and demanding ' groynes ' or barriers running out into the sea in order to prevent absolute denudation. But when we arrive at Sandwich we find ourselves confronted by different and more complicated phenomena, which can only be stated here, and left for elucidation by historical facts as we proceed.

For the protection of the southern portion of the passage to London by the Thames the Romans relied upon the fortresses at either end of the Rutupian Channel (famous even in those days for its oysters), Regulbium and Rutupiæ, afterwards Reculver and Richborough. This channel, called by the English the Wantsum, though it had begun to shrink before the Romans left Britain, afforded for many centuries so fine a passage to London as to be in constant use for ships making their way to the Thames from the southward. Several rivers flowing from the Kentish high-lands and meandering towards Dover Straits by the eastern port, towards the Thames by the northern, maintained Thanet in the character of an island, even when no longer separated by a considerable arm of the sea from Kent. The Stour, though a broad and shallow river, was navigable, and it was at Ebbsfleet, a creek of the estuary used as the landing-place for Thanet, that the Jute invaders, and later on, St. Augustine, first touched our shores.

Such a condition of land and water would certainly have lasted longer than it did if the improving hand of civilization had not here again reclaimed the marshes or 'salts,' as they were called, just as at Romney, Rye, and Winchelsea. An archbishop, Cardinal Morton, again set the example; but it must be admitted that in the nature of things the channel could not have been permanently kept open. Meeting the flood tide twice a day, the rivers would certainly at some time or other have been checked in their flow, and forming innumerable eddies, could not but have deposited alluvial soil in the channel, thereby diminishing the volume of tidal water required to keep it clear. The inning of the 'salts' powerfully aided the process, and the tides were gradually excluded; while at the same time the rivers were also reduced in volume by the clearance of Andred Forest, and were easily bridged. Thus Thanet ceased to be insular, and the towns which had flourished on the Wantsum shrank away with its waning waters.

The effect on Stonor and Sandwich was only too palpable. Those places, when Richborough was deserted by the tides, became the natural ports of the fine bay at the head of which they stood. The instinct which preferred the closer neighbourhood of the open sea was justified by the prosperity of centuries, but the course of nature could not be arrested. The fatal influx of choking sand may be said to have waited upon the growth of London. As long as its two Kentish outposts were of real importance for that growth, the sea was their obedient vassal, but when the great city had risen beyond the need of such help, by the time that Sandwich had proved its superiority over its rival, and become the chief rendezvous for royal fleets, the Eastward Drift began to produce its ruinous effects. Co-operating with the causes which were acting on the Wantsum, the sand, which was held in suspension by the tides long after they had deposited their burden of shingle, washed more and more into the bay, till in its progress to the East the mouth of the Stour, which had been at Sandwich, was driven mile by mile in the same direction as the sand. The river, helplessly yielding to compulsion, having long ago reached the limit of endurance, debouches, after a course of nine miles, under the cliffs of Thanet by Pegwell Bay, and the famous Bay of Sandwich has long become one expanse of sand, which cuts off from the sea by some two miles or more of dreary waste, one of the most interesting towns in England. Yet the place had time to make a figure—no small one—in English history.

The dates of these changes, or rather the centuries which measure them, will come out as we proceed. Everything will now fall into its place.

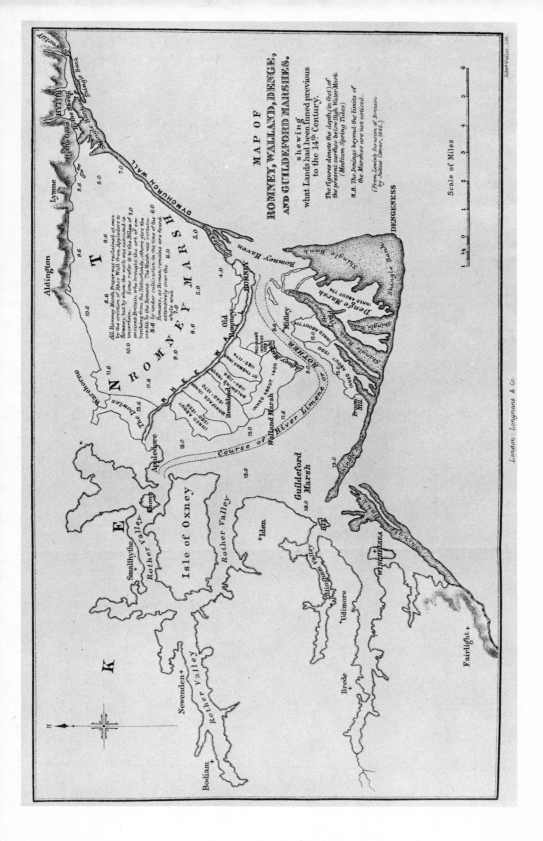

MAP OF
ROMNEY, WALLAND, DENGE,
AND GUILDEFORD MARSHES,
shewing
what Lands had been Inned previous
to the 14th Century.

The figures denote the depth (in feet) of
the present surface below High Water Mark.
(Medium Spring Tides)

N.B. The Innings beyond the limits of
the Marshes are not noticed.

(From Lewin's Invasion of Britain
by Julius Cæsar, 1862.)

Scale of Miles

London: Longmans & Co.

Edwd Weller, lith.

367

A Map of the
RUTUPIAN PORTS
the ancient Course of the Wantfume
and the present Course of the
River Stour.

*The white space between the Island of
Thanet and the County of Kent formerly
covered entirely with water, being now
all of it dry land, as far as the Eastern
Shore at Peppernesse.*

(From Harold's History of Kent.)

Εμιθ.Walker, lith.

London: Longmans & Co.

368

B. Soil Conservation

The series of five articles that comprise this unit are designed to indicate different aspects of man's attempts to conserve soil during his utilization of it as a resource.

The three best known Roman agronomists were Marcus Porcius Cato (234–149 B.C.), Marcus Terentius Varro (116–27 B.C.), and L. Junius Moderatus Columella (1st century A.D.). All wrote books on farm husbandry and those by Cato and Varro are reviewed by Hooper and Ash (1960). Although Gras (1946) feels Varro's contributions were greatest, Columella wrote more material, with a more elegant style, and was more concerned with the soil and its maintenance as well as what was happening to agriculture. Therefore selections from his book are more appropriate for this volume. Along with other important ideas he refutes the theory prevalent in his time that soils go through an aging process during man's use of them. Instead, he shows how through proper conservation their fertility can be maintained. Columella was born in Gades (now Cadiz, Spain) but moved to Rome and wrote at least 16 books on husbandry. Twelve are contained in this 1745 translation. His writings of about 60 A.D. were abridged by Palladius during the 4th century and were forgotten until rediscovered in the 18th century. They aided in serving as a base for the English husbandry books.

The brief selection from one of Sir John Sinclair's (1754–1835) books is used as an entree to conservation methods as practiced in the British Isles about 200 years ago. Handley (1953) reported:

> The English traveller Topham, writing from Edinburgh in 1775, asserted that 'the Scotch are by no means good farmers. Agriculture is one of those things of which they seem to have but a very indifferent idea, and which the learned here have never thought of studying.' Thirty years later the Scots had learned their lesson so well that they could in turn give instruction to the English farmers who crossed the Border for that purpose and elicit a eulogium from Curwen, the English agricultural writer, to the effect that the beauty and regularity of the crops and the extreme cleanness of the fallows in East Lothian struck him more than anything he had ever before beheld in any other country; that he did not know a farmer who might not learn something in that district; that in regard both to excellence of soil and management it exceeded anything he had ever witnessed in any other part of Great Britain. (pp. 286–287)

The man most instrumental in educating the Scotch to the importance of soil conservation, and showing by example on his own fields, was Sinclair. He became their leading authority on agriculture and in addition produced a 21 volume series (1791–1799) on the "Statistical Account of Scotland" which contained data on farming, industry, natural history, and demographic considerations. Sinclair was also active in politics and carried on a correspondence with George Washington, and in a September 10, 1796 letter to him stated: "I hope that you will recommend some agricultural establishment on a great scale before your quit the reins of government."

L. JUNIUS MODERATUS COLUMELLA

OF

HUSBANDRY.

IN

TWELVE BOOKS:

AND HIS

BOOK

CONCERNING

TREES.

Translated into *English*, with several Illustrations from PLINY, CATO, VARRO, PALLADIUS, and other antient and modern AUTHORS.

Ecclesiastes, Chap. V. Ver. 9. *The Profit of the Earth is for All ; the King himself is served by the Field.*
Ecclesiasticus, Chap. VII. Ver. 15. *Hate not Husbandry, which the Most High hath ordained.*

Virg. Georg. Lib. I. ———— *Pater ipse colendi*
Haud facilem esse viam voluit, primusque per artem
Movit agros, curis acuens mortalia corda.

LONDON:

Printed for A. MILLAR, opposite to *Catharine-street* in the *Strand.*
M.DCC.XLV.

370

28

L. *JUNIUS MODERATUS COLUMELLA*

OF

HUSBANDRY.

BOOK FIRST.

The PREFACE. *To* PUBLIUS SILVINUS.

I frequently hear the principal men of our city blaming, sometimes the unfruitfulness of the ground, at other times the intemperateness of the weather, as hurtful to the fruits of the earth for many ages now past : some also I hear mitigating, in some measure, as it were, the foresaid complaints, because they are of opinion, that the ground, being, by its overmuch fruitfulness during the former part of its duration, become barren, and worn out of heart, is not now able, with its wonted bounty, to afford sustenance to mortals. Which causes, *Publius Silvinus*, I am fully persuaded, are very remote from the truth; because it is neither lawful to think, that the nature of the ground, which that original Former and Father of the universe endowed with perpetual fecundity, is affected with barrenness, as with a certain disease; nor does it become a wise man to believe, that the earth, which, having a divine and everlasting youth bestowed upon it, is called the *common parent* of all things, because it has always brought forth, and will henceforth bring forth, all things whatsoever, is grown old, like a woman.

B

(1) Nor,

(1) Nor, after all, do I think, that thefe things befal us from the diftemperature of the weather; but rather from our own fault, who commit our Hufbandry to the very worft of our fervants, as a criminal to a public executioner, which all the beft of our anceftors were wont to treat with the greateft gentlenefs : and I cannot enough wonder, why they, who defire to learn eloquence, are fo nice in their choice of an orator, whofe eloquence they may imitate ; and they, who fearch after the knowledge of furveying or menfuration, and of numbers, look out for a mafter of the art they delight in ; and they, who are defirous of fome fkill in dancing and mufic, are exceeding fcrupulous in their choice of one to modulate their voice, and teach them to fing agreeably ; and no lefs of a dancing-mafter, to regulate the geftures and motions of their body ; alfo they, who have a mind to build, fend for architects, mafons, and carpenters ; and they, who refolve to fend fhips to fea, fend for fkilful pilots ; they, who make preparations for war, call for men, who underftand the art of war, and are acquainted with military affairs ; and, not to men- tion every particular, in that ftudy which every one refolves to pro- fecute, he makes ufe of the wifeft and ableft director he can find ; finally, every one fends for a perfon from the fociety and affembly of the wife, to form his mind, and inftruct him in the precepts of virtue : but Hufbandry alone, which, without all doubt, is next to, and, as it were, near akin to wifdom, is in want of both mafters and fcholars. For hitherto I have not only heard, that there are, but I myfelf have feen, fchools of profeffors of Rhetoric, and, as I have already faid, of Geometry, and of Mufic ; or, which is more to be wondered at, academies for the moft contemptible vices, for deli- cately dreffing and feafoning of victuals, for contriving and making up dainty and coftly difhes for promoting gluttony and luxury ; and I have alfo feen head-dreffers and hair-trimmers; but, of Agriculture, I have never known any that profeffed themfelves either teachers or ftudents.

For, even fuppofe the city fhould want profeffors of the forefaid arts, neverthelefs the commonwealth might be in a very flourifhing condition, as in antient times ; for, of old, cities were happy enough, and will hereafter ftill be fo, without ludicrous arts, yea, even without

---

. (1) *Pliny*, in his *Natural Hiftory, lib.* 18. *cap.* 2. fays, that the caufe of the former plenty was, that the ground was at firft cultivated by the hands of Generals, Confuls, Tribunes, and Senators ; but afterwards by Slaves, Criminals, and Malefactors, who bore upon their bodies the marks of their infamy, and did not cultivate it fo carefully as thofe men of honour and virtue did.

advocates

advocates alfo (2) : but without Hufbandmen, it îs manifeft, that mortals can neither fubfift, nor be maintained. For which reafon, what is come to pafs, is the more like a prodigy, that a thing fo necef-fary and convenient for our bodies, and the advantages of life, fhould, to this very time, of all things whatfoever, have had the leaft con-fummation ; and that this perfectly innocent way of enlarging and preferving one's patrimony fhould be defpifed. For thofe other different, and, as it were, repugnant ways of doing this, are contrary and difagreeable to juftice ; unlefs we think it more agreeable to equity to have acquired booty by a military profeffion, which brings us nothing without blood and flaughter, and the ruin and deftruction of others. Or, to fuch as hate war, can the hazard, uncertainty, and danger of the fea, and of trade, be more defireable ? That *Man*, a terref-trial animal, breaking through the boundary and law of nature, and expofing himfelf to the rage of the winds and fea, fhould dare to commit himfelf to the waves, and, after the manner of the fowls of the air, always a ftranger upon a far diftant and foreign fhore, wan-der over the unknown world ? Or is ufury, which is odious, even to thofe whom it feems to relieve, more to be approved? Or is, forfooth, that canine ftudy and employment, as the antients called it, of fnarling, and barking at, and flanderoufly accufing every man of the greateft fubftance ; and that open robbery of pleading againft the innocent, and for the guilty, which was neglected and defpifed by our ance-ftors, but even permitted and allowed of by us within the walls, and

(2) *Caufidicus*, an appellation not very honourable amongft the *Romans*. *Quintilian*, in his *Inftitutions*, *lib.* 2. avoiding harfher terms, calls him *vocem mercenariam, inutilem litium advocatum*, a mercenary tongue, a promoter of law-fuits, a wrangling advocate. Our author feems to have had men of this character in great contempt, who employed their eloquence either in pleading for the notorioufly wicked, or againft innocent per-fons. If the word *Caufidic* were as well known as the word *Advocate*, it would be more expreffive of the thing.

In our author's days, the *Romans* had loft their liberty, and were under a very tyran-nical government ; and, no doubt, many of them, being greatly diffatisfied with their prefent ftate, by their murmurings, and otherwife, made themfelves obnoxious to the difpleafure and refentment of their oppreffors, who, by profcriptions, endeavoured to deftroy all they fufpected to be their enemies ; and many of the orators of thofe days became informers and accufers ; and, it feems, always pitched upon the richeft, with a view to a fhare of the plunder. It is this *canine* eloquence, as they called it, which our author cenfures : *eloquence* employed in defence of innocence, and againft the guilty, in fupport of truth againft falfhood and calumny, and efpecially in directing the public counfels, appeafing popular commotions, and correcting public errors, is a divine endowment ; in all ages had in the greateft reputation by the wifeft nations, and juftly promoted to the greateft honours : otherwife it is a very dangerous talent, efpecially in countries where haranguing and pleading at the bar is much in ufe, if the judges are not very fharp-fighted, to difcern true reafon from fophiftry.

B 2   in

in the very *Forum* itself (3), more excellent and honourable ? Or,
should I reckon more honest and honourable, the most deceitful, lying,
and beggarly hawking of a mercenary levee-haunter, who is constantly flying about from the threshold of one great man in power
to that of another, and guessing, by the report of others, whether
his patron is awake, or not ? Nor, indeed, do the servants vouchsafe
to answer him, when he asks what is a doing within-doors : or,
should I think it more fortunate, after having met with a repulse
from the porter with his chains upon him, to loiter and hang about
the ungrateful and hateful doors, oft-times till it be late at night,
and, by a most mean and pitiful servitude and attendance, purchase
with disgrace the honour of the *Fasces* (4), or a government, or a
command in the army or navy, and, after all, squander away one's
own patrimony ? For honour is not bestowed, as a reward, upon
disinterested service and attendance, but upon such as make presents,
and give bribes.

Now, if all good men ought to avoid these very things, and others
like to them, there is still remaining, as I said, one way of increasing
one's substance, worthy of a freeman, and a gentleman ; which arises
from Husbandry, of which if the precepts were put in practice, suppose it were but imprudently, by such as have not been instructed in it,
provided nevertheless they were possessors and proprietors of the lands,
which they cultivate, as was the antient custom, rural affairs would
suffer less damage ; for the industry and diligence of the masters,
would, in many things, compensate the loss occasioned by ignorance ;
and they, whose own interest lay at stake, would not appear to be all
their life-time willingly ignorant of their own business ; but thereby
becoming more desirous of learning, would attain to a thorough knowledge of Husbandry.

Now we disdain, and think it below us, to live upon, and cultivate
our own lands ourselves, and look upon it as a matter of no moment,
to make choice of a man of the best sense and skill we can find, for
our Bailiff ; or, if he be ignorant, at least, of a man of vigour, vigilance, and activity, that he may learn the more speedily what he is
ignorant of. But, whether he be a rich man that purchases a piece
of ground, he picks, out of his crew of footmen and chairmen, one
that is the feeblest, and the most worn out with years, and banishes

---

(3) *Forum* signifies the building, or place, where public courts of justice were held ;
and matters of judgment pleaded and decided ; or the court of justice itself.

(4) *Fasces* were the public ensigns of magistracy among the *Romans*, being a bundle
of rods, with an ax, tied together, and carried before the magistrate.

him

him into the country : whereas that bufinefs requires, not only knowledge, but green age, and ftrength of body, to bear labour and fatigue :
or if he be mafter of a middling eftate, he commands one of his hire-
lings, who now refufes to pay that daily tribute of fervice required of
him, and cannot thereby increafe his income, to be director and over-
feer, who is ignorant of the bufinefs he is to have the overfight
of (5). Which things when I obferve, frequently confidering and
revolving in my mind, with how bafe and fhameful an agreement and
confent rural difcipline is deferted, and worn out of ufe, I am in
dread, left it fhould be accounted villainous, and, in fome meafure,
fhameful and difhonourable, for free-born men. But when, by the
records and writings of many authors, I am put in mind, that our
worthy anceftors looked upon it as their glory, to take care of their
rural affairs, and to employ themfelves in Hufbandry, from which (6)
Quintus Cincinnatus came, and refcued the befieged Conful and his
army, being called from the plough to the Dictatorfhip; and again,
having laid down the *Fafces*, which, *when a Conqueror*, he more
haftily furrendered, than he had affumed them when he was made
General, he returned to the fame fteers, and his fmall manor of four
jugera of land, left him by his anceftors (7): and *CaiusFabricius* alfo,
and

(5) *Ex mercenariis, aliquem jam recufantem, quotidianum illud tributum*, there feems to
be fomething wanting in this fentence, to make it more intelligible, which I cannot pre-
tend to fupply : the intention of it muft either be what I have expreffed, or perhaps it
may fignify, that one of the hired fervants, who refufes to ferve for common wages, is
promoted to the office of a Bailiff.

(6) *Quintus Cincinnatus* was made Dictator during the Confulfhip of *L. Minutius
Carbetus*, and *C. Nautius Rutilius* III. *Anno* 296. from the building of *Rome*. The mef-
fenger from the Senate found him ploughing his four *jugera* of land, which he had in
the *Vatican*, and which, from him, were called the *Quintian Meadows*. It is faid, he was
naked, and all covered over with fweat and duft. The occafion of his being chofen
Dictator, was, becaufe the Conful *Minutius*, and his army, were befieged in their camp
by the enemy, and were in danger of being made prifoners of war. This ftory is
elegantly told by *Livy, dec.* I. *lib.* 3, who fays, it is worth their while to hear it, who
defpife all human things, in comparifon of riches ; and think, that there can be no
place, either for great honour, or for valour and virtue, but where there is great affluence
of riches.

(7) *Columella* calls thefe four *jugera* of land, his *prædiolum avitum*, as if they came to
him from his anceftors; which is contrary to what *Feftus* fays, *viz. That the* Quintian Meadows *were fo called, from* Quintus Cincinnatus, *becaufe, after his Son was condemned, he
fold all that he had, and purchafed four* jugera *of land beyond the* Tyber. They made
near two *Englifh* acres and a half.

The *jugerum*, which many of our *Englifh* tranflators render *Acre*, was much fmaller
than the *Englifh* acre ; and it only impofes upon the reader, and gives him a falfe
idea of this meafure, to tranflate it thus ; fo that I think it better to retain the original
word, and give an explication of it in a note, than, by tranflating it *Acre*, convey a falfe
notion to the mind of the reader.

The

and *Curius Dentatus* (8) ; the one, after having driven *Pyrrhus* (9) out of the confines of *Italy* ; and the other, after he had subdued the *Sabines*, did no less industriously cultivate, than they had bravely gained with their swords, their dividend of seven *jugera* of land a man, which they received of the land they had taken from the enemy.

And that I may not now unseasonably make mention of them one by one, when I behold so many other renowned and memorable Captains of the *Roman* nation, who were always in great reputation for this two-fold study ; either of defending, or of cultivating, their paternal or acquired estates ; I perceive, that the antient custom, manners, and manly life of our ancestors, are disagreeable to our luxury, and voluptuous delicacy. For (as *Marcus Varro* (10) formerly complained in our grandfathers times) *all we, who are masters of families, having abandoned the pruning-hook, and the plough, have, in a sneaking manner, crept within the walls ; and rather move our hands in the Circus* (11) *and Theatres, than in our corn fields and vine-yards :* and with astonishment we admire the postures of effeminate wretches ; because, by their woman-like motions, they counterfeit

---

The *Roman jugerum*, as our author informs us, consisted of 28,800 square feet, whereas the *English* acre consists of 43,560 square feet, which is about a *Roman jugerum* and a half ; and, according to the nearest computation, the *jugerum* consists of 2 roods, 18 *square poles*, 250,05 *square feet* ; and the proportion it bears to the *acre*, is very near as 10 to 16 ; and the *Roman* foot, according to the *English* standard, is 11,604 inches.

(8) *Curius Dentatus, an. urb.* 479. conquered *Pyrrhus*, and drove him out of *Italy*, and triumphed over him. *Plin. Nat. Hist. lib.* 8. *cap.* 16. *Florus, de Bello Tarentino* describes this war, victory, and triumph, very elegantly ; and, *lib.* 1. *cap.* 18. says, that, *Curius* preferred his own earthen ware to all the gold of the *Samnites* ; and that *Fabricius* rejected the offers of *Pyrrhus*, who would have made him Partner in the Government, if he would have betrayed his country. *Pliny* says, that they had but one saltseller, and the bottom of it was of wood.

Fabricius, when Censor, removed *Ruffinus*, a man of consular dignity, from the Senate, because he had ten pounds of plate, judging it great luxury ; and forbid the most warlike Generals to have more silver plate than one goblet, and a saltseller. In those days, the Generals baggage cost the public very little, and was no great incumbrance to the army. *Plin. Nat. Hist. lib.* 23. *cap.* 12. *Val. Max. lib.* 4. *cap.* 3. The seven *jugera* these two Generals possessed, amounted to 4 ⅝ *English* acres.

(9) *Pyrrhus*, King of *Epirus*, was called by the *Tarentinians* to their assistance against the *Romans* : he fought with them several times very successfully, and reduced them to very great danger.

(10) *Marcus Terentius Varro* has these words in his second book of Husbandry : he was a famous philosopher and historian, and reckoned the most learned man among the *Romans*. Besides his books *de Re Rustica, et de Lingua Latina*, which are still extant, he wrote forty-one books of Antiquities, and several other tracts mentioned by several authors. He lived a few years before *Cicero*.

(11) The *Circo's* were places set apart by the *Romans*, for the celebration of several sorts of games, generally of an oblong figure, walled round, with ranges of seats for the conveniency of the spectators.

a sex-a fex which nature has denied to men ; and deceive the eyes of the fpectators. Then, prefently after, that we may come in good plight to public places of riot and debauchery, we confume and dry up our daily crudities in bagnio's ; and, by fweating out the moifture of our bodies, we endeavour to procure an appetite for drinking; and fpend the nights in libidinous gratifications and drunken-nefs, and the days in gaming, or fleeping ; and account ourfelves happy, becaufe we neither fee the rifing nor the fetting of the fun. Therefore the confequence of this idle and flothful way of living is *bad health* : for thus the bodies of young men are fo unbraced, relaxed, and enfeebled, that *death* will not feem to make any alteration or change in them.

But, verily, that true and genuine progeny of *Romulus*, being con-ftantly exercifed in, and inured to hunting, and no lefs to country bufinefs and labour, excelled in, and were highly efteemed for their exceeding great ftrength and firmnefs of body ; and, when the fervice of their country required it, in time of war, they eafily fupported the fatigues of a military life, being hardened by their laborious exer-cifes in times of peace ; and they always preferred the country com-monalty, to that of the city. For, as they, who ftill kept within the inclofures of the manor-houfe, were accounted more flothful and faint-hearted, than thofe who laboured the ground without doors ; fo they who fauntered, and fpent their time idly within the walls, under the fhade of the city, were looked upon as more lazy and unactive, than thofe who cultivated the fields, and managed bufinefs relating to Hufbandry. It is alfo evident, that their ninth-day Fairs or Markets (12), where they affembled themfelves together, were eftablifhed, and kept up, for this very purpofe, that city affairs might be tranfacted every ninth day only, and rural affairs on the other days. For, in thofe times, as we faid before, the people of quality, and principal men of the city, lived in the country, upon their own lands ; and when their advice about public affairs was wanted, they were fent for from their villas, to attend the Senate ; from which thing, they who were fent to fummon them were called *viatores* (13); and while this cuftom was obferved, and kept up,

(12) There was a Fair or Market at *Rome* every ninth day, for the country people to meet and fell their goods, and tranfact other bufinefs in town ; fo that their *Nundina* were not idle days, but appointed for bufinefs.

(13) *Viatores:* It feems by their firft inftitution they were to be fent by the Senate to the country, to fummon fuch as lived there, to attend the public fervice, and to conduct them to town: afterwards they were a fort of Beadles, or Sergeants, who went before the Tribunes of the people, and fome other officers of leffer dignity.

4   by

by a moſt perſevering deſire of cultivating their lands, thoſe antient *Sabines* (14), who became citizens of *Rome* ; and our old *Roman* an-ceſtors, tho' expoſed on every hand to fire and ſword, and to have their corns, and other fruits of the ground, waſted by hoſtile incur-ſions, notwithſtanding, laid up greater ſtore of them, than we, who, by the permiſſion of a long-continued peace, have had it in our power to inlarge and improve our Huſbandry.

Therefore things are now come to ſuch a paſs, that in this *La-tium* (15) and country where *Saturn* lived, where the gods taught their own children the art of cultivating the ground ; even there we let, by public auction (16), the importation of corn from our pro-vinces beyond ſea, that we may not be expoſed to a famine ; and we lay in our ſtores of fruits and wines from the *Cyclad* iſlands (17), and from the regions of *Bætica* (18) and *Gaul*. Nor is it any wonder, ſeeing the vulgar opinion is now publicly entertained and eſtabliſhed, that Huſbandry is a ſordid employment ; and that it is a buſineſs which does not want the inſtruction of a maſter. But as for myſelf, when I conſider and review, either the greatneſs of the whole thing, reſembling ſome vaſtly extended body ; or the number of its parts, as ſo many members in particular ; I am afraid, leſt my laſt day ſhould ſurpriſe me, before I can acquaint myſelf with the whole of rural diſcipline.

For he that would profeſs himſelf to be perfect in this ſcience, muſt be exceedingly well acquainted with the nature of things ; muſt not be ignorant of the ſeveral latitudes of the world ; that he may be ſure of what is agreeable, or what is repugnant, to every climate ; that he may perfectly remember the time of the riſing and ſetting of the ſtars, that he may not begin his works when winds and rains are coming upon him, and ſo fruſtrate his labour. Let him conſider the temperature and conſtitution of the weather, and of the preſent year ; for neither do they, as it were by a ſettled law, always wear the ſame dreſs ; nor does the Summer or Winter come every year with the ſame countenance : nor is the Spring always rainy, nor the Autumn moiſt : which I cannot believe any man can know beforehand, without an enlightened mind, and without the moſt excellent arts and ſciences.

Now very few have the talent to diſcern the great variety itſelf of the ground, and the nature and diſpoſition of every ſoil, what each of them may promiſe or deny us. Yea, when has any one man whatſoever had the opportunity to contemplate all the parts of this art, ſo as throughly to underſtand the uſe, advantage, and management of all forts of corns, and of tillage, and the various and different forts of earth, moft unlike to one another ? of which, fome deceive us by their colour, fome by their quality : and, in fome countries, the black earth, which they call brown, or dufky, deferves to be commended ; in others, that which is fat, and red-coloured, anfwers better : in fome countries, as in *Numidia* in *Africa*, the rotten fands furpafs, in fruitfulnefs, the ftrongeft foil whatfoever ; in *Afia* and *Myfia* (19), thick glutinous earth produces the greateft abundance of any.

(19) *Myfia*, a country in *Leffer Afia*, extending moftly weftward, towards the *Hellefpont*. It was divided formerly into the Leffer and Greater. Both parts are now called *Natolia*, fubject to the *Turks*.

C yield

C H A P. V.

Of Water.

AND let there be either within the manor-houſe a ſpring that never dries up, or let it be brought into it from without. Let wood for fire, and forrage, be near at hand. If running-water cannot be had, let well-water be ſought for hard-by, which may neither lie too deep, and be difficult to draw, nor be of a bitter or brackiſh taſte. But if theſe alſo fail you, and the ſmall hopes of ſpring-water force you, let large ciſterns, after all, be provided for men, and ponds for cattle, for gathering and keeping rain-water, which is the moſt proper and ſuitable to the health of the body; and this you may have exceeding good, if you convey it, in earthen pipes, into a covered ciſtern. Next to this is running-water, which has its ſource upon the mountains, provided it tumbles down headlong over the rocks, as at *Guarcenum* (1) in *Campania*. Well-water is the third, either that which is found upon riſing ground, or not in the loweſt part of the valley. The worſt of all is marſh-water, which creeps and ſlides along with a ſlow motion. That which always ſtagnates in a marſh, is peſtilent; nevertheleſs this ſame water, tho' of a hurtful nature, yet, in winter, being ſoftened and allayed by the ſhowers of rain, abates of its bad quality: from which we underſtand, that rain-water is exceeding wholſome, becauſe it alſo purges out the pernicious quality of poiſonous water (2): but this we have ſaid to be the moſt approved for drinking. But rivulets, that have a ſtrong current, and a fall, contribute very much to moderate the heats, and to the delightfulneſs of places, which, if the ſituation of the place will allow it, whatever quality they may have, provided they be ſweet, ought, by all means, in my opinion, to be brought into the villa.

But if the river be at a greater diſtance from the hills, and if the wholſomeneſs of the place, and the higher ſituation of its banks, ſhall allow you to place your houſe upon the current, nevertheleſs you muſt

(9) *Bæotia*, a country in *Greece*, bordering upon *Attica*, of a foggy unwholſome air, but good for cattle. The inhabitants were, by the antients, reckoned dull and ſtupid. The chief city of it was *Thebes*, now called *Stibes*, and a ſmall village. *Bæotia* borders upon *Doris*, *Phocis*, *Attica*, and *Corinthus*, now called *Stramulipa*, and ſubject to the *Turks*.

(10) *Eubæa*, an iſland eaſt of *Achaia* in *Greece*, now called *Negroponte*, ſeparated from *Achaia* by a narrow ſea (*Euripus*). Its chief city is *Chalcis*. They ſay it is about 130 miles long, and 30 broad. It was long ſubject to the *Venetians*; but now in the hands of the *Turks*. The *Euripus* is now called the *Streight of Negropont*, and is ſo narrow, that *Eubæa* is joined to *Achaia* by a bridge.

take care, that it have the river rather behind than before it ; and that the front of the building be turned from the troublefome and hurtful winds peculiar to that country, and turned towards thofe that are moft friendly ; for moft rivers are covered and hid from you with hot mifts in fummer, and with cold mifts in winter, which, unlefs they be carried off by the greater force of the winds that blow upon them, prove deftructive both to men and cattle.   But, as I faid, in fuch places as are wholfome, it is beft to turn the front of the manor-houfe towards the eaft or fouth ; and, in fuch as are unwholfome, towards the north. And a villa looks always rightly to the fea, when it is beat upon and fprinkled with the waves thereof, but never from the bank, or when it is a little removed from the fhore : for it is better to have fled back to a great than to a fmall diftance from the fea ; for the intermediate diftances are of a groffer air.   Nor indeed muft there be a marfh near the buildings, nor a public highway adjoining : for the former always throws up noxious and poifonous fteams during the heats, and breeds animals armed with mifchievous ftings, which fly upon us in exceeding thick fwarms ; as alfo fends forth, from the mud and fermented dirt, envenomed pefts of water-fnakes and ferpents, deprived of the moifture they enjoyed in winter ; whereby hidden difeafes are often contracted, the caufes of which, even the phyficians themfelves cannot thoroughly underftand : and alfo, at all times of the year, the dampnefs and moifture rots and fpoils the implements of hufbandry, houfhold furniture, and the fruits of the ground, that are either laid up in ftore, or not as yet brought into the houfe.   And the latter is a burden to your eftate, by the plunderings of travellers that pafs by, and the conftant entertainment of thofe that come to lodge with you.

Wherefore I advife you to avoid thefe inconveniencies, and to build a manor-houfe neither by the highway, nor in a peftilential place, but

(1) *Guarcenum* in *Campania.* There is no mention of this place by *Pliny,* or any other author I have feen.   Probably there is an addition or tranfpofition of one or two letters. *Pliny* mentions feveral times *Mons Gaurus,* and *vinum Gauranum* in *Campania.* This mountain lies near to *Baiæ* or *Puzzuolo* ; and, on the fide of the hill looking towards thefe places, there is excellent wine ; fo that our author perhaps means fome town that ftood near this hill, and took its name from it.

(2) Rain-water, by moft authors, is accounted the wholfomeft.   *Vitruvius* fays, that the lighteft and moft fubtile particles are extracted from all the fountains, and carried up into the air, by the conftant motion of which, it is agitated, ftrained, and liquefied ; and then it falls to the earth.   *Hippocrates, Galen,* &c. commend it, becaufe it is light, fweet, clear, and thin.   Some authors fay, that fummer rain-water, which falls in time of thunder, is better than that of common fhowers ; and that water of melted fnow or ice is the worft of any.   *Cornelius Celfus* ranks them thus, with refpect to their weight ; rain-water, fpring-water, river-water, well-water ; next to thefe, that of fnow and ice ; that of a lake is weightier, and of a marfh is heavieft of all.

at a great diftance from them, and upon a higher fituation ; and that the front of it be directed to the rifing of the fun at the time of the equinox ; for this kind of fituation keeps an equal balance, and a well-adjufted medium between the winter and fummer winds.   And the more declining towards the eaft the ground is, on which the building ftands, the more freely will it receive the cool paffing breezes in fummer, and be lefs incommoded or hurt with ftorms in winter, and fo be thawed with the rifing fun, that the frozen dews may melt : for that ground is reckoned almoft peftilential, which is not within the reach of the fun, and not expofed to breezes warmed with the fame ; which if it want, there is no other thing of any efficacy to dry up and wipe off the nocturnal hoar-frofts, and any fort of ruft, mildew, or filth, that fixes upon it.   And thefe things are not only deftructive to men, but alfo to all forts of cattle, and to every green thing whatfoever, and to their fruits.

But whofoever has a mind to build upon a floping area, let him always begin at the lower part ; becaufe when the foundations are begun from the more depreffed place, they will not only eafily fupport their own fuperftructure, but alfo ferve as a butteridge and under-propping againft fuch things, as fhall afterwards be applied to the upper part, if peradventure he has a fancy to inlarge the villa : for the buildings that have been raifed before from the lower part, will powerfully refift and bear up againft thofe that, being placed above them, fhall lean and reft upon them.   But, if the uppermoft part of the rifing ground, being made the foundation, fhall have received the weight of its own fuperftructure, whatever you join to it afterwards from the lower part, will become full of clifts and chinks ; for a new building, when it is built and joined to an old, and that which is frefh to what is full of chinks, it, as it were, ftruggling againft the weighty load that preffes upon it, gives way ; and that, which was firft built, will prefs upon that which gives way, and, being gradually weighed down, will be pulled down headlong with its own weight.   Therefore this fault, in the way of building, muft be avoided when the foundations are firft laid

CHAP. I.

That the Earth neither grows old, nor wears out, if it be dunged.

YOU afk me, *Publius Silvinus*, what I don't refufe to inform you of without delay; Why, in the very beginning of the firft book, I immediately confuted the opinion of almoft all the antients, who have fpoken of Hufbandry; and rejected, as falfe and erroneous (1), their judgment, who think, that the earth, being wearied and worn out by a long-continued cultivation, and become barren by the filth, naftinefs, and mouldinefs it has contracted, in a long fucceffion of years already paft, is now become old? I am not ignorant, that you have a great veneration for the authority, both of other illuftrious writers, and efpecially for that of *Tremellius*; who, after having, in an elegant and learned manner, written and publifhed very many precepts of Hufbandry, being certainly carried away and allured by too great a regard for the antients, who treat of the like fubject, did, without any foundation, believe, that the *earth*, the *parent of all things*, like the female fex, being now fpent and worn out with old age, was become unfit for the production of fruits. Which thing I myfelf would alfo acknowledge, if fhe produced no fruits at all: for a woman is then reckoned to be arrived at barren old age, not when fhe ceafes to bring two or three children at a birth, but when fhe is neither able to conceive or bring forth at all. Therefore, after the days of her youth are paft and gone, tho' a long life ftill remains, yet bearing of children, which is denied to years, is not reftored to her: but, on the contrary, when the earth is abandoned, and left deftitute of men, either by their own choice, or by fome accident, yet, when they return to it again, and cultivate it, it pays the Hufbandman with a very large ufury for the time it ceafed. Therefore the earth's old age is not the caufe of the fmall quantity of her fruit, feeing that, when once old age has invaded and come upon her, fhe has no regrefs, no way to recover herfelf, to take heart, and grow young again.

Nor indeed does the wearinefs and faintnefs of the ground diminifh the fruit that is due to the Hufbandman; for it does not become a wife man to be induced to believe, that, as in men *wearinefs* follows upon, and is occafioned by, too violent exercife of the body, or the weight of fome burden, fo it is with land, by its being toffed and tumbled by

(1) *Pliny* alfo, in his *natural hiftory*, confutes the opinion of thofe, who think, that the earth is become old, and lefs fruitful than formerly; and charges its unfruitfulnefs upon its want of due cultivation, *lib.* xvii. *c.* 5. and in other places.

old.

frequent cultivation. Why is it therefore, say you, that *Tremellius* positively affirms, that woodlands, which were never tilled, when they are first cultivated, bring forth abundantly; but, soon afterwards, they don't thus pay the labour of the Husbandman? He sees, no doubt, what comes to pass; but why, it is so, he does not throughly understand. For land, which has lain long uncultivated, and which, from being all covered over with wood, has been lately reduced into corn-land, ought not therefore to be reckoned the more fruitful, because it has lain untilled, and is younger; but because, being fattened, as it were, with the more plentiful nourishment, which it received from the leaves and herbs, which it naturally produced, during the course of many years, it has strength enough to bring forth, educate, and bring to perfection, the fruits that grow upon it. But when the roots of the herbs, which are torn up and broken with spades and ploughs, and the woods which are cut down with the ax, have left off nourishing their *mother* with their leaves, and when such leaves as fell down from shrubs and trees in the autumn, and lay upon her, are, presently after, turned over with the sock, and mixed with the lower ground, which, for the most part, is leaner, and afterwards consumed, it follows, that the ground, being deprived of its former nourishment, grows lean.

It is not therefore from weariness, as very many have believed, nor from old age, but indeed from our own slothfulness, that our cultivated lands don't so bountifully answer our expectation as formerly; for we might receive a greater product, if the earth were refreshed and cherished with frequent, seasonable, and moderate stercoration: of the culture of which we shall now discourse, as we promised in the first book.

CHAP. II.

Of the several Kinds of Land.

THEY who had the greatest skill and experience in Husbandry, O *Silvanus*, have said, That there are three kinds of land (1), *champaîn*, *hilly*, and *mountainous*. They approved most of a *champain*,

(1) *Varro, lib.* i. *cap. 6.* describes the conveniencies and inconveniencies of these three different situations of land: ' In champain lands, he says, the heat is greater, as in *Apulia*, ' where it is very grievous. Lands that are mountainous, as those of *Vesuvius*, are lighter, ' and so more wholsome. They who cultivate low lands, suffer greater inconveniency ' in summer; but high lands more in winter. Low grounds are both sown and reaped ' earlier in the spring, than those that are high. Some things grow taller and stronger upon ' mountains, because of the cold, as firs and oaks, *&c.* Other things thrive best below, ' because it is warmer, as the *almond-tree*, and the *Marifcan fig-tree*. Corn-lands are most

fituated not upon a perfectly equal and even plain, nor exactly upon a level, but fomewhat declining; of a *hill* rifing gently, and by degrees; and of a *mountain* not lofty and rugged, but covered with plenty of wood and grafs. And to each of thefe kinds they affign fix different fpecies of land; *viz.* that of a fat or lean, loofe or denfe, moift or dry foil; which qualities, compounded and mixed alternately with one another, make very many varieties of land. To enumerate them, is not the bufinefs of the ingenious Hufbandman; nor indeed is it the bufinefs of any art to wander over all the different fpecies, which are innumerable; but to begin with generals, which can be eafily joined together by the thoughts of the mind, and brought within the compafs of words.

Therefore we muft have recourfe to certain conjunctions, as it were, of qualities, that are unlike or contrary to one another, which the *Greeks* call συζυγίας ἐναντιοτήτων, and we fhall tolerably well call the *matching* or *joining together of difcordant things*. And we muft alfo inform you, that, of all the things which the earth brings forth, there are more of them which thrive better upon a champain, than upon a hill, and in a fat foil, than in a lean. As to things growing in foils naturally dry, or well watered, we don't find out, which of them exceed in number, feeing it is certain, that fuch as delight in dry places are almoft infinite, as are alfo thofe that delight in moift; but there is not any one of them, that does not grow up better in loofe and open ground, than in that which is clofe and denfe; which our countryman *Virgil* alfo, after he had reckoned up the other commendable qualities of fruitful land, added (2),

> ' A loofe and crumbling foil; for, with the plough,
> ' We ftrive to make it fuch.'

For to cultivate is no other thing but to open, and loofen, and ferment the earth; therefore the fame land, which is both fat, and loofe, and crumbling, yields the greateft profits, becaufe, at the time that it yields the moft, it requires the leaft, and what it requires is done with very little labour and expence. Therefore fuch a foil may very juftly be faid to be the very beft of any.

' efteemed upon plains; vineyards upon little hills; and woods upon mountains. They
' who inhabit champains, are beft accommodated in winter, becaufe then the meadows
' have plenty of grafs, and trees can then be tolerably well pruned. On the contrary, it
' is more convenient living upon mountains in fummer, becaufe then there is plenty of
' forrage there, when all things are withered and burnt up below; and the culture of trees
' is more commodioufly performed, becaufe there the air is colder. A champain, which
' tends or declines equably towards one part, is better than that, which lies exactly upon
' a level.' With feveral other obfervations too tedious to mention.

(2) *Virg. Georg. lib.* ii. 204.

Then, next to this, is the *fatty-thick dense soil,* which rewards, with great increase, the charges and labour of the farmer. A *place that is well watered* is reckoned in the third rank, because it can yield fruit without any charge. *Cato,* who preferred the product of meadows to all other products of lands whatsoever, called this the best. But we are now speaking of moving and agitating the earth, and not of letting it lie still.

There is no kind reckoned worse, than that which is dry, and likewise dense and lean ; because it is both cultivated with difficulty, and, when it is cultivated, it does not so much indeed as thank you : nor does it turn to good account, when you turn it to meadows or pastures. Therefore this land, whether it be tilled, or lies fallow, will always give the Husbandman reason to wish he had never meddled with it, and is to be avoided as if it were pestilential ; for *this* brings forth *death,* but *that, famine,* death's most frightful and cruel companion, if we give credit to the *Grecian* muses, which cry aloud (3),

' With famine to consume and pine away,
' And slowly die at last, what wo so great ? '

But now we shall rather take into consideration that kind of land which is more fruitful, which must be considered under two different views ; *viz. as cultivated,* and *as covered with wood.* We shall first speak of reducing woodlands into the form of arable ground ; because clearing of land is of an older date than the cultivating of it. Let us therefore consider a place that is not cultivated, whether it be dry or moist, full of wood and trees, or rugged and craggy, and full of stones ; whether it be covered with rushes or with grass, and encumbered with fern-plots, and nurseries of other shrubs. If it be wet, let the abundance of moisture be first drained and dried up by ditches. Of these we have known two sorts, *blind* or *hidden,* and *open.* In thick and chalky grounds they are left open ; but, where the ground is more loose, some of them are made open, and others of them are also shut up and covered ; so that the gaping mouths of such of them as are blind may empty themselves into those that are open. But it will be proper, that the open ones be wider towards the upper part, and sloping and narrow towards the bottom, like ridge-tiles inverted ; for such of them, whose sides are perpendicular, are presently spoiled with the water, and filled up with the falling down of the ground that lies uppermost.

Moreover, these blind works ought to be made by sinking furrows three feet deep, which, after they are half-filled with stones and bare

(3) Λιμῷ δ᾽ οικ]ισω θανέων κỵ τότμοͷ ἐπισπῶͷ,

gravel, are made even, by throwing upon them the earth that you digged out of them ; but, if you have neither ftones nor gravel, you muft make, as it were, a rope of fprays tied together, of fuch a thicknefs, as the bottom of the narrow ditch may receive it when it is preffed together, and, as it were, exactly fitted to it. Then it muft be ftretched all along the bottom; and, after treading cyprefs or pine-boughs upon it, or, if thefe cannot be had, any other boughs, let it be covered with earth, having placed at the head and mouth of the ditch two great ftones only, inftead of pillars, and one fingle ftone above thefe, after the manner of little bridges, that this kind of ftructure may fupport the bank, that it may not be fhut up, and the water hindered either to run into it, or out of it.

There are two ways of managing tracts of land that are covered with wood, fhrubs, and bufhes, either by extirpating the trees by the very roots, and removing them ; or, if they be thin, by cutting them down, and fetting them on fire, and plowing up the ground. But it is eafy to clear ftony ground, by picking up the ftones ; and, if there be a great number of them, fome parts of the ground muft be taken up with building them into certain piles, that fo the other places may be clear of them ; or the ftones muft be buried in furrows dug very deep: which neverthelefs is only to be done, in cafe the low wages of the labourers engage you to do it.

The deftruction of bulrufhes and grafs is *trenching*; and of fern, frequently plucking them up by the roots, which may be done even with the plough; for, when they are often pulled up, within the fpace of two years they die, and the more fpeedily alfo, if, at the fame time, you dung, and fow with lupines or beans, that, with fome return and profit, you may cure the diftemper of the ground; for it is certain, that fern is the moft eafily killed by fowing and dunging: but, if you cut it with a weeding-hook, as it grows up from time to time, which is bufinefs for a very boy, its livelinefs is deftroyed within the forefaid time.

But now, after the method of clearing rough uncultivated land, follows the care of lands, that are newly broken up and cultivated; of which I fhall prefently declare my opinion, after I fhall have given fuch precepts and directions to fuch as defire to inform themfelves of the nature of corn-lands, as muft be firft learned.

I remember, that very many of the antients, who have written of Hufbandry, have declared, that the peculiar *fweetnefs* of the ground, the *abundance of herbs and trees, and the fruit*, they produced, and its *black or afhy colour*, were, as it were, acknowledged uncontefted and undoubted figns of land that was fat, and would bear corns in abundance. As to the reft, I am doubtful; but, as to the *colour*, I cannot enough admire, that both other writers, and also *Cornelius Celsus*, a man not only well acquainted with Husbandry, but also with universal nature, should have been so much mistaken, both in their judgment, and also in their eye-sight, that so many marshes, and so many fields also full of salt-pits, which, for the most part, are of the foresaid colours, did not occur to them: for we scarcely see a place, which is not either of a black or ashy colour, provided it contain any water that moves slowly; unless I myself perhaps am deceived in this, that I don't think, that exceeding good corn can grow or thrive well either in a marshy or slimy, or in a bitter and ousy soil, or in plains lying upon the sea-side, which are full of salt-pits. But this error of the antients is too manifest to want to be confuted by many arguments.

The colour therefore is no certain authority, nor sure evidence, of the goodness of arable lands; and therefore *corn-land*, that is, *rich fat land*, must rather be judged of by other qualities; for as the strongest cattle have different and almost innumerable colours, so also the strongest lands have a great number and variety of them. Therefore as we must take care, that the ground, which we mark out by its colour for cultivating, be fat, yet this is but of very little importance by itself, if it want sweetness; both which we may inform ourselves of in a manner expeditious enough: for you sprinkle a very little water upon a clod of it, and knead it with your hand; and if it be glutinous, and if, when pressed with the gentlest touch, it sticks to your fingers, and, as *Virgil* says (4),

   ' When handled, clammy grows, and sticks, like pitch,
   ' Fast to the fingers;'

And if, when the same is thrown against the ground, it does not crumble, and fall into small bits, this tells us, that, in such matter, there is a natural inherent juice and fatness; but also, if after having thrown the earth out of some trenches, you would replace and put it up very close, and tread it down again, when, with some kind of ferment, as it were, there is more than enough of it for filling up the trench, it will be a certain sign, that it is fat; and when there is not enough, but somewhat wanting, we may be sure, that it is poor and lean; and, when it exactly fills them, that it is middling: tho' these things I have now mentioned may possibly seem not to be so true signs, as if the earth were somewhat of a blackish colour, which is best tried and approved by the increase of the fruits it produces.

We shall also know it by its taste, if out of that part of the land, which displeases us most, there be clods dug, and soaked in an earthen vessel, and thoroughly mixed with sweet water, and carefully strained, in the manner of dreggy wine, and then carefully examined by the taste; for whatever taste the water shall have, which it has derived from the clods, such we shall say the ground has.

But, besides this experiment, there are many things, which may shew, that the earth is both sweet, and fit for corn, as *the rush, the reed, grass, the dwarf-elder, bramble-bushes, wild plum-trees,* and many other things, which are also known to them that search for water, and are not nourished but by the sweet veins of the earth. Nor must we be contented with the appearance of the surface of the earth, but carefully search to find out the quality of the matter that lies below, whether it be earthy, or not. But it will be sufficient for corns, if the ground below be equally good two feet deep. The depth of four feet is abundantly enough for trees.

AN
ACCOUNT
OF THE
SYSTEMS OF HUSBANDRY
ADOPTED IN THE MORE IMPROVED DISTRICTS
OF
29   ## SCOTLAND;

WITH

SOME OBSERVATIONS ON THE IMPROVEMENTS OF
WHICH THEY ARE SUSCEPTIBLE.

———

DRAWN UP FOR THE CONSIDERATION OF THE BOARD OF AGRICULTURE, WITH A
VIEW OF EXPLAINING HOW FAR THOSE SYSTEMS ARE APPLICABLE TO
THE LESS CULTIVATED PARTS IN ENGLAND, AND SCOTLAND.

———

BY THE RIGHT HONOURABLE
SIR JOHN SINCLAIR, BART.
PRESIDENT OF THE BOARD OF AGRICULTURE.

———

" Knowledge is power."   BACON.

———

EDINBURGH:
PRINTED FOR ARCH. CONSTABLE AND COMPANY, EDINBURGH;
G. & W. NICOL, BOOKSELLERS TO HIS MAJESTY, PALL-MALL, AND
LONGMAN, HURST, REES, ORME & BROWN, LONDON;
AND JOHN CUMMING, DUBLIN,

By Abernethy & Walker.

———

1812.

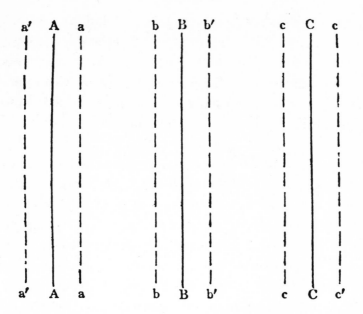

It is evident, in addition to every other consideration, that the breadth of ridges must also depend upon the mode of culture. Where the broad-cast system
is followed, the size must be calculated for enabling the
sower to scatter the seed, in the manner the most likely to yield a productive crop *. Whereas, when the drill
system is adopted, the breadth must be adjusted to the size
of the machine. In wet or tenacious soils, it is an excellent plan, to have the horses walking in the furrows of a
ridge, and drilling the whole at once.

The only other point that remains to be mentioned is,
the method of ploughing wet land, where the ridges have
been gathered high for the preceding crop. Some cross
the ridges, and open the old furrows afterwards, but that is
not so good a plan as cleaving the ridges, and opening the
old furrows, after going a round or two, which leaves the
old ridges divided in the middle. This method keeps the

* It is said, that a good sower will scatter the seed sufficiently
correct in ridges of any breadth; but they are not always to be
met with.

field equally dry, levels the land better, and gives an opportunity for crossing in the spring if necessary. But if the land is wet, it would not be advisable to risk cross ploughing, unless when the land is summer fallowed. I am informed, however, that few good farmers ever hazard the clearing of clay soil, except in the summer months.

3. *Straightness of ridge.*—It is extremely material to have the ridge as straight as possible. Mr Curwen justly remarks, that it is the very essence of good ploughing to hold the plough even, which it never can be, if it has to work in a curve. It is calculated that ridges, when much crooked, measure one-fifth more in the serpentine direction, than when taken in a straight line, and consequently they must take one-fifth more labour in ploughing, harrowing, &c. than if they had been perfectly straight. That does not imply that there is more land in the field. No form of ridges can alter the quantity within the same boundary ; but their form tends to impede the operations of the plough as much as that addition to the land. In ploughing such ridges, every farmer who has had a plough in his hand, knows how awkwardly the plough moves in them. In the convex side it constantly inclines to take too narrow a furrow, and in the concave side the reverse, owing to the direction of the draft being different from the direction of these sides.

In regard to crooked ridges, many ridges, in the best cultivated parts of Scotland, were formerly very broad, much raised, and greatly curved. Levelling such ridges, in very stiff wet clays, was a very difficult operation, and unless executed with considerable skill and judgment, productive of loss. It should never be attempted but in a year of fallow, and the straightened land should get a full dose of calcareous manure, and much cross ploughing, to mix the old and new staple, and to rouze the fertility of the new soil.

4. *Height.*—It is highly necessary that ridges, on wet land, should be well rounded, so as to form the segment of a circle. This is effected by gathering the soil once or twice, according to its dryness or wetness, in the course of ploughing the ridge. Indeed, Mr Rennie of Phantassie has often gathered the soil thrice, with much success, especially for a spring crop, as it not only lays the land dry through the winter, but enables the farmer to get sooner at it in the spring. The height, however, should not be too great, only sufficient to furnish a declivity to let off the water; for when the crown is raised too high, one half of the ridge is always covered from the sun, (a disadvantage which is far from being slight in a cold climate), and the crop, which is always best on the crown, is more easily shaken by the wind, than where the whole crop is of an equal height *. In arable culture, the more the equality of the soil, (which cannot happen where the ridges are high raised), the more equal will be the crop, and the more abundant will be the produce †.

5. *Line of direction.*—The last point regarding ridges, which it is necessary to consider, is, the line of direction, more especially in steep grounds. In such situations, it has been found a great advantage, both for the facility of ploughing and for draining, to plough diagonally from left to right: the furrow going up the hill, falls off from the plough, the horse has better footing, and less pull, and the furrow catches the running springs ‡. This is particularly to be attended to in the case of drilled turnips; for

---

* Gentleman Farmer, p. 74.

† Remark by Mr Charles Alexander, Easterhaprew. It is a great disadvantage, when ridges are too much rounded, that the sun cannot act equally upon the crop.

‡ Remarks by Mr Stewart of Hillside.

owing to the many furrows between the drills, when the turnips are eaten off by sheep, not only the soil, but their dung and urine, are carried off, which greatly augments the evil. Besides, where the field is steep, the dung for the turnips can be much easier carted on diagonal ridges *.

In regard to steep banks or declivities, there are four modes in which the ridges may be laid out.

1. *When they are planned on the same line or level, thus :*

This is done partly with a view of preventing the soil and manure from being washed down, and partly from the idea, that it is easier for the cattle to work it. But it keeps up the water in the furrows, and is an awkward mode of ploughing. Sometimes this sort of ridge is carried all round a small hill in a spiral form, beginning at the bottom.

2. *When the ridges are straight up and down.*

This is a very improper mode. The soil and manure are both apt to be washed down, and when the plough is going up, the earth makes such a resistance, that it is extremely difficult for the cattle to cleave the ground without the utmost exertions.

3. *From the top of the bank sloping to the left.*

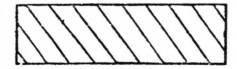

* Remark by Mr Charles Alexander.

This mode also does not answer, for when the plough is going up, the ploughman is obliged to force the earth against the bank, which makes but very indifferent work; and it cannot be done without injury to the cattle.

4. *From the top of the bank sloping to the right.*

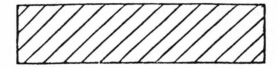

This is the proper plan to be adopted, for when the ridges are laid in this manner, the ground always falls from the plough, as it goes upwards, without any great exertions on the part either of the ploughman or cattle. The ground is not forced against the bank, until the plough is coming down, and then it is done with so much more ease, that one-third less strength of cattle will plough an equal quantity of land.

Some farmers, however, when a field is very steep, plough only down hill, the plough being drawn up hill empty. By this method the horses travel up hill in less than half the time they could go with a furrow, and by being quite fresh at the top, they come down with spirit; and by giving the direction a little to the left in going down, the furrow falls away from the plough freely, every inch of the soil is perfectly raised, and lies so close together, that lying in that state for one year in some soils, and in others for two years, the sod rots, and being all laid one way, cuts easily by the plough; whereas, when attempting to plough against hill, the ploughing is not half done, grows up in grass, and, when cross ploughed, makes a bad appearance. The fighting against the hill also, hurts a horse, in one day, more than three days' ploughing in the way pointed out. Only one-fourth of the time is lost, but that is doubly repaid, by getting the work properly done, and the advantage in the after ploughing. Mr

Blackie of Holydean in Roxburghshire, who makes this remark, states, that he has cultivated a great deal of ground on this principle, and that he is never afraid of any land, however steep, if there is soil enough ; *and that by this mode land may be ploughed, which would otherwise be impracticable.* In similar situations other judicious husbandmen prefer ploughing in diagonal ridges, so constructed as to admit of ploughing up hill without material injury to the horses ; and in this way the furrows are much less apt to be run away or sanded by heavy rains. Where the land is excessively steep, it is often necessary to plough directly across, throwing the plits or furrow slices all down hill ; and, with the ordinary plough, going back empty. But where there is much land of this excessive steepness to cultivate, a plough with a shifting mould-board, usually called a *turn-wrest* plough, admits of ploughing both backwards and forwards, shifting the mould-board in such a manner as always to throw the furrow-slice down hill. These two last methods have been suggested by Mr Kerr of Ayton, in his Berwickshire Report, who has seen both practised, and executed the latter himself *.

Another rule regarding this point is, to direct the ridges north and south, if the ground will permit. In this direction, the east and west sides of a ridge divide the sun equally between them, and will ripen at the same time †. In clay soils, however, ridges must be regulated by the run of the water, so that no rule can be applicable to that particular case.

---

* The Turn-wrest Plough, with a shifting mould-board, is certainly adapted to ploughing across the slope of hills, as it enables the farmer to turn the furrow always downwards. It is, however, attended with this disadvantage, that it brings, lower and lower, the staple of the soil.

† Gentleman Farmer, p. 79.

The articles by Hall, Sorsby, and Nickols provide a combined historical approach and a status summary of the soil conservational art used in the eastern United States prior to 1900. It would also be of interest to indicate even much earlier use of landscape skills during prehistory agriculture in the New World. Cook (1916) shows how the Incas built banks of 20 to 30 terraces in many places, and even occasionally as many as 50 in order to conserve land and water, and develop an agrarian culture. He reports a special case of transporting earth 700 miles for the gardens at Cuzco. The Incas also straightened river banks and stream beds, and had 12-ft deep aqueducts that carried waters more than 300 miles.

At least as early as revolutionary times, several patriots were very concerned about soil erosion and its prevention, including Patrick Henry, who remarked, "He is the greatest patriot, who stops the most gullies." The following samples of letters by George Washington also illustrate his interest:

> My favorite objects, as I have often repeated to you, are to recover my land from the gullied and exhausted state into which it has been unfortunately thrown from some years back. (letter to William Pearce, July 13, 1794 in Fitzpatrick, 1940, v. 33, p. 430)

And of how to accomplish this he wrote:

> I am glad to find you are engaged in so useful, and desirable a work as that of filling up gullies in the fields . . . (letter to William Pearce, January 25, 1795 in Fitzpatrick, 1940, v. 34, p. 104)

> [in preventing gullies] drive in stakes to catch and retain the trash that is swept down with the torrent. They also serve to break the force of the water . . . (letter to William Pearce June 21, 1795, in Fitzpatrick, 1940, v. 34, pp. 217–218)

Such matters were even on Washington's mind four days before his death when he wrote:

> The washed and gullied parts . . . ought to be levelled and smoothed . . . covered with litter, straw, weeds, corn stalks, or any other kind of vegetable rubbish, to bind together, and to prevent the earth from gullying. (Lord, 1938, p. 30)

Additional writings occur in Brooke (1919).

It is interesting to compare Sinclair's work, who was still suggesting diagonal slope cultivation, with some of Jefferson's letters and early practices in America, which were among the first in horizontal (contour-farming) methods. Introduction of the horizontal method in America is attributed to T. M. Randolph, who was Jefferson's son-in-law. Letters by Jefferson as reported in Lord, 1938, p. 31, state:

> Mr. Randolph's farm was the only one which has not suffered [from a devastating rain], as horizontal furrows arrested the water at every step

until it was absorbed ... Everybody in this neighborhood is adopting his method of ploughing, except tenants who have no interest in the preservation of the soil. (from 1810 letter)

[the horizontal furrow method] has already become very general, and has entirely changed and renovated the face of our country. Every rain, before that, while it gave temporary refreshment, did permanent evil by carrying off our soil and fields were no sooner cleared than washed. At present we ... lose none of our soil, the rain not absorbed at the moment of its fall being retained in the hollows between the beds until it can be absorbed. (from 1817 letter)

Hall's article provides a generalized approach to the problem of soil erosion, men who were aware of it, and methods and recommendations for its solution. Sorsby provides details on construction techniques for horizontal plowing and indicates the importance of hillside ditching. He is so ecstatic about the methods that he feels their discoverer deserves "a place upon the tablet of memory next to that of the father of our country."

The book by Nickols is written in a rather chatty and informal style by a farmer scientist who has observed various methods of hillside ditching, and has experimented and discovered an improved technique. This rather obscure publication contains information that was adopted by later conservationists, such as deep plowing. This is one of the few contemporary books written on the theme of erosion and methods for its prevention.

United States Department of Agriculture, 1937, Miscellaneous Publication No. 256, 31 pp.

30

EARLY EROSION-CONTROL PRACTICES IN VIRGINIA

By A. R. HALL, *assistant soil conservationist, Division of Climatic and Physiographic Research, Soil Conservation Service*

CONTENTS

FOREWORD

During recent years, for the first time in American history, various governmental agencies have given serious and concentrated attention to the problem of culturally induced erosion. For this reason it is commonly assumed that the problem is a new one. Mr. Hall's study reveals that, on the contrary, American farmers individually have been fighting soil erosion for at least a century and a half.

It is probable that the Virginia planters were troubled with soil wastage as soon as they began to till lands with any considerable degree of slope. By the end of the eighteenth century culturally induced erosion had made great inroads into the agricultural resources of the State, and attempts to control it were beginning to be made. Most of the erosion-control practices in use at the present time, such as the use of legumes and grasses, deep plowing, contour plowing, and hillside ditching, the prototype of modern terracing, were either developed by the Virginia farmers or became known to them during the first half of the nineteenth century.

If these various practices have been known for so long a time, why is it that they have not been more effective in promoting soil conservation? The answer to this question is found in the lack of agricultural organization of this earlier period. Farming was then the most highly individualistic of enterprises. Coordinated effort in agricultural research was in its embryonic form, and its representatives were the several voluntary county and State agricultural societies. Among the documents of the Virginia legislature for the period of the 1830's and 1840's are a number of petitions from these societies for governmental aid to farmers. As early as 1803 Thomas Jefferson recommended the introduction of agricultural education, and when plans were drawn up for the curriculum of the University of Virginia he urged the establishing of a chair of agriculture. However, no effective assistance was given to the farmers, and plans for the teach-

399

1

ing of agriculture at the University of Virginia were not approved by the State legislature. Each farmer was left to his own resources and conducted his own experiments in erosion control. Others might advise, but he alone was responsible for his methods and the judge of his results. Such attempts to prevent or control erosion as were made were often haphazard or superficial. Contour plowing, hillside ditching, or proper crop rotation might be given a hasty trial and discarded, not because they were inherently defective, but because the experimentation necessary to perfect the technique had not been performed, or merely because of prejudice in favor of the old methods. Many were unconcerned about soil wastage because of the relative abundance of land. Thus the community was either indifferent or divided in opinion as to the best soil-conservation practices.

Little headway could be made against erosion under these conditions. Soil wastage has accordingly proceeded until the problem has reached a crisis. The State agricultural experiment stations and the Federal Department of Agriculture began to study erosion about the beginning of the present century. The work of these different agencies has now been brought together and expanded by the Soil Conservation Service, in cooperation with landowners and operators. A coordinated and unified defense against culturally induced erosion, an ideal never realized by the early agricultural societies of Virginia and other States, is now possible of achievement. No longer is the vital question of erosion left to be solved by the sporadic efforts of scattered individual farmers.

H. H. BENNETT.

THE EROSION PROBLEM AND ITS RECOGNITION IN COLONIAL AND EARLY NATIONAL TIMES

Patrick Henry is said to have remarked on one occasion soon after the Revolution that " 'since the achievement of our independence, he is the greatest patriot, who *stops the most gullies*' " (*66, p. 586*).[1] The statement was indicative at once of the existence of a serious erosion problem by that date and of its recognition by farmers and statesmen. Abundant agricultural land in proportion to a sparse population, a type of farming based on one staple crop, and a theory of commerce that subordinated the needs of the colony to the desires of the mother country all combined to bring about a "mining" of Virginia's soil in the colonial period

Tobacco, the great staple of commerce, and Indian corn, the great feed crop, were both clean-tilled crops. In both tobacco and corn cultivation the soil was hilled up about the plants with the hoe, or for the latter crop stirred superficially with the light, one-horse shovel plow. In either case the tillage left the soil in a condition susceptible to washing by the heavy summer rains. Virgin lands just cleared of the forest were planted to tobacco for 3, 4, or 5 years until they would no longer yield a profitable crop. They were then either abandoned at once or planted to corn for a number of years until that crop would no longer pay for the labor devoted to it. After this ruinous course the lands were abandoned to broomsedge,

---

[1] Italic numbers in parentheses refer to Literature Cited, p. 27.

thickets, and gullies. In the meantime new lands were being cleared only to be subjected to the same exploitation. By the process of clearing and abandonment, this destructive tobacco economy marched through Tidewater Virginia and most of the Piedmont during the century and a half of the colonial period.

Although soil exhaustion came to be regarded as normal by Virginians, complaints against it were not lacking. Some substitute for tobacco as a staple crop was constantly being sought. Toward the end of the eighteenth century many sections of the State where virgin tobacco land was growing scarce or where the soil was unsuitable for tobacco found this substitute in wheat. Although it was less exacting in its soil requirements than tobacco, the Virginia farmers were just as injudicious in its cultivation. Lands were cropped in wheat and other small grains or wheat and corn continuously until they were considered completely worn out (*43, v. 1, pp. 445–446; 49, p. 108; 73; 51. v. 3, p. 142*).

It is more than likely that the soil exhaustion complained of by Virginians from the earliest times was due as much to erosion as to other factors. The planters who early settled along the James River had occasion to complain of the destructive freshets of that stream. In 1685 the first William Byrd described one such deluge that carried away the tobacco hills "with all the top of the manured land." Concerning a flood in 1771 another observer (*61*) wrote:

* * * Worst of all is the Loss of Land—in many places on the low grounds the soil is entirely gone—all the Fences, together with the Tob'o that was planted thereon * * * Mr. Walter King of Bristol has lost in soil only at least nine thousand pounds.

Throughout the latter part of the eighteenth and the beginning of the nineteenth centuries there were increasing comments on the destructive effects of erosion. As early as 1769 George Washington was conducting experiments at Mount Vernon to determine "whether the land was not preserved more by harrowing than by lying in furrows" (*35, v. 1, p. 347*). Nevertheless the Father of his Country continued to be troubled by soil washing during the remainder of his career as a planter. Referring to the Mount Vernon estate a quarter of a century later, he wrote (*22, p. 83*):

The soil of the tract * * * is a good loam, more inclined however to clay than sand. From use, and I might add, abuse, it is become more and more consolidated, and of course heavier to work. * * * A husbandman's wish would not lay the farms more level than they are; and yet some of the fields, but in no great degree, are washed into gullies, from which all of them have not as yet been recovered.

This letter was written for the purpose of attracting English tenants to his land. The measure of his discouragement with farming may be judged by his writing thus in a sales letter! In fact, much of the land of Fairfax County was a drug on the market during the last decade of the eighteenth century because of its gullied condition (*7*).

Richard Parkinson, an Englishman who traveled through the seaboard section of Virginia about this time, noticed other gullied and washed lands on the Potomac in the vicinity of Mount Vernon. This phenomenon of soil wastage was quite novel to Parkinson. He noted that it was caused by the frosts of winter followed by the hasty showers or "gusts" of summer, and that the land was often cut into gullies 10 feet wide and 10 feet deep, or was eroded into the form of a hole having the appearance of a stone quarry. This stranger to American agricultural requirements had some disheartening experiences with erosion on a farm that he purchased near Baltimore. He found that the land in tillage could not be pulverized. On land treated in this way (*70, v. 1, p. 45; v. 2, pp. 481–482, 489, 493–494*) :

* * * the whole of the soil [moved], for an acre together, when a heavy rain fell, from the current in some places cutting gullies, and carrying part of the manure away; and the soil seemed to press in or slip after it.

The Tidewater areas were faced not only with the problem of washing on the uplands and flooding in the stream valleys, but also with that of silting in the stream channels themselves. Very little was done in the way of draining or improving the lowlands. Instead, the uplands were farmed in such a way that the productive silt was washed downhill, thus ruining both uplands and lowlands. John Taylor of Caroline County, an acute observer of things agricultural as well as things political, writing in 1813, deplored this condition (*84, p. 246*). He said that few of the channels of the seaboard streams retained any appearance of their natural state, "being everywhere obstructed by sands, bogs, bushes, and rubbish, so as to form innumerable putrid puddles, pools, and bogs upon the occurrence of every drought * * *." Taylor (*84, pp. 172–173*) saw clearly that there was more than one reason for viewing the erosion problem with alarm.

The disaster is not terminated by the destruction of the soil, the impoverishment of individuals, and the transmission of a curse to futurity.—Navigation itself is becoming its victim, and in many parts of the United States, our Agriculture has arrived to the insurpassable state of imperfection, of applying its best soil to the removal of the worst farther from market.

As the farmers of Virginia advanced from the Tidewater into the more rolling land of the Piedmont they made few agricultural adaptations to the different environment. Corn continued to be "cross plowed" regardless of the situation of the field, one furrow being conducted up and down the slope for every one that crossed it (*24, p. 11*). The results were not long in becoming apparent. An English officer held captive at Charlottesville and Richmond during the Revolution noted in 1779 that soil washing in the lands of the upper Piedmont caused the James River to look like a "torrent of blood" in times of high water (*17, v. 2, p. 360*).

We may infer that by 1790 the process similar to that by which Cecil sandy loam has been converted into Cecil clay loam over large areas was largely completed in Amelia County. Such an interpretation might be placed upon the remarks of Meriwether (*57, pp. 35–37*), who said that the gray surface soil of much of that county had been swept away, leaving the subsoil of hard, tenacious, red clay exposed.

The inroads of erosion in the region adjacent to the Blue Ridge notably on soils of the Davidson series (the "red lands"), was especially disquieting to those early Virginians, because this region had the reputation of being one of the richest agricultural areas in the State. William Strickland, an Englishman sent over to examine the agriculture of the United States, had this to report of the area in 1796 (*83, p. 205*) :

A richer district by nature there cannot be, than all those counties which lie at the eastern foot of the Blue Ridge; but, like whatever on this continent has been long cultivated they are nearly exhausted.

Years later those remarks were confirmed by Craven (*29*) of Albemarle County. He wrote that in 1799, when he first came there, the "red lands" were worn out, washed, and gullied, and presented an impression of nakedness.

In 1817 Thomas Jefferson,[2] of the same county, commented that "fields were no sooner cleared than washed" (*36, v. 12, p. 56*). Madison (*55*) declared 2 years later that without the use of soil-saving methods of cultivation, the ownership of "red lands" was little more than a lease for years. Nevertheless, farmers of the lower Piedmont could also make the same complaint. That voiced by one (*89*) from Prince Edward County in 1838 is less striking but more specific than Madison's. He estimated that the destruction by washing had been so general that very little hilly land cleared for more than 20 or 30 years was of any value.

There was some difference of opinion as to which crop, if any particular one, was most destructive of soil resources. Corn, tobacco, and even wheat, each received a share of the blame for soil wash, but the first named was usually declared the major villian. Washington, Jefferson,[2] and others complained of the "ravages" of corn on the soil. To be sure, tobacco was very exacting in its chemical requirements, but it was generally planted in small patches, whereas cornfields took up a larger part of the area of the farm. Tobacco was often "manured" with decaying leaves and trash, whereas corn was plowed frequently and the ground left bare (*72*). Perhaps the practice in Halifax County in the 1830's was typical of the entire tobacco region in the early nineteenth century. No land except that intended for tobacco was manured because of the danger that rains would wash the manure away. A small, level place free from erosion was accordingly selected to be planted to tobacco year after year, while the unmanured crops were left to the more exposed hillsides (*23*). Thus, the nature of the crop practice prevented tobacco from wreaking the destruction attributed to corn. The opinion was widely held that tobacco was harmful principally because it took most of the farmer's attention, leaving little time for the improvement or preservation of land in other crops. At any rate it was believed that land in tobacco rarely showed signs of washing, one author holding that the "vegetable mold" or topsoil of the tobacco patch disappeared more by a process of evaporation than in any other way (*41*).

It was an easy and popular attitude that blamed the principal crops for the soil wastage, but there were at least two writers who declared that the farmers and planters themselves were not entirely guiltless. One of these was John Taylor. The other was Thomas Moore, of Maryland. Moore (*60*) was among the first to take a comprehensive view of culturally induced erosion and its causes in the South. His voice was raised in warning against the insidious process of sheet wash that was depriving the farmers of the cream of their soil. Freshly cleared lands did not lose much soil the first year, he said, since the undecayed vegetable matter held it in place; but because of the prevailing practice of shallow plowing, rolling lands were usually attacked by erosion the second year. The plowing

---

[2] Thomas Jefferson to T. M. Randolph, Philadelphia, Aug. 11, 1793; George Washington to Thomas Jefferson, Mount Vernon, Oct. 4, 1795; Thomas Jefferson Papers, Library of Congress.

referred to did not extend to a depth greater than 4 inches and did not afford sufficient loose earth to absorb the water. Each successive plowing brought up fresh mold to be swept off in its turn, according to Moore, the result being that throughout the hilly country of the Southern States the surface of the soil was then (1801) the whole depth of plowing lower than when the land had been first cleared. The proofs cited for this assertion were the half-buried posts in low places and the silting taking place in creeks, millponds, and the heads of rivers.

Thus the land becomes sterile not so much from the vegetable nutriment being extracted from the soil by the growth of plants, as by the soil itself being removed; that this is a necessary consequence of *shallow ploughing*, on lands that are in any degree hilly, in this climate, I trust, has been satisfactorily proved. * * * what further proofs need we, to convince us that the practice of agriculture, particularly in the southern states, is miserably defective, than the deserted old fields that so frequently present their disgusting surfaces from Susquehanna to Georgia? Some years ago, I was of opinion that this speedy reduction of soil, was althogether occasioned by the nature of the crops cultivated thereon; but, on attending more accurately to the subject, I am of a different opinion, and believe * * * it is more from the manner of cultivation than from the exhausting properties of the crops * * * (*60, pp. 13–16, 27–28*).

Enough has been said to show that the erosion problem was present in colonial times and that by the beginning of the nineteenth century it had become a matter of considerable concern to some agricultural writers. The erosion problem in itself would perhaps not have caused so much perturbation, had it not been for the prolonged agricultural depression of the close of the eighteenth and the beginning of the nineteenth centuries. The increasing scarcity of virgin tobacco lands, the declining yields from the old areas, the low price of tobacco, and the highly unstable character of the wheat market forced the Virginia farmer to make readjustments. He could either abandon his tired and worn fields for fresh lands in the West, or he could begin a course of improved and more intensive farming on these same old fields.

Far too many agriculturists chose the former course. The existence of the vast unoccupied West thus acted as a deterrent to any improvement at home. "* * * the scratching farmer's cares and anxieties are only relieved by his land soon washing away. As that goes down the rivers he goes over the mountains" (*1. p. 25*).

Nevertheless, certain forward-looking members of the agricultural community initiated a reform movement in agriculture. This movement stressed proper crop rotations, the use of animal, vegetable, and mineral fertilizers, and the prevention and control of erosion. Farmers of liberal education who operated on a rather large scale were the principal leaders in this movement (*28*). They were the moving spirits in the agricultural societies, as they were the founders and supporters of the agricultural press. It is their records which the modern agricultural historian must consult, for the great body of small farmers did not write of their operations. To a very great extent the latter group seems to have been content to continue in the old way of doing things, professing a great contempt for the "book farmers." No doubt it was also true that soil wastage was especially bad on the smaller holdings, since the larger estates had a greater

112157—37——2

amount of uncleared land or other surplus ground reserved for future exploitation (*25, p. 147–148*). If the resources of a large estate were wasted the improvident management of the overseer was generally blamed.

On the other hand, one must not get the impression that all the great landholders were bearers of the light while all the small farmers and the overseer class were content to remain in darkness. The small Quaker farmers of Loudoun County gained the reputation of being among the best agriculturists of the State. Nor could overseers be blamed if absentee or amateur owners demanded large immediate returns regardless of the ultimate results to the land.[3]

Stated generally, the problem of renovation was to restore productivity to old worn-out and eroded fields and to maintain productivity on these fields. The problem of restoring gullied surfaces had been brought to the public attention at least as early as 1788 in Pennsylvania. In that year the Philadelphia Society for Promoting Agriculture published a list of prize awards, one item being the following (*91, v. 3, p. 269*):

For the best method, within the power of common farmers, of recovering old gullied fields to a hearty state, and such uniformity or evenness of surface as will again render them fit for tillage; or, where the gullies are so deep and numerous as to render such recovery impracticable, for the best method of improving them, by planting trees or otherwise, so as to yield the improver a reasonable profit for his expenses therein, founded on experiment, a gold medal; and for the next best a silver medal. To be produced by the 1st of January, 1790.

Similar to this was the questionnaire published by the Richmond Agricultural Society (*76*) in 1811 asking for information on these subjects:

1st. The best mode of restoring worn out land, filling gullies, and bringing it in order for the plough.
2nd. The best rotation of crops in which Indian corn, wheat and clover are included. * * *
3rd. Do. In which tobacco, wheat and clover are included. * * *
7th. The best mode of preventing lands under the plough from washing.
* * *
9th. The best method practicable on a large scale, of bringing exhausted lands into a condition to bring clover.

There were 84 questions in this list. That the problems of restoring worn-out and gullied fields and of preventing other cultivated fields from washing further should occupy first places on this list indicates their importance in the minds of these Virginia farmers. Forward-looking members of the agricultural community attacked this problem with intelligence and ingenuity, with the result that many devices for the prevention and control of erosion were worked out. Some of these devices had their American beginnings in Virginia. The State became a great laboratory in which many different methods of restoring washed lands were tested. Many workers then discovered facts that the erosion experiment stations, by more careful methods, are rediscovering today. The remainder of this publication deals with the various techniques developed at this early time.

---

[3] See, for instance, correspondence between plantation owners of Amherst County and their overseers, Ambler deposit of mss. University of Virginia Library, 1823–24.

ELIMINATION OF GULLIES AND GALLS

If crops were again to be raised on fields where broomsedge had taken the place of corn, and gullies had replaced furrows, some means must be found to restore the land so that washing would not be resumed. With progressive farmers and planters this was an important desideratum. George Washington informed his overseer in 1795 that immediate profit was not so much an object as the bringing of worn-out and gullied fields into a condition to bear grass (*27, p. 158*). Much of the land at Mount Vernon would not yield grass "kindly",[4] but the General did not wait for grass to take a field without aiding the process of recovery in other ways. When fields became broken and washed they were retired from cultivation, smoothed with the harrow, covered with straw, weeds, or other "vegetable rubbish" to prevent further gullying, and left to resume the process of natural recovery (*22, p. 109*).

In the filling of gullies the great difficulty was to hold the material in place and to prevent further washing. Gully dams of various types were tried. Some were of stone, some of woven limbs or wattle, and some of transverse logs. Such contrivances, unaided, were open to the criticism that water, in falling over them, cut the earth below, and so accelerated the gullying. Some farmers seem to have regarded stone dams as especially open to this objection (*64*). Wheat straw, brush, and small dead trees might also be placed behind the dams in the larger gullies or used alone when the gullies were of smaller dimensions. Evergreens, still having the needles on the limbs, placed with the branches pointing up the gully, were recommended for this purpose. Care was taken not to destroy or break with the plow any grass which might begin growth in the gully.

Farmers not content to wait for the slow natural process of gully healing could speed the work by partially filling small gullies with dirt, rubbish, or ashes. An effective way of accomplishing this was to plow the sides parallel to the gully and throw the dirt inward. The method adopted by one enterprising farmer was perhaps typical of many others. He hauled dirt from fence ways, turning rows, and other vacant places to fill his small gullies and other barren spots (*11, 26, 56, 69*).

The term "gall" or "gald" has long been applied to barren, unproductive spots from which the topsoil has been washed. Plowing and harrowing were often not enough to restore these spots to productivity. Thick coatings of straw or leaves were frequently left to rot on the galls and then plowed in to aid in producing a new tillable soil on the barren area. Edmund Ruffin, the advocate of lime as a cure-all for the agricultural ills of eastern Virginia, admitted that lime alone would have little effect on the "acid hilly land" of that section, for good done would diminish in proportion to the amount of soil previously removed. To restore fertility to galled spots, he (*77, p. 53*) recommended a combination of lime with putrescent manure. This, he said, would aid soil to form on such spots from vegetation brought in by the wind.

---

[4] George Washington to Thomas Jefferson, Mount Vernon, July 6, 1796. Thomas Jefferson Papers, Library of Congress.

The most conspicuous culturally induced erosion features of the Piedmont area are the gullies caused by old roads. The sites of many of these are now marked by ravines completely covered and healed over by matured forest growth.

Gullying, both on public and on farm roads, was a source of trouble at all times. To combat it Meriwether (*57, pp. 19–20*), of Amelia County, devised a pair of cart wheels with 10-inch treads to be used for hauling crops out of the field, carting manure, and performing similar tasks. Two narrow-wheeled carts and a wagon were also used, but the broad-wheeled cart always followed the others to level their tracks. Meriwether began using these wheels about 1798 and not only succeeded in preventing gullying in roads but smoothed over several roads that had previously been gullied.

At a later date, when interest in public roads had become more widespread, some attempt was made to prevent the wearing away of these thoroughfares. Brush was sometimes placed in the ditches on either side of the road but it was found that this might result in the gullying of the road itself, until it was lower than the ditches. This difficulty prompted the novel suggestion that a hillside road cut should be allowed to wash deeper and deeper until the road on the hill was level with the road in the valley (*16*). Roads were thus to be allowed to grade themselves.

THE USE OF GRASSES AS SOIL BINDERS

Eighteenth century Virginia husbandmen, in common with those of England, believed that it was undesirable to leave the ground exposed to the rays of the sun. Those who attempted to improve their land used various legumes, grasses, and clovers primarily as shade crops. Those crops were also esteemed because they were thought to draw "atmospheric manure" into the soil and because their roots and straw prevented the soil from washing.

John Taylor incorporated the idea of grasses as soil binders and improvers into his famous system of agriculture. Others had deplored the damage done by clean-tilled crops such as corn, but Taylor was the first to work out a constructive plan to ameliorate the evils. He advocated a rotation of crops to consist of corn, wheat, and 2½ years of rest, or "enclosure", on any one field. While the field was enclosed it was not, in Taylor's mind, lying idle, for it was to be allowed to grow up to white clover and other volunteer perennials. When plowed under, the fibers of these plants would create "covered drains" and prevent washing while the land was in corn.[5] Later he came to regard meadow oat as the best grass to prevent erosion (*85*).

Clover and redtop, or as it was often called in Virginia, herds grass, were the two most popular soil-preserving crops of ante-bellum Virginia. Taylor considered that the clovers were more satisfactory in the section just east of the Blue Ridge than in the exhausted lands of the lower country. White clover the farmers already had at hand. It was the first plant to cover a newly abandoned field, although it was succeeded the second year by sassafras and brier bushes (*83, p. 263*). Red clover was apparently introduced from Pennsylvania and was first used by the Quaker farmers

---

[5] John Taylor to Thomas Jefferson, Caroline, Mar. 5, 1795. Jefferson Papers, Library of Congress.

of Loudoun County. Israel Janney and John A. Binns started raising
it with the aid of gypsum as a fertilizer in the late 1780's (*25, p. 164*).
By the 1830's the use of these twin improvers, red clover and gypsum,
had spread throughout the upper Piedmont counties of Fauquier,
Orange, Albermarle, Nelson, and Amherst. By their aid and by the
practice of deeper plowing much was done in the way of restoring
fertility, smoothing over old washed fields, and preventing the formation of new gullies (*56*). Gypsum was thought of not only as a
fertilizer for the clover but was itself considered as an agent for
preventing the soil from washing. Thomas Moore believed that
its effect was to a certain extent the same as that of deep plowing
in that it opened the soil to a sufficient depth to permit the absorption
of heavy rains.

Jefferson placed great hopes in clover. In order to reduce the
acreage devoted to corn he tried substituting potatoes, red clover, and
sheep for corn and hogs. He found that this could not be done in
any economy in which corn meal and pork were the principal items
in the diet of the laborers. Nevertheless, clover sown with gypsum
remained an important part of the rotation on the Jefferson estates
after 1794 (*52, v. 18, pp. 187–200*).

A system of rotation akin to that of Taylor's was developed in
the upper Piedmont area. It consisted of corn the first year, wheat
the second, and red clover the third and fourth. Probably here, as
in Halifax and Mecklenburg Counties, tobacco was reserved for one
particular spot on the farm, but it was recognized that a rotation
on tobacco lots was a desirable type of management. A system of
rotation recommended by one writer for Nelson and Amherst Counties in 1837 consisted of tobacco the first year, wheat the second,
and clover for 2 years thereafter. This, together with various mechanical devices for conserving the soil, was believed necessary if
tobacco was to continue as a staple commodity of that section. The
forested land could no longer be relied upon to furnish virgin
tobacco soil for even then, in many instances, the wood lots were too
small for the support of the farm (*10*). However, this farmer may
have taken too pessimistic an attitude, for others believed that the
old fields cleared of their second growth of pine, if given a judicious
rotation, produced the finest quality of tobacco (*56*).

Redtop was another crop introduced from Pennsylvania. Senator
Abraham Venable, of Prince Edward County, is said to have sent a
parcel of seed to Virginia from Philadelphia while the Federal Government was located there. In the Piedmont it could be used on
highlands too badly exhausted for clover (*92*); it was believed that
redtop prepared the ground intended for tobacco better than did
clover (*53*); as a soil binder it was also found superior, since its roots
gave the land a stronger turf and it would continue to thrive for a
longer period (*63*).

Other grasses were used or recommended as the particular "pets"
of certain farmers. Orchard grass was found to do well near Beaver-
dam, Hanover County, but was not to be recommended for the "red
lands" or the light sandy soils of lower Virginia (*71*). In Prince
Edward County it was observed that the spontaneous growth of
crabgrass did much to retard the destruction of land brought about
by shallow plowing. The principal draw-back to the use of this
as well as other grasses native to the section was that they were

annuals. Hence, it was necessary to raise the introduced perennials (*89, p. 754*). For the sandy rolling lands of eastern Virginia one correspondent (*12*) of the Southern Planter recommended the wire grass (Bermuda) as a soil binder, remarking that "Virginia farmers can kill every thing else with which dame nature has furnished them, except mules and wire grass * * *."

LAND RETIREMENT

In 1834 the complaint was made that the tendency to till as many fields as the planter's labor supply would permit, regardless of the fertility of those lands, had resulted in much unprofitable farming, especially in the hilly lands. Why should uplands be manured when the first rain might sweep both soil and manure away (*65*)? To cultivate more of the bottom lands and allow the hillsides to rest, then, was the object of many. In the 1820's Minor, of the Albemarle Agricultural Society, conducted some experiments in manuring corn with a view to establishing permanent manured cornfields on the flats so the hillsides could be relieved of this exhausting crop (*57, pp. 44–45; 58*). It seems that the practice of limiting corn to the lowlands was carried out by other farmers as well (*14*). One farmer (*72*) of Wardsfork, Charlotte County, advocated the planting of hillsides in grass, orchards, or wheat and reserving the valleys for the cultivated crops.

What was to be done with the hillsides retired from cultivation? The history of agriculture shows that a succession of lands have been retired from cultivation in Virginia—not for the purpose of preventing washing, indeed, but simply because they were already too badly gullied or otherwise exhausted to bear more crops. However, there were those who advocated a deliberate policy of turning out fields that were too steep for profitable cultivation that they might reclothe themselves with forest growth by the natural process of plant succession (*19*). Such a policy of permanent retirement had its strict limitations, at best, for farming must continue to be profitable.

The use of this land for pasture naturally suggested itself, but doubts were entertained that this would be a better way to preserve the soil than was cropping. One writer believed that the hoofs and teeth of cattle were second only to the washing rains as destroyers of land (*66*). Taylor had emphasized the point that livestock should be kept out of the enclosed fields that were resting under a grass cover. Nevertheless, he would have had the farmers maintain permanent pastures, to provide for fertilizing the cultivated fields. Some agricultural writers, on the other hand, advocated that farmers should reduce their number of livestock and depend upon artificial fertilizers and grasses to restore their land (*21*). Perhaps part of the distrust of livestock was due to the traditional colonial habit of keeping only a small number of cattle.

As time went on an important school of opinion grew up, holding that properly conducted grazing was the best use for grass crops. In 1847 a writer declared that low stream bottoms and steep hillsides should be kept in perpetual grass to prevent the soil from washing away and that these situations should be used only for pasture. The pastures should be periodically restored by the application of gypsum, ashes, salt, lime, or crushed bone to return to them the substances taken away by the animals and the washing rains (*13*).

The advantages of pasturage were eloquently set forth in a speech of Morton (*63, p. 131*) before the agricultural club of Mecklenburg County in 1843:

> Is there not something humiliating in having our eyes, whenever we ride or walk into our fields, greeted with the yawning gall, or the more hideous gully? Or meeting by the wayside, the kine of Pharaoh, who, having devoured all the miserable trash and weeds, which mar the beauty of our fields, are themselves, just about to be devoured by the buzzards? How do these scenes contrast with the verdant grass springing up in all its vigor and luxuriance, and clothing our fields in its beautiful habiliments; with the cattle of a thousand hills grazing bountifully through the day, and returning home at eve laden with deposits, richer than those of the *mammoth bank*, and laying their grateful tribute at the master's feet, and causing his table to groan under the teeming abundance of milk, butter, cheese, and beef?

INTERPLANTING

Various ways of leaving parts of the field in grass while the remainder was cultivated were tried out, but they do not seem to have been successful. In 1814 a certain James Hall secured a patent for a method of planting corn in an unplowed field. He marked off the land in squares, each square being of certain dimensions and a certain distance from its neighbors and containing a given number of cornstalks. Only these squares were cultivated, manured, and mulched, the rest of the field being allowed to remain in grass. A number of Albemarle County farmers found this method a complete failure because of the inability of the corn to withstand dry weather. Jefferson's was the only experiment that approached success, but even his corn suffered from drought.[6] Some farmers left a strip of turf unplowed between the corn rows, throwing the dirt to the row by the operation of listing the corn in cultivating it. This was done not only to prevent washing but also to lessen the danger from cutworm, since it was believed that the insects would eat the grass and to a certain extent spare the young corn. However, this practice was frowned on by others as being a slovenly method of cultivation and as being open to the same objection as was Hall's method (*20, 65*). Washington and Jefferson adopted the practice of alternating rows of potatoes or some other vegetable with rows of corn (*35, v. 3, pp. 187, 377–378*).[7]

METHODS OF PLOWING AND CULTIVATING

Progressive farmers realized that the customary methods of cultivation should be improved greatly if erosion was to be minimized. The object of Thomas Moore in writing his book was to combat the prevailing practice of shallow plowing.

Shallow plowing was partly the result of poor implements. The principal type of plow used in colonial and early national times was the light, one-horse shovel plow. After the introduction of heavier two- and three-horse moldboard plows made of iron the plowing could be deeper, but many farmers continued with the old instruments and in the old ways. They believed that to plow deeper than 3 or 4 inches would mean the turning up of the "dead earth" of the subsoil, thereby injuring the topsoil. Nevertheless, most of the systems

---

[6] Hall's patent and specifications, Nov. 19, 1814. P. Minor to General Cocke, Ridgeway, July 15, 1815. Cabell Mss., Va. State Library; Jefferson to Charles W. Peale, Monticello, Mar. 21, 1815. Jefferson papers, Library of Congress.
[7] Thomas Jefferson to T. M. Randolph. See footnote 2.

of farm improvement, such as Taylor's or that practiced in Loudoun County included deep plowing as one of the remedies for soil washing. Jefferson wrote (*52, v. 18, p. 278*) to a friend:

Ploughing deep, your recipe for killing weeds, is also the recipe for almost everything good in farming. The plough is to the farmer what the wand is to the sorcerer. Its effect is really like sorcery.

The Davidson soils of Jefferson's county were found to be admirably suited to deep plowing. In 1825 it was said that the average maximum depth of plowing in Albermarle was 6 inches, but that a depth of from 8 to 10 inches was preferred where the strength of the horses and the type of plows would permit it (*59*). In Loudoun County 12-inch plowing was attained with plows drawn by three, four or even five horses (*30, 68*).

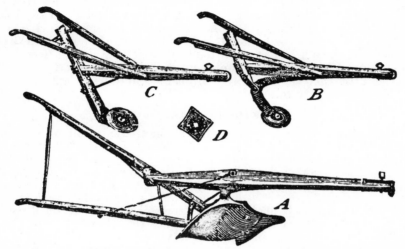

FIGURE 2.—Plows manufactured by Gideon Davis: *A*, Bar-share plow; *B*, substratum plow; *C*, shovel plow; *D*, square type shovel for plow.

A simple turning plow designed to penetrate to such depths was not considered adaptable to much of the soil of the tobacco districts of Halifax County or the wheat districts of the northern part of the State. In general these soils were described as having a thin sandy topsoil with a clayey subsoil (*75*). To bring this stiff clay to the surface was considered as merely accelerating erosion, since the clay would form a cement when the first heavy rain fell, thus preventing the water from being absorbed. If some means could be found by which the tough substratum could be broken without bringing it to the top, the water-absorbing capacity of these soils would be greatly increased and erosion lessened. Some farmers ran a colter deeply in the furrow following the turning plow to effect this object. The substratum plow designed by Gideon Davis, an implement maker of Georgetown, D. C., was simply a refinement of this colter. This plow consisted of a long tongue of iron to which was attached a cutting disk or point (fig. 2). This, like the colter, was to follow in the furrow made by the turning plow. The topsoil was in this way turned over and the subsoil broken without disturbing the relative position of either. The two plows together were supposed to break the ground to a depth of about 1 foot (*31, 32*). The substratum plow was introduced in Virginia about 1822 and soon became a popular farm tool.

The method of plowing and cultivating was as important as the depth of plowing. By the end of the eighteenth century some farmers were discontinuing the old method of ridging or hilling their crops. Jefferson and his son-in-law, Thomas Mann Randolph, decided that the washing of land in corn, potatoes, or peas would be lessened by dressing the ground out flat. John Taylor also practiced this method in cultivating corn on his Caroline County farm. To prevent washing on hilly potato land he ran his drills across the face of the hill with a double moldboard plow, trod manure into the furrow on top of the potato slips, and covered the furrow in the direction opposite to the one in which it had been opened. When laid off in this manner the potato rows themselves served as drains to carry off excess water.[8] Meriwether of Amelia County was another advocate of flat tillage. Writing in 1818 he recommended that on "gray land", such as his, the soil be broken 6 inches deep and after planting, harrowed out smooth. A straight-toothed triangular drag 3 feet wide containing 13 teeth was the implement used for this operation. Meriwether attributed the disposition of his ground to wash less than that of his neighbors to this method of cultivation (*62*).

HORIZONTAL PLOWING

Horizontal or contour plowing was another method of plowing and cultivating appropriated and developed by early Virginians in order to prevent erosion. The customary usage of cross plowing the corn was poorly adapted to the rolling country of the Piedmont. Plowing up and down slope was open to at least three objections: It was so difficult that it caused the ground to be worked very superficially; it opened channels by which the soil was carried off directly down the slope; and it failed to preserve the moisture. For these reasons the summer rains were doubly destructive when followed by drought, as was often the case. Some farmers modified the cross-plowing practice by inclining the furrows at an angle of 45° from either direction, but this was insufficient to prevent soil and moisture losses (*24, p. 11*).

Plowing horizontally or at a slight inclination down the slope seems to have been a very old practice in Europe. It was referred to in Roman literature and was advocated by a number of eighteenth century English and Scotch writers on husbandry. Taylor observed in Arator that the "ignorant highlanders" of Scotland had practiced contour plowing for a century. Even the type of hillside plow, supposed by many of his Virginia contemporaries to have been invented by T. M. Randolph, had been used in Great Britain in the eighteenth century. Richard Peters, of Pennsylvania, found that a Hessian soldier who had settled in his State after the Revolution used a heavy hillside plow with a turning moldboard to lay his furrows horizontally, diagonally, or in curves along the hillside. This was the type of plowing with which he had been familiar in the hilly parts of his native land[9] (*8, 88*).

---

[8] Jefferson to Randolph. See footnote 2. Taylor to Jefferson, Caroline, Mar. 5, 1795, Jefferson Papers, Library of Congress.
[9] Peters to Jefferson, Belmont, Pa., Mar. 25, 1816, Jefferson Papers, Library of Congress.

112157—37——3

There is one mention of horizontal plowing having been practiced as early as 1785 in Essex County, by a Mr. Spindle and his neighbors (*67, p. 744*). Thomas Moore was familiar with the practice and recommended it to overcome the three objections to cross plowing since it aided in deeper plowing, prevented washing, and prepared the land to take advantage of sudden showers. In plowing horizontally on a hillside field the furrow should be turned downhill and the plow returned empty to its starting point to begin the new furrow, advised Moore. If the hill had a conical shape the plow should begin at the bottom and ascend spirally, throwing the furrow slice down all the time.

About 1804 Slaughter (*89, 81*) of Culpeper County, commenced horizontal plowing with the bar-share plow, an implement in common use at that time (fig. 2, *A*). The corn was listed in rows about 7 feet apart, after which a harrow laid the surface smooth. Slaughter considered that by this means the water was allowed to run over the surface without collecting in channels that would later wash into gullies.

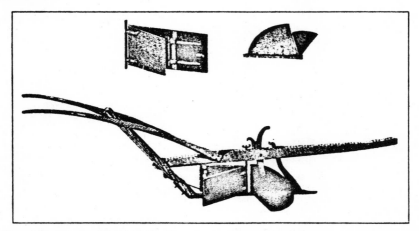

FIGURE 3.—The Randolph hillside plow.   Inserts show moldboard (left) and share (right).

Jefferson and Randolph may have received their ideas of horizontal plowing from reading British works on agriculture. If Jefferson observed the practice in France,[10] as has been suggested frequently, he seems to have made no mention of it in his writings. He, himself, always gave the credit to Randolph. The latter, according to his own testimony, commenced the practice of plowing curvilinear furrows for his corn crop in 1793. He adhered to the practice from that time forward, except in the year 1799, when he made one experiment in the old method. Jefferson is said by Randolph to have tried horizontal plowing in 1794 but to have abandoned it after that for a good many years in favor of the old rectilinear furrows. In 1808 Randolph constructed his first hillside plow with a shifting moldboard (fig. 3) (*74*).

[10] WARD, J. E., JR. THOMAS JEFFERSON'S CONTRIBUTIONS TO AMERICAN AGRICULTURE, p. 56. Ph. D. diss., Univ. Va. Library. 1935.

By 1810 Jefferson had become an ardent believer in horizontal plowing. Describing the results of the method during a certain heavy downpour, he said that on Randolph's farm "horizontal furrows arrested the water at every step until it was absorbed, or at least had deposited the soil it had taken up", whereas on other property the torrents had swept everything before them and greatly injured the fields (*37, pp. 193-194*).

A complete picture of horizontal plowing and bedding as practiced by Jefferson and Randolph is given in a letter from Jefferson to Tristram Dalton, dated Monticello, May 2, 1817 (*36, v. 12, pp. 56-57*).

A method of ploughing our hillsides horizontally, introduced into this most hilly part of our country by Col. T. M. Randolph, my son in law, may be worth mentioning to you. He has practiced it a dozen or 15 years, and it's advantages were so immediately observed that it has already become very general, and has entirely changed and renovated the face of our country. every rain, before that, while it gave a temporary refreshment, did permanent evil by carrying off our soil and fields were no sooner cleared than washed. at present we may say that we lose none of our soil, the rain not absorbed at the moment of its fall being retained in the hollows between the beds until it can be absorbed. our practice is when we first enter on this process, with a rafter level of 10.f. span, to lay off guide lines conducted horizontally around the hill or valley from one end to the other of the field, and about 30. yards apart. the steps of the level on the ground are marked by a stroke of a hoe, and immediately followed by a plough to preserve the trace. a man or a lad, with a level, and two small boys, the one with sticks, the other with the hoe, will do an acre of this in an hour, and when once done it is forever done. we generally level a field the year it is put into Indian corn, laying it into beds of 6.f. wide with a large water furrow between the beds, until all the fields have been once levelled. the intermediate furrows are run by the eye of the ploughman governed by these guide lines. the inequalities of declivity in the hill will vary in places the distance of the guide lines and occasion gores which are thrown into short beds. as in ploughing very steep hillsides horizontally a common plough can scarcely throw the furrow up hill, Colo. Randolph has contrived a very simple alteration of the share, which throws the furrow down hill both going and coming. it is as if two shares were welded together at their straight side and at a right angle with each other. this turns on its bar as on a pivot, so as to lay either share horizontal, when the other becoming vertical acts as a mouldboard. this is done by the ploughman in an instant by a single motion of the hand at the end of every furrow * * * horizontal and deep ploughing with the use of plaster and clover are but beginning to be used here will, as we believe, restore this part of our country to its original fertility, which was exceeded by no upland in the state.

The rafter level was an instrument commonly used in the South at that time for running drainage ditches, laying off roads in hilly country, and similar work. It was made of two scantlings fastened together at their ends to form an acute angle, a horizontal crosspiece between them, and a plumb line suspended from the apex. The crosspiece was often graduated so that a measured grade could be maintained with each "step" of the instrument if necessary. In order to run hillside furrows exactly horizontally it was, of course, necessary to keep the line on a center mark on the crosspiece as the instrument was "stepped" around the hill (fig. 4).

The prestige of Randolph's name seems to have aided him in securing credit for originating the horizontal culture and inventing the hillside plow. In 1822 the agricultural society of his county awarded him a "piece of plate with an appropriate device and inscription" for this service to agriculture (*87. p. 299*). It has been noted previously, however. that others were practicing horizontal plowing in Virginia about the same time that Randolph started. The real contributions of Jefferson and Randolph were not to originate, but to perfect and publicize this improvement. By doing this work scientifically they left room for others to discover defects and make adaptations to differing situations. By means of his wide correspondence with agriculturists, including among others William Dunbar, of Mississippi, and the members of the Philadelphia Agricultural Society, Jefferson spread the knowledge of horizontal culture to other States (*90, p. 153*).

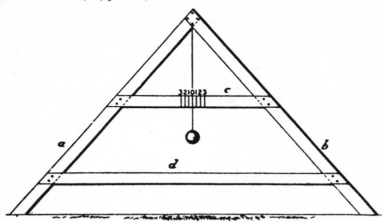

FIGURE 4.—The rafter level : *A* and *B*, Legs of the level ; *C*, scale ; *D*, rafter or cross beam.

Jefferson might write enthusiastically about this new practice and presidents of agricultural societies might declaim sonorously about its virtues, but unless the generality of farmers took it up it would do little to preserve the land. The literature indicates that the practice of horizontal plowing had a wide vogue in Virginia. In determining the extent of the practice it is necessary to distinguish between the perfectly leveled horizontal beds such as Randolph used and the less perfect systems similar to Slaughter's.

The care taken by Randolph and Jefferson was not exercised by most farmers. Randolph seems to have been a prophet without honor in his own country for many years. At first the lack of good plows prevented his system being sufficiently successful to induce others to try it. Many criticisms were directed at the hillside plow after its introduction. It was more costly than other plows; it was commonly thought that it would get out of order easily, that time would be lost in shifting the moldboard, and that there were few hills so steep as to make its use absolutely necessary (*5*). Nevertheless, the hillside plow was to be seen before long over a wide geographic range, and improvements were constantly being made in it (*18*).

Various methods were used by those who preferred the less perfect system of horizontal or near-horizontal plowing. Sometimes in laying horizontal furrows with the ordinary plow. when running the plow back in the same furrow it was tilted in such a way that the point would scoop under the unbroken surface. By this means a greater width than the actual furrow could be turned when the next bout was made. Many did not use the water furrow, but adopted Slaughter's method of combining horizontal rows with flat tillage. This method was open to question, for some farmers believed that by allowing the water to sweep over the flat tilled land in a sheet, erosion was merely facilitated, in spite of the fact that the rows were run on the contour (78). Those who were not willing to take the pains to use the rafter level trusted to the eye to preserve the contour line. Where fields lay on one side of the hill only and were bordered on either side by narrow depressions running up into the hill the farmer might turn his furrows downhill across the upper part of the field, drag the plow down one depression, turn his furrows uphill across the lower part of the field, and ascend the other depression to the starting point to make the next bout. A serious objection to this way of plowing was that it was very laborious where the furrows had to be turned uphill, and it tended to steepen the slope in this part of the field (5).

J. M. Garnett, Jr., of Essex County, noted that horizontal plowing was coming into general use in 1822 but deplored the fact that its efficacy was often counterbalanced by inaccurate methods. In the interests of more accurate leveling he (39) suggested a new type of instrument. This consisted of two pieces of timber in the form of a cross. At the top of the longer upright piece a ring was fastened and at its bottom a weight, while sights were placed on the side and near either end of the shorter crosspiece. A long stake could be driven in the ground at a position near the foot of a hill, this instrument suspended from the top of it, and a number of points on a contour on the hillside could be determined by sighting along the crosspieces.

During the 1830's the various methods of horizontal plowing were esteemed by progressive upper-Piedmont farmers as among their most valuable improvements. One Loudoun County farmer believed that deep and horizontal plowing had done as much as clover and gypsum to raise the productivity of the soil there (68). In 1834 T. J. Randolph, the son of T. M. Randolph, said that horizontal plowing had assisted in reclaiming the red lands from the desolation wrought by tobacco planters. The surface was again beginning to be smoothed and to produce vegetation. On the other hand, said the younger Randolph, the system was inadequate in many respects. Where exactly horizontal beds were used, sudden rains caused the more soluble lands to become compacted to a degree that hindered absorption, the water furrows soon filled, overflowed into the next water furrow below, and a body of water collected which swept down the hillside, starting a gully. He predicted that the growing practice of cultivating corn on land that had been in clover or grass the previous year would lead to the complete abandonment of horizontal plowing (6). Similarly in Fauquier County deep plowing, gypsum, and clover were the main reliances in preventing washing; plowing across the hill slope being considered of only minor importance (56).

In spite of the increasing popularity of horizontal plowing, the old method of cross plowing still retained its hold on farmers, while many others tried the new system only to give it up. After a few trials the question was properly raised as to "whether in some climates and soils it has not been so far to fail its purpose as to produce great and lasting injury and if there should not be a slight change in the mode" (*3*).

The criticisms of T. J. Randolph, who lived in the upper Piedmont, have been noted. The Tidewater farmers found the method even less adapted to their soil. Arator recommended horizontal plowing very highly, suggesting that on steep hillsides the ridges or beds should be narrow, their width increasing on more moderate slopes. But later he condemned the horizontal method with faint praise, pointing out that filling the land with vegetable fibers was so far superior to horizontal plowing in guarding against erosion that he considered the latter as an auxiliary only (*86*). A decade and a half after this statement was written Edmund Ruffin was finding that narrow contour beds were entirely unsuited to the sandy soils with low organic content in the Tidewater. More destruction was wrought than if horizontal culture had not been attempted (*9*). In 1837 DuVal, of King and Queen County, wrote the following (*34, p. 180*):

In riding through the country, ask the date of the enormous gullies which everywhere intrude upon your notice, and compare it with the date of horizontal ploughing, and you will be satisfied as to the source of the evil.

In summary it may be pointed out that exactly horizontal plowing was criticized because the capacity of the water furrows was often not great enough to hold the water of a heavy rain. When this circumstance did occur and the ridges broke, the accumulated water caused accelerated washing. By tilling the ground flat or by giving the ridges and furrows an inclination this difficulty was in part overcome. Nevertheless, the rainfall during the thundershowers of summer was often too great to be absorbed or carried off clean-cultivated fields. Some other device was needed to take care of the excessive amounts of water falling in a short time.

HILLSIDE DITCHING

The device adopted by Virginia farmers to conduct the excessive rainfall from the field was the hillside ditch. This term was applied to a variety of structures, the essential feature of which was a graded gutter or ditch running across the face of the hill paralleled by an embankment on the downhill side. As used in this publication, the term "hillside ditch" will denote a waterway made with a spade and having a sharp embankment. The term "hillside furrow" will denote a similar structure made with the plow and hoes and having a more rounded embankment, or bed. As used by these Virginia farmers and their contemporaries the words "ditch", "furrow", and "trench" were interchangeable. These hillside structures were the ancestors of the modern terrace.

The same difficulty is encountered in attempting to trace the origin of hillside ditching as is found in the case of horizontal plowing. One southern writer speaks of it as a strictly southern invention, but this statement may be looked upon with considerable skepticism. The Duc de La Rochefoucauld-Liancourt evidently had some such device in mind when he criticized Jefferson's idea of dividing fields by a row of peach trees rather than by ditches. The latter were especially good in a declivitous situation where the soil was constantly being washed down (*51, v. 3, p. 148*). Gov. James Barbour, of Orange County, claimed that he put hill ditches on his farm after an extremely heavy rain in August 1813 had proved to him that horizontal furrows were not always adequate (*20*). Another statement credits a certain Delaplane with having brought the practice to notice about the year 1818. Soon after this, one farmer of Amherst County is said to have tried the plan, given his ditches too great an inclination, and caused gullies in his land 10 feet deep.[11] Humberston Skipwith, who owned a large estate in Mecklenburg County, was given the widest publicity as the originator of the hillside ditch. He seems to have been a lone laborer at this undertaking from about 1815 until about 1831, however.

Skipwith employed the method outlined below. Using the rafter level, ditches 3 feet wide and 2 feet deep were conducted from the center of the hillside field to ravines on either side. These ditches were dug with the spade and the dirt placed on the embankment on the lower side of the ditch. The ditches were placed 20, 50, or 100 yards apart, according to the steepness of the slope. In plowing and cultivating, the furrows were made parallel with the ditches if the hill was very steep but were made on a contour if the declivity was not so great.

James C. Bruce, of Halifax County, began hillside ditching in 1830 and laid claim to an improvement on Skipwith's method. His hillside furrows were made with the plow and hoes. Three rows were plowed on the lower side of the line run by the rafter level, throwing the dirt uphill. Four rows were then plowed on the upper side, throwing the dirt downhill. The hoes then drew the dirt of the four rows onto that of the three and an embankment was completed with a trench on its upper side 3 feet wide at the bottom. Bruce gave his hillside furrows a fall of about three-fourths of an inch in 12 feet and placed each furrow some 30 yards from the next. If a ravine in which to empty the water was not near at hand, he thought it well to dig a spade ditch 3 feet wide and 2 deep directly down the slope to receive the water of all the furrows (*23*). Some writers suggested that this device was not desirable, but that the hillside furrow should be conducted to the nearest branch or ravine, even though it were half a mile away (*64*).

There was some difference of opinion as to which of these two methods, Skipwith's or Bruce's, was the better. The hillside ditch was objectionable on several grounds: (1) It was more difficult to construct than the furrow; (2) it offered obstructions to the carts carrying off the crops; and (3) the sharp embankment could not be cultivated but must be left to briers and weeds. The hillside furrow seemed designed to meet these objections and ultimately gained in popularity over the Skipwith method (*4; 65, p. 681*).

The rafter level continued to be the most popular instrument for grading ditches. For this purpose it was gaged beforehand by placing it on some level floor, slipping blocks of 1-, 2-, or 3-inch thickness under one of the legs, and marking the position of the plumb line on the crossbar. The proper fall could be given the ditches by using these marks. By tacking a block of the desired thickness to

[11] William Massie to N. F. Cabell, Pharsalia, Nelson County, Feb. 8, 1854, Cabell mss., Va. State Library, Richmond.

the bottom of one of the legs and by keeping the plumb line on the center mark a uniform grade could also be maintained (79). There were other less popular leveling instruments in use. One, described as especially adapted to gently undulating land, was made by securing two pieces of board of the same length at right angles to each other and placing these horizontally on a strong staff. This staff was to be driven into the ground. It had a mortise in its center in which a plumb bob was hung. A modification of this instrument to secure it against warping was a box with diagonal braces in which the plumb line was suspended, the whole supported by a tripod (67). There was at least one water level on the market. It was a U-shaped tin tube 3½ feet long, having two upright glass vials at either end, fixed on a staff. An unbroken column of colored liquid filling the tube and coming up into the vials was the medium whereby the horizontal position was determined. This instrument sold in Richmond for $1.25. These leveling devices were to be used with the aid of a rod in the same way as modern levels (45).

As the practice of hillside ditching spread it became evident that no rigid rules as to the size of the ditches, their distance apart, or the proper fall, could be given for all situations. Each one of these three factors was of vital importance if the system of ditching was to be a success, and each aroused much discussion in the agricultural press. There was general agreement that ditches should be as short and straight as possible. The grade of three-fourths of an inch in 12 feet used by Bruce in Halifax County seems to have been considered too little by farmers in other parts of the Piedmont, but on the more gentle slopes of the Tidewater even less of a grade was required. DuVal (34) of King and Queen County, finding that a 2- or 3-inch fall for ditches spaced at intervals of 30 yards was satisfactory, could not understand why Thomas B. Gay, of Goochland County, should find it expedient to give a fall of 3 inches in 12 feet in ditches spaced at intervals of 40 or 50 feet. Gay (40) explained that he lightened the burden required of the ditches not only by placing them as close together as this but also by plowing his land into 12-foot beds. The water was divided by these beds and was conducted from each into the trenches without causing gullies. Although Gay recognized that the fall in the ditches should vary with the slope of the land, he considered that the amount of the incline was not as important as providing a fall throughout the entire length of the ditch.

In Nelson and Amherst Counties a grade of 1 inch in 10 feet was recommended for hillside furrows spaced from 40 to 60 yards apart. From Waterloo, N. C., came the advice to give a much greater fall to the ditches or furrows than was the common practice. If they showed a disposition to wash too deeply, stones, blocks of wood, or similar trash could be thrown into them at intervals of about 100 yards (44). After the practice of hillside ditching had been in vogue some 30 years, one farmer pointed out that for long ditches the fall should increase toward the lower end so that the greater volume of water collecting there could be carried off readily. The bottom of the ditch would then scour enough to prevent the ditch from silting up (79).

An overseer on a plantation in the lower South wrote on this problem in the year before the Civil War. He believed that in order to be preserved a hillside furrow should be increased in size by one plow furrow for every 100 yards in length. Thus, for the first 100 yards it should be four plow furrows wide, for the second hundred, five furrows, and so on. In spacing the hillside furrows consideration should be taken of the surplus water. At the point below the first hillside furrow where this surplus water started to carry off the soil, another furrow should be placed. There should be 9 inches fall in the first 36 feet and 1½ inches per 12 feet thereafter if the ditch was to be not over 200 yards long. If it were necessary to make it longer the fall for the first 100 yards should be 1 inch per 12 feet and for the second 100 yards, one-half inch (*93*). Another farmer of the deep South pointed out that the grade of the ditches should also depend upon the character of the soil. If there was a firm clay foundation the ditch could have more fall without danger of causing a gully, but for coarse, sandy land the fall should be less (*15*).

Certain interesting adaptations to local or special conditions were made. For instance, one Halifax County farmer found that mole holes in his embankments caused the water to seep through and form gullies. He avoided this by making his embankment of the clay subsoil (*47*). In order to prevent accumulations of water from breaking over from an upper ditch and destroying the one below, a Charlotte County farmer ran small water furrows at a gently sloping angle from the bank of the upper into the lower ditch.

The common practice in providing outlets for the hillside ditches or furrows was to discharge them into the nearest convenient depression, fence row, or road cut. Some farmers advocated digging a special ditch for this purpose. The overseer of the deep South, quoted above, recommended this very strongly. He would have these conductors made with a spade and large enough to hold the water of all the tributary hillside furrows. It was important, he said, that the furrows should not be emptied under the fence into the road, since by this means a "hog hole" would soon be formed and the road ruined. Unless some precaution was taken with the outlet the process of gullying might be accelerated rather than prevented by hillside ditches. For this reason the early Virginia exponents of ditching often sowed redtop in the hillside ravines used for outlets. This served the double purpose of preventing gullying and securing a hay crop from an otherwise unproductive strip of land (*4*). One farmer who had a gently rolling piece of land affording few convenient outlets for ditches believed that a rock-paved ditch running straight down the declivity would serve the purpose. If a scarcity of rock made this impossible, he recommended that on land of such gentle slopes as his a perfectly level hillside ditch or furrow would be reliable (*67*).

The spaces between the hillside furrows should be cultivated with a view to preventing the accumulation of water in any one place before its discharge into the furrows. One way of accomplishing this was by making each corn and tobacco row carry off its own water into the hillside furrow (*48*). The bedding method of wheat culture used by Gay (*40*) has been noted. To prevent giving too much or too little fall to the land between the hillside furrows he plowed alternately parallel to the upper furrow and then to the lower, finishing the plowing midway between them. In order to secure accurate spacing in his plowing he attached a measuring stick at right angles to the beam of the plow with a switch to drag the ground at the outer end of the stick. This aided in maintaining the same distance from the next plow furrow.

Perhaps the most complete and scientific exposition of the engineering methods used to prevent soil erosion written before the Civil War was that of Sorsby (82). Although his pamphlet was not written primarily for Virginians, his conclusions are of general application. He summarized the various practices of cultivating to prevent washing. The first, he said, was the method of running crop rows horizontally. The second was the grading method, whereby crop rows were given a slight inclination downhill in order to drain the land of the excess water. Hillside furrows or ditches could be used to supplement both the horizontal or the grading method, said Sorsby; however, the horizontal method was much to be preferred and hillside ditches used as little as possible. Variations in method should be used to suit different situations.

The size of drains and ditches should be determined by reference to a variety of circumstances, the combined influence of which may generally be estimated in practice, although not reducible to any very exact rules, viz: 1st, we must consider the annual quantity of rain; 2d, the quantity which falls on the land during a heavy rain; 3d, the nature of the soil as to porosity or compactness; 4th, the inclination of land; 5th, the length of slopes and extent of surface to be drained. Every horizontaler must take into consideration these things, and judge for himself.

He gave the following table (table 1) of recommendations for the construction of soil-saving structures:

TABLE 1.—*Sorsby's table on soil-saving structures*

Character of soils	Drains			
Not subsoiled	Depth of soils	Depth of drains	Kind of drains	Distance apart
POROUS	*Feet Inches*	*Feet Inches*		*According to the Declivity of Land*
Light loam (fresh land)	} 1 00	0 10	Guard-Drains	Wide apart
Sandy " " "				
Light gravelly sand	} 0 10	1 00	Guard-Drains	Wide apart
Coarse gravelly sand				
MEDIUM				
Clayey loam	0 8	1 00	Guard-Drains	Not so wide apart
Gravelly loam	} 0 10	0 10	Guard-Drains	Not so wide apart
Friable loam				
COMPACT				*Need Subsoiling*
Tenacious clay	0 6	1 00	Hill-Side ditches	Close together
Friable clay	0 8	1 00	" " " "	" "
Soft Free Clay	0 10	1 00	" " " "	Not so close

By "depth of soil" Sorsby evidently meant the depth of plowed soil. It will be noted that for soils of coarser texture he recommended that the bottoms of the drains should not extend as deep as this plowed soil, while for the finer soils they should be lower than the plowing. These recommendations were for land on which the substratum plow was not used, as is denoted by the phrase "not subsoiled." By "guard drain" Sorsby meant a small hillside furrow, since, according to his definition a hillside ditch had a greater water capacity.

With most farmers approaching the erosion-control problem by the trial and error method there was bound to be considerable dissatisfaction with the various techniques. In the vicinity of Wardsfork, Charlotte County, hillside ditching seems to have been tried and found wanting. To prove its ineffectiveness dams were built across the bottoms serving as outlets on a well-ditched field. It was found by the farmer (72) who did this that great quantities of his own runaway soil as well as that of his neighbor's were caught by these traps, hillside ditches to the contrary notwithstanding. The conclusion was drawn that hillside ditching and horizontal cultivation were so contrary to nature that she showed her disapproval by "sending destroying rain storms." The hillside ditches could not withstand these torrents, and the "ropes of sand had snapped in ten thousand places." A sojourn in this part of the State in 1836 convinced Edmund Ruffin that the trouble lay more in the manner of constructing and caring for the ditches and furrows than in the system itself. He found that the grade lines were often carelessly and incorrectly marked off, and that none of the ditches seemed large enough to accommodate the heavier rains. Furthermore, land in clover fallow resisted washing so well 'that agriculturists were tempted to dispense with a system requiring much trouble and more skill than most overseers were willing to exercise.

A perusal of volumes 4 and 5 of the Farmers' Register, for the years 1837 and 1838, discloses that there was much dissatisfaction with the ditching system. There were repeated warnings that great care must be used in the construction of the furrows, warnings that were heeded or unheeded according to the inclination of the individual planter. In general, ditches or furrows, being either too small or too long or having too little fall, or combining all three faults, overflowed and broke during heavy rains. If given too little fall, they would clog with sand and rubbish and, unless cleared out, were utterly useless. Even those farmers who were most conscientious in their work often found that ditches did more harm than good.

Hillside ditching appears to have been talked about much in Virginia in the 1830's but never very extensively practiced. What vogue it did enjoy seems to have died down somewhat by about 1852. In that year a young farmer (38) sought information on the subject through the correspondence column of the Southern Planter. Two persons whose advice he asked orally had opposed hillside ditches; one had been in favor of them, and others had "uttered mere empty incoherences." The editor replied that although he lived in the midst of mountains, he had seen very few hillside ditches and no good ones. He confessed to a preference for deep plowing as a substitute. About the same time the owner of a James River Piedmont plantation wrote of hillside furrowing as if it had been the practice of the previous generation. He said that he had filled up many of these furrows made originally by his father but later washed into gullies. Under deep plowing the same lands showed no disposition to erode.[12] On the other hand, it seems that hillside ditching was fairly popular in

---

[12] Peyton Harrison to William B. Harrison, Clifton, Dec. 30, 1853, Cabell ms., Virginia State Library, Richmond.

the Cotton States in the decade before the Civil War. Most of the communications on the subject to the Southern Planter in that period were from the deep South.

Even if hillside ditches and furrows were not generally used, there were certain individuals in Virginia laboring to improve the system. Richard N. Venable, of Prince Edward County, made hillside furrows very nearly on the modern design. In order to eliminate the small ditch with its unproductive bank he made a rounded bed 10 or 12 feet wide with a water furrow of corresponding size on the upper side. This bed was to be tilled with the rest of the field and was to remain in the same place year after year. In other respects it was like the hillside ditch. The size of this structure gave it a greater water capacity than a ditch and its shape made it less likely to break when full (*89, p. 753*).

Among the first men to use the word terrace to describe this type of hillside bed was John H. Cocke, of the Bremo estates, Fluvanna County. In 1840 Cocke's overseer, evidently not a very literate person, kept a journal of work performed on the plantation. In it the building of "Terris's", "Terryss", or "Terresses" is referred to. These terraces were beds raised some 4 to 6 inches above the level of the waterway. The waterway itself was about 3 or 4 feet wide. On gentle slopes Cocke threw the dirt out of the waterway to either side, but on the steeper slopes the terrace was made on the lower side. A fall of 2½ inches for every 16½ feet was given these terraces. Cocke also claimed to have developed a horizontal terrace as a means of irrigating hillsides.[13]

CONCLUSIONS

The problem of erosion on agricultural land is not new, nor are the means of controlling it new. All of the methods in use today with the possible exception of strip cropping were known to the Virginia farmers of the early part of the last century. They used legumes and grasses to restore fertility and to bind the soil. They increased the capacity of the soil to absorb water by turning these green crops under and by deep plowing. They developed horizontal or contour plowing to conserve moisture and to prevent washing. They cultivated the land "flat" rather than in ridges to prevent the accumulation of water. They introduced the system now known as terracing to make the most effective use of the excess water of heavy summer rains. Even the suggestion of strip cropping is contained in the practice of some farmers of leaving strips of sod unplowed between the corn rows or alternating rows of corn with rows of some other crop. While some farmers, finding one particular method successful, urged it as a panacea for all erosion ills, it was generally recognized that the method must vary with different types of soil and different slopes.

With these means at hand, with other improved general farm practices, and with improved farm equipment, it was possible for the Virginian of the 1850's to conserve his soil much more successfully than did his predecessors. Nevertheless, many did not avail them-

[13] Journal of General Cocke's overseer, January–April 1840; J. H. Cocke to Edmund Ruffin, Bremo, July 1854; COCKE, J. H., SR. AN ESSAY ON AGRICULTURE. Bremo Bluff Fluvanna Co., Va. n. d.

selves of the new practices, and soil conservation still seems to have been the exception rather than the rule.   In 1856 a writer could still complain that Virginia was "bleeding from a thousand wounds inflicted by improvident husbandry", and that "we behold everywhere around us stunted vegetation, scanty crops, poverty of soil, and innumerable gullies and galds" (*46*).   Another author (*42*), after quoting the passage from Taylor given above (p. 5), declared that—

Nothing has yet been done to wipe from our agriculture the reproach of Arator. The alluvial treasure, annually washed from our forests and badly cultivated soils, and floated down our rivers, continues to serve no other purpose but to obstruct our navigation and poison our atmosphere. Not one scientific effort has been made to arrest it, in its progress to tidewater, and none to appropriate it below.

Although great progress had been made in the developing of soil-conservation practices during the first half of the nineteenth century, the perfecting of these techniques remained for future generations. The individual efforts of a few, no matter how intelligent these might be, could not solve the widespread erosion problem.   The problem required not only accuracy and eternal vigilance in the application of erosion-control techniques but also a Nation-wide, coordinated program for preventing soil wastage.

LITERATURE CITED

(1) ANONYMOUS.
    1831. ON PLOUGHING. By De Rustica. (Letter to editor). Amer. Farmer 13 : 25–26.
(2) ———
    1831. DE RUSTICA NO. II. ON HORIZONTAL PLOUGHING. By De Rustica. (Letter to editor). Amer. Farmer 13 : 43–44.
(3) ———
    1833. HORIZONTAL PLOUGHING AND HILLSIDE PLOUGHING AGAIN. By a Virginian. (Letter to editor). Amer. Farmer 15 : 82–83.
(4) ———
    1834. ON HILLSIDE DITCHES—TO PREVENT THE WASHING OF BROKEN LAND. By Wardsfork. Farmers' Register 1 : 562–564. (Comment by editor, pp. 563–564).
(5) ———
    1834. A GLANCE AT THE FARMING OF ALBEMARLE. By a Gleaner. Farmers' Register 2 : 233–238.
(6) ———
    1834. OBSERVATIONS ON THE RED LANDS OF THE SOUTH WEST MOUNTAINS. By A Furrow Turner. Farmers' Register 2 : 315–316.
(7) ———
    1834. THE MOUNTAIN REGION OF VIRGINIA. By Jeremiah. (Letter to editor). Farmers' Register 2 : 390.
(8) ———
    1835. INQUIRY INTO ORIGIN OF HORIZONTAL PLOUGHING. By Farmer. (Letter to editor). Farmers' Register 2 : 667–669.
(9) ———
    1836. IMPROVEMENT OF THE APPOMATTOX RIVER. By E. Farmers' Register 4 : 377.
(10) ———
    1837. ON THE AGRICULTURE OF NELSON AND AMHERST NO. II. Farmers' Register 5 : 7–9.
(11) ———
    1842. GALDS. (Quotes letter from James T. Jones). South. Planter 2 : 56.
(12) ———
    1846. [WIRE GRASS.] By Observer. South. Planter 6 : 182–183.
(13) ———
    1847. GRASS. South. Planter 7 : 285–287.

(14) ——
    1849. AGRICULTURAL CLUB IN ALBEMARLE. South. Planter 9: 252–255.
(15) ——
    1851. HILL-SIDE DITCHING, PRESERVATION OF LAND, &C. By a Cotton
        Planter. (Letter to editor). South. Planter 11: 268–270.
(16) A.
    1848. ROADS. (Letter to editor). South. Planter 8: 107–108.
(17) [ANBUREY, T.]
    1791. TRAVELS THROUGH THE INTERIOR PARTS OF AMERICA, IN A SERIES OF
        LETTERS. By an officer. New ed., 2 v., illus. London.
(18) B., R. R.
    1834. ROTATION SUITABLE FOR ROCKBRIDGE CO. (Letter to editor). Farm-
        ers' Register 1: 485–487.
(19) B., T.
    1831. RE RUSTICA NO. III. PLOUGHING—ADDITIONAL REMARKS. (Letter to
        editor). Amer. Farmer 13: 65.
(20) BARBOUR, J.
    1835. ON THE IMPROVEMENT OF AGRICULTURE, AND THE IMPORTANCE OF LEG-
        ISLATIVE AID TO THAT OBJECT . . . (Essay by Gov. Barbour, sent
        by A. Broadhead, Secretary, Agricultural Society of Albemarle).
        Farmers' Register 2: 703–706.
(21) BONDURANT, T. M.
    1835. PROCEEDINGS OF THE BUCKINGHAM AGRICULTURAL SOCIETY. Farmers'
        Register 3: 502–507.
(22) BROOKE, W. E., ed.
    1919. THE AGRICULTURAL PAPERS OF GEORGE WASHINGTON. 145 pp., illus.
        Boston.
(23) BRUCE, J. C.
    1833. HORIZONTAL TRENCHING TO PREVENT THE WASHING OF HILLY LANDS.
        (Letter to editor). Farmers' Register 1: 334–335. (Comment
        by editor, p. 335).
(24) CABELL, N. F.
    18——. EARLY HISTORY OF AGRICULTURE IN VIRGINIA. 41 pp. Washington.
(25) ——
    1918. SOME FRAGMENTS OF AN INTENDED REPORT ON THE POST REVOLUTIONARY
        HISTORY OF AGRICULTURE IN VIRGINIA. William and Mary Col-
        Quart. Hist. Mag. 26: [145]–168.
(26) CONWAY, C.
    1835. IMPROVEMENT OF WORN LAND BY CLOVER AND PASTURE. (Letter to
        editor). Farmers' Register 3: 443–444.
(27) CONWAY, M. D., ed.
    1889. GEORGE WASHINGTON AND MOUNT VERNON, A COLLECTION OF WASHING-
        TON'S UNPUBLISHED AGRICULTURAL AND PERSONAL LETTERS. Long
        Island Hist. Soc. Mem. 4, 352 pp., illus. Brooklyn.
(28) CRAVEN, A. O.
    1925. SOIL EXHAUSTION AS A FACTOR IN THE AGRICULTURAL HISTORY OF
        VIRGINIA AND MARYLAND, 1608–1860. Ill. Univ. Studies Social
        Sci. v. 13, no. 1, 179 pp.
(29) CRAVEN, J. H.
    1833. SYSTEM OF FARMING. (From Amer. Farmer, letter to Mr. Smith).
        Farmers' Register 1: 150–152.
(30) ——
    1836. AN ESSAY READ BEFORE THE AGRICULTURAL SOCIETY OF ALBEMARLE.
        Farmers' Register 3: 611–612.
(31) DAVIS, G.
    1823. IMPROVEMENTS IN THE BARSHARE, SUBSTRATUM, AND SHOVEL PLOUGHS;
        AND MANNER OF USING THEM EXPLAINED. Amer. Farmer 5: 1–3,
        9–10, illus.
(32) ——
    1832. TILLAGE. (Third prize essay, Agricultural Division). Amer.
        Farmer 13: 369–370.
(33) DRUMMOND, Z.
    1831. MANAGEMENT OF GULLIES. Amer. Farmer 12: 396.
(34) DUVAL, J.
    1837. HORIZONTAL PLOWING—HILL-SIDE TRENCHES—HAND RAKES—USE OF
        GYPSUM. (Letter to editor). Farmers' Register 5: 180–181.

425

(35) FITZPATRICK, J. C., ed.
    1925. THE DIARIES OF GEORGE WASHINGTON 1748–1799. 4 v., illus. Boston
        and New York.
(36) FORD, P. L., ed.
    1904–5. THE WORKS OF THOMAS JEFFERSON. 12 v., illus. New York.
(37) FORD, W. C.
    1916. THOMAS JEFFERSON CORRESPONDENCE, PRINTED FROM THE ORIGINALS IN
        THE COLLECTIONS OF WILLIAM E. BIXLEY [BIXBY], 322 pp., illus.
        Boston.
(38) FOOTE, R. H.
    1852. HILLSIDE DITCHES. (Letters to editor). South. Planter 12:151.
        (Comment by editor).
(39) GARNETT, J. M., JR.
    1822. [A NEW LEVELING INSTRUMENT.] Amer. Farmer 4: 60, illus.
(40) GAY, T. B.
    1837. ON HORIZONTAL PLOUGHING—HILL-SIDE DITCHES AND HANDRAKES
        USED IN CULTIVATING CORN. (Letter to editor). Farmers'
        Register 5 : 302–303.
(41) GOOCH, C. W.
    1833. ON AGRICULTURE IN VIRGINIA. (Prize Essay). Amer. Farmer 15:
        138–141.
(42) GORDON, W.
    1856. ESSAY ON IRRIGATION. South. Planter 16: [161]–172, illus.
(43) GRAY, L. C., assisted by THOMPSON, E. K.
    1933. HISTORY OF AGRICULTURE IN THE SOUTHERN UNITED STATES TO 1860.
        2 v., illus. Washington, D. C. (Carnegie Inst. Wash. Pub. 430).
(44) GREGORY, W. O.
    1838. SASSAFRAS, RAT-PROOF MEAT-HOUSES, CLOSE GRAZING, HILL-SIDE DITCHES.
        (Letter to editor.) Farmers' Register 6: 109–110.
(45) H., F.
    1835. DESCRIPTION OF A CHEAP WATER-LEVEL AND THE MANNER OF USING IT.
        (Letter to editor.) Farmers' Register 3: 59–60.
(46) HURT, J. M.
    1856. IMPROVEMENT OF LAND FROM ITS OWN RESOURCES. South. Planter
        16: [325]–326.
(47) J., R. B.
    1837. TRENCHING ON HILL-SIDES. Farmers' Register 5: 143–144.
(48) KEY, R. D.
    1834. ON WATER FURROWING. (Letter to editor.) Farmers' Register
        2: 320.
(49) KNIGHT, F.
    1847. LETTERS ON AGRICULTURE FROM HIS EXCELLENCY GEORGE WASHINGTON
        . . . TO ARTHUR YOUNG . . . AND SIR JOHN SINCLAIR . . . 198 pp.,
        illus. Washington, D. C.
(50) L., N.
    1837. REMARKS ON RAKES AND HOES—NARROW BEDS. (Letter to editor.)
        Farmers' Register 5: 33–34.
(51) LA ROCHEFOUCAULD LIANCOURT, F. A. F., Duc de
    1800. TRAVELS THROUGH THE UNITED STATES OF NORTH AMERICA, THE
        COUNTRY OF THE IROQUOIS AND UPPER CANADA IN THE YEARS 1795,
        1796 AND 1797. Ed. 2, 4 v., illus. London.
(52) LIPSCOMB, A. A., ed.
    1904. THE WRITINGS OF THOMAS JEFFRESON. Mem. ed., 18 v., illus. Wash-
        ington, D. C.
(53) M.
    1834. IMPROVEMENT OF WORN LAND. Farmers' Register 2: 382–383.
(54) M., S. D.
    1836. IMPROVEMENT OF WORN LAND. Farmers' Register 4: 260–261.
(55) MADISON, [J.]
    1837. AN ADDRESS BEFORE THE AGRICULTURAL SOCIETY OF ALBEMARLE, (VA.)
        ON TUESDAY, MAY 12, 1819. Farmers' Register 5: 412–422.
(56) MARSHALL, T.
    1820. ON IMPROVING LAND GENERALLY . . . (In a letter . . . to Geo. W.
        Jeffreys). Amer. Farmer 2: 261–262. (Comment by editor,
        Amer. Farmer, p. 262, illus.)

(57) MERIWETHER, W.
    1820. [LETTERS]. Nos. III, V, and VI of a series of Agricultural
        Essays, communicated by Geo. W. Jeffreys . . . Amer. Farmer
        2 : 19–20, 35–37, 44–45, illus.
(58) MINOR, P.
    1822. MEMORANDUM OF THE RESULT OF A NEW MODE OF PLANTING CORN.
        Amer. Farmer 4 : 73.
(59) ———
    1825. CORRESPONDENCE OF THE EDITOR—ON THE HILL-SIDE AND HORIZONTAL
        PLOUGHING IN ALBEMARLE, VIRGINIA. [Includes letter from P.
        Minor.] Amer. Farmer 6 : 355.
(60) MOORE, T.
    1801. THE GREAT ERROR IN AMERICAN AGRICULTURE EXPOSED : AND HINTS FOR
        IMPROVEMENT SUGGESTED. 72 pp. Baltimore.
(61) MORRISON, A. J., ed.
    1908. LETTERS OF ROGER ATKINSON, 1769–1776. Va. Mag. Hist. and Biog.
        15 : 350–352.
(62) ———
    1914. VA. AGRICULTURAL HISTORY. NO. 9. South. Planter 75 : 757–760.
(63) MORTON, A. C.
    1843. ON THE COMPARATIVE ADVANTAGES OF HERDSGRASS AND CLOVER, AS
        GENERAL IMPROVERS OF THE SOIL. South. Planter 3 : 129–131.
(64) N., C. F.
    1834. ON HORIZONTAL PLOUGHING AND HILL-SIDE DITCHES. (Letter to edi-
        tor). Farmers' Register 1 : 449–450.
(65) ———
    1834. ON THE SEVERAL PLANS TO PREVENT WASHING OF HILLY LANDS. (Let-
        ter to editor). Farmers' Register 1 : 680–682.
(66) N., M.
    1834. ON IMPROVEMENT OF LANDS IN THE CENTRAL REGIONS OF VIRGINIA.
        Farmers' Register 1 : 585–589.
(67) ———
    1835. ON HORIZONTAL PLOWING. Farmers' Register 2 : 558–560, 744. (Re-
        marks on paper, p. 744).
(68) NOLAND, W.
    1838. LOUDOUN FARMING. (Letter communicated by Geo. W. Jeffreys,
        esq.). Farmers' Register 5 : 593–596.
(69) PALMER, R. D.
    1843. GALLS AND GULLIES. (Letter to editor). South. Planter 3 : 279.
(70) PARKINSON, R.
    1805. A TOUR IN AMERICA IN 1798, 1799, AND 1800 EXHIBITING SKETCHES
        OF SOCIETY AND MANNERS, AND A PARTICULAR ACCOUNT OF THE
        AMERICAN SYSTEM OF AGRICULTURE, WITH ITS RECENT IMPROVE-
        MENTS. 2 v. London.
(71) PLEASANTS. T. S.
    1828. ORCHARD GRASS, SUITABLE TO A SOUTHERN CLIMATE. Extract of a
        letter . . . to a friend in Maryland. Amer. Farmer 10 : 217–
        218.
(72) R., I.
    1836. THE CORN CROP THE GREATEST LANDKILLER. Farmers' Register
        4 : 33.
(73) RANDOLPH, T. J.
    1842. REPORT OF THE BOARD OF AGRICULTURE OF VIRGINIA TO THE SENATE
        AND HOUSE OF REPRESENTATIVES OF VIRGINIA. Va. House of Dele-
        gates Jour., sess. 1842–43, Doc. 12 : 51–53.
(74) RANDOLPH, T. M.
    1883. FARMERS AND FARMING IN VIRGINIA IN THE OLDEN TIME. NO. 12.
        (Letter from Col. T. M. Randolph, July 20, 1820, quoted).
        South. Planter 44 : 318–319.
(75) RICE, I. B.
    1838. DEEP PLOUGHING INJURIOUS ON CERTAIN KINDS OF SOIL. (Letter to
        editor). Farmers' Register 5 : 755–756.
(76) [RICHMOND SOCIETY FOR PROMOTING AGRICULTURE]
    1811. QUAERE. Richmond Enquirer, v. 7, no. 10, Apr. 9, 1811.
(77) RUFFIN, E.
    1835. ESSAY ON CALCAREOUS MANURES. Ed. 2, 116 pp., illus. Shellbanks,
        Va. (Farmers' Register, v. 2. Supplement).

(78) Ruffin, F. G.
1844. THE CULTIVATION OF INDIAN CORN. (Letter to editor). South. Planter 4 : 230–232. (Comment by editor, pp. 231–232).

(79) Shepherd, W. P.
1851. HILL-SIDE DITCHING—AGAIN. (Letter to editor). South. Planter 11 : 335–336. (Comment by editor, p. 336).

(80) Slaughter, J. S.
1811. [PREVENTING LAND UNDER THE PLOUGH FROM WASHING—CULTIVATION OF INDIAN CORN.] (Letter to Geo. Hay). Agr. Mus. 2 : 150–152.

(81) ———
1820. [LETTER.] No. II, of a series of papers communicated for the Farmer, by Geo. W. Jeffreys, Esq. Amer. Farmer 2 : 14–15.

(82) Sorsby, N. T.
1860. HORIZONTAL PLOWING AND HILL-SIDE DITCHING. [45] pp. Mobile, Ala.

(83) Strickland, W.
1835. OBSERVATIONS ON THE UNITED STATES OF AMERICA. Farmers' Register 3 : 201–210, 262–269.

(84) Taylor, J.
1813. ARATOR; BEING A SERIES OF AGRICULTURAL ESSAYS, PRACTICAL & POLITICAL, IN SIXTY-ONE NUMBERS. By a citizen of Virginia. 296 pp. Georgetown, D. C.

(85) ———
1820. OBSERVATIONS ON SOWING WHEAT AMONG INDIAN CORN . . . HORIZONTAL PLOWING . . . (Letter to G. W. Jeffreys, Esq. . . .). Amer. Farmer 2 : 212.

(86) ———
1821. [LETTER.] Communicated for the American Farmer by G. W. Jeffreys, Esq. Amer. Farmer 2 : 397–398.

(87) True, R. H., ed.
1921. MINUTE BOOK OF THE ALBERMARLE (VIRGINIA) AGRICULTURAL SOCIETY. Amer. Hist. Assoc. Ann. Rept. (1918) 1 : 261–349.

(88) Tull, J.
1829. THE HORSE-HOEING HUSBANDRY: OR, A TREATISE ON THE PRINCIPLES OF TILLAGE AND VEGETATION . . . TO WHICH IS PREFIXED AN INTRODUCTION ... . BY WILLIAM COBBETT. 466 pp., illus. London.

(89) Venable, A. W.
1838. ON HILL-SIDE DITCHES. (Letter to editor). Farmers' Register 5 : 752–753.

(90) Wailes, B. L. C.
1854. REPORT ON THE AGRICULTURE AND GEOLOGY OF MISSISSIPPI . . . 371 pp., illus. Philadelphia.

(91) Wiley, H. D.
1909. THE CONSERVATION OF THE FERTILITY OF THE SOIL. In Natl. Conserv. Comn. Rept. 3 v., illus. Washington. (60th Cong., 2d sess., S. Doc. 676).

(92) Williams, C. B., rec. secy.
1853. ANNUAL MEETING OF THE VIRGINIA STATE AGRICULTURAL SOCIETY. Va. State Agr. Soc. Jour. Trans. 1 : 103–119.

(93) Woffard, D.
1860. HORIZONTAL CULTURE. (Letter to Dr. Cloud). South. Planter 20 : 379–382, illus.

AN ESSAY

ON

Horizontal Plowing and Hill-Side Ditching

By NICHOLAS T. SORSBY, M.D.

OF ALABAMA.*

DEDICATION.

This unpretending production is respectfully dedicated to the Farmers and Planters of the State of North Carolina, as a testimony of his tender regard for them, and love for his native State, by

THE AUTHOR.

FORKLAND, GREEN COUNTY, ALABAMA,
October, 1857.

TO THE COMMITTEE ON ESSAYS:

Gentlemen: You perceive from the length of this Essay, that it has cost me a good deal of *time* and *labor* to write it. Rest assured, I would not have written such an Essay for any other than the Agricultural Society of North Carolina.

I was induced to write it from the interest I feel for the progress of the Society, and the advancement of the Agriculture of the State, and as the only and best way I am able to assist them.

If awarded the Premium, the Society is at liberty to publish all, or any part of it, and as many copies as they desire, but I beg leave to reserve the copyright; and as I have no copy of it, I would be under many obligations to them to return it, when it has served them in the manner they desire.

By so doing they will much oblige,

Very respectfully,

Their ob't serv'nt,

N. T. SORSBY.

FORKLAND, Ala., Oct. 13th, 1857.

---

* A Premium of $50 was awarded by the Society to this Essay.

HISTORY OF HORIZONTAL CULTURE.

We regret to state that we have not been able by a careful research of all the Agricultural works that we have been able to examine, in the English and French languages, to find the origin of this system of culture.

Mr. Thomas Jefferson, who was a close observer of improvements in Agriculture, in a letter dated "Monticello, 6th March, 1816," says, "My son-in-law, Colonel Thomas M. Randolph, is, perhaps, the best farmer in the State ; and by the introduction of the Horizontal method of Plowing, instead of straight furrows, has really saved this hilly country. It was running off in the valleys with every rain, but by this process we scarcely lose an ounce of soil.

"A rafter level traces a horizontal line around the curve of the hill or valley, at distances of thirty or forty yards, which is followed by the plow ; and by these guide-lines the plowman finishes the interval by his eyes, throwing the earth into beds of six feet wide, with large water furrows between them. When more rain falls than can be instantly absorbed, the horizontal furrows retain the surplus until it is all soaked up, scarcely a drop ever reaching the valley below.

"Mr. Randolph has contrived also, for our steepest hill-sides, a simple plan which throws the furrows always down hill. It is made with two wings welded to the same bar, with their planes at a right angle to each other. The point and the heel of the bar are formed into pivots, and the bar becomes an axis, by turning which, either wing may be laid on the ground, and the other then standing vertically, acts as a mould-board. The right angle between them, however, is filled with a sloping piece of wood, leaving only a cutting margin of each wing naked, and aiding in the office of raising the sod gradually, while the declivity of the hill facilitates its falling over. The change of the position of the share at the end of each furrow is effected in a moment by withdrawing and replacing a pin."

It seems Colonel Randolph introduced this method of plowing into Virginia, previous to 1816, as Mr. Jefferson states he was acquainted with it two or three years previous to writing this letter.

430

This is the earliest notice that we have seen of the use of the horizontal culture, as practiced in the South at the present day. It would be gratifying to know from whence he introduced it, and where it originated.

In " Taylor's Arator," published in Virginia the beginning of this century, on the subject of plowing hilly lands, it is stated " that such lands will admit of narrow ridges, as well as level, by a degree of skill and attention so easily attainable, that it has existed in Scotland above a century past under a state of agriculture otherwise execrable, and among the ignorant Highlanders ! It is effected by carrying the ridges horizontally in such inflections as the hilliness of the ground may require, curved or zigzag, preserving the breadth. The preservation of the soil is hardly more valuable than that of the rain water in the successive reservoirs thus produced to refresh the thirsty hill-sides, instead of its reaching to and poisoning the valleys."

It is very strange, if this system was pursued in Scotland so very long ago, that there is no mention made of it in English works.

During an extensive tour, and residence of over three years in Europe, from Great Britain to Naples, Italy, through Holland, Belgium, France, Switzerland, and parts of Germany, we never saw, heard or read of its being pursued in any of those countries as it is done here, and we cannot conceive how it could have ever been practiced in Scotland and not kept up now-a-days.

In our travels throughout the United States, we have seen it pursued from Mississippi to North Carolina. We have been to Monticello several times, when a student at the University of Virginia, and though remarking the productiveness of the soil there, and around Charlottsville, we were too young to notice the mode of culture, but we are sure we never saw a rafter-level or any other level applied to land in Virginia. Had we seen it we should have noticed it, because we had followed it before we went there to school, in 1836.

In "Thaër's Principles of Agriculture," a standard German work, in speaking of plowing ridges, he says : " The most advantageous disposition of them that can be made on an inclined surface, is to give them a horizontal or standing direction ;" but he says nothing more on the subject. Had he been acquainted with the method as pursued in the South, he would have written considerably on it.

We are inclined to believe the Horizontal system of plowing is of Southern invention. We are astonished at the fact, since the Southern planters and farmers have the reputation of being such careless and wasteful cultivators of the soil.

We consider it the most important discovery of the modern agricultural era. So important is it to the South, and to the soil in every part of the world where it rains like it does here, that the discoverer of the method deserves the lasting gratitude of the Southern people, and a place upon the tablet of memory next to that of the father of our country.

Hill-side ditching and guard-drains, were discovered subsequent to the origin or introduction of the horizontal system into Virginia. They were first introduced into that State soon after the introduction of the horizontal method, about 1815 or 1816 ; by whom, we do not know.

The first written notice of the horizontal culture and hill-side ditching that we ever saw, was in the pages of the " Southern Cultivator." Major E. D. W., our step-father, first introduced the method of Horizontal Plowing on the level system into this county, in the spring of 1834. He had read a notice of it in some paper, which induced him to try it on some hilly land at the DIAL PLACE.

He used the rafter-level and plummet-line, and ran off rows to be plowed four feet apart into beds for corn and cotton. We were a boy then, and carried the hoe and made the chop marks for him. He was so well pleased with the results of it, and with his experiment, that he has continued it ever since with great success on two plantations. He has a thousand or more acres under the plumb. He has tested it thoroughly, and has preserved the fertility, retained the soil, and improved his lands, aided by a proper application of manures, under a severe course of cropping. Without this system, all the manure he could make would not preserve half of the land in its present state of fertility for five years. He would as soon abandon planting as to abandon the horizontal system of culture.

We have assisted him in the work a good deal, and induced him to try guard-drains and hill-side ditches about 1851 or 1852, in order to lighten his labor and lessen his care and attention to it, as he is getting old and the confinement to the field and exposure to the cold during the winter and spring, are injurious to his health. But, he says, he could dispense with the drains and ditches if he could attend to the plowing in person every spring, and direct the work and correct the errors of the previous year's work.

An old negro horizontaler lays off the rows, and attends to one plantation where there are between six and seven hundred acres under the plumb ; and manages it astonishingly well for a man of his understanding.

His lands were originally of a good quality, and are of a mixed character. On one plantation, the grey and mulatto sandy land prevails, the subsoil being yellow and red clay a foot, and eighteen inches originally, in parts of it, beneath the surface soil.— The balance of the land is a chocolate loam on a red clay subsoil.

432

Some of it is considered stiff red clay land. On the other plantation, the chocolate loam prevails with a close, stiff red clay subsoil, requiring a long and sharp pointed plow to penetrate it when moderately dry. The rest of the land on this plantation, is grey and gravelly sandy soil, loose and porous. Most of the land on both places, is gently undulating ridges. Some of it hilly, and some knolls. The stiff red clay land is the most difficult and expensive to cultivate, and is the best land for grain. It is also the most difficult of his land to manage on the level method of culture.

I took my first lessons under him in the science, and owe him a debt of gratitude which can never be paid. He taught me the level culture, and I taught him the grading method. I commenced planting in 1844, in Hinds county, Mississippi, near Jackson, in copartnership with a brother. The *level culture* No. 1, and the *grading method* No. 1, both combined, without drains and hill-side ditches, had been in use a few years on that plantation. The soil, a close, tenacious, marly clay, of a yellow color, changing into an ashy colored soil, when thoroughly disintegrated and cultivated a year or two. I was partial to the level culture, and he to the grading method. I found out after a better acquaintance with the land, that the level culture retained the water too long, and made the land too wet for cotton. The grading method drained, but washed the land a good deal. After testing both methods to my satisfaction, I gave into his views rather from an avaricious motive than otherwise, to make better crops, though at a sacrifice of some land that took the streams and disappeared. From one to three inches fall were given to each row, when practicable, and the short inside rows plowed on a level. The land was rolling, and drains between the ridges conveyed the water into ditches and branches. We continued both systems until I left in December, 1850, and moved back to this place. The grading method has been kept up by him. I commenced a mixed system here in 1851, and have practiced both of them to a certain extent.

My land is chocolate and grey sandy land on a red and yellow clay subsoil. The grey land is of a fine texture, and much of it runs together and bakes. The chocolate land is loose and porous. It is generally a little undulating, some rolling, and some flat basins and ponds. It requires much ditching and surface drainage, and some under-draining. Forest growth, pine, oak, hickory, chestnut and poplar, with a variety of undergrowth.

My experience and observation teaches me, that the *level culture* is the best method ever discovered to prevent arable land, of the majority of soils in the South, from washing by rains, but not the best always to secure good crops. The grading method is the safest as a general rule for the culture of cotton, and can be pursued to great advantage on many soils that could be cultivated well on the level method, when one is willing to lose a little soil to make a better crop, by draining the land. No one system of culture is, then, applicable to all soils ; and on large plantations of mixed soils, both the level and grading systems should be applied. He is a fortunate man who understands the different methods well enough to apply them to the best advantage to the different soils, on a large plantation. It requires close application to field study, a good knowledge of the geology of the soil and the agricultural character of the land, with years of experience, to know how to cultivate land to the best advantage to the soil, and to the increased size of the purse.

SECTION I.

DEFINITION OF HORIZONTAL CULTURE.

Horizontalizing, Circling, and Leveling land are different terms employed by *Agriculturists*, in the *South*, to mean the same thing ; viz.: cultivating land in parallel lines run by a leveling instrument to direct and control rain water with the plow.

SECTION II.

ITS OBJECTS.

The objects of the System of horizontal culture are, to irrigate, to drain, and to preserve arable soil, in the simplest and most economical manner.

1st. By collecting, maintaining. and distributing rain water, on the surface of arable land, it effects natural irrigation.

2d. By conveying it away, by artificial channels, it effects drainage.

3d. By a proper system of irrigation and drainage, the soil and the food of plants are retained, and the fertility of the land is preserved.

SECTION III.

GENERAL CONSIDERATIONS.

Rain water being a solvent of the food of plants, and the medium of supplying them with many of their elements, the system of horizontal culture teaches us to control, and diffuse it in the soil, and distribute it in such a manner that the food of plants it contains, may be made available to the utmost degree, in promoting their growth ; and, when it exists in excess, to remove it without injuring, or washing away the soil.

Hence, we conclude that a correct system of manuring and improving land, depends greatly upon a proper regulation of water by the horizontal culture.

We perceive, then, that the horizontal culture is a beautiful branch of the science of Agriculture ; that it is a mixed art, a combination of irrigation, drainage, and manuring. We cannot, therefore, study it well, appreciate it properly, and practice it successfully, without some knowledge of agricultural engineering, of the geology of the soil, and hydraulics, and the application of them to irrigation and drainage.

We can then realize and appreciate the several advantages and connections of these branches of science with each other, in developing the chemical and physical properties of soils, and in the improvement of the fertility of land. To practice it scientifically, and successfully, we must study and understand the geological formation, and the agricultural character of the soil, and ascertain by observation and experiment what plants grow on it best, and are most profitable to cultivate.

Drill-husbandry, that is, the cultivation of crops in drills, by the ridge and furrow method, is indispensable, and the check and hill-culture are inadmissible except on level lands, as a general rule, by the system of horizontal culture. Of course, the broadcast method can be employed, as well with one method as with the other. The horizontal culture, by the ridge and furrow method, conflicts with the practice and opinions of many farmers, in the oldest of the Southern States, who advocate the check and hill culture ; but an acquaintance with the horizontal culture changes their practice and opinions.

SECTION IV.

THE DIFFERENT METHODS OF HORIZONTALIZING LAND

Are divided into two principal systems : viz :
1st. The level Method of Culture.
2d. The Grading Method of Culture.

The Level Method, (*or Irrigating System*,) is divided into two methods ; viz :
1st. Horizontaling with an instrument, on the level culture, without the aid of guard-drains, and hill-side ditches ; and,

435

2d. The level culture, aided by those drains and ditches.

The Grading Method, or Draining System, is divided into four different systems, viz :

1st. Horizontaling with an instrument, giving a grade to the rows, without the assistance of guard-drains, and hill-side ditches.

2d. With a grade to the rows, the same as that given to the drains and ditches, accompanied by those drains and ditches.

3d. With a grade given to the rows so as to empty their water into the drains and ditches.

4th. The straight-row method. The rows run up and down hills, and empty into hill-side ditches.

Besides the above methods, there is the old mode of horizontaling with the eye, without the aid of an instrument, or guard-drains, or hill-side ditches.

SECTION V.

THE DIFFERENT METHODS EXPLAINED.

The old method of hill-side plowing by running the rows around hill-sides with the plow, directed with the eye, is mere guess work, and only an approximation to accuracy, and of course is very imperfect.

It is done with the object of retaining the rain water in some instances, and of removing it in others ; in either case, it cannot effect the object in as perfect a manner as the new methods of level and grade work done on correct principles, by the leveling instrument.

When the object is to retain the rain water, it answers tolerably well in some countries, on porous, poor, sandy soils, where the showers are not frequent and are light, and where the luguminous crops are cultivated mostly on high beds and lands, as a substitute for artificial irrigation, and where the spade and hoe are used, generally, for the purpose of forming the ridges.

When adopted to drain hill-sides by the plow, unless the soil it not disposed to wash, it is very liable to do more injury to the land by washing it away than benefit by removing the water.

It should not by any means be resorted to now, since we can substitute better methods for it. It is the first step towards the horizontal culture from the straight-row method ; and was perhaps invented for the purpose of retaining instead of removing water.

1. *Level Culture or Irrigating System.*—By this method the rows are laid off with a leveling instrument on a perfect level, and the land cultivated without the aid of guard-drains, or hill-side ditches.

436

Here, science steps in to correct the imperfections of the eye.
It is impossible to lay off a level row by the eye. The most
skillful horizontaler cannot judge with accuracy the degree of inclination of lands, and discover all the inequalities of surface well
enough to horizontal land on a level by the eye. But, with a
rafter-level properly made and adjusted, it can be done, on an
even or uneven surface with perfect accuracy, on a dead level ;
and if the land be properly plowed the rows will hold all the
water that falls on them.

It is the best and only system ever invented to prevent comparatively level, and gently undulating lands, from washing.

It is intended to retain all the water that falls on land just
where it falls : this is natural irrigation. We all know the value
of water for the nourishment of animals and plants. They cannot live without it. Crops often fail for the want of it. By this
method none is wasted. Enough water is absorbed during winter and spring rains by land cultivated on this system, to almost
make some crops, especially when aided by light summer showers,
that would fail to do so, cultivated by the grading method.
This method is most applicable to all poor, thirsty, porous sandy
soils, whether they rest on clay or sandy subsoils ; and to many
varieties of clay soils not too compact and retentive of water.

We think we may say with truth, that we never knew, in this
country, but one kind of clay soil, on uplands, that this system
was not applicable to, on the ground of making it too wet for
profitable culture. That is the fine, close, tenacious, marly-clay
soil, resting on a retentive yellow clay subsoil, of the black-jack,
post-oak, and hickory ridges of Hinds, Madison, Yazoo, Carrol,
Holmes, Warren, and other parts of Mississippi.

Besides this kind of soil to which the level culture is objectionable, are the compact red and yellow clay soils of some hilly
lands, and the blue and white clays of low-lands.

The red and yellow clay lands may be cultivated by it, if they
admit of subsoiling to advantage. It is seldom that the level
culture is objectionable for corn and small grains, and the root
crops. But when it causes the soil to become too wet during
the cultivation of crops, to plow well, and hastens a rapid growth
of grass and weeds that destroy the crops, it is an evidence that
it should be abandoned, and a grading method substituted for it.

2. *Level Culture with Guard-drains, or Hill-side Ditches.*—
The rows are plowed on a level, and guard-drains, or hill-side
ditches are added, with a slight grade to correct the evil of the
excess of water, and remove it, should the ridges break. Some
soils, such as close tenacious clays, though plowed deep, may absorb a great deal of water during heavy and repeated rains, until
the plowed soil becomes well saturated ; the water will then sink
until it reaches the impervious strata, not broken by the plow,

and move along that strata on steep hill-sides, until it accumulates in such quantities as to break the ridges, and flow downhill, carrying the soil with it.

Again, in clay soils, plowed shallow, a heavy rain succeeding another heavy rain, that had run the land together, and baked by the sun, and closed its pores, may cause the water to accumulate in level rows until the volume and weight of water makes a breach, and some of the ridges give way, and the water is precipitated from row to row till it reaches an outlet.

A mole, a stump, bad plowing, the wheels of a cart or wagon, and other causes may break the ridges, and cause the land to wash. To prevent such a disaster, guard-drains and hill-side ditches have been invented, to aid and protect the level culture, and to correct the ignorance and errors of the inexperienced horizontaler, and save his time, labor, and soil. But, in many instances, they encourage careless work, and are sometimes evils to the system. They should not be relied upon too much ; the remedy is sometimes worse than the disease.

1. *The Grading Method, (or Draining System.)*—The great object of this method is surface drainage, of arable land : hence it is divided into,

1st. Horizontaling with a grade given to the rows, without the aid of guard-drains and hill-side ditches.

Every row is designed to drain itself, and of course the other drains are unnecessary. It is a kind of self-sustaining system, and a substitute for straight rows. It is beautiful in theory, but difficult to practice in a general system, on all soils. Some fields, and parts of fields, no grade is necessary, whilst different grades are required according to the inclination of land, and the physical properties of soils, and the length of rows. The length of rows is very irregular by this method, and short rows emptying into long ones, pouring their water into them, force them to wash into gullies. Hence, it is impossible to prevent the soil from washing by this method. It should be confined to close clay soils. This method, combined with level culture, answers a better purpose.

2d. *Horizontaling with a grade given to the rows* the same as that of guard-drains and hill-side ditches. This method was adopted, doubtless, to correct the evils of the preceding method.

When the drains are well made, they check the flow of water descending down the hills from the broken rows, and thus convey it away and protect the land beneath them. Without their aid much mischief might take place, but if the work by the preceding method be well done, there is no need of the drains to aid it. Imperfect work, then, excuses their employment. But they are indispensable evils to the system they are used to protect, and are much employed.

3. *Horizontaling with a grade given to the rows* so as to empty their water into guard-drains and hill-side ditches.

This is truly a draining process, employed on clay-up-lands, and low-lands, and answers a good purpose when the rows are not too long, and the fall is correct. Of course the drains and ditches require considerable fall, and to be very capacious. It is popular with those planters who have clay soils, and trust much to overseers, and negroes, and kind Providence for gentle showers, to make them crops. But overseers make mistakes, plowmen do bad work, and the clouds pour down heavy rains, and the soil, as it were, melts and runs rapidly away. To answer a good purpose, the overseers, plowmen, and drains require strict attention, or the land will be injured by this method.

4. *The Straight row Method, with Hill-side Ditches.*—The ditches in this instance are cut on hill-sides with considerable fall, and the land is plowed on the old straight-row method, the plowman raising his plow over the ditch banks as he passes them. It is evidently a troublesome business to raise the plow over the ditches, and keep them clean. If the soil be sandy, and disposed to wash, the ditches must be deep and large, the fall great, and the plowman careful, which is contrary to negro character, or else every heavy rain will fill up the ditches with sand, break their banks, and cut the land into gullies and galls. However, it has the recommendation of being simple, and better than the old up and down hill method, without the protection of ditches.

Experience will soon teach any one that it is a bad system for hilly lands ; for low-lands it answers a good purpose for quick and effectual drainage, and enables some low-lands to be cultivated that could not be without this kind of drainage.

On the rich low wet lands, and the rolling up-lands, in the prairie or lime lands of Alabama and Mississippi, when too wet, this kind of expeditious drainage is the *sine qua non,*—the proper method to remove the water, and dry the land in time to prepare it for a crop, and to save the cotton from damage by excess of water.

SECTION VI.

PHILOSOPHY OF THE LEVEL METHOD.

It is true there are deep, sandy, alluvial soils that absorb all the water that falls on them during the heaviest rains ; but again, there are other soils when cultivated on the straight-row method, that are injured by the irregular distribution of water, one part of the field being drained too much, whilst the land below it is being drowned ; thereby, both parts sustaining an injury.

439

The crops on such land grow and mature irregularly in consequence of the irregular distribution of the water and the culture. The level culture corrects these evils. It retains the water and soil in its proper place, and when the land is cultivated alike, all remains nearer the condition of dryness, and the crops grow off more uniformly on the same quality of land and mature nearer the same time.

Should the land be manured, the elements of the manure remain where deposited, and not removed by the first rain to the nearest ditch or branch. It irrigates and preserves the soil, when properly done. It is the best method to employ to aid in restoring exhausted lands.

It is very difficult to lay down any set of rules by which to do the work ; because, the physical properties of soils are such, and the inequalities of land vary so much, no one rule or set of rules would apply to any great extent of surface. One part of a field might require the level culture, and another part the grading method. Hence, we are forced to adopt the one or the other, according to circumstances, and to do the work correctly, we must be acquainted with all the different methods.

It matters but little, where the work begins or terminates in the field, so the rows are laid off accurately, on a level. The most important rule is to follow the level, let it lead to whatever point it may. It will run at every point of the compass, and form rows of every imaginable form and length, terminating any where in the field. It will lead the new beginner in the art, into a maze from which he can scarcely extricate himself, but he should have patience and perseverance, and all will come out right and no land be lost. He must be content to follow the level, but not try and make it follow him, and force it to any particular place or termination. The only way to terminate a row at a certain point, is to start the level at that point ; but ten chances to one, in returning, if the next row does not go off at an angle, and terminate at some distance from the first starting point. It is immaterial whether the rows be long, short, straight or crooked, or where they begin and terminate, so they are on a level, and the land be well plowed in rows or ridges. This should ever be borne in mind. The horizontaler will make mistakes, and be awkward at first, but will learn to do the work correctly.

SECTION VII.

ADVANTAGES OF THE LEVEL METHOD.

This system is the best mode of cultivating land ever invented to prevent the devastating effects of rain water washing away the soil and the manures put upon it. It enables the soil to absorb more water, and retain it better, and give it back to plants when needed, more effectually and regularly than any other mode, thus preventing the deleterious effects of drought. It makes the soil more uniform in production; improves its fertility by retaining the manures; makes it easier to work, with less labor; causes the crops to grow faster, more uniform in growing and maturing; and as the rain water is evenly distributed on all parts of the field alike, when one part can be plowed, all can be done at the same time, and saves time turning around at wet land.

DISADVANTAGES OF THE LEVEL METHOD.

It seems in the order of things in this world, there is always an evil attached to almost every good. So it is in this instance, but we shall find that the disadvantages disappear by practice, and are counterbalanced by the advantages.

The disadvantages are, the unavoidable necessity of having so nany short rows terminating at any part of the field, forcing the plowman to turn around often, and lose time by so doing: (this time, however, is made up in the greater number of long rows.) The injury to the crop, done by the plow, the mule and the hand in turning around at the end of the short rows. The difficulty at first of doing the work well, and of plowing the rows out without breaking up the work, and deranging the rows. The constant care and attention, by the overseer or employer, to maintain and keep up the system. The necessity of using the ridge and furrow system and abandoning the check and hill culture.

SECTION VIII.

PHILOSOPHY OF THE GRADING METHOD.

Surface drainage is one of the most important operations connected with the tillage of the Southern soil. The value of the grading method cannot be over-estimated. It has to contend with a troublesome element, that is a moveable element, always seeking its level, whose particles have a great affinity for each other, and running together whenever they can, thus accumulating in a mass, and increasing its volume and velocity when in motion. This element we wish to control with a level and the plow on the surface of arable land, and derive all the advantages of it we can as a feeder of plants, and at the same time, get rid of the excess that would prove injurious to the soil and growing plants. Nature does this for us in some soils and teaches us how to do it in others. It sinks the water in porous soils, and stores it up for future use of plants, and removes it when superabundant, from undulating close clay soils before it does injury to the plants that do not require it, teaching us to level porous thirsty soils, and deepen and drain compact close soils. We should study carefully the operations of nature, and apply its beautiful principles to the present subject, and conform them to the limited capacity of the uneducated minds of men. Very few fields of one hundred acres have the same inclination of surface, and one variety and depth of soil. Land slopes in every direction, and each hill-side or plane of inclination requires sometimes a different mode of drainage and a different method of culture.

In examining a field, we may find some acres requiring the level culture, others again, one method of grading, and another a different method, and so on perhaps, through the whole list of the different methods of grading. It would be improper, then, to employ one system alone for every part of the field. The different methods should be applied according to the demands of the land. Science should guide us, and the one-system horizontaler is led into error by his efforts to apply it to all localities and inclinations of surface of land. We should be acquainted with all the systems, and not make a hobby of any one. Better try first one and then another, in experimenting, and select those that are best and most applicable to the land. If we find a straight row more convenient and better than a crooked one, if it be correct, adopt it, without sticking to the idea that the horizontal culture consists of a system of crooked rows. Experience will soon teach the new beginner the degree of grade necessary to give to his rows and drains, and the number of drains or ditches to use, to drain a certain area of land. The grade to the rows and drains is governed by the kind of soil, the declivity of the land, the extent of the surface to be drained, and the method of horizontaling they are intended to aid. If the level culture, with drains, be adopted, a few shallow guard-drains with a fall of from one to two inches for every span of the level, may answer in moderately close clay soils, and less fall in porous sandy soils. If the grading method be adopted, the fall of the rows and the drains depends upon the kind of method of plowing used, and the nature of the soil cultivated. We should recollect, that the washing power of water descending a hill recently plowed, is dependent upon the declivity and the length of the hill, the depth of the plowing, the character of the soil, and the quantity of water in motion. Hence, the greater the fall, the longer the hill, the shallower the plowing, the more porous and light the soil, and the greater the volume of water, the more the land will be washed. If the grade be not sufficient and the dimensions great enough, the rows are apt to be chocked and broken. A regular and proper grade must be given, and if an error be com-

442

mitted, it should be on the side of too little fall.   If the grade
be too much the rows will wash into gullies.   Guard-drains and
hill-side ditches should have grade and capacity enough to drain
the land speedily and effectually, without having their sides and
bottoms washed too much.   With a proper fall and dimensions,
they may be used to convey sand to fill up gullies, basins, and
deposit it convenient to cover galled places.

SECTION IX.

ADVANTAGES OF THE GRADING METHOD.

It possesses all the advantages of surface drainage of arable
soils in a simple and the best possible manner without doing
serious damage to the land.   It is the best method ever invented
to assist in breaking up galls and gullies, and filling up depressions in the land, and the beds of old ditches and branches, as
well as ponds, basins and bogs, and in aiding the plow and the
hoe in restoring worn-out soils.

It possesses, also, many of the advantages of the level culture.

DISADVANTAGES OF THE METHOD.

By careless construction of drains, and neglecting to attend to
them afterwards, they are liable to choke and break, and wash
the land below them into gullies.   When they have too much
fall, each row or drain is apt to wash into a gully, and do harm
to land below their mouths by covering it with sand.   They distribute water irregularly, and where not demanded, drying the
ridges and hills too much, and drowning the bottoms.   Upon
the whole, they are of minor importance compared to the benefits
of drainage.

SECTION X.

SUBSOIL PLOWING

Means loosening the subsoil with a plow without any mould-
board to turn it up.

We have seen, Nature teaches us three important operations
that are essential to the perfection of the horizontal culture, viz:
to open, to deepen and to drain the soil.

An open, deep and dry soil, we all know, can be cultivated to
better advantage and profit, by either the level culture, or grading method, than a close, shallow and wet soil by any method.

443

32

PRESERVATION and PROTECTION

OF

Cultivated Lands

FROM SURFACE WASHING.

A NEW SYSTEM OF HILLSIDE
DITCHING.

By DAVID NICKOLS, Allatoona, Ga.

ATLANTA, GEORGIA:
JAS. P. HARRISON & CO., PRINTERS.
1883.

INTRODUCTORY.

In presenting this subject to the careful investigation of farmers I am prompted solely by the influence it bears upon the success of the agriculture of our country. It is a plain fact that no one who is blessed with eyesight can fail to see the general and rapid depletion of Southern farms caused by the surface washing and leaching of the soil. Go in any direction you may, the unsightly gully, or the naked and denuded surface of mother earth, greets our vision. Farms that were once rich and productive are to-day cultivated in patches, and more or less of them turned out to gullies, exhausted, and the soil washed off. In a great many cases we see the signs of the old and abandoned hillside ditches marked by rows of briars, broomsedge and bushes, and very often large gullies where formerly were hillside ditches.

A most lamentable fact that close observation and careful investigation discloses, is the sad truth that there is scarcely one farmer out of a thousand who has not washed his soil away through the channels of his ditches. This has not been done in every instance by letting the ditches break over and wash gullies up and down the hills, but in very many cases where the farmer has used great care in giving his ditches a gradual fall, and when exceedingly diligent in keeping them cleaned out so that all the water, soil and valuable vegetable debris could have a safe and rapid transit out of the field into the nearest ravine, or creek, or public or private road. The late Dr. Lavender once asserted that the washing of the soils impoverished the farmers of Georgia more than all the lien laws, guano bills and credit systems combined.

In his address before the Georgia State Agricultural Society Mr. Furman said:

"The scientific trouble is gone, but the mechanical difficulty remains. Shall I say what it is? Do you not all recognize it? It is the fearful loss of the top soil with it's valuable elements of fertility, caused by our tropical washing rains and the shallow system of culture to which we are driven in the cultivation of our standard crops, corn and cotton."

In the Scientific Manual, issued from the Department of Agriculture of Georgia, the author says:

"The principal products removed from the farm in Georgia, and sent to market, carry off very little plant food. If, therefore, all refuse products are either returned directly to the soil or fed to animals whose manure, solid and liquid, is applied to the soil, it will require many years, *if surface washing is prevented,*

445

to become exhausted, even if no artificial fertilizers are used."

Again, "A single heavy rain in winter or early spring, when the surface is finely pulverized by recent freezes, often causes greater injury to the naked fields of the South than would the removal of a dozen crops of lint cotton."

We refer the reader to these high authorities as corroborative evidence of the fact of the fearful exhaustion of Southern soils by surface washing and leaching, owing, in a great measure, to the nakedness of the lands necessarily resulting from cotton culture:

"Just here some of the results obtained by Mr. J. B. Lawes, at his celebrated experimental farm at Rothamstead, in England, are exceedingly instructive and interesting. He finds that where land is kept perfectly clean by repeated ploughings, no crop being allowed to grow upon it, that fifty pounds of nitrogen are annually taken away and lost from one acre by the rain water which drains through it, that is, leached out of it, whilst on adjoining land, sowed in wheat, only some twenty-five pounds are annually removed from an acre, viz: fifteen (15) pounds in the wheat crop and ten (10) in the rain water which sinks through the soil. It is just at this point that grass and grain growing regions have a most decided advantage over those that grow cotton and tobacco; in the latter the land leaches and washes terribly, in the former the washing is almost nothing, and the leaching is very greatly reduced, scarcely exceeding in the matter of nitrogen that which is annually supplied to the land through the rainfall—eight to ten pounds per acre."

It is not the purpose of the writer to go into all the details of exhaustion of Southern farms and to give a sure and perfect remedy for such exhaustion, for he candidly confesses his inability to do so, but it is his object to call attention to the great importance of his subject and give such light and relief as he has been able to gather from a number of years of careful and patient experiment. Exhaustion of soils is generally admitted to be caused by three agencies, viz: surface washing, leaching and removal of crops, the chief of which is surface washing.

I will here state that the subject of how to prevent the surface washing of our soil has engaged the most earnest attention of the author for the last thirty years. He has read every available article on the subject with great interest and practiced to some extent most of the plans suggested, as well as every plan that his own

brain could originate, but alas, all his efforts in that
direction have been far from satisfactory, and seemed
only to mock him until he was upon the very verge
of despair. The loss sustained by the surface washing
of the soil is entirely different from that caused by the
removal of exhaustive crop, for in the latter there is
something to show for the injury done to the land in
the way of crops taken from the soil, but in the
former, nothing is left in payment or rebuttal, but
it is an entire clear, frightful loss. I feel that the
subject has impressed its importance upon me as
though the fate of nations depended upon it.

Notwithstanding I made my ditches large and gave
them a regular fall so that they carried all the water
that would accumulate in them during the heaviest
rains; yet they were far from satisfactory; for I discovered that my soil was surely and rapidly leaving
me through the channel of my ditches, and the more
I examined the operations of my own ditches and
those of my brother farmers the more thoroughly I
became convinced that the attempt to prevent surface washing by the general system of hillside ditching was a deception and a snare. The question then
presented itself in another form: How shall I so construct a ditch as to carry off all surplus water, and at
the same time retain the soil? I then fell upon my
present plan, which I have never since changed.

HILLSIDE DITCHING.

MY PLAN STATED.

In laying off my ditches, I run them at intervals
on a perfect level, varying from thirty to ninety yards
in length, according to the location and length of the
ditch, making them from six to ten inches deeper in
those level places than anywhere else, so that the
water in passing over those sags or level spaces will
deposit most of the elements of fertility held in solution or suspension, as it passes over these level areas
very slowly.

In the spring of 1877, after some experiment and
much reflection upon the plan, I commenced its general adoption on my farm. The more I thought it
over the more thoroughly I became convinced of its
superiority. Only one objection presented itself, and

that was the rapid filling up of those sags or levels, but I determined to keep those places shoveled out, much preferring to save it on my own land than to have it washed off into the creek or carried to my neighbor's land.

LOCATING HILL-SIDE DITCHES.

This operation is perhaps by far more difficult to describe or perform than any of the operations pertaining to hill-side ditching.

First, there is such variety in the topography of different farms that only an outline can be given, so that one may, by adapting general rules laid down to his surroundings, approximate correctness. Secondly, as a general rule the line or incline or grade should run up in the reverse direction from that of the stream whi.h drains the land, that is, the water in the ditch should often be made to empty up stream, but not always, as it sometimes happens that there is a public or private road which forms a good outlet, and in many cases the course of ditch will be that of the stream below. Again, in many instances, there will be old gullie, which will do to empty into, but always with a view to filling them up. Just here let us impress the reader with one idea never to be forgotten, and that is, to improve the spot on which you empty your ditch by catching what is held in suspension in the water; of course we do not desire to add to the fertility of public roads neither do we wish the cream of our soil to drift up into the fence corners bordering our public road, which, to be utilized at all, must be hauled back to our fields, or the fence must be torn down and the old fence row cultivated. This many of our friends are doing where the stock law is in force, but this accumulated fertility along many of the road-sides is being rapidly exhausted as the mode of culture practiced is such as to rapidly move it into ditches or gullies to be washed away. Therefore, whenever the ditch is to empty into a public road there should be particular attention given to the filtering of the water before it is allowed to pass into the road-ditch or outlet. We mean by so constructing our ditches as to cause the water to pass off in as purified a state as possible, because, as a general thing, we must and do give a final farewell to all the elements of fertility contained in it.

The first and general rule will apply with more force to fresh lands, for when first cleared is the most favorable time to commence improving and preventing our lands from surface-washing. It is a prevalent idea among farmers that surface washing amounts to almost nothing the first two years of its cultivation, but I apprehend it is a great deal more than is generally supposed, and a careful investigation will sustain my opinion.

I never did cut ditches in a new ground, but if I did I would not make a great mistake, but I do urge the construction of ditches in the second year's cultivation. Here the operator is likely to become very much puzzled about where to locate and where to empty his ditches, for the reason that there are no gullies or denuded surface upon which to empty his ditches, but in almost every field in broken countries there are ravines or hollows, some of which we term wet and some dry hollows.

First construct dams of rock if they exist on the field, (no one ought ever pile them up for they are too much in the way) across these dry hollows every three, four or six feet fall; that is to say, you construct the first dam near the head of the ravine, then go below until you reach a point that is three, four or six feet below, and so continue until you reach the mouth of the ravine or outside of the field. Be sure always to leave the dams lower in the center than at the sides, for if the water is forced around at either side of the dam it will be sure to wash a gully on the lower end of the dam. In a great many instances, these hollows should have a blind ditch running up through them, or more correctly stated, underdrained. When these hollows are so fixed, all the soil carried into them will lodge against these dams, so that instead of having large gullies that you cannot drive a cart over, you will have rich deposits, making the best crops in the field and affording an easy passage for wagon and team. A striking illustration is where a fence has been built across hollows.

Hollows so arranged afford the most favorable outlets for ditches, these dams catching what little soil may have escaped through the ditches.

These dams can be constructed out of logs and brush also, but I prefer rock if in easy access. The rapid growth of vegetation will add greatly to their upbuilding (the common plumb bush is especially adapted to such locations.) These dams may be raised by degrees as circumstances demand, being quite sure that you always leave them lower in their centers so that water will pass over them in the middle of dams. They will ultimately, by proper care, extend to a considerable length, owing altogether to the steepness or grade of the hillside on each side of the bottom.

On old lands where there exist gullies and naked surfaces of earth, these afford many more favorable outlets for ditches than on fresh lands where they are not so numerous. In the first named, the ditches can, with great advantage, run in parallel directions with adjoining streams, run to one of these gullies and discharge into it. By having the gully well filled with brush, and letting it pass down the gully for some distance, after which intercept it by commencing another ditch and carrying it some distance and discharging it into another gully, and letting it flow down the line of the gully through brush and rubbish of any kind. This will gradually fill them (the gullies) up, if care is taken to catch all soil and suspended particles in every conceivable way possible. After water has been conveyed in this direction near the foot of the hill, there should be an extra ditch run in a reverse direction to convey the water to the nearest water-course. This can and should often be done by underdrains. We mean, that after we have controlled and conveyed the water to low or bottom lands by passing the water through underdrains we would rob it of most of its fertilizing elements, because the water in its passage to tile will have to sink through a considerable depth of soil, thereby purifying it almost entirely.

By this process there would be but little of the coarser sands reach the foot of the hill which is so rapidly filling our streams, forming in many instances insurmountable barriers to the profitable drainage of some of the finest lands in the country. This difficulty can only be removed by special legislation. The subject demands the serious attention of our political advisers. I know of more than one interruption or falling out between neighbors on account of one allowing the sterilized sand from his lands to flood those of the other. This could have been obviated by an intelligent practice of drainage. Would that every farmer in the land fully realized the great truth that it is impossible for them to wash sand from their farms without carrying off vast quantities of plant food. The coarse sand is the last to leave and travels much slower than any of the other part of the soil. In truth, it may be termed the rear guard of our soil in its march seaward. The natural formation of many hillsides require very long ditches. In such cases we should endeavor to divide the direction of the water, letting a portion run one way and the other another, but instead of running one long line of ditch and letting it discharge at both ends, would prefer two short ditches, or by dividing the long ditch into two, commencing as near as possible in the center of the line and running in opposite directions, but observing to commence each line above or below and letting the ends or starting points of each extend some distance beyond the other, forming a sort of zig-zag passage for wagons and teams in moving from one plat to another without having to cross any ditch.

I have found it convenient in some instances to extend a line of ditch from one slope to that of another. In this case what would be the lower side of the hill on my right on one slope would be the lower side on my left on the other. By this I mean we will cross a point where there is as much need of the dirt to be thrown out on one side as the other, and at these particular locations the ditch should always be made deeper than the general line of the bottom of the ditch, for it affords very favorable conditions for these level spaces, which are of great importance, acting somewhat like a reservoir or silt basin.

In several instances we have caused the ditches of the whole field to finally discharge upon one spot or space of land not exceeding one acre, which was greatly worn, and by laying plenty of brush, poles, logs and other rubbish of every conceivable kind, it is fast improving by catching the washings of other portions of the field, and by again intercepting the water at the foot of the hill in an extra large ditch and conveying it to the main stream.

Be careful to put ditches close enough together to hold the water that may accumulate in them. If you have any doubts about this, be sure to give the ditch the benefit of the doubt, ordinarily not nearer than twenty yards, nor further than eighty or one hundred yards apart. Old fields well set in briars and sedge and woods form good outlets for ditches, but the practice of running a ditch along the side of a hill and turning it out down the hill by the side of a fence and washing out a gully, or that of cutting out small ditches directly up and down hills, is very objectionable; far better turn out a considerable space and by well covering with old logs, brush and such like, allow the water to pass down through it, where it will not wash out gullies. Indeed, under no circumstances should there be great gullies even on the most rolling land that I have ever seen under the plow, if proper care and attention is bestowed at the right time, and that is when the land is fresh. Correct judgment as to proper outlets is of great importance, but, in the language of David Dickson, "It is hard to transfer knowledge, and much harder to transfer art and judgment." But one of the greatest benefits is realized by the filling up of these and cultivating their former locations every four or five years. By close observation one may be able to remedy all defects both as to outlets or lines of ditches in the second cutting or construction of new ditches.

Be sure always to commence near enough the top of the hill, or the source from whence the waters gather. I have in quite a number of instances, gone outside of a field and laid out lines through woods in order to intercept the water before it gathered in too large volumes, and turned it off in more favorable directions, and by that means avoiding the extra labor it would have required to have let it come into the field. One should always take into account the amount of land above each ditch and its absorptive powers, as some soils possess this quality in a much greater degree than others.

As to the proper grade, that is dependent on circumstances, perhaps more on the kind of outlet or jump-offs than any other. By this I mean where the water gets away very fast, as falling into a deep stream, some six or ten feet to its bottom, or bounding down a steep cliff or hill. Where such outlets or jump-offs are to be had, I prefer the line of ditch to be on a perfect level if not more than a hundred yards long and the bottom of the ditch below a level, that is, make the whole line of ditch deeper than the last fifteen or twenty feet, but make the fifteen or twenty feet wider than the long and deeper portion of the ditch.

On very steep lands the ditches require some more fall than on a moderate grade, but even on steep hillsides the ditches should at intervals run on perfect levels from twenty to sixty yards in length, always observing to locate these perfectly level places on the straightest part of the lines, never on sudden curves, but always give some fall where the curves exist. The grade of fall depends entirely on location, sometimes it may run as high as three or four inches in twelve feet, but it is hardly ever necessary to give such fall for more than one or two rods at a time.

The theory is, to have lines of ditches so arranged that for the first five or ten yards some fall, then say from twenty to sixty yards if the line is tolerably straight on a level, again some fall, and then level, and so on through the entire length of the ditch, observing always to locate the level spaces on the straightest and least abrupt part of the hillside, and to give the fall on all sudden curves and steeper portions of land.

My readers perhaps will be greatly astonished that I can show thousands of farms or lands upon which, lying in such a shape, the line of the ditch may be laid off by the use of a perfect instrument on a perfect level, and yet when the ditch is cut and finished, it will be found by applying the level to the bottom of the ditch that it has considerable fall. For instance, if you commence where the slope of the hill is not more than three feet fall in fifty yards and gradually approach a point where it is ten feet in twenty yards, it will be found that the construction of the ditch where the slope is greatest, necessarily causes it to be deeper upon the upper side than where the grade of the hill is not so steep. I call attention to this very important fact for fear that with a good level the operator might make a mistake, but such mistake is not liable to occur except where the operator commences a ditch on a moderate grade and soon arrives where it is very steep, or where the hillside is very steep, and then passes on to where the grade is about the same as it was at the starting point.

In locating lines of ditches it will often pay the farmer in his first attempt to employ the services of some one who has had some practical and successful experience in the matter, but as a general thing it will be the best for him to carefully study the peculiar topography of each and every one of his fields, and apply the rules laid down as near as possible, and constantly watch their general application, after carefully locating all lines, and having them marked by one good furrow with a good common plow. The line of furrow should always indicate the upper edge of the ditch.

A SLOW PROCESS OF DEEP PLOWING OR CUTTING HILLSIDE DITCHES WITH A VIEW OF FILLING THEM UP AGAIN.

Yes, a rotation or change of ditches is as essential as rotation or change of crops. Indeed it is by filling up the ditches and cultivating the spaces allotted to them that the highest degree of success can be reached. First, the deep plowing out and removal of the earth, especially the clays deposited on the lower bank of the ditch in constructing it exposes considerable surface of clay to the action of air, water, freezing and the sun, generally termed weathering, which gradually improves it, unlocking the mineral elements of plant-food existing heretofore in a locked up or inert condition and by the absorption of valuable gases from the atmosphere. Most farmers have noticed the gradual improvement of clays dug and piled out from cellars, and wells. A very noticeable instance is seen in the embankments of breastworks thrown up during our late war. These ditches should be filled up and new ones cut every three or four or six years; a cheap and rapid process of doing this is to take a two-horse plow, commence on lower bank and turn the dirt from lower bank into the old channel of the ditch, coming back on upper side, a kind of sandwitching, that is, first a furrow of clay from lower side, next a furrow from the upper side of the deposits of rich vegetable matters, continuing the process until the old channel of the ditch is completely filled up, and if the instructions are carefully carried out this line or space occupied by the ditch will be higher or elevated above the general surface of the land joining it, and in a very improved condition for the growth of succeeding crop. *The writer is aware that then, and only then, will this system be fully appreciated by most farmers, for it will be then and there that they will see the truth of my theory, existing in the most simple, plain and undeniable facts.* The favorable effects of deep and thorough preparation of lands are so well understood, and have been in practice so long in the older countries, that it seems amazingly strange that it should be overlooked by so many farmers in the South, especially since it has been repeatedly demonstrated that deeply pulverized soils will stand drouth so much better than those subjected to shallow plowing. It gives plants a deeper and wider range to gather plant food and hastens and prepares food for plants that otherwise lie dormant or locked up. It is strongly argued by some very prominent writers that it is the cheapest and surest way to increase our area of land instead of buying more by the side of it, to send our plows and spades deeper down and pulverize to the depth of twelve inches. One acre broken twelve inches would be equal to three stirred to the depth of four inches. Be this true or not, I have an abiding faith in the future indorsement of my system of filling up or changing locations of my ditches. Prof. J. P. Steele of Mobile, Alabama, thus sums up the reasons in favor of deep pulverization of soil. He says: " Deep plowing enriches the soil by preparing it for rapidly absorbing the rains that fall, charged with ammonia, etc., from the atmosphere and filtering the important fertilizing elements from them. Soil not thoroughly pulverized does not do this. On the other hand the waters run off over the surface not only carrying the ammonia with them, but also a large per cent of the fertilizing elements already on the land." These reasons, were there no other, ought to decide us in favor of deeply working the soil, but there are many other good reasons for doing so, as for instance:

1st. It gives full scope to the roots of plants, causing them to become more fibrous than they would in a packed soil, hence to afford the growth for better opportunities for feeding.

2d. It admits the air directly to the spongioles of the roots, without which no plant can have a healthy growth.

3d. It raises the temperature of the soil in spring by admitting the warm air and warm rains.

4th. It enables the soil to absorb large quantities of fertilizing gases from the atmosphere.

5th. It acts as a drain in excessive wet weather, causing the water to settle down and escape through the subsoil or immediately along its surface.

6th. It leads to more rapid decomposition of dead vegetable matter in the soil, by bringing it directly in contact with the decomposing gases, thus speedily converting it into plant food.

These ditches when filled up act as underdrains for several years; the writer has noticed water running out of the mouth of these old ditches for several days after excessive wet spells of rainy weather, and could locate the line of the old ditch several hundred yards distant by the general appearance of the land through which they run, the surface appearing to dry off much sooner than where no ditch was cut.

By continuing this process for a number of years, that is change location every four years, which is the maxium, we would doubtless gain a point in the distant future where we could dispense with them altogether, but that is for the future generations to decide.

C. Environmental Planning

The study of ancient civilizations reveals different patterns in the Old and New World. Near Eastern societies grew and flourished in desert-like regions whereas American civilizations such as the Inca chose more humid climates. In both cases little remains that indicates future environmental planning. This will comprise a large component in Volumes 2 and 3, but it is fitting that the last selection in this volume should bridge the gap. Furthermore, the works and influence of John Wesley Powell are so great that his foresight must be singled out and form the finale. The reader is referred to the many fine biographies that give details of his life, but some comments upon his stature will aid in providing the setting for his article.

Powell (1834–1902) was born in what is now New York City and spent his early life in Ohio, Wisconsin, and Illinois. He is remembered for such exploits as his classic voyage down the Grand Canyon in 1869, and his leadership of the Powell Survey. He was Director of the Bureau of Ethnology and the second Director of the U.S. Geological Survey (1881–1902). He initiated the irrigation surveys of the West which led to the establishment of the Bureau of Reclamation in 1902. The condensed reproduction presented here is a classic as are many of his publications such as *The Colorado River of the West* (1874) and the *Canyons of the Colorado* (1895). It was G. K. Gilbert, speaking before the Washington Academy of Sciences on February 16, 1903, who best summed up Powell's accomplishments:

> The glow of his enthusiasm, the illumination of his broad philosophy, the warmth of his friendship, are still with us . . . It was through this personality too that he accomplished much of his work for science. Gathering about him the ablest men he could secure, he was yet always the intellectual leader, and few of his colleagues could withstand the influence of his master mind. Phenomenally fertile in his ideas, he was absolutely free in their communication with the result that many of his suggestions—a number which can never be known—were unconsciously appropriated by his associates and incorporated in their published results . . . The scientific produce which he directly and indirectly inspired may equal, or even exceed that which stands in his own name.

33

REPORT

ON THE

LANDS OF THE ARID REGION

OF THE

UNITED STATES,

WITH A

MORE DETAILED ACCOUNT OF THE LANDS OF UTAH.

WITH MAPS.

BY

J. W. POWELL.

APRIL 3, 1878.—Referred to the Committee on Appropriations and
ordered to be printed.

WASHINGTON:
GOVERNMENT PRINTING OFFICE.
1878.

CHAPTER V.

CERTAIN IMPORTANT QUESTIONS RELATING TO IRRIGABLE LANDS.

THE UNIT OF WATER USED IN IRRIGATION.

The unit of water employed in mining as well as manufacturing enterprises in the west is usually the inch, meaning thereby the amount of water which will flow through an orifice one inch square. But in practice this quantity is very indefinite, due to the "head" or amount of pressure from above. In some districts this latter is taken at six inches. Another source of uncertainty exists in the fact that increase in the size of the orifice and increase in the amount of flow do not progress in the same ratio. An orifice of one square inch will not admit of a discharge one-tenth as great as an orifice of ten square inches. An inch of water, therefore, is variable with the size of the stream as well as with the head or pressure. For these reasons it seemed better to take a more definite quantity of water, and for this purpose the *second-foot* has been adopted. By its use the volume of a stream will be given by stating the number of cubic feet which the stream will deliver per second.

THE QUANTITATIVE VALUE OF WATER IN IRRIGATION.

In general, throughout the Arid Region the extent of the irrigable land is limited by the water supply; the arable lands are much greater than the irrigable. Hence it becomes necessary, in determining the amount of irrigable lands with reasonably approximate accuracy, to determine the value of water in irrigation; that is, the amount of land which a given amount of water will serve.

All questions of concrete or applied science are more or less complex by reason of the multifarious conditions found in nature, and this is eminently true of the problem we are now to solve, namely, how much water must an acre of land receive by irrigation to render agriculture thereon most successful; or, how much land will a given amount of water adequately supply. This will be affected by the following general conditions, namely, the amount of water that will be furnished by rainfall, for if there is rainfall in the season of growing crops, irrigation is necessary only to supply the deficiency; second, the character of the soil and subsoil. If the conditions of soil are unfavorable, the water supply may be speedily evaporated on the one hand, or quickly lost by subterranean drainage on the other; but if there be a soil permitting the proper permeation of water downward and upward, and an impervious subsoil, the amount furnished by artificial irrigation will be held in such a manner as to serve the soil bearing crops to the greatest extent; and, lastly, there is a great difference in the amount of water needed for different crops, some requiring less, others more.

Under these heads come the general complicating conditions. In the mountainous country the areal distribution of rainfall is preëminently variable, as the currents of air which carry the water are deflected in various ways by diverse topographic inequalities. The rainfall is also exceedingly irregular, varying from year to year, and again from season to season.

But in all these varying conditions of time and space there is one fact which must control our conclusions in considering the lands of Utah, namely: any district of country which we may be studying is liable for many seasons in a long series to be without rainfall, when the whole supply must be received from irrigation. Safety in agricultural operations will be secured by neglecting the rainfall and considering only the supply of water to be furnished by artificial methods; the less favorable seasons must be considered; in the more favorable there will be a surplus. In general, this statement applies throughout the Arid Region, but there are some limited localities where a small amount of rainfall in the season of growing crops seems to be constant from year to year. In such districts irrigation will only be used to supply deficiencies.

The complicating conditions arising from soil and subsoil are many. Experience has already shown that there are occasional conditions of soil and subsoil so favorable that the water may be supplied before the growing season, and the subsoil will hold it for weeks, or even months, and gradually yield the moisture to the overlying soil by slow upward percolation or capillary attraction during the season when growing crops require its fertilizing effect. When such conditions of soil and subsoil obtain, the construction of reservoirs is unnecessary, and the whole annual supply of the streams may be utilized. On the other hand, there are extremely pervious soils, underlaid by sands and gravels, which speedily carry away the water by a natural under drainage. Here a maximum supply by irrigation is necessary, as the soils must be kept moist by frequent flowing. Under such conditions the amount of water to be supplied is many fold greater than under the conditions previously mentioned, and between these extremes almost infinite variety prevails.

Practical agriculture by irrigation has also demonstrated the fact that the wants of different crops are exceedingly variable, some requiring many fold the amount of others. This is due in part to the length of time necessary to the maturing of the crops, in part to the amount of constant moisture necessary to their successful growth. But by excluding the variability due to rainfall, and considering only that due to differences of soils and crops, and by taking advantage of a wide experience, a general average may be obtained of sufficient accuracy for the purposes here in view.

In examining the literature of this subject it was found that the experience in other countries could not be used as a guide in considering the lands of Utah. In general, irrigation in Europe and Asia is practiced only to supply deficiencies, and the crops there raised are only in part the same as in Utah, and the variation on account of the crops is very great. Certain statements of Marsh in his "Man and Nature" have been copied into the journals and reports published in the United States, and made to

459

do duty on many occasions; but these statements are rather misleading, as the experience of farmers in the Arid Region has abundantly demonstrated· From that statement in general the writers have overestimated the quantitative value of water in irrigation.   The facts in Italy, in Spain, in Grenada, and India are valuable severally for discussion in the countries named, but must be used in a discussion of the arid lands of the United States with much care.   It seemed better, under these circumstances, to determine the quantitative value of water in irrigation in Utah from the experience of the farmers of Utah.   Irrigation has there been practiced for about thirty years, and gradually during that time the area of land thus redeemed has been increased, until at present about 325,000 acres of land are under cultivation.   A great variety of crops have been cultivated—corn, wheat, oats, rye, garden vegetables, orchard trees, fruits, vines, etc., etc.; and even the fig tree and sugar cane are there raised.

During the past six or seven years I have from time to time, as occasion was afforded, directed my attention to this problem, but being exceedingly complex, a very wide range of facts must be considered in order to obtain a reasonably approximate average.   During the past year the task of more thoroughly investigating this subject was delegated to Mr. Gilbert.   The results of his studies appear in a foregoing chapter, written by him; but it may be stated here that he has reached the conclusion that a continuous flow of one cubic foot of water per second, i. e., a *second-foot* of water, will, in most of the lands of Utah, serve about 100 acres for the general average of crops cultivated in that country; but to secure that amount of service from the water very careful and economic methods of irrigation must be practiced.   At present, there are but few instances where such economic methods are used.   In general, there is a great wastage, due to badly constructed canals, from which the water either percolates away or breaks away from time to time; due, also, to too rapid flow, and also to an excessive use of the water, as there is a tendency among the farmers to irrigate too frequently and too copiously, which is corrected only by long experience.

The studies of Mr. Gilbert, under the circumstances, were quite thorough, and his conclusions accord with my own, derived from a more desultory but longer study of the subject.

AREA OF IRRIGABLE LAND SOMETIMES NOT LIMITED BY WATER SUPPLY.

While, as a general fact, the area of arable land is greater than the area of irrigable land, by reason of the insufficient supply of water, yet in considering limited tracts it may often be found that the supply of water is so great that only a part of it can be used thereon. In such cases the area of irrigable land is limited by the extent to which the water can be used by proper engineering skill. This is true in considering some portions of Utah, where the waters of the Green and Colorado cannot all be used within that Territory. Eventually these surplus waters will be used in southern California.

METHOD OF DETERMINING THE SUPPLY OF WATER.

To determine the amount of irrigable land in Utah, it was necessary to consider the supply; that is, to determine the amount of water flowing in the several streams. Again, this quantity is variable in each stream from season to season and from year to year. The irrigable season is but a small portion of the year. To utilize the entire annual discharge of the water, it would be necessary to hold the surplus flowing in the non-growing season in reservoirs, and even by this method the whole amount could not be utilized, as a great quantity would be lost by evaporation. As the utilization of the water by reservoirs will be to a great extent postponed for many years, the question of immediate practical importance is resolved into a consideration of the amount of water that the streams will afford during the irrigating season. But in the earlier part of the season the flow in most of the streams in this western region is great, and it steadily diminishes to the end of the summer. Earlier in the season there is more water, while for the average of crops the greater amount is needed later.

The practical capacity of a stream will then be determined by its flow at the time when that is least in comparison with the demands of the growing crops. This will be called the critical period, and the volume of water of the critical period will determine the capacity of the stream. The critical period will vary in different parts of the region from the latter part of June until the first part of August. For the purposes of this discussion it was only necessary to determine the flow of the water during the critical period. This has been done by very simple methods. Usually in each case a section of the stream has been selected having the least possible variation of outline and flow. A cross-section of the stream has been measured, and the velocity of flow determined. With these factors the capacity of the streams has been obtained. In some cases single measurements have been made; in others several at different seasons, rarely in different years. The determination of the available volume of the several streams by such methods is necessarily uncertain, especially from the fact that it has not always been possible to gauge the streams exactly at the critical period; and, again, the flow in one season may differ materially from that in another. But as the capacity of a stream should never be rated by its volume in seasons of abundant flow, we have endeavored as far as possible to determine the capacity of the streams in low water years. Altogether the amount of water in the several streams has been determined crudely, and at best the data given must be considered tolerable approximations. In considering the several streams experience may hereafter discover many errors, but as the number of determinations is great, the average may be considered good.

METHODS OF DETERMINING THE EXTENT OF IRRIGABLE LAND UNLIMITED BY WATER SUPPLY.

In the few cases where the water supply is more than sufficient to serve the arable lands, the character of the problem is entirely changed, and it becomes necessary then to determine the area to which the waters can be carried. These problems are hypsometric; relative altitudes are the governing conditions. The hypsometric methods were barometric and angular; that is, from the barometric stations vertical angles were taken and recorded to all the principal points in the topography of the country; mercurial and aneroid barometers were used, chiefly the former; the latter to a limited extent, for subsidiary work. Angular measurements were made with gradientors to a slight extent, but chiefly with the orograph, an instrument by which a great multiplicity of angles are observed and recorded by mechanical methods. This instrument was devised by Professor Thompson for the use of the survey, and has been fully described in the reports on the geographical operations.   To run hypsometric lines with spirit levels would have involved a great amount of labor and been exceedingly expensive, and such a method was entirely impracticable with the means at command, but the methods used give fairly approximate results, and perhaps all that is necessary for the purposes to be subserved.

THE SELECTION OF IRRIGABLE LANDS.

From the fact that the area of arable lands greatly exceeds the irrigable, or the amount which the waters of the streams will serve, a wide choice in the selection of the latter is permitted.   The considerations affecting the choice are diverse, but fall readily into two classes, viz: physical conditions and artificial conditions.   The mountains and high plateaus are the great aqueous condensers; the mountains and high plateaus are also the reservoirs that hold the water fed to the streams in the irrigating season, for the fountains from which the rivers flow are the snow fields of the highlands.   After the streams leave the highlands they steadily diminish in volume, the loss being due in part to direct evaporation, and in part to percolation in the sands from which the waters are eventually evaporated. In like manner irrigating canals starting near the mountains and running far out into the valleys and plains rapidly diminish in the volume of flowing water.   Looking to the conservation of water, it is best to select lands as high along the streams as possible.   But this consideration is directly opposed by considerations relating to temperature; the higher the land the colder the climate.   Where the great majority of streams have their sources, agriculture is impossible on account of prevailing summer frosts; the lower the altitude the more genial the temperature; the lower the land the greater the variety of crops which can be cultivated; and to the extent that the variety of crops is multiplied the irrigating season is lengthened, until the maximum is reached in low altitudes and low latitudes where two crops can be raised annually on the same land.   In the selection of lands, as governed by these conditions, the higher lands will be avoided on the one hand because of the rigor of the climate; if these conditions alone governed, no settlement should be made in Utah above 6,500 feet above the level of the sea, and in general still lower lands should be used; on the other hand

463

the irrigable lands should not be selected at such a distance from the source of the stream as to be the occasion of a great loss of water by direct and indirect evaporation. For general climatic reasons, the lands should be selected as low as possible; for economy of water as high as possible; and these conditions in the main will cause the selections to be made along the middle courses of the streams. But this general rule will be modified by minor physical conditions relating to soil and slope—soils that will best conserve the water will be selected, and land with the gentlest slopes will be taken.

In general, the descent of the streams in the arid land is very great; for this reason the flood plains are small, that is, the extent of the lands adjacent to the streams which are subject to overflow at high water is limited. In general, these flood-plain lands should not be chosen for irrigation, from the fact that the irrigating canals are liable to be destroyed during flood seasons. Where the plan of irrigation includes the storage of the water of the non-growing season, by which all the waters of the year are held under control, the flood-plain lands can be used to advantage, from the fact that they lie in such a way as to be easily irrigated and their soils possess elements and conditions of great fertility.

Other locally controlling conditions are found in selecting the most advantageous sites for the necessary water works.

These are the chief physical factors which enter into the problem, and in general it will be solved by considering these factors only; but occasionally artificial conditions will control.

The mining industries of the Arid Region are proportionately greater than in the more humid country. Where valuable mines are discovered towns spring up in their immediate vicinity, and they must be served with water for domestic purposes and for garden culture. When possible, agriculture will be practiced in the immediate vicinity for the purpose of taking advantage of the local market. In like manner towns spring up along the railroads, and agriculture will be carried on in their vicinity. For this and like reasons the streams of the Arid Region will often be used on lands where they cannot be made the most available under physical conditions, and yet under such circumstances artificial conditions must prevail.

In coloring specific areas on the accompanying map of Utah, it must be considered that the selections made are but tentative; the areas chosen are supposed to be, under all the circumstances, the most available, chiefly governed by the physical facts; but each community will settle this problem for itself, and the circumstances which will control any particular selection cannot be foretold. It is believed that the selections made will be advantageous to the settler, by giving him the opinions of men who have made the subject a study, and will save many mistakes.

The history of this subject in Utah is very instructive. The greater number of people in the Territory who engage in agriculture are organized into ecclesiastical bodies, trying the experiment of communal institutions. In this way the communal towns are mobile. This mobility is increased by the fact that the towns are usually laid out on Government lands, and for a long time titles to the land in severalty are not obtained by the people. It has been the custom of the church to send a number of people, organized as a community, to a town site on some stream to be used in the cultivation of the lands, and rarely has the first selection made been final. Luxuriant vegetation has often tempted the settlers to select lands at too great an altitude, and many towns have been moved down stream. Sometimes selections have been made too far away from the sources of the streams, and to increase the supply of water towns have been moved up stream. Sometimes lands of too great slope have been chosen, and here the waters have rapidly cut deep channels and destroyed the fields. Sometimes alkaline lands are selected and abandoned, and sometimes excessively sandy lands have caused a change to be made; but the question of the best sites for the construction of works for controlling and distributing the water has usually determined the selection of lands within restricted limits.

To a very slight extent indeed have artificial conditions controlled in Utah; the several problems have generally been solved by the consideration of physical facts.

INCREASE IN THE WATER SUPPLY.

Irrigation has been practiced in different portions of the Arid Region for the last twenty-five or thirty years, and the area cultivated by this

12 A B

means has been steadily increasing during that time.   In California and New Mexico irrigation has been practiced to a limited extent for a much longer time at the several Catholic missions under the old Spanish regime. In the history of the settlement of the several districts an important fact has been uniformly observed—in the first years of settlement the streams have steadily increased in volume.   This fact has been observed alike in California, Utah, Colorado, and wherever irrigation has been practiced.   As the chief development of this industry has been within the last fifteen years, it has been a fact especially observed during that time.   An increase in the water supply, so universal of late years, has led to many conjectures and hypotheses as to its origin.   It has generally been supposed to result from increased rainfall, and this increased rainfall now from this, now from that, condition of affairs.   Many have attributed the change to the laying of railroad tracks and construction of telegraph lines; others to the cultivation of the soil, and not a few to the interposition of Divine Providence in behalf of the Latter Day Saints.

If each physical cause was indeed a *vera causa*, their inability to produce the results is quite manifest.   A single railroad line has been built across the Arid Region from east to west, and a short north and south line has been constructed in Colorado, another in Utah, and several in California. But an exceedingly small portion of the country where increase of water supply has been noticed has been reached by the railroads, and but a small fraction of one per cent. of the lands of the Arid Region have been redeemed by irrigation.   This fully demonstrates their inadequacy.   In what manner rainfall could be affected through the cultivation of the land, building of railroads, telegraph lines, etc., has not been shown.   Of course such hypotheses obtain credence because of a lack of information relating to the laws which govern aqueous precipitation.   The motions of the earth on its axis and about the sun; the unequal heating of the atmosphere, which decreases steadily from equator to poles; the great ocean currents and air currents; the distribution of land and water over the earth; the mountain systems—these are all grand conditions affecting the distribution of rainfall. Many minor conditions also prevail in topographic reliefs, and surfaces favorable to the absorption or reflection of the sun's heat, etc., etc., affecting in a slight degree the general results.   But the operations of man on the surface of the earth are so trivial that the conditions which they produce are of minute effect, and in presence of the grand effects of nature escape discernment.   Thus the alleged causes for the increase of rainfall fail.   The rain gauge records of the country have been made but for a brief period, and the stations have been widely scattered, so that no very definite conclusions can be drawn from them, but so far as they are of value they fail to show any increase.   But if it be true that increase of the water supply is due to increase in precipitation, as many have supposed, the fact is not cheering to the agriculturist of the Arid Region.   The permanent changes of nature are secular; any great sudden change is ephemeral, and usually such changes go in cycles, and the opposite or compensating conditions may reasonably be anticipated.

For the reasons so briefly stated, the question of the origin and permanence of the increase of the water supply is one of prime importance to the people of the country.   If it is due to a temporary increase of rainfall, or any briefly cyclic cause, we shall have to expect a speedy return to extreme aridity, in which case a large portion of the agricultural industries of the country now growing up would be destroyed.

The increase is abundantly proved; it is a matter of universal experience.   The observations of the writer thereon have been widely extended. Having examined as far as possible all the facts seeming to bear on the subject, the theory of the increase of rainfall was rejected, and another explanation more flattering to the future of agriculture accepted.

The amount of water flowing in the streams is but a very small part of that which falls from the heavens.   The greater part of the rainfall evaporates from the surfaces which immediately receive it.   The exceedingly dry atmosphere quickly reabsorbs the moisture occasionally thrown down by a conjunction of favoring conditions.   Any changes in the surfaces which receive the precipitation favorable to the rapid gathering of the rain into rills and brooks and creeks, while taking to the streams but a small amount of that precipitated, will greatly increase the volume of the streams themselves, because the water in the streams bears so small a proportion to the amount discharged from the clouds.   The artificial changes wrought by man on the surface of the earth appear to be adequate to the production of the observed effects. The destruction of forests, which has been immense in this country for the past fifteen years; the cropping of the grasses, and the treading of the soil by cattle; the destruction of the beaver dams, causing a drainage of the ponds; the clearing of drift wood from stream channels; the draining of upland meadows, and many other slight modifications, all conspire to increase the accumulation of water in the streams, and all this is added to the supply of water to be used in irrigation.

Students of geology and physical geography have long been aware of these facts. It is well known that, under the modifying influences of man, the streams of any region redeemed from the wilderness are changed in many important characteristics. In flood times their volumes are excessively increased and their powers of destruction multiplied. In seasons of drought, some streams that were perennial before man modified the surface of the country become entirely dry; the smaller navigable streams have their periods of navigation shortened, and the great rivers run so low at times that navigation becomes more and more difficult during dry seasons; in multiplied ways these effects are demonstrated. While in the main the artifiicial changes wrought by man on the surface are productive of bad results in humid regions, the changes are chiefly advantageous to man in arid regions where agriculture is dependent upon irrigation, for here the result is to increase the supply of water. Mr. Gilbert, while engaged during the past season in studying the lands of Utah, paid especial attention to this subject, and in his chapter has more thoroughly discussed the diverse special methods by which increase in the flow of the streams is caused by the changes wrought by man upon the surface of the earth. His statement of facts is clear, and his conclusions are deemed valid.

IRRIGABLE AND PASTURE LANDS.

UINTA-WHITE BASIN.

The Uinta-White Valley is a deep basin inclosed by the Uinta Mountains on the north and the Tavaputs highlands on the south. Eastward the basin extends beyond the limits of Utah; westward the Uinta Mountains and West Tavaputs Plateau nearly inclose the head of the Uinta Valley, but the space between is filled with a section of the Wasatch Mountains. From the north, west, and south the Uinta Valley inclines gently toward the Duchesne River. Many streams come down from the north and from the south. In the midst of the valley there are some small stretches of bad lands.

Along the lower part of the Uinta and the Duchesne, and the lower courses of nearly all the streams, large tracts of arable land are found, and from these good selections can be made, sufficient to occupy in their service all the water of the Uinta and its numerous branches. The agricultural portion of the valley is sufficiently low to have a genial climate, and all the crops of the northern States can be cultivated successfully.

Stretching back on every hand from the irrigable districts, the little hills, valleys, and slopes are covered with grasses, which become more and more luxuriant in ascending the plateaus and mountains, until the peaks are reached, and these are naked.

On the north of the Uinta, and still west of the Green, the basin is drained by some small streams, the chief of which is Ashley Fork. Except near the lower course of Ashley Fork, this section of country is exceedingly broken; the bad lands and hogbacks are severed by deep, precipitous cañons.

From the east the White River enters the Green. Some miles up the White, a cañon is reached, and the country, on either hand stretching back for a long distance, is composed of rugged barren lands. But between the highlands and the Green, selections of good land can be made, and the waters of the White can be used to serve them. From the White, south to the East Tavaputs Plateau, the grasslands steadily increase in value to the summit of the Brown Cliffs. Many good springs are found in this region, and eventually this will be a favorite district for pasturage farms.

Fine pasturage farms may be made on the southern slope of the Yampa Plateau, with summer pasturage above and winter pasturage below. Altogether, the Uinta-White Basin is one of the favored districts of the west, with great numbers of cool springs issuing from the mountains and hills; many beautiful streams of clear, cold water; a large amount of arable land from which irrigable tracts may be selected; an abundance of fuel in the piñon pines and cedars of the foot hills, and building timber farther back on the mountains and plateaus.

The whole amount of irrigable land is estimated at 280,320 acres.

THE CAÑON LANDS.

South of the Tavaputs highlands, and east and south of The High Plateaus, the Cañon Lands of Utah are found. The lower course of the Grand, the lower course of the Green, and a large section of the Colorado cuts through them, and the streams that head in The High Plateaus run across them. All the rivers, all the creeks, all the brooks, run in deep gorges, narrow, winding cañons, with their floors far below the general surface of the country. Many long lines of cliffs are found separating higher from lower districts. The hills are bad lands and alcove lands.

The Sierra la Sal and Henry Mountains are great masses of lava, wrapped in sedimentary beds, which are cut with many dikes. South of The High Plateaus great numbers of cinder cones are found.

On the Grand River there are some patches of land which can be served by the waters of that river. On the Green, in what is known as Gunnison Valley, patches of good land can be selected and redeemed by the waters of that river.

Castle Valley is abruptly walled on the west, north, and northeast by towering cliffs. East of its southern portion a region of towers, buttes, crags, and rocklands is found, known as the San Rafael Swell. In this valley there is a large amount of good land, and the numerous streams which run across it can all be used in irrigation. Farther south, on the Fremont, Escalante, and Paria, some small tracts of irrigable land are found, and on the Kanab and Virgin there are limited areas which can be used for agricultural purposes. But all that portion of the cañon country south of Castle Valley and westward to the Beaver Dam Mountains is exceedingly desolate; naked rocks are found refusing footing even to dwarfed cedars and piñon pines; the springs are infrequent and yield no bountiful supply of water; the patches of grass land are widely scattered, and it has but little value for agricultural purposes.

A broad belt of coal land extends along the base of the cliffs from the Tavaputs Plateau on the northeast to the Colob Plateau on the southwest. At the foot of the cliffs which separate the lowlands from the highlands, many pasturage farms may be made; the grass of the lowlands can be used in the winter, and that of the highlands in summer, and everywhere good springs of water may be found.

The extent of the irrigable lands in this district is estimated at 213,440 acres.

THE SEVIER LAKE DISTRICT.

This district embraces all the country drained by the waters which flow into the Sevier Lake, and the areas drained by many small streams which are quickly lost in the desert. The greater part of the irrigable land lies in the long, narrow valleys walled by the plateaus, especially along the Sevier, Otter Creek, and the San Pete. The arable lands greatly exceed the irrigable, and good selections may be made. Most of the irrigable lands are already occupied by farmers, and the waters are used in their service. In the valleys, among the high plateaus, and along their western border, the grasses are good, and many pasturage farms may be selected, and the springs and little streams that come from the plateau cliffs will afford an abundant supply of water. The summits of the plateaus will afford abundant summer pasturage.

Westward among the Basin Ranges feeble and infrequent springs are found; there is little timber of value, but the lower mountains and foot hills have cedars and piñon pines that would be valuable for fuel if nearer to habitations. The cedar and piñon hills bear scant grasses. The valleys are sometimes covered with sage, sometimes with grease wood, sometimes quite naked.

The amount of irrigable land in this district is estimated at 101,700 acres.

14 A E

THE GREAT SALT LAKE DISTRICT.

This district has already become famous in the history of western agriculture, for here the Latter Day Saints first made "a home in the valleys among the mountains".

The rivers and creeks bring the waters down from the Wasatch Mountains on the east. The high valleys among the mountains have to some extent been cultivated, and will hereafter be used more than at present for meadow purposes. In general the people have selected their lands low down, in order to obtain a more genial climate. Yet the irrigable lands are not very far from the mountains, as a glance at the map will reveal. Utah Lake constitutes a fine natural reservoir and discharges its waters into Salt Lake by the Jordan, and from its channel the waters may be conducted over a large area of country. The waters of the Weber and Bear Rivers, now flowing idly into the lake, will soon be spread over extensive valleys, and the area of agricultural lands be greatly increased. Westward the influence of the mountains in the precipitation of moisture is soon lost, and beyond the lake an irreclaimable desert is found.

Near to the mountains the grass lands are fair but they have been overpastured and greatly injured. Out among the Basin Ranges few grass lands of value are found.

The amount of irrigable land in this district is estimated at 837,660 acres.

The lofty zone of mountains and table lands with arms stretching eastward, with its culminating points among summer frosts and winter storms, is the central region about which the human interests of the country gather. The timber, the water, the agricultural lands, the pasturage lands, to a large extent the coal and iron mines, and to some extent the silver mines, are all found in these higher regions or clinging closely to them, and this wonder land is the home of a strange people.

Table of irrigable lands in Utah Territory.

	Square miles.	Acres.	Cultivated in 1877. Square miles.	Cultivated in 1877. Acres.
Salt Lake drainage system.				
Base of Uinta Mountains	2.5	1,600	1.6	1,024
Yellow Creek and Duck Creek	2.0	1,280		
Woodruff Valley, Randolph Valley and Saleratus Creek	69.0	44,160	9.6	6,344
Shores of Bear Lake	9.0	5,760	5.0	3,200
Cache Valley	250.0	160,000	50.0	32,000
Delta Plain, Malade Valley and Connor's Spring Valley	218.0	139,520	22.0	14,080
Box Elder Valley (Mantua)	1.5	960	1.1	704
Kamas Prairie (northern edge)	3.0	1,920	.7	448
Peoa to Hennefer, inclusive	9.0	5,760	8.5	5,440
Parey's Park	3.2	2,048	3.2	2,048
Uptown	2.0	1,280	.5	320
Echo Creek	0.9	576	.3	192
Croydon	0.5	320	.4	256
Round Valley	0.5	320	.5	320
Morgan Valley	6.9	4,416	6.0	3,840
Ogden Valley	8.0	5,120	4.1	2,624
Delta Plain	219.0	140,160	91.0	58,240
Kamas Prairie	10.0	6,400	4.0	2,560
Hailstone Ranche and vicinity	2.0	1,280	2.0	1,280
Provo Valley	16.0	10,240	6.0	3,840
Waldsburg	2.0	1,280	2.0	1,280
Utah Valley	190.0	121,600	59.0	37,760
Goshen, Mona, Nephi } Salt Creek	16.0	10,240	14.0	8,960
Salt Lake Valley (including Bountiful and Centerville)	192.0	122,880	89.8	57,412
Tooele Valley	45.0	28,800	5.4	3,456
Cedar Fort	1.5	1,000	1.2	800
Fairfield	1.5	900	1.2	800
Vernon Creek	2.0	1,200	1.5	960
Saint John's	1.1	700	1.1	700
East Cañon Creek; Rush Valley	1.5	900	.8	500
Stockton	.3	500	.3	200
Skull Valley	4.0	2,500	1.6	1,000
Government Creek	.5	300	.5	300
Willow Spring, T. 10 S., R. 17 W	.4	250	.4	250
Redding Spring	.1	50		20
Dodoquibe Spring	.1	50		
Deep Creek, T. 9 S., R. 19 W	1.6	1,000	.8	500
Pilot Peak	.3	200		
Grouse Valley	2.4	1,500	.8	500
Owl Spring	.1	10		
Rosebud Creek	.6	400	.2	150
Muddy Creek, T. 10 N., R. 15 W	.5	300	.5	300
Park Valley	3.5	2,300	1.1	700
Widow Spring	.1	20		
Indian Creek, T. 13 N., R. 12 W	.2	100		
East base Clear Creek Mountains	.2	150		5
Cazure Creek	.3	200		
Clear Creek, T. 15 N., R. 12 W	.3	200	.1	80
Junction Creek	.7	500		
Goose Creek	.3	200		

Table of irrigable lands in Utah Territory—Continued.

	Square miles.	Acres.	Cultivated in 1877.	
			Square miles.	Acres.
Salt Lake drainage system—Continued.				
Pilot Spring	.1	15	....	....
Deseret Creek (or Deep Creek)	4.5	3,000	.5	300
Crystal Springs, T. 14 N., R. 7 W	.2	100	.1	60
Antelope Spring, T. 9 N., R. 6 W	.1	30	....	30
Hanzel Springs	.1	15	....	15
Promontory, east base	.9	600	.5	300
Blue Creek	2.3	1,500	....	....
Brackish Springs, near Blue Creek	1.5	1,000	.3	200
Antelope Island	.1	50	....	....
The valley of the Sevier River.				
San Pete Valley	31.2	20,000	17.0	10,880
Gunnison	6.2	4,000	44.4	2,800
Sevier Valley, above Gunnison	54.7	35,000	16.5	10,500
Circle Valley	6.3	4,000	1.1	750
Panguitch and above	10.9	7,000	2.8	1,800
Irrigable lands of the desert drainage of southwestern Utah.				
Cherry Creek	.2	100	....	....
Judd Creek	.2	100	....	....
Levan	3.1	2,000	....	....
Scipio	2.6	1,700	....	....
Holden	1.6	1,000	....	....
Fillmore and Oak Creek	5.5	3,500	....	....
Meadow Creek	1.9	1,200	....	....
Kanosh	3.1	2,000	....	....
Beaver Creek and tributaries	21.9	14,000	....	....
Parageonah	1.6	1,000	....	....
Parowan	1.6	1,000	....	....
Summit	.6	400	....	....
Cedar City, Iron City, and Fort Hamilton ...	3.6	2,300	....	....
Mountain Meadows	.3	200	....	....
Pinto	.3	200	....	....
Hebron	1.6	1,000	....	....
Irrigable lands of the Colorado drainage.				
Virgin River	30	19,200	11.0	7,040
Kanab Creek	2.5	1,600	1.1	700
Paria River	6	3,840	....	....
Escalante River	6	3,840	....	....
Fremont River	38	24,320	....	....
San Rafael River	175	112,000	....	....
Price River	11	7,040	....	....
Minnie Maud Creek	3	1,920	....	....
Uinta River	285	182,400	.5	300
Ashley Fork	25	16,000	.1	50
Henry's Fork	10	6,400	....	....
White River	75	48,000	....	....
Brown's Park .... ⎫	10	6,400	....	....
Below Split Mountain Cañon ...... ⎬ Green River .... ⎰	50	32,000	....	....
Gunnison Valley .... ⎭	25	16,000	....	....
Grand River	40	25,600	....	....
Total	2,262.4	1,447,920	....	....

References

Bailey, R. W. 1935. Epicycles of erosion in the valleys of the Colorado Plateau province: *Jour. Geol.,* v. 43, p. 337–355.

Barnes, H. E. 1921. The relation of geography to the writing and interpretation of history: *Jour. Geog.,* v. 20 n. 9, p. 321–336.

Bell, B. 1971. The Dark Ages in ancient history: *Amer. Jour. Arch.,* v. 75, p. 1–26.

Beverley, Robert. 1722. The History of Virginia in Four Parts: London. 284 p.

Brooke, W. E. (Ed.). 1919. The Agricultural Papers of George Washington: Boston, 145 p.

Brunhes, Jean. 1952. Human Geography: George G. Harrap & Co., London, 256 p.

Bryan, Kirk. 1925. Date of channel trenching (arroyo cutting) in the arid Southwest: *Science,* v. 62, p. 338–344.

Bryson, R. A. and Baerreis, D. A. 1967. Possibilities of major climatic modification and their implications: Northwest India, a case for study: *Amer. Met. Soc. Bull.,* v. 48 n. 3, p. 136–142.

Bryson, R. A. 1967. Is man changing the climate of the Earth?: *Sat. Review,* Apr. 1, p. 52–55.

Burrows, A. J. 1885. Romney Marsh, past and present: *Royal Inst. of Surv., Trans.,* v. 17, p. 336–368.

Burrows, M. 1888. *Cinque Ports*: London, 261 p.

Cadwell, H. M. 1929. Land reclamation in Forth Valley: *Scottish Geog. Mag.,* v. 45, p. 7–22.

Carman, H., and Tugwell, R. G. 1934. In Essays upon Field Husbandry in New England 1748–62 by Jared Eliot: Columbia Uni. Press, New York, 261 p.

Carman, H. J. (Ed.). 1939. American Husbandry (1775): Columbia Uni. Press, New York, 582 p.

Cathey, C. O. 1966. Agriculture in South Carolina before the Civil War: Raleigh, 45 p.

Coates, D. R. (Ed.). 1971. Environmental Geomorphology: Publications in Geomorphology, New York, 262 p.

Columella, L. I. M. 1785. Columella's Husbandry: Anonymous translation, London, 600 p.

Cook, O. F. 1916. Staircase farms of the ancients: *National Geog. Mag.,* v. 29, p. 474–534.

Cooke, C. W. 1931. Why the Maya cities of Peten District, Guatemala were abandoned: *Wash. Ac. Sci. Jour.,* v. 21, p. 283–288.

Cowgill, U. M. and Hutchinson, G. E. 1963. Ecological and geochemical archaeology in the southern Maya lowlands: *Southwestern Jour. of Anthr.,* v. 19, p. 267–286.

Craven, A. O. 1926. Soil Exhaustion as a Factor in the Agricultural History of Virginia and Maryland, 1606–1860, Uni. Illinois Press, 179 p.

Cutright, P. R. 1969. Lewis and Clark; Pioneering Naturalists: Uni. of Illinois Press, 506 p.

Denevan, W. M. 1967. Livestock numbers in Nineteenth-Century New Mexico, and the problem of gullying in the Southwest: *Assoc. Amer. Geog. Annals,* v. 57, n. 4, p. 691–703.

DeVoto, B. (Ed.) 1953. The Journals of Lewis and Clark: Houghton Mifflin Co., Boston, 504 p.

Durand, J. D. (Ed.) 1967. World Population: *Amer. Academy Pol. Soc. Sci., Annals,* v. 369,

Evenari, M. et al. 1961. Ancient agriculture in the Negev: *Science,* v. 133, p. 979–996.

Evenari, M., Shanon, L. and Tadmor, N. 1971. The Negev: Harvard Uni. Press, Cambridge, 345 p.

Eyre, S. R. and Jones, G. R. J. (Eds.) 1966. Geography as Human Ecology: St. Martins Press, New York, 308 p.

Fairbridge, R. W. (Ed.) 1968. The Encyclopedia of Geomorphology: Reinhold Book Corp., New York, 1295 p.

Fitzpatrick, J. C. (Ed.) 1940. Writings of George Washington (in 36 Volumes): Gov. Printing Office.

Frank, Bernard. 1955. The story of water as the story of man, In Water: The Yearbook of Agriculture: Gov. Printing Office, p. 1–8.

Galbraith, V. H. 1961. The Making of Doomsday Book: 242 p.

Geikie, Sir Archibald. 1905. Landscape in History: Macmillan Co., Ltd., London, 352 p.

Gilbert, G. K. 1877. Report on the Geology of the Henry Mountains: U.S. Geog. and Geol. Sur. Rocky Mtn. Region, 160 p.

Gilbert, G. K. 1917. Hydraulic-mining Debris in the Sierra Nevada: U.S. Geol. Survey Professional Paper 105, 154 p.

Gras, N. S. B. 1946. A History of Agriculture: F. S. Crofts & Co., New York, 496 p.

Gregory, H. E. and Moore, R. C. 1931. The Kaiparowits Region, a Geographical and Geologic Reconnaissance of Parts of Utah and Arizona: U.S. Geol. Survey Professional Paper 164, 161 p.

Hack, J. 1942. The changing physical environment of the Hopi Indians of Arizona: Harvard Uni. Peabody Mus. Arch. and Ethn. v. 35, n. 1, p. 70–80.

Hall, A. R. 1937. Early erosion-control practices in Virginia: U.S.D.A. Misc. Pub. No. 256, 31 p.

Handley, J. E. 1953. Scottish Farming in the Eighteenth Century: London, 314 p.

Hayden, F. V. 1872. Preliminary Report of the United States Geological Survey of Montana and Portions of Adjacent Territories: Fifth Annual Report of Progress, Gov. Printing Office, 538 p.

Hayden, F. V. 1876. First, Second, and Third Annual Reports of the United States Geological Survey of the Territories for the Years 1867, 1868, and 1869: Gov. Printing Office, 261 p.

Hodge, C. and Duisberg, P. C. (Eds.) 1963. Aridity and Man: Amer. Assoc. for the Advanc. of Science, Pub. No. 74, 584 p.

Hooper, W. D. and Ash, H. B. 1960. Cato and Varro de Re Rustica: Cambridge, Harvard Uni. Press, 543 p.

Huntington, E. 1917. Climatic change and agricultural exhaustion as elements in the fall of Rome: *Quart. Jour. Econ.*, v. 31, p. 173–208.

Jacobsen, T. and Adams, R. M. 1958. Salt and silt in ancient Mesopotamian agriculture: *Science* v. 128, p. 1251–1258.

Jones, W. H. S. (Ed.) 1957. Hippocrates, Vol. 1: Cambridge, Harvard Uni. Press, 361 p.

Kedar, Y. 1957. Water and soil from the deserts: some ancient agricultural achievements in the central Negev: *Geog. Jour.* v. 123, p. 179–187.

Kedar, Y. 1967. Ancient Agriculture in the Negev Mountains (in Hebrew): Bialik Institute, Jerusalem, 124 p.

King, C. 1880. First Annual Report of the United States Geological Survey: Gov. Printing Office, 62 p.

Knight, Franklin (Ed.) 1847. Letters on Agriculture from His Excellency George Washington; To Arthur Young and Sir John Sinclair: Washington, D.C., 198 p.

Leopold, Aldo. 1949. A Sand County Almanac: Oxford Uni. Press, 226 p.

Leopold, L. B. 1951. Rainfall frequency: an aspect of climatic variation: *Trans. Amer. Geophys. Un.* v. 32, p. 347–357.

Lord., R. 1938. To Hold This Soil: U.S.D.A. Misc. Publ. No. 321, 122 p.

Lowdermilk, W. C. 1943. Lessons from the old world to the America's in land use: *Smithsonian Inst. Ann. Report,* p. 413–427.

Maclure, William. 1817. Observations on the Geology of the United States of North America: Amer. Phil. Soc. Trans., May 16, 91 p.

Marsh, G. P. 1877. The Earth as Modified by Human Action: A New Edition of Man and Nature: Scribner, Armstrong & Co., New York, 674 p.

McGee, W. J. 1893. Genetic classification of Pleistocene deposits: *Internat. Geol. Congress V*, Washington, p. 198–207.

Mulkearn, L. 1949. A Topographic Description of the Dominions of the United States of America by T. Pownall: Uni. of Pittsburgh Press, 235 p.

Nevins, Allan. 1928. Fremont the West's Greatest Adventurer (in two Volumes): Harper & Brothers publishers, New York, 738 p.

Nickols, D. 1882. Preservation and Protection of Cultivated Lands from Surface Washing: Atlanta, Georgia, 69 p.

Olson, G. W. 1970. Examples of ancient and modern use and abuse of soils: *N.Y. Food and Life Sciences*, v. 3 n. 2, p. 27–29.

Olson, G. W. 1971. Some implications of soils for civilizations, *N.Y. Food and Life Sciences*, v. 4, n. 4, p. 11–14.

Peterson, H. V. 1950. The problem of gullying in western valleys: In Applied Sedimentation, P. Trask, Ed., John Wiley & Son, New York, p. 407–434.

Pillai, V. R. and Panikar, P. G. K. 1965. Land Reclamation in Kerala: Asia Publishing House, New York, 197 p.

Powell, J. W. 1878. Report of the lands of the arid region of the U.S. with a detailed account of Utah: 45th Congress, House Exec. Doc. 73, 195 p.

Rich, J. L. 1911. Recent stream trenching in the semi-arid portion of southwestern New Mexico, a result of removal of vegetation cover: *Amer. J. of Sci.*, v. 32, p. 237–245.

Sears, P. B. 1947. Deserts on the March: Uni. of Oklahoma Press, 178 p.

Sears, P. B. 1953. Climate and Civilization: In Climatic Change, H. Shapley, Ed., Harvard Uni. Press, Cambridge, p. 35–50.

Semple, E. C. 1911. Influences of Geographic Environment: Henry Holt & Co., New York, 683 p.

Semple, E. C. and Jones, C. F. 1933. American History and its Geographic Conditions: Houghton Mifflin Co., Boston, 541 p.

Sherlock, R. L. 1931. Man's Influence on the Earth: T. Butterworth, London, 256 p.

Simkhovitch, V. G. 1916. Rome's fall reconsidered: *Pol. Sci. Quart. Jour.*, v. 31, p. 201–243.

Sinclair, Sir John, 1812, An Account of the Systems of Husbandry Adopted in the More Improved Districts of Scotland: Edinburgh (var. pg.)

Smucker, S. M. 1856. The Life of Col. John Charles Fremont and His Narrative of Explorations and Adventures in Kansas, Nebraska, Oregon and California: Miller, Orton & Mulligan, New York, 493 p.

Sorsby, N. T. 1860. Horizontal Plowing and Hill-side Ditching: Mobile, Alabama, 45 p.

Stamp, L. D. 1964. Man and the Land: London, 272 p.

Toynbee, A. J. 1950. Greek Historical Thought from Homer to the Age of Heraclius:Beacon Press, Boston, 256 p.

Tuan, Yi-Fu. 1966. New Mexican gullies: A critical review and some recent observations: *Assoc. Amer. Geog. Annals*, v. 56, n. 4, p. 573-597.

Veen, J. V. 1962. Dredge Drain Reclaim, The Art of a Nation: Martinius Nijhoff, The Hague, 5th ed., 200 p.

Volney, C. F. 1804. A View of the Soil and Climate of the United States of America: Philadelphia, 446 p.

Weld, Isaac. 1807. Travels Through the States of the United States of North America 1795–97: London, Vol. 1, 427 p.

Wheeler, G. M. 1889. Report Upon United States Geological Surveys West of the One Hundredth Meridian: Gov. Printing Office, 780 p.

Wheeler, W. H. 1902. The Sea-coast: London, p. 333–352.

Wittfogel, K. A. 1956. The hydraulic civilizations: In Man's Role in Changing the Face of the Earth, F. Thomas (Ed.), Chicago Uni. Press, p. 152–164.

Woodbury, R. B. 1961. A reappraisal of Hohokam irrigation: *Amer. Anthro.* v. 63, p. 550–560.

Worthington, E. B. 1946. Middle East Science: H.M. Stationery Office, London.

Index

Numbers in *italics* indicate pages with illustrations.

485